JAMAICAN FOOD

JAMAICAN FOOD
HISTORY BIOLOGY CULTURE

B. W. HIGMAN

The University of the West Indies Press
Jamaica • Barbados • Trinidad and Tobago

The University of the West Indies Press
7A Gibraltar Hall Road, Mona
Kingston 7, Jamaica
www.uwipress.com

A catalogue record of this book is available from the National
Library of Jamaica.

ISBN: 978-976-640-911-1 (paper)

Book and cover design by Heather Whitton.
Cover photograph of ackee fruit by Julian Dadag.

Printed in the United States of America

For Sandra

CONTENTS

PART 1: PLANTS

PART 3: INORGANIC MATTER

ILLUSTRATIONS

FIGURES

COLOUR PLATES

PREFACE

This is not a cookbook. Although readers will occasionally encounter a recipe sufficiently complete to be prepared in the kitchen, for the most part I have suggested only the broad outlines of how to make a dish, without being precise about proportions, measurements and cooking times or even necessarily listing all of the ingredients. If you want to know how to cook Jamaican food, I recommend that you consult the several excellent cookbooks that have appeared in recent years. I must confess, however, that over the decades this volume has been in the making, when friends asked me what I was going to call it and I responded simply, *Jamaican Food*, several counselled me that such a title could identify only a cookbook. They told me I would need to think of something different. I'm afraid I did not take their advice, but these comments do show clearly the extent to which the story of food has become dominated by the practical cookbook. The other side of the coin is that modern people have often lost touch with the sources and origins of their food, and lack a knowledge of the global food chains that deliver their meals. These are the dominant themes of this book, and I hope that the subtitle, pointing to the historical, biological and cultural focus of the text, is sufficient clue to these concerns.

I chose to write this book, rather than a cookbook, because I am interested in trying to understand why Jamaicans eat what they eat, how they define Jamaican food and how their choices have changed over time. These are important questions that provide insight into the social, cultural, agricultural, economic and political history of Jamaica. In everyday life, these choices are at least as important as decisions about whom to vote for and what to have faith in. Although it may appear transient, food is not just essential to bodily survival but vital as a driver of culture and identity. At one extreme, when meals are purchased as fast food, there is hardly any space between deciding what to eat and eating, and little knowledge of how the food has been constituted. In the past, by contrast, the sources of food grew in fields and forests, sea and stream, for weeks and months; they were observed from birth to maturity, and were watched closely as they came to ripeness or fatness. The apparent transience of food was equally an omnipresence.

For most of Jamaica's history, people lived in the midst of plants and animals recognized as potential foods. Food crops were by far the most important component of the economy, whether for local consumption or for trade. Decisions about what to eat, whether these decisions were made in Jamaica or in other places, determined the pattern of agricultural economy and had ramifications for systems of land and labour exploitation, the environment, and indeed every area of social and political life. Only in recent times, and only in some parts of the world, has the production of food become abundant and assured, so that people can be concerned more about overeating, obesity and exotic taste experiences than about hunger and food security. Historically, where the next meal was coming from was a well-justified concern.

This book is particularly concerned with the sources of the food – the plants and animals – consumed by Jamaicans. I recognize that my approach leaves out much and that readers may wish for more on the sociology of consumption, on the role of food in society and religion, in festivals and rituals, and in politics and culture. There is enough in these subjects to make another book. Another alternative would be to focus on nutrition, in which case it would be best to begin with the diet, show how it has changed over time and trace it backwards to its components and their contributions to well-being. Yet another way of organizing the discussion would be to start with the different styles of food preparation or "dishes" and their combination in meals. This has much in common with the structure of cookbooks, but it makes difficult an analysis of origins and the story of particular ingredients, which is my primary objective.

The two main sections of the book deal separately with plants and animals. Plants are grouped together according to the parts of them used as food: roots, stalks and leaves, fruits and seeds. Generally, all aspects of a particular plant have been discussed together, and the plant as a whole has been located with the part that dominates its use. Animals are treated in the same way, putting all of their uses in a single place but grouping them into biological families. These accounts are not watertight but overlap and interact in many ways, most obviously where separate ingredients are combined, as in ackee and saltfish or rice and peas. A practical outcome of this arrangement is that occasionally it is has been hard to decide where something should best be placed. Soup, for example, typically combines diverse ingredients. My solution here is to discuss such subjects where they first appear in my scheme or where they seem to have the greatest weight. So, ackee and saltfish appears in the chapter on fruits under ackee, and the patty is in the chapter on seeds, giving priority to pastry and flour. In the event that picking where something might be found in the book is less than intuitive, I recommend the index.

The sources available for the study of Jamaican food history are diverse. I have depended on a number of essential reference works for basic information. The most substantial of these are F.G. Cassidy and R.B. Le Page, *Dictionary of Jamaican English*;

C.D. Adams, *Flowering Plants of Jamaica*; Alan Davidson, *The Penguin Companion to Food*; *The Cambridge World History of Food* edited by Kenneth F. Kiple and Kriemhild Coneè Ornelas; Harold McGee, *On Food and Cooking: The Science and Lore of the Kitchen*; *The New Oxford Book of Food Plants* edited by J.G. Vaughan and C.A. Geissler; Jonathan D. Sauer, *Historical Geography of Crop Plants: A Select Roster*; and Olive Senior, *Encyclopedia of Jamaican Heritage*. These works are arranged alphabetically or have detailed indexes. I have provided precise citations for them only when I have quoted directly. For statistical data after 1961, I have relied on the statistical website of the Food and Agriculture Organization of the United Nations (FAO, at http://www .fao.org/waicent/portal/statistics_en.asp), and I have not attempted to cite this source in every case.

This book was written in the History Program of the Research School of Social Sciences, at the Australian National University. Before joining the university in 1996, I lived for near thirty years in Jamaica, but I began systematic research on the history of food only in the middle of the 1980s. For funding my research, I thank first the Research and Publications Committee of the University of the West Indies. A fellowship from the John Simon Guggenheim Foundation facilitated early progress, as did an exchange visit to Johns Hopkins University. A short-term residency at the John Carter Brown Library provided an opportunity to work through its excellent collection of seventeenth- and eighteenth-century literature. Some material was collected in the course of research for another project, supported by the Australian Research Council. Research assistance was given by Verity Archer, Gregory Bowen, Marsha Coore, Kirsty Douglas, Nick Fuller, Paul Halloran, Michele Johnson, Mathew Johnston, Murna Morgan, Elizabeth Pigou-Dennis and Karen Riley. I am particularly grateful to Daryl Adair, who alerted me to the recent construction of an online searchable version of the *Gleaner*, Jamaica's oldest newspaper, founded in 1834. For advice and information, I thank Karl Aiken, Gordon Briscoe, Laurence Brown, Carollin Carol, Lizzie Collingham, Desley Deacon, Stanley Engerman, Valerie Facey, Ivan Goodbody, Jerry Handler, Ken Ingram, Howard Johnson, Joyce Johnson, Trevor McClaughlin, Charmaine McKenzie, Jill Matthews, Brian Moore, Veront Satchell, Barry Smith, Margaret Steven and Swithin Wilmot. Howard Johnson provided me with a copy of the indispensable 1957 *Farmer's Food Manual*. Kay Dancey prepared the maps and diagrams. William Murray created the illustrations, using the real materials wherever possible, together with the author's photographs and published examples. Samantha Hallett, Curator of Natural History at the Bristol Museum and Art Gallery, facilitated my use of the John Lindsay papers. I thank the directors of the museum for permission to reproduce as colour plates a selection of Lindsay's images. In Jamaica, I benefited from numerous field trips, particularly botanical and ethnobotanical ventures with John Rashford and Thera Edwards. Farmers and gardeners contributed much to my knowledge, many of them now forgotten, but including Mr Barrett at Castleton, Basil Burke, Theophilus Gayle, Douglas Hall, Jerry Harrison, Fay Sylvester and Cyril Vassell. Many cooks – far too many to mention here – made possible my experience of Jamaican food. For readings of the manuscript and parts thereof, I thank Merle Higman and Linnette Vassell.

CHAPTER 1

WHY DO JAMAICANS EAT WHAT THEY EAT?

Eating and drinking are as essential to survival as breathing, but we can do without food the longest. Awake or asleep, we breathe by reflex, taking into our nasal passages more or less whatever happens to be in the enveloping atmosphere. There is no real choice because a few minutes without oxygen will kill. We can, in contrast, be more choosy about what we put into our mouths and what we swallow. The ingestion of food and drink can be postponed for days, giving ample time to make decisions about what to consume and how and when to prepare it. The materials we choose to ingest are drawn from nature, ultimately from soil and water, though often substantially transformed. Only a small proportion of what might be efficiently eaten is consumed; most of what is available in nature is rejected. Different peoples choose to include different things in their diets and will regularly express disgust at the foods consumed by others, making food choices a defining characteristic of cultures and cultural difference. Thus food and drink have become part of elaborate systems of production and distribution, and have given rise to "national", "regional" and "ethnic" cuisines. People proudly identify with the foods said to define them. Cookbooks codifying these cuisines have become numerous and popular.[1]

Within the Caribbean, the cultures and societies scattered across the islands and rimland have generally been defined by language and, since European colonization, by political association. Projects of unification and federation have been few. Similarly, although the idea of "Caribbean food" has sometimes been advanced as a unifying feature of life, and although this regional definition has sometimes been located within a broader idea of "creole food" or "creole taste", individual islands and states have clung to – even created – notions of difference and uniqueness.[2] "Jamaican food" is one such variety.

WHAT IS JAMAICAN FOOD?

"Jamaican food" means at least three different things. First, it means the food commonly consumed by Jamaican people, the major items of the diet. Second, it refers to foods, whether common or uncommon, that are more or less uniquely associated with the island. Third, it denotes those foods which have been attributed a defining role in the creation of national identity. The three meanings overlap, but each has its own particular significance. The first is fundamental and points directly to the central question of why Jamaicans choose to eat what they do. The second and third are not necessities, and are wholly missing in some societies. Jamaicans, however, aggressively assert the uniqueness and superiority of some of the island's foods and enjoy having the label "Jamaican" attached to them. Modern Jamaicans have also embraced the idea of iconic "national" foods and accept them as part of their identity.

Jamaica has given its name to a variety of products, almost all of them food items. The index to the *Cambridge World History of Food*, published in 2000, includes eleven "Jamaica" or "Jamaican" items: Jamaica banana, Jamaica cherry, Jamaica ginger, Jamaica pepper (pimento or allspice), Jamaican Blue Mountain coffee, Jamaican cucumber, Jamaican gherkin, Jamaican hot pepper, Jamaican plum, Jamaican red pepper and Jamaican sorrel. Jamaica's eleven items compare to thirteen Italian, nine French, eight Scotch (this number including the Scotch bonnet pepper), six English, four Barbados, three Cuban and sixty Chinese. Every one of the Jamaican items derives from a plant and, with the exception of ginger and coffee, every one is a fruit. This matches the weight given to fruit in this book. Although Jamaicans might find several of the items in the list unfamiliar or might know them better without the "Jamaican" label, the frequency with which the eponymous label occurs would not surprise. It fits neatly with the people's readiness to assert the superiority of the island's products and to claim them as the best of their type in the world. Such claims, particularly for ginger and banana, were common already by the nineteenth century.[3] Jamaicans believe that an orange grown in Jamaica tastes better than an orange grown anywhere else, and "Jamaica orange" is not even included in the list. Nor is "Jamaica rum", which gained its reputation even earlier.

Around the world, it is possible to find the "Jamaican" label attached to food products such as chocolate, biscuits and buns the ingredients of which have nothing to do with the island. Thus "Jamaican" has a visibility in the world food system, derived from its unique products and its status as an exotic, tropical-flavour icon.

The idea of national Jamaican foods is relatively recent. When independence was achieved in 1962, Jamaica had for over three hundred years been a colony of the British and, more immediately, part of the short-lived West Indies Federation. Constitutional independence went together with a search for the symbolic trappings of nationalism, including a national anthem and a flag. The ancient coat of arms was retained but given a new motto: "Out of Many, One People", a sentiment shared with other societies but having peculiar significance for Jamaica's creolized population. National heroes, first proposed in 1952, were identified and embodied in statuary. Four national emblems were installed, one of them a food: a national bird (the doctor bird, a species of humming-bird), a national flower (the lignum vitae), a national tree (the blue mahoe) and a national fruit (the ackee). The lignum vitae was indigenous to much of tropical America, the blue mahoe was originally shared with Cuba and the doctor bird was uniquely Jamaican. Of the ackee, a committee reported: "This fruit selected itself and whilst not indigenous to Jamaica, has remarkable historic associations. It was originally imported from West Africa, probably brought here in a slave ship, and now grows luxuriously producing each year large quantities of edible fruit." Furthermore, although the ackee tree was grown elsewhere in the Caribbean and Central America, only Jamaicans recognized its fruit as an edible crop.[4]

What characteristics made the ackee such an obvious choice and how did they relate to its role as a food? All of the national emblems, including the ackee, were chosen for their natural beauty or aesthetic appeal. According to the committee, "The ackee tree produces a rich, savoury fruit, consisting of an outer pod of vivid scarlet which opens in a petal-like fashion when mature, displaying two or three bright cream-coloured arils topped by a shiny black seed." It was a prettier fruit than most of its potential rivals, with its multicoloured components, but there was a sinister side to the ackee that went unmentioned. Eaten before properly ripe, before the pod opens out and exposes its arils, the ackee can be poisonous, even fatal. It is rarely eaten raw but entered the food system of Jamaica in combination with other ingredients, notably saltfish.[5]

The set of national emblems introduced in 1962 did not include a national dish, though the idea was occasionally proposed. In the longer term, many – perhaps most – Jamaicans came to believe that the combination of ackee and saltfish held this status. In part, the dish achieved this status by association with the ackee's new-found symbolism, but the idea had much deeper roots. In the decades leading up to Independence, the development of concepts of national identity was driven by ideologies, notably Garveyism and Rastafarianism, but was also in ambivalent opposition to the "foreign" and the metropolitan. The growth of the tourist industry contributed to a separation between what were often called "native dishes" and the European and North American meals commonly served by hotels. Occasionally, from the 1910s to the 1930s, tourists even complained that they were denied the chance to sample native dishes, including local fruits and vegetables – and ackee and saltfish. Comparison was made with the Bahamas, where visitors enjoyed "such delectable dishes as baked turtle, the national dish of the Bahamas". One visitor, having spent some months in Jamaica in 1935, complained of the lack of "distinctively Jamaican" offerings and argued that the island's "national dishes", national dances, national music, and national costumes and festivals were hidden from the tourist because Jamaicans were ashamed of them. Questions also emerged about the distinctiveness and uniqueness of the dishes. In 1936, the director of agriculture, A.C. Barnes, commented that "our two most charac-teristic dishes in Jamaica – saltfish and ackee, and rice and peas – were composed mainly of imported foods".[6]

The political and cultural movement towards self-government, along with the great labour disturbances of 1938 that pushed Jamaica to universal suffrage, contributed substantially to the making of Jamaica's national dish. Discontent was traced to malnutrition, and popular taste linked to creole culture. In August 1939, the black middle-class reformer Amy Bailey published a key statement in support of the Jamaica Progressive League's slogan "Jamaicanising Jamaica". Bailey accepted the view that "things Jamaican were despised, unhonoured and unsung", and that "Jamaican foods were in the main apologised for if they had to be set before foreigners". It was only when "the foreigners found them delightful and delicious, and said so loudly, that their status rose". Bailey understood these negative attitudes as those of "snobs" rather than "the ordinary people", and felt that many in the middle class refused to eat local foods "simply because they had not on a foreign label". She focused her argument on food, she said, "because not only is it the maintenance of life, but it is true also that the kind of food we eat and our attitude to it does much to develop and reveal our national character". One practical means of Jamaicanizing Jamaica was to eat more "Jamaica foods": it was therefore essential not to "despise our yams, our cocoas, our plantains, our bananas, our bush-tea, etc.". Bailey went on to say, "It is significant that our two national dishes – ackee and saltfish, and rice and pease, should depend on two imported materials for their composition. This entirely sums up our national consciousness. I should like to be told of another country where its national dish has a foreign element. The thing is a contradiction in terms; and yet we have complacently accepted this attitude year in, year out. It may be difficult, but we shall have to find national dishes that are wholly Jamaican. Let the pepper-pot be one, boiled with native pork or beef." She called on schools and entrepreneurs to create "an appetising Jamaica dish".[7]

Bailey's reference is the earliest identified to ackee and saltfish as a national dish of Jamaica. It is important for that fact, coming almost twenty-five years before Independence and the declaration of the ackee as national fruit, but Bailey made the claim only to criticize the status of the dish, and to pair it with another national dish, rice and peas. Her use of the label went little beyond the earlier discussion of native dishes, though associating the dish with national character and consciousness was original.

Rice and peas seems never to have been in the running for national dish, probably because it was insufficiently unique, but these two dishes – ackee and saltfish, and rice and peas – had great longevity as the iconic foods of Jamaica. As early as 1930, writers had acknowledged the status of rice and peas by calling it "Jamaica Coat of Arms".[8] Other "national dishes" were also mentioned from time to time. In 1944, for example, it was said that curried goat had "long become a national dish in Jamaica", but when it was served at a United Nations Fair held at King's House, it was supplied from the "Indian" rather than the Jamaican stall. In February 1962, shortly before the announcement of the national emblems, Desmond Henry wrote from college in Pittsburgh reflecting on the role of the traditional turkey dinner in the American celebration of Thanksgiving and proposing that Jamaicans should consider "the eating of a common dish to be regarded as our national dish of independence". He promoted curried goat for the role, but realized that many would think ackee and saltfish a more obvious choice. Although ackee and saltfish was sometimes still referred to only as "a Jamaican national dish" rather than as *the* national dish, its position was already firmly established.[9]

After Independence, ackee and saltfish was commonly called Jamaica's "national dish", and repetition proved enough to convince many that the dish had in fact been formally installed. The usage persisted strongly.[10] Although a few maintained the idea that "curried goat and rice" or "curried goat and rice and fried plantain" could claim the role, most quickly accepted statements that claimed boldly, "Jamaica's national dish is ackee and codfish", or that referred to "our national dish of salt-fish and ackee". Even the most cautious were comfortable declaring "salt fish and ackee is almost a national dish". Some claimed that ackee and saltfish became the national dish because of its "taste", but also because it symbolized the bringing together of the dangerous ackee with saltfish, "the food of slavery", through "the ingenious creativity of the transplanted Africans". Thus "the gastronomic lesson of ackee and saltfish" was seen as the Jamaican's capacity to turn "difficult, negative situations into something positive and constructive".[11]

The promotion of ackee and saltfish and the persistence of rice and peas emphasized the combination of elements from other places, a combination often referred to as symbolic of Jamaica's population history and reflected in its national motto. Each of the dishes combines imported and naturalized ingredients – ackee and saltfish sui generis, and rice and peas as a version. Both include other ingredients, but the dishes are distinguished by their combinations, sometimes referred to as a marriage, suggestive of a bringing together of contrasted elements in a complementary and rewarding fashion.[12] Plants provide the larger part of the ingredients, with rice and peas combining two kinds of seeds, and ackee and saltfish combining fruit and fish. With the exception of the fish, the ingredients came from domesticated plants; and with the exception of the ackee, the ingredients sometimes arrived as imports. The saltfish almost always came through the ports and the rice generally did so as well. Not one of the elements is endemic, meaning indigenous and unique to the island, though ackee (and, to a lesser extent, peas) is naturalized. These facts led some to dispute the choice, echoing Bailey's complaint of 1939, and to propose fresh alternatives, such as jerk pork and roast yam, fried fish and bammy, or the Jamaican patty, and even to ask, "Why have a National Dish at all?"[13]

The idea, advanced by Bailey and others in the 1930s, that the middle classes of Jamaica disparaged local foods is only a partial truth for earlier periods. In spite of the colonial, dependent status of the island, many enjoyed the local foods and promoted their qualities. During the period of slavery, down to 1838, it was the wealthy whites, with access to resources and leisure, who most often declared their favourite foods, and these were to some extent shared with other inhabitants. This might be called a "creole" taste. Contemporaries generally thought in terms of "delicacies", meaning the particular treats that set Jamaica off from other places and cultures. Maria Nugent, famous for the journal she kept as wife of the colony's governor, recorded that when visiting Montego Bay in 1802, they were served an abundant dinner that "consisted of every Jamaica delicacy: and we were pressed to taste of so many things that it was scarcely possible to avoid being stuffed into a fever".[14] The enthusiasm of the creoles for their foods was great.

What were the "delicacies" of Jamaica? The English naturalist Philip Henry Gosse said in 1847 that "of the three superlative delicacies of which the natives of Jamaica boast, the Ringtail [pigeon] holds the undisputed pre-eminence. The others are the Fresh-water Mullet, and the Black Land-crab".[15] These three featured regularly down to the end of the nineteenth century, though not all commentators placed the ringtail at the top of the ranking (Figure 1.1). Edward M. Earle, in 1895, claimed that the ringtail pigeon had been "associated by a once famous governor with the black crab and the mountain mullet, as the three great delicacies of Jamaica". The governor has not been identified, and may be confused with Gosse, but these three certainly gained strong symbolism. Visitors to the Jamaica International Exhibition of 1891 could purchase a handkerchief depicting, in its four corners, "the mountain mullet, the black crab, the ringtail pigeon, and the turtle". Into the 1930s, the ringtail pigeon and "the famous mountain mullet" were paired as treats of the Blue Mountains, along with "the well known 'jerked-pork', than which there is no finer delicacy to be had anywhere".[16] Individual references to delicacies, discussed in the following chapters, added to the list manatee, iguana, macaca, coco plum and banana fig. Most of these are no longer on the menu and some are indeed now regarded with disgust. Twentieth-century additions included oyster, conch, lobster, cowfoot, cow tail, tripe and the patty.

It is striking that all three of the delicacies named by Gosse were animals, and specifically identified as such: a bird, a fish and a crustacean. They were known for themselves, not as meat or as elements of prepared dishes. They were also, more particularly, all wild animals that had to be hunted in their natural habitats. None was domesticated, and all were endemic. This endemism contributed powerfully to an identification as truly "Jamaican", a characteristic lacking in the later national dishes. Furthermore, down to the middle of the nineteenth century and the introduction of refrigeration and canning, none of these three delicacies was transportable. Anyone who wanted to taste them had to travel to Jamaica, the only place where these animals were to be found, dead or alive. As cooked and eaten, the ringtail, the mullet and the crab were little transformed; they were not generally combined with other substantial ingredients. One important rival was the turtle (a reptile), but it was not endemic to Jamaica, could be shipped live to Europe and was the subject of elaborate transformation in preparation for the table. Similarly, the pig, once barbecued or jerked, might be considered a Jamaican food, but its status as such came from the mode of its preparation rather than from the animal itself, which was introduced and feral rather than endemic.

Only in the later nineteenth century did delicacies begin to emerge that were not endemic and not animal in origin, and that were identified as dishes rather than as

Figure 1.1 Ringtail pigeon, black crab and mountain mullet

animals or plants. This broadening of the concept of the Jamaican delicacy was closely associated with the development of tourism, contrary to the later view that tourists ate only foreign food. Visitors at this time were encouraged to sample "Jamaican food" and even to take some of it home with them. "Jamaica Delicacies" promoted by a Kingston agency beginning in 1878 included turtle soup in canisters, roast cashew nuts, tamarinds in kegs and an extensive range of "Jamaica Preserves". The latter consisted of fruits in syrup (ginger, lime, orange, pineapple, tamarind, mango, cashew, coco plum and water-melon), guava jelly, syrups, pickles (including mountain cabbage), peppers (including Scotch bonnet) and crystallized ginger, cashew, coconut and tamarind. These delicacies were offered alongside natural specimens or "Jamaica Curiosities", such as fern albums, ornamental seeds, fish-scale work and hummingbirds. To these were soon added solid-ified turtle soup in tablets, Jamaica black crab paste, Jamaica pepperpot, Jamaica honey and cassava cakes. In 1900 an advertisement declared, "Tourists and others visiting Jamaica should take away with them, some of the world renowned Blue Mountain Coffee and Special Reserve Rum." The coffee and the rum have remained favourites of the duty-free shops, but plant products, particularly fruits, came to dominate the list. By 1906, tourists were being encouraged to purchase a box of "Jamaica Oranges" as the best possible souvenir.[17]

As well as the shift from animals to plants, an increasing proportion of the foods thought characteristic of Jamaica came to derive from naturalized or imported sources rather than the endemic or indigenous. This shift went together with an increasing tendency, beginning in the later nineteenth century, to identify the delicacies of the island in dishes of "Jamaican food" that combined disparate ingredients in unique ways. Since the fundamental elements were not unique to Jamaica, it was necessary to distinguish the "Jamaican" contribution as the manner of preparation and the character of the combinations. The change can be seen in the foods tourists were encouraged to sample. For example, in 1905 the English visitor Bessie Pullen-Burry said of the Rio Cobre Hotel in Spanish Town that "island delicacies are often served up here to innocents abroad – turtle steaks, turtle soup, snooker [snook], calepeva, or jack-fish cooked in various ways; of cod-fish and ackie let the stranger beware! Jamaican vegetables are numerous and good; cho-cho, garden egg, ochra, plantain, yams, and yampis are frequently given. Guava jelly served with cocoanut milk is delicious, so too are the fruit salads; cassava biscuits, and cake sometimes flavoured with island ginger are by no means despicable; a cup of Blue Mountain coffee will complete a typical Jamaican meal."[18] Similarly, a tourist guide produced by the Jamaica Tourist Association in 1911 listed, as "Jamaica delicacies" that the visitor should try, "pepper pot soup, salt fish and ackee, turtle, in its various forms, mountain mullet, black crab, bald pate and ringtail pigeons".[19]

Independence and the informal crowning of ackee and saltfish as Jamaica's national dish pushed that dish to the fore in touristic promotion, with rice and peas hanging on tenaciously to second place. As one 1968 vacation guide said, "Continental [North

American] cuisine is everywhere but some local dishes worth sampling are rice and peas, salt fish and ackee (an exotic tree vegetable); curried goat and rice, jerked pork, run down (made from salted shad and coconut oil), mackerel and bananas, pepperpot soup, fricasseed chicken (actually a thick stew) and roast pig. Jamaica also has a wide variety of the usual and unusual in fruits." In 1984 tourists were told, "No one should leave Jamaica without tasting our pepper pot soup, ackee and saltfish, rice and peas, run-dung and curried goat, to name a few."[20] By now, Gosse's three delicacies – ringtail pigeon, mullet and crab – had largely disappeared, and introduced plants and animals dominated. The creole had displaced the indigenous.

The indigenous survived best among the fruits of Jamaica, and to a lesser extent among the seafood. For example, in a particularly enthusiastic guidebook published in 1973, Government Archivist Clinton Black told tourists that Jamaican meals "derive a peculiarly exciting character from the local fruits and vegetables served". His emphasis was on "exotic" ingredients rather than on methods of preparation. At breakfast, he said, the tourist could "discover a new world of delight in the bowl of fruit which usually accompanies the breakfast tray – the citrus and banana, pineapple and golden pawpaw, the strange, pimply sweetsop, the rich, purple, milky starapple, the sweetcup, naseberry, . . . and, of course, the mangoes". Lunch and dinner offered avocado, chocho, okra, callaloo, eggplant, ackee, plantain, green banana, peas and beans, cocos, sweet potato, yam and breadfruit. Black then explained that among the "truly Jamaican dishes", the "best known and best loved" were the two combinations ackee and saltfish and rice and peas. Other "esteemed local dishes" mentioned were "curried goat, roast suckling pig, turtle stew, black crabs baked in their backs, curried lobster . . . ; and a very local quartet: dip-and-fall-back, stamp-and-go (also called bragadap – a fish fritter), Solomon Gundy, and mackerel run-down". Of Jamaican soups, Black thought particularly delicious those prepared from gungo and red peas and from pumpkin, and he placed pepperpot soup "in a class by itself". He continued:

> Visitors should also try such local taste-sensations as cassava wafers; the bulla, a big, round, flat, gingery cake; the plump, pink, plantain tart; the delicious, grated-coconut tart, sweetened with brown sugar and flavoured with nutmeg which goes by the odd name gizada; the cut-cake and grater-cake, both coconut and sugar confections; the tasty concoction of parched Guinea corn, heated with sugar, coloured and rolled into balls called coction; the crisp biscuits; the sugar cake called wangla, because they were made originally with sesame seeds; tie-teeth, made by boiling sugar syrup until it becomes tightly elastic; stagger-back, a candy noted for its toughness, hence its other names iron-cunny and Busta-backbone, in compliment to Sir Alexander Bustamante; finally "the big, soft, glittering, molasses-scented, almost chocolate-brown richness and lingering sweetness upon the tongue" of wet sugar, the cheapest grade of Jamaican sugar.[21]

As to drink, Black promoted Jamaica rum – "the world's best" – but also encouraged the tourist to go beyond it: "Meet your favourite fruits again in drink form: coconut water (not milk), fresh, cool from the green nuts; orange juice, lemonade, ginger beer and pineapple drink; rich nectars made from the tamarind and granadilla, the guava, soursop, mango and pawpaw."

Alongside the shift towards characteristic dishes as the defining icons of Jamaican food, a number of food festivals were established near the end of the twentieth century, designed to promote particular foods or food places. Most celebrated a single food. A yam festival was held first in 1997, in Trelawny, followed in 1998 by a spice festival in Ocho Rios. In 2000, breadfruit festivals were held both at Bath and in Hanover, a busu festival in Portland, a fish festival at Port Royal and a jerk festival at Boston. A curry festival was initiated at Savanna la Mar in Westmoreland in 2001 and, the following year, a sugar cane festival at Petersfield, in the same parish, and a sweet potato festival in Manchester. The Jamaica Tourist Board promoted some of these events and advertised the Jamaica Spice Festival held in the tourist town of Ocho Rios as a "culinary festival" that celebrated "the best of Jamaica's cuisine through the ages". The promoters claimed that the "traditional foods" of Jamaica were "often spicy and national favourites include ackee (from Ghana), saltfish, curried goat and bammy cake, an irresistible pepper pot soup and very spicy jerk pork and chicken which is a Jamaican invention that has become a worldwide favourite". The St James Pineapple Festival was established at Stone-henge in 2004, and 2005 saw the Bakers and Pastry Makers Fiesta inaugurated in Kingston, as well as an ackee festival in Linstead and a third breadfruit festival, this time in St Mary.[22]

Another indicator of the character of "Jamaican food" is which items are carried by Jamaicans when visiting family and friends overseas and which are craved by Jamaicans of the diaspora. There are no systematic studies of these things, but it is at least certain that food items have been prominent in the Jamaican products taken on board ships and aeroplanes. From the seventeenth century, English absentees appreciated turtles and preserved fruits, as well as Jamaica rum. Rum has remained important, but the speed of air travel and the post-1945 diaspora encouraged the carrying as well of roast breadfruit, fried fish, ackee, hard-dough bread, water crackers, bun, cheese, spices, season-ings and fresh fruit. Few of these items derive from endemic species; most gain their "Jamaican" character from their methods of preparation as much as from their essential ingredients. Often the items have equivalents in the places to which they are carried but the Jamaica version is thought superior and thus worth the trouble of transporting: a fish seasoned and fried in Jamaica tastes better than one fried in London or New York. Here can be seen an emphasis on pure preparation that supplanted to a large extent the earlier focus on the endemic and unusual and on the animals of the wild.

The period since Independence was marked by a continuing struggle between local and foreign tastes and styles. The era of democratic socialism in the 1970s saw a political move towards the local. Thus the minister of agriculture, Percival Broderick, declared in 1977 that "as a nation, we need to acquire tastes and preferences for our locally produced foods, which are always available, and to be well versed in the ways of preparing traditional as well as new and interesting dishes".[23] There was a clear feeling that the "traditional" dishes of the island were being lost and that it was these long-established specialties that truly constituted Jamaican food. This philosophy faced severe challenges in the following decades, particularly as a consequence of changes in the regulation of overseas trade, but at the same time "Jamaican food" demonstrated a good deal of fight. Towards the end of the twentieth century, this domestic struggle was assisted by a growing enthusiasm for the cuisine by outsiders and by the nostalgia of Jamaicans in the diaspora. A local cookbook published in 1998, *Jamaica: Finest Taste for All Seasons*, told readers, "The popular Jamaican trend in cooking is to revive our grandparents' favourite recipes."[24] In 2000, Minister of Agriculture Roger Clarke advocated production of the ingredients needed to make "the forgotten indigenous recipes of our traditional palate", because the "old-style Jamaican foods and herbs enhance the healthy lifestyle". Brave attempts were made to encourage Jamaicans to "eat what we grow and grow what we eat", a slogan reminiscent of the 1930s and 1940s, though in a pure form this was increasingly difficult and historically it did not neatly match the traditional foods of the island.[25] There was a disjunction between what was considered characteristic of Jamaican food and what Jamaicans actually consumed.

Today the most popular food of Jamaicans is chicken, generally fried. By 2005 the status of chicken was such that "in some circles it is referred to as the 'national meat'".[26] Chicken had, in fact, achieved this status by the 1980s. As early as 1965, school caterers found chicken "in any form" proved a favourite, whereas the "national dish" of ackee and saltfish had to be removed from the lunchtime menu for lack of takers – an indication of generational change. In the island's markets at the same time, ackee and saltfish and rice and peas were the foods most eaten by vendors, with ackee and saltfish served at any of breakfast, lunch and supper, and rice and peas at every meal other than breakfast. Yet the new popularity was insufficient to qualify chicken as truly "Jamaican food", because it was a popularity shared with many other modern countries and because chicken failed to connect with any unique element of Jamaican food culture.[27] One way of cooking chicken, jerk, can be regarded as truly Jamaican, but it remained relatively marginal to total consumption. Although fried chicken was not, therefore, proposed as a national dish or as an island delicacy, it could be declared good-tasting, and highly desired, because it referenced the Jamaican taste for salt and spice.

Popularity is interesting, but it does not necessarily help in identifying the common foods and dishes of a community. The food systems of most nations contain hundreds or even thousands of items. Only a small number of these are defined as delicacies or favourites and, more surprising perhaps, a small proportion of the total available items accounts for the majority of the food actually consumed. Studies from the late 1990s showed that the most commonly eaten foods in Jamaica were, in descending order, orange, cabbage, ripe banana, carrot, chicken, rice and peas, callaloo, sardine, tinned mackerel, plain rice, yellow yam, corned beef, tomato, green banana and lettuce. The most common dishes prepared at home were chicken (fried, brown-stewed or curried), rice and peas, plain rice, beef (roasted or stewed), fish (brown-stewed), pork (stewed), stew peas (made with kidney beans), boiled yellow or sweet yam, dumplings, green bananas, soups, and porridges (cornmeal, oats, rice or banana).[28] In this ranking, there was some association between the popularity of a food and its frequency of consumption, but the association was far from perfect. Although oranges, ripe bananas, cabbages and carrots played a large role, they did not constitute a meal or dish of "food". Necessity shines through as a vital driver of what people actually ate. Only chicken and rice and peas were both common and popular, and only rice and peas belonged to the more exclusive class "Jamaican food". Ackee and saltfish was completely missing, defeated by the high cost of the imported fish.

This disjunction between popularity, commonness and identity was equally strong in earlier periods, though the pattern was different, with chicken notably absent. For example, in 1936 Dr Dahlia Whitbourne, school medical officer, described "the ordinary diet in Jamaica", saying, "Rice and cornmeal are apparently our cheapest foods and most used, because they swell in cooking and provide large quantities of food at a cheap rate." She also found a heavy reliance on "starchy foods of vegetable origin", with yam, potato, coco, breadfruit and green banana "consumed in large amounts" and generally eaten with only "a piece of some salted fish as a savoury" rather than with meat and vegetables. Other common foods of the 1930s were mango, callaloo, susumber and okra. Among the "favourite dishes" were rice and peas and stew peas. A quantitative estimate of the wartime diet in 1942, prepared by the economist Frederic Benham, showed by comparison with contemporary nutritional ideals that Jamaicans consumed large amounts of "ground provisions" (the starchy staples) and pulses, average amounts of fruit, vegetables and sugars, and inadequate portions of milk, eggs, fats, grains and meat.[29]

Substantial change occurred over the following twenty years, so that at Independence the consumption of cereals had increased to such an extent that they began to rival the steeply declining roots and starchy foods. Pulses and nuts also declined, but these were of minor importance. Big increases occurred in the consumption of sugars, fruits and vegetables, and smaller increases in meat, fish, eggs, dairy products and fats and oils. Food by this time accounted for about 60 per cent of total household expenditure in working-class households. Although root crops still contributed the larger weight, bread and flour provided more calories to the diet and took a larger proportion of household expenditure. The "poor man's staple diet" consisted of yam, green banana, breadfruit, sweet potato, maize, rice, white bread, sugar cane, fruit and a little saltfish or salt pork and fresh beef.[30]

Earlier descriptions, from about 1900, distinguished between the diet of town and country. In town, the "average" food of the common people – the poor – consisted of, "on two evenings of the week[,] herring, yam, bananas, sweet potatoes or breadfruit; on two other evenings salt fish, with the same ground provisions, soup on one evening and, perhaps, tripe on the other; then on Sunday there may be rice and pease, or a little beef". In the country, herrings were eaten four times and saltfish three times a week, or occasionally a vegetable soup with salt beef: "Now and again these people taste fresh pork; fresh beef they scarcely ever eat. Anything will do for their breakfast, a roasted potatoe, a few bananas or so. In the town the people may eat three farthings' worth of bread flavoured with a little sweetened water for breakfast. People in the country prefer bush-tea and chocolate – generally bush-tea – to coffee, not generally from taste but from its general cheapness."[31] It is only rice and peas that seems to have had continuity in its status, and only in town. However, there was an underlying continuity in the use of salt to season savoury foods. The salt came together with cured fish in 1900 but was later added as free salt. It was this saltiness that bridged the gap between affordability and taste.

During the period of slavery, the taste for salt was satisfied most often by salted and pickled fish, the one major food item imported and distributed as rations by the masters. Salt meat was uncommon, and fresh beef and pork were rare. The basis of the plantation slave's diet was the starchy staples yam, coco and plantain, most of the produce coming from grounds cultivated by the enslaved. Cassava, the root that had been the foundation of Taino diet, declined in importance. These staples were eaten with small quantities of saltfish, in much the same way as at the end of the nineteenth century. Rice and flour were rarely available to the enslaved, but Guinea corn (sorghum) and corn (maize) were important in some parts of the island. The now-classic dishes rice and peas and ackee and saltfish seem to have been unknown. Most dishes were prepared by slow cooking in an iron pot. Legumes and vegetables also went into these pots, but just how much is hard to know. Fruit was relatively abundant, and its range and variety significantly expanded in the later eighteenth century, but once again it is hard to know how much was consumed. Enslaved people living in towns generally received rationed allowances or cash in lieu of food, so they may have had greater access to items such as bread. Overall, the dependence on starchy staples and saltfish was similar in town and country. Shortages of salt provisions particularly caused complaint.[32] It was this taste for salt that most obviously provided continuity through to the twentieth century.

JAMAICAN COOKERY

To what extent is it plausible to talk of "Jamaican" methods of food preparation that might stand beside a taste for particular dishes and ingredients? Does it make sense to talk of Jamaican cooking or cookery as well as Jamaican food? The Jamaican motto, "Out of many, one people", adopted in 1962, was derived from the Latin *e pluribus unum* ("out of the many, one"), which, in turn, had its origin in a poem ascribed to Virgil, in which a ploughman prepares his lunch, grinding together green herbs and white garlic in a mortar, the original ingredients losing their individual properties and merging into a single, new colour.[33] The food metaphor is as strong in this blending as it is in the idea of the "melting pot". In Jamaica, the analogy was not lost, and the motto was quickly turned around to read "Out of one country, many cuisines". In an article published in 1964, Chinese cooking was said to be characterized by its "unusual sauce combinations", Syrian cooking by its lavish use of olive oil, French cooking by its "seasonings" and Indian cooking by its curry. In this model, both African and English modes were put to one side. On the other hand, the Culinary Arts Competition, established at the first anniversary of Independence, was seen as "an unusual, benign form of nationalism", bringing to the fore fufu, callaloo and pepperpot – "Jamaican" dishes.[34]

Does the preparation of Jamaican food require distinctively Jamaican tools and technologies? Some of the food items identified as "Jamaican" have been simply unique – the mountain mullet, the black crab and the ringtail pigeon, for example – and have been defined directly by their existence and use in the island. None of these require a method of preparation to give them their status. Other Jamaican foods have gained their character as dishes – ackee and saltfish and rice and peas – but the status of these similarly depends more on combination of ingredients than on their mode of preparation or cooking. Common ingredients can be cooked in combination or by themselves, and can be given a special character by the mode of preparation. But distinctive taste can indeed be derived from the materials used in the process of cooking and from the nature of the cooking process itself.

Naturally, foods consumed raw and fresh were subject to the least complicated technologies of preparation. The mango eaten beneath its tree required nothing more than a stone thrown to knock it to the ground. Some foods could be stored and eaten later in their raw state, but generally raw and fresh went together. Many fresh ingredients are not palatable raw, however, and in some significant cases they are positively unhealthy. Instead, physical and chemical transformations are required before they can be eaten. Historically, the most important agent of transformation is heat, producing food cooked on a fire. To "cook" is to transfer energy from a heat source to food ingredients. Heat is the essential element, making digestible and palatable things that would otherwise not be safe or attractive to consume.

Heat can be applied to food in several ways, enabling a variety of styles or methods of cooking. The three mechanisms of heat transfer are conduction, convection and radiation. Conduction involves the direct exchange of thermal energy, from one particle to another, the efficiency of the transfer being determined by the materials of the vessels used. Convection is the mixing of warm and cold particles, as in the boiling of liquids. Radiation is pure thermal energy, received direct from the sun or from microwaves. In cooking, all three mechanisms often work together, though one will dominate and create a distinctive product and taste, the result determined largely by the level and speed of heating.[35] The range of possible methods is extended by the use of different combinations of water, air and oil and by the physical qualities of the vessels in which the cooking is done. Thus the choice of cooking methods is determined by the available technology, by the available vessels and cooking materials and by the available heat sources, as well as on the available ingredients and the cook's work-time regime.

The most ancient cooking method is probably the roasting of food over an open fire or glowing coals. Jamaica is closely associated with two methods of roasting: barbecue and jerk. *Barbecue* is supposedly a Taino word; the earliest citation in the *Oxford English Dictionary* comes from Hickeringill's *Jamaica Viewed* of 1661.[36] To barbecue was to roast or broil meat, sometimes stuffed and basted, over a smoky fire. A "barbecue" might also be a raised wooden platform above a mosquito-repelling smoky fire, for sleeping on outdoors or for drying and preserving meat. Further, in a Jamaican English usage also dating to the seventeenth century, "barbecue" is the open paved terraces on which green crops, especially coffee beans, are spread to dry. The historical use of the word in Jamaica thus relates both to the cooking of meat by radiation and smoking, for immediate consumption and also as a means of preservation. Smoke was originally used when salt was not available. As well as a method of low-temperature slow cooking, smoking introduces complex chemicals that inhibit the growth of microbes and gives a characteristic flavour.

Jamaica's best-known contribution to cooking methods is "jerk", a technique derived directly from the barbecue and roasting of meat. Again, the word is believed to be of Amerindian origin, perhaps reaching Jamaica through the Spanish *charqui*. In this form it relates to "jerky", or dried meat, cured in long, thin strips, sometimes without salt. Cuba and Argentina were among the important producers of "jerked beef" into the nineteenth century. In Jamaica, "jerk" was applied traditionally to pork (as discussed in chapter 10) and, down to the early twentieth century, involved smoke-drying and salting. Soon after 1900 the technology of jerk began to change, the meat being more heavily seasoned and brought closer to the radiant heat of a partially enclosed bed of glowing coals. New meats, particularly chicken, were introduced, and were cooked as urban street food using a 44-gallon (200-litre) metal drum cut down the middle to make semi-circles, hinged on one side, with a grate or wire mesh fitted over the bottom section, the whole mounted on a stand. Thus jerk came closer to high-heat barbecuing than to slow smoking. Preservation or curing ceased to be an important objective and the street version became a variety of fast food. In the later twentieth century, as a result, the essence of jerk was attributed more often to the unique seasoning than to the technology. Bottled wet and packaged dried "jerk seasoning" appeared on supermarket shelves and was soon promoted as a Jamaican food taste that could be applied in kitchens across the world.[37]

Jerk and barbecue may have a distinctively Jamaican character, but for most of the island's people, for most of their history, the roasting and broiling of meat was relatively insignificant in the repertoire of cooking methods. Roasting is not an efficient use of fuel or ingredients. It is also risky. The food may be overdone or, worse, charred beyond edibility. When enslaved people ate meat it was generally stewed. Only planters and penkeepers had the resources to consume large quantities, roasted and broiled in their kitchens using metal gridirons and spits over glowing coals in brick or stone fireplaces or fried in skillets and iron pans.

Frying in oil at a high temperature cooks by both conduction and convection. As with roasting and broiling, the foods most commonly fried are meat and fish. Because of this, and because special iron pans and cooking oils were required, frying was a method used in Jamaica mainly by the elite before the twentieth century. Braising and fricasseeing were popular variants, the latter using more elaborate sauces. In Jamaica, by the 1970s, frying in shallow fat was the most popular method of cooking whole or filleted fish. In the last decades of the twentieth century, fried foods became more generally popular, especially deep-fried foods produced on a commercial scale. Fried chicken emerged as the favourite food. As a technique, deep frying is nearer to boiling than to pan frying, but in each case the cooking temperature is high.[38] At the household level, deep frying requires a profligate use of oil.

Some of the cooking oils and fats used in Jamaica were imported. Olive oil has been the most important of these over the long term, and was favoured by the Spanish. The British also imported lard, butter and, after its invention in 1869, margarine. By the twentieth century, locally produced coconut oil predominated. Coconut oil is highly saturated and therefore stable and an excellent source of fat.[39] Although unsaturated fats are advocated as healthy, saturation is a benefit in preventing the deterioration and rancidity of food after cooking. Fats and oils in general produce crisp textures and attractive flavours and they can be heated to high temperatures and so serve to efficiently transfer the heat from the pan to the food. Different fats give different flavours. The use of oil as a cooking medium has the disadvantage that it begins to decompose if the temperature becomes too high – at the smoke point – with disastrous results.

These deleterious effects – rancidity, decomposition and deterioration – are aggravated by particular interactions between food and fat (or other cooking mediums) and the materials from which the utensils have been made. Iron, for example, speeds up the decomposition of fats and makes frying difficult, but iron pots and skillets were the only vessels available for most of Jamaica's history, for rich and poor alike. Coarse handmade pottery could not be used successfully in frying, and ceramics came generally to be used only as ovenware, subjected to diffused heat. Stainless steel, invented in 1912, became popular because it resists rusting, but it conducts heat less efficiently than iron and is more expensive. To hinder rusting, iron may be seasoned with cooking oil, giving the material a continuing role among the poor. The local availability of aluminium in Jamaica after 1950 led to the casting of a variety of cheap utensils with good conductivity. When the material is unalloyed, however, the interaction between cooking food and aluminium tended to discolouration and gave such pots a negative reputation by the 1980s. Non-stick (Teflon) surfaces, which reached Jamaica soon after Independence, were applied to Dutch ovens as well as to frying pans; these pre-empted many of the problems but were slow to find acceptance.[40]

Baking (in ovens) depends on radiation from the walls of the enclosure and on air convection. The temperature may be much lower than for roasting, making baking the more energy-efficient oven method, though still less efficient than boiling. In addition to this relative lack of efficiency as a means of heat transfer, baking needs an air-tight container, heated externally, with easy access. These requirements make it a complex cooking technology – yet one to which simple solutions were sometimes attempted.

In the long term, the most common cooking method in Jamaica was boiling, with its variants steaming and stewing. It was these three processes for which the handmade clay yabbas and iron pots of the enslaved, and of the peasantry well into the twentieth century, were used. Boiling could be achieved even without a pot. For example, today's Maroons boil food in bamboo joints. A small hole is dug, a fire is built in it and a green bamboo joint filled with water is placed upright in the centre of the fire. The water quickly comes to the boil and vegetable food is rapidly cooked. The disadvantage of the method is that the bamboo burns from the outside, so that it can be used only once. A more complex method, called "earth boiling", was used by enslaved people who escaped from their masters to "take refuge in remote and uncultivated mountains". The first step was to make a hollow in clayey soil and smoothe the surface of the cavity. This was lined with plantain leaves; water was poured in and food added; the contents were covered with plantain leaves, sticks and a layer of earth; and a fire was lit on top to cook the food. This method seems largely lost to memory in modern Jamaica, but experimental cooking has shown it to be viable. Boiling, whatever the technology, cooked much of the food eaten by Jamaicans, over the long term. Claude McKay described a "formidable" celebratory dinner of the early twentieth century in the novel *Banana Bottom*, in which almost every dish had been produced by boiling – "a great old-fashioned platter of akee and codfish done in butter, boiled ham, a boiled chicken in rich sauce and a selection of the many vegetables that feature the peasants' table: two kinds of yam, the yellow afou and the delicious starchy white; boiled breadfruit; boiled plantains and boiled sweet cassava".[41]

Boiling depends on convection currents and requires only a low temperature. Because the entire surface of the food is in contact with the turbulent boiling water or its steam, this is a highly efficient method of applying heat. Boiled food also has the advantage of needing little monitoring. It is hard to spoil because once water has been brought to the boil, it maintains a constant temperature. All of this, and the simplicity of the materials needed, made boiling the preferred method in many circumstances. It was, in particular, one of the most popular ways of cooking the flesh of mammals: stewing enabled the use of old animals and salted meat, making the meat tender and the coarse "food" and vegetables palatable, for which long simmering, rather than strict boiling, was essential – hence the saying "A stew must smile but never laugh".[42]

JAMAICAN TASTE

Modern Jamaicans are considered excessive consumers of both salt and sugar, with a craving for salty foods and a highly developed sweet tooth. The taste for sweetness they share in particular with the British, and indeed it was the development and strength of this taste that fuelled the imperial project, slavery and the plantation. The origins of the Jamaican taste for salt may similarly be traced back to the period of slavery and remained firmly in place, giving way only reluctantly in the later twentieth century when salt acquired an increasingly unhealthy image. The attack on salt began in the 1930s, when nutrition came to the fore as an issue of public policy. In October 1938, after the disturbances, it was noted that Jamaicans had long eaten and liked "salted things" and that "now, however, we are hearing that some of these foods are full of malnutrition, which may be the case. But the difficulty is how to prevent a man from eating what he enjoys, and to induce him to take instead to tomatoes, cucumbers and cabbages."[43]

Sweetness has grown to become an even stronger component of Jamaican taste than saltiness. At the end of the twentieth century Enid Donaldson could claim, "To say that most Jamaicans have a sweet tooth is an understatement." This taste is reflected in the island's many recipes for sweets and desserts, and Jamaicans often have eaten their fruit combined with sugar and lime, with milk and sugar (sometimes combined in sweetened condensed milk), or stewed in tarts, pies, trifles and ices. A cookbook published in 1998 contended that "a variety of desserts are used to accompany our local spicy and often highly seasoned local dishes, because Jamaicans, on the whole, have a weakness for sweets". Sweet-tasting snack foods are more popular than salty items. Traditionally, sugar came from an abundant consumption of fruits in season: as the cookbook said, "The sweeter the fruit, the more it is liked." Even Jamaica's citrus was more sweet than sour. Donaldson argued that "Jamaica's sunny climate seems to develop the sucrose in the citrus, giving rise to the Jamaican phrase 'so sweet it scratch yu throat', which describes sweet citrus".[44]

In spite of the central roles played by sweetness and saltiness in the diet, these tastes have not been used to characterize Jamaican food. Rather, Jamaican food is most often described as "spicy", with the variations "very spicy" and "spicy hot".[45] These terms point directly to pungency as the central principle, whether connected with salt or with sweet. In 1963 Mary Manning Carley said the "Jamaican working man . . . considers 'white man's' food to be dull and tasteless, and likes his meal to be well seasoned with hot red peppers (chili) and native onion (scallion)". She said also that "creole cooking has long been famous – though to some English palates it is rather rich and too peppery". Here she meant the delicacies that only the rich and the middle class could afford, rather than the "tasty meal from simple ingredients" eaten by "the poorer people". The Jamaican cook's "liberal application of spices and peppers" was "originally introduced to disguise the taste of preservatives", thus adding a further dimension to the saltiness of much of this food. At a world food fair held in Germany, in 1997, Jamaica was represented by Blue Mountain coffee, coffee liqueur, Pickapeppa sauce, spices and teas, as well as rum cakes, biscuits, "our typical Jamaican seasonings" and "the traditional jerk seasoning".[46] It was the pepper, spice and seasoning that seemed characteristic.

Jamaicans' enthusiasm for spicy, peppery, highly seasoned food was not always shared by outsiders, and this helped construct the uniqueness of Jamaican taste and

Jamaican food. For example, Esther Chapman, an Englishwoman who came to Jamaica in 1935 to edit the *Jamaica Times* and who founded the *West Indian Review*, declared in her 1952 tourist guide that "there are two distinct diets in Jamaica. The native taste is for a limited number of special dishes. The European (and American) taste rarely adapts itself to these eating habits. As in most tropical countries, there is a preference for highly seasoned dishes, complemented, oddly enough, by a taste for heavy starch foods. These will not please the visitor as a rule and, while some of the Jamaican dishes are very good indeed, they are usually regarded by the outsider as giving spice to the normal menu rather than as the basis for a steady diet."[47] Other, earlier, outsiders were more broadly disparaging, dismissing Jamaican food without reference to spice and pepper. Thus Bessie Pullen-Burry said she could not "acquire a taste" for avocado (which she thought tasted like "soft soap"), pawpaw, or mango (with "the flavour of turpentine"), and she abstained from eating saltfish and ackee.[48]

Whereas *bourgeois visitors often failed to appreciate the island's foods,* Jamaican taste was shared broadly across Jamaica's highly segmented social structure. Even in the period of slavery, Creole whites often included food among the things Jamaican that defined them. Bryan Edwards, for example, at the end of the eighteenth century, found that many of the food crops of Europe thrived in Jamaica and were often "of superior flavour to the same kinds produced in England", yet he also declared, "To my own taste, however, several of the native growths, especially the chocho, ochra, Lima-bean, and Indian-kale, are more agreeable than any of the esculent vegetables of Europe." Green plantain roasted was "an excellent substitute" for wheaten bread, he said, "and universally preferred to it by the negroes, and most of the native whites". As to fruit, he thought "perhaps no country on earth affords so magnificent a dessert", the largely indigenous "elegant fruits" being as varied as they were excellent.[49] When a coachman told Pullen-Burry he would like to go to England with her, she responded that he would not like the cold weather or the food, perhaps recognizing a mutual incompatibility. The coachman declared, said Pullen-Burry, "Give a man out yar salt-fish and akee and roasted bread-fruit far breakfast, and he trow away all de ham and eggs into de street." Travelling in England in the early 1930s, H.G. De Lisser found that "salt fish and ackee is like Greek" to the English, whose style of cooking was "not quite the Jamaica style". Foods prepared in England, said De Lisser, "do not taste as well to the Jamaica palate as do our Jamaica dishes".[50]

Jamaicans were also said to share a preference for "putrid" beef and saltfish. This, it was claimed, was common to Maroons, domestic servants and local whites. Dolf Wyllarde, another Englishwoman visiting Jamaica at the beginning of the twentieth century, said of saltfish and ackee that this "Jamaican confection can reach a suggestion of decay and rotting flavour which is enough to drive a European out of the room", though it was a favourite with the creole planter class. The American writer Edmund Wilson, visiting in 1969, was equally disparaging of the food and people of Jamaica, and when poisoned by his first plate of saltfish and ackee, reflected that "the fish – cod, probably imported – did smell rather rank". Criticism was not confined to foreign visitors. When Rastafarians rebuked meat-eaters amongst their ranks, they singled out the "man wha get dem terrible mackrel from de middle a de barrel – de one yuh coulda smell from a distant". On the other hand, it has to be recognized that in some societies (including some today), premium prices have been paid for "high" meat and people have taken trouble to make their own fermented fish sauces. Putridity can be a matter of taste, rather than something that needs to be smothered by spice.[51]

What does the Jamaican appreciation of spice and pungency imply? Some argue that spiciness or pungency is not enough to distinguish the taste of Jamaican food because West Indian food in general shares this characteristic, because it is equally true of the food of West Africa, or because indeed all of the food of the tropics is highly spiced. Subtleties of difference, however, are found in the Jamaican use of "seasoning" derived particularly from Scotch bonnet pepper, combined with thyme, scallion, garlic, onion, tomato, black pepper, lime juice, pimento and salt. In terms of the human capacity to appreciate taste, though, this may be just too subtle. Fresh hot peppers are seen as "the hallmark of Jamaican cooking", and it would seem fair to say that overall the "spicy hot" label is appropriate enough. Again, this is a characterization shared with modern West Africa, the ancestral home of most Jamaicans and the recipient of hot peppers from the West.[52]

FLAVOUR

The concept of Jamaican "taste" has thus far been considered in everyday terms, pointing both to choice and preference and to the sensory experience of consuming food. In food science, however, "taste" is a precise technical term. The more comprehensive experience is called "flavour". As P.A.S. Breslin puts it, "Our perception of flavour is comprised of the sensory combination and integration of odours, tastes, oral irritations, thermal sensations and mouthfeels that arise from a particular food." In this way, flavour brings together the "chemical senses" of smelling and tasting with the senses of feeling (including chemical irritation) and seeing. It is the pleasure associated with eating that brings enjoyment and contributes to the development of specific preferences and tastes.[53]

The study of the complex components of flavour extends into many technical areas, with important nutritional, psychological and commercial implications. It is necessary here only to explore some of the major features that can contribute to a more complete understanding of the characteristics of Jamaican food.

In deciding whether or not to eat something, we are directed first by the eyes, then by the nose and finally by the mouth. Our responses determine whether to try the food at all, to have a second bite or take the chance again on another day.[54] At one extreme, we experience the emotion of disgust (literally, an offence to good taste), which serves the valuable survival purpose of preventing contact with toxic, diseased and unwholesome matter, and induces a feeling to retch even without actual contact or eating. At the other end of the scale, the stimuli can be so positively powerful that we eat excessively, perhaps even leading ultimately to the stomach's rejection of the seductive, tasty food. Fortunately, most of what we assess for its food value and flavour falls somewhere between these extremes.

Because food comes from soil and water, it contains a complex mix of nutrient and non-nutrient substances, whether processed or consumed raw. Even a banana contains more than three hundred non-nutrient chemicals. In order to cope with the ingestion of all these elements, the human gut or gastrointestinal tract is necessarily a large, complex and dynamic organ. As is now well known, physiological responses can vary significantly. Some individuals are allergic or sensitive to common foods (as in those for whom drinking milk leads to diarrhoea), others suffer metabolic food reactions to common foods only when those foods are consumed in excessive quantities or are poorly processed (as in unripe ackee leading to vomiting), while yet others experience pharmacologic reactions (such as hallucinations after eating nutmeg).[55]

Appearance and colour are vital. For example, we generally reject fruit with an "unripe" or false colour. An ackee that has not opened to display its arils is potentially deadly. Unripe sugar cane and sorghum may also be toxic, as may yam and some of the common pulses, sometimes even leading to death. Rejected with less logic are oddly shaped or sized items. Modern food producers and marketers use these principles quite strictly, in deciding what customers will select from their shelves. Much good food is dumped because it is wrong in size, shape and colour, or, alternatively, it is enhanced and modified to match consumer preferences. Meat is displayed under fluorescent light to make it appear more attractive. The characteristic red-pink colour of uncooked cured, salted meat similarly serves as a test of its attractiveness and edibility. Modern Jamaicans readily reject foods offered for sale that look strange, particularly frozen meat.[56]

Of all the elements that combine to create flavour, the most powerful is aroma. Whereas taste is confined to the tongue's responses to just five sensations, humans discriminate between several thousand different odours, and the nose can detect substances in truly minute concentrations. The logic of this contrast is that it is efficient for survival to be able to smell food before we taste it. The volatile constituents of food that make up aroma evaporate rapidly or pass off as vapour, coming up into the nose, whereas the non-volatile chemical compounds are trapped in the food substance, waiting to be sensed by the tongue. It is the volatiles that give foods their "unique, personal identity and character".[57]

Aroma is grounded in culture as well as biology, leading to olfactory typologies that classify substances as either edible or inedible, raw or cooked. Roasting is the most obvious example. The characteristic aroma of roasted coffee beans, for instance, is formed largely by the process of roasting; the aroma is almost completely missing in green beans.[58] The same principle applies to roast beef or jerked chicken. The enticing aromas that waft mid-morning from Jamaica's country bakeries speak of freshly baked bread – soft and crisp, hot and delicious even without butter or (avocado) pear – a complex set of perceptions reaching the nose, surpassing by far the blandness of a bag of flour.

Volatile aroma compounds interact with non-flavour food components to create flavour perceptions. Simple carbohydrates represented by sugars and starches, for example, can, through binding, serve as the carrier substances for flavours, and particular foods and food ingredients interact in complex ways to release the volatile constituents. When food is chewed, chemicals from its surfaces dissolve in the saliva and make contact with sensory receptors in the tongue and the mouth. Warmed to body temperature, the volatile chemicals are pumped into the retronasal cavity and thence to the nose, contributing to overall flavour perception.[59] Hence the intense nasal sensations experienced when drinking soup in which a hot Jamaica pepper has burst.

In humans, the anatomical aspect of taste is found in the sensations elicited by the chemical stimulation of specialized taste receptor cells on the edges of the tongue, the soft palate and the throat (Figure 1.2). As already noted, taste is more easily segregated than aroma, with sweet, salty, bitter and sour long having been thought to constitute the complete range. Since the 1980s, the existence of a unique fifth taste has been accepted. This is umami, identified prototypically as MSG (monosodium glutamate) and indicated by a savoury, meaty, brothy taste, present in natural foods such as tomatoes, mushrooms, milk, meat and tuna. Umami-specific receptors have been identified in taste buds at the back of the tongue.[60] Although Jamaicans consume MSG, the concept of umami as a separate taste has little currency. A vegetarian cookbook published in Jamaica in the 1980s argued, without mentioning umami, that "fat" needed to be added to sweet, salt, sour and bitter, "because fats add a certain sense of satisfaction with a meal that most people interpret as a taste". Sweet and salty were the appealing tastes, it was observed, but had to be used in moderation, with natural sources always preferred.[61]

When we eat, we typically encounter a diversity of tastes produced by chemical stimuli, including sugars (sweet), amino acids (umami), sodium chloride and other salts (salty), alkaloids (bitter) and acids (sour). In general, humans willingly accept and ingest the sugars and amino acids, whereas bitter-tasting substances provoke rejection reflexes. The preference for sweet taste is present at birth, serving to lead the infant to sources of nutrients and energy.[62] Sweet and bitter serve as metaphors for nutritious and toxic,

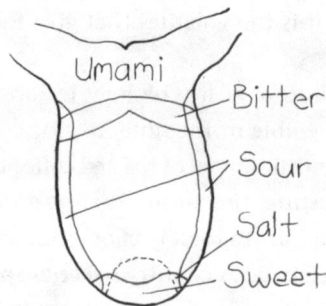

Figure 1.2 Taste zones of the human tongue

but the messages the tongue sends the brain are not always clear and sometimes are mixed. Studies show a relationship between sweet and bitter taste mechanisms and compounds, suggesting a connection between sweet and bitter taste receptors. A wide range of chemical compounds taste sweet, stretching far beyond the sugars (sucrose, fructose, glucose), and these compounds vary in the quality of their sweet taste. There is also great diversity of compounds that taste bitter. This occurs in the perceived "sweetness" of bitter cassava, as discussed in chapter 3. Interactions among salty, sour and bitter tastes are also important. Saltiness can suppress bitterness, whereas salts and acids (sour) enhance one another at moderate concentrations and bitter and sour combine erratically, varying with particular foods and concentrations.[63]

In psychological terms, although taste is identified by the qualitative descriptions salty, sweet, sour, bitter and umami rather than by terms such as hot, pungent or astringent, it is difficult to separate the elements. This is why a person who loses the sense of smell will say food has no "taste". Taste can vary according to the physical state of the eater. For example, pregnant women experience physiological changes in thirst and appetite and a reduced acuity of taste, driving cravings and aversions.[64]

Pungency lies outside taste and smell, and is closely associated with chemical sensitivity to temperature and pain in the cutaneous membranes of mouth and throat. Hot peppers create a burning sensation, citric acid has a sting and tartness, peppermint has a sharp coolness, and carbonated drink tingles and prickles. All of these sensations can be broadly termed *chemesthesis*. They are not mere chemical irritants but, says John P. Bartley, possess "a qualitative richness that may even surpass taste". The classic pungent spices used to flavour food, such as ginger and pepper, each delivers a quite different sensation, but it is their characteristic irritants that help make them some of the best-liked flavours. While more than one hundred aroma compounds have been detected in ginger, for example, these "contribute only partially to the flavour impact since fresh ginger is valued both for its aroma and for its pungency".[65]

A general feature of these chemesthetic stimuli is that at low concentrations they produce tastes and odours, and only at higher concentrations do they trigger pungency. It is also significant that individuals experience desensitization over time, leading to the consumption of larger doses to maintain the level of perceived pungency. The eating of hot peppers in quantity, a practice much loved by Jamaicans, is a clear case of this relationship, a variety of "benign masochism". Historically, where spices were scarce and expensive, the serving of pungent, almost painful food was seen as an indication of the wealth and status of the host.[66] This was less true of Jamaica, however, where the taste for pungent spice was shared across social classes from quite early in the colonial history of the island. The poor and enslaved were effectively denied certain categories of meat, but pungent spices were readily available.

Because the most important function of spices is to flavour food and drink, the label "spice" is sometimes attributed to all the aromatic vegetable products used in this way, whereas more technical definitions restrict it to the "hard or hardened parts of plants, usually originating in the tropics and mostly used in a pulverized state, which impart an agreeable flavour and aroma to food and drink". Spices also serve as medicines, as fumigants and as preservatives, their odours overcoming the smell of unfresh food. Only thirty-six different herbs and spices are said to be generally recognized and commonly used in the modern world. In terms of money value, globally the most important are white and black pepper, followed by cloves, nutmeg, cardamom, cinnamon, ginger, mace and pimento.[67]

In recent times, the role of spices in seasoning otherwise insipid food has been replaced by the "artificial" creation of flavour by biotechnology. The practical methodology for this can be traced back to the manipulation of microbes in fermentation for the making of bread and beer and rum, but the science of these fermentations was not understood until the nineteenth century, and the isolation and controlled cultivation of microbes that could be applied to the production of flavour chemicals became possible only in the 1970s. When recombinant DNA technology became a central part of biotechnology it was applied first to pharmaceuticals, but then, in 1994, it was used to create the first genetically engineered whole food, the FlavrSavr tomato. Biotechnology was increasingly applied in the flavour and fragrance industries, though consumer resistance led to the development of more "bioflavours" derived from plant sources by fermentation and the cultivation of fungal spores, ones that could be distinguished from the feared "chemical" and "synthetic" products.[68]

CHOICE AND NECESSITY

In deciding what to eat, whether at an individual or a social level, "taste" is only one of many powerful influences. In theory, people should rationally choose those foods that deliver the best returns in nutrition and energy, but this does not always happen: the most nutritious foods may be the most expensive or the least palatable. Economic efficiency is equally important as a determinant of choice, as people balance the cost (in time and money) of acquiring particular items against the quantity and quality delivered. Storage and preservation properties are part of the measure of efficiency. Again, choices about what and what not to eat depend on cultural rules governing the acceptability of particular items. These rules may be broadly shared by a whole society or confined to smaller communities and sects. They are not a matter of individual preference but the product of group choice.[69] Overall, social and national food choices (and preferences) are controlled by a range of sometimes contradictory influences, including ecological, economic, political, social, cultural, psychological and physiological conditions that extend far beyond nutritional need and the sensory experience of eating and drinking. The idea that consumers are free to choose their own diets is an illusion, whatever the political and legal system in which they live, even though we are said now to live in an unprecedented era of choice.[70]

Materials ingested as food are chosen because of their capacity to provide nourishment to the body, but such choices are mediated by an appreciation of particular plants and animals for their medicinal qualities as well as of their characteristic taste and contribution to nutrition. Defining "food" is not as simple as it might seem, particularly because nutritional and medicinal attributes often overlap in a general concept of physical well-being. As Marjorie Grant Whiting has observed, it is common to find "not even a thin line of differentiation between food plants, toxic plants and medicinal herbs". For example, the bush tea traditionally consumed at the beginning of the day in rural Jamaica was often the major component of the morning meal but was regarded more as a treatment for indigestion or fever than selected for its taste or energy value. The fruits soursop, grapefruit, breadfruit and avocado are all believed to aid the treatment of hypertension. A willingness to risk the ingestion of "wild" plants or "weeds" finds its justification in the search for new and wonderful cures and tastes. Spices have often been appreciated for both their medical and dietary benefits – even while differing from other foods simply by being more powerful – and understood as a means of adjusting the diet. The overlap between the spicery and the pharmacy remains strong, even though *spices can sometimes be harmful as well as helpful, serving "dangerous tastes".*[71] The combined business "druggist and grocer" remained common in Jamaican commerce well into the twentieth century.

Who made the choices that determined the composition and character of Jamaican food, and why did they make the choices they did? It was a process that both demonstrated and tested the power of the imperial state and its agents. Plants and animals were introduced to the island, but their insertion into the food system depended on the reactions and the initiatives of the colonized people at the bottom of the social hierarchy. In Jamaica, especially during the period of slavery, the system of food production and the introduction of plants and animals were controlled by the planter class. At the same time, enslaved people sometimes took an active role in plant introductions and, because they dominated the actual processes of production and supply and served as the island's cooks, they were in a position to make decisions that ultimately proved influential in creating the character of Jamaica's cuisine.

As well as seeking new sources of food and regulating production, since the middle of the nineteenth century governments have increasingly intervened to regulate the purity and safety of food. Here we are talking strictly about the self-conscious and intended preparation and consumption of particular organisms. Occasional cases (like a tooth in a patty) may be well publicized when they occur in public eating places, but these are far outweighed by the fly in the soup or the cockroach in the rice and peas that cause only minor unpleasantness. On the other hand, people have always consumed small amounts of unwanted materials, unnoticed. Modern industrial food systems are unable, or find it too costly, to remove all of these unwanted things and attempt only to meet acceptable standards. Even the US federal Food and Drug Administration, often regarded as a model for Jamaica and elsewhere, merely sets out maximum allowable counts of, for example, insect parts and rodent excreta in cornmeal and numbers of maggots in canned mushrooms. Most of this material is not harmful, so long as it is subjected to heat during processing.[72]

Government regulation distinguishes between the many toxic substances that occur naturally in common foods in non-threatening proportions and the "contaminants" added to foods that make it potentially hazardous by adulteration. The former are tolerated more readily than the latter. Traditional and common foods that have been consumed for many generations are generally assumed to be "safe" and are not subject to the close toxicological scrutiny that is applied to, for example, new pharmaceuticals. Attempts to prohibit traditional foods meet with strong resistance, however hazardous the chemistry of the substances, as demonstrated clearly by the banning of ackee by the United States. Yet Jamaicans do follow high standards of household food safety and, by the beginning of the twenty-first century, concerns had led some to discontinue the purchase of animal products such as chicken, beef, pork, milk, yogurt and ice cream.[73] Such decisions were based on external knowledge or on the appearance of foods rather than on flavour. The items were left on the shelves.

Compared to most other animals, humans have learned to select from a wide range of plant and animal species and varieties. Some choose to eat only plant material. Few are strict carnivores. As Marvin Harris puts it, humans share with other omnivores, "such as pigs, rats, and cockroaches", the ability to "satisfy our nutritional needs by ingesting a very broad variety of substances". Humans are also unusual in often eating dead rather than living plants and animals, and in cooking their food. At the same time, they are quite selective about which parts of plants and animals they consume, rejecting much of what is included in the harvest. For example, potentially edible parts of plants are regularly discarded in processing, and fisheries throw away "nonconventional" species rather than attempt to encourage their consumption or have them made into processed fish products.[74]

Looked at from the point of view of the vast range of potential foodstuffs found in nature, the dietary choices of most humans are very narrow, in spite of human omnivory. Some potential foods are ignored because they offer too little return for the effort or cost required to exploit them. In other cases, exploitation may seem to involve unacceptable damage to the natural or social environment. Further, markets may be distorted by political or entrepreneurial decisions, imperial policies and international trade agreements.

Plants and animals enter the human food system in different ways. They may be hunted and gathered from the wild, or farmed and domesticated. Thus there are essentially three levels of choice involved: whether a plant or animal is good to eat, whether it can be efficiently farmed or reared, and whether it is worth the trouble of domesticating. Farming and rearing mean simply the creation of appropriate environments in which plants and animals can be grown productively and harvested easily. For example, plants can be cultivated on chosen soils and fenced, or fish raised in ponds. Domestication requires more active human intervention and is the first step towards selection. Genetic change in plants is controlled through the choice of seeds and planting material, and it is humans who make the choices about which animals can reproduce, how they are cared for, and how and on what they are fed. Domesticated plants and animals supply the greater part of the food consumed by modern humans, but it is striking that of all the possible plants and animals that might have been chosen for domestication the number actually chosen is so small. Of approximately 7,500 species of grasses worldwide, only 30 have been subjected to human production strategies. Of the roughly 100 species of cassava spread through the neotropics, just 1 was ever domesticated. Of the extant species of large non-carnivorous mammals (about 150), 1 in 10 has been domesticated, of birds (10,000 extant species) about 1 in 1,000; for fish the proportion is even smaller. Further, although the domestication of some animals has been highly successful (as, for example, cattle and poultry), in other cases (such as the manatee and the mountain mullet) it has been much less so. The major domestications that matter for the Jamaican food system all took place far away and long ago, most of them complete more than five thousand years before the present, in Asia, Africa, Mesoamerica and South America.[75]

Decisions to eat particular plants and animals have something to do with nutritional efficiency and much to do with culture. For example, most grasses, mosses, algae and bark are eaten by humans only in extremis, in times of starvation and catastrophe, because they deliver little in nutrition and energy relative to effort. Distinctions between "weeds" and "vegetables" are harder to explain. Most difficult of all are cultural differences in the use of animals as food. One man's meat is another's poison. Hans Sloane, pondering the question in the first volume of his *Voyage*, published in 1707, acknowledged the relativity of taste and noted that, for example, "persons not us'd to eat whales, squirrels, or elephants, would think them a strange dish; yet those us'd to them, prefer them to other victuals".[76] Once a pattern of preferences has been learned, it can become quite rigid and long-lasting. It is this conditioning that enables the development of distinctive diet and cuisine, shared by all or most members of a community. It provides the basis for "Jamaica food" as a unique experience, however scattered and diverse the origins of its ingredients.

Food taboos, particularly cultural variations in the consumption of particular animals and of animals generally, seem hard to explain once viewed on a global scale. Although most living creatures are defined as inedible and their consumption is prohibited either consciously or unconsciously, a small number are eaten by humans on a large scale. Pig, cow, chicken, horse, camel, dog and fish, for example, have all been eaten with avidity by some cultures and avoided by others. Goat, on the other hand, is effectively free of prohibitions but nonetheless has only a small role in world consumption. It is impossible to explain these choices simply in terms of availability, cost, nutritional and health values, physiology or even taste. In practice these factors come into play only after an animal has jumped the cultural hurdles of prejudice and customary rules. Once established, prohibitions are difficult to overcome because they are associated with disgust and revulsion, and eating such disgusting food is likely to be a highly emotional experience, associated with nausea and even vomiting.[77]

Jamaica has found a small role in recent studies of strange and exotic eating practices around the world. On a relatively mild note, Robb Walsh, the American author of *Traveling Jamaica with Knife, Fork and Spoon*, opens his book *Are You Really Going to Eat That?* with a search for the world's hottest peppers, and finds most of them in the Caribbean, including Jamaica, with its Scotch bonnet. More confronting is the selection of foods covered by Jerry Hopkins in his *Extreme Cuisine*, many of which would disgust Jamaican taste. In his section on poisonous plants, Hopkins includes both cassava and the ackee, describing the latter as "a sort of 'national dish' in Jamaica" – one that can kill if not treated properly. People ate the fruit, he said, simply "because it tastes good", like most of the other items on the "extreme" list that were so readily rejected.[78]

Few Jamaicans are strict vegetarians, and the Jamaican Vegetarian Society was not established until 1984. Many prohibitions and choices are almost universal, based on learned cultural attitudes rather than nutritional value or economics. Religion plays a role in these choices, but only ambiguously. For example, the Jewish community of Jamaica has not remained faithful to its strict tradition, whereas the new religious movements of the twentieth century have proved more successful in raising varieties of prohibition and preference.[79] Seventh-Day Adventists avoid pork and shellfish. Among Rastafarians, it is commonly argued that "ital" – "natural", "organic", "fresh" and "living" – foods should be consumed "in their natural state without any artificial ingredients or chemicals", rather than dead things. Rastafarians consider all meat harmful, but revulsion is particularly provoked by the eating of unclean animals, notably pigs and scavengers such as poultry and goats. Fish is included in the prohibition but less strictly. The long association of salt with meat and fish in Jamaica results in a related rejection of salt as seasoning – as a dead thing – to be replaced with fresh hot peppers and other herbs. The most important provision is that everything consumed should be of "natural, organic origin". Rasta may argue that "the Creator 'sweeten' and 'salt' dose ting Himself. So de mango doan need no sweeten, de yam doan need no salt." Nature did all this perfectly, and Rasta respected this "naturality" by using pepper to "sweeten" their food. They came to apply a broad understanding of the wholeness and wholesomeness of the natural world, rather than pursuing theological directives such as the lesson offered by Lot's wife's being turned into a pillar of salt. Within these rules, individuals practise considerable freedom in making their choices.[80]

Alongside vegetarianism and similar food-prohibition practices is the concept of "meat hunger", in which a craving for flesh foods is strong, specific and unrelated to general shortages of food. Meat hunger is generally found in Africa, where some societies may regard a meal lacking meat as hardly worth eating and as a social failure. The appetite for meat has come to be associated, both by science and more broadly, with the physiological desire for fat in the diet, but this connection is relatively recent, forming part of a "nutrition transition" characterized by a shift away from starchy roots and coarse grains to meat, milk, sugar and oil.[81] In modern Jamaica, the question "What's for dinner?" generally implies "Which animal, or part of an animal prepared in a particular way, are were going to eat today?"

CHAPTER 2

SYSTEMS OF SUPPLY

Choices about what and what not to eat and drink are made within the context of availability and existing technologies. What is available to be consumed depends in turn both on taste and on systems of supply. The modern supermarket presents an extreme example of availability and potential choice, offering in a single space a vast array of food items in various stages of preparation – from the raw to the cooked – set out temptingly for the consumer to handle and select. The construction of this seeming cornucopia is based on complex chains of supply that bring together the products of local and distant agriculture and industry separated from their original producers, environments and seasons of production. Before the introduction of the supermarket to Jamaica in the 1960s, systems of supply were more diffuse and more closely identified with individual producers and places, and they were more closely governed by the seasons. Generally, they delivered more limited choices, but this assessment must be qualified because modernization has often led to concentration on a single successful plant (such as wheat) or animal (such as the chicken) and to a reduction in the diversity of diets. In the longer term, the content and character of what came to be identified as "Jamaican food" depended on the peculiar construction of the systems of supply that developed in the island, governed by economics, knowledge, attitudes and taste. Thus, in order to understand the choices made by Jamaicans, it is necessary to set out these systems of supply.

Food can be obtained in three principal ways. First, people can choose to consume strictly from resources available in their immediate environments, eating what they collect, hunt or grow. Second, they can seek sources in other places, introducing alternative domesticated plants and animals but producing and raising them in their own locations. Third, they can trade in order to obtain food items that cannot be produced in the home region or that cannot be produced there as efficiently as they can be elsewhere. In the case of Jamaica, agricultural settlement and colonization, together with modern modes of transport and preservation, tipped the balance to the second and third modes. This was a pattern typical of many colonial places, but the actual choices of food sources and methods of preparation depended on factors beyond the crude fact of imperialism. While the island environment remained a factor, plant and animal introductions altered the available store of potential ingredients. Over time, technological change affected the relative costs of imported foods, preservation and preparation. Equally important were the settlement history of the island and the cultural contributions of its varied immigrants. However, human agency is only part of the story. Long before people came to the island, before they even knew of its existence, the food resource was being put in place by nature.

ISOLATION

Jamaica is an oceanic island, never connected to the American mainland or to its island neighbours (Figure 2.1). It emerged from the sea ten million years ago and gradually moved eastwards, away from the mainland. This isolation was a vital factor in determining the range of biotic resources Jamaica might support in the great sweep of time

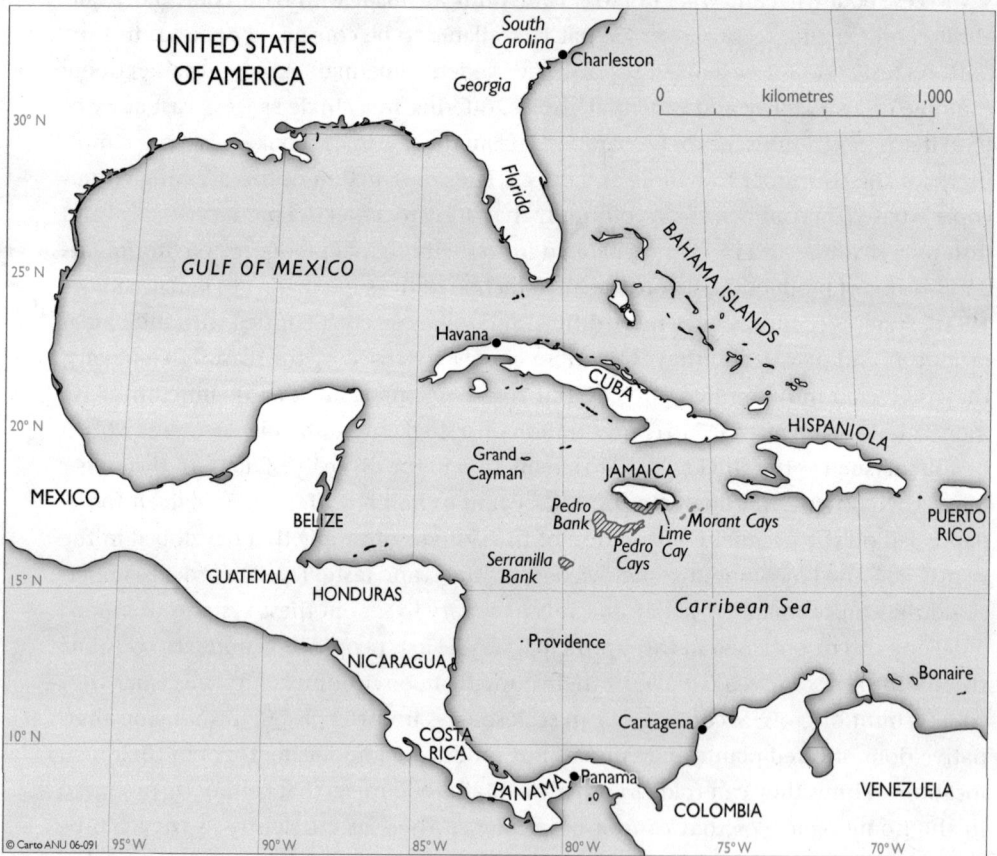

Figure 2.1 Jamaica in its region

before long-distance human voyaging. Sea fish and mammals were there before the island and evolved within the marine environment, but the emergence of the island altered marine conditions and created niches for new varieties of aquatic life. Marine species invaded land and freshwater sites and underwent surprisingly rapid transitions in lifestyle and speciation. Indeed, Jamaica provides an outstanding example of this process, the island's geographic isolation and highly varied ecological niches enabling the adaptive development of amphibians, crustaceans and reptiles and the evolution of many endemic species of animals and plants. Jamaica has a larger number of floral endemics than any other island in the Greater Antilles, only weakly related to the flora of Central America. The island hosts about 2,800 species of flowering plants (angiosperms) and 55 species of ferns (pteridophytes), with a high proportion of endemics.[1]

Winds and ocean currents carried birds, seeds and a variety of flotsam to the island, depositing their cargoes along the seashore. Land animals and plants had to cross the water to reach the island. This happened almost always by chance, and the difficulty of the crossing meant that survival was highly selective. The only plants and animals with a chance of reaching Jamaica were those already established in the coastal environments of the Caribbean rimland. Their chances of surviving the passage and successfully establishing in Jamaica were determined by physical and biotic characteristics. For example, could a seed float, and could it survive exposure to salt water over a prolonged period? Further, small islands generally support limited numbers of species of animals and plants because of the islands' limited ecological diversity and because of competition between species. The outcome for Jamaica was a surprisingly substantial level of biodiversity.[2]

Changes in sea level extended Jamaica's surface somewhat, but for the last ten thousand years the coastline has been effectively fixed and its area close to the modern measurement of 11,700 square kilometres. Around most of the coast, the offshore shelf slipped away steeply, though coral reefs continued to grow along parts of the north coast, and cays and banks provided relatively good conditions for fish and bird populations on the south. Streams were numerous but rarely substantial in spite of localized heavy annual rainfall.

The surface of Jamaica is characterized by considerable internal topographic variation associated with differences in soil and climate. To simplify, level alluvial lands occur as a narrow strip along most of the north coast and more extensively in the south. The eastern third of the island is dominated by the Blue Mountain range, which rises to 2,257 metres. The mountains are composed of metamorphic rocks, with thin soils on steep slopes, and experience heavy rainfall. Before the arrival of human beings, mountain forest and tropical rainforest covered this zone, down to the sea. The western interior regions are largely made up of elevated limestone, with rich, level soil in constricted interior valleys and with complex drainage systems. Seasonal rainforests, adapted to the soils, grew here. Some areas have highly developed karst landforms (the best known being the Cockpit Country); here the soil resources for agriculture are extremely limited. Elsewhere, as, for example, in the Hellshire Hills, minimal rainfall created harsh, serrated limestone surfaces, dominated by cacti and thorn bush (Figure 2.2).

Although Jamaica is a small and recent island on the world scale, by Caribbean standards it is large and old. The consequence is a relatively large proportion of endemic (unique) plant and animal species compared to the islands of the eastern Caribbean, though substantially smaller than is found in the larger neighbouring islands of Cuba and Hispaniola. Of the frogs found in Jamaica, 90 per cent of species are endemic, of lizards 71 per cent, of birds 22 per cent, of flowering plants 25 per cent and of ferns 13 per cent. The birds of Jamaica largely derive from North America but have a high rate of endemism due to genetic isolation. The endemism of land-bird species is greatest in the mountains, while endemism is relatively non-existent among water and shoal birds. Most of Jamaica's plants derive from Central and South American sources.[3]

Before the arrival of human beings in Jamaica, mangrove swamps and the marshes and lagoons on the coastal fringes created a rich environment for aquatic life. Birds and

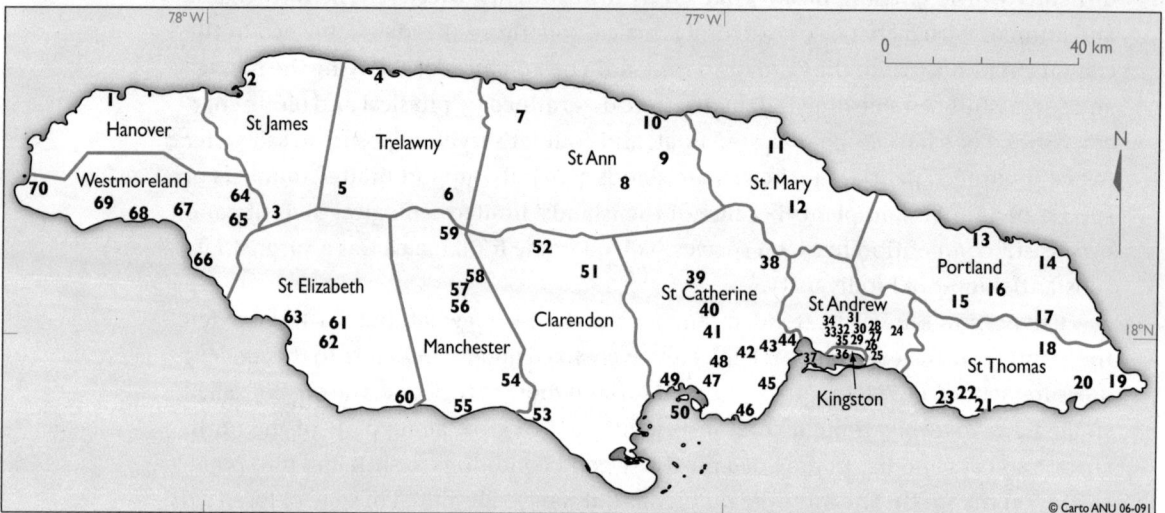

Figure 2.2 Jamaica parishes and places mentioned in the text. Key: Albert Town 6; Albion 23; Alligator Pond 60; August Town 25; Bath 20; Black River 63; Bluefields 66; Blue Mountains 15; Bog Walk 40; Boston 14; Brown's Town 7; Bushy Park 47; Cabarita River 69; Caymanas 43; Christiana 59; Cockpit Country 5; Constant Spring 34; Content 48; Corn Puss Gap 18; Cross Roads 35; Cuna-Cuna 17; Darliston 65; Falmouth 4; Ferry 44; Fullerswood Park 62; Glengoffe 38; Goat Island 50; Golden Grove 19; Gordon Town 28; Great Salt Pond 45; Gut River 55; Half-Way-Tree 33; Hellshire 46; Highgate 12; Hope Gardens 29; Hope River 30; John Crow Mountains 16; Kendal 57; Kingston 36; Lacovia 61; Lamb's River 64; Liguanea 32; Linstead 39; Longville 51; Lucea 1; Mandeville 56; Milk River 53; Mona 26; Montego Bay 2; Negril 70; Newcastle 31; Ocho Rios 10; Old Harbour 49; Papine 27; Pedro 8; Petersfield 67; Port Antonio 13; Port Maria 11; Port Royal 37; Port Royal Mountains 24; Rio Cobre 41; Salt Ponds 21; Savanna la Mar 68; Shooter's Hill 58; Spanish Town 42; Spring Plain 54; Stonehenge 3; Trout Hall 52; Walkerswood 9; Yallahs 22

manatee thrived, along with turtle, lobster, crab, oyster and inshore fish. Reptiles were also relatively successful in crossing the water; Jamaica has a rich variety of lizards, as well as alligators (caiman) and non-poisonous snakes. Land mammals, on the other hand, rarely survived the sea. Only a rodent, the hutia, seems to have arrived before human beings. Freshwater fish were also limited, compared to the variety of the marine community. In terms of potential food for human exploitation, the coastal zones of Jamaica were by far the richest resources.[4]

Human populations were slow to settle in Jamaica. The first identified groups arrived as late as AD 700 and represented the final stage of a migration from Asia, through the American land mass and, beginning around 7000 BP (before the present) in Trinidad, along the Caribbean island chain. These first people are commonly known as Island Arawak, for their language, or as Taino, for their culture. Those who first settled in Jamaica depended little on trade with the peoples and places they had left behind. Their settlements clung close to the coast, and they concentrated on exploiting the resources of the sea, particularly the mangrove marshes and littoral areas. Turtles, sea fish, shellfish and manatee were central to the diet. Wild land animals, including the hutia and a variety of birds, were eaten but played a minor role. Taino exploitation of the fauna of Jamaica depended on resources found in and around the island. None of these animals was introduced by the people and none was domesticated for food. On the other hand, the Taino arrived as fully formed agriculturalists rather than foragers or hunter-gatherers. They brought with them to Jamaica a range of plants of long-term significance, particularly tubers. These plants came from ecological niches similar to the environment encountered in Jamaica, having been domesticated and established in the Caribbean rimland. Adaptation was simple and cultivation practices easily transferred.

Taino agriculture, using a system of shifting cultivation known as *conuco*, was directed mainly at the production of root crops such as cassava and sweet potato but also included corn and cucurbits. Forest was cleared and the earth worked into large mounds of loose, aerated soil, arranged in patterns that facilitated drainage and sustained cropping on a long-term crop-fallow system. The *conuco* farming system proved productive and efficient. Other foods were produced in gardens, notably fruits such as sweetsop, soursop, hog plum, guava, mammee apple and pineapple. Together with wild vegetables and wild fruits, these root-crop carbohydrates and the aquatic foods rich in fats and proteins combined to deliver a healthy diet. The Taino population of Jamaica was small, probably never exceeding sixty thousand, so the demand on resources was satisfied without significant impact on sustainability.[5]

Taino food production and consumption were localized within the village community. What the community collected and cultivated it ate. Some of the wild plants the Taino used had seasonal cycles, but the major items of diet were available year-round, so that storage and preservation were not crucial factors. Opportunities for exchange were limited, as were needs. Processing technologies, however, were sometimes quite elaborate and did result in a long-lasting product, as in the preparation of cassava.

Taino griddles, or burens – thick, circular, flat platters of low-fired clay with an average diameter of about 45 centimetres – were specially designed for baking cassava. Ceramic vessels used to boil liquids were more highly fired.[6] The Taino had learned the qualities of many plants, by observation and by trial and error. They knew which to avoid because of their deleterious effects, which had medicinal value, which tasted good and which bad. Within their own specific ecological niches, the Taino had developed a healthy diet, and they suffered from few endemic diseases. It was isolation that enabled most of these advantages, but isolation also made them vulnerable to intruders.

INSERTION

The coming of Europeans thrust the Caribbean into a wider world, initially defined by the limits of the Atlantic but eventually global. Food supply and consumption patterns followed the path of demographic, economic and technological change. New foods and new plants and animals accompanied waves of immigrants with new tools and knowledges. The highly localized food supply of the Taino was rapidly, though not immediately or completely, replaced.

Jamaica was first sighted by Columbus in 1494, and Spanish occupation began in 1509. The invaders found little gold but saw in the Tainos' productive *conucos* a source of provisions for the richer Spanish colonies and quickly began to use forced labour to enable the export of food. This system established the pattern for the next three centuries. The forcing of the Taino to labour, the Tainos' vulnerability to introduced diseases and the brutality of the Spanish, as well as forced migration to Cuba and Hispaniola, led to the rapid decline of the indigenous population, particularly of its males. Taino women were fully incorporated into the domestic life of the towns of early Spanish America and played a central role in the maintenance and transmission of Taino ways of food preparation. The influence of the Spanish was relatively slight initially, but the introduction of large animals – cattle, horses and pigs, which quickly multiplied on the savannas – was devastating. The animals' trampling and foraging contributed to the destruction of the *conucos*.[7]

After only a decade of desultory attempts to cultivate sugar and temperate grain crops, the Spanish effectively abandoned Jamaica. The Taino were reduced to a remnant population, and enslaved Africans were brought in to support the marginal system of subsistence agriculture that struggled amidst the roaming herds of feral animals. Food supply depended heavily on cassava. Plants introduced from Europe, Africa and mainland America included garden vegetables, citrus, yams, pigeon peas, plantains and pawpaw, but Jamaica was much less important as a site of agricultural innovation than other islands of the Spanish Caribbean. Jamaica's major export was cowhide, along with horses and salt pork, produced at semi-sedentary sites. Throughout the period from 1520 to 1650, the people of Jamaica had abundant supplies of meat, fish and root crops, yet most of the island was clothed in forest. The vestigial population, numbering no more than five thousand, lived in impoverished, scattered settlements; they were highly vulnerable but rarely hungry.[8]

In the middle of the seventeenth century, English imperial promoters painted seductive pictures of Jamaica's resources, seeking to attract potential planter-colonizers from the booming sugar islands of Barbados and St Kitts, where the land was already fully occupied. In 1657, two years after Cromwell conquered the Spanish, one propagandist said of Jamaica, "This island excels the others for the goodness both of the ayr, and bounty of the soyl, it is the most part a plain and even country, yeilding in great abundance whatsoever is necessary for mans life." In addition to the vast stock of horses, cattle and hogs, Jamaica's output of cassava made it "the granary of the rest of the islands". In 1661 Edmund Hickeringill praised the "pregnant and fertile" soil of Jamaica, as proved by its abundant groves of orange, lime, guava and pomegranate. The wild hogs were "fat and large", feasting on the "bountiful commons, as falls from the trees in a very liberal contribution". Hickeringill recommended that English colonists establish themselves on the border lands between the savannas and the "woods" (the rainforest) to enjoy the benefits of both, the "woody ground producing the best provisions for a family, as corn, potatoes, plantanes, cassauder, sugar canes, &c.". He also advocated cocoa and coconuts as special "improv'd productions".[9]

In the long term, the English colonization of Jamaica followed the fundamentals established in Barbados. Sugar plantations spread across much of the level land and up the gentler slopes, to reach their maximum geographic extent by the end of the eighteenth century. These plantations were founded on the labour of enslaved African people, who made up 90 per cent of the population by the time the British abolished the Atlantic slave trade in 1807. The total population of Jamaica was then about 370,000, compared to 20,000 in 1670, when the plantation economy was in its infancy and the numbers of blacks and whites were roughly equal.

Although the early promise of a diversified economy producing sugar, cocoa, indigo, pimento and livestock was overtaken by the aggressive growth of the sugar plantation, Jamaica did not follow the monocultural path laid out in Barbados. Livestock pens prospered on the savannas, producing not for export but to meet the needs of the planters in their mills and fields. Meat was a by-product of working animals. Indigo and cocoa dwindled, but pimento and ginger flourished as minor export crops, and from the 1790s coffee quickly became a major resource, cultivated in areas not suited to sugar, particularly the high mountains.[10]

The environmental outcome of the sugar and slavery period was extensive clearing of the rainforest and destruction of animal habitats. The English introduced few new animals, and the feral populations of the mid-seventeenth century were reduced. Wild hogs came to be confined to the natural woodlands. Fences and walls protected crops from marauding livestock, and efforts were made to exterminate vermin, particularly rats. The English did, however, introduce a number of significant plants during the period of slavery. Botanical gardens were established to test the viability of exotics, both as potential export crops and as food resources. These attempts formed part of the larger British imperial enterprise of scientific discovery and economic botany. Plants came from all parts of the world, temperate as well as tropical; some prospered only in the cooler uplands. Efforts to attempt grain crops such as oats and barley failed. The consequence was a substantial modification of the vegetation of the settled regions of the island. Sugar cane, a grass, occupied large areas previously covered by forest, while exotic trees quickly entered the woods and became elements in a "creole" pattern.[11]

The food supply during the period of slavery had unique features that distinguished Jamaica from other Caribbean colonies and had a significant effect on developments after the abolition of slavery in 1838. Rather than provide rationed allowances or prepared meals, Jamaican planters chose to designate areas of their lands as gardens and as more extensive "provision grounds", on which the enslaved were required to produce their own food. In some cases, the land was precisely surveyed and allocated to enslaved families, households and individuals, but more often the people were expected to make their own choices about where to plant within the boundaries of the gardens and grounds. Certainly they had to decide for themselves what to plant, how to tend their crops and what animals they might raise. Occasionally the planter provided planting material. More important, the enslaved could choose what from the produce of their gardens and grounds to consume, and what to exchange. The major products of the provision grounds were "ground provisions", the staple carbohydrate crops that supplied the foundation of the diet on which the enslaved had to depend. In 1818 "A Planter" said "provisions" included everything from plantain, coco and yam to "the humblest bean", and argued that all these deserved the attention of the botanist and cultivator, "food being the ground-work of all labour, and the strength and happiness of the labouring classes depending on the abundance and quality of their provisions".[12]

Although some slaves refused to participate in this system, a surplus was soon produced that enabled participation in public markets. The enslaved quickly became the principal suppliers of fresh food to the free population and held most of the small coin circulating in the island. In this way enslaved people were able to supplement the planters' meagre distributions of imported salted and pickled fish and the occasional cut of fresh beef. The enslaved could sometimes also hunt, trap and fish on the plantations, but time for such activities was limited. In the towns, meanwhile, enslaved people rarely had access to gardens and grounds and depended instead on rations or on "board-wages" paid in cash, as well as on scavenging. In the late eighteenth century, self-hired people were sent by their owners "to work out as it is called, for which liberty they are obliged to pay a certain rate per week or month". In order to cover their obligations, it was complained, such people engaged in fraud and theft, "the most honest part of their employment being to monopolize roots, greens, fruits, and other edibles, which they purchase from the country negroes, and retail at exorbitant rates".[13]

The provision-ground system did not necessarily deliver a nutritious diet to the enslaved. Social and psychological factors meant that food was exchanged for non-food items rather than consumed by the producer, and the demographic health of Jamaica's enslaved was no better than those subsisting on rationed allowances elsewhere. Further, plantation slavery exploited labour fiercely, leaving only limited time for any activities other than the master's work.[14] Plants and animals that required close attention were difficult to monitor and secure, especially when the provision grounds were distant from the slave village, and this limited the range of choice. For these reasons, the most common plants grown in the grounds were yams, cocos and plantains. Time and tools for the preparation of meals were similarly limited, resulting in a preponderance of "soups" and stews.

Whatever the social and nutritional disadvantages of the provision-ground system, it laid the foundations for peasant development after 1838 and created a role for the internal marketing system that continues today. The peasants were the great producers of "fruits and roots" for the local markets.[15] Most of the nineteenth century saw decline in sugar and coffee production as well as in the plantation-dependent livestock sector. Smallholders, meanwhile, increased their output of ground provisions. The peasants *had disposable income that enabled some consumption of beef and pork, while the* richer white plantation-based population dwindled and became less rich. Population growth was rapid and the people much more healthy, though epidemic disease remained a killer. People drifted to the towns, particularly after 1870, and a small external migration commenced.

The period from 1838 to 1900 was marked by a shift to a more internally oriented economy, though imported foods remained important in the diet. Large areas of Jamaica grew up in "ruinate", or secondary vegetation. The peasantry, freed from the time demands of plantation labour, could think afresh about the most productive mix of plants and animals raised in gardens and grounds. With time to attend and harvest tree crops, the concept of the "food forest" gained ground and contributed to the development of a viable and sustainable agriculture. In the food-forest model, as many as fifty useful species of plants might be grown together in three or four tiers, with ecological, economic and agronomic advantages.[16] Some areas of major food-crop production, as, for example, northern Manchester, were densely settled for the first time following the abolition of slavery.

When the planters' stores of imported and locally harvested foods were closed down, new towns sprang up to serve the productive interior regions of the island. Markets were built or refurbished, and shops became common. Groceries and bakeries joined the public markets, selling mostly imported drygoods, such as flour, rice and canned foods, as well as cured fish and meat. This trade depended on large-scale merchant wholesalers, established in the main towns, who distributed to the retailers. In the larger towns, hawkers walked the streets selling fresh fruit and vegetables, fish and poultry, while the more specialized offered yam, sweet potato, plantain, ackee, eggs, black crabs, wood or charcoal. Other hawkers sold cooked foods, such as cakes and "Jamaica sweetmeats". Some set up semi-permanent stalls on the pavements outside the public markets. By 1900 the larger stores in Kingston offered a wide range of imported foods, from salmon and lobster, sardines, herrings, canned fruits, canned meats to French

and other vegetables, soups, potted meats, pickled hams, marmalades, sauces, confectionery and dried fruits. Cookshops, rum shops, restaurants and hawkers sold cooked
food, ready to eat, and handcarts offered drinks and sweets.[17]

Technologies of preservation remained limited. For the long term, salting, pickling
and drying were still the best options. In the short term, competition from cockroaches,
rats, birds and other animals was relentless. In the 1790s, one writer noted that "as rats
are very numerous and rapacious, the negroes guard against their devouring the meat,
fish, and other provisions, which they hang over the fires in the middle of their huts,
by placing a little above the same, an half cylinder of bark with the round side
uppermost, the rope to which their food is appended passing thro' this up to the ridge-
pole".[18] Bread could be kept in a basket hung from the rafters. In the longer term, wire
mesh and metal safes did service, but the battle against weevils and maggots was finally
won only with the development of freezing and canning. For most of Jamaica's history,
the best method of preservation was to keep materials alive until the last moment.
Animals were slaughtered on the day they were to be eaten, and root crops were kept
in the ground as long as possible. This had important consequences for the types of foods
consumed, placing an emphasis on items that could be dried or cured, that could be
kept long in the ground or that were not too big to be consumed quickly.

Changes in cooking technologies were few until the late nineteenth century. Local
potters continued to contribute to the range of utensils. The round-bottomed yabba,
placed on a trivet made of three large stones, remained a common cooking pot. Large
ceramic vessels serving as water jars, often with similarly rounded bottoms, were "raised
from the ground, on a stem of a small tree with three prongs, fixed in one corner of
their house." The ceramic yabba competed with the three-foot pot, made of cast iron,
that was issued by the planters during slavery. Sometimes known as a "Dutch pot" or
"dutchy", with a two- or four-gallon capacity (nine or eighteen litres), it came with a
cover and handles to permit lifting and suspension from a hook above a fire (Figure
2.3). A rim around the cover was designed to contain hot coals so that food could be
baked as well as stewed. Similar pots were used in the kitchens of the planters, but
there they were used alongside a wider range of metal cooking utensils, particularly
skillets and frying pans. For example, in 1814 the "household furniture" of Harmony
Hill Pen, St Ann, included five iron pots, a tea kettle, two spits, a gridiron and a skimmer,
as well as a corn mill and a coffee mill. This suggests that plantation cooks had to
make do with few tools; however, items such as yabbas, calabashes (gourds) and bamboo
utensils made by the cooks themselves may have been deemed unworthy of listing in
an inventory.[19]

The calabash was a widely used small vessel – used by Tainos, Africans and Europeans
– but it served most often for the storage or consumption of food and drink rather than
for preparation or cooking. The gourds were carved and decorated to be "dishes, cups,
and spoons, of several shapes, bigness, and fashion". The planter Edward Long, in his
1774 *History of Jamaica*, observed that the thin, tight, firm texture of the shell of the

Figure 2.3 Cooking and storage pots: yabbas (top), water jars (bottom) and three-foot iron pot (centre right)

calabash enabled its use as "an earthen-pot" to boil water or broth. During slavery and into modern times, bamboo similarly supplied spoons and stirring sticks, cups and containers, only occasionally being used as a substitute for a cooking pot.[20]

Heat for cooking was fuelled almost entirely by wood, generally in an open fire. Stoves and ovens remained rudimentary. In the 1790s it was reported that "ovens are occasionally made by scooping hollows in perpendicular sides of a bank; and covered with a shade of sticks and leaves to keep off rain; the lower edge of the shade being farthest from the mouth of the oven. By frequent heating the cavity acquires sufficient hardness and answers the intention."[21] As well as these, some households had outdoor bake-houses or ovens, large brick and stone structures that rivalled those of commercial bakeries before factory mechanization and mass production. The modern cast-iron box oven, with its own chimney and enclosed fire, was not available until the late nineteenth century, and "ovenproof" ceramic vessels date only from the 1850s. The "American stove" reached Jamaica in the 1870s and became commonly known by brand names such as Dover, Caledonia and Carron or by numbers indicating size. In 1880 it was claimed that "cooking stoves have now completely superseded fire places, 'kitchen places' and brick ovens". The new stoves were portable, used less fuel and created less smoke, and could be used for "boiling, baking, roasting, frying, grilling, and every other kind of cooking". Portability was enhanced by the use of fluid fuel. Kerosene became available in Jamaica in 1866, imported in cans, but kerosene stoves did not become popular until the 1880s. In 1900 a fifteen-shilling "kerosene burning gas stove" was advertised as "No dirt. No smoke. No smell. No wick. Non-explosive."[22]

Plant and animal introductions were few between 1838 and 1900. Attempts to find new export crops were generally directed at non-food products such as silk and quinine. Tea was tried and abandoned. New food crops did emerge, notably bananas and copra, but they did not derive from unknown crop plants.[23] But while new plants were few, new people contributed significantly to the development of taste and tradition in Jamaica's food culture after 1838, particularly the Indians and Chinese who were brought to save plantation agriculture but who soon joined the ranks of the peasants and traders. These new peoples were a small proportion of the total population, which reached 700,000 in 1900, but they were influential. By the end of the nineteenth century, Jamaican food was beginning to be less obviously "African" and "British", with fresh elements added to the creole mix.

INTEGRATION

Nineteenth-century inventions such as canning and refrigeration had their real impact after 1900, when they enabled the global transfer of preserved and prepared foods on a significant scale. As early as 1858 Anthony Trollope could note that breakfast among the planter class always included "half a dozen 'tinned' productions, namely, meats sent from England in tin cases". Alfred Leader, writing in 1907, said that "a good deal of tinned and bottled food, chiefly American, is used in the island (though not by the negro), including bottled bacon, which was a novelty to me – the quality being good".

In the United States, the freezing of fish and poultry began as early as 1865, of fruit in 1908 and of vegetables in 1929, but development was slow at first and took off only after World War II. In Jamaica, canned, chilled and frozen foods gradually displaced salted, dried and pickled items, and enabled the import of new varieties of fruits and vegetables. By the 1930s, local penkeepers complained of the increasing import of chilled meat, and there were fears that imported fresh and frozen meat and poultry would wipe out the local livestock industries.[24] But the new methods of preservation could be applied to a wider range of foods, and consumption shifted from local to imported sources.

Speedier transportation had a similar effect, as did liberalized international trade, which beginning in the 1980s allowed freer entry to foreign food products. In 1991 subsidies on several basic foods were removed, to meet agreements with the World Bank, pushing up prices alongside a devalued dollar. Local production of many common vegetable crops declined, beginning with the importation of onions in 1990 and speeding up from 1995, when imported cabbage, tomato, carrot, Irish potato, red peas, lettuce and beetroot came to dominate the market. Equally important, Jamaican consumption shifted significantly after about 1950 from carbohydrates derived from local roots and tubers to imported cereals, particularly wheat, rice and corn.[25]

Even after Independence in 1962, the pattern established during slavery of selling rather than consuming the most valuable products of the grounds was said to persist among small farmers. Thus crops like carrots, turnips, beets and string beans, along with eggs, chickens and goats, were sold in markets, while the peasant household ate starchy foods, either grown in their own grounds or bought from shops. Attempts were made to make the system more efficient, through the Agricultural Marketing Corporation (established in 1963), and the democratic socialist government of the 1970s promoted local production through a variety of systems of land tenure, including Food Farms and Self Help, under the umbrella project GROW (Growing and Reaping Our Wealth). Most of these state-managed agencies and projects were overtaken in the 1980s, when free market principles and structural adjustment initiatives were adopted. In 1990 the government set up the Rural Agricultural Development Authority, with one of its objectives being the stimulation of food production for local consumption, through (beginning in 1997) the Domestic Food Crop Production and Marketing Project. The government also sought to encourage consumers, through its Home Economics programmes and by publishing cookbooks devoted to "traditional Jamaican dishes".[26]

The island's population quadrupled in the twentieth century to reach 2.6 million by its end. Heavy outmigration made the experience very different from that of previous periods and created a Jamaican diaspora, especially in the United States, Canada and the United Kingdom. The diaspora contributed to the development of new attitudes to the foods of those nations, though tastes often remained conservative. In the later twentieth century, these traditional tastes were to some extent satisfied by the increasing availability in the northern metropolitan centres of generic Jamaican-type foods, such as yams and plantains, and of more specifically Jamaican food items, such as canned ackee, fish tea and cock soup mixes, hard-dough bread and water crackers.[27] Within Jamaica, population growth was associated with heavy migration to the urban centres, especially Kingston, which had a population of 575,000 in 2001. More and more land was taken up by non-agricultural uses, fewer people were able to grow their own food, and fewer youth chose to take up agriculture.

In the kitchens of Jamaica, a long-term shift occurred, away from handmade ceramics such as the yabba to metal pots and pans with milled bases and smooth-bottomed ceramics and glass. Direct contact between stove top and pot bottom maximized heat transfer by conduction. Flat cooking surfaces generally went together with heat sources that could be more closely controlled by the cook. This combination facilitated cooking styles such as frying, braising, fricasseeing and what came to be called brown-stewing. Cooks with stoves or brick fireplaces found it "easy to keep the fire the right size, or simply to simmer the stew at the side of a larger fire".[28]

Somewhere between the extremes of the yabba simmering over an open fire and the metal stew-pan on the glass-top electric stove was the charcoal-burning coal-pot. F.G. Cassidy and R.B. Le Page, in 1967, described the coal-pot as a "black, cast-iron, charcoal stove, having a round foot (about 8 in. diameter and 6 in. high) and a shallow pot-like top with a metal grill". Such coal-pots were, they said, widely used in Jamaica. Six years earlier, Cassidy had mentioned "a six-inch circular base and a bowl-like top with a grate". The coal-pot was long-established at that time. Annie Manville Fenn, an Englishwoman setting up house in Jamaica in 1893, said her black cooks found the American stove too hot and preferred to use either "a wood fire on an open hearth, or a 'coal-pot,' – a basin-shaped stove for charcoal", along with "a brick oven for baking large joints". Phyllis Clark recommended in 1945 that households have several coal-pots, to suit pots and pans of different sizes and also to heat the irons used to iron clothing. She also recommended coal-pots have "a good arch to allow for plenty of draught".[29] The glowing coals of the fire were contained in the top or bowl of the coal-pot, resting on the grill or grate that fitted into the top of the neck (Figure 2.4). Ashes fell through the grate to be scraped out through the arch. Some foods could be roasted directly in the coals, and pots and pans could be placed on wire racks. Much heat was lost, but the coal-pot had the advantages of portability and relatively clean operation. It remains in common use for particular purposes, such as roasting breadfruit, and for situations and occasions when alternative fuel is not available, such as after hurricanes.

The coal-pot is not unique to Jamaica. It is common, historically and today, in most of the anglophone Caribbean. Richard Allsopp traces the origin of the word *coal-pot* to the Dutch homophone *koolpot* and argues that these "Dutch stoves" were probably introduced to the English Caribbean in the seventeenth century. But references to coal-pots occur relatively late in Jamaica, the earliest citations occurring in the 1870s.[30] The coal-pot or Dutch stove is not to be confused with the portable but covered and fully enclosed "Dutch oven", "Dutchy pot" or "dutchy", which had to be placed on a fire.

Figure 2.4 Coal-pot

The coal-pot has in Jamaica sometimes been called a "coal-stove" but, used as equivalent for the portable item, the term "*coal-stove*" did not emerge until the 1930s.[31] The context of the coal-pot was typically rural, whereas the coal-stove was identified first in the overcrowded tenements of Kingston and lower St Andrew.

Coal-pots were a fire hazard, and a hazard to the body as well: cooks were encouraged to place them high enough to avoid stooping. By the 1930s, some country kitchens had a brick or concrete range with holes for a series of portable coal-pots, the fire introduced at one end and a chimney at the other, thus economizing the use of fuel and getting smoke out of the kitchen; but such technologies were quickly overtaken by alternative heat sources. The pots themselves also changed: by the 1970s Jamaicans began to cast coal-pots in aluminium; these new pots generally replaced the imported iron versions, but ceramic coal-pots were rare. In 1992 the Dutch government contributed to the development of an improved "coalpot", said to use 30 per cent less energy in cooking.[32]

Individuals occasionally produced the charcoal used in coal-pots themselves, but most charcoal was produced by the professional, specialist charcoal-burners whose smoky coal-pits dotted the wooded landscape. Wood was cut from the forests or scavenged from the streets and fields. Sellers of wood and charcoal had their own special markets in Kingston, the coal sold by the bag or drum. In the larger towns, carts roamed the streets, bringing fuel right to the door. In the 1980s, charcoal was identified as a "cheap renewable energy source" and used in some households, hotels and restaurants to replace kerosene, gas and electricity for cooking. Improved kiln technologies were investigated, using chimneys, to produce more charcoal more rapidly, and fast-growing trees were planted.[33]

Wood and charcoal were the dominant fuels for cooking throughout most of Jamaica's history. Systematic data were collected beginning with the 1982 census and provide a useful *terminus post quem*. In that year 50 per cent of Jamaican private households used wood, charcoal or both as fuel for cooking. In St Elizabeth the proportion reached as high as 80 per cent; only in Kingston and St Andrew were other fuels more important. Wood-fuelled stoves were rapidly disappearing, but down to the 1950s box ovens were recommended for baking and roasting; these were made from large wooden crates lined with zinc or tin, with wires as shelves and with a door, and were fed with coals from a nearby fire.[34] By 1982 gas accounted for the cooking fuel in 30 per cent of households overall, and in St Andrew it was the most popular. Sold in metal cylinders of various sizes, gas could be purchased in small quantities, enabling the mobility of stoves. Kerosene was used by 18 per cent of households and was the dominant fuel in Kingston parish. In Kingston and St Andrew, kerosene-using households outnumbered the users of wood and charcoal, as did the users of gas, but elsewhere this was never the case. Kerosene had some of the same advantages as gas: it could be purchased in small amounts (from shops and petrol stations with specialized pumps, though sometimes not after 6 p.m.) and was portable. For cooking, both kerosene and gas burners could be more closely regulated than wood or charcoal fires, and they were cleaner. Gas was superior to kerosene in all respects. Gas stoves were first promoted in 1940 but entered the market only after 1955, when gas became available as a by-product of local oil refining.[35]

Electricity was used for cooking in a mere 1.2 per cent of households in 1982 and was the least popular fuel in every parish. Although electric stoves were clean, they lacked the rapid heating and regulation possible with gas, particularly pre-1960s models, fitted with a heavy boiling plate that was slow to heat and slow to cool. They were also expensive. More importantly, electric stoves required connection to a public supplier and payment of periodic bills. Failure to pay risked disconnection. On top of that, the supply of electricity was erratic and unpredictable; scheduled and unscheduled outages lasting for hours troubled cooks in most periods. Thus, whereas electricity had become the principal source of power for lighting by 1982 (with kerosene a close second), it was not favoured for cooking. Most Jamaican cooks felt more confident with supplementary technologies at hand – small gas burners or coal-pots – that could be relied on in an emergency. Microwave ovens had but a limited market outside the commercial sector.

In the decades after 1982, the use of wood, charcoal and kerosene declined dramatically. The 1991 census showed wood and charcoal to be still the most common fuel for cooking, at 46 per cent, but by 2001 they had fallen to just 12 per cent. Kerosene fell from 18 per cent in 1982 to 5 per cent in 2001. The great gainer was gas, which increased its share to 43 per cent in 1991 and 80 per cent in 2001. The proportion using electricity as cooking fuel changed little, reaching a mere 1.6 per cent in 2001, even though 87 per cent used electricity for lighting – a massive increase over 1982 as the result of an aggressive rural electrification programme. Gas quickly became the dominant fuel for cooking in the most urbanized parishes, eclipsing the traditional sources in all of the rural parishes by the end of the twentieth century. Beginning in 1992, efforts were also made to encourage the use of solar ovens, manufactured in Jamaica. There were two types: a small portable version and a larger commercial one, constructed as an insulated cardboard box, using aluminium foil, tempered glass or polyester film. Both versions were capable of baking and roasting as well as steaming, but the adoption rate remained low.[36]

Whereas electricity struggled to find a place as a source of energy for the cooking of Jamaican food, it proved much more popular as a means of refrigeration. At first it was used more often to cool or chill than to freeze. Householders employed ice-chests to cool their food, using ice purchased from an ice factory established in Kingston in 1884, which in turn depended on electricity. This technique remained important into the 1960s. Freezing depended on industrial and domestic refrigeration, and was used in large hotels by 1920. Electric refrigerators for private homes, such as the Frigidaire, were first promoted only in the late 1930s. By 1939 the Jamaica Public Service Company had for sale electric refrigerators, as well as electric cooking ranges, toasters, coffee percolators, hotplates and blenders.[37] For those lacking access to electricity, the kerosene refrigerator offered a moderately successful cooling technology.

The freezing of fresh and cooked foods began to replace drying and canning soon after the Second World War as the dominant mode of preservation, especially for meat and vegetables. The domestic refrigerator remained relatively expensive and uncommon. The spread of electricity made a difference, replacing kerosene and making freezing a viable option. The transformation was easier than for cooking, because even lengthy interruptions of power supply could be tolerated much more readily by the refrigerator than by the stove. The refrigerator also made possible a whole new variety of leftovers of relatively great longevity.

Before the refrigerator and local factory production of ice, methods of food preservation were more limited. Ice was imported beginning in the 1840s but was too expensive to have much general significance. Meat could be preserved by being placed in a container of wire or sticks (commonly known as a kreng-kreng) and hung above a smoky fire. Corned fish, pork, beef and tripe were hung for drying and smoking in the bricked chimney of an outside hearth, with the coal-pots below. Uncooked yams could be cured to last for a year or more, the cut ends covered with ashes and carefully stacked. By the early twentieth century, some fruits and vegetables could be preserved by home sterilization and bottling. Canning could also be done at home but required a special machine to seal the lids. The 1957 *Farmer's Food Manual* offered detailed directions on home canning, and this was roughly the high-water mark for this process within the household economy.[38]

The industrialization of food preparation saw mechanized factories replace small-scale kitchens in the production of many foods, with the capacity to package as well as cook. The effect of factory production was to partially replace cooking in home kitchens and outdoor sites by providing ready-to-eat foods. Fast food outlets had a similar effect; their kitchens also increasingly took on an industrial aspect, using modern utensils and machines, almost all of them imported and operated to international standards. Food-processing plants developed strongly in Jamaica after 1950, building on earlier local enterprise in brewing and biscuit-making. Some of these activities, such as the canning of ackee and the bottling of jerk seasoning, were directed at new export opportunities, particularly within the Commonwealth Caribbean, but most served the domestic market. A flour mill, using imported grain, began operation in 1968. In that year there were about sixty bakeries in Kingston alone, but large-scale modern bakeries expanded to replace village and backyard versions, producing brand-named bread, biscuits, buns and pastries.[39]

From 1968 retort techniques were used to produce a "meal in a bag" that did not require refrigeration. Jamaica Way brand vacuum-sealed plastic pouches, in which the cooked food was sealed in a pouch and sterilized at 212 degrees Fahrenheit, needed only to be boiled for five minutes to prepare for serving. But consumers demonstrated conservative taste in packaging and left much of it on the shelf. Meals offered in this format included curried goat, curried chicken, beef stew and stew peas. Jamaican taste continued to govern demand, so that the products were often peculiar to the island rather than shifting to the dominant styles of the northern nations. This technique was reintroduced in the late 1980s, this time using aluminium pouches to store such favourites as curried goat, stew peas, beef stew and "ackee and salt fish dinner". Using more traditional packaging, a new range of "Ready A Ready" canned goods was launched in 2005, including carrot drink, Irish moss, red peas soup, ketchup, hot sauce, Scotch bonnet pepper sauce and seasoned callaloo.[40]

The new technologies of preservation, processing and transportation made possible new systems of distribution. They affected not only the bringing of foods to markets, but also the mobility of the consumer and the capacity of the household to store food. Large-scale wholesalers emerged to feed local and foreign goods into the retail market. Supermarkets first appeared in Kingston in 1954 and quickly became common. Smaller versions were found in country towns and villages by the early 1960s, putting pressure on the small shopkeeper.[41]

The supermarket was an important innovation because it brought together all of the food ingredients previously found in separate specialized sites. It replaced the butcher, the grocer and the higgler, making possible one-stop shopping; the consumer could travel to just that one site by car, taxi, bus or foot. To compete, groceries installed freezers and stands for fresh fruit and vegetables, cutting into the higglers' and hawkers' markets. Small-scale bakeries survived better but sold less bread and concentrated more on pastries, patties and cakes. Hawkers of fruits and vegetables, who formerly roamed city streets singing and calling their wares, became rare. In their place, new-style handcarts distributed fruit and vegetables and milk on a smaller scale, and street-side sellers of local and imported fruit and vegetables set up on the footpaths, as near as possible to the supermarket doors and car parks. Equally important, the public markets continued to serve a wide clientele, often providing sections for specialist butchers and sellers of fish and charcoal. By 2000 the market system had adjusted to the new high level of imported fresh foods by incorporating these products into the existing structure developed to distribute locally grown produce. Local carrot and onion became "almost obsolete", but the imported items were often sold by higglers, who simply re-sourced their supplies. Even at the Coronation Market in Kingston, it was reported, "many of the vendors are selling more imported than local fruits and vegetables". Local produce became scarce and expensive.[42] Produce specialization largely disappeared, with everyone – from higgler to supermarket – selling a little or a lot of everything. Cooperative community food shops became big business in town and country.

One of the largest enterprises, Grace Food Processors, was formed in 1973 after an older firm, Grace, Kennedy and Company, acquired the operations of the DaCosta Brothers. (Grace, Kennedy and Company had been established in 1922 as a wholesaler and distributor importing "general provisions" and exporting "island produce".) The merged canning and bottling plants produced a wide range of juices, jams, jellies, beans, vegetables, ketchup, "hot and spicy" Vienna sausages and much else, using both local and imported inputs. In 1984 Grace acquired one of the leading supermarket chains, Hi-Lo, which had been established in the early 1950s, thus creating a fully integrated system of production and supply. Food crops were purchased from contractors, to be sold fresh or processed, the company providing support and advice to farmers.[43]

These developments paralleled the emergence of fast food outlets of various sorts, some of them multinational, others local. Restaurants, particularly Chinese restaurants, were already popular and widespread. In 1968 Kingston alone had about three hundred restaurants of various sizes and styles.[44] The first international chain (Tops) opened in the early 1970s, followed by Kentucky Fried Chicken in 1975, Shakey's Pizza, Burger King in 1984, Popeye's in 1992, Pizza Hut in 1993, TCBY Yogurt in 1993 and McDonald's in 1995. The local company King Burger opened in 1981, along with Mother's, which by 1991 had become "the largest Jamaican fast food chain".[45] Shakey's began home delivery of pizza in Kingston in 1986. Foreign firms did not always have an easy entrance: McDonald's was criticized for not using local beef, and fears were raised over the possibility of the dumping of inferior and diseased product. The company "never established itself in Jamaica as a strong brand" and left the island in 2005. Local patty businesses, on the other hand, prospered, and some of the largest, such as Tastee, Juici and Island Grill, began to broaden their menus to a wider range of "Jamaican foods".[46] In these various ways, Jamaica was drawn into a globalized food culture in which a plural diet became increasingly typical. Jamaica was not unique in this experience, of course, but the process worked itself out in unique patterns that allowed international taste to thrive alongside the self-conscious identification of "Jamaican" food.

Street food, cooked and consumed on site, competed with more traditional cookshops and restaurants but emphasized foods derived from the Jamaican tradition in contrast to the offerings of the fast food chains. Sidewalk cookshops sold cheaply but were regarded as a health hazard, and attempts were made to remove them. But increasingly, vendors of street foods included in their stock commercially prepared and pre-packaged items, because of their convenience and popularity. The tools and technologies of street food derived from a mix of traditional and recycled materials.

Changes in diet and methods of food preparation and processing after 1900 were not associated with significant introductions of plants and animals. The flora and fauna remained essentially unchanged, though the populations of some animal species, such as turtles, were severely depleted. Hybrids and clones were produced by scientific breeding, however, notably the citrus fruits ortanique and ugli, and the Jamaica Hope and Jamaica Red cattle.

At the beginning of the twenty-first century, Jamaica's system of food supply and distribution incorporated a variety of elements inherited from the deep past that sometimes meshed, sometimes conflicted, with the modern. This is a pattern typical of most contemporary food systems, though the inequality of wealth and income that characterizes Jamaica operates to retain the traditional, pre-modern foods and methods of preparation more than in some countries. The modern middle-class kitchen of suburban Kingston or Mandeville has all the appliances and tools and utensils typical of its equivalent in New York or London. A few additional items might be present, but they are not essential to the preparation of modern Jamaican food or of any national dishes. The roots of the coexistence of ancient and modern in foodways generally are to be sought in the fundamental absence, until very recent times, of significant modification of the raw materials. Hybridization and genetic manipulation have, thus far, been directed at increasing yields and resistance to vermin and disease. Organic farming began to become popular in the late twentieth century but spread slowly in Jamaica, with demand for products such as organic ginger far exceeding supply.[47] The tools and techniques applied to the preparation of food may change, and new choices can be made about what to consume from the standard offerings, but the ingredients remain in themselves relatively constant.

KNOWLEDGE

Jamaican cooks' practice was rooted in knowledge acquired through experience, demonstration, observation and listening to lore. The precise measurement of weights, cooking times and temperatures was rarely possible, and dishes with the same name might vary in ingredients and taste. Cookbooks written by Jamaicans with the intention of explaining Jamaican ways of cooking were few and far between until Independence. Before that, advice might be sought in up-to-date cookbooks published by English and North American writers (an early edition of Mrs Beeton's cookbook was available by 1869), but these rarely showed much interest in the ingredients and dishes that characterized Jamaica. They regularly described roasting, boiling, frying, broiling, stewing and baking, and sometimes took trouble to explain how to prepare turtle, pepperpot or barbecued pig. Often, however, the advice was not useful and was even contrary to island practice.[48]

The earliest known local cookbook is *The Jamaica Cookery Book*, first published in Kingston in December 1893 by Aston W. Gardner and Company. Its author was identified only as "C.S. of St Andrew", who had "collected" the 312 recipes in the book, saying she had "confined myself entirely to the every day dishes which come under immediate notice in this island". However, the collection was explicitly directed at "newcomers", meaning Europeans, and the "native" dishes described were by no means restricted to those that could be afforded by the island's poor. The author had begun collecting recipes aware that "up to the present time a book on native cookery has never been produced in Jamaica"; a contemporary reviewer noted, "The art of cookery in these islands has hitherto been carried on by tradition and empirical rule and we welcome an attempt to place it on a definite basis and to introduce some method and principle as a point from which future conquests on behalf of tropical humanity may be made."[49]

A second, "revised and enlarged edition" of *The Jamaica Cookery Book* was published in November 1897, with 364 recipes and hints. The collector was now identified as Caroline Sullivan. This was probably the Caroline Sullivan who died in 1904, widow of Frederick Sullivan, Postmaster General for Jamaica from 1870 until his death aged fifty-five in 1892. She had lived at Drominagh, St Andrew, part of Eastwood Park Pen, and her funeral was held at Half-Way-Tree. Frederick Sullivan had come to Jamaica as a child, with his English-Irish parents, and spent his career in the public service.[50] In 1906, following Caroline Sullivan's death, the *Jamaica Cookery Book* was advertised by Gardner's Tourist Agency as the work of "Mrs. Sullivan". In 1908 the agency brought out a "third edition", with the author once again identified as Caroline Sullivan and the recipes and hints still numbering 364. This seems to have been a response to demand, the earlier editions having become hard to find. The *Gleaner* greeted the publication with enthusiasm, saying, "It is a splendid book, and one that should have an important place in every regulated household." Soon after, it was advertised as *Gardner's Jamaica Cookery Book*, and for most of the twentieth century authorship slipped away from Caroline Sullivan.[51] She was not rediscovered until the 1990s. A version of her 1897 edition was published in Jamaica in 1990, followed by a slight adaptation of the 1893 edition, published in England in 1996, and a much-transformed 1997 German translation.

Sullivan's cookbook was directed at a middle-class audience and based on urban middle-class experience. Talking of rural Jamaica in the early twentieth century, Claude McKay described "pure native cooking and serving", and noted that Europeans living in Jamaica "had many of the native foods prepared in their own way, different from the native style".[52] How someone like Sullivan fitted this mould is hard to say. She sometimes distinguished her methods from "native" cookery and used ingredients in ways that fit poorly with what is otherwise known, but at the same time she systematized a culinary range that reflected Jamaican cookery at all social levels. Sullivan often cooked with ingredients beyond the means of a poor family, but this did not make the recipes she offered for those rare items unauthentic. Her cookbook is a vital source because of its pioneering role and its broad coverage. She remains a crucial figure in the narrative of Jamaican food, and appears often in this book.

Between the publication of Sullivan's *Jamaica Cookery Book* and Independence, only a handful of cookbooks were produced in the island. Nutritional education was advanced after 1945, particularly through Jamaica Welfare and the Food for Family Fitness programme, and in 1957 the Jamaica Agricultural Society published *The Farmer's Food Manual: A Recipe Book for the West Indies*, within the context of Federation. After 1962, the idea of national, rather than native, dishes, came together with a sudden outpouring of cookbooks. Some of this activity was encouraged by government, through publications by the Jamaica Information Service and the annual Independence Festival Culinary Arts competitions. Starting in 1961 the island's leading newspaper, the *Gleaner*, included a weekly Food Supplement, which changed its name to Supermarket Supplement (including a Market Basket section) in 1989, Home Living and Food Guide (including Food Basket) in 1990, What's Cooking (including Food Basket) in 1995, Food (including Food Basket) in 2000, and Food (including You in Your Kitchen) in 2001. A substantial proportion of the supplements' material consisted of local contributions that emphasized Jamaican ingredients and styles, but many of the recipes and methods described came from overseas sources, mostly syndicated columns and cookbooks. Most of these were published originally in Great Britain and the United States, thus helping to install those traditions as a kind of standard. The newspapers also published Caribbean-generated material from the Caribbean Food and Nutrition Institute and the institute's periodical *Nyam News*, most of this information didactic. Even the local recipes were often intended to promote particular goods or ideas rather than to reflect everyday practice.

In 1969 Grace, Kennedy and Company Limited established Grace Kitchens and Consumer Centre, "to develop recipes which emphasise economic and innovative use of locally-grown foods and, of course, products from the Grace Brand". A regular television programme – *Creative Cooking* – followed, and booklets and pamphlets introducing some of the recipes promoted there.[53] These ventures combined well-known Jamaican recipes with borrowings from other countries. Many of the cookbooks published in Jamaica did the same, and some devoted themselves to introducing ideas from around the world. Bookshops also sold cookbooks from other places, particularly Britain and North America. As early as 1938 Jamaicans could listen to Betty Crocker on the radio; local cooking programmes became popular after Independence. Each year Festival celebrations included competitions in National Culinary Arts, and the publication of recipes resulting from these initiatives were a significant influence in promoting the local over the foreign. After Independence, the slow trickle of locally published cookbooks fairly quickly became a small flood.[54]

Down to the 1890s, in the absence of cookbooks, readers seeking instruction on Jamaican food and cookery could turn to the works of the island's botanists, zoologists and historians. Although many of the men who wrote natural histories of Jamaica in the English colonial period lacked formal training and worked in other professions, they did attempt to be systematic and to be accurate in their descriptions. Natural history was often combined with other subject matter, but this is an advantage rather than a limitation in terms of the food history of Jamaica. Modern scientific studies of plants and animals generally ignore their use as human food.

Works on the Jamaican flora, particularly those of Hans Sloane, who lived in Jamaica from 1687 to 1689 as a medical practitioner and whose collections formed the initial core of the British Museum, were important sources in the establishment of botanical classification, and were relied on heavily by Linnaeus in the binomial system he developed in the middle of the eighteenth century. Another doctor, Henry Barham, who came to Jamaica from England early in the eighteenth century and married into the plantocracy, produced an extensive botanical manuscript before he left the island in 1740. Most of this work seems to have been complete by about 1725, but Barham's *Hortus Americanus* remained unpublished until 1794, when a Linnaean index was added (although Edward Long's 1774 *History of Jamaica* had already included a large proportion of the *Hortus*).[55] Some works remained permanently unpublished and little known. One of these, compiled by the Reverend John Lindsay in the 1760s and 1770s under the general title *Elegancies of Jamaica*, included numerous illustrations of plants and animals. A selection of Lindsay's images is included among the colour plates in this book, together with a smaller number from W.J. Titford's *Sketches towards a Hortus Botanicus Americanus* of 1811.

The naturalist Philip Henry Gosse spent eighteen months in Jamaica, from December 1844 to June 1846; he published his classic *The Birds of Jamaica* in 1847 and four years later published a more general account of his observations, *A Naturalist's Sojourn in Jamaica*. Gosse included in these works much information supplied by Richard Hill, the first coloured stipendiary magistrate in Jamaica and a member of the House of Assembly in 1837–38. Like those before him, Gosse depended on young black men to guide him through the country and to find and identify many of the plants and animals that he described. Often the names applied in the Jamaican vernacular differed from those used by naturalists, though the sometimes highly localized versions and folk taxonomies were always of interest.[56]

The concept of natural history refined its principles of inclusion and exclusion over time. The question is essentially whether to include the many plants and animals brought to Jamaica from other places or to consider only those that can be defined as indigenous or endemic. Gosse raised the issue in 1851, in connection with his discussion of the "land tortoise", saying that some of the "old writers" such as Patrick Browne mentioned it among the animals of Jamaica but said that whether it was "actually indigenous or imported, is doubtful". Gosse argued that those animals of a country existing in "an independent feral state, have a right to a place in the local Fauna, even though the race has been originally introduced". He opposed, however, the enumeration of every variety that could possibly be seen in a place, "though confessedly imported and preserved in confinement".[57] The development of this exclusive approach has meant that many of the most common plants and animals of colonial and independent Jamaica, such as the banana and the chicken, have been largely ignored in modern inventories even when feral. Whereas there are good scientific grounds for this exclusion, the history of food must be inclusive, taking in every variety exploited for human consumption.

In modern Jamaica, the presence of the Caribbean Food and Nutrition Institute at the University of the West Indies, Mona, has created a vast store of information. The historical study of food, on the other hand, has found relatively few adherents. The Englishman John Parry, the first Professor of History at the University College, did take an interest. In 1956 he read to the Jamaica Historical Society a paper published the year before, a "historical sketch on the introduction of food crops into Jamaica". Parry declared that Caribbean history should be written to explain the experiences of the people themselves, rather than as a part of the larger history of the Atlantic economy. The peoples' history, said Parry, "should be the story of yams, cassava and salt fish, no less than of sugar and tobacco".[58] This admonition, now fifty years old, bore little fruit. It is time to return to those roots.

PART 1: PLANTS

CHAPTER 3

ROOTS

Jamaicans often use the word "food" to refer specifically to starchy carbohydrates, especially those derived from roots and tubers. Until quite recent times, a meal without "food" hardly counted as a meal, however appetizing its ingredients. If asked the meaning of *food* in the 1950s, Jamaicans' answers might have ranged no further than yam, coco and potato. In the 1960s, Jamaica's "food crops" were said to include "yams, yampies, sweet potatoes, Irish potatoes, breadfruit, cassava, etc.", all but breadfruit being "roots". A cookbook published in 1990 included a section titled "foods", following soups, fish and seafood, and meats; the recipes for "foods" matched closely the definition of food crops. This usage is shared with only a few other places, such as Barbados and Cuba, where *vianda* ("food") comprises root crops such as cassava, coco and sweet potato, as well as the starchy fruit staples plantain and banana.[1] Although the Jamaican equation of "food" with roots is not strictly unique, its survival into the twenty-first century points to the centrality of these foods and to the importance of roots in Jamaican food culture.

The older term "food-kind" was similarly limited in definition, and its relative "bread-kind" was used into the early twentieth century to identify "tuberous rooted plants producing starch foods" or, more liberally, "all such vegetables as are used as staples, like yam, coco, sweet potato, and plantain".[2] Even older usage, before the arrival of the breadfruit tree in Jamaica, linked "bread-kind" to "bread-fruit" and "ground-fruit". Peter Marsden in 1788 used "ground-fruit and bread-fruit" to refer to the starchy staples. Hans Sloane, writing about the late seventeenth century, said the people fed on "cassada bread, yams, and patatas, which they eat as bread, and is the natural product of the country". Charles Leslie, in his 1739 *New and Exact Account of Jamaica*, observed that "the common bread here is plantane, yams or cassava". The following year, the author of *The Importance of Jamaica to Great-Britain* noted that Jamaica imported flour and bread from North America but said of "bread" broadly, "Of their own product, they make use of yams, red, white and purple, roasted or boil'd, the cocoa root, potatoes, sometimes the cassada and bread-nut; but plantane is the most generally used in times of scarcity." The consumption of these roots and fruits was considered by some a "substitute" for bread made from imported flour. Cassava, yam and plantain might not have been "so elegant, or agreeable to strangers", wrote Patrick Browne in 1756, but they were "not much inferior in wholesomeness or degree of nourishment".[3]

Analogous to the tightly specified usages of *food* and *bread-kind* is the phrase *ground provisions*. Modern Jamaicans sometimes use "ground provisions" to identify locally produced crops such as yam, coco, potato, cassava, plantain, banana and breadfruit, contrasting these with the mostly imported starches like wheat, rice and corn. Earlier definitions were confined to crops drawn from the ground (such as yam, coco, potato and cassava) or "roots". These were products of the plantation provision grounds during slavery but were cultivated along with plantain and corn, both of which were classed among the bread-kind. In the final decades of slavery, the three crops that dominated the provision grounds were yam, coco and plantain, the rest appearing only erratically. Yam, coco and plantain maintained this relative ranking down to the end of the twentieth century.[4] Broadly, "food" and "ground provisions" came both from the provision grounds and from the ground, the archetypal examples growing underground, together with the roots of the plant. It was the association of these staples with the roots that made them "roots" and "root crops".

What made roots good to eat? We think of the roots of most plants as tough and straggly, like those of a weed, or immense and woody, supporting a tree – almost always unappetizing. The primary function of the root system of a flowering green plant (an angiosperm) is to absorb minerals and moisture from the soil and to transport these elements to the shoot system (stem, leaves, flowers, seeds) of the plant above ground (Figure 3.1). To achieve this, roots have to be able to push their way through unpredictably resistant materials, using their conical growing tips to find ways through and around impediments. Roots are most efficient when they have a large surface area relative to volume, in order to maximize the interface with the soil and moisture, and this makes them long, thin, cylindrical, hairy and sometimes fibrous. Roots also need to be strong enough to resist pressures that might crush them, and this means that they need to have tough skins. The second function of roots is to physically support the plant's above-ground growth. To support a plant that is very tall or very large, the roots must be extensive, strong and woody. The many roots of a coconut palm, for example, resemble steel cables sent down deep into the earth in a spreading conical pattern. Many green plants, however, have a single vertical taproot with numerous smaller lateral hairy roots. With all these various functions to serve, roots that do so efficiently are rarely good to eat. The exceptions are those plants which develop soft, nutritious, swollen taproots, such as carrots, turnips, beetroots, parsnips and radishes, but these are not the "roots" of the Jamaican food system.

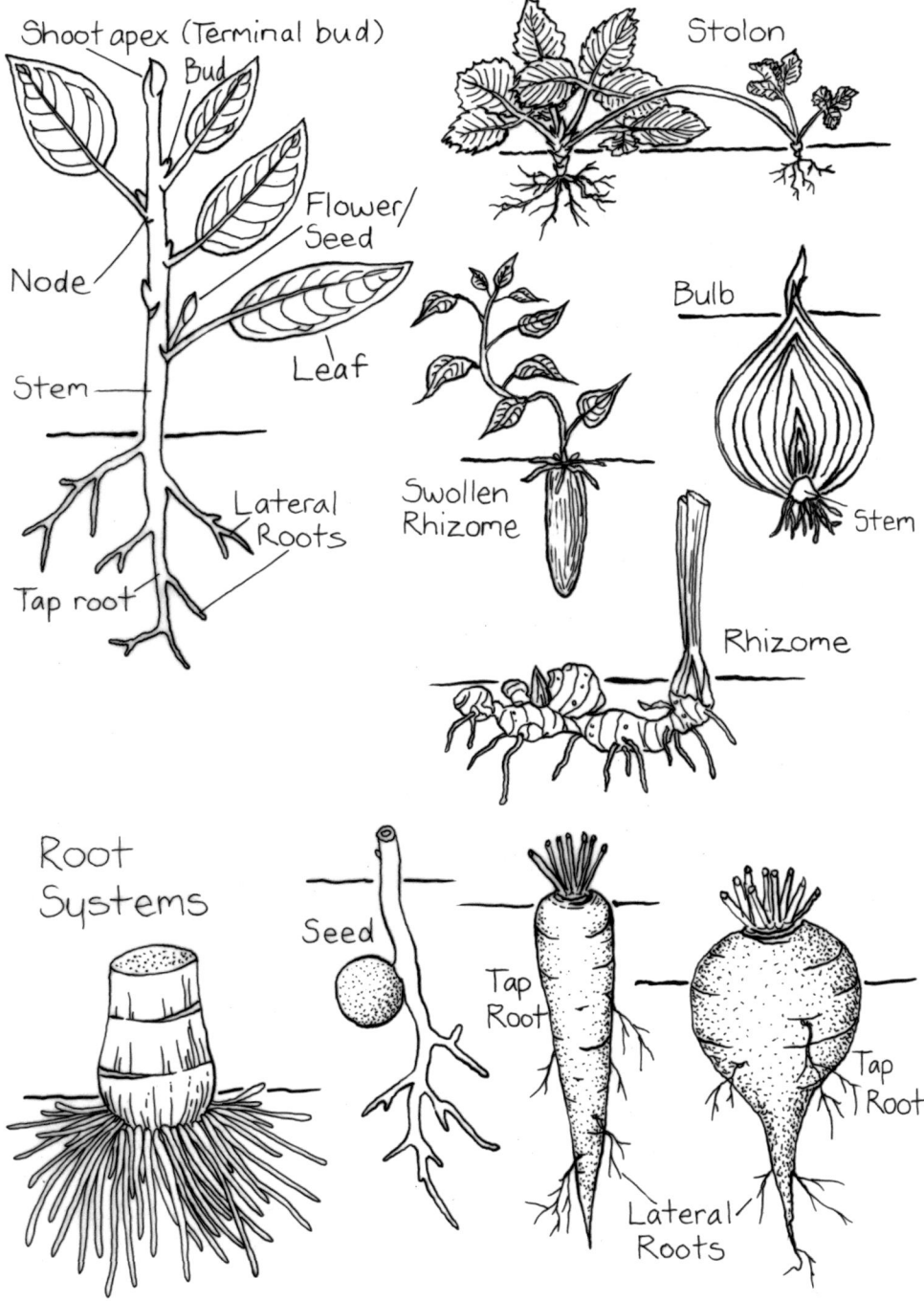

Figure 3.1 Plant structures: roots, stolons, rhizomes, tubers

Technically, most of the "roots" and root crops of Jamaican agriculture and diet are not true roots or true parts of root systems. Rather, they are modified stems, with important roles in the storage of food for the plant (just as roots store nutrients) and in propagation. Such modified stems take four main types (Figure 3.1). Some plants produce stolons, or "runners", that send out shoots above ground to root in new places, such as the strawberry plant. Others, such as ginger, have horizontal stems that grow by elongation below the surface. These stems are called *rhizomes*, and like the stolons their primary function is the propagation and spread of the plant. The rhizomes of some plants are swollen and grow very large, not to aid propagation, but to store nutrients and water in significant amounts in order to supply food to the plant as required. These are the tubers, and they account for most of the "roots" – cassava, yam, coco, sweet potato, Irish potato – that are important in the Jamaican food system and that are discussed in this chapter. The fourth type of modified stem is strictly a bulb, such as an onion. *Bulbs are vertical shoots formed underground; they consist largely of the swollen bases of leaves attached to a short stem. Like the tubers, their function is the storage of food for the plant.*[5] Although it is botanically incorrect to speak of rhizomes and tubers as "roots", practical everyday nomenclature – both Jamaican and international – persists in lumping them together. That error is perpetuated here: the principal roots of this chapter are all strictly rhizomes and tubers (bulbs will be postponed to the next chapter, where they are at home with the leafy green vegetables).

Almost certainly, the major roots (really tubers) used as food in Jamaica came to the island by human agency, selected with an eye to food value and agricultural advantage as well as to transportability. The physical characteristics of the plants and their mechanisms of propagation made it unlikely that any of them reached the island on the water or in the wind, or that they might have been carried by birds. Thus the roots came to Jamaica only by self-conscious human intent and knowledge of their value as food and of methods of their preparation. On the other hand, none of the introductions can be securely attached to a particular individual, ship or date, in the way that can be done for several fruit. Nor were any of the roots the object of large-scale imperial botanical enterprises: none of them occupied an important place in the botanical gardens of Jamaica. In general, the roots arrived in Jamaica along with people who already knew their qualities, their advantages and disadvantages, and who cultivated and ate them; indeed, they often came because they were being eaten on the same voyage that brought them. In this way, the roots generally arrived unremarked and became part of the diet in a natural and unremarkable fashion.

Among these root crops, cassava and sweet potato dominated Taino consumption but declined after European colonization, to be replaced by yam and coco, and these in turn were often overshadowed by the fruit of the plantain. In 2004 Jamaica produced 148,000 tonnes of yam, 24,000 tonnes of coco, 22,000 tonnes of sweet potato, 15,000 tonnes of cassava and 4,000 tonnes of Irish potato. Small proportions of the yam, coco and sweet potato crops were exported, while 9,000 tonnes of Irish potato were imported. The net consumption of 210,000 tonnes of roots was, however, overwhelmed by 633,000 tonnes of grain – wheat, rice and corn – virtually all of it imported. The balance between the roots and the cereals has shifted back and forth, but ultimately the trend has been away from roots grown in Jamaican soil and towards seeds that grew on the stalks of plants waving in the air of foreign fields.[6]

In addition to the decline of the roots, there have been significant changes in the relative importance of the different root crops in Jamaica. Between Independence and the end of the twentieth century, yam increased its dominance from 60 to 70 per cent of total production, while sweet potato and coco remained stable at 10 per cent each and cassava and Irish potato lost ground. Thus the range of root crops consumed by Jamaicans became increasingly limited to yam, at the same time as the roots were overwhelmed by imported grains. Cassava struggled to maintain its place and became an occasional food for most consumers rather than a staple. By the 1980s cassava was rarely seen in the markets and was rarely thought of except when other staples, such as rice, were in short supply or when price rises threatened. In these changes, Jamaica followed its own path. Root crops are staple foods for one-third of the world's population, cassava and sweet potatoes accounting for more than 90 per cent of root production in the tropics. Jamaicans eat less roots than the typical inhabitant of the tropics and have largely discarded the indigenous cassava for introduced species. The Jamaican pattern is closest to that of Africa, but Africans now consume less yam than cassava, which was introduced from the Americas.[7]

Most of the fall in the consumption of roots and tubers in Jamaica occurred in the second half of the twentieth century. It can be explained partly in terms of availability and price, but the transition was underpinned by nutritional opinion, beginning in the 1930s, that strongly favoured cereals, particularly wheat flour, over root crops because the "flesh-forming proteins" of yam and cassava cost five times as much as flour. The roots also did not lend themselves to modern packaging and continued to arrive in the kitchen untidy and bulky, covered with dirt and needing to be peeled and processed. Further, leaving part of a root uncooked generally meant loss, as the cut surface dried out and had to be discarded. And because roots have a high water content (often as much as 75 per cent), they have a relatively short shelf-life and are expensive to transport, and they can easily rot or sprout during storage and transport.[8] Overall, roots were not regarded as highly flavoured, though some were preferred to others and they performed better as a group than the cereals. It was rare for roots to feature in the colourful photographs of foodstuffs published in glossy cookbooks, and botanical illustrators ignored them as well. Roots were strong on texture, but it was sometimes a "woody" texture that did not appeal to all consumers. In these ways, even though the roots were really tubers, they had something in common with the true roots, as a consequence of their formation underground. Essentially, the basic root food crops were regarded as the foundation of a meal rather than contributing the spicy-hot flavour that helped define Jamaican taste, and generally they needed salt to be made palatable. None of the roots were ever promoted as elements of Jamaican national dishes, or given the "Jamaican" label, in spite of their status as "food".

At the beginning of the twenty-first century, roots were thought to be "'low esteem' products". Even when cooked and served on a plate, they were hard to make attractive, because they retained their bulky, rough-hewn appearance. For example, Virginia Burke's 2005 cookbook *Eat Caribbean* put "ground provisions, rice, breads and plantains" towards the back of the volume, and recognized "how awkward a plate of boiled green bananas, hunks of yellow yam and a fat grey dumpling might appear to someone who is unaccustomed". Burke offered her dishes "in more refined versions", with attention to presentation and appearance. She herself claimed to find "the earthy blandness" of roots and their staple relatives "comforting" and indeed believed them to be essential to traditional dishes. However, with the exception of a recipe for "creamed cassava with roasted garlic", all of her offerings were for the plantain, the breadfruit and the cereal-based foods, ignoring the fundamental earthy ground provisions, and she told readers that "rice, flour and cornmeal are at the heart of every kitchen".[9] This lack of enthusiasm for the roots spread, with imported rice and flour, from an overseas, non-Jamaican audience to infect Jamaicans living in Jamaica, sending the roots to the sidelines.

In the light of this shift away from the roots of Jamaican food and the apparent growing distaste for them, it is necessary to ask why roots had dominated for so long and what advantages they possessed over alternatives. What were the conditions that made roots so much more vital a part of the Jamaican diet in the long period before the recent transition to dependence on cereals?

In the first place, there were advantages of culture and cultivation. Root crops grown within the ecological niche of the food forest are less demanding on the available supply of plant nutrients than are cereal crops, permitting the longer cultivation of individual plots and a relatively slow decline in yields before fallowing is needed. Soil erosion and weed invasion are also lesser problems for root crops under substantial canopies, enabling longer periods of settlement without relocation. Within the provision ground system, as practised during slavery, these were attractive features. In addition, although the root crops require a relatively long growing period (compared to the cereals), yields and edible energy produced per hectare are good. In more recent times, it was an advantage that the manual character of cultivation and harvest made less demand on fossil fuels than mechanized types of agricultural production, however more productive the latter may appear in man-hours.[10] This helps account for the "rootedness" of the Jamaican peasantry and their enslaved plantation ancestors, evidenced by their strong attachment to particular grounds. This attachment was not only spiritual; the grounds were also containers of stored resources, long-term investments of labour and time.

The common characteristic of the roots is the storage of food and water in specialized underground organs, naturally adapted to survival through dry seasons yet capable of rapid growth when moisture becomes available. It is the reserves of food and water stored by the underground organ during the period of dormancy, the dry season, that predisposes the roots to attack by humans and animals. As a defence, some plants seek to fend off attack by burying their tubers deep in the ground, though domestication selected shallow-rooting types with large tubers, making harvest easier.[11] The hidden quality of the tubers gives the roots some protection against theft, and few animals dig for their food. The underground storage of nutrients is equally valuable in enabling root crops to withstand the devastation resulting from hurricane winds. Thus the planter faces fewer competitors for the produce of the soil and the food stored in the root or tuber is relatively secure until harvest. On the negative side, the harvesting of root crops is necessarily hard manual work, and the roots generally require substantial processing before they can be eaten – few are palatable raw and some are indeed toxic. This toxicity is another element in the armoury of roots. Human consumers had to learn how to remove or reduce this potential poison, which added yet another element to the task of preparation. Why should people choose such hazardous plants as staple foods?

CASSAVA

Sloane, pondering the cultural diversity and perceived strangeness of human taste in 1707, reflected, "It was some matter of wonder to me, to think how so many people, perhaps one fourth part of the inhabitants of the whole earth, should come to venture to eat bread, made only by baking the root of cassada, which is one of the rankest poisons in the world, both to man and beast, when raw." It may indeed seem strange that the Amerindians should choose as a favoured domesticate a plant so potentially dangerous and so demanding on labour. But the choices available to them were limited, and bitter cassava does have the great advantages of bearing on poor soils where other crops would fail, being drought resistant, giving several harvests from one planting and storing efficiently once processed. In the ground, the roots can be kept for long periods, safe from herbivores because of their very toxicity. As a modern crop, cassava has been assessed "highly suitable for low input, low risk, ecologically and culturally appropriate subsistence agriculture in the tropics".[12]

The status of cassava as a basic food crop of the Taino raises a number of intriguing questions about the decisions underlying food choices. The Taino balanced the hazards of cassava with its advantages (including that it can deliver a caloric yield three times that of maize) and found the plant to be a winner, but their assessment required a careful weighing of risks and benefits rather than the simple selection from nature of a self-declared winner. It was not simply an adaptation or a matter of making do from a narrow range of possibilities. Once the Taino had developed their techniques of cultivation and preparation, they carried these along with the cassava plant as they migrated through tropical America and the Caribbean.

The cassava plant, *Manihot esculenta*, is a single species, domesticated in Brazil (and probably also in Central America) at least four thousand years ago.[13] Originally a crop of the upland tropical forest, it succeeded in a variety of marginal environments. The name *cassava* is Arawakan, bestowed on the plant by the people who carried it to the Caribbean. Another name for it, *manioc*, from Brazil, never had currency in Jamaica. A distinction is generally made between two varieties of the species, sweet cassava and bitter cassava, the latter requiring processing before it can be eaten. Although sweet cassava is not poisonous, it yields much less than the bitter variety, and was less often planted. Bitter cassava's superior fermentation qualities also deliver better-quality flour and starch. In modern, post-Columbian, times, many cultivars have been moved from place to place; by Independence, Jamaica had perhaps one hundred varieties, some of them developed in the island but most brought from South America by the Department of Agriculture.[14]

Bitter cassava contains in its roots substantial concentrations of toxic cyanide. Thus it is "an exception to the general rule that humans select the less toxic cultivars of a given food plant", and is perhaps "the only staple crop in the world that is highly poisonous". The amount of cyanide varies with the cultivar, the age of the plant, and soil and climate; it increases with the age of the plant but peaks and then declines. Traces of cyanide remain in most processed cassava, though research has been directed at achieving complete detoxification. Untreated cassava root contains linamarin, a cyanogenic glucoside which releases hydrogen cyanide on contact with stomach acid. Chronic ingestion of linamarin may slow down neuronal processes, leading to spastic paralysis.[15] Many compounds contribute to the taste of cassava, however, and the degree of bitterness is not always an accurate measure of the cyanide potential: bitterness is not a perfect warning system. Indeed, bitter cassava is not bitter in taste once processed; it is perceived instead as "sweet" because of the glucose released from the cyanogenic glucosides. Further, the perception of bitterness is partially confounded by the presence of other compounds with a sour taste. Much effort has been put into creating low-cyanide or cyanide-free varieties of cassava. On the other hand, it has been argued that because the secondary compounds in the plant play a role in protecting it from pests and pathogens, reducing the cyanide in cassava may carry hidden costs.[16]

The cassava, a perennial woody shrub, grows to three metres (Plate 3). Starchy roots up to a metre in length radiate from the base of the stem, just under the surface of the soil (Figure 3.2). An individual plant can yield six to eight harvestable roots, weighing about one kilogram each. By the 1940s, Jamaican farmers were producing about four tonnes of cassava per acre. Roots used for food are best harvested at about seven months. The plant is hardy, highly resistant to drought and hurricane, but when exposed to the air the roots deteriorate quickly (within one to three days) and so they tend to be left in the ground until required. Cropping of the perennial plant can continue for up to fifteen months. This practice occupies potential crop land but was a great advantage before storage and preservation became relatively easy.[17]

The Taino propagated cassava from stem cuttings planted in mounds on the *conuco* system. They dug the roots anywhere from ten months to three years after planting. The skin was peeled off using a seashell, and the edible fleshy portion pulped by grating – probably, in Jamaica, using a stone covered with shark skin or a piece of hardwood inset with stone chips. The pulp was left in a wooden trough overnight then placed in a woven cylinder two to three metres long but only about ten centimetres in diameter, made from palm leaves or bark. At each end of the cylinder was a loop, one end attached

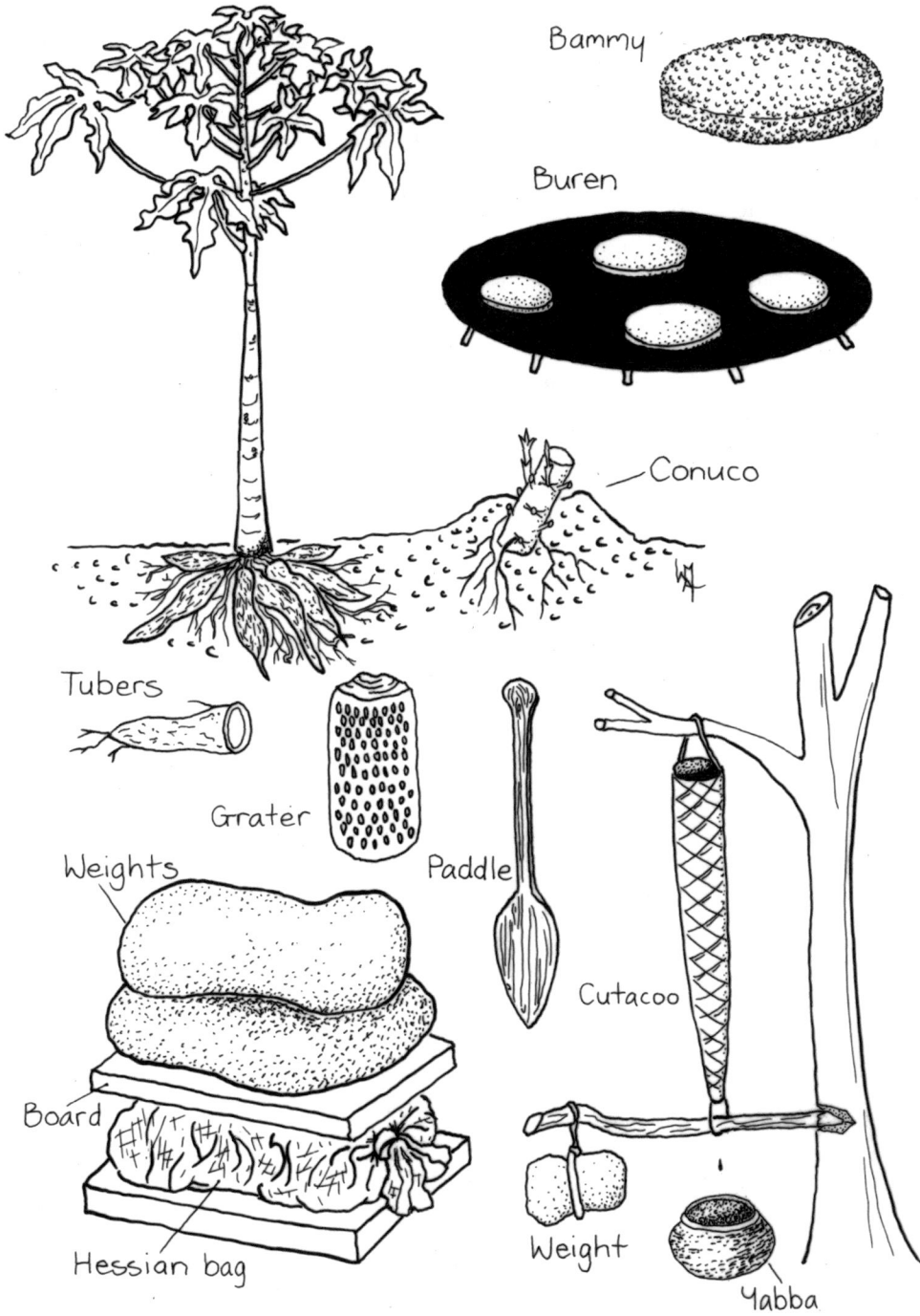

Bammy

Buren

Conuco

Tubers

Grater

Paddle

Weights

Cutacoo

Board

Hessian bag

Weight

Yabba

Figure 3.2 Cassava plant, tubers and processing technologies

to a tree and the other drawn down by a weight, using stones or the leverage of a pole (Figure 3.2). The poisonous juice was squeezed out but could be collected and boiled to produce a sauce. The damp pulp was sifted and heated on a buren. As it cooked, the meal formed cakes about three centimetres thick; these were turned with a wooden paddle, and left for fifteen minutes on each side. Sometimes the cakes were made thinner, wafer-like. The cassava cakes were sun-dried for several days and could be stored for two to three years. The Taino ate the cakes broken into pieces and dipped in a sauce.[18]

The cultivation and processing practices of the Taino were followed closely by the Spanish colonists, who depended on cassava as a major food resource. The English and Africans in Jamaica generally did the same. Sloane said that the cassava root was peeled, grated and put in a bag and the juice squeezed out; the dried "farina" was "spread in the sun to dry further, then put on a gridiron set on coals, and there bak'd as oat cakes are in Scotland". These cakes could keep for three years. The English sometimes used a different method, without a woven cylinder to squeeze out the poisonous liquid. According to William Hughes, writing in 1672, the English planters grated "manyoc" using a wooden wheel with a metal jacket, laid the grated cassava on "a plain [flat] thing they have for the same purpose, as broad as the bottom of a bushel or sive; and then press[ed] forth the juyce or moisture thereof very clean and dry". The resulting cakes, pressed to about one centimetre thick, were put on "an iron pan of a suitable circum-ference, being placed on bricks; . . . making a moderate fire under, and turning them, and baking them leisurely, till they are very hard and dry; and then they lay them up in their houses for daily bread". These lasted for three to six months, said Hughes. By the 1680s cassava was termed the "common bread" of planters and servants, and Charles Leslie claimed in 1739 that the cakes were "white and crisp, and much in request here, being preferred by our creoles to any other bread whatsoever".[19]

Enslaved Africans brought to Jamaica initially learned techniques of cassava culti-vation and preparation directly from the Taino (Figure 3.3). In time, however, Africans began to reach Jamaica with a pre-existing knowledge of cassava, because the plant had been taken by the Portuguese from Brazil to Africa in the sixteenth century. In this way cassava became a common food in the slave trade, particularly from Central Africa. Jamaica received relatively large numbers of people from this region before 1700 and again after 1790. British imperialists carried cassava to India, but it remained confined to a limited region in the nineteenth century. Few of the indentured Indians who came to Jamaica knew the crop, and most immigrant peoples readily accepted the established processing technologies, descended from those of the Taino, that had been developed to deal with the peculiar physical and chemical qualities of cassava. Occasionally people died from poisoning, but whether as a result of inadequate knowledge of processing or of the different types of cassava is uncertain.[20]

In the eighteenth century, cassava cakes became a market item, produced and sold by enslaved people with developed expertise. Modern Jamaicans call cassava cakes *bammy*, a term unique to the island. F.G. Cassidy found the etymology "puzzling" but

BITTER CASSAVA

LEAF   TUBER

BOIL   PEEL   ROAST → PEEL

WASH

GRATE

FERMENT

PRESS → JUICE

DRY   STARCH   BOIL

SIFT   CASSAREEP

BAKE   PEPPERPOT

FARINA

PORRIDGE   POUND   MOULD

BAKE   BAKE → DUMPLING

MEAL   DRY ——→ CAKES

PUDDING   BAKE

PORRIDGE   BAMMY   BREAD   LACE   PUDDING
CAKES

SOAK   CRUMBLE   TOAST
GRILL

BAKE   TOAST   STEEP
FRY   STEAM
GRILL

PERINOE

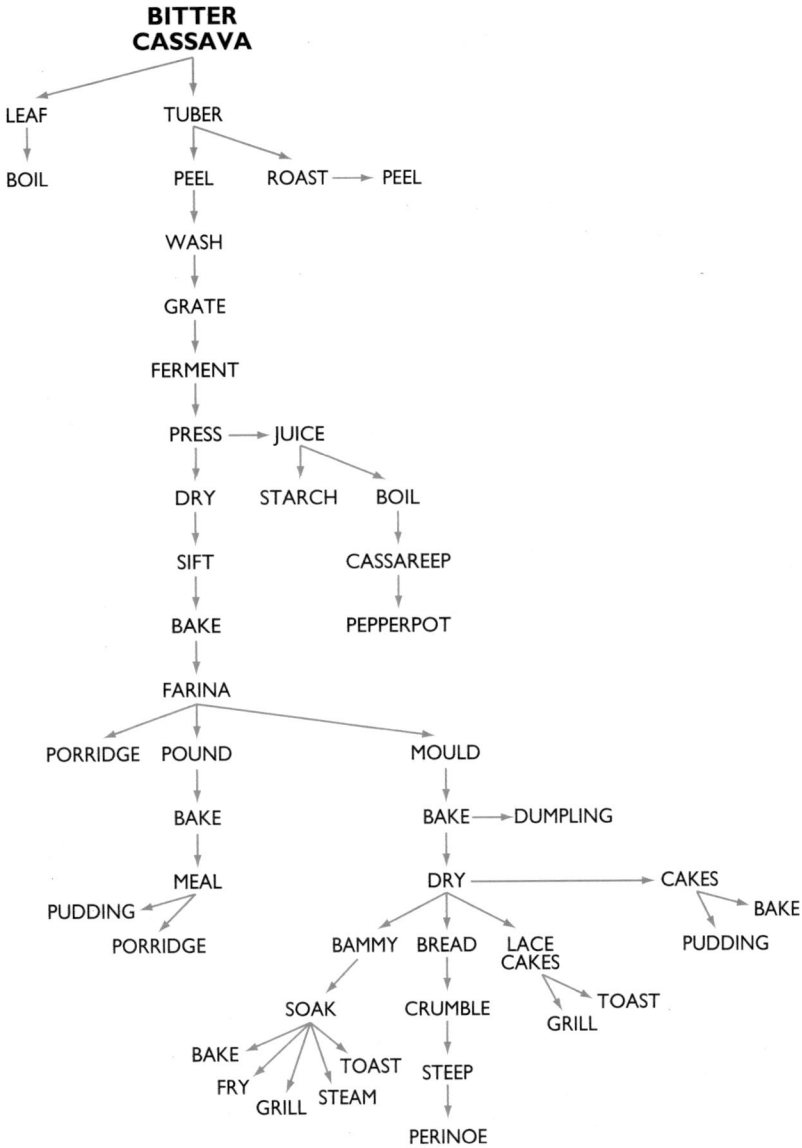

Figure 3.3 Cassava: processing flow chart

believed it was "unlikely to be anything but Indian" (meaning Taino/Arawakan). This seems unconvincing, as the first citations come late. Cassidy was undeterred by the fact that the earliest reference he could identify to *bammy* came from Caroline Sullivan's *Jamaica Cookery Book* of 1893. Some earlier citations have come to light, but none from the period of slavery. The first found in the *Gleaner* is from 1866, when a Mrs Amelia Josephs won a prize of ten shillings for her "cassava in bammy or thin cakes" at an agricultural show held at Cumberland Pen, near Spanish Town. Richard Allsopp offers an African source: *bami*, "cakes or bread of cassada", from an 1858 Ga-Adangme dictionary. This is a tantalizing suggestion. The Ga-Adangme community, on the dry coastal plain of Ghana, came to depend much more heavily on cassava in the twentieth century than most other regions of West Africa.[21] The spread of cassava probably occurred after these peoples were sent to Jamaica through the slave trade but perhaps in time for the dictionary of 1858, when they were part of a British protectorate.

Sullivan said, "bammys are sold ready for cooking and are a sort of muffin", and she explained that they did not keep long and were best eaten fresh. To cook, they were "put on the gridiron till done, turning them till both sides are brown, then split open and buttered". The reference is reminiscent of an earlier description by Henry Barham, who said, "they make the cakes as broad as a hat, which, buttered while hot, eat like an oat-cake". Oatmeal lacks gluten and so, in Scotland and Wales, was formed into flat cakes, the dough heated on a griddle or baking stone. When eaten, the oatcakes were toasted on a fork, opened and buttered inside, much like a modern "English" muffin. The practice of opening and buttering the bammy disappeared sometime in the twentieth century. A letter to the editor of the *Gleaner* in 1914, from a Manchester correspondent, said, "nothing can be nicer than toasted bammies cut in halves and buttered while hot". Phyllis Clark, in 1945, said only that "cassava bread" should be browned or toasted and buttered before serving.[22]

To prepare bammy "cakes", Sullivan explained in 1893, "the bitter cassava is grated, pressed, and then put into iron hoop moulds". She distinguished these thick "bammy cakes" from "cassavas", which were thin and made with less butter at the bottom of the moulds. Sullivan also offered a bammy recipe using sweet cassava, grated and squeezed in a cloth then baked "between stones or in a pan until firm". When the time came to eat these bammy, they were soaked in milk, toasted, cut in half and buttered. These "bammy cakes" were "much liked", but Sullivan recommended buying them ready-made, saying a packet sufficient for breakfast, "unless the party is a large one", could be bought for a penny halfpenny. A packet of "cassava cakes" could be bought for three pence. Sullivan proposed these for breakfast or tea, saying they should be buttered on one side and put on a gridiron, doubled over when half done, and served "light brown and very crisp". In 1899, John Tully opened a bakery on Matthews Lane in Kingston, offering "cassava cakes or bammy".[23]

In the second edition of her cookbook, Sullivan added a distinct recipe for "cassava cake" made from eight or nine "thin cassava cakes", soaked in sweetened milk, combined with sugar, butter, eggs, cinnamon and currants, and baked in a tin. She also introduced a recipe for "cocoanut and cassava pudding" that used six cassava cakes placed in a pie dish, buttered and soaked in milk, sugar and egg yolks; grated coconut was spread on the dish and baked, with a meringue on top.[24]

The *Dictionary of Jamaican English* finds "cassava lace cakes" in St Andrew around 1915, and common in the 1950s: "A very thin wafer made of cassava meal; toasted, buttered, folded in two, and served for tea." Lace cakes were a novelty still in 1918 when a *Gleaner* correspondent saw them in Brown's Town, displayed in a glass case and labelled "lace cakes made from cassava, etc.", a product of the Spring Plain Cassava Factory in Clarendon. They cost four pence a package and were "really and absolutely unsurpassed as a dainty toast for tea and breakfast". "Wafer" bammy were known commercially in the 1950s as "lace cakes" or "bammy chips, thin as paper – not made by Quashie". They were still around in the 1960s. In 1938 "bammies" were sold at penny halfpenny and three pence each, "cassava wafers" at four pence per pack.[25]

Martha Beckwith's ethnographic observations provide a detailed account of household practice in about 1920, including further distinctions in the types of bammy. After grating, Beckwith said, "the meal is mixed with water and the whole strained through a towel held between two persons". Left to settle for an hour or two, the water (with the poison) could be separated from the starch, and the "trash" that was left in the towel could be used for food. If the trash was allowed to dry in the breeze for two hours then mixed with salt and baked, it was called *pot bammie*. Alternatively, it could be dried in the sun for several days, "beaten in a mortar, sifted, and mixed with flour to make dumpling". However, said Beckwith, "for the choicest dish of all, the cherished 'bammie', the starch must not be washed out at all". Following ancient practice, grated cassava was "put into a 'cutacoo', or long, flat basket, shaped like a wall pocket and woven of thatch". This was suspended "in a press extemporized out of a couple of boards, the lower of which rests on a pile of stones, the upper fitting at one end into the hollow of some tree, and weighed down by a rock". Alternatively, the cutacoo might be folded over and placed between boards with rocks on top, or replaced with a hessian bag (Figure 3.2). After a night under pressure in the bag or cutacoo, the meal was beaten and sifted, "mixed with salt and water and baked and turned like a flapjack on a hot griddle (called an iron)". Finally, the edges were cut "round like a wheel". According to Beckwith, "The Negroes are extravagantly fond of this delicacy. No choicer offering can be made to an exile to the wet north side of the island, where cassava is not grown, than a package of homemade 'bammie' from the drier south."[26] St Elizabeth was already, in 1920, the home of the bammy.

The major change in the preparation of bitter cassava over the long term seems to have been the gradual reduction of the diameter and thickness of the cassava cakes. The circular shape itself, however, has remained standard, partly because it gives a structural strength not found in squares or rectangles, which might lose their corners, and partly because of tradition. As cassava became an occasional food, it shrunk in size and needed to speak instead to nostalgia. In the cassava-growing districts of the south side of the island, said Beckwith, "every market has its row of old women, with trays on their knees or at open stalls, selling flat white 'bammie' cakes as big as a plate, folded up in white napkins as protection from the dust". Clark recommended using a hoop or "bammy ring" about thirteen centimetres in diameter and making the cakes thin so they would be crisp and digestible. Larger, thicker bammy tended to dominate until factory production began to overtake the handmade version in the later twentieth century.[27] By the 1980s, somewhat thicker bammy –

five centimetres in diameter – became popular, but these were still vastly reduced from the initial thirty or more centimetres.

In 1993, one hundred years after Sullivan, Enid Donaldson's cookbook *The Real Taste of Jamaica* found the making of bammy dying out, "because many feel it can only be made in the parish of St Elizabeth by the experts". She did offer brave cooks a recipe using bitter cassava, wrung out in a muslin cloth, the prepared bammies to be soaked in milk, water or coconut milk, then fried, grilled or steamed, and buttered (but not sliced in half). The bammy thus cooked was to be eaten with fried fish or with saltfish and ackee. By the 1990s the cassava dumpling was almost forgotten but could be made from a grated bammy if the cook did not wish to begin with grated wet or dried cassava. These dumplings went well in peas soup or with ackee and saltfish but remained a rarity. By 2005 Jamaica Producers was making chips from cassava, as well as banana and potato, branded St Mary's Best, but other companies' plans to make cassava chips commercially were abandoned due to a failure of supply.[28]

The "farina" described by Sloane in the seventeenth century survived into the 1950s, but it was no longer easily available, some of the technology forgotten and driven from the market by the entry of three-minute breakfast cereals. Farina was described as "a product of the bitter cassava obtained by grating the tubers, thoroughly pressing out the liquid, and gently cooking the crumbled and thinly spread 'dough' in a wide, heavy, flat pan over a very slow fire, until the meal attains a light biscuit-brown colour, then sifting to obtain the coarser particles". Prepared this way, it lasted for a long time. It could later be made into a porridge by mixing with water and pouring the mixture into boiling milk, stirring for a few minutes, adding salt and nutmeg, and sweetening to taste. In 1908 Yucacelli brand cassava meal or starch was sold in Kingston, advertised as "a new and perfect food, unrivalled for puddings, porridges, etc.". The pudding was made by boiling the meal in milk, adding eggs, sugar, butter, grated coconut and vanilla, and baking. It was hard for these elaborate processes to compete with quick oats.[29]

Sullivan gave a recipe for "pepper pot" of the Guyanese variety, using "pure casseripe", salt, bird peppers, meat and hard-boiled eggs, adding something each day and warming the earthenware pot in which it was stored. This was an uncommon notion for Jamaicans. In 1938 the *Gleaner* explained how to make "cassareep", saying it was "used as the base in making many well-liked English sauces". No connection was made with the Amerindian or contemporary Guyanese use of cassareep in the making of pepperpot. Readers were told to grate bitter cassava and add water, extract the starch and "boil down the remaining juice until it is the consistency of syrup".[30]

Sweet cassava had few advocates in the twentieth century. Donaldson observed that it was "eaten as yam or potato" but gave no recipes. In the eighteenth century, however, sweet cassava had been enjoyed roasted or, less often, boiled. Edward Long favoured boiling because "in this state, the outward part is commonly brought almost to the state of a jelly, and is extremely delicate and agreeable". He also thought it made a fine flour. Sullivan offered a basic method for making "cassava flour (Quaco)". The sweet root was grated and washed "as for starch", dried in the sun, pounded in a mortar and sieved, squeezed, and dried a second time. She also offered "mussa" and "quaqua" as forms of cassava flour made into a thick paste or gruel, under the broad umbrella "couscous". Sullivan proposed two methods for tapioca made from grated sweet cassava, strained into a pan or yabba, and a recipe for tapioca pudding. Much later, in the 1970s, there were attempts in St Elizabeth to make bread from cassava flour mixed with wheat, but this failed because of the relative cheapness of imported wheat. Unusually, a 2001 prize-winning dish was "cassava veggie pizza", made with cassava meal.[31]

In the seventeenth and eighteenth centuries, cassava was sometimes recommended for use in drinks, but these seem to have disappeared and indeed were not strongly advocated even by their best promoters. Hughes said that some people used it "to thicken chocolate: it is not very clammy; and therefore nourisheth not very much, neither hath it a very grateful taste alone". In the 1680s it was said that cassava was used to make a drink "which they call perinoe". Sloane believed "perino" was unwholesome because it quickly became sour. To make it, he said, "Take a cake of bad cassada bread, about a foot over, and half an inch thick, burnt black on one side, break it to pieces, and put it to steep in two gallons of water, let it stand open in a tub twelve hours, then add to it the froth of an egg, and three gallons more water, and one pound of sugar, let it work twelve hours, and bottle it, it will keep good for a week."[32] Browne claimed that the matter "expressed from the farine" could be boiled and skimmed, and noted, "the remaining fluid (being found by long experience to be both wholesome and agreeable) is sometimes diluted and kept for common drink". Some people used it in "sauces for all sorts of fish as well as many other kinds of foods".[33]

In Jamaica, the only part of the cassava plant commonly used as food was the tuber or root. The green leaves are rich in protein but, because over-harvesting inhibits the development of roots, they are generally seen as a food only in extremity. Long did claim in 1774 that "the Negroes boil and eat the leaves as a green". Another eighteenth-century writer said of the "wild cassada" (distinguished from the bitter and the sweet), "the leaves . . . are boil'd and eaten with oil for the gripes, the water it is boiled in is drank after it". This was a medicinal rather than a food use.[34]

ZAMIA

Least known and least understood of the Jamaican roots is zamia, *Cycas megacarpa*. As it is even more hazardous than bitter cassava, its consumption as human food is even more puzzling. A cycad, the zamia plant resembles a stubby palm and is indeed sometimes called a sago palm (Figure 3.4). Unlike the true palms, cycads do not flower but bear naked seeds, literally gymnosperms, like their relatives the conifers (such as pine trees). Beneath the zamia's crown of spiky evergreen leaves lies a subterranean tuberous stem rich in starch. All parts of the plant are toxic; the pulped stems have to be washed and fermented to make them fit for human consumption. Simple squeezing, as is done for cassava, is not enough. Cycad flour can induce sclerosis (hardening of tissue), caused by membrane destruction or the inactivation of enzyme systems.[35]

About thirty species of zamia occurred in the Americas, from Florida to Brazil, and also in other parts of the world. Las Casas identified zamia roots as a significant food source for the Taino of Hispaniola in the early sixteenth century, and this was probably the case throughout the Greater Antilles, including Jamaica. The plant was cultivated by the Taino, not merely collected wild. They shaped the pulp into small cakes and baked them on a buren, like cassava. Zamia was sold in Jamaican markets in the nineteenth century, but it is not certain how much was local product and how much imported from the Cayman Islands, where it was used to make a porridge. It remained a food into the twentieth century, though it was more often used for starching clothes. In the 1950s, there were reports from western Jamaica of zamia prepared as a gruel, cooked with sugar, milk and water.[36] The plant is now little known and, for good reasons, absent from Jamaica's cookbooks.

Figure 3.4 Zamia plants and seed cone

ARROWROOT

The arrowroot plant, *Maranta arundinacea*, was a less lethal source of starch than cassava or zamia. A perennial herb with leafy growth up to one metre above ground, the arrowroot's roots are strictly rhizomes, with a starch content of more than 20 per cent (Figure 3.5 and Plate 1). In parts of Southeast Asia, the whole rhizome is used as food, boiled or roasted. Elsewhere, including Jamaica, it is just the refined starch that is eaten. The arrowroot's main virtue was the fine grain of its starch, making a very smooth paste that is easily digestible and therefore particularly suitable for invalid and infant diets. Its disadvantage was that obtaining the starch required much labour, as for cassava. It was necessary first to peel off the acrid scales with which the tough rhizomes are covered and grind or pound them to release the grains. Before the 1840s, when rotary hand mills were introduced to grate the dried rhizomes, they were generally pounded to a fine white powder in "large deep wooden mortars".[37]

M. arundinacea was brought to Jamaica from tropical South America, along with cassava, but there is no certain evidence that it was actually cultivated by the Taino, and it may have remained part of the wild economy. Two main cultivars are found in Jamaica, the creole arrowroot and the banana arrowroot, which must be processed within seven and two days of harvest respectively. Successive ratoon (regrowth) crops can be achieved for five to six years, and indeed it is a complaint that arrowroot can be difficult to eradicate from a field.[38] It prefers rich sandy loam and a good supply of moisture during growth, without waterlogging.

In the eastern Caribbean, particularly St Vincent, where arrowroot is more common than in Jamaica, the plant has been used to make arrowroot pap, a "porridge or thick drink" produced by mixing the starch with boiled milk and regularly fed to babies. Long called *M. arundinacea* "Indian arrow-root" and retailed a popular account of its etymology (following Barham and Sloane) as an antidote to the poisoned arrows of the Taino. He expatiated on the merits of arrowroot in counteracting spider bite and other poisons, as well as malignant fevers, but said little to suggest its use as a food. John Lunan, in 1814, was more expansive. He emphasized that arrowroot made "excellent starch" but added that "boiled with milk and water, it is a most nourishing and extremely palateable food, which may be retained by the weakest stomach". Lunan thought that "for many domestic purposes" arrowroot was "preferable to the best wheaten flour, especially in making puddings".[39]

Arrowroot entered English cooking during the eighteenth century, particularly in the making of biscuits, cakes and puddings. These foods generally contained only small quantities of the starch. Sullivan's 1893 recipe for "arrowroot cakes", which called for flour and arrowroot in equal proportions, was unusual. A "snow cake" was made by beating arrowroot with sugar and butter, then mixing in beaten eggs and vanilla essence, and beating all of this for up to thirty minutes, before baking in a "pudding pan". Sullivan encouraged the use of "Jamaica arrowroot" because of its superior whiteness and lightness. Phyllis Clark's 1945 *West Indian Cookery* offered only a recipe for

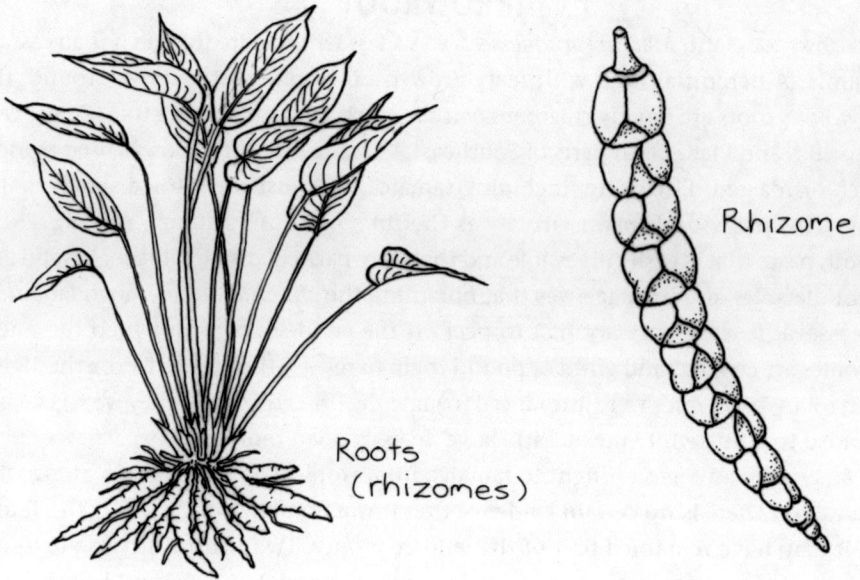

Figure 3.5 Arrowroot plant and rhizomes

"arrowroot drink (or porridge)", in a chapter on "diets for sick people". The 1957 *Farmer's Food Manual* gave a recipe for "arrowrootporridge", using boiled milk, sugar and flavouring, as a breakfast dish. Once ready, it was to be served immediately to prevent its becoming "thick and unappetising". Later cookbooks generally ignored arrowroot, employing alternative thickeners such as cornflour, though arrowroot remained significant in commercial baking.[40]

In contrast to the major root crops of Jamaica, which served a largely internal market, arrowroot emerged at the beginning of the nineteenth century as a minor export staple. Jamaica was the leading British West Indian exporter of arrowroot down to about 1840, when it was overtaken by St Vincent. Local production persisted into at least the 1870s, when barrels of "Manchioneal arrowroot" could be purchased in Kingston. But by 1918 arrowroot was almost forgotten and an advocate could claim it had not been "cultivated to any extent on the Island" while contending that arrowroot flour might be a useful wartime substitute for wheaten flour. In the 1980s even imported arrowroot was "found only by diligent search of shop shelves and occasionally in Kingston's Coronation Market".[41]

YAM

Whereas cassava is a single species with a single region of origin, there are hundreds of species of yam within the genus *Dioscorea*, widely scattered through the tropical world. Yet although there are numerous indigenous New World species – in fact more than there are Old World species – the Amerindians "paid little attention to them as potential crop plants", argue John Alexander and D.G. Coursey, "because of the availability of more easily cultivated 'root' crops" such as cassava, coco and sweet potato. Only one American species, *D. trifida*, came to achieve importance as a food, and its cultivation is limited to the West Indies. This species' centre of origin was in northeastern South America, along the Guyana/Brazil border, where it was domesticated by about 5000 BP (before the present). Cultivation spread through Trinidad and along the island chain, "becoming progressively more highly selected, until in Jamaica only one or two forms are known".[42]

Around the world, as many as sixty species of *Dioscorea* are used as food, but just four account for the majority of consumption, and these do not include *D. trifida* in their number. The four leaders are *D. rotundata* (the white Guinea yam) and *D. cayenensis* (the yellow Guinea yam), both of which were domesticated in West Africa; and *D. alata* ("water yam" or "greater yam") and *D. esculenta* ("Chinese yam" or "lesser yam"), domesticated in Southeast Asia. The greater yam produces tubers of up to fifty kilograms, whereas the lesser yam typically weighs less than one kilogram. The African and Asian species are much more closely related to one another than they are to *D. trifida*. The two species dominant in the modern world, *D. rotundata* and *D. alata*, are regarded as true cultigens – unknown in the wild state – and are artifacts of ancient domestication. Yam was central to the food culture of many West African societies, where it established its dominance long before rival plant introductions from Asia and the Americas. Domestication of the yam in Africa, by perhaps 10,000 BP, argues Coursey, was "an essentially indigenous process based on wild African species".[43]

Tracing the diffusion of the yam is difficult and sometimes controversial. The spread of *D. alata* is the most important piece in this puzzle. There is documentary evidence of its introduction from Asia to the west coast of Africa by Portuguese and Spanish traders by the early sixteenth century, and it came to Jamaica by that route, with the traders.[44] The Portuguese brought the word *yam* to the New World along with the tuber, but the true source of the word is generally regarded to be the Senegalese *nyami*, meaning "to eat". *Nyam* has long been used in this sense in Jamaica, making firm the association between yam, "food" and consumption.

It has sometimes been argued that yams were "brought to the West Indies by African slaves". Although such direct agency seems improbable, yams were indeed major foods in the slave trade and in much other long-distance voyaging, and yams certainly travelled along with the people. Yams were loaded by the people traders, often in large quantities – up to fifty thousand yams per ship. Slaving voyages were directed particularly at the West African yam-farming regions and were planned to match the seasonal availability of yams on the coast.[45]

Once in Jamaica, the yam rapidly overtook cassava, much more quickly than cassava supplanted the yam in West Africa. The reasons for this swift shift are several. Firstly, yam was central to the food culture of a large proportion of the people brought from Africa. Fresh contingents of people were poured into the island for three centuries, bringing with them knowledge that constantly renewed and sustained the culture. Secondly, most yams, consumed in standard portions, lack the toxic hazards associated with cassava and thus are easier to prepare. This advantage was particularly important during the period of slavery, when people had little time to devote to elaborate technologies of food preparation. Thirdly, yam yields are high, almost as high as those of the cassava. Fourthly, although their harvest season is short, yams could be stored uncooked, whereas cassava required elaborate preparation. And fifthly, yam is amenable to a wider range of styles of preparation.

Jamaicans have a large lexicon for the different species of yam. The 1988 *Farmer's Guide* claimed that there were more than two hundred varieties but reduced this to a short list very similar to that used by Jamaica's official statisticians, who identified and collected data for eleven varieties: hard, Lucea, Negro, renta, St Vincent, sweet, tau, white, yellow and mozella yam, and yampie.[46] New names continue to emerge as older ones fade. "Guinea science" is one neologism, derived from the older "Guinea yam", with its broad reference to Africa. Folk names also abound. Not surprisingly, the common names do not match species exactly and some varieties have more than one name. Some of the variants are regional, others have fallen into disuse, and new names continue to gain currency. The latter are local inventions but many of the traditional names have direct African sources.

In modern usage, *D. alata*, now the most extensively cultivated yam in the West Indies, is commonly called "white yam", but it is also known as "sweet yam", "moonshine", "renta" and "St Vincent"; *D. cayenensis* is "yellow yam"; *D. rotundata* is "Negro yam" (a white yam); *D. trifida* is "Indian yam" or "yampie" (known locally in Jamaica as "a-mi-du", meaning "it is I who do it", and planted in grounds to discourage thieves); and *D. polygonoides* (a wild variety) is "bitter yam". Although *D. alata* became common, it was argued in the 1960s that Jamaicans favoured the African species. Certainly, modern cookbook recipes are more likely to mention *D. cayenensis* than other varieties, and it has become the most popular of all the yams exported.[47]

Yam names from the eighteenth century introduce many more varieties. Barham distinguished several types, saying one white yam was "called the seed-yam, which is extraordinary white, and makes an admirable fine flour for making of bread or puddings, and thickening broth". Another variety was "a coarse sulphur-colour or yellowish yam, called negro-yam, whose stalks are prickly, and are of the convolvulus kind". Others were purple or purplish. Browne distinguished "Negro yam" from "yam" but did not explain the distinction. He said, "Both of these plants are cultivated for food, the roots, which grow very large, being mealy and easy of digestion: they are generally both dry and palatable, and not inferior to any of those [roots] now in use, either in delicacy, flavour, or matter of nourishment." Long distinguished "Negro-yam" and "White-yam", the first yellowish, coarse, stringy "and not so much in esteem as the second, vulgarly called, by the Negroes, *bochara-yam*". The term *backra yam* persisted into the twentieth century, for higher-grade tubers, perhaps referring to their whiteness but also, more broadly, to a general notion of superiority not necessarily associated with the white man, or *backra*. Sullivan observed that the white yam was "sometimes called 'flour yam' from its floury nature". Beckwith believed that "the whites prefer the soft, meally white yam which matures slowly, generally coming in about Christmas time, and which may, like our own potatoes, be kept six months after digging as against a few days for the yellow and a few weeks for the 'negro'".[48]

Lunan identified two kinds of "negro yam", known as "cassada-yam" and "man-yam". The man-yam was thought to be superior, "as being of a mealier better taste, and drier texture, but is not so productive". It had stringy fibres over the skin, whereas the cassada-yam was smooth. "The inside of both of these yams is white, of a viscous or clammy nature", said Lunan, and "when roasted or boiled they are meally like a potatoe but of a closer texture, they are a very pleasant and nourishing food, in much esteem among the negroes". Thomas Roughley, in 1823, said that "the negro and white yams" were the most cultivated, producing the largest, most nutritious and longest-lasting tubers. The "Indian yam" was floury and delicate but difficult to cultivate.[49]

In her 1893 cookbook, Sullivan listed "the white yam, the guinea yam, the hard yam, the yellow or affoo yam, the negro yam, the Lucea yam, and the Indian yam". Lunan had earlier identified "Afou yam" as *D. aculeata*, a small tuber of yellow colour. By about 1920, Beckwith could claim that, "as the Negro prefers hard food to soft, the yellow or 'afoo' yam is the favorite and next to this the yam called the 'negro'". Cassidy and Le Page, in the 1950s, traced *afu* (or *afu yam*) to the Twi word *afuw*, meaning "plant" or "cultivated ground". The Twi language group was centred in Ghana, northwest of the Ga-Adangme group, the possible source of *bammy*. As well as being used for the common hard yellow yam, the name *afu* was sometimes applied to the hard white yam, the "white afu". The Lucea yam derives its name from the town of Lucea in Hanover, the western centre of the yam trade, and is a white yam. Varieties were sometimes called "afu Lucea", mixing the African and toponymic references. Other yams were called "red afu" and "afu pumpum", the pumpum yam being round and lumpy rather than elongated; the word *pumpum* derived, like *afu*, from Twi. By the 1990s Lucea yam had become scarce in the market, even in Lucea. Farmers attributed its disappearance to the growing use of fertilizer and manure, which produced large force-ripe tubers that were red rather than white in colour. In 1996 one lover of the Lucea yam was reported saying, "long time me nuh si it . . . but when a used to eat it a couldn't mek it cold else it woulda scratch out me daylight".[50]

In 1940 the Jamaica Agricultural Society distinguished the following, proposing minimum prices: yellow yam (six shillings per hundredweight, or fifty-one kilograms), Negro yam (eight shillings and six pence), Lucea yam (ten shillings), white yam (twelve shillings) and yampie (thirteen shillings). This hierarchy matched Clinton Black's 1973 statement that the "aristocrat" of all the tubers was the yampie, "a delicious, fine-textured variety, superior, many claim to the best Irish potato".[51] But by the early 1990s yampie also had become hard to find in the market; yellow yam was now "the most favoured of the yam family" but sold at the same price as the St Vincent yam, and both of these were substantially cheaper than the "most costly and finest-eating . . . sweet yam". St Vincent has recently been shown to contain high levels of phenols (carbolic acid), which give foods bitterness and astringency, as well as high levels of cyanoglucoside (like bitter cassava), though its potentially toxic doses are much reduced in their effect by boiling in salted water. Beckwith, however, reported an informant calling the St Vincent yam "'Come-here-fe-help-we' because it keeps so long in the earth and propagates itself by seed, so that one planting will sometimes perpetuate itself for fifteen years and serve the people in hard times".[52]

Why so many names for the yam? The texture and flavour of the tubers varies significantly, and individual taste is often quite specific, but the different plants that produce them are not always distinguished easily by their habit. In spite of the myriad names and varieties, the pattern of growth is generally similar. Each year the perennial yam plant produces a climbing vine that dies at the end of the growing season, while the tubers below ground store up nutrients for the next year (Figure 3.6). The plants grow best in well-drained soils. Although they can tolerate drought, yield is much reduced if insufficient water is received over the season. Yams therefore need high-quality soils, and do not prosper in the marginal soils that might support cassava or sweet potatoes. Many species of *Dioscorea* contain toxins, designed to protect the tubers from rooting animals, as well as prickly stems and roots. Others bury their elongated tubers deep in the soil, making removal difficult. The tubers are stem tubers but with a rhizomatous end, called the "head", from which the twining vines, roots and tubers arise. It is from the head that propagation is most commonly achieved, but other sections of the tuber can also be used as planting stock, and tissue culture was developed in the 1980s. However, propagation of edible yams by tuber cuttings or setts, practised for thousands of years, has reduced the sexual fertility of many cultivars to the extent that they rarely produce fertile seed or even flower. Thus the yam has become completely dependent on agroecological systems.[53]

The planting of yams was described by Browne in the eighteenth century. Pieces of the root with skin attached were "put into convenient holes (two or three in each) which are generally dug pretty regular, and about a foot and a half or two feet square: these are afterwards filled from the adjoining banks, and the whole piece covered with cane-trash; which serves to keep the ground cool and fresh, and to prevent the growth of weeds". For plantation use, Roughley recommended lining the ground in four-foot squares, dug out with a hoe, in order to "raise yam hills", and planting the Negro yam around Christmas time. Mould was dug in around each peg, to a diameter of twenty inches, then formed into a cone until the hills were "high, bulky, and pervious". Yam heads with "lively eyes" were planted two to each hill by pushing an arm into "the bosom of the hill" on opposite sides. Once the budding vine had emerged, "stiff prongy stakes" were driven into the ground to carry the creeping tendril. When the vine died off, the yam was nearly ripe and almost fit to dig.[54]

Roughley recommended cutting half the plantation yam piece in August, for heads; the head was cut underground, near the vine, and this small part of the yam was left to produce more tubers while the remainder of the yam was dug out. The latter were "young" and needed to be used quickly. Roughley said that these Negro yams were

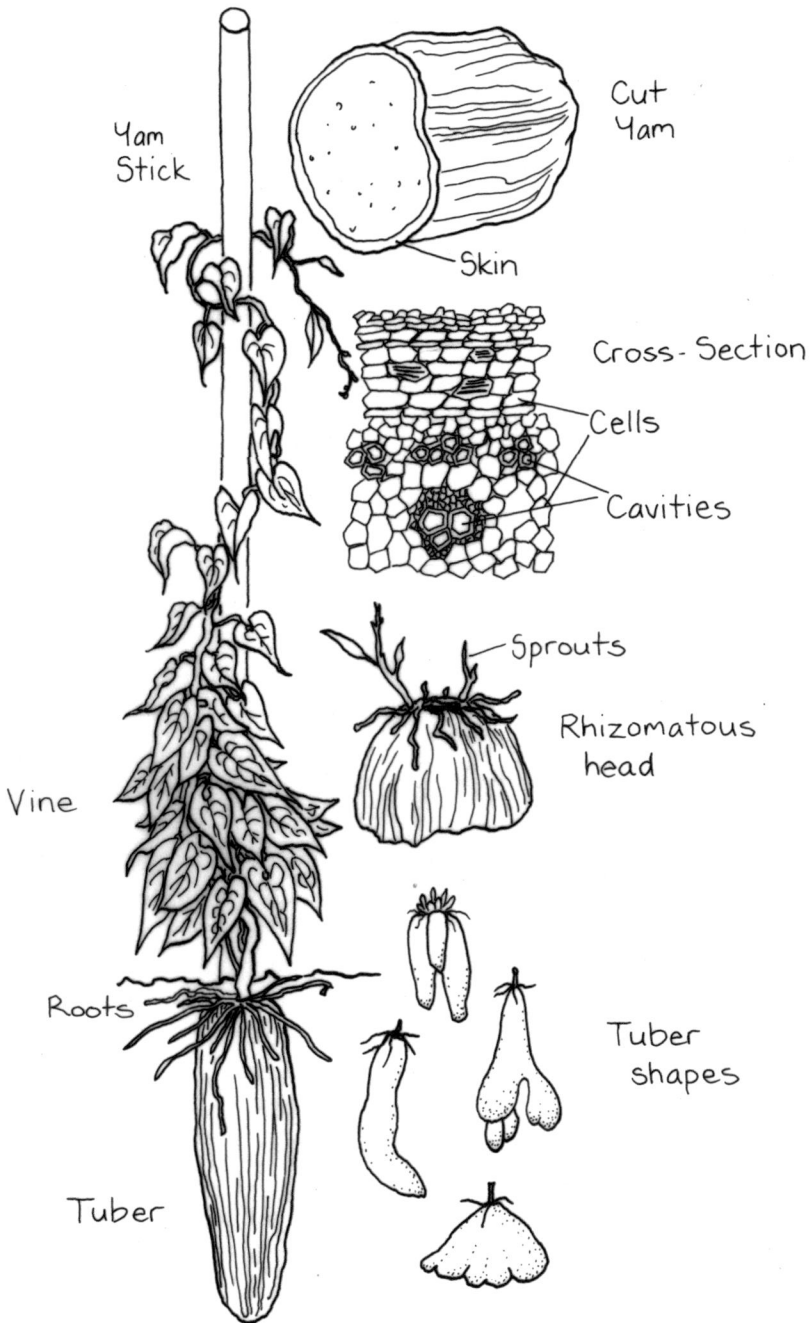

Figure 3.6 Yam plant and tubers

"similar to young potatoes at this time, being rather soft, moist, and will not keep long; however, they are esteemed a rarity". By Christmas, all of the yam vines withered and the yams were harvested, cleaned and stored. These directions were specifically for the Negro yam, but much the same applied to the white yam, said Roughley, except that it was not cut for heads or plants in August, but planted in February or March to be dug twelve months later. In the long term, yams were essentially a smallholders' crop, very visible in the provision grounds. In modern Jamaica, production of *D. alata*, *D. cayenensis* and *D. trifida* peaks around February, and *D. rotundata* around October, so that output is at a minimum overall in the middle of the year.[55]

Preservation and storage took a variety of forms. Browne said that the harvested yams were "rubbed over with ashes, from the copper-holes, or other fires, and piled regularly on convenient beds, or hurdles, raised above the floor, so that the air may come easily between them: but where they are heaped in great quantities, care should be taken to strew some ashes between the layers". Alternatively, the yams could be exposed to the sun for a few days to harden after the coating of ashes had been applied, then stored, carefully stacked to avoid bruising, in a cool place away from moisture. Lime was sometimes used rather than ashes. Once the yams had dried, they remained good eating for more than a year. Modern accounts of these methods suggest that the yams best suited to curing include renta, St Vincent, white and mozella yam. "Dry, waxy" yams are generally preferred. One disadvantage is that, while the tubers are rarely attacked by insects or rodents, loss by respiration can be 25 per cent in six months, and the same amount can be lost to rotting. There is also significant loss in peeling off the thick skins.[56]

Methods of preparing yam have ranged from roasting to pounding, with very different demands on labour and technology. Roasting and boiling were quick and simple, and were therefore the most common methods both during slavery and in the modern kitchen. Roasting took the least preparation, the complete tuber being placed in the coals. The charred skin was then scraped off, and the tuber cut in half and eaten, by itself or with some sauce or oil. Boiling was easy but required a pot, a yabba or the digging of a pit for earth-boiling; the yams were boiled with the skin peeled off and were then cut into large slices. Boiling time differed with variety but could be as short as ten minutes. Sullivan declared white yam "excellent roasted or boiled and mashed with butter", and she thought the skin when roasted "delicious". Yellow yam was more variable, she said – sometimes waxy, sometimes floury. Its skin was "bitterish" yet "some people like it". Claude McKay noted that the preparation of yam heads for planting left many small "toes" that were kept for home consumption, saying "no part of the yam was more valued than a fresh 'toe' rich in starch. Such a 'toe' well roasted and eaten hot (sometimes with butter or a piece of meat or fish) with the morning's coffee was manna to a peasant." Roast yam was already in decline. During World War I it was said that Jamaicans would be forced "to go back to roast-yam, to go back to an article in high favour some forty or fifty years ago".[57] By the early twenty-first century, roast yam had become an occasional treat rather than a common food.

The soup of Jamaica is most often a bulky, chunky soup in which the roots are not mashed or pureed but retain their integrity as substantial pieces, in the midst of a well-seasoned but relatively transparent liquid. Yam is fundamental, and a dry, woody tuber is frequently favoured over something that can turn mushy. Botanically true "roots", such as carrot and turnip, may be included in this soup and these are often bundled together for sale in the market, called "leggins" or "leginz" (derived from the French *legumes*). These bundles might contain scallion, pumpkin, thyme, cabbage, chocho and parsley, along with the roots carrot and turnip, in various combinations and quantities. By the late twentieth century, the term itself had largely disappeared from the vocabulary, but the bundles were still sold, and nostalgic recipes for "leggins soup" or "Saturday soup" were sometimes still published, adding to the yam and the bundle of vegetables such items as country pepper, garlic, pimento, breadfruit, Irish potato, cabbage, paprika, salt and chicken feet.[58]

Boiled yam could be subjected to further processes, requiring more tools and time. Sullivan said the yellow yam was sometimes grated and sent to table. Mashed boiled yam could be formed into "yam balls" and fried in lard. Alternatively, the yam could be sliced thin and fried in a pan or buttered and cooked on a gridiron. As well as these, Sullivan offered a recipe for yam stuffing (for a roast pig), yam pie (mashed yam spread over minced meat and baked) and yam pudding (using white yam).[59] The "Guinea people" of Hanover made a dish called *agidi* (derived from the Yoruba) using grated yellow yam mixed with flour and fried in oil. The same name was sometimes given to a dish made with cornmeal.

In 1902 the Imperial Department of Agriculture for the West Indies published a pamphlet titled *Recipes for Cooking West Indian Yams*, in an ambitious attempt to promote the tubers in North American and UK markets. The pamphlet included the usual recipes for roasted, baked and boiled yams, along with yam chips, yam rice (pressed through a colander), yam rissoles, yam border (mashed, mixed with eggs and butter, moulded and baked, then filled with meat or fish and served in a sauce), yam *au choux* (boiled yam and cabbage rubbed through a sieve, mixed with butter, cream and seasoning, and served hot with fried croutons), porcupine yam, yam fritters, yam pudding and yams *en brun* (sliced boiled yam, fried with parsley, shallots or mushrooms, pepper, salt and lime juice). Several of these concoctions had no known Jamaican parallels and seem much more the product of English cookery, but the advocacy and inventiveness were unusual. Yam pudding did survive; a 1955 recipe using white yam called it a "Jamaican dessert". In this recipe, the yam was boiled, mashed with butter and spices, rosewater and milk, eggs and sugar, and baked in a pie dish. A recipe for "an old-fashioned yam pudding" published in 1991 used grated raw yellow yam, flour, breadcrumbs, baking powder, nutmeg, cinnamon, butter, brown sugar, vanilla, grated orange rind, soaked fruit and egg. The result was "a pudding not unlike Christmas pudding", beginning with the creaming of the butter and sugar, adding the wet and dry ingredients, and baking.[60]

Twentieth-century cookbooks offered less and less on how to cook yam as it lost favour to other foods. Clark, in her 1945 guide for the everyday cook, had no reference to yams in her index and said only that "ground provisions" could be boiled, stewed, steamed, baked or grilled. Donaldson, in 1993, also omitted any recipes specific to yams, saying only that they could be boiled or roasted or used in soup (though they did appear as an ingredient in nine of her recipes).[61] Even in soup, yam became an ingredient rarely mentioned in cookbooks. Whereas green banana and Irish potato belonged in fish or chicken soup in the 1980s, yam might appear only in "hard time soup", created from a range of starches and vegetables and a pack of chicken noodle soup mix. Vegetarian cookbooks similarly sidelined the tuber. Yellow yam might be used to make a salad, but in this role it was a substitute for the more usual Irish potato. It was occasionally used to make a dessert, as in yellow yam pudding – mixed with sugar, soaked fruits, nutmeg and vanilla, and steamed. Mashed and sieved, it could be mixed with vegetables, flour, seasoning and raisins to be moulded into a "yam hill", imitating the cultivation mound. Increasingly, yam became associated with "traditional" Jamaican cookery.[62]

When the inaugural Yam Festival was held at Albert Town, Trelawny, on Labour Day 1997, there were complaints that the yam itself was hard to find, but displays included yam-based fruit puddings; one-pot dishes that combined yam, vegetables, sausages, butter and seasoning; and "'Emancipation', a kind of yam salad, created with a combination of diced yam with mackerel sticks as well as whole kernel corn and seasoning". Other dishes exhibited were "yam cup cakes, yam chips, fruity yellow yam cake, yam bread, yam corn dog, yam fritters, yam dumplings, yam/veggie meat, yam pudding, yam 'blue drawers', yam muffins, yam salad, yellow yam and callaloo, yam cocktail patties, yellow yam gizzada, rich yam fruit cake, yam and potato pudding, yellow yam pie, luscious yam in fancy style and yam dip". Drinks offered included "yam beverage delight, nog, yam shake, yam punch, southern yam quencher and yam drink".[63]

Missing from most cookbooks, with the exception of Sullivan in 1893 and Norma Benghiat in 1985, was any reference to the preparation of yam by pounding, a process directly derived from African practice. According to I.C. Onwueme, pounded yam is "the most popular and most traditional form in which yam is eaten in West Africa". In the African tradition, boiled yam is pounded in a large mortar using a heavy pestle until it forms a paste, which is then "rolled into small balls, dipped in a sauce or stew ('soup'), and swallowed without being chewed". Different yams produce different consistencies. As Coursey wrote in the 1960s, "In African households probably the most important culinary utensil, after the cooking pot or pots, is a large wooden mortar, with a wooden pestle, which is used for the preparation of the carbohydrate component of the meals, by a protracted and usually very laborious process of pounding." Such impressive mortars and pestles, made from a solid length of tree trunk, hollowed out and standing sixty to eighty centimetres from the ground, and requiring the use of both hands, were made and used in Jamaica during slavery.[64] What is striking here is that enslaved people, probably men, found the time to laboriously hollow out timbers to make the mortars and that enslaved women found the time to pound their roots and tubers in order to prepare them in African styles. The pounding process was generally performed outside, the sound echoing among the hills. The product of this hard labour was highly valued, the true food and centre of culture.

Pounded yam is well known from Jamaica in the eighteenth and nineteenth centuries. For example, an observer in the 1770s said that some enslaved people "beat their boiled roots in a mortar, which gives the mass nearly the cohesion of a boiled pudding, this they call foo-foo, and is generally eaten with broths". *Fufu* is derived from the Twi and Ga-Adangme languages, and the word is used in the same sense in several Caribbean territories, often applied to pounded plantain and cassava as well as yam. Occasionally, in Jamaica, fufu was called *tumtum*, imitating the sound of the pestle in the mortar, and the mortar was called a "tumtum mortar". The accompaniment with soup and pepperpot persisted. At the Culinary Arts Competition of 1968, it was reported that an eighty-year-old woman from Waterworks in Westmoreland contributed "a Tum-Tum, a kind of thick, highly seasoned soup, which is traditionally served in her village with Foo-Foo, both very African recipes".[65]

Sullivan's recipe for fufu was introduced in the context of her section on "soups", and Benghiat did the same. After giving a series of recipes using different kinds of peas, Sullivan noted that "the natives do not strain their peas soup: they eat the whole thing boiled with yam, coco and dumplings and often with a remarkable concoction called 'foo-foo' which consists of yam or coco boiled and beaten and then added to the soup". This created "a decidedly substantial repast". Benghiat said fufu remained, in the 1980s, familiar to Jamaicans in the country areas, but the recipe she offered was "more of a sauce than a soup" and quite elaborate, including kale, callaloo, okra, salt beef and seasoning.[66]

The general omission of fufu from twentieth-century Jamaican cookbooks may be explained by a reluctance to encourage the long and noisy process of pounding in a mortar, which could take fifteen to thirty minutes. The manual process has now been replaced to some extent by blender-like machines, but this technology became available only when fufu was already less popular. Clark gave a recipe for "foo foo" in 1945 but said it was made with green plantains. A collection of "African recipes" published in Jamaica in 1980 included a method for "fufu" beaten in a mortar and made from any of yam, green plantain, green banana or corn, to which might be added cooked vegetables, salt pork and scallion. Another 1980s cookbook gave a recipe ("from Barbados") telling its readers that "foo foo" was "a well known African dumpling made with starchy foods such as green bananas, green plantains and sometimes mixed with cornmeal and seasoned" – but recommending that cooks use green bananas. This was a long way from the traditional product. By the 1990s fufu was a matter of nostalgia among the Maroons, a dish "once much loved" and "made by pounding roasted breadfruit (without the crust) or yellow yam".[67]

COCO

In Jamaica, "coco" is used both to identify a specific tuber and a larger group. In Africa, "cocoyam" serves as the comprehensive term, while "taro" is the general label applied in Asia and the Pacific. Neither of these terms has currency in Jamaica. Rather, in Jamaica "coco" is used broadly to comprehend tubers from two distinct plants – *Colocasia esculenta* and *Xanthosoma sagittifolium* – but applied specifically to the tubers of *X. sagittifolium*. The latter are also known as "tannia", while the tubers of *C. esculenta* may be classified as "eddoe", "dasheen" or "badoo". These varieties are not always easily distinguished or recognized.[68]

C. esculenta originated in Asia, most probably in India, Burma or Malaysia. There is strong evidence that it was domesticated early and cultivated in terraced flooded-field systems even earlier than rice. It spread through the Philippines to New Guinea around 4000 BP, and then through the Pacific. Long-distance trade from Indonesia and India brought the plant to Africa by AD 100. *C. esculenta* reached the West African coast before Europeans did, and travelled from there to Jamaica with the slave trade. It was probably used as food on slave ships, though it was less important than yam. As in the case of the yam, the contention that slaves were active agents in bringing *Colocasia* from Africa and installing it in gardens in tropical America is unsupported and seems improbable.[69]

X. sagittifolium is a New World plant, cultivated in the Greater Antilles before Columbus. Early Spanish writers reported seeing the plant in Hispaniola and Puerto Rico, using the Arawak word *yautía*, and it seems certain that it grew in Jamaica as well. It was taken from tropical America to Africa in the nineteenth century, perhaps earlier, and spread from there to Asia and the Pacific, following in reverse the route taken by *C. esculenta*. In Africa, the Yoruba refer to *koko*, and the Twi word *kóokó* is believed to be derived from the Jamaican *coco*, reversing the pattern for *yam*. The presence of *X. sagittifolium* in the Caribbean at the beginning of European colonization makes difficult a precise dating of the arrival of *C. esculenta* in Jamaica,[70] and the continuing terminological confusion is no doubt related. Other edible species of *Xanthosoma* have been exploited in the West Indies, but *X. sagittifolium* is the most widely cultivated and consumed.

All of the cocos are perennial herbs. The two species *C. esculenta* and *X. sagittifolium* are the most important of the edible aroids, belonging to the Araceae, or arum, family, which has hundreds of genera and more than a thousand species. Most of the aroids are tropical plants, growing in moist and shady habitats. Some are vines, creepers and climbers, but *C. esculenta* and *X. sagittifolium* are arum lilies. *C. esculenta* has a central corm or rootstock from which the shoots grow as tall as two metres, with large, rounded leaves shaped like elephant ears at the ends of stiff stems (Figure 3.7). The shoots appear two to three weeks after planting, the leaves and stems constantly declining and being replaced for some six months. In the next phase of growth, the corm becomes more active. Flowering is rare, varying between the eddoe and dasheen types but always taking the form of an arum lily. The corm itself is spherical or barrel-shaped, up to thirty centimetres long and fifteen centimetres in diameter in dasheen, and smaller in eddoe

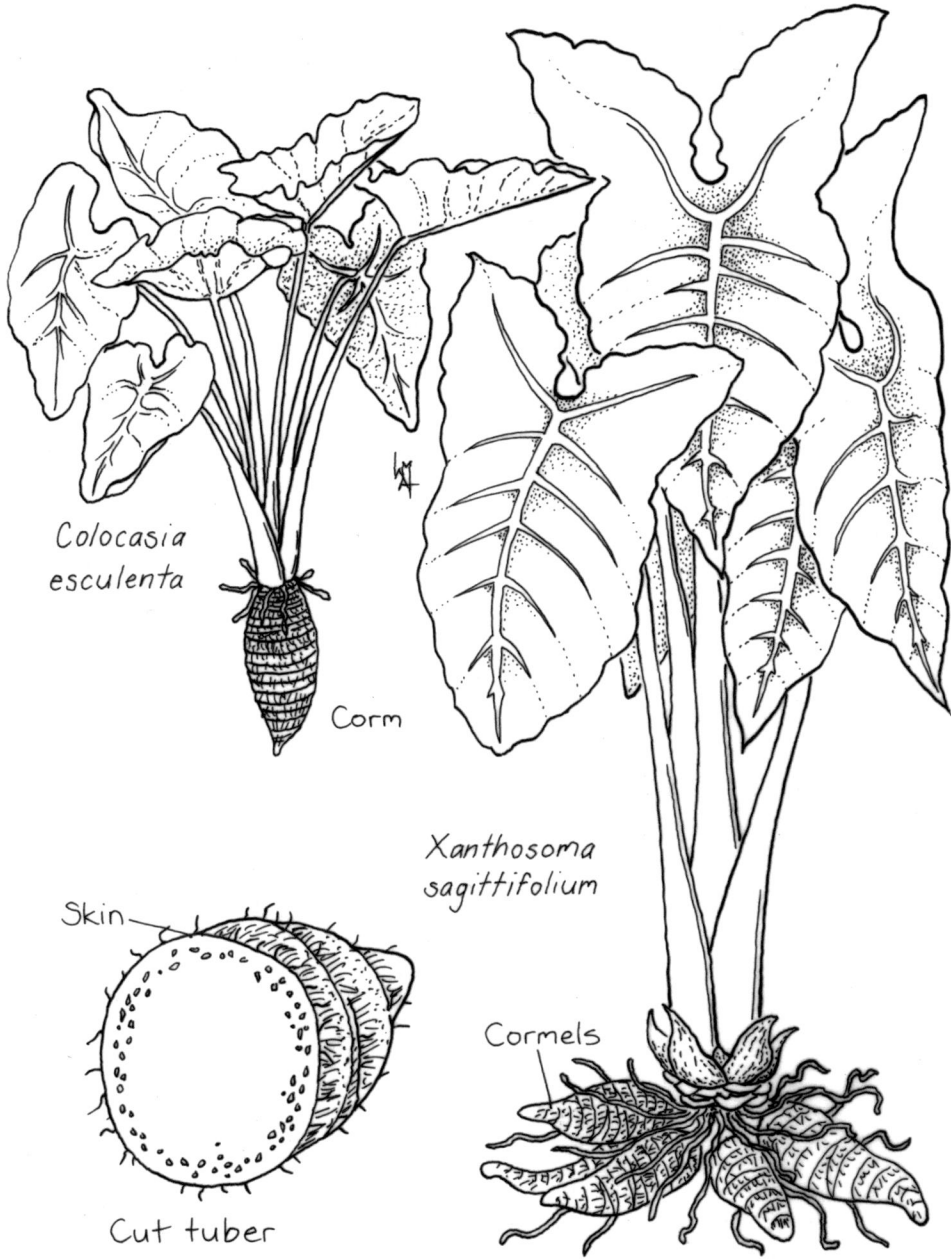

Colocasia
esculenta

Corm

Xanthosoma
sagittifolium

Skin

Cut tuber

Cormels

Figure 3.7 Coco plants and tubers

types. As well as the corm, small lateral branches, or "cormels", develop as stem tubers, particularly in the eddoe. *X. sagittifolium* has similar characteristics but is generally more robust, and its cormels are larger and more numerous, more elongated and flask-shaped. The difference is seen most clearly in the leaves, those of *X. sagittifolium* taking a distinct heart shape.[71]

It is hardly surprising that terminological complexity surrounded efforts to identify the different varieties produced by the two species. Europeans coming to the Caribbean struggled first of all to distinguish the tuber (*coco*) from the fruit of the tree (*cocoa*) and of the palm (*coconut* or *cocoanut*). More confusing was the fact that the tuber was spelled *cocoa* before it became *coco*. By 1740 the tuber was being called "ground-cocoa" or "cocoa root" in order to elucidate the difference. The spelling *coco* emerged sometime after this. To add to the complication, many other terms had been used earlier in Jamaica to comprehend coco – "tannie", "tannier" or "taya", "eddo" and "eddoe". Barham placed the "tayas" among the "eddos", saying they were "the largest sort". Even in the early twentieth century, Beckwith still found a "great variety of names attached to the coco in different localities". In St Mary she was told of the hard "Duke" or "Commander", the "Sally", "Minty" and "Green 'talk", and in Mandeville "were enumerated the 'Lef' Hand' as the hardest, the 'Jeremy' as the biggest, and the 'White Stalk', 'Too Good', 'Sinket', and 'Burban' (Burbank), each with its own peculiar merit".[72]

By the late twentieth century, official Jamaican sources were sometimes putting together coco and tannia, distinguishing them from dasheen, or else combined "tanias, cocoes, dasheens" as a single category. The agricultural censuses made no attempt to count the number of farms growing coco, though they managed for the other major tubers. A committee that reported on the costs of production of local "food crops" provided close detail for most of the tubers but found that "cocoes (dasheens, baddoes, etc.) . . . and similar crops of the *Xanthosoma* and *Colcocasia* [sic] genera" were "almost invariably grown in 'mixed' cultivation as a secondary crop" and hard to count.[73] Viewed globally, and within the wider Caribbean, the confusion of names is compounded, and coco has come to simply be placed in the "other" category.

The 1988 *Jamaica Farmer's Guide* offered advice only for "dasheen". Propagation of dasheen was achieved by dividing the corm or head into setts, each with an eye, and planting these into prepared holes. The tubers could be ready for harvest in anywhere from six to eighteen months, and were harvested by pulling, in the drier upland soil types, or by digging, in wetter grounds.[74] Historical descriptions of the cultivation of coco in Jamaica are rare. Simon Taylor, attorney for Golden Grove Estate in St Thomas, said in 1786 that cocos would grow only in newly cleared land, but that once established and allowed to remain undisturbed for a year or more they proved highly productive. He thought cocos a great hedge against shortages caused by hurricanes, but said "all cocos are exceedingly watery and bad food unless they are very old indeed from the month of July until Febry and March". Lunan said cocos (*Colocasia*) were "very generally and largely cultivated", bearing in about nine months and producing tubers every four or five months for up to three years, after which the head was lifted. The most common varieties in Jamaica at that time were the purple, white, Surinam, San Blas, St Kitts and "baboon hog coco or taya". The San Blas had been in cultivation "for some years past", producing large heads and roots – cocos weighing three to four pounds each. According to Lunan, "when full they are dry and very palateable, forming a hearty and nourishing food". Cultivation of the San Blas variety dominated, he said: "It is very rare to see a field of any other description. The negroes are particularly partial to them."[75]

Overall, Lunan claimed, cocos formed "a principal part of the subsistence of the negroes, who prefer them even to yams, though not so light nor so agreeable a food, yet very wholesome and nourishing, either boiled or roasted". Several features of the coco made it an attractive food for enslaved and poor people in Jamaica. Yield per hectare was substantial, and indeed greater by a wide margin than for any other Jamaican tuber, including yam and cassava. Once planted, little attention was required apart from occasional weeding, and pests were few. The labour of digging the tubers made the crop *relatively secure in provision grounds. The above-ground leaves were more easily* harvested, but their rapid growth and replenishment made them a plentiful resource. Like yam and cassava, the availability of coco could be extended by prolonging the harvest. Beckwith explained that "one year after planting, the first 'breaking' is ready, but the head may be moled [*sic*] up for nine months more for a second breaking, and eight months later the whole is pulled up for cuttings and the rubbish fed to the pigs". Such multiple-harvesting, removing the cormels and secondary cormels, is more common for *X. sagittifolium* than for *C. esculenta* and requires careful digging. The plant does have some disadvantages: once removed from the soil, coco stores poorly, though three months' storage can be achieved in Jamaica in a cool and dry storage environment.[76] Recent experiments with the canning and freezing of coco have demonstrated the viability of the processes, but commercial production in Jamaica seems improbable even for an exile market.

Coco is eaten in much the same way as yam. The tuber can be roasted or boiled and used to make soup or potato pudding, or added to the coconut-based dish pakassa (discussed in chapter 5). Sullivan included "coco soup" in the second edition of her cookbook, saying it was "a favourite dish amongst the peasantry, especially in the country parts where fresh meat is scarce". In her recipe, the cocos were boiled and mashed fine, with a penny halfpenny each of salt pork and beef, seasoning, scallion and tomatoes, and served with flour dumplings. Boiled coco could also be served mashed with butter, and grated coco made good fritters. Sullivan thought "roasted coco skin . . . very nice eaten with butter". A century later, Donaldson encouraged her readers only to try coco fritters, omitting the flour and egg used by Sullivan but adding baking powder and evaporated milk. Only the occasional modern cookbook mentions the coco, as an ingredient in soup, vegetarian meals or puddings. Dasheen makes a rare appearance, in vegetarian cookbooks, in croquettes and as a pudding. General lists and glossaries published in cookbooks regularly omit the whole range of cocos and universally ignore badoo.[77]

Modern cookbooks do occasionally contain recipes for "coco" referring specifically to *X. sagittifolium*, which comes closest to the yam in terms of shape, surface and texture.

In West Africa too, *X. sagittifolium* is now regarded as superior to taro. Dasheen and badoo are gummier, stickier than the more floury *X. sagittifolium*. In 1987 "white eddoes or coco" were recommended as an accompaniment to salt meat or fish. The eddoes were prepared by boiling them in their skins, then, when the eddoes were soft, cutting off their tops and squeezing out the pulp into a pickle made of hot water, pepper, salt and lime juice. The pulped eddoes were kept hot and put into another dish to serve, spread with butter. In the 1990s a distinction was made simply between "soft" white coco, the cheaper variety, and the purple "hard coco", which was "more favoured", particularly for soups. In this, the taste of the majority has conquered. Roughley was among the few who would have recommended, for the plantation managing class, "the bourbon, which is large, but rather soft, less nutritious, but more palatable to white people, and sooner becomes fit to dig in; and the country white and black cocoas, which are small, more prolific, more nourishing, drier, and more agreeable to the negroes, but which take a longer time to become ripe".[78]

In the 1980s dasheen was thought "unknown to many Jamaicans who live in our drier districts", but its cheapness made it attractive for soups, dumplings and puddings, or as an accompaniment to ackee and saltfish, and it was soon called the "fast-becoming favourite tuber". In the 1990s "the lowly dasheen" increased in popularity and price, and was promoted as a "tasty accompaniment for the kidney, salt-fish, pork as well as a number of other meats". The Rural Agricultural Development Authority began manu-facturing dasheen chips in Hanover, the chips sold in half-ounce sized plastic bags. An export market opened up for dasheen, and it was promoted for deep-fried chips, flour, powder and paste.[79]

Little use is now made of the leaves of the coco, though they occasionally appear in vegetarian dishes and soufflés. In the eighteenth century, however, Dovaston said, "the leaves as well as the stalk that supports ye flower are eaten by the Negroes as a salad". Long claimed in the late eighteenth century that the tops of the "white coco" were sometimes used as greens but were generally thought to be inferior to Indian kale. In the early twentieth century, the peasantry used coco shoots, while in their folded state, as an ingredient in pepperpot soups and steamed finely shredded coco shoots like callaloo to eat with rice or bread.[80]

One reason why the eating of coco leaves has effectively disappeared is that the older leaves of both *C. esculenta* and *X. sagittifolium* contain needle-like crystals of calcium oxalate, designed to defend the plant from being eaten, that can puncture the mouth and throat. Only the young, folded leaves are consumed, and they must be cooked. Modern writers generally contend that the irritating effect found in the tubers as well as the leaves is removed by boiling. In the eighteenth century, Long said that the old roots of "scratch coco and eddyes or eddoes, . . . though boiled for a long time, still retain a degree of pungency, which affects the throat". He found that all of the coco tubers possessed "an extraordinary acrimony; but after being dried and kept for some time, they lose all this quality, and become insipid to the taste". The Westmoreland overseer and planter Thomas Thistlewood planted "scratch toyer" in the 1780s but noted that "Toyer heads require boiling 8 or 10 hours, and the water to be several times shifted else they will scratch and itch the throat abundantly. The fingers are better than the heads and don't take so long boiling."[81]

Barham said that "tayas" were "apt to cause a heat in the throat, which they call scratching the throat, so that only negroes and hogs eat them; and they must be well boiled to correct that peccant juice". The tops of some of the plants were only good for feeding to hogs, said Long, as were the tubers of the "baboon or hog coco".[82] The notion that coco tops and tubers were fit for pigs, along with the need for extended boiling, helped place the crop low in the ranking of favoured foods. Roots as a group generally fall near the bottom of the pecking order, in terms of artistic representation, taste and agricultural research priorities; and among the roots, cocos occupy the lowest rungs. Even within the cocos, some varieties are spurned even more decidedly than others. In Jamaica, of the cocos considered fit for human food, the badoo is perhaps the least favoured, with dasheen struggling to keep ahead, and the eddo or strict coco most favoured. Yet in spite of the disparagement and general decline of the cocos, the expression "one one coco full basket" remains in common use, indicating the virtues of persistent industry and incremental capital accumulation, and referring to the tuber's former glory.

SWEET POTATO

For Jamaicans, the generic potato is the sweet potato, *Ipomoea batatas*, rather than its distant white relative *Solanum tuberosum*. Only in the late twentieth century did Jamaican cookbooks begin to affect the international usage of "potato" for "the ordinary potato", which had previously been called the "Irish potato". In terms of both production and consumption, the sweet potato remains the more important crop in Jamaica, with superior yield per hectare and an output five times greater than its rival the Irish potato. The sweet potato is valued for both its flavour and its versatility. Indeed, in the 1980s, the sweet potato was called "Jamaica's supreme tuber: a tuber whose cuisine demonstrates refined taste seldom experienced in much else of our highly spiced recipes". The overall output of sweet potato is a little less than that of coco, and substantially less than that of yam, but this valuation does not translate into consumption; and even though the sweet potato has long been considered more nutritious, it cannot rival hard yam and coco in Jamaican taste. In the 1990s, in spite of the sweet potato's purported refinement, it was claimed that "sweet potatoes are not a favourite among Jamaican men" because "it had nothing in it" and is thought to "interfere with nature".[83]

I. batatas is the only economically significant species of the morning-glory family (Convolvulaceae). In Jamaica, its leafy stems trail or twine up to five metres, with pink or purple flowers (Figure 3.8). Sweet potato cannot tolerate waterlogging or prolonged drought and grows best on a well-drained sandy loam. Whether it is planted in ridges or mounds, composting and good drainage are essential and, since the 1930s, planting on the contour has been advocated. Although a perennial plant, it is generally grown as an annual. Propagation is by slips, taken as stem cuttings, or by shoots, pulled from

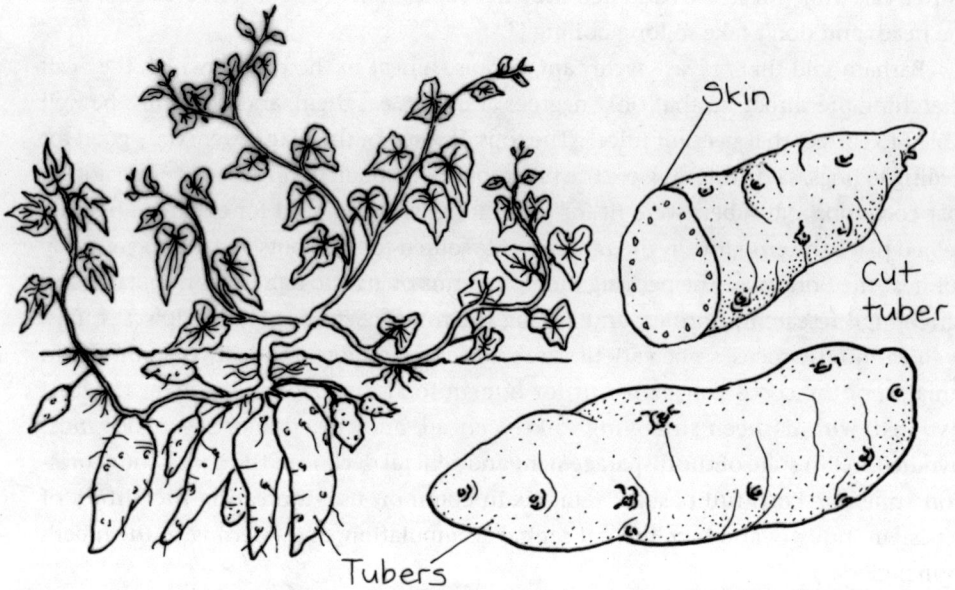

Figure 3.8 Sweet potato plant and tubers

sprouting tubers, and this adventitious vegetative reproduction is one of the plant's attractions for the grower. After planting, weeding is essential to allow full growth of the vines. The tubers come to maturity in four to six months but are usually harvested progressively. If the harvest is too early, yields are poor, and if too late, the plants may be attacked by weevils and suffer rot, making the tubers less palatable. Most of the crop is found where the slip was inserted into the ground, but secondary crops occur along the vine. Yields of twenty tonnes per hectare were normal in Jamaica in the 1940s, individual tubers rarely weighing more than two kilograms. Overall yields remain less than for yam but better than those achieved by Irish potato.[84]

Storage of the sweet potato can be problematic. Soft rot appears as fungal growth and quickly turns the tuber into mush, particularly if it is placed in a humid environment. Tubers damaged during harvest are most at risk, hence the practice of keeping them in the ground as long as possible. Another problem is the condition known as "cacoon", in which the texture and flavour of the cooked sweet potato prove unpleasant and uncharacteristic because the tuber has become overripe and started to produce new shoots, though these could not be observed on the surface of the uncooked root.[85]

Sweet potato originated in the modern region covered by Mexico, Ecuador and Peru. Domestication occurred by 5000 BP, probably from wild Mexican progenitors, and spread early through the Greater Antilles. Columbus found *I. batatas* in the islands and took the plant back to Spain on his first voyage. Peter Martyr found eight varieties of "patatas" in Jamaica before 1520, so there is no doubt that the species was indigenous to the island. The sweet potato came second only to cassava as a *conuco* crop for the Taino, with a lower caloric yield but the advantage of rapid growth to maturity.[86] Columbus, who knew yams *(Dioscorea)* from West Africa, initially called the sweet potato a yam. This confusion continues in North America, where the true yams did not grow. Wrong from the other direction were those who thought the yam "a kind of potatoe". The Spanish, however, quickly understood the difference, and accepted the Arawakan *batata* for the reddish-orange tuber. By 1600 it was growing in England, and *batata* became *patata* and, soon enough, *potato*. *I. batatas* had already been taken to Africa, but the sweet potato's relatively poor storage qualities made it a poor substitute for yam, especially *D. alata*, in provisioning slave ships.[87]

In Jamaica, as in England, the phrase "Spanish potatoes" was used occasionally in the seventeenth and eighteenth centuries to refer to sweet potatoes, but most often they were simply called "potatoes". Sloane called them "Spanish patatas", and said they were available with both red and white roots. Long talked only of "sweet or Bermudas potatoe", which he clearly distinguished from "Irish potatoe". At the same time, a rich inventory of local names emerged for particular varieties. "According to a Mandeville informant", wrote Beckwith around 1920, "the 'Lewis Daley' is long and big; the 'Sarey', round and red; the 'Stewart', white 'right through'; 'Prison Farm', white outside and pink inside; 'Police' is a round potato 'with peg-peg all over'; 'Costa Rica' is a white potato; 'Scissors Tail' (named from the shape of the leaf) bears a whole bunch of tubers". In the 1950s Cassidy found "brass cannon", "pigeon neck", "yellow coby", "red-white", "dog-blood", "dog-liver", "yellow-belly", "punkin", "bunch-a-key", "giant", "full-pot", "flour-barrel", "flog-all" and "pickny-mumma", as well as a series of personal and place names. The 1988 *Jamaica Farmer's Guide* included among the popular varieties "Flog-All", "Blue Bud" and "Mother Edwards".[88]

Knowledge of the superior taste of *I. batatas* in the islands spread rapidly amongst the European colonizers. The English came to regard sweet potato both as a common food and as "one of the best, most wholesome, and delicious roots in the world", especially when eaten fresh from the soil. They were "easie of digestion, agreeing well with all bodies, especially with our hot stomacks . . . ; they breed very good nourishment; they corroborate or strengthen exceedingly; they chear the heart, and are provocative of bodily lust". The English also used the sweet potato to make "a pleasant cool drink" known as "mobby" or "mobbie", by boiling, mashing and fermenting the roots.[89] Mobby disappeared after the eighteenth century.

Sweet potato was roasted and boiled, in much the same ways as yam and coco, but added less often to soup, because of its relative softness. Hughes, in 1672, said, "I have eaten them; either roasted under the ashes, and then peeled, pulp't and buttred, or boiled and buttred, or eaten alone, or with girk't beef and pork instead of bread; the driest of them they bake either in pots or pies, hardly any way comes amiss." Sloane thought they tasted like chestnuts, roasted or boiled, providing "extraordinary good and nourishing food, and because of their speedy attaining their due growth and perfection, they are believed to be the most profitable sort of root for ordinary provision". Sweet potatoes also made "an excellent bread mixed with flour". To make this bread, wrote Long, the potatoes were boiled, skinned and bruised in a mortar, then diluted with hot water and kneaded into a dough with the leaven and flour. He recommended using "at least one third part flour to make it eatable". He claimed the bread would "retain its moisture many days longer than other bread; a circumstance which recommends it particularly to common use in this climate". At the end of the nineteenth century, Sullivan made no mention of sweet potato bread but, in the second edition of her *Jamaica Cookery Book* she did offer a recipe for "sweet potato buns", made in similar fashion.[90] Both the bread and the buns have vanished from the Jamaican repertory.

The baked dish that did become "a perennial favourite" in Jamaica was (sweet) potato pudding. It was the answer to the riddle, "Hell a top, hell a bottom, hallelujah in the middle", the pudding baked in a dutchy with live coals on top of the pot cover as well as underneath the pot. The origins of the pudding date back at least to the eighteenth century, but there have been substantial changes in the ingredients since that time. Pounded in a mortar, said Long in 1774, the roots "are often made into a kind of pudding, called here a pone, which is baked, and, with the addition of a few ring-tailed pigeons, justly esteemed a nourishing and relishing dish". Following Long, Sullivan said the "natives" cooked "an excellent pudding . . . which goes by the name of potato pone". Her recipe required a large boiled and grated sweet potato, a tablespoon of yam or coco, an egg, butter, grated coconut, milk, black pepper and sugar. This mix was baked "in a 'pudding pan' as they call the little round baking tins". By the 1940s the dish was commonly called "potato pudding", and the name "pone" became less common. The recipe also changed: potato pudding was increasingly a sweet, spiced dish. Clark introduced orange juice and sherry, and decorated the pudding with cherries, leaving out the yam, coconut and black pepper (not to mention the pigeons). Later cooks added raisins, condensed milk, vanilla, nutmeg, cinnamon and rum. These modifications reflected eighteenth-century English practice, in which "potatoe pudding" was made with Irish potato, butter, sugar, brandy, wine, currants, orange peel and the juice of Seville orange. This was a dish not far removed from the orange pudding and lemon pudding of English cookery,[91] but the use of the sweet potato changed its character.

Apart from the evolution of the pudding, sweet potato was used for few new dishes in Jamaica in the twentieth century. Some candied it; others made fritters or muffins, stuffed it into orange skins or combined it with callaloo in a pie or casserole. Most often, it was boiled, roasted or fried in thin slices, much as in the nineteenth century, when, as Sullivan observed, the cheapness of sweet potatoes had made them "a substantial assistance to the food of the people". The tuberous roots are the only part of the plant used as food. Jamaicans do not eat the leaves as greens in the way they are consumed in parts of Latin American and Southeast Asia.[92]

IRISH POTATO

The Irish potato, *Solanum tuberosum*, has only a marginal role in Jamaican food culture. This marginality contrasts strongly with the global pattern of consumption. In the world at large, the Irish potato is the fourth most important food crop, following the cereals wheat, rice and maize. It is easily the most important tuber. It is known as *the* potato, and it has been the subject of more historical research than any other root or tuber. Indeed, Redcliffe N. Salaman's classic work *The History and Social Influence of the Potato*, published in 1949, provided a model for the writing of commodity history. More recent studies of the role of crop plants in world history similarly give a central place to the Irish potato and say little about the other roots and tubers. Further, the superior culinary qualities of the Irish potato are often taken as broadly agreed upon, contrary to much Jamaican opinion.[93]

Why have Jamaicans been relatively unenthusiastic about the Irish potato, and what explains their apparent reluctance to follow global opinion and trends? Initially, the Irish potato was seen as unsuited to Jamaica's climate, and the tuber remains uncommon in the tropical lowlands. Whereas yam and coco had indigenous Caribbean roots and the introduced species of yam and coco came from similar environments, the Irish potato was a temperate-zone crop. Long observed in 1774 that in Jamaica the Irish potato was "thought to degenerate". It grew "what is commonly called *waxy*, and acquires in time a more saccharine taste than those which are imported from Europe".[94] Modern Jamaicans persist in complaining of waxy Irish. The *Oxford English Dictionary* reports the use of *waxy* in this sense, for "boiled potatoes that have not become 'mealy'", though the earliest example given comes from 1841. Yet such "degeneration" did not occur in all of the fruits and vegetables introduced into Jamaica from temperate climates, and several were thought to achieve superior qualities, so the simple fact of temperate origin was not necessarily problematic.

The Irish potato's journey to Jamaica was circuitous. Wild potato species occurred in an extensive zone stretching from the southwest of North America into South America, but always at medium to high altitudes – up to four thousand metres. Many of these species were toxic. Domestication and clonal propagation took place in the high Andes, resulting in the cultigen species *S. tuberosum*, which was cultivated as early as 7000 BP. *S. tuberosum* was taken in the sixteenth century from there to Spain, where cultivars emerged that were adapted to a range of high-latitude European climates. At first, Europeans regarded the potato as a decorative flowering garden plant rather than as a food crop (Figure 3.9). It was in Ireland, where the moist, light, well-drained soils were ideally suited to the plant, that the transition took place. As Jonathan Sauer notes, "The name Irish potato for these cultivars is apt, because Ireland was the first region outside South America to take the species seriously as a food crop." Colonial Americans and West Indians began to call *S. tuberosum* the "English or Irish potato", to distinguish it from the Spanish or sweet potato, and during the eighteenth century "Irish potato" became established as the prime colonial term.[95]

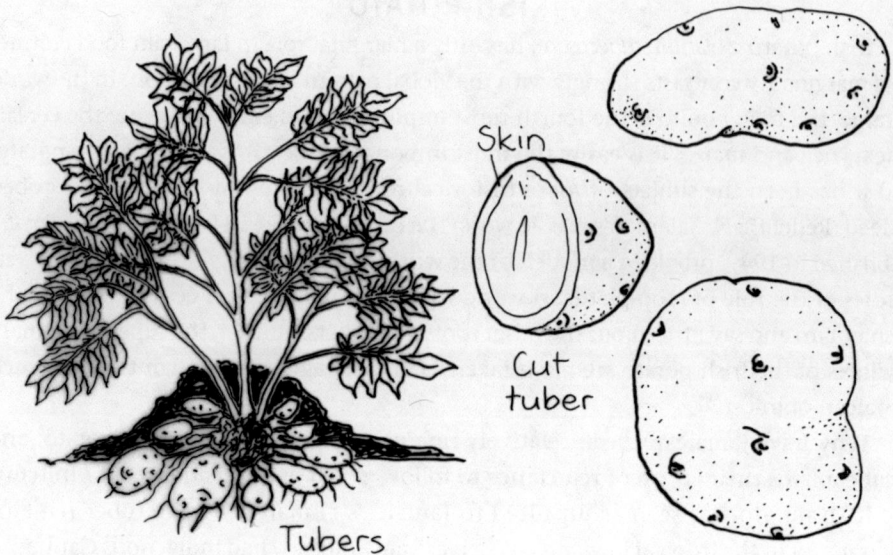

Figure 3.9 Irish potato plant and tubers

Exactly when *S. tuberosum* reached Jamaica – whether introduced by the Spanish, perhaps through Cartagena, or by the English – is uncertain. But by the middle of the eighteenth century, the plant was firmly established and known strictly by the name "Irish potato". This was quickly reduced to "Irish", while "potato" was reserved for *I. batatas*. Hawkers walked the streets crying "Irish! Irish!" And unlike yam, coco and sweet potato, the Irish potato was endowed with few local names. Most varieties retained the names of their foreign sources, especially in the twentieth century, when seed stock was imported from Britain and North America. In the 1980s, the most common varieties were Pontiac, Sebago, Red Lasado, Kennebec, Arran Consel, Green Mountain and Cobbler.[96] None of these names had currency in the provision markets.

Before the mid-twentieth century, the Irish potato had few advocates in Jamaica. Anthony Trollope found, in the 1850s, that the yam was "with the negro somewhat as the potato is with the Irishman". Sullivan offered no recipes. In 1912 Algernon Aspinall said of the yam, "soft and floury to the palate, it would soon put the potato to shame if the two could meet on even terms in this country [England]".[97] Only later in the twentieth century did the Irish potato establish a toehold in the Jamaican market. In part, this new status resulted from the more efficient exploitation of superior agricultural environments. The cool upland regions of northern Manchester, where cultivation became concentrated, had been settled only sparsely during the period of slavery, thus limiting the possibility of Irish potatoes playing a significant part in the provision ground system. In 1938, when land settlements were extended, the Jamaica Agricultural Society sought recipes to "encourage the wider use" of the expected increased output of "ground provisions and ground food-stuffs", noting that "there were as many as 16 or 17 ways of preparing Irish potatoes as food". Clark promoted the Irish potato in her 1945 cookbook, sometimes calling it simply "potato", and offered recipes for fried potato chips, potato cream soup (using Irish potatoes as a substitute for tannia or eddo), "potato surprise" (a potato baked in its skin with an egg inside), "grilled potatoes or other ground provisions" and roast potatoes with meat, as well as an East Indian recipe for "talkari".[98]

Local cultivation remained limited until World War II, when the government took control of the importation of seed potatoes in order to prevent "the debilitating effect of accumulated viruses on successive crops". By 1965 a Darliston, Westmoreland, farmer could call for an increase in the price of potatoes in the local market, claiming, "Irish potato is no longer a luxury food. It is as necessary and vital a food as meat and fish, and is now being used to a greater extent than rice." Festival 1968 made the Irish potato the "special product" of the Culinary Arts Competition, and the Irish Potato Board contributed a trophy. Nonetheless, the Irish potato remains at the bottom of the heap in terms of output and Jamaican consumers persist in disparaging its taste and texture. Modern Jamaican cookbooks provide few recipes in which the tuber is a key ingredient, sometimes even fewer than for the much-maligned coco.[99]

In spite of efforts to encourage local production, Irish potato became the one root to be imported into Jamaica in substantial quantities (see Appendix 1). The pattern was erratic, with minor peaks centred on the years 1845, 1915 and 1960, but by far the largest growth in imports occurred after 1990, when they rose dramatically from a historically low level to reach six kilograms per capita by 2002 (Figure 3.10). Before 1950, Irish potatoes were imported in barrels from diverse sources such as Ireland, Malta, Bermuda and Canada.[100] The surge of the 1990s was supplied from North America and arrived primarily as frozen processed potato chips (North American "French fries").

It is an irony that Jamaica now imports more Irish potato than it produces locally. A root once rejected for its lack of flavour has been made acceptable, even desirable, by deep frying and the application of salt, in the chips and French fries offered by fast food enterprises. When multinational chains entered the Jamaican market in the 1990s, they used imported Irish potato, claiming the Jamaican product lacked the needed qualities. Local growers sometimes complained of this, but the restaurants generally refused to make contracts after early failures in the 1980s, saying processors would need to be involved in the chain of supply because the production of French fries resulted in much wastage, creating by-products that needed to be converted into potato powder or hash browns. The farmers, on the other hand, said that without contracts and certainty of demand, they were better off growing "a table potato for Jamaican housewives". By 1995 it was claimed that "French fries, fried chicken and hamburgers have become almost staple diet for many Jamaicans as fast-food restaurants are becoming increasingly popular". French fries are popular partly because of their characteristic aroma, described technically as "deep-fried, boiled, potato-like, earthy, malty, and caramel-like". The aroma owes much to the exposure to heat in cooking, sharing odours with roast beef, coffee and cocoa.[101] These pungent characteristics are appealing even though they do not match the fundamental elements of spicy-hot Jamaican taste. All of the

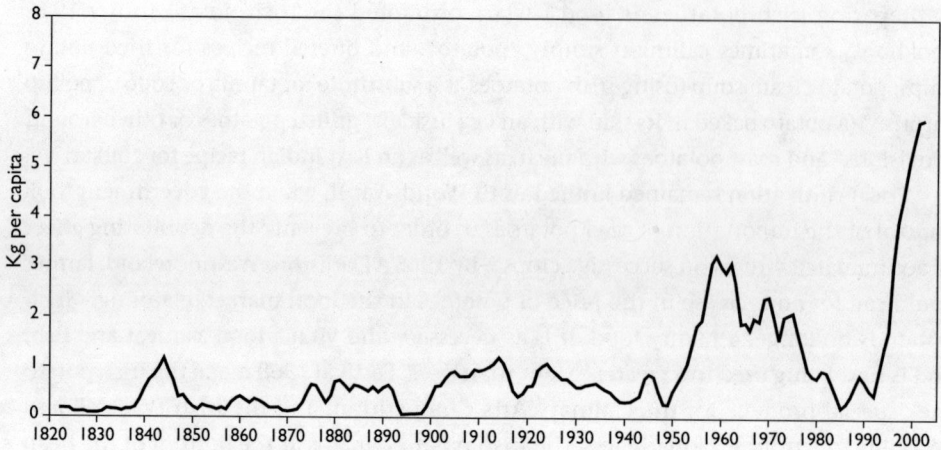

Figure 3.10 Irish potato imports per capita, 1822–2004. Source: Appendix 1.

roots need help to attain these characteristics but it is odd that it was the blandest and least favoured – the Irish potato – that had so much technology bestowed on it. Probably it was the added salt, sprinkled liberally on chips and fries, that accounted for much of the appeal.

ARTICHOKE

One tuber that never achieved popularity in Jamaica was the Jerusalem artichoke, *Helianthus tuberosus* – the American sunflower. Even less well known in Jamaica has been the thistle-like globe artichoke, *Cynara scolymus*, of the Mediterranean. Long did say, in 1774, that three varieties of the globe artichoke were cultivated in Jamaica: the common small French, the chardon, and the large French. The third, said Long, had only recently been introduced from Hispaniola and was commonly called the Hispaniola artichoke. He thought it far superior, with bottoms up to fifty centimetres in circumference, propagated from slips or suckers. Hispaniola artichokes could be eaten fresh or pickled, and proved "profitable articles for the town markets", brought to Kingston by growers in the Liguanea mountains. Artichokes continued to be grown in the cooler, higher areas in the nineteenth century, and, wrote Lunan, "very fine ones may be met with in the Kingston market, the produce of Port Royal, Liguanea, and St. David's, mountains". Rampini, in 1873, saw a Kingston higgler selling "magnificent artichokes, which had . . . been grown amongst the mountains".[102] Globe artichokes were also imported in the nineteenth century. Later references have not been found, however, and the artichoke has no place in the modern Jamaican cookbook or at the table.

GINGER

The one root that does deliver the pungency of hot-spicy Jamaican taste is ginger, *Zingiber officinale*. But "Jamaica ginger" is not any old ginger. It is "the world's finest" and provides the international industry standard, in recognition of "the long history of consistently high quality of the Jamaican ginger". As early as the 1870s, it could be argued convincingly that there was consensus that "Jamaica ginger is superior to any in the world". This special reputation continued to the end of the twentieth century. In 1990, for example, it was declared that Jamaican ginger was famously distinctive, "more pungent than any other" and brighter in colour with its "earthy brownish-yellow".[103]

Pungent qualities sharply affect the organs of taste and are biting and acrid, piercing and pricking, but they are clearly distinguished from tastes such as bitterness and the prickliness of some of the toxic roots. The "pungent principles" of ginger were first isolated chemically in the 1870s, and a number of pungent compounds were later extracted (notably gingerol and the less important shogaol and zingerone). Pungency can decline with storage, as the gingerols transform into shogaols and then degrade, and with cooking, if excessive heat is applied. Knowledge of the relative pungency values of the compounds in ginger remains limited, though measurement advanced rapidly at the end of the twentieth century.[104]

In spite of the close association between Jamaica and ginger, *Z. officinale* is not indigenous to the island or even to the region. Its distinctive types result from characteristic variations in soil, climate and cultural practices. *Z. officinale* originated in tropical Asia, and the ginger plant was brought to Jamaica from India by the Spanish about 1525. By the late seventeenth century it was observed that ginger grew specially well in the island's soils, and Jamaica quickly became a substantial exporter, maintaining a high level of output to the present. The plant was dispersed within Jamaica, though plantation production in the eighteenth century was mostly in the north-central parishes. From the middle of the nineteenth century, the region of greatest specialization was in the Christiana Mountains, the home of Irish potato, above six hundred metres.[105] Around the world, ginger is typically intercropped with other root and tree crops.

A perennial herb with a fibrous root and aerial shoots to about one metre, the ginger plant produces fleshy creeping underground tuberous rhizomes (Figure 3.11). It is propagated vegetatively from cuttings of these rhizomes, and it is the rhizomes that provide "root ginger". Long, in 1774, believed that in the best soils each ginger plant could produce a spreading root or hand weighing up to one pound. Modern farmers can produce as much as six thousand kilograms of green unpeeled ginger, or up to one thousand kilograms of dry ginger, per hectare.[106]

Planting generally took place between March and May, and the root was ready for harvest in January or February, about six months after planting. When dug from the ground, the stools of the plant were "tangled clumps of interconnecting rhizomes" – the hands and fingers – which had to be broken up for processing. Whole rhizomes from which the corky skin had been removed were called "peeled" or "scraped" ginger. "Black ginger" was made by scalding and sun-drying before peeling, a process that killed the rhizome and made peeling easier but that darkened the final product. "White ginger" was scraped or clean-peeled, then washed and dried – a more labourious process that

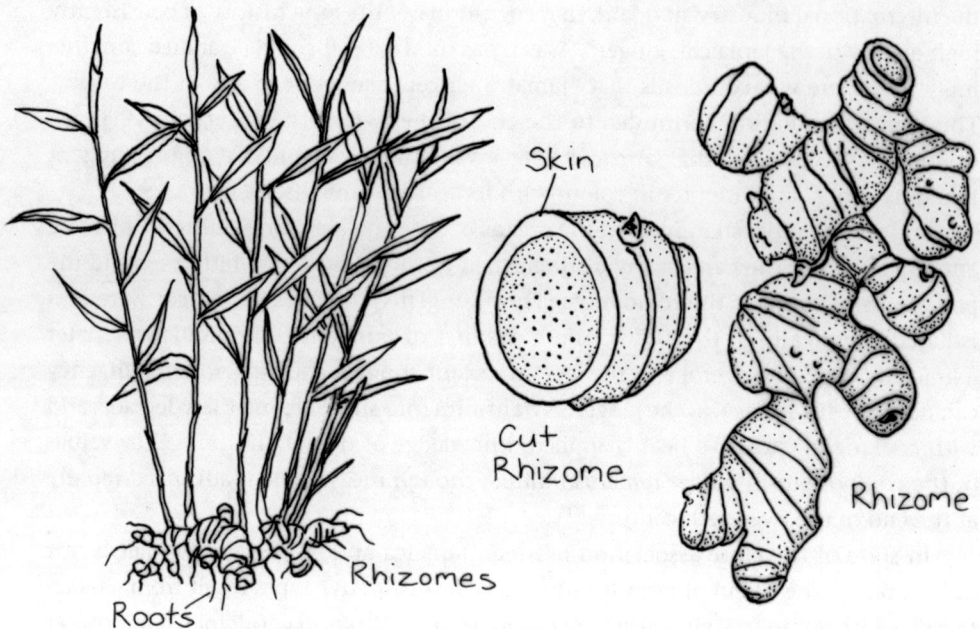

Figure 3.11 Ginger plant and rhizome

fetched higher prices. Both processes – for black and for white ginger – were already practised in the late seventeenth century, and fully described by Sloane. By the beginning of the twentieth century, peeling was done using a special "ginger knife" with a narrow blade and drying was achieved on special "ginger mats".[107]

By the 1980s, Jamaica was also producing Oriental ginger. Oriental ginger was "more succulent and less fibrous", and was "used as a fresh food in oriental cooking". It was washed and air-dried, then exported as a fresh product. The attraction of this other ginger was that "when grown in Jamaica", it had "a more enhanced flavour because of the potency of the soil". Jamaican ginger, on the other hand, "because of its strong flavour", was exported as a liquid concentrate. This was produced by slicing and drying on the farm, followed by processing in Kingston, where the ginger was made into "an oleoresin or a semi-liquid concentrate". The product "Jamaican dried ginger" is "generally considered superior to other sources owing to its good appearance and to it its delicate aroma and flavour". It is marketed in the clean-peeled, whole form and graded according to size and colour (bold, medium or small). Ratoon ginger is the lowest grade, being more fibrous and lacking the fine flavour of the other forms.[108]

For use to make sugar preserve, ginger was dug while still tender and juicy. In modern times, writes D.W. Rodriquez, "ginger preserved in syrup or crystallized in sugar is regarded by some individuals as a delicacy of the choicest kind". These forms are not particularly popular in Jamaica; most of the ginger consumed in the island finds its way into food as flavouring for bread, cakes, sausages, cookies, sauces, puddings, pies and chocolates or as a substantial spice in meat dishes, such as curries and stir-fries. It is blended with other spices, such as pepper and pimento, to create a distinctive "spicy Jamaican" character. In the eighteenth century, some of the liquor poured off in making this sugar preserve was used in cool drink, diluted and mixed with chewstick, lignum vitae and sugar. In modern times, ginger is used in ginger tea, steeped in hot water. In 1971, Rodriquez mentioned "ginger sugar" as "a local delicacy manufactured by a small number of cane farmers", and as an item of trade. Modern commercial food production also uses "oil of ginger" in flavouring many foods, notably sauces and confectionery.[109]

Finally, ginger is used to make ginger beer (notably "Jamaica ginger beer") and ginger ale, which can be mixed with rum or used to settle the stomach. Medicinal claims have long been made for ginger. For example, A. Cooper, in 1757, claimed that ginger was "an excellent carminative and stomachic; it assists digestion, dispells flatus's, and takes off cholic pains almost instantaneously". Recent scientific research has shown the validity of such claims, and indeed has suggested broader benefits, including the control of nausea, the healing of stomach ulcers and the prevention of coronary artery disease.[110]

TURMERIC

In Jamaica, turmeric is known best as an ingredient in curry powders, making up about one-quarter of the weight of curry powder and providing its characteristic golden-brown colour. The powder is made from the rhizome of the turmeric plant, *Curcuma domestica*, which was domesticated in south Asia (Figure 3.12), where India remains by far the largest producer. The plant reached Jamaica in the 1780s and became naturalized. An erect herb, with a habit much like ginger, turmeric is a perennial but is generally grown

Figure 3.12 Turmeric plant and rhizome

as an annual. Jamaica became a significant exporter in the 1950s, sending most of its product to the United States, and the preparation of the root was modernized into a factory operation, but Jamaican turmeric (and that of the Caribbean generally) is regarded as inferior in quality and value to that of India.[111]

SARSAPARILLA

Jamaican sarsaparilla, *Smilax regelii*, is a large indigenous climbing shrub. Its root or rhizome is used most often to produce a tonic drink, distinguished by its bright red colour and made by boiling in water and sweetening. The extract was used as early as the seventeenth century, in England, as the base of some of the first soft drinks. Sarsaparilla became an erratic item of export and in the later nineteenth century was re-imported under proprietary labels, such as "Wilkinson's essence of fluid extract of Red Jamaica Sarsaparilla", advertised as "the only preparation recognised by the faculty as a wonderful purifier of the human blood". "Jamaica" or "red sarsaparilla" maintained its popularity well into the twentieth century and was declared superior to other varieties. In Jamaica, it was commonly combined with roots, barks and vines, such as Chainy Root (*S. balbisiana*), ginger, nerve wiss, sage, pimento, strong back and four-man-strength root, to create "high potency roots wine" and aphrodisiac potions, as discussed under "wiss" in the next chapter. In 2005, Tru-Juice Vitalizer was advertised as "the ital riser", combining vegetables, roots and fruits such as carrot, cucumber, apple, beetroot, sorrel, strong back, celery, spinach, parsley, ginger and sarsaparilla.[112]

CHAPTER 4

STEMS, LEAVES

Stems and leaves belong to the shoot system of a green flowering plant, growing above ground in the sunlight though dependent on and supported by its roots. Nodes on the stem support branches, leaves, flowers and fruits (Figure 3.1). At the tip of a shoot is the terminal bud, the main growing point of the shoot. In some plants, such as trees, the stem is erect and woody. In others, such as runners, it may be soft and horizontal. In plants such as cabbages and lettuces, the stem remains short and hidden by enclosing leaves until the seeding stage. The purpose of the stem – regardless of its characteristics – is to hold up the branches, leaves, fruit and seeds of the plant, to allow the leaves to soak up sunlight and the seeds to scatter, and to provide a conduit for nutrients supplied by the roots.

Because the stem needs to be unattractive to foraging animals, it may be inedible except when young. In its vegetative phase, the plant consists essentially of root, stem and leaf, and this is the stage at which stems and leaves are most attractive as human food – before the plant enters its reproductive phase, when it bears flowers, fruit and seeds. Thus some crops, such as cabbages and spinach, are harvested before they reach the reproductive stage, while others, like broccoli and cauliflower, are allowed only to just enter this stage, and still others, like peas and beans, are harvested during the reproductive stage but before their seeds ripen.[1]

Woody stems are generally unattractive to humans as food sources because of their hardness, dryness and poor nutritional potential. Neither the relatively moist core nor the desiccated bark of such woody plants is consumed often except in times of great hardship.[2] Their leaves are not much more palatable, only the fruits – if anything – being valued as food. The stems and leaves of grasses are equally unattractive, and they are generally fed to grazing animals, at an intermediate point in the food chain. The major exception is the sugar cane, its sucrose-packed stem the source of much of the food energy produced in Jamaica over several centuries.

Herbaceous plants, in which the above-ground stem does not become woody or persistent, are green throughout and are valued primarily for their leaves, though the stems may also be eaten when still young. They reproduce more rapidly than the woody plants, bearing fresh shoots frequently and enabling speedy cropping. Modern Jamaicans tend not to eat the soft young shoots of such plants, at least not to the extent found in other tropical places. Pumpkins, for example, are valued in Jamaica exclusively for their fruit. The shooting tips and the flowers of the vine are generally ignored, though in the past it was much more common to eat these young shoots.[3] It is the leaves of herbaceous plants that are most often eaten in Jamaica.

The nutritional importance of leaves is not surprising, since they are the true working part of any plant, vital to its growth. They are the main sites of photosynthesis, using energy from the sun and water to convert carbon dioxide found in the air into organic matter. In this way, leaves produce carbohydrates, mostly in the form of sucrose, which they then supply in solution to the other parts of the plant. They do not themselves store carbohydrates, and so contain relatively few calories, but because they have a high moisture content, their nutrient value is in fact considerable. Leaves are flat and thin (forming a blade), and are arranged optimally on the plant in order to capture the maximum possible amount of sunlight. Most leaves are joined to the stem by a stalk, or petiole, at a node, though some plants, such as grasses, lack petioles, and the base of their leaves instead form a sheath that wraps around the stem (Figure 4.1). Generally, leaves are rigid in order to maintain the firm skeleton needed to hold liquids in the assimilating cells. The food obtained from leaves comes from the protein, carried in the inner tissues, rather than from the fibre or cellulose that support the structural characteristics of the leaf. The leaf proteins represent "the largest store of all food proteins in the world" and leafy crops yield more protein than any other farmed plant, as well as essential vitamins and minerals. Best of all, are the thin-leaved dark-green leafy plants.[4]

In spite of their dietary importance, leafy vegetables tend to be neglected in the world food economy. This is true in Jamaica as elsewhere, though with important exceptions. On the one hand, cooked meals eaten at home or sold in markets and on the streets often came without any sign of leafy food. On the other, it has been said that "Jamaicans are adept in leaf cuisine", particularly in the use of herbs such as thyme, basil, marjoram and oregano as seasonings, as well as scallion and parsley, and above all in using callaloo in pepperpot soup and other dishes.[5]

CALLALOO

Callaloo has long dominated the thin-leaved dark green herbaceous leafy vegetables consumed in Jamaica. Often compared to spinach, or even called "spinach", by the 1960s callaloo had become "the most versatile and widely used green leafy vegetable in Jamaica". One reason for the popularity of callaloo is that it grows rapidly even in poor soils, reaching half a metre – ready to harvest – in just six weeks. Some species can grow even in saline conditions, and all are hardy, needing only warm bright sunlight

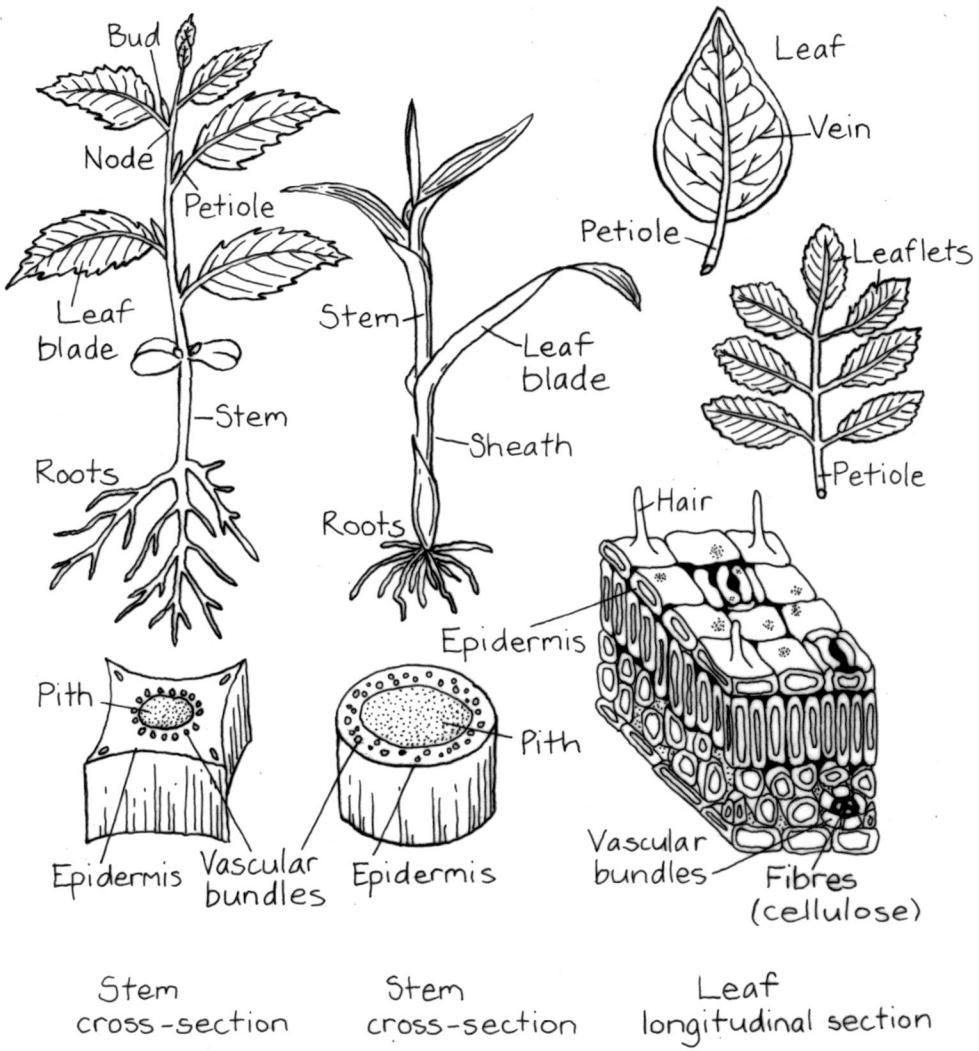

Figure 4.1 Plant structures: stems and leaves

and adequate moisture to thrive. Thus John Stewart could declare in 1823 that Jamaicans hardly missed the European esculents and thought "the Indian kale and calalu (the latter growing spontaneously in the fields), are equal to spinage". Callaloo has an iron-like, earthy flavour, and has since the 1940s been known to be rich in iron and vitamins A and C. It is often cut from the kitchen garden or yard and when the branches are cut, fresh growth appears rapidly.[6] In markets and supermarkets it is sold in bundles, priced by size and weight (Figure 4.2). But however it is obtained, it needs to be used quickly or refrigerated, because its high moisture content means that it wilts soon after harvest.

The prominence of callaloo in the Jamaican scheme of vegetables is interesting in several ways. To begin, callaloo is rare in offering food from both stalk and leaf. It has a protein content of about 5 per cent. In addition, the plants included in the callaloo bundle are mostly weedy types that can survive in wastelands and poor soils, flour-ishing after rain. Their leaves could be found in the wild and in disturbed environ-ments, and collected in quantity without attention to cultivation. Careful watering and weeding in a kitchen garden might produce superior, smoother leaves and softer stalks, but the essential choice came with the introduction to the diet of plants broadly considered rough and weedy. But because of its recent origin in the realm of the weeds, and in spite of its importance in everyday cookery and having quickly become a permanent resident in the island's kitchen gardens, callaloo has often been neglected or sidelined. Agricultural censuses have generally ignored callaloo or identified it simply as "spinach". Manuals for Jamaican farmers similarly overlook callaloo, while giving detailed directions for the cultivation of other (introduced) vegetable crops.[7] Cookbooks have tended to neglect callaloo or to include it under spinach, though one whole booklet has been devoted to it. Only in the late twentieth century did callaloo enter overseas trade from Jamaica, and only in that period did it reach local markets in more refined, ready-to-cook forms.

Preparation was always time consuming, because it was generally considered necessary first to peel off the cortex or outer layer of the stalk. In older stalks, the cortex peeled easily but had to be taken off in a series of five or six strips without cutting deeply. Younger stalks might be harder to peel, but they, at least, were less in need of the operation. Some cooks discarded the shoots and seeds, though these enhanced the nutritional value of the plant. Others saved themselves the trouble of sorting and simply chopped up everything. Although the seeds are very small, they are numerous and have higher levels of protein than most commercial grains. They can be milled to produce baking flour and, when added to wheat flour, make pleasant nutty breads. This remains essentially an experimental finding, not coming into use. Once peeled, the callaloo was usually sliced finely across the stalks, especially when the latter were woody, and the most woody stems were first split longitudinally in a cross. By the 1990s, plastic bags of chopped callaloo were being sold in supermarkets, saving much labour but risking staleness.[8]

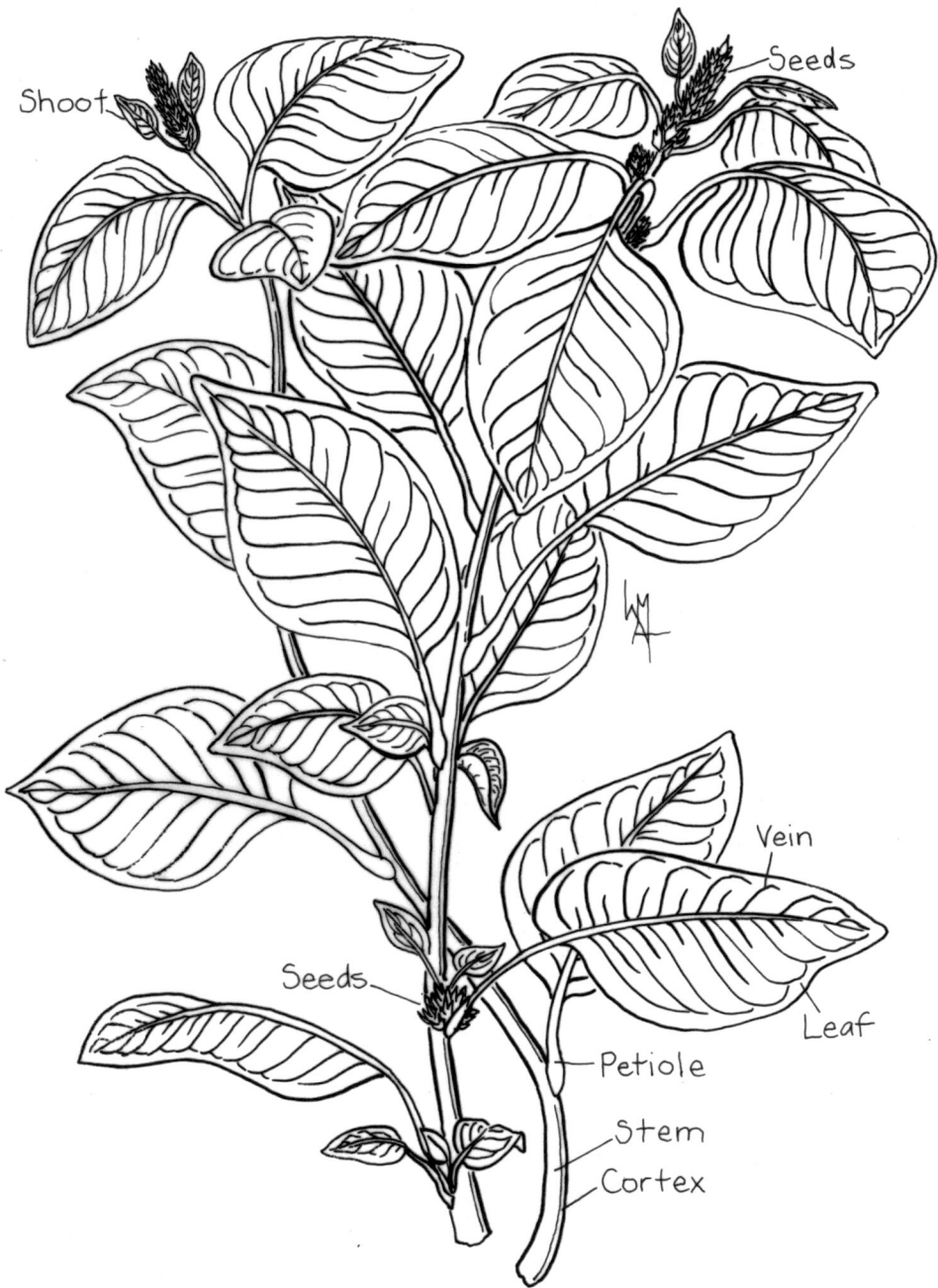

Figure 4.2 Callaloo stems and leaves

Identifications and classifications of callaloo have been complex and confusing, particularly because of varied usage in different regions of the Caribbean. At the end of the seventeenth century, the word *callaloo* was being used in Jamaica to refer to a number of different herbaceous plants with leaves that could be eaten as greens. This is a Jamaicanism, derived from the American Spanish *calalú*, a soup or stew in which the green leaves from such plants constituted fundamental ingredients. Jamaicans identify such a soup as "callaloo soup" and extended the prime use of *callaloo* to comprehend almost any kind of leafy green vegetable. Sometimes it is simply referred to as "spinach", with other types of spinach but distinguished from, for example, "English spinach". In this sense callaloo has become both the generic green leafy vegetable of Jamaica and a particular plant. In 1995 cooks were told that young callaloo could be substituted for any recipe that called for "spinach" and some bemoaned the disappearance of "'real spinach', the flat leafed variety" that had earlier been available in supermarkets.[9]

In 1740 the author of *The Importance of Jamaica to Great-Britain, Consider'd* found that the island's kitchen gardens contained "callaloe of three sorts, top-a-top, or the cocoa-callaloe; another sort grow like brocolli, and eats like spinage; and the mountain-callaloe". "Cocoa-callaloe" was probably the leafy tops of the coco tuber, what Thomas Thistlewood, in 1767, called "toyer callaloo". Patrick Browne, in 1756, found only two types of callaloo, both of them native to Jamaica. "Spanish calaloe" he described as "a palatable wholsome green, and, as such, commonly used at most people's tables: the tender stalks are frequently served up for young sperages, and often prove a very agreeable succedaneum [substitute]". The second type Browne termed "mountain calaloe, or poke-weed", its "leaves and more tender shoots" being "frequently used for greens, by the negroes, instead of the other sort". As suggested by its name, the second variety was most common in the hills and mountains, growing there to 1.2 to 1.5 metres, whereas the Spanish callaloo was much more widely distributed.[10]

In his 1774 *History of Jamaica*, Edward Long offered four types of callaloo. The first he called "branched calalue" (which he styled "*Solanum humilius diffusum, Br.* 174; *Solanum somniferum, Thes. Zey*"), a plant he believed common in Europe, where it had a "heavy strong smell" and "very narcotic quality". These characteristics were lacking when the plant was cooked in Jamaica. But there, the branched callaloo was "in daily use", "the leaves found by long experience to be a pleasant wholesome green". Long added that "the *smooth red calalue*, or *atriplex*, has the same use and good quality when boiled" (Figure 4.3 and Plate 2). He seems to have regarded this as a variety of the branched callaloo. His second type was the "prickly calalue" (*Amaranthus aculeatus refuscens*), but about this he said only that it was "frequent in the mountains and lower hills, and used as a green, being universally esteemed a wholesome agreeable vegetable". Third, Long referred to the "Spanish calalue" (*Phytolacca erecta simplex*), which, like Browne, he considered "a palatable wholesome green" in common use and found in most kitchen gardens. Long saved his most detailed entry for the fourth type, "mountain calalue, pokeweed, Surinam or juckata calalue" (*Phytolacca assurgens ramosa*). This variety

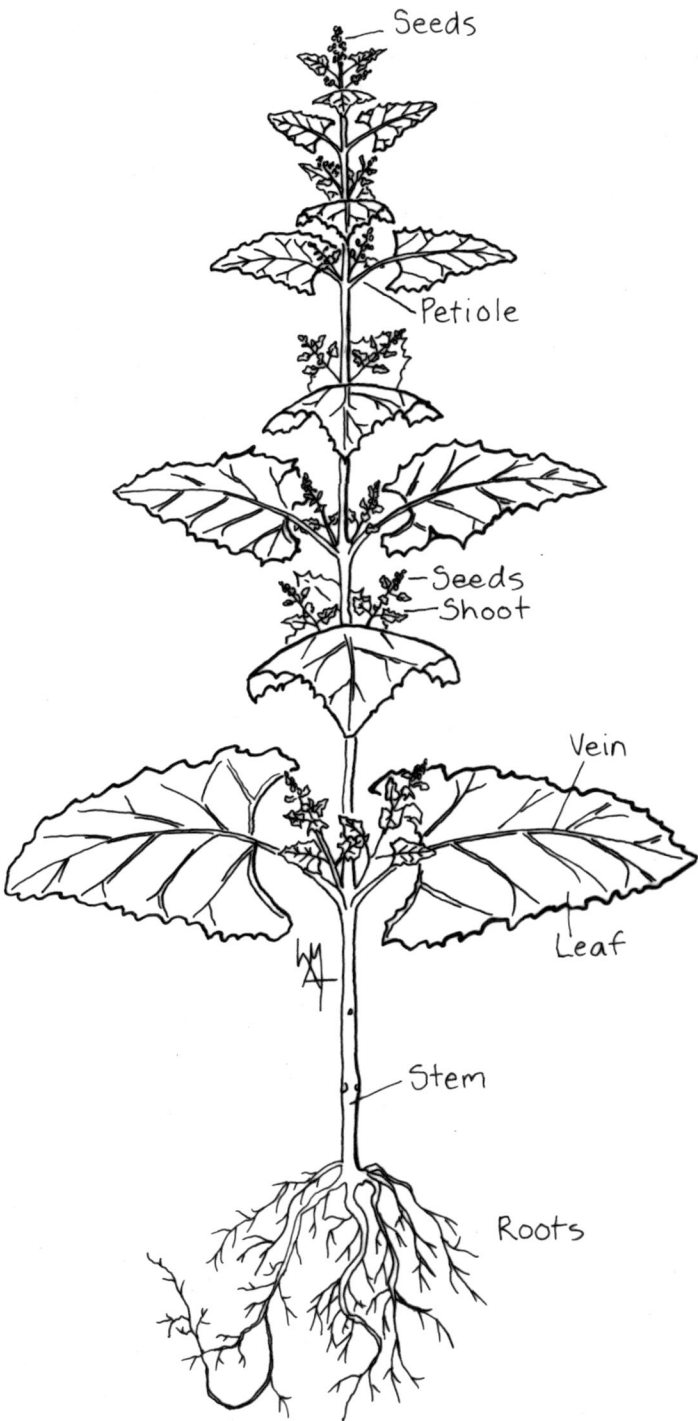

Figure 4.3 Atriplex plant

he thought indigenous to Jamaica, as it grew luxuriantly in the cooler hills and mountains. The plant reached 1.5 metres, dividing at the top, and was "called either red or white, from the colour of the flower-stalks, for all the branches terminate in long and tender spikes of those colours". Long said that the "leaves and tender shoots" were frequently used for greens, and he noted that the plant's juice and root could be used to cure ulcers and cancers, and as a purge. It also yielded a dye.[11]

It is clear from these eighteenth-century texts that the botanical identification of callaloo was problematic, partly because of the variety of plants included in the category and partly because of difficulties of classification. In 1814, John Lunan, following Browne and Long, classified "calalu, prickly" as an amaranth, saying it was "frequently used as a vegetable, and is perfectly wholesome and agreeable". He made no attempt to classify the only other variety he mentioned, "calalu, branched", though it was "commonly called *gooma* or *goomer* calalu". This variety grew "very luxuriantly in new grounds", said Lunan, and had "an agreeable bitter taste", being "much esteemed as a green, pot-herb, and purifier of the blood, and is generally aperient [purgative]". In 1864 Grisebach classified callaloo as *Phytolacca*, as Long had done for Spanish and mountain callaloo. In 1893 Caroline Sullivan, in her cookbook, distinguished two types of callaloo, saying "the broad leafed one is used as a table vegetable like spinach, being boiled and chopped very fine, then mixed with butter and a little milk and black pepper". What the second type was, she did not say.[12]

In 1971 the Scientific Research Council specifically identified callaloo as *Amaranthus viridis*. Spinach was properly classified among the Chenopodiaceae, a family with only rare species in Jamaica (including the atriplex mentioned by Long), rather than the Amaranthaceae. Long had called only the prickly callaloo an amaranth. Dennis Adams, in 1972, identified *A. viridis* as "garden calalu" and described it as an annual herb growing to a metre or more, with ovate-rhomboid leaves up to five centimetres in length with inflorescences and tiny seeds at their ends. It was "common as a weed of grassy places and open ground", growing best in lowland areas during wet periods, flowering and fruiting most of the year. Although the term "garden calalu" is an uncommon usage, it is nonetheless certain that when Jamaicans talk about "callaloo" with specificity, they mean *A. viridis*. Adams also offered descriptions for "prickly calalu" (*A. spinosus*) and "Spanish calalu" (*A. dubius*). The prickly variety was a perennial herb, common as a weed in pastures and waste places and extending higher into the hills than *A. viridis*, with leaves tending to "lanceolate". It was this prickliness that made it less likely to succeed as a food plant. The Spanish callaloo was an annual or a short-living perennial, sometimes growing larger than the other varieties but having much in common with *A. viridis* and growing to higher elevations, approaching one thousand metres above sea level. By the twentieth century, extensive cross-breeding meant that several varieties could be grown year-round. Variations in the size and colour of the plants, in leaf and stalk, were relatively minor, contributing to the generic description of callaloo.[13]

Although Adams, in his definitive work of 1972, firmly placed callaloo among the amaranths, he identified Jocato (Long's "mountain calalue") as *Phytolacca rivinoides*, a tough-stemmed bushy herb growing to 120 centimetres and springing up in cleared land and disturbed waste grounds. Modern popular discussions call "jutkuto" or "jokotoh" a close relative of the callaloo, with larger bodies and leaves, and some claim it offers "a finer texture and quality for eating". "Sipple callaloo" (or "slippery callaloo") is sometimes said to be a distinct variety – "Indian kale" or "coco-callaloo" – and other times is identified as a special dish made by cooking chopped callaloo in coconut milk, rundown fashion, to form a "custard" to be eaten with meat or rice or food.[14]

Hans Sloane, in 1707, wrote in praise of "caterpillers or culilu", saying that the leaves were stripped from the stalk and boiled as a "sallet", making "one of the pleasantest I ever tasted, having something of a more fragrant and grateful tast, than any of these herbs I ever knew; when likewise 'tis shred and boiled in pottages of all sorts, and so eaten, is emollient, loosning, and provokes to a stool". It was also "eat[en] as spinage". It grew throughout the lowlands, said Sloane, and was "gathered very plentifully every where after rain". Barham similarly declared "colilu or culilu . . . much the same as English spinage; some say it exceeds it, especially young and fresh gathered". Because it grew wild and plentifully, he said, callaloo was "of great service to poor slaves, who, if they can get salt to season it (otherwise it is apt to purge them, if they eat too much of it), they will live upon it weeks together".[15]

The best-known use of callaloo in the eighteenth century was in the preparation of a dish called "pepperpot" (quite distinct from callaloo soup), sometimes termed a Sunday dish. In the 1760s, the Reverend John Lindsay declared "pepper-pots – the favourite pottage of this hot climate – being a soop made very thick with tender greens of any sort, and meats of any sort, generally indeed salt meats, or salt fish – but always highly seasoned with the peppers of this climate, to make it agreeable to the tone of relax'd stomach's".[16] The anonymous author of the "Characteristic Traits of the Creolian and African Negroes in this Island", published in the *Columbian Magazine* in Kingston in 1797 but written in the 1770s, said, "The soup known by the name pepper-pot, is a favourite dish; in the composition of which they [enslaved people] use calilue of several sorts, ochros, plantanes, yams, cocos, salted meat and fish, and kayan pepper:- the young sprouts of the large cotton tree, and the tender leaves of the prickley-pear are sometimes used as ingredients."[17] Richard Briggs's 1792 American cookbook provided a recipe for "West India pepper pot" under soups, using veal, mutton, ham and beef stewed with a variety of vegetables and herbs, including pimento; this was boiled gently for three hours before adding "a dozen heads of greens boiled tender" and walnut-sized flour dumplings, all seasoned "very hot with Cayan pepper and salt".[18]

Charles Rampini was introduced to pepperpot at Chapelton in 1873, describing it as "a rich succulent potage, a very Meg Merrilees [the gypsy of Sir Walter Scott's novel *Guy Mannering*] broth of pork and beef and fowl, ochroes and calaloo (the West Indian spinach), peppers, crayfish and negro yam; in colour a dark green, with the scarlet prawns appearing through the chaotic mass not unpicturesquely". He contrasted this with "the Demerara pepper-pot with its evil-smelling and still more evil-tasting Cassareep sauce and its hereditary pipkin". This version seems to have been from the hand of a white creole, since Rampini went on to say that "with the negroes, pepper-pot is a compound of the most heterogeneous description. Prawns or crayfish of some kind are *de rigueur*, but bamboo tops, cotton-tree tips, cabbage, pimpernel, pulse, and even the buds of the night-blowing cereus, occasionally find a place in this concoction."[19]

Both varieties of pepperpot reported by Rampini were richer than that which Martha Beckwith described in the 1920s: "a kind of vegetable soup composed of a leaf or two of cabbage, callalu, young chocho vine (a kind of cucumber), pumpkin, broad and sugar beans, tomato and okra, boiled with salt beef or pork and flavoured with red peppers". Callaloo continued to be considered the fundamental element in Jamaican pepperpot soup throughout the twentieth century. In 1993 it was said, "by tradition we are made to believe that callaloo cooked with or without other edible green leaves must be used in making pepperpot soup". However, a canned version using pumpkin led to the interpretation that "pepperpot soup can be any thick soup providing it is acrid (peppery) in taste". Versions using yam and breadfruit were proposed, completely without callaloo.[20]

Further uses for callaloo were promoted after World War II. Esther Chapman, writing in 1952, said that callaloo was "practically a weed", with "thick but delicate stalks almost like asparagus, but because it is common and cheap it is not regarded as the delicacy it really is". The Jamaica Agricultural Society recommended "calaloo and rice" as an ideal one-pot dish, boiled up with salt pork (or crabs in season), hot pepper, okra, onion, black pepper, scallion, tomato, garlic and margarine. In the 1970s, the Scientific Research Council proclaimed callaloo "a good mixer", combining well with meat, fish, eggs, cheese, roots, fruits and cereals, or eaten together with stews, soups and salads.[21] It was also recommended as an addition to breads, such as banana bread and corn bread.

Steamed – the most common method of cooking – callaloo could be eaten with butter, or with onions and country pepper. By the 1970s it was being used as a filling for patties (enclosed in pastry and baked), the first reputedly sold on the Spanish Town Road in Kingston. Its creation can be understood both as cost-saving and as catering to meat-avoidance. Callaloo sandwiches appeared on the breakfast menus of Kingston restaurants as well as on the tables of small farmers. Refined versions of the callaloo sandwich were made with brown bread, spread with butter, mayonnaise or even peanut butter, and steamed callaloo. Callaloo fritters, along with callaloo patties, were served as hors d'oeuvres.[22]

Steamed callaloo makes an excellent eggs Florentine, though that name was not used in Jamaica. Sullivan, in 1893, had included callaloo in the title of only one of her recipes, "callilu and eggs", with poached eggs resting on top of steamed callaloo. A 1970s recipe for "callalu sunnyside" similarly recognized the potential but had the eggs and callaloo cooked separately and set side by side on the plate rather than combined. By the 1980s, callaloo omelette and "spinach and soft boiled egg" began to be recognized as delicacies. Cream of callaloo is made by bringing saved liquid to the boil, adding celery, oregano and scallion, simmering with salt, and thickening with coconut milk (or evaporated milk) and cornflour. When the rest of the dish is ready, butter and black pepper are stirred in and the dish served with toast or bread.[23]

Callaloo is also used to make a cleansing drink, "callaloo juice", blended with string bean, cucumber, orange juice and sugar. Alternatively, the vitamin- and iron-rich liquid drained from the callaloo steamed to make patties can be drunk neat or with "a dash of celery".[24]

PUSSLEY

A native of the Old World tropics, pussley, or purslane (*Portulaca oleracea*), now grows freely over much of North and South America, occurring most often as a weed in cultivated ground and waste places. It is a sprawling annual, with thick fleshy leaves (Figure 4.4). In spite of its abundance, it was rarely eaten in Jamaica, but was believed to possess medical benefits. Unusually, Sullivan said the young shoots of "pursley, or purslane", could be boiled and that "the natives eat it with their salt fish, or chopped and put in ochro soup, or chopped fine and mashed like spinnach, and mixed with butter and salt and sprinkled with black pepper".[25] In 1963 it was bemoaned that Jamaicans neglected purslane, "a weed we call pig weed", although it was rich in vitamin C and could be "used raw in salads or cooked with spinach". In 1968 the Trident Hotel of Port Antonio offered "a lovely smooth, almost Irish-green chilled soup, flavoured with blenderized seaside purslane (pussley), a very common shore plant on most of our beaches which is also delicious raw in salads, or intriguing as a hot pureed vegetable". A "sea pussley mayonnaise" was also promoted, to be eaten with lobster. But these were directed at the tourist and the adventurous Jamaican, rather than being thought acceptable as common foods. Pussley shares the wild, weedy habit of callaloo, and is readily and cheaply available, but it can have toxic effects if eaten in quantity, which has effectively discouraged its use as a potherb.[26]

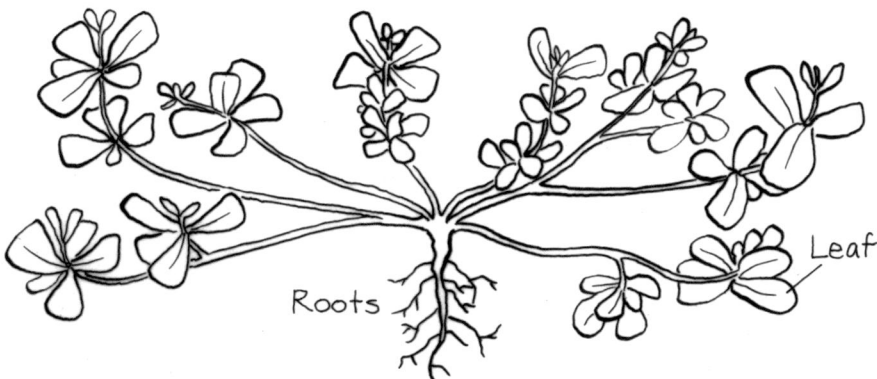

Figure 4.4 Pussley plant

CABBAGE, KALE, LETTUCE, ASPARAGUS

Although the indigenous callaloo rose to prominence among the leafy green vegetables of Jamaica, the island's European colonists tried hard to produce the vegetables of the Old World, and regularly imported seed (in the same way that Irish potato seed was continuously imported) to provide fresh crops of cabbage, lettuce, turnip, carrot, radish and the like from their kitchen gardens. Some of these did not succeed, particularly on the hot dry plains, but as James Phillippo wrote in 1843, "Most of the European vegetables grow in the mountainous regions at comparatively little trouble and expense, and a succession of crops may be produced throughout the year." He included among these cabbage, turnip, parsnip, artichoke, cucumber, leek, radish, carrot, lettuce, celery, asparagus and peas.[27] This ecological division privileged the eastern end of the island, with the mountains above Kingston well placed to supply the city, and worked to introduce many of these vegetables to the provision grounds as well as to the kitchen gardens of the Europeans.

Opinions differed on the quality of the crops. For example, some said cabbages grown in Jamaica had a "much mellower and sweeter taste than in Europe" whereas others believed them inferior. Long claimed that kale offered a "wholesome palatable green" when boiled and that it was widely cultivated across Jamaica. But kale was generally rejected in favour of callaloo. And where Barham claimed that "the common garden asparagus never grows so large in Jamaica as they do in England", Lunan thought it yielded good shoots as early as twelve months after planting (compared to the three or four years required in temperate climates).[28] The enthusiast Thistlewood took the trouble to properly prepare extensive asparagus beds in his Westmoreland garden and was willing to wait while the plants came to bearing. In 1772 his patience bore fruit, and he was able to supply "a large calabash full of asparagus" when the governor had dinner in the parish. Thistlewood also recorded giving enslaved people of his plantation "plenty of cabbage, savoy and broccoli plants to plant in their grounds".[29] The planting of these European vegetables not only contributed to the marketing potential of the people, but also introduced them to these foods for their own table and eventually made these vegetables important elements of Jamaican diet.

Green, leafy cabbage came to be a "vegetable favourite" and, as seen in chapter 1, one of the common foods of modern Jamaica (Figure 4.5). When local cabbages were plentiful and cheap, in the late 1960s, cooks were encouraged to try new ways with them, from raw and shredded to steamed with saltfish, bully beef, boiled eggs or sausages, cooked in milk, or sweet and sour. Lettuce was more likely to be imported. In 1931, in the Great Depression, the Plaza Store of Kingston offered "delicacies for your Christmas table", including "American lettuce" at 1 shilling 3 pence per pound (454 grams), as well as "American celery" and "American tomatoes".[30] These were luxuries, imported in quantities too small even to figure in the official statistics. Only beginning in 1992 were cabbage and lettuce imported in substantial, visible quantity. Cauliflower joined this

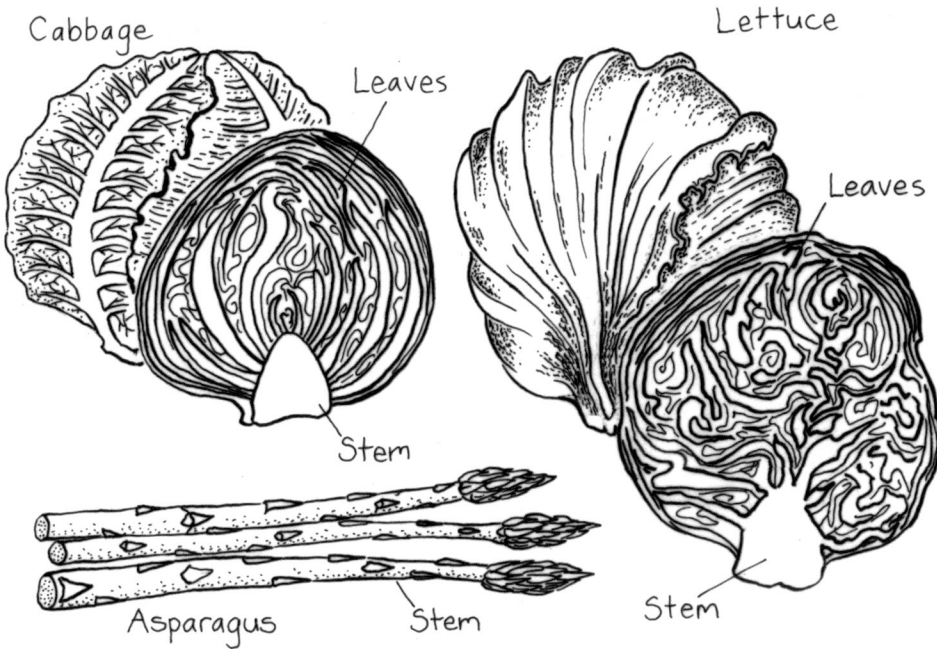

Figure 4.5 Cabbage, lettuce and asparagus, stems and leaves

stream, along with a dribble of asparagus (and spinach). Asparagus remains little known and more likely to come from a tin than to be cooked fresh.

ONION, SCALLION, GARLIC

Importation of onions and garlic began early in Jamaican history but remained at low levels down to 1950 (Figure 4.6). There was a great surge between 1950 and 1975, but imports again returned to low levels until the new surge of the 1990s. Changes in the level of local production are not known for the period before 1960, but output was then low, at only one-quarter of total consumption. The decline in imports between 1975 and 1990 was more than balanced by growth in local output, and even when imports picked up again at the end of the twentieth century, they were outstripped by product from Jamaica's farms. This local production was directed not so much at (dry) onions and garlic, but at "green shallots and onions", or what Jamaicans call scallion, skellion or escallion. Particularly in the parish of St Elizabeth, scallion came to occupy broad fields and niches, including the front gardens of many households. As early as the 1820s, it was remarked that the lack of a local supply of onions caused little concern, "there being abundance of echallots, far surpassing them in flavour".[31]

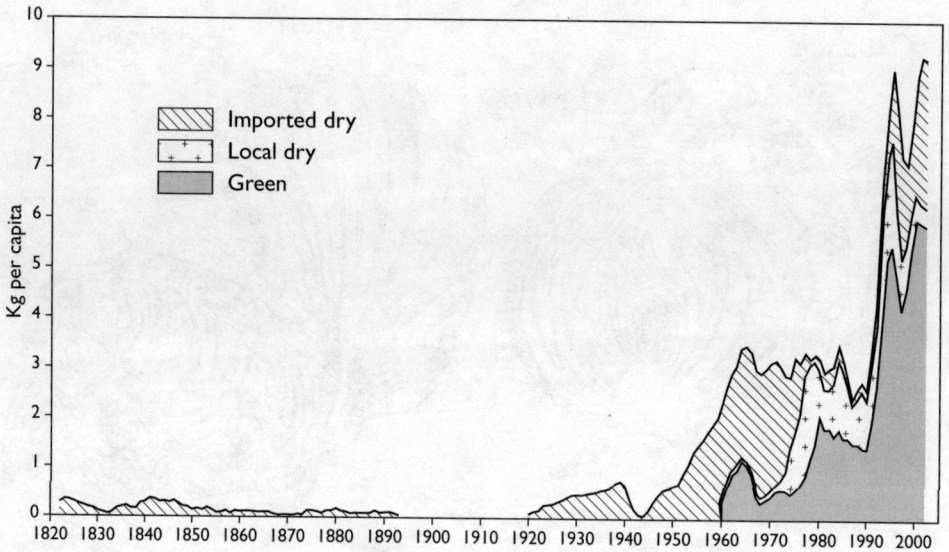

Figure 4.6 Onion production and imports per capita, 1822–2004. Source: Appendix 1.

Onions and their relatives are bulbs with very short stems and vertical underground shoots that are largely made up of the swollen bases of leaves. They store food and water in much the same way as the tuberous roots and rhizomes. In food culture, the different varieties produce bulbs and above-ground leaves of different qualities, and these are valued differently by different peoples (Figure 4.7). Variations in the rate of importation and in the proportion of local production depend on these differences. In the case of Jamaica, it is the green and white soft tops or above-ground leaves that are most favoured, thus ensuring the long-term supremacy of the domestic product. Without refrigeration, green onions can be stored only for a few days, whereas "dry" onions and garlic can survive much longer, the bulbs having been allowed to reach a state of dryness in the field before harvest and the outer shells becoming stiff and hard.

All of the onions belong to the *Allium* genus and are characterized by their allicins, substances that produce volatile chemical compounds containing sulphur, with a distinctive aroma and the capacity to make us cry when cutting the bulbs. They were long valued more for their medicinal than for their food values. Thus W.J. Titford in 1811, referring specifically to "Jamaica garlic, (*Allium gracile*)" – but adding that "many species of Allium, as common garlic, leek, onion, scallion, cives [chives] and shalotts are very common, and particularly wholesome in Jamaica" – discussed the onions in medical terms, though he also noted that "the Jews use garlic considerably, and particularly season with it a sort of smoked sausage, called chorisas, which are very good". Similarly, Lunan observed that garlic thrived in Jamaica but devoted his lengthy discussion exclusively to its medicinal uses.[32]

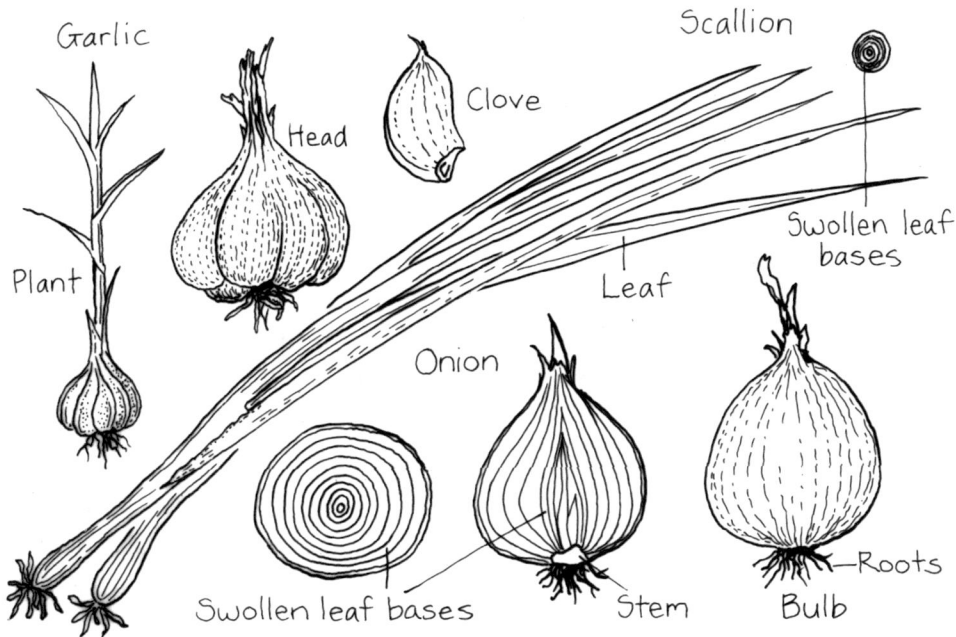

Figure 4.7 Garlic plant, head and clove; scallion plant and leaves; onion bulb, stem and leaves

The *Allium* genus has about five hundred species, making the overlap and resulting confusion in naming and classification hardly a surprise. The onion, *Allium cepa*, itself makes up a good proportion, including the "green shallots and onions" of modern official statistics. This class includes varieties in which the bulb is almost non-existent, as in the favoured smoothly upright scallion of Jamaica that most closely approaches what is called elsewhere spring onion or the thinner-leaved chive. Scallion, *Allium fistulosum*, grows like an onion but never forms a distinct bulb and is effectively harvested immature. It is less pungent than onion or garlic (*Allium sativum*) but subtle and well flavoured. The scallion has more in common with the leek (*Allium ampeloprasum*), though this plant is little known in Jamaica. All of these probably originated in southwest Asia and were widely domesticated in ancient times, to be brought to Jamaica from the Old World by Columbus, though the garlic seems to have arrived ahead of him.

Jamaicans rarely eat any of the onion family raw but generally introduce it finely chopped in seasoning for meats. The great increase in the output of scallion in recent decades seems to have been largely a result of patty-making and jerk seasoning. Both the green and the white parts of the stem are used, for seasoning or even as decoration. In 1993 scallion was called "one of the most favourite seasonings for Jamaicans". Recipes with scallion as a main ingredient, in contrast, are few and far between, and scallion is therefore rarely eaten in quantity in the way it might be used, for example, to dominate in a scallion scrambled egg dish.[33]

HERBS

Jamaicans have long used a wide variety of herbs, as seasoning (often combined with scallion and garlic) and as medicine (Figure 4.8). Richard Blome in 1687 said the gardens of the planters' houses included "medicinal herbs" and "all manner of summer-garden-herbs and roots common to us in England; as, pease, beans, cabbage, carrots, turnips, radishes, onions, lettuce, pursley, colli-flowers, cucumbers, melons, parsley, and other pot-herbs". Another writer, in 1740, said Jamaican kitchen gardens included "sage, rosemary, winter-savory, marigolds, mint, scallions, leeks, parsley, beet, radishes, turnips, carrots, parsnips, sallary, horse-radish" and much more. One herb, not mentioned by these writers, that became very common and popular was thyme, the best quality being thought to be produced in St Andrew and St Elizabeth. Patrick Browne, in 1756, observed that "marjorum" thrived in "the mountains of New Liguanea".[34] Along with marjoram and oregano, thyme was introduced fresh into soups and stews and used dried to stuff meats.

Basil and parsley were generally used fresh and green. Basil long remained a medicinal rather than a food herb, and was recognized in several varieties. Browne said of the "great basil" that there was "no plant more common . . . in the gardens of Jamaica". Titford thought "common parsley" was used as a remedy for dropsy in its early stages.[35]

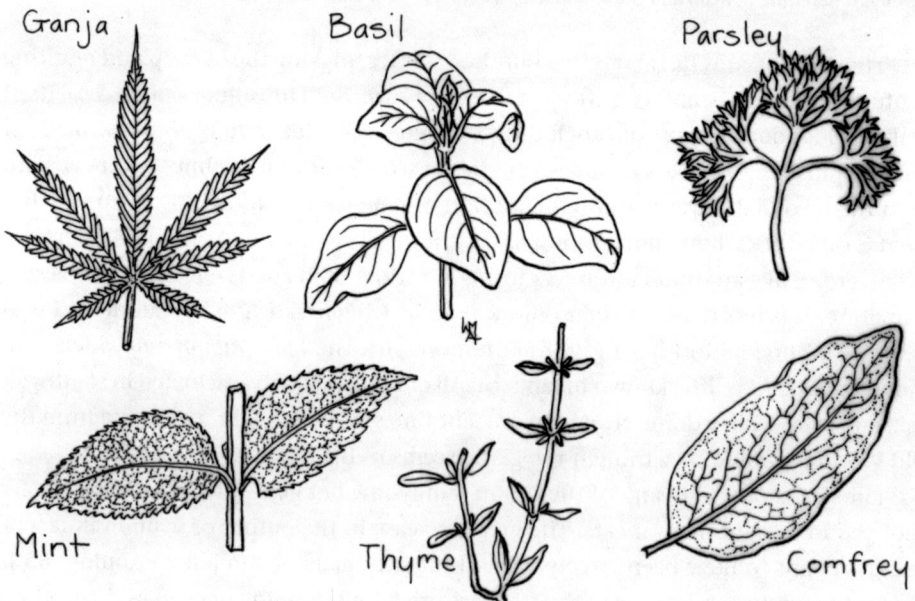

Figure 4.8 Herbs: ganja, basil, parsley, mint, thyme and comfrey

Mint, likewise, was most often used as a tea, to cure various maladies. Thus Alfred Leader in 1907 said that imported tea was too expensive for "the negro" and that "he drinks chiefly what is called bush tea, i.e., infusions of a variety of herbs, mint, sorrel, etc., some of which are pleasant beverages enough, and said to possess valuable medicinal properties". Sullivan believed Jamaicans had great faith in herbs, using a wide range in preference to tea or coffee: "Jack-in-the-bush, cerasee, mint, elder, ochro, vervine, sage, search-my-heart, ackee, lime-leaf, ginger, fever-grass: there seem no end to them – each appearing to them to possess qualities either nourishing, cooling, or medicinal." For a fever, the ideal drink was "fever grass tea" made from the "fragrant smelling lemony grass". Mint remained one of the most popular bush teas throughout the twentieth century, along with cerasee, cold bush (leaf-of-life), lemongrass, orange peel and the twining parasite love bush (*Cuscuta Americana*). In the 1980s "a blend of Jamaican peppermint leaves and green tea" was packed in tea bags for both local and export markets.[36]

The use of herbal "bush" teas in Jamaica can be explained partly in terms of heritage and partly by the continued importation of the leaf teas of China and India, plucked from the tree *Camellia sinensis*. The leaves of other trees, such as lime, lemon and soursop, are commonly used in Jamaica to make tea, but *C. sinensis* has not become a plant in the gardens of the island or in any other part of the Americas. In the eighteenth century, Barham, Long and others identified *Capraria*, common on savannas, as "West India tea", the leaves of which some "extolled as the very best green tea they ever drank in their lives".[37] However, imported tea dominated. By the end of the nineteenth century, branded blends such as Lipton's and Tetley's had begun to come to prominence. Loose-leaf tea was gradually displaced by tea bags, introduced to Jamaica in 1948 but at first, down to the 1960s, placed in the pot rather than the cup. However brewed, modern Jamaicans liked their cup of tea loaded with sugar and sweetened condensed milk, to make a heavy drink quite unlike a clear herbal tea. By the 1980s imported varieties began to offer herbal tea-bag blends, using material unfamiliar to Jamaican gardens. When tea bags became expensive, drinkers "deserted tea for mint, cerasee and other so called bush teas from their own backyard supply".[38]

Some herbal teas came to be associated with ill effects, the toxic elements overriding the benefits. For example, in the 1980s Jamaicans were warned that comfrey – popular as a herbal tea and as an aphrodisiac or medicine, using both the roots and leaves – was a potential cause of liver failure, caused by toxic concentrations of alkaloids.[39]

Ganja, or marijuana (*Cannabis sativa*), has similarly been used most often in Jamaica as a therapeutic bush tea or tonic. The plant is known only from the later nineteenth century and was probably introduced along with indentured Indian workers, who regarded it as a holy herb and smoked it in special pipes. Before 1900, some Europeans used *C. sativa* seeds as fatty oil in food and fed the whole seeds to animals.[40] Consumption and trade were made illegal in Jamaica in 1913. Although ganja is an established element in folk medicine, it is equally true, as Henry Lowe and Errol Morrison observe, that "many Jamaicans . . . have cooked with marijuana or used it in baking". The leaves can be used in soup, generally pepperpot or callaloo soup, or crushed and pureed to prepare a ganja butter, to spread on bread or bake in cakes and cookies. These food products can be "quite potent". Outside Jamaica, cookbooks devoted to the use of ganja began to appear in the late twentieth century, recommending the use of either fresh or dried leaf in biscuits, cakes, sweets and drinks, the ganja preferably first ground into a fine powder. Cookbooks originating in Jamaica or with Jamaican authors tend to be much more cautious or to ignore ganja completely. Restaurants rarely offer dishes that include ganja. In 1993, however, two policemen who "feasted on 'herb cakes' at an ital restaurant in Kingston . . . fell unconscious immediately after their meal and were rushed to the Kingston Public Hospital". Forensic reports showed the herb cakes were "laced with ganja".[41]

BAMBOO

A native of the East Indies, the bamboo (*Bambusa vulgaris*) was introduced to Jamaica via Hispaniola, and was apparently plentiful by 1700. It was used most often for fuel, cooking utensils, fencing and ornamental purposes, though the occasional writer noticed that in Asia it was used also as a food. Lunan, for example, observed that in the East bamboo shoots were, "when very tender, . . . put up in vinegar, salt, garlic, and the pods of capsicum, and thus afford a pickle, which is esteemed a valuable condiment", and were "said greatly to promote the appetite, and assist digestion". Mature bamboo, however, is not a potential food: it contains large amounts of cellulose that humans cannot digest. In this respect bamboo is like the leaves of most trees and most blades of grass, which can be eaten only very selectively in a raw state or substantially processed. By the 1870s, Rampini could report that in Jamaica "bamboo tops" were used in pepperpot soup, and in modern times the shoots are said to have been eaten as a vegetable in parts of St Elizabeth.[42] In the twentieth century, bamboo shoots entered the Jamaican diet through Chinese cuisine, but most often in tinned, imported forms rather than locally cultivated. Overall, this apparently abundant food resource has been neglected in Jamaica, by all classes.

CABBAGE PALM

The cabbage palm is the source of what are now known as "palm hearts" or "hearts of palm". As an element of Jamaican food, the cabbage palm has proved more successful and persistent than bamboo shoots in spite of difficulties of harvest. Hearts of palm are the edible apical meristem, or "cabbage", of the tree, extracted from a green, tubular leaf sheath that forms an erect crown shaft of 1.5 metres. Jamaica has two endemic species, *Roystonea altissima* (mountain cabbage palm) and *R. princeps* (morass royal, swamp cabbage palm), but these are very similar and perhaps simply ecological variants. The former is the more common, growing to 20 metres, particularly on the mountain slopes of the central and eastern regions of Jamaica. Lindsay drew *R. princeps* in 1761, in a

Plate 1

"Habit and characteristic appearance of plants" (part 1), W.J. Titford, 1811. Original key: 1 Indian shot; 2 Indian arrow root; 3 wild clary; 4 Jamaica vervain; 5 sugar cane; 6 Bahama grass; 7 tamarind tree; 8 Guinea grass; 9 Scotch grass; 10 adrue; 11 sweet potatoes; 12 star apple; 13 coffee tree; 14 pine apple; 15 American aloe; 16 red lily; 17 oyster plant; 18 cinnamon tree; 19 yellow hogplum; 20 Occidental cassia; 21 common cashew nut; 22 mangrove; 23 melon thistle; 24 four-sided torch thistle; 25 cochineal Indian fig; 26 mammee apple; 27 cashaw; 28 sweet sop; 29 sour sop. From W.J. Titford, *Sketches towards a Hortus Botanicus Americanus* (London: Sherwood, Neely and Jones, 1811), plate 1. Cambridge University Library.

Plate 2

"Habit and characteristic appearance of plants" (part 2), W.J. Titford, 1811. Original key: 30 narrow-leaved calabash; 31 spear-leaved oily pulse; 32 five-leaved silk cotton tree; 33 red sorrell; 34 chocolate nut tree; 35 forbidden fruit; 36 esculent coco; 37 common Indian corn; 38 bread fruit tree; 39 red colilu; 40 bitter cassada; 42 cocoa nut tree; 43 pumpkin gourd; 44 oil nut tree; 45 esculent yam; 46 Jamaica pepper; 47 Guinea corn; 48 Indian jack fruit tree; 49 plantain tree; 50 common papaw tree; 51 palmetto thatch; 52 mango tree; 53 Spanish dagger; 54 anchovy pear; 55 abbay tree or oily palm; 56 wood ants nest. From W.J. Titford, *Sketches towards a Hortus Botanicus Americanus* (London: Sherwood, Neely and Jones, 1811), plate 2. Cambridge University Library.

Plate 3
Cassava, by Rev. John Lindsay, c. 1770. Bristol Museum and Art Gallery.

Plate 6
Avocado, by Rev. John Lindsay, 1770. Bristol Museum and Art Gallery.

Plate 7
Coconut tree, by Rev. John Lindsay, 1766. Bristol Museum and Art Gallery.

Plate 8
Coconut, by Rev. John Lindsay, 1767. Bristol Museum and Art Gallery.

coastal setting (Plate 4). It now occurs at Negril in small "pure stands", growing 5 to 15 metres tall. Since the 1980s this palm has been protected by a tree preservation order.[43]

As early as the 1670s, the "Indian cabbage tree" was recognized to be unique to Jamaica. An English writer observed that the soft white "cabbage" at the top of the palm, "when boiled, is very good aliment, eaten with butter and vinegar, and doth very well agree with our hot stomacks". Sloane similarly reported of the cabbage tree that "the Germen, sprout, top, bud or unexpanded leaves . . . are boil'd, and eat like our cabbage, or pickl'd". In pickled form, hearts of palm quickly became an item of export from Jamaica. Browne said of the "Barbados cabbage tree" that "the lower part of the inward ribs, and the embryo leaves, are very tender; and, when boiled, become a delicate wholesome green, which is generally called cabbage in all the colonies".[44] Long believed this to be the same species as the Jamaica cabbage tree, or mountain cabbage, and said these were cut down to obtain the "baluster or cabbage" found at the top of the trees. *According to Long, "the cabbage stripped of its outer green coat appears perfectly white, cylindrical, and formed of several concentric laminae. The inner tunicles are sliced, and either eaten raw, with onions, pepper, and vinegar, or boiled, and served up with butter; in which way, it most resembles the European cabbage in flavour"* (Figure 4.9). Philip Henry Gosse noted in the 1840s that the palms generally grew only in height, "by the progressive development of one great terminal bud". It was the bud that was "eaten as a delicacy, either boiled, or raw as a salad", in which "the young unexpanded leaves are wrapped over each other so closely, as to acquire a crispness and a tenderness, which with the delicate whiteness produced by the exclusion of light, somewhat resemble those of the heart of a large cabbage".[45]

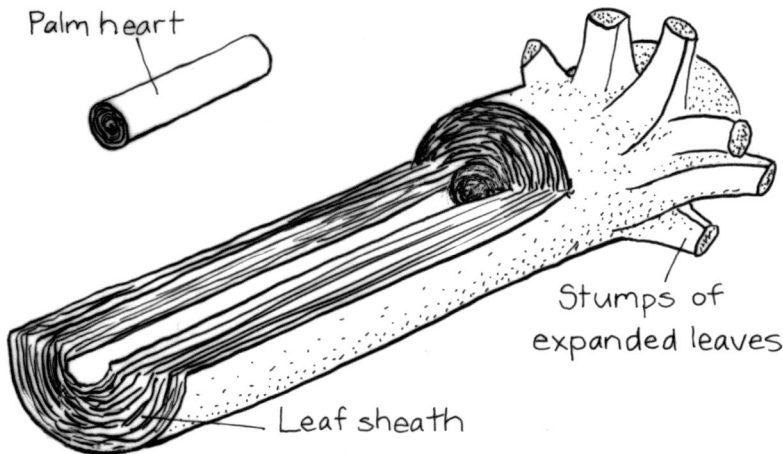

Figure 4.9 Extraction of hearts of palm

Later observers sometimes compared cabbage palm to asparagus "in appearance and taste". Sullivan gave recipes for boiled mountain cabbage, served with a thick white sauce, and for pickled mountain cabbage. She said also that the cabbage palm was "extremely nice even eaten raw, but it is then decidedly indigestible". Herbert Thomas, venturing into the mountain fastnesses of eastern Jamaica in the 1880s, reported enjoying a breakfast of mountain mullet, ringtail pigeon, jerked pig and "fresh mountain cabbage heart" – all island delicacies.[46]

It has often been remarked that the extraction of hearts of palm is destructive of the plant itself and that the practice is therefore not viable, though small-scale exploitation has continued for centuries. Maria Nugent, in 1802, claimed that the trees "grow wild in the woods, are eighty years coming to perfection, and for a dish of cabbage you cut down the whole tree, as the top of it is the only part eaten, and the tree dies when that is taken off". Fortunately, the trees are in fact fast-growing and reach harvestable maturity within ten years, though commercial exploitation adds pressure. In 1880 a Kingston preserving company advertised that "mountain cabbage will be purchased in any quantity and preferably by the load of fifty at one time".[47]

In recent times, the cabbage palm has experienced a resurgence in local and overseas markets, with commercial enterprises concentrated in Portland. In 1985 a Hearts of Palm Project was established at Passley Gardens to supply "Pejibaye palm" seeds and seedlings to satellite farms, but the enterprise was quickly declared a "debacle". Individual private entrepreneurs were more successful. At Negril, it was said, locals "had over the years been destroying the species by harvesting the 'hearts' of the palm for gastronomical purposes", which led to the tree preservation order.[48] Most of the hearts of palm consumed in modern Jamaica – in salads, soups and other dishes – come from imported, canned product. The Dominican Republic, one of the world's largest canners, exploits *R. oleracea*, and in Brazil the trees used have been the single-stemmed *Euterpes edulis*, which has to be killed in order to extract the heart, and the multi-stemmed *E. oleracea* of the Amazon estuary. Illegal cutting in Brazil threatens natural stands, and *E. edulis* is already locally extinct.[49] Jamaica, in contrast, has conserved its natural resource, helped in part by the lack of an extensive local demand for hearts of palm.

TRUMPET TREE

The trumpet tree, *Cecropia peltata*, is common in the lower forest and cleared lands of Jamaica. It grows quickly to thirty metres, with a light, hollow trunk and few branches. References to its use as food come mainly from the eighteenth century. According to Barham, at the top of the tree "there is a soft pappy substance, which some will eat". Further, he said, "The holly on the top of the tree contains a white, fat, and juicy pith, which some eat; but the negroes, with this, and with the young tender soft leaves, cure their wounds and old ulcers." Long claimed that the leaves and flowers of the trumpet tree were "eaten by the Negroes in their broths". The large fingers of fruit that emerge from the flowers are reputed to taste like a ripe fig but are rarely eaten in modern Jamaica (Figure 4.10). When "a vegetable dish made with the heart of a trumpet tree" was entered in a competition in 1965, it was greeted with surprise.[50]

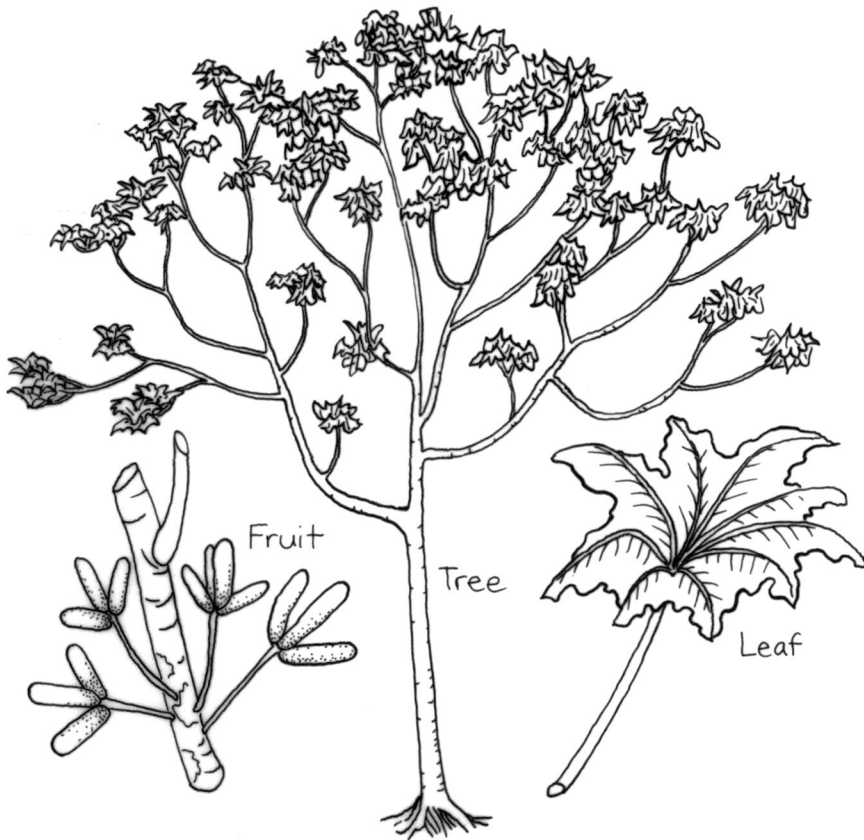

Figure 4.10 Trumpet tree plant, leaf and fruit

CINNAMON

An exception to the consumption of bark from trees is the use of cinnamon stick, though only to flavour certain foods such as rice and peas, porridges and curries, and as a spice in baking and pickling. The leaves are used in chocolate tea. Cinnamon, *Cinnamomum verum*, is native to Sri Lanka. The Portuguese found it there in its wild state in the sixteenth century, but it was not until about 1770 that it was brought into cultivation, by the Dutch. By the 1780s Jamaica was importing cinnamon. The plant thus moved quite quickly around the world, but commercial production remains concentrated in Sri Lanka, the Seychelles and the Malagasy Republic, and little work has been done since to improve the cultivars.[51]

In Jamaica, Browne identified a wild cinnamon, *Canella winterana*, in 1756, one common in the lowlands and arid rocky hills. The aromatic outer bark of the tree produced a version of cinnamon but with something like the flavour of cloves. A less common plant was the endemic *Cinnamodendron corticosum*, known as "mountain cinnamon" and found only in the wet forests of the eastern end of the island. Long claimed that the best bark came from the branches of the wild cinnamon, this bark being thinner, milder and closer to the true cinnamon, but he directed his attention to its medicinal rather than its culinary qualities. Titford, however, said that the "Negroes" used the leaves and young buds of the cinnamon to season their vegetable food (Plate 1), and Lunan believed that the bark was "a common ingredient with capsicums in the food of the negroes".[52]

As well as the importation of the bark and the promotion of indigenous varieties, efforts were made to cultivate the Eastern plant in Jamaica. In 1788 Thomas Dancer, the newly appointed superintendent of the botanical garden at Bath, sent Long "a specimen of our cinnamon bark, which notwithstanding my want of experience in separating and curing it, will I flatter myself be found to vie, in point of quality, with *the best pieces of Ceylon cinnamon". Dancer claimed the cinnamon had been presented* to the garden by Admiral Rodney, who had taken it from a French ship bound from Isle de France to Hispaniola. Although the plant proved slow-growing in Jamaica, and though the inner bark (the skin used as spice) had to be carefully separated in order not to "vitiate the flavour", Dancer believed the cinnamon to be highly "aromatic" and "much more retentive of its virtues than any of the other spices". By the early nineteenth century, the cinnamon plant could be said to thrive throughout the island. Indigenous cinnamon, however, maintained a presence. In 1850, for example, cinnamon from trees in the Port Royal Mountains was declared equal to the finest imported product "in point of flavour and substance". The cinnamon was "brought down from the mountains wrapped in leaves of the plant by an African", one newspaper reported, "and we were assured that the trees grow luxuriantly, and is abundant throughout the mountainous districts".[53]

LIGNUM VITAE

Another tree exploited for its bark is the lignum vitae (*Guaiacum officinale*), the tree that bears the national flower. In 1739 Leslie said the "Negroes" made "cool drink" from the bark of the lignum vitae tree. The author of the "Characteristic Traits of the Creolian and African Negroes" said, "Their common drink is water; but they prefer cool drink, a fermented liquor made with chaw-stick, lignumvitae, brown sugar, and water." In 1759 Thistlewood tried to revive a sick enslaved man with a "diet drink" made of "lignum vitae, sarsaparilla and senna".[54] As with cinnamon, the bark of the lignum vitae was used only to flavour.

CHEWSTICK

The chewstick, *Gouania lupuloides*, is a large vine commonly found climbing over trees in the woodlands of the eastern end of Jamaica. Short sections cut from the vine have long been used as a toothbrush. Similar practices are found in West Africa, where a wider range of sticks is used for dental hygiene. In the eighteenth and nineteenth centuries, chewstick was also used in Jamaica to flavour and ferment drinks, as in the version of cool drink made with lignum vitae. Lunan said in 1814 that chewstick was "generally put in those cool-drinks often used in Jamaica, to which it yields an agreeable flavour". Long called it "chaw-stick", saying it gave "flavour to the small diluting drinks in common use".[55]

WISS

The water withe ("water wiss"), or wild grape (*Vitis tiliifolia*), is a climbing vine with stems as thick as an arm, reaching into the tops of tall trees in the forest and occasionally draping over fences. Barham said this was also known as "wild vine" or "true travellers joy" because, "by cutting off a piece about a yard long, holding it up, and sucking one end, a great deal of refreshing water will come into the mouth". This quality was known from the seventeenth century, and wiss continues to be used by modern Maroons as a source of cool water in the Blue Mountains. Gosse described the water withe as "a valuable plant, for the resource it affords to thirsty travellers". He found it equal to "pure cold water", a metre's length yielding half a litre of liquid.[56] There is no need even to suck; the cool water flows naturally from the cut vine held above the mouth.

Other significant climbing plants include chainy (China) root (*Smilax balbisiana*) and bridal wiss, which are components of "high potency roots wine", with a relatively large proportion of iron. Chainy root is also used to make iced drinks, in combination with ginger, lime peel, evaporated milk, vanilla, strawberry syrup and sugar.[57]

JUNJO

Jamaicans use the word "junjo" or "junja" to identify fungus, whether edible or not, growing on wood or, less often, on the ground. It flourishes on the trunks of cotton and fig trees and in damp spots. In the eighteenth century, junjo was pounded and boiled in soups with salt beef or combined with saltfish. By the end of the nineteenth century, it was disparaged, regarded as fit only for the desperately poor. In consequence, mushrooms of more refined quality were also often summarily rejected as poor eating. In 1990, when mushroom-growing was tested in Jamaica, it was acknowledged that Jamaicans were not used to eating fresh mushrooms and knew them mostly from cans.[58] There was fear of poisoning, because Jamaicans lacked the knowledge of when and what to eat of the mushroom.

Fungi are not in fact plants, though they were once grouped with them and it is probable that fungi and animals have a common ancestor. Unlike plants, fungi do not live by photosynthesis but rather absorb energy from organic matter, such as the dead trees on which they grow. Fungi digest their food outside their bodies by secreting powerful and sometimes poisonous enzymes into the food, hence the potential danger for humans.

SEAWEED

Seaweed are true plants, but they are algae rather than the angiosperms that dominate food history. As marine algae or aquatic chlorophyll-containing plants, they can be thought of as sea vegetables, with poorly organized cells and tissues. In parts of east Asia, notably Japan, several species of seaweed are eaten fresh or processed and are praised for their nutritional value. In modern Jamaica, seaweed is rarely used in these ways, except in Chinese cookery. It does feature in a popular drink, Irish moss, made from seaweed or its extract mixed with milk and sugar.[59]

In earlier times "Irish moss" referred directly to the edible seaweeds *Chondrus crispus* and *Gracilaria*, which could be harvested around the coast of the island and bought in the markets. The strained liquid of boiled seaweed could be combined with sugar, rum, vanilla, nutmeg and colouring and chilled in a mould until firm. This version of Irish moss "emits delicate flavours as it melts in your mouth". Others said the jelly had "a very delicate and subtle flavour". Enid Donaldson, in 1993, observed that the "gelatinous cream-coloured liquid . . . sweetened with condensed milk and flavoured with nutmeg and vanilla" was popular as a health food and was "believed to aid sexual prowess". Alternative ways of using seaweed were occasionally recommended, one such being a "sea weed soup (Irish moss)" made with chicken broth, chopped onion, beaten egg, salt and pepper.[60]

SUGAR

Of the basic tastes, sweetness is the most attractive, and sweetness is most directly associated with sugar. Although sugar – the chemical sucrose – can be obtained from a variety of sources, notably fresh fruit, in Jamaica it was the sugar cane, *Saccharum officinarum*, that dominated and was most visible. The stalks of this perennial tufted grass, which grows to five metres in flower, when crushed yield a substantial quantity of juice and sucrose (Figure 4.11). Sugar cane dominated the landscape of plantation Jamaica throughout most of the three hundred years from 1670 to 1970, and the plant remains a prominent feature in some regions. Its agriculture and commerce are well known and central to the economic history of the Caribbean generally. The sugar cane was a cornerstone of the Atlantic economy and fundamental to the trade in people and commodities that shaped Jamaica.[61] Most of the plant's products – cane sugar, molasses and rum – were exported, feeding overseas populations rather than Jamaicans. But from the standing crop to the finished product, sugar represented a vast store of calories and, one way or another, a proportion always entered the diet of the island's people.

Once the hard outer skin has been removed with a knife or strong teeth, sugar cane can be sucked and chewed in the mouth, the juice flowing freely from the cellulose until a dry mass of trash is left. This juice is rich in sucrose. Since the seventeenth century, canes cut in the field have been used in this way, both legally and illegally.[62] In the factories, the juice flowed more freely as the canes were passed through the heavy rollers, and some of this juice was allowed to the workers before it was sent to the boilers

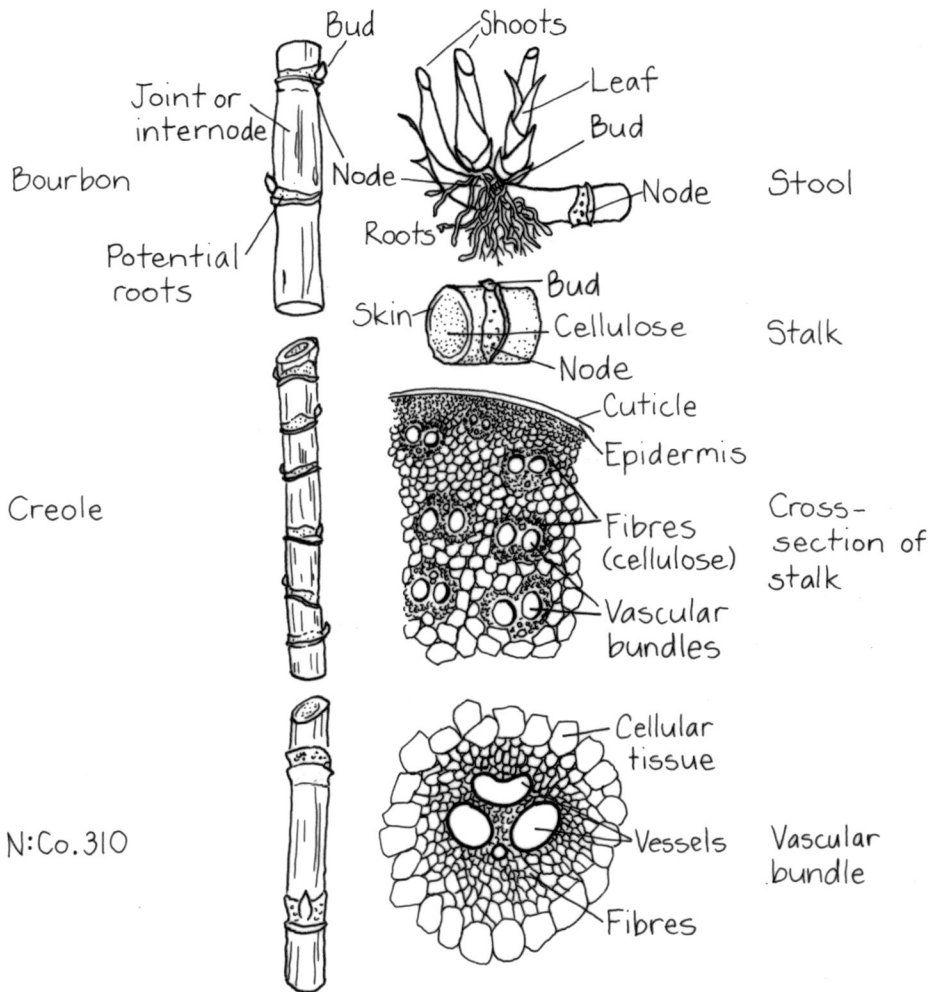

Figure 4.11 Sugar cane varieties, stalks and cross-sections

SUGAR CANE

CHOP ← STALK → CHOP → PEEL → RAW

POUND IN MORTAR — CRUSH → TRASH/BAGASSE

BOIL JUICE — JUICE → DRINK

COOL — SCREEN

STRAIN — FILTER

CANE DRINK — CLEAR JUICE

CLARIFY

HEAT → CANE LIQUOR

RAW SYRUP → FANCY MOLASSES

EVAPORATE

CRYSTALLIZE → BOTTOMS

PACK ← DRAIN → MOLASSES → ANIMAL FEED / FERTILIZER / FERMENT

CLAY — RAW SUGAR (MUSCOVADO) — DISTILL — FERMENT → YEAST / ETHANOL

DRAIN — RUM

CLAYED SUGAR — DRAIN — NEW / AGED → PUNCH / LIQUEUR

REFINE — DRINK / DRINK

BROWN SUGAR — WHITE SUGAR CRYSTALS — GOLDEN SYRUP

FERMENT

BEER STOUT — CUBES SWEETS

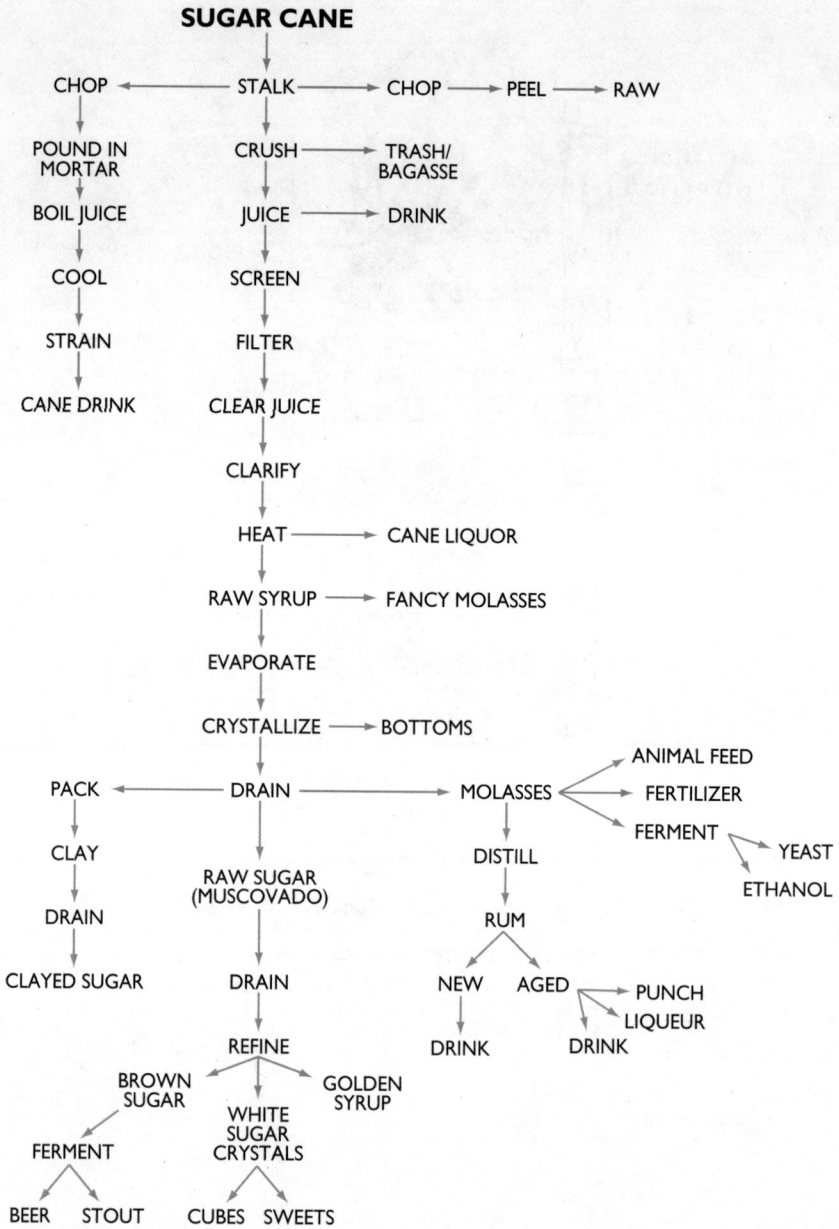

Figure 4.12 Sugar: processing flow chart

(Figure 4.12). In modern times, street sellers have sold whole sticks of cane and also, more recently, shorter, peeled lengths in plastic bags. They have also used portable rollers to squeeze fresh juice, sold by the glass.

Imperial legislation and tariffs long made it unprofitable to produce highly refined sugar in Jamaica. Some sugar was "clayed" to a first stage of purity, but most of the exported product was "raw" muscovado. In the eighteenth century, some sugar estates even imported loaves of "single refined sugar" from Britain for use by white people.[63] Local consumption was largely confined to cruder forms of sugar and – at least from a modern perspective, with highly refined sugar now understood as a cause of tooth decay, diabetes, obesity and hypertension – this was not so much a loss as a gain, for both health and taste.

Sugar was not a regular part of the rations of the enslaved but was given out on special occasions. Thus Thistlewood at Egypt plantation in 1752, "served the Negroes . . . 2 large bottoms of sugar to make them merry, now crop over". These "bottoms" were the sugar formed in the coppers or pans after boiling was complete and crystallization had begun but before the sugar was packed in barrels, to be drained of its molasses in the curing house in order to produce the muscovado grade typically exported. It was better known as "pan sugar" or "new sugar". Nugent recorded receiving a gift of pan sugar in 1802, on the second day of January, when the crop was barely begun, commenting, "The new sugar is excellent, drank in cold water; and I like the pan sugar of all things." Sullivan in 1893 said that "new sugar" was "infinitely preferred by the natives to even 'shop sugar'". By then it was "made in the island at their small settlements and is sold in its unrefined state either as molasses, or, firmer, as pan sugar".[64]

As early as the Apprenticeship, small-scale crushing became associated with the emerging peasantry, for household consumption as juice or boiled as sugar. In 1929 Beckwith said, "The Jamaica Negro is fond of sugar and generally grows a small patch of sugar cane for home consumption, which he grinds in a small hand mill." She also thought that "many" small settlers had mills powered by a mule, and poured the boiled sugar into kerosene pans or "little clay forms about the size of a pint can". Such sugar was often sent from country in five-gallon (twenty-three-litre) pans, to be retailed in smaller amounts by town higglers.[65]

In the 1930s, "wet sugar" was described as unrefined sugar, "heavy and moist with molasses, very sweet, of a flavour dear to those well accustomed to it and not to be found in any other sort of sugar". Nutritionists condemned new sugar because it contained few vitamins, but it was widely consumed. Visitors sang the praises of "the big, soft, glittering, molasses-scented, almost chocolate-brown richness and lingering sweetness upon the tongue, of the cheapest grade of Jamaican sugar". By the end of the twentieth century, nutritional opinion had shifted, and "unrefined sugar, deep brown and moist" was considered superior to the refined variety because it contained "all the rich nutrients found in cane juice".[66]

Claude McKay, in *Banana Bottom*, described a "sangaree concocted of plain sugar and bitter oranges, ginger and chewstick". The peasant's favourite beverage, said McKay, was "crude cane sugar and water with the juice of bitter oranges". Sullivan's 1893 recipe for sangaree – drawn from the elite tradition – was more conventional, combining sherry, water, nutmeg, lime peel and sugar. Her "cool drink" or "beverage" was mixed from new sugar, water and a little lime juice. "Sugar water" remained popular throughout the nineteenth century and beyond, until replaced largely by commercial "sweet drink".[67] To make "cane drink", said Sloane at the beginning of the eighteenth century, "take six or seven long sugar-canes, cut them to pieces, beat them in a mortar, put them into a kettle, with about three gallons of water, boil them for a pretty while, then put as many fresh canes, and about a gallon of water more; boil them again. When 'tis cool, strain your drink, set it in a jar, and put to it the white of an egg beat to froth, to which some of the liquor is added. Let it work twelve hours, then bottle it, it looks very clear."[68] During slavery, sugar workers were sometimes permitted to take "calabashes full of the hot purified cane juice" or "cane liquor", which, when "fermented in bamboos with the chewstick withe", produced "tolerable beer".[69]

In spite of the persistent appreciation of the pleasures of wet sugar, demand for the dry, crystallized, white refined product was strong, partly because it was thought superior and partly because it served different purposes. By the late nineteenth century, Jamaica's sugar factories worked hard to produce more highly refined sugars to compete with the "clear crushed sugar" imported in barrels. In 1880, for example, local "Bybrook sugar" was sold in barrels and tierces as vacuum pan "white" or "canary colour", and was advertised as "manufactured with the greatest cleanliness and care and . . . worthy of patronage for private use particularly". In 1893 Lascelles De Mercado and Company offered sugar in "barrels centrifugal, barrels muscovados, barrels brown vacuum pan, barrels white vacuum pan, cases of cube sugar, bags of granulated sugar". At the beginning of the twentieth century, when the Jamaican sugar industry was at its lowest point, locally produced Brown Albion and White Albion sugars came from St Thomas, but white crystal and fine castor sugars were imported. Throughout the century, the sugar industry experienced highs and lows, production peaking at 500,000 tonnes in the 1960s only to decline again. By the 1980s the island was struggling to maintain self-sufficiency and in some years was forced to import raw as well as refined sugar. The import duty on refined sugar was high, putting pressure on the prices of manufactures such as confectionery and condensed milk. By 2005 annual output was down to 124,000 tonnes.[70]

After sugar, the most important product of the sugar cane was rum, produced from the molasses drained from the muscovado and the skimmings from the coppers. In the long run, Jamaican rum had more character and visibility than did the island's sugar. Highly refined sugars are difficult to tell apart once they approach pure sucrose. Rum, on the other hand, is made distinctive by its particularity of fermentation and additives. It has been boldly claimed that "Jamaica produces a greater variety of types and flavours than anywhere else in the world", and rum has been called Jamaica's most famous export. In 1938 the Sugar Manufacturers' Association proclaimed, "Jamaica Rum is a distinctive type of rum, with geographical significance. For in no other part of the globe has it ever been possible to produce a spirit with quite the same characteristics of flavour and aroma." The "genuine 'Old Jamaica'", the association claimed, offered a "wholesome and delightful" drink, a "delicious flavouring for puddings and sauces" and a "restorative and stimulating" medicine or "first aid" for fevers, colds and chills.[71]

In the late seventeenth century, the first skimmings from boiling were regarded as poor quality, said Hughes, but were used to make "a very good drink . . . called Locusale, much used by the servants" or were sent to the distillery to make "a sort of strongwater they call rum, or rum-bullion, stronger than spirit of wine, and not very pleasant until a man is used to it". In the early eighteenth century, treatises on fermentation used rum as their prime example. One such author, George Smith of England, said in 1729 that rum took longer to ferment in the West Indies than in temperate climates, and that this "greatly contributes towards the exaltation of the principles and perfection of the subject, which is allowed to be a much finer product than what can be obtained here, tho' attempted with the same materials".[72]

Rum could be drunk "new" or, preferably, allowed to mature for a number of years, taking character from its barrel. Aging was an expensive operation, so the rougher new rum was used in some circumstances. Most of the rum distributed to enslaved people on plantations seems to have been of this quality. For example, in 1752 Thistlewood, at Egypt, "served the Negroes 15 quarts of rum out of the butt a filling in the curing house".[73]

The rum produced by particular estates was at first known simply by the names of the plantations. In 1880, for example, a Kingston merchant offered puncheons of "Rock River rum 1877 crop", and in 1890 another merchant had "dozens of Appleton Estate 1880 crop – Old Rum – at 5 shillings per bottle". Other rums became associated with the name of the blender. John Wray, founder of the long-lived firm J. Wray and Nephew Ltd, began experimenting with rum purchased from the "best" estates in 1825, and created "a blend that pleased his palate and that of the customers to whom he offered it". By 1918 Wray and Nephew were advertising themselves as "Jamaica's leading rum merchants", and in 1938 the firm claimed to be "the largest rum dealers in the world growing their own cane, distilling their own rum and controlling the output of Appleton, Monymusk and Bernard Lodge [Estates]". Wray and Nephew had five million litres of rum aging in its warehouses.[74] The firm competed with Daniel Finzi (founded in 1843) and with Edwin Charley's wide range of brands (founded in 1892), which included White Label, Red Label, Black Seal, Gold Seal, White Rose, Light Coloured, Coronation, Diamond, Punch Bowl and Royal Reserve (a liqueur), advertised as offering the best value in "flavour, aroma and strength". In 1935 the range of "Myers's fine old Jamaica rums" included Green Seal (over four years old), Old Kingston (over five years), Light Vatted (over eight years), Planters' Punch brand (over eight years), Jamaica Liqueur Rum (over thirteen years), Mona (distilled in 1906), and Mount Eagle (distilled in 1895). Daniel Finzi had registered the word "amber" in 1915 and claimed that "this rum (colour of whisky) has made a name for itself, and for those that like a light coloured rum, it is unexcelled".[75]

The earliest reference to "white rum" in the *Gleaner* comes from 1866 when Peter Desnoes and Son offered some puncheons for sale, followed later in the year by Daniel Finzi and Co. Throughout the twentieth century, white rum – the strong, overproof variety, not the etiolated, weaker version – was the most popular alcoholic drink in Jamaica, and the island was said to rank high in the world in consumption of alcohol generally.[76] By the 1980s Wray and Nephew held 90 per cent of the liquor market. In 1985 the company launched a new drink, "Sugar Ray Light Rum Punch", that it claimed was "truly indigenous to Jamaica", based on the traditional formula (one of sour, two of sweet, three of strong, four of weak), with "the addition of spices, pimento and Jamaican fruit juices". The following year the firm introduced Coconut Rum, "a pure white spirit made from aged rum and natural coconut extract", which could be mixed with pineapple juice to produce a piña colada or drunk with milk or soda. The company soon added Rum Cream, combining smooth cream with overproof rum, and Sugar Ray and *Cane Dew*.[77]

Rum can be drunk straight, or with water or ice, or mixed with some other drink. One common mixed variety, since as early as the seventeenth century, has been rum punch. Sloane said rum punch was made of "rum, water, lime juice, sugar, and a little nutmeg scrap'd on the top of it". He believed it was unhealthy because it was "made usually of the sugar-pot bottom". In May 1938 the *Gleaner* offered an "authentic recipe for planters' punch", mixing in a glass one dessertspoonful of sugar or syrup, two dessert-spoons of fresh lime juice, three tablespoons of cold water and four tablespoons of Myers' Fine Old Jamaica Rum. Plenty of cracked ice was added to the glass, along with slices of pineapple, orange and lemon, a cherry and a sprig of mint. The traditional rhyme called for one of sour (lime juice), two of sweet (sugar syrup), three of strong (rum) and four of weak (water). Some writers attributed this formula to rum punch, which they distinguished from planters' punch, but the essentials were the same. In the 1980s, a more elaborate recipe for planters' punch called for dark rum, sugar syrup, fresh lime juice, cold water and crushed ice, stirred in a tall glass, with added slices of orange, lemon and pineapple, and adorned with a maraschino cherry and a sprig of mint. Degraded versions, from the 1980s, substituted strawberry syrup, pineapple juice, bitter lemon, rum and Angostura bitters.[78]

Further rum mixtures began to emerge in the twentieth century. By the 1930s "rum and ginger ale" was already "one of the most popular and refreshing rum drinks", and "rum and coca cola or konut [kolanut]" was "rapidly taking a high place in the hall of famous drinks". Drinkers were also encouraged to try "a rum cocktail" mixed with French vermouth, sugar syrup and bitters, or "a rum Collins" with lime juice, sugar syrup and soda water. Effervescing soda water, lemonade and gingerade were available as mixers by 1870, in bottles imported from London.[79]

Rum-based liqueurs using local fruits were long produced on a small scale. In 1974 Sangster's Old Jamaica Spirits began commercial operations, particularly for export, and developed varieties such as Blue Mountain coffee, wild orange, coffee-orange, coconut rum, pimento dram and banana. These were marketed with a nostalgic emphasis, using containers modelled on old Port Royal decanters and labels with prints of scenes from the years before 1850.[80]

Some of the blenders and wholesalers of rum also became producers and marketers of other drinks – alcoholic and not – that made plentiful use of sugar. For example, the firm Desnoes and Geddes, founded in 1918, imported liquor and manufactured aerated waters. The Desnoes were descended from a family of rum blenders, having won a medal in London in 1862 for their Jamaica Old Rum. Desnoes and Geddes took over the West Indies Mineral and Table Water Company, and in 1960 introduced the foreign brands Schweppes Tonic, Bitter Lemon and 7-Up. They also produced their own lines of ginger beer, ginger ale, soda and soda water, along with five varieties of soft drinks; developed Ting, a grapefruit-based sweet drink, in 1985; and in 1992 introduced Malta and Dandy Shandy.[81]

Jamaican beer was also closely associated with Desnoes and Geddes, and with sugar. Beer is largely made of water and grains, but sugar is the most significant of the local ingredients. Jamaica long imported beer, mostly from Britain, and it continues to do so. In 1928, however, Desnoes and Geddes opened the Surrey Brewery and commenced making Red Stripe, the beer that would become most closely identified with Jamaica. In 1935, it was later claimed, the governor observed that "this local industry turns out a beer so excellent and at so cheap a price that the English beers are unable to compete". Red Stripe was at first a light ale, but the modern lager formula replaced the ale in 1938. Desnoes and Geddes adopted few foreign beers, but did introduce McEwan's Strong Ale and Heineken in 1973.[82]

Equally popular with Jamaicans was stout, imported and local, particularly respected by men for its supposed capacity to deliver power and vigour, and "put it back". Generic stout was imported by the 1820s, Guinness's Stout by 1870. Mackeson's Milk Stout was introduced in 1913, and Gilmour's Oatmeal Stout the next year.[83] Desnoes and Geddes launched Dragon Stout as a "wholly Jamaican enterprise" in 1961, and it became the most popular brand. Although it was thought sweetish, Dragon appealed to the Jamaican taste, some mixing it with condensed milk or even white rum. In 1985 Desnoes and Geddes acquired Guinness (Jamaica) Limited and began to brew the famous – and "good for you" – stout at Central Village. An Extra Stout was developed, "stronger and sharper to the tongue than the regular Guinness", created by using "a second fermentation that is encouraged by the introduction of a little old stout to the new brew late in the brewing process". In 1993 the family-owned company Desnoes and Geddes sold out to Guinness.[84]

Rum, both dark and overproof, formed the basis of many of the mixed drinks promoted along with beachside tourism, often with an aphrodisiac promise and a touch of James Bond. One mainstream example is the "naked lady", comprised of white rum, sweet vermouth, apricot brandy, Grenadine and lemon juice, shaken well with ice and strained into a cocktail glass. Tonic wines were also popular in the twentieth century, either imported or produced locally under licence. For example, Sanatogen Tonic Wine, made by Edwin Charley for Whiteways of Whimple, was promoted as doing "a power of good" when taken "in conjunction with a programme of regular exercise, balanced diet and ample sleep". Jamaica spawned many and varied indigenous drinks designed to sustain and support, directed particularly at male sexual performance. In 1991, for example, Coction was named the big drink at Sunsplash: "Made with equal parts of Supligen (Vanilla) and Stallion and Mare Roots Wine with nutmeg and crushed ice, Coction keeps you going (they say)."[85]

Sweetened drinks also blended into the emergence of self-consciously "natural" juices. During World War II, shortages led to the adoption of carrot as a sweetened drink, and its popularity continued, particularly as a drink with Sunday dinner. It became available in cans, but the "conventional" way to prepare this drink was to grate carrots and ginger, add water and squeeze through a strainer, then flavour with sugar and lime juice. Sometimes it was made with sweetened condensed milk. An alternative "Culture Drink" of the 1990s used canned carrot juice, water, condensed milk, sugar, white rum or brandy, and stout. Beets were also used. In 2005 Tru-Juice Vitalizer offered "the energy and power of nine vegetables, fruits and roots in one ital juice". Even more natural was "Ital Cool-Aid" – simply chilled coconut water served over ice.[86]

Rum also found its way into Jamaica cookery, most obviously in the steeping of fruits for cakes and puddings. The same applied to beer and stout. In 1993 a Red Stripe cookbook was published, using the beer in peas soup, stamp and go, and Easter bun, for example. Beer also appeared in independent cookbooks, beginning in the 1960s. Red Stripe was used to stew beef, or combined with rice, shrimp, lobster and crab meat to create "beer seafood creole". Stout was also used in cooking – in buns, for example.[87]

The most obvious way of cooking with sugar was the making of "sweets". Homemade sweets, such as peppermint sticks, were retailed along with imported items in the nineteenth century. A local industry emerged in the early twentieth century, partially replacing the imported article and taking advantage of the increased availability of refined sugar, the major ingredient. Lannaman's Sweet Factory was established in Kingston in 1932, and Desnoes and Geddes Confectionery produced "lolly-pops", "candy drops", "Jamaica paradise plums" and "ju-jub-jellies", all "made in Jamaica by Jamaicans with Jamaican sugar". The manufacture was claimed to be distinguished by cleanliness, from the "pure sugar stage" to the final product, untouched by naked hand. Forty pounds of sugar at a time was melted in a boiler, with just a quart of water and a teaspoon of cream of tartar, then poured onto a metal table, mixed with flavouring, moulded through a machine and packed in tins or glazed paper packets. Before modern packaging, mint balls and icy mints, ginger sweets and "sweet-sour Chinese sweeties" filled bottles and jars in small shops and decorated the shelves of handcarts. Small-scale manufacturing persisted to the end of the twentieth century, producing many unique items. In the 1960s, common Jamaican sweets included wangla, stretcher, guava cheese, paradise plum and peppermint stick. Bustamante backbone, characterized by its toughness, used wet sugar and grated coconut.[88]

CHAPTER 5

FRUITS

In 1890 Jamaica was described as "the paradise of the fruit lover". Luscious, tantalizing fruit seemed to be everywhere in every season, dangling temptingly before the eye, asking to be plucked and eaten on the spot, fresh, raw and juicy. Temptation was almost impossible to resist. Even the most testy visitor, having perhaps disparaged creole cookery and complained broadly of the meat, fish and roots of the island, was forced to concede that "the fruits of Jamaica are delicious indeed".[1] Since the eighteenth century, a heap or basketful of representative fruit, with their contrasting colours, shapes and textures, has been a prime image of abundance and desirability (Plate 5).

As human food, fruits are readily distinguished from seeds. Whereas fruit is most often eaten raw and is typically thought of as juicy and sweet, seeds are generally cooked, because they are hard and dry. But botanically, fruit and seed are united in the single objective of reproducing the species, and their development is intimately connected. The pollination and fertilization of a plant's flower results in the development of both the embryo and the much larger surrounding multicellular endosperm, which stores food in its tissue to nourish the growing embryo that will become the seed. In order to serve this purpose, the endosperm is rich in nutrients and starch, and may be either solid or liquid. As the embryo's cells begin to divide, it gradually consumes the endosperm. Some seeds, such as those of legumes, effectively consume all of the endosperm, whereas others, such as the cereals, retain a large quantity of endosperm in the mature grain in order to supply energy for germination. The example of the orange, sketched in Figure 5.1, is only one of the possibilities. It illustrates the cycle for the most common of Jamaica's foods.

However constituted, the growth of the seed is paralleled by the swelling of the flower's ovary, and it is this that becomes the fruit. Other parts of the flower, such as petals, sepals and flower stalks, may swell and fuse with the ovary. In its developed and ripened form, the fruit is essentially a container of seeds (formed in turn from the ovules), prepared for dispersal and growth as new plants. The ripening of fruit and seed leads to

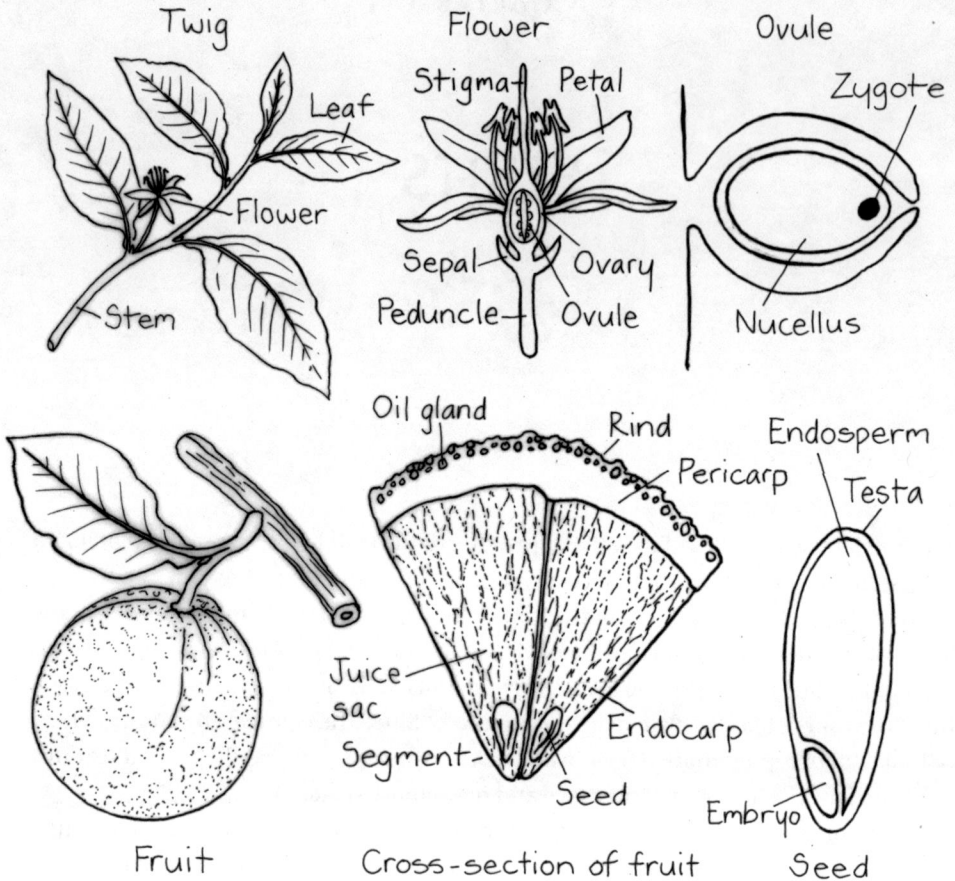

Figure 5.1 Plant structures: fruit and seed, as in the orange

a loss of water in the seed and to the onset of dormancy while the seed awaits the arrival of suitable conditions for germination. The seeds (or seed) within a fruit may be eaten or not, depending both on the size and hardness of the seeds and on the edibility of the container. For example, the pod of a pea may be eaten when young, before the seeds are ready to germinate, but once the seeds are mature, the pod may become dry and unattractive as human food, the pod snapping open and shooting its seed across the ground. In this case, the fruit is effectively a protective barrier. In other plants, such as rice, only the mature seed is consumed as human food.[2]

The fruits most attractive to humans and other animals are the fleshy, succulent varieties, and these tend to have a relatively complex structure. The degree of their complexity is determined by the organization of the ovary itself and by the way it develops after fertilization. The exterior wall, or pericarp, of the fruit derives from the wall of the ovary. Some fruit, such as the plantain and the mango, have a hard wall, or rind, separate from the flesh, whereas others, like the cherry and the tomato, have no rind and may be bitten into directly. In some fruit, such as the coconut, the pericarp is differentiated into layers. Overall, the most fragrant, succulent and best-tasting fruits are the most likely to be dispersed by animals, including humans. Not all fruiting plants are propagated by the dispersal of seeds, and the development of fruit survives from earlier stages of evolution in seedless varieties that are preferred by consumers. Bananas and tangerines are good examples of this. In recent times, seedless varieties of some fruits have been produced by growth-regulating chemicals as well as by selection. It is also striking that, with some exceptions, humans select carefully either the fruit or the seed as food, and often spit out seeds embedded in juicy flesh.

Attractiveness is also controlled partly by colour, the unripe fruit generally being green and often bitter – even poisonous, like ackee – whereas ripe fruits with seeds ready for dispersal turn red, yellow or purplish black to signal that the fruit is full of sugars and ready to eat. *Discrimination is thus needed in choosing what to eat and what not.* In assessing stages of ripeness, Jamaicans talk about fruit (and other food crops) as "fit", or ready to gather and harvest though not quite ready to consume. A "fit" fruit can be picked with the expectation that it will continue to mature to ripeness. A "force-ripe" fruit is one picked too early and forced to ripen prematurely in the sun or the dark, and therefore potentially bad-tasting or even hazardous.

In food science, a fruit can be defined as "the edible part of a plant normally eaten raw".[3] This applies to most of the fruits eaten by Jamaicans and considered sweet and juicy. On the other hand, some important fruits, such as the plantain and the bread-fruit, do require cooking and belong to the "food" category of ground provisions. These need salt and sauce to be eaten, just as roots do. Still other fruits, notably the banana, can be consumed in different states in different ways, some of which require cooking. From the point of view of human nutrition, the succulent golden fruits that dangle temptingly seem to offer an easy return to effort. Their disadvantage is that they rot rapidly and often deliver their harvest over a short period, making dependence on them strictly seasonal. In Jamaica it became a common expression – one still used today – that during mango season the cook could turn down her pot.[4] Fruits are also subject to depredations from thieves of all sorts, who often work on the assumption that fruits are part of the commons. More importantly, above-ground fruiting plants are vulnerable to storm and hurricane. An entire harvest can be lost and the long-term resource damaged in a single night's high winds. Particularly at risk are those plants that are top-heavy when in fruit, borne on unstable stems and weakly rooted, which is most obvious in plantain and banana.

PLANTAIN

Botanically, the plantain is closely related to the banana, and for this reason many texts treat the two plants together. Jamaicans, however, distinguish clearly between the two and employ them differently in food culture, so they are discussed separately here. Both plantain and banana belong to the family Musaceae, and almost all of the edible varieties share a single wild ancestor, *Musa acuminata*, which was domesticated in antiquity. But the edible *Musa* cultivars are all hybrid forms – sterile and effectively seedless. For this reason, the nomenclature applied by Linnaeus, based on a description of hybrids and calling the plantain *M. paradisiaca* and the banana *M. sapientum*, has been abandoned. Some writers have even argued for the complete abandonment of formal Latin names until the taxonomy is better understood.[5] With this caution in mind, the two plants and their fruits will be referred to here simply as "plantain" and "banana". In most texts, the plantain is given a secondary role, but historically it has been the more significant food in Jamaica.

Domestication of the wild species of both plantain and banana led to the selection of mutations that replaced fruit full of hard, stony seeds with fruit full of edible pulp. This process occurred for plantain in the ancient gardens of rainforest Malaysia, while hybridization was more broadly spread through Southeast Asia. Some argue for a specific origin in Papua New Guinea. The plantain (as well as the banana) was carried to Africa in prehistoric times and reached the coast of West Africa before Europeans. Both plantain and banana were in Spain by the tenth century and were introduced to the Canary Islands in the early fifteenth century. From these sites, both banana and plantain were taken to the West Indies by the Spanish and quickly became an important food source.[6] The plantain was probably well established in Jamaica by 1520.

The plantain is a tree-like perennial herb. It stands up to five metres above the ground, with a dense mat of roots near the ground surface and an underground corm that suckers (Figure 5.2). The shoots that develop from these suckers produce large leaves, replacing one another in spiral succession. Each shoot flowers just once and produces a single stem of fruit, but fresh suckers keep rising from the corm. Strictly, what is called the fruit is actually a berry, with seeds lying free in the pulp. The stem hangs downward while the flowers and fruit grow upwards, with as many as fifty fingers of fruit to a stem, or bunch. John Lunan, in 1814, said a spike of fruit could weigh up to eighteen kilograms. The fingers form into about five "hands", the most substantial being at the top and the fingers splayed out rather than closely arrayed as on the banana. The hydrolysis of starch to sugar is slower in the plantain than in the banana, so that when "fit" it has a relatively starchy and acid flesh that requires cooking to be palatable.[7]

Varieties of plantain are recognized, though consumers are often not aware of their differences. They have also changed over time. In 1933 H.A. Bloomfield of St Andrew wrote to the *Gleaner* seeking "a dozen good strong suckers of the Tiger Plantain" – a species of plantain, he said, that used to grow abundantly in the Dry Harbour Mountains of St Ann but had since become rare. According to Bloomfield, "in size and quality they are much like the maiden plantains, only that each plantain is covered with black spots", and its bunches had up to twelve hands. The tiger plantain got its name from its "spreckle-spreckle" spots. The maiden plantain's name came from its small size, bearing large bunches with many small fruit. Hans Sloane ranked the maiden plantain the

Banana

Plantain

Hand

Bunch

Bunch

Finger

Stem

Flower

Finger

Cross-section

Cross-section

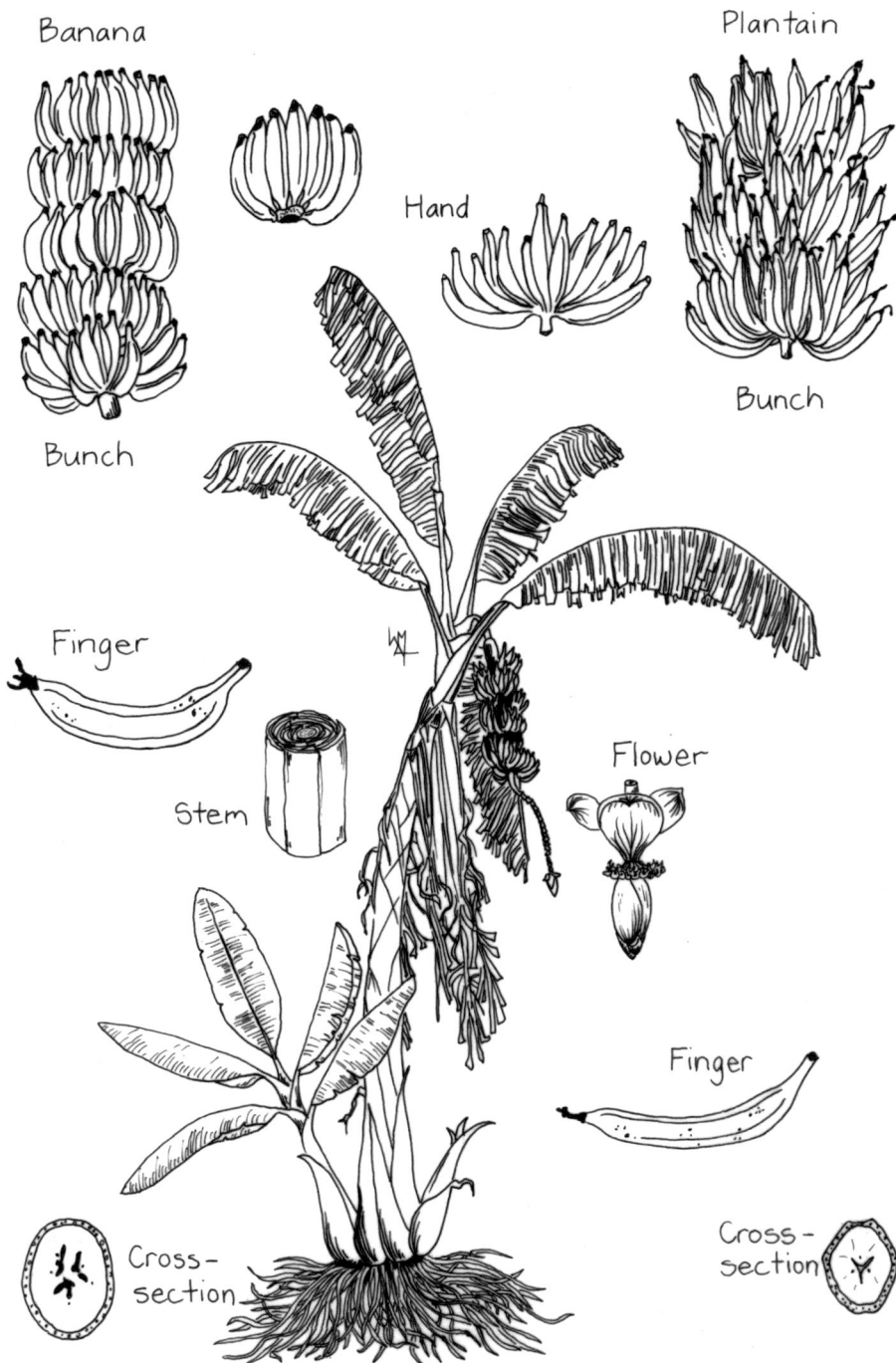

Figure 5.2 Plantain and banana: plants and fruit

smallest and best of the varieties, followed by the larger "Pleasant-Plantain" and the biggest of all, the "Horse-Plantain".[8]

During the period of slavery, the plantain was one of the most important sources of food in Jamaica. Writing of the 1680s, Sloane thought that, after cassava, plantain was "the next most general support of life in the island". As cassava declined in importance during the eighteenth century, plantain joined coco and yam among the leading foods of the enslaved. Plantain was also widely consumed by free people. It was grown not only in provision grounds but also on plantation land as a crop to provide food for the population, especially in times of scarcity. Thomas Roughley, in 1823, for example, recommended planting three hectares, in the most sheltered location possible, and planting wide – in rows three metres apart with two metres between each plant – to give the plantain space to grow and sucker, but with cocos between the rows. Carefully weeded and drained, this plantain walk would bear in twelve months, he said, "amply *repaying for the labour and trouble of planting it, and giving an almost inexhaustible* supply of fine provisions", if spared hurricanes and storms. Earlier writers were sometimes critical of the planters' husbandry, arguing that the "plantain-walks are so crowded with trees, that storms shake them down".[9]

The plantain's vulnerability to high wind is a function of its shallow rooting and mechanical inadequacies, so the problem persisted in the long term. Because the plantain is not a woody tree, "the aerial stem is entirely dependent upon the surrounding mass of leaf sheaths for its support", making "a limp structure incapable of supporting itself". Once a bunch of fruit emerges, the weight can be enough to bring down the plant and the trees are commonly propped up with bamboo poles and sticks.[10]

Plantain can be consumed at different stages of development but is always cooked, never eaten raw (Figure 5.3). One eighteenth-century observer did claim that the fruit was delicious when ripe and, "fresh from the tree, eats like a pear, but of a more pleasing flavour". Perhaps he simply conflated plantain and banana. Equally uncommon was the early observation that, sliced and steeped in water, the plantain made "a fine cool drink" which could intoxicate. This drink became rare in the nineteenth century. Caroline Sullivan, in 1893, offered a recipe for "plantain drink" but said she had borrowed it and noted that it was "an old recipe and no mention is made of proportions of plantains to water". It was made from "*quite* ripe" plantains, peeled, mashed and steeped in boiling water overnight. Strained into bottles, it was ready to drink in a week. Sullivan warned, "It is a very pleasant and strong drink; but it should be drunk sparingly, as it is stronger than sack, and apt to mount to the head."[11]

Sloane had earlier observed that the plantain was picked "a little green; they ripen and turn yellow in the house, when, or before they are eaten". Generally, plantains were peeled and roasted under hot coals, or "boil'd in oglio's or pepper-pots, and prepar'd into a past[e] like dumplins, and several other ways". Henry Barham said, "Roasted before they are ripe, they eat like bread; they are eaten boiled or roasted, and one roasted that is ripe, and buttered, eats very delicious." In 1788, the plantain was called "the principal and most esteemed bread-fruit", having a mealy taste when boiled or baked

PLANTAIN

↓

FRUIT

[Flow chart branches]

GREEN — TURNED — RIPE

GREEN:
BOIL → REMOVE SKIN
REMOVE SKIN → BOIL, SLICE, FRY, POUND, DRY
SLICE → ROAST → CHIPS
POUND → FUFU → MOULD
DRY → BEAT → FLOUR → BOIL, CONCANTINE → PORRIDGE, DUMPLING

TURNED:
REMOVE SKIN → FRY, ROAST, BOIL, MASH
MASH → MOULD → BOIL → DUMPLING

RIPE:
REMOVE SKIN → FRY, ROAST, MASH
MASH → BAKE, STEEP
BAKE → TART, WRAP in LEAF → BOIL → DOKUNU
STEEP → STRAIN → DRINK

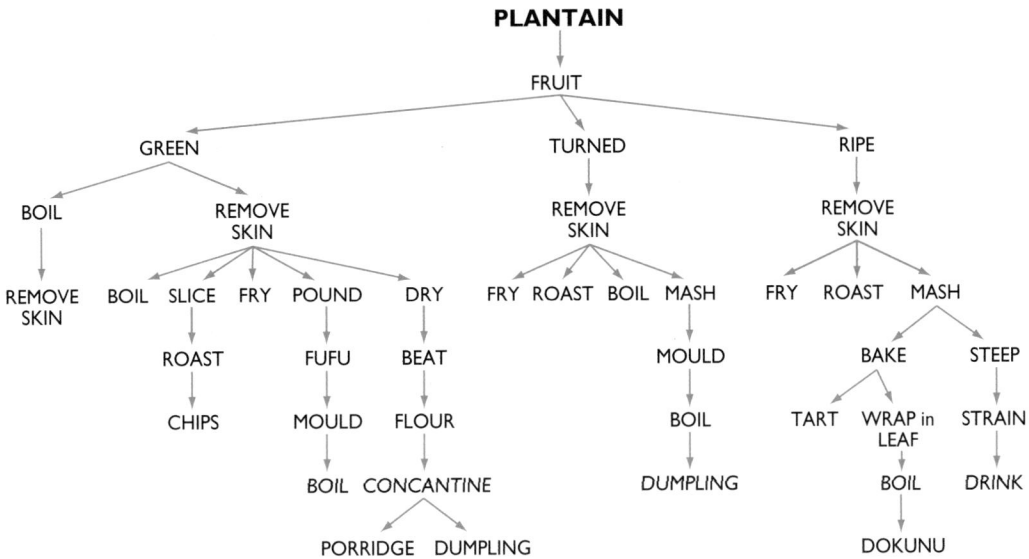

Figure 5.3 Plantain: processing flow chart

before it was ripe. Patrick Browne gave these same descriptions in 1756, adding that "the negroes generally boil them with their other messes, as salt-fish, beef, pork, pickle, or crabs, &c. and find them a hearty wholesome food". The occasional British voice declared roast plantain a "tasteless substitute for wheaten bread", but the more common view was that, as Edward Long expressed it, "many white persons, after being accustomed to it for some time, actually prefer it to bread, especially when young and tender".[12]

At the end of the nineteenth century, Sullivan was just as enthusiastic, dealing with plantains first in her section on vegetables. She distinguished "plantains green, plantains ripe" and "plantains turned", the latter equivalent to what Long called "full-grown", as indicated by the colour just beginning to change from green to gold. In this state the fruit was combined with saltfish or "eaten boiled or roasted with butter put inside them". The green plantain, said Sullivan, could be boiled or roasted; "the people" ate it with soup or saltfish. Roasted plantain was served in a folded napkin, "with the planter's cheese". Even ripe plantain could be served, roasted or fried, with vegetables and other "food". Early in the twentieth century, Martha Beckwith could say that "because of their preference for hard food over soft, the Jamaica Negroes eat both plantains and bread-fruit green by choice, either boiled or roasted".[13] Most of these methods remain common, though modern cookbooks say little about them.

Plantain could be pounded in a mortar to make fufu, like the more common coco and yam. Thomas Thistlewood in 1750 ate "tum tum of plantain and fish beat together". Its use continued into the nineteenth century and beyond. Phyllis Clark offered a recipe in 1945 for "foo foo or pound plantain", using boiled green plantains to make balls served in soup. But Clark was unusual in associating fufu with plantain rather than with roots. Few twentieth-century cookbooks said much about the plantain in its green state, though a rare recipe did describe "foo foo (pounded plantain)" using three green and one ripe but firm plantain.[14] In most texts, the green plantain was replaced by the green banana. Plantain chips were also produced commercially but had to compete with those made locally from green banana and with imported varieties that used Irish potato.

By the 1930s it could be said that "plantains are not much in demand as a breadfood now; they have been superseded chiefly by [imported wheaten] flour". Earlier, plantain had itself been used to produce a flour. This was first done by enslaved people in the early eighteenth century, the flour made by slicing the plantain and drying it in the sun, then pounding it.[15] This practice was later adopted by the planters. In 1785 the planter-attorney Simon Taylor observed that following the storms of that year, many planters had "cutt off all the plantains that were nearly full, sliced them, dryed them extremely well, ground them, and rammed them down into casks as flour, it has kept well for some months, and is a very strong healthy good food". Taylor had not done this himself but proposed to do so in the future, having learned from "fatall experience". There were times of the year when plantains were in great surplus, he said, and he now believed the plantations should attempt to establish a "magazine of dried plantains . . . , which the negroes call coor cuntine [concantine]". In the *Dictionary of Jamaican English*, F.G. Cassidy and R.B. Le Page identify *kongkonte* or *kongkote* as "flour made from cassava, plantain, or green banana", and note that it was eaten as porridge and dumplings. They trace the roots of the word to Twi and Gã, but the earliest citation is from only 1873, when Charles Rampini talked of "*conquintay*", or the flour made for porridge by pounding slices of plantain that had been dried on sun-baked stones. Taylor's use of the word almost one hundred years earlier suggests an African origin for the technology as well as the word. Taylor thought the plantain flour to be "as wholesome and nourishing as wheat flour" and believed that "if we can get the plantain flour to keep I really think it will be the best thing that ever has yet been thought of".[16]

Ripe plantain retained its status more easily than did green plantain. Eighteenth-century writers described the ripe fruit as "lusciously sweet" and ideal for making "tarts and sweet-meats". Browne said, "As the fruit ripens, it becomes soft and sweetish, and is then generally made into tarts; or sliced and fryed with butter, and thus served up in plates."[17] By the end of the twentieth century, the "plantain tart" was dominating the cookbooks, calling for "very ripe" or "well ripe" plantains, the fruit almost liquid. The plantains were boiled and mashed, combined with sugar, nutmeg, vanilla and red food colouring, and encased in pastry and baked. Sullivan had a similar recipe, using "the juice of the prickly-pear squeezed out" to obtain a deep red colour.[18] Plantain tarts became a common commodity of pastry shops and a rare example of the use of the ripe fruit in commercial baking.

Dokunu, another sweet pudding, was originally made with the plantain, but the fruit lost ground to other starchy ingredients. The word *dokunu*, another Twi derivation, means boiled maize bread, but as early as 1740 it was said the plantain "boil'd in its leaves" was called "duckano". One Maroon variation baked the dokunu in an iron pot, enclosing the mixture in leaves and covering with ashes. Later descriptions, including Sullivan's, identified the principal ingredient as cornmeal, following the Twi terminology, or as green banana, coco, sweet potato or cassava. Modern versions generally use either cornmeal or sweet potato and offer the alternative names "blue drawers" and "tie-leaf". One recent recipe specified cornmeal, mixed with salt, nutmeg and grated coconut, and blended with vanilla. This mixture was dropped, half a cup at a time, into the centre of rectangles of banana leaf, twenty by thirty centimetres. Banana leaf used for this purpose must first be "quailed" (a Jamaicanism meaning to make limp and pliable) over a fire. The sides of the rectangles are folded up to form parcels and tied with thin strips of banana bark, then boiled for an hour. Recipes like this have sometimes been called "corn tie-a-leaf".[19] In these versions, the plantain is completely missing, replaced even to its leaf by the banana.

BANANA

How was it that the banana became more significant than the plantain in the Jamaican food system, and why did it happen so slowly? In the provision grounds and house gardens of enslaved people, the banana had only a minor place. Certainly the banana was included in general contemporary descriptive accounts of gardens and grounds, but such lists were long and contained many uncommon plants. Wherever more precise data are available, the banana is never prominent, whereas the plantain is ubiquitous. One important reason for this preference may have been the relative roles of plantain and banana in West Africa, where the plantain was an established staple food and the banana insignificant down to the nineteenth century. Until recently it was thought that the plantain had reached West Africa in pre-colonial times and the banana later, as a colonial introduction. Now it is generally agreed that the two fruits arrived together, before the Europeans. The preference for the plantain would have been carried from Africa to Jamaica, and its survival indicates the ability of the enslaved to maintain this aspect of their system. Further, there is nothing in the record to suggest that the planters sought to overturn the choice and much to confirm their fundamental agreement. Browne, for example, having devoted much space to the plantain and having waxed lyrical on its merits, dismissed the banana summarily. All he could find to say was that the banana was "seldom cultivated by any but those that have a particular fancy for the fruit of it, which, when ripe is sweet, clammy, and soft; but it lies heavy upon the stomach".[20]

What accounts for this broad general preference – among enslaved and free, in Jamaica and in Africa – for the plantain over the banana? One explanation can be found in the higher productivity of the plantain. Ease of preparation may also have something to do with it. Certainly the plantain was superior as a food to be pounded, for the making of fufu. The plantain also delivers more energy and carbohydrate, and contains less water, though it is inferior to the banana in protein. The principal difference was one of utilization, the plantain being used at all stages of ripeness but the banana, down to the nineteenth century, eaten most often only when ripe (Figure 5.4).

BANANA

```
                          BANANA
                   /                \
               NAVEL               FRUIT
                 |                /       \
              NAVEL          GREEN         RIPE
              STEW          /     \           \
                      REMOVE       BOIL      REMOVE
                       SKIN          |        SKIN
                /    |   |    \    REMOVE   /  |  |  |  \        \
             BOIL  FRY GRATE DRY   SKIN  RAW FRY ROAST BAKE MASH  SUN-DRY
             /  \   |    |    |                              /  | | \    /    \
      PUDDING SOUP DRY  BOIL POUND                       BAKE SAUCE FRY STEEP BOIL BANANA
                   |     |    /  |  \                     |    |    |    |     |    FIG
                CHIPS  MUSSA FLOUR PAP PORRIDGE        BREAD PUDDING FRITTER WINE PRESERVES
                             |                        PANCAKE
                           BAKE
                             |
                           BREAD
```

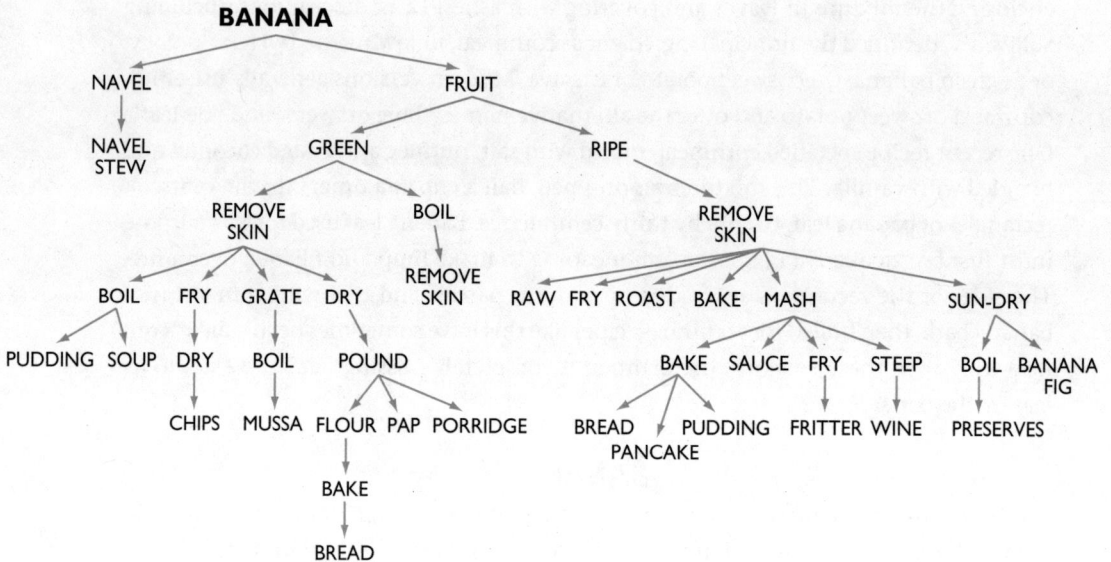

Figure 5.4 Banana: processing flow chart

Long, in 1774, said the banana was "generally used when ripe"; it resembled the plantain but had "a softer, mellower taste, and more proper for tarts and fritters". He said nothing of the use of green banana, boiled or otherwise. Neither did Barham or Browne, who allocated the banana to the realm of sweet dishes rather than including it among the starches. W.J. Titford, in 1811, similarly ignored the green banana, saying only, "This fine fruit, when ripe, has a rich, yellow, sweet, mealy pulp, very agreeable and nourishing, raw, baked, or sun-dried. It makes a drink exceeding cider." Roughley, describing the laying out of a plantain walk, merely noted that "a few banana suckers" might be included because "sometimes they are much in request, as a luscious, wholesome fruit". Historians have sometimes claimed a larger role for the green banana during slavery. Thus Douglas Hall argued in 1964 that bananas were an important market commodity for the post-slavery peasantry, "which the upper and middle classes generally consumed in their ripe state, but which, from the days of slavery, had been eaten by workers, as a staple item of diet, green and boiled or roasted".[21] It may be that contemporaries conflated banana and plantain when observing the cooking of the green fruit, but there seems to be no evidence to support Hall's contention that the banana was a staple, and it is more likely that both slave and free ate the banana ripe rather than green.

One reason for the late general adoption of the banana may be found in the varieties available during slavery. It was not until after the abolition of slavery that the Gros Michel variety was introduced to Jamaica from Martinique. First planted in St Andrew in 1835, the Gros Michel quickly spread to parishes with more fertile soils and higher rainfall levels, especially in the north and east of the island, where sugar land was being abandoned. The Gros Michel was long called the "Martnick but came to be known simply as "Jamaica banana".[22] In 1912 Claude McKay referred to it in his poem "King Banana":

> Green mancha mek fe naygur man;
> Wha' sweet so when it roas'?
> Some boil it in a big black pan,
> It sweeter in a toas'.[23]

What accounts for this apparent new-found enthusiasm for the banana, and specifically for the Gros Michel, "green mancha"?

The role of the banana changed dramatically in the 1870s when it emerged as a profitable new commodity in Jamaica's languishing export economy. The growth of the banana trade depended on changes in shipping technology and on the establishment of rapid and regular steamship services between Jamaican ports and the booming coastal cities of the northeastern United States, which offered massive markets for fresh fruit and vegetables. In the late 1860s, small American schooners began to carry bananas as well as pineapples, coconuts, oranges and yams from northern Jamaican ports, especially Port Antonio, to New York and Boston. From this mix it was the banana that emerged supreme, appealing to a taste for the exotic by supplying a previously unavailable food. In such markets the banana began life as a luxury good, but it quickly became relatively cheap.[24]

As late as 1876 the Englishman Sir Sibbald David Scott could complain of the Jamaica banana that it combined "the taste of butter, tallow-candles, and sleepy-pears". But ten years later the *Gleaner* reported that the yellow or Martinique banana had become "known in the United States as the Jamaica banana to distinguish it from the large red banana formerly exported in large quantities from Cuba. The Cuba banana has now been almost entirely replaced by the brighter and more attractive as well as the luscious fruit from Jamaica." Local and American merchants – the active agents in the banana trade – initially had trouble filling the holds of their ships because the banana was not in plentiful supply in Jamaica. Promoters had to be sent into the countryside to encourage small settlers to produce Gros Michel for the trade. At first, large planters were not interested. Lord Olivier later reflected on this stage of development, recalling that "banana-growing was still despised as backwoods 'nigger business,' which any old-time sugar planter would have disdained". Nonetheless, the trade to North America developed rapidly after 1880, and direct shipment to the United Kingdom commenced in 1897. Large corporations, notably the United Fruit Company in the United States and Elders and Fyffes in the United Kingdom, emerged to control both production and trade. United Fruit absorbed Elders and Fyffes in 1910 and reigned supreme down to 1940. In 1902/3, Jamaica shipped 13 million bunches of bananas to the United States and 1 million to the United Kingdom, drawing on greatly expanded plantings.[25]

Overseas trade in bananas had a significant impact on local consumption, developing in a way different from other export crops. One fundamental reason for this effect can be found in the growth cycle of the banana itself. In order to get fruit to North American markets in top condition to be consumed ripe, the shippers of the 1880s sought to purchase fruit as near as possible to eighteen days short of ripeness. Cut too soon, the fruit failed to ripen properly and had a "force-ripe" or "force-fit" mealy quality. Cut too late, the banana was overripe when it reached market, black and soft.[26] With this narrow window of opportunity, Jamaican banana growers found themselves with unsold fruit on their hands, forcing them to push their product onto local markets and into their own cooking pots. This was especially the case before 1900, when shipping schedules were uncertain and when competition between shippers meant erratic demand.

Bananas are fragile fruit, requiring particular care for long-distance trade. Damaged bananas are not marketable. From the very beginning of the trade, merchants learned to refuse fruit that fell short of the standard. The Gros Michel was favoured in part because it could be shipped as whole bunches, without special wrapping or cutting off hands, and because it could withstand rough handling relatively well. Rejected fruit found itself on the local market but had to compete with perfect product that had simply missed the cycle. It had to be sold at lower prices or be consumed by the farmer's own household.

These factors had their most direct and significant effect on local consumption in wartime. Shipping of bananas to the United Kingdom was interrupted during World War I and unwanted bananas given free or sold cheaply to consumers. In 1917 the boiled green banana was still being called "a hard time food", but it was a cheap one, and one of "the staples of the poorer classes' diet". The important factor was that these wartime bananas were not "wingey" or "reject" quality, but rather fruit that had been prepared for export. The same applied in World War II, when the fingers were "big and fat; the fruit has been well-fed and its quite respectable: it is not of an inferior banana status". Bananas were sold cheaply in Kingston and elsewhere, and people were encouraged to purchase them as a patriotic duty. Yet it was complained that many were not taking advantage of the offer "due perhaps to no previous particular desire for green bananas or 'iron soup', or for other delicacies made from this marvellous fruit". Bananas were also given away, beginning in 1940, in large quantities. Boiled green banana was advocated as a substitute for rice. Growers of yams and potatoes complained that this depressed the market for other "native foodstuffs", but the effect was a greatly increased general demand for green banana, rather than a depressed market for yams and the like, and by 1942 "the people had, on account of having had cheap bananas for so many months, developed the habit of eating bananas, and are now buying them".[27]

For these several reasons, the rapid increase in banana production created a substantial local supply at the same time as it served the export trade. The banana's local availability contrasted to that of the traditional export staples, such as sugar, rum, coffee and pimento, which could be stored efficiently and so did not spill over onto the local market. Yet the "reject banana" became a symbol of inferiority – an underdeveloped, overripe or imperfect fruit that failed to satisfy. It may also be that the current Jamaican taste for the ripe banana at a stage of ripeness well beyond that preferred in foreign markets stems from the ready availability of the luscious fruit in the reject basket. Low prices also contributed directly to the growing popularity of the banana, in both its green and its ripe states, making the fruit a powerful competitor with the traditionally preferred plantain.

In the midst of these developments in taste and trade, the Gros Michel was struck, around 1910, by Panama disease (a fungus) and by leaf spot, and was gradually replaced by the resistant Cavendish variety. In 1924, Jamaica established one of the earliest banana-breeding programmes, and produced many new varieties. Cavendish clones became even more productive than the Gros Michel; one of them, Lacatan, emerged as the main crop in the period after World War II, when the United Fruit Company stranglehold was broken. Production peaked at about 200,000 tonnes in 1965, then fell to 25,000 tonnes by 2005.[28]

The repertoire of recipes for dishes using banana quickly outgrew that for the plantain, in spite of the banana's slow progress to dominance. In 1893, Sullivan, with the banana trade flourishing around her, offered twelve recipes in her section on puddings and preserves, and another recipe under ices, probably to introduce her readers to new possibilities. Under vegetables, Sullivan mentioned bananas only in association with plantains, but in her section on fruits she said the banana "can be cooked in various ways, besides being an agreeable and much sought after edible in its raw state". The green banana could be dried and pounded to produce a pap. "The natives", wrote Sullivan, "eat it in its green state boiled, added to their salt-fish or meat or soups; and it makes a dainty preparation in the form of puddings". For dessert, "Slice bananas and pour cream and sugar over them." She also suggested a banana ice cream made by mashing bananas into a custard of eggs, milk and sugar, then freezing. Her other "pudding" recipes were for fried, roasted and baked bananas, banana fritters, two boiled banana puddings in a mould, and a baked banana pudding with an egg custard on top. Bananas could also be used, she said, as a substitute for preserves or in "imitation strawberries and cream". Set in the sun for five to six days, peeled bananas could be dried, and when boiled in sugar syrup they could be preserved. The dried version was generally known as "banana fig" and made in factories for export in the 1890s. These "sun-dried bananas" were promoted during World War II as a substitute for imported dried fruit, and some believed these home-made figs might become "a favourite dish" and a "delicacy".[29]

Phyllis Clark's 1945 cookbook similarly allocated the banana to fruit (and the plantain to ground provisions), but offered recipes only for banana fritters (sprinkled with sugar), banana ice cream and banana sauce (a sweet sauce made with guava jelly). The now-popular banana bread, said to have been invented by an American housewife during the Depression of the 1930s, appeared in Jamaican cookbooks only after Independence. It was among many new possibilities. When the Culinary Arts Competition associated with the Jamaica Festival highlighted the banana in 1965, six hundred entries were received. A selection of these recipes were published, in the following categories: appetizers (including Playboy banana canapés), soups (consommé Gros Michel), with seafood (kingfish "look behind"), with meats (chicken à la William Gordon), as a vegetable (banana au gratin), in salads (banana nut salad), for dessert (banana ska), preserved (crystallized banana peel), in breads (banana bread), in batters (banana pancake) and in snacks (banana home-style), and beverages (banana wine).[30]

Modern cookbooks sometimes include a variety of recipes for drinks using bananas, such as the banana daiquiri (with rum, sugar and lime juice) and banana chiffonade (blended with honey, milk and vanilla). Banana wine and nectar have also been proposed, connecting with much older potions. Hughes, in 1672, said that "when they are full ripe, the planters peel them, and macerate the meat, either alone, or with boiled potatoes and water, &c. and make very good drink thereof". Long said similarly that "the juice of the ripe fruit fermented" made a "very excellent drink".[31] A more modern use is as banana tea, for the nerves, made by infusing the withered black fibres at the end of the fruit, the remains of the flower.

Recent contributions to the range of green-banana dishes include "cheezy bananas", "duchess green bananas" (moulded with a forcing bag), "fried green bananas" (pressed down with a fork, along the lines of the Hispanic *tostones*) and "green banana sticks" (fried like chips). Green banana, boiled and cubed, has also been offered as a substitute in potato salad.

Banana chips were first produced commercially in the 1960s. Native Food Packers, founded in 1964, used surplus bananas to develop what became a "fashionable snack" under the Chippies brand. By the end of the 1980s, it was claimed that "our locally produced banana chips have displaced the vogue of the British 'crisps'". By 2000 the company produced both banana and plantain chips, as well as cheese curls, fruit pops, onion bits, nuts and popcorn.[32]

The occasional recipe in the 1990s used the navel stew, which, in Jamaican English, refers to the pink sheath at the end of a fruiting stem of bananas, containing the blossoms and undeveloped fruit. The navel could be introduced to gungo peas soup or combined with string beans. One recipe began with cutting the navel stew into small sections and seasoning the pieces with salt, MSG (monosodium glutamate), black pepper and garlic, rubbing in sliced onion and chopped tomato, and coating the whole with curry powder. The seasoning was scraped from the navel stew sections, which were then browned in oil. Soy sauce and water were mixed with the seasonings and poured over the navel stew, and the whole was cooked in a covered skillet, with chopped string beans added just before it had been stewed to tenderness.[33]

The green banana has also, at times, been promoted as a dessert, as in green banana pudding and banana custard (using grated green banana and baked). Banana porridge, following an older recipe, was made by combining green bananas with coconut cream, flour, milk and sugar, spiced with cinnamon, vanilla and nutmeg; it was served as a hot breakfast cereal. Although violating the standard definition of a cereal, this porridge recipe followed the tradition of "pap" and the even earlier "mussa", made from green banana grated and boiled with coconut milk as a "hasty pudding", and in its name indicating the genus *Musa*.[34]

Bananas were also assimilated to the cereals and to "bread-kind" through proposals to use banana flour in baking. The idea first surfaced in the 1890s as a means of using the great quantities of fruit rejected by the trade. Banana flour was promoted as a competitor with cereal flour for both its cost and its nutritional advantages. In 1912 a Banana Food Manufacturing Company was established in Montego Bay to turn surplus and rejected stems into banana flour, for export as well as local consumption, and particularly for infants and the unwell. Banana flour was advocated again during World War I, when the external markets for bananas were largely closed off.[35] The idea resurfaced in June 1938, in the midst of the labour disturbances, when a factory was established in Kingston to produce "banana meal" out of varieties not grown for export and out of Gros Michel rejects, selling it for use in porridge. During World War II, experimenters claimed to have used banana flour successfully in dumplings and journey cakes, porridge and baby food. Some argued that mixing banana flour with wheat flour merely spoiled both; others said it was "entirely a matter of taste". By the 1990s the banana dumpling, made from grated dried fruit, was almost forgotten.[36]

BREADFRUIT

Long before these attempts to make bread from banana, and long before the acceptance of green banana as an important food, other attempts had been made in response to natural disasters and interruptions of trade to reduce reliance on imported wheat flour and rice. These efforts were first prompted by the great famine of the 1780s, caused by a series of hurricanes that overlapped the war with the American colonies. As a result of the storms, said the House of Assembly, "the plantain walks, which furnish the chief article of support to the negroes, were generally rooted up, and the intense droughts which followed, destroyed those different species of ground provisions [the tubers] which the hurricanes had not reached".[37] Relaxations of trade restrictions were sought, and efforts made to encourage the cultivation of plantains and yams. A search for alternative food crops began.

This perceived urgent need for more reliable resources emerged in the midst of a bourgeoning imperial European interest in economic botany. The French and the British in particular were actively engaged in expanding their power and knowledge into new realms, including actively experimenting with new crops in new environments. Botanical gardens were being set up throughout the British Empire, as commercial experiment stations. Kew, in England, was established as the metropolitan centre in 1759, and Jamaica's first public botanic gardens followed soon after: Enfield (Spring Garden) in 1774 and Bath in 1776.[38] These gardens sought to trial almost every possible plant in every possible environment, but more self-conscious choices were made to fill particular needs. What the planters desired was a solution to the problem of food supply that ensured that the best land remained planted in export crops. In the 1780s, the solution seemed to lie in a gift from the South Seas: the breadfruit. Its introduction to the West Indies resulted entirely from choices made by the planter class and by imperial authority. Whereas the dominant ground provisions – yam, coco and plantain – were all well known from Africa and had travelled effectively with the people on the slave ships, the breadfruit was a mystery.

The fruit of the breadfruit tree, *Artocarpus altilis*, is an ancient staple food of Polynesia. The tree grows up to twenty metres, with a spreading canopy and large dark green leaves (Figure 5.5 and Plate 2). It prefers rich, light soils and good rainfall, at elevations below five hundred metres. In the right conditions, growth is rapid. Propagation is by root suckers or root cuttings, and fruiting can occur in three to four years from planting, after which trees normally bear two crops a year. The fruit is round or ovoid, about twenty centimetres in diameter and weighing up to two kilograms, with a tessellated green or yellow skin. It contains a high proportion of starch – up to 20 per cent – and is rich in protein. When the fruit is roasted in its mature state, the skin chars black, while the fleshy pulp remains a creamy white. When the fruit is boiled and peeled in its immature state, its pulp becomes more yellowy and transparent. Most of the fruits are seedless and sterile, so the tree needs to be vegetatively propagated.[39] This enabled the important capacity of the breadfruit to survive long-distance journeys, as a cutting or as a potted plant, though the tree's inability to yield easily moved seeds also made necessary the elaborate voyages that spread the plant through the Pacific and brought it to Jamaica.

Most accounts attribute the first European description of the breadfruit to the English voyager William Dampier, who saw the tree growing on Guam in 1688. More important was James Cook's voyage in the *Endeavour* (1768–1771) accompanied by the influential botanist Joseph Banks, who was much impressed by the breadfruit's qualities as a food crop. Banks romantically believed that the Tahitians were almost "exempt from the curse of our forefather; scarcely can it be said that they earn their bread with the sweat of their brow when their chiefest substance bread fruit is procurd with no more trouble than that of climbing a tree and pulling it down". In view of this assessment, David Mackay has argued that it "may well have been Banks who suggested to the West Indians the idea of transplanting breadfruit".[40]

By the beginning of 1787, after a number of false starts, Banks had convinced the British government to finance an expedition to bring the breadfruit to the West Indies. An enterprise was put together with William Bligh as master of the *Bounty*. A large number of breadfruit plants were collected in Tahiti, but the mutiny of the crew prevented them reaching Jamaica.[41] In spite of this expensive failure, the British government quickly tried again. An expedition even grander than the first was assembled, and in 1791 Bligh sailed with two vessels under his command, the *Providence* and the *Assistance*. Two gardeners were on board, James Wiles and Christopher Smith. With the help of the Tahitians, 1,686 breadfruit plants were raised and taken on board, along with 350 other useful and "curiosity" plants. Replacements for some had to be acquired in Timor, but in the end enough of the breadfruit survived for 333 to be delivered to the botanic garden in St Vincent and 346 to Jamaica, in February 1793. The gardener Wiles stayed in Jamaica to tend the plants, but because the public nursery at Bath had space for only a small proportion, he quickly began distribution to planters throughout the

Figure 5.5 Breadfruit tree and fruit

island. Wiles was joined by a Tahitian man, Bobbo, who had helped the botanists collect and care the breadfruit plants, and had stowed away on the *Providence*. Bligh believed that Bobbo would be "happy and well taken care of" in Jamaica and wrote, "I really think he will be the means of the breadfruit being brought early into use, and on that account his life is valuable to Jamaica."[42]

How was the breadfruit received by Jamaicans, slave and free? The *Royal Gazette* reported the arrival of Bligh's ships in Kingston harbour, predicting that "in less than twenty years, the chief article of sustenance for our negroes will be entirely changed:- plantains, yams, cocos, and cassava, will be cultivated only as a subsidiary, and be used merely for change; whilst the bread-fruit, gaining firm hold in the earth . . . will afford in the greatest abundance, for nine months of the year, the choicest and most wholesome food".[43] Equally optimistic and grateful, the Assembly was quick to vote Bligh one thousand guineas for his trouble and thanked Banks for "promoting the introduction of the bread fruit and other valuable plants".[44]

Modern historians, however, have delivered a broadly negative judgement on the introduction of the breadfruit. John H. Parry argued in 1955 that "the Jamaican slaves at first refused to eat a plant which bore no resemblance to anything they had known in Africa or Jamaica". The fruit, he said, "was fed to pigs for fifty years", and it was only after 1838 that it became "an important source of food for communities of free peasants". In 1956, Parry, together with Philip Sherlock, offered a harsher assessment, saying, "the slaves perversely refused to eat the breadfruit, preferring the more familiar yams and plantains". Later writers have repeated these views. Thus David Watts in 1987 said that "for 50 years, workers refused to eat it, preferring instead the more familiar Afro-indian combination of maize, yams, plantains and cassava, and leaving the breadfruit to be fed to pigs and other animals". Richard Sheridan argued much the same, though with irony: "Alas, the men who projected and carried out the breadfruit scheme made no allowance for the unpredictable palate of the lowly slave."[45]

Contemporary observers did sometimes deplore what they saw as a "want of industry in cultivating the breadfruit tree", or claim that it was grown only as "an ornamental tree, or a fruit tree of secondary importance". Some said the breadfruit was regarded with "cold apathy" by the enslaved, who preferred "his more productive and substantial plantain, and his more palatable and nutritive yam".[46] On the other hand, there is little doubt that the breadfruit trees were well distributed and flourishing within a decade of reaching Jamaica. John Lunan said in 1814 that the breadfruit had been "cultivated in every part of this island with great success, though not in so extensive a manner as they deserve". The trees grew "as large a size as in their native soil, bearing abundance of fruit, and forming an excellent addition to the many other articles of subsistence which the island possesses".[47]

The breadfruit also had to stand the test of the storm. Hurricanes were less frequent in the years following the arrival of the breadfruit than they had been in the 1780s, but the test came soon enough and the tree proved vulnerable, not only by comparison with the roots and tubers, but even in competition with the fragile plantain. A "tremendous storm" struck the island in October 1812. The agricultural reporter for *The Jamaica Magazine* commented that the effects were less serious than feared, particularly "with respect to the plantain-walks, which yield their bread-fruit in a continued succession". He drove home the point: "We say bread-fruit, because the product of this valuable tree is much more deserving the appellation than that of the far-famed South-sea plant of that name, imported some eighteen or twenty years ago into this island, and from which such wonders were expected." The plantain enjoyed "a quick perpetual reproduction, so that if the parent trees are blown down, the suckers which replace them will bear in from nine to twelve months after, and the soil, if naturally good, is rather enriched than impoverished by it". By contrast, once uprooted, the "East Indian breadfruit" took years to recover. In any case, the breadfruit was less productive than the plantain and exhausted the soil. As a result the slaves were "not only indifferent about the breadfruit tree, but averse to the employing their time, and occupying and impoverishing their grounds, with the cultivation of it".[48] And though the tree survives in former plantation village sites, descriptions of Jamaican provision grounds during slavery make no mention of the breadfruit.

There was also the matter of taste, and of the breadfruit's equivalence to bread. Titford said in 1811 that "gathered green, parboiled, and afterwards baked, the inside very nearly resembles new bread". When used as "bread kind", said Lunan, the fruit was picked before fully ripe, roasted whole, and the rind scraped off, when "the inside is then soft and white, tasting much like sweet cassada, to which its texture has also considerable resemblance". Alternatively, "if the outward rind be taken off, and the fibrous flesh dried, and afterwards boiled with meat, as we do cabbage, it has then the taste of artichoke bottoms". It was necessary to eat the roasted fruit quickly, said Lunan, because it was "not palateable if kept for any length of time after being cooked". Less positive was John Stewart, who in 1823 declared the breadfruit "an insipid and not very substantial food". Similarly, the naturalist Philip Henry Gosse reported in 1845 being "disappointed in the fruit; it has a sort of wooliness not agreeable". On the other hand, he also described the breadfruit as "a foreigner made to feel himself at home", cultivated more often by the "Negroes" than by the "higher classes".[49]

Certainly the breadfruit faced stiff competition from the existing "food" crops consumed in Jamaica. It was outside the experienced taste of the enslaved, and perhaps too reminiscent of the spurned Irish potato. Banks, in Tahiti, said that the breadfruit when baked in a pit between layers of hot rocks became "soft and something like a boild [Irish] potatoe, tho not quite so farinaceous as a good one yet more so than the midling sort".[50] Equally important, the breadfruit suffered by being promoted explicitly as a food for slaves and as one imposed by the masters. Seen in this way, reluctance to accept the breadfruit at the expense of the long-established roots and fruits of the provision grounds was not simple conservatism (something common enough in the history of taste) but rather a vehicle of resistance to the will of the slave-owning class.

If there was perversity and unpredictability in the response to the breadfruit, this was its source.

Methods of storage and of preparing the breadfruit as practised by the people of the Pacific travelled less easily than did methods of cultivation. The Tahitian man Bobbo died within months of reaching Jamaica. Wiles survived for many years, until the late 1830s at least, but how much he knew about breadfruit storage and preparation is uncertain. Storage to provide for the three months without a harvest was a difficult task. The Tahitian method of fermenting mature fruit below ground to ensure a steady supply of *mahi*, or "sour paste", seems not to have been transmitted to Jamaica. Nor did Jamaicans adopt the Tahitian method, described by Banks, of pounding baked bread-fruit in a mortar to make a paste that could be mixed variously with coconut milk, ripe plantains, bananas and sour paste.[51] This is more difficult to account for, since the African tradition of pounding fufu in a mortar was so firmly established in Jamaica.

Although the breadfruit never became the basis of the diet of the enslaved in Jamaica and was never cultivated on a large commercial scale in "breadfruit walks" or orchards, it did, by the end of the nineteenth century, enter the repertoire. In 1917 the breadfruit could be called a staple food for the poor and an "integral part" of Jamaican cuisine. By 1945 it was "one of the most popular items in the average daily Jamaican diet", and in the 1970s, claimed Dulcie Powell, it was "absolutely relied upon in rural areas, where breadfruit, in its season, is eaten three times a day". Although the breadfruit never fully entered either the "food" or "ground provision" category, it became sufficiently well implanted to be a favourite food carried (roasted) by travellers visiting family overseas, and air transport enabled a trade in the uncooked fruit. In the 1980s, however, a rapid decline was observed in production of the "popular staple", as the roots of many trees were attacked by parasites. Jamaica had at least eight varieties of breadfruit, but a further twenty-nine were introduced from Hawaii in an effort to defeat the onslaught.[52]

Sullivan, in her 1893 cookbook, said "various opinions" were expressed on the breadfruit, "some liking it extremely and others not liking it at all". But the latter was elite opinion, for she followed it by noting, "The natives are very fond of it." According to Sullivan, "The people often put it in their soups." This was the boiled version; roasted, it was eaten in wedges, with or without butter. She did not mention frying but did suggest cutting the fruit in thin slices and toasting it on a gridiron, buttering it and eating it hot. Sullivan also described breadfruit flour, which was known at least by the 1860s, made by drying slices of the green fruit, and pounding and sifting. When prepared this way, said Sullivan, "the people boil it up into a pap which they sweeten, and it forms one of their favourite breakfasts". During World War I, breadfruit flour was mixed with cornmeal to make porridge. Much later, in the 1980s, a pure breadfruit porridge was made using a mature breadfruit with skimmed milk powder, water, vanilla and brown sugar.[53]

The ripe fruit, mashed with nutmeg, cinnamon, rosewater, butter, sugar, sherry and eggs, made breadfruit pudding. Lunan had said the roasted fruit could be used in puddings and fritters. Clark, in 1945, added to the list of possibilities creamed bread-fruit (using boiled ripe fruit), stuffed breadfruit (with fresh beef or pork, and ham or pickled meat, in a "full but not ripe" fruit), fried breadfruit (either almost ripe or green, and first boiled or steamed) and "breadfruit pie or soufflé" (using boiled fruit and baked in pastry).[54] By the 1960s, baked breadfruit, done in the oven, offered a cleaner method than roasting over coal pot or ashes, while "breadfruit with coconut milk" created a version of pakassa (discussed under coconut). In 1971 Judy Cuninghame offered a savoury breadfruit pudding (with onions, pepper and salt), stuffed breadfruit (following Clark) and, at last, "foo foo (Jamaican style)". For the fufu, a roast breadfruit was beaten in a mortar to a smooth consistency and spoonfuls placed in a bowl, to be covered with a soup made of salt pork, okra, scallion, callaloo and coco. Norma Benghiat, in 1985, offered an even larger range of recipes, among them roast breadfruit stuffed with ackee and saltfish, and "breadfruit chips". Others mentioned breadfruit salad (yet another variation of potato salad), breadfruit croquettes, breadfruit soup and pickled breadfruit. A 1993 collection of breadfruit recipes from around the Caribbean found more than forty variations.[55]

Generally, only the fruit was thought appropriate as food. Occasionally, however, recipes were offered for "crystallised breadfruit 'sword' or blossom", using the inflores-cences plucked from the tree before the fruit could develop. A recipe from the 1950s described boiling the just-ripe swords with grated ginger, cooking with granulated sugar and drying in the sun for two days. A 1992 attempt to promote the dish said the bread-fruit swords should be boiled slowly, first with lime and ginger, and then with sugar, until tender, and when cooled served with chilled coconut cream.[56] This was an item that had little success in Jamaica.

The breadfruit nonetheless found a home for itself in Jamaican food culture, providing the basis for a few special dishes, resting comfortably beside the roasted roots and tubers, and joining plantain and banana in soup and pakassa. It was a small achieve-ment, a significant but relatively minor reversal of an initial rejection. By 2001 an annual "breadfruit festival" had been inaugurated, partly as a tourist attraction, held in August at Bath, where "each year, the party-loving community focus on the use of this ubiq-uitous Jamaican food". William Bligh and the heroic voyaging that gave the breadfruit a place in global food transfers and world ecological history have only a minor place in Jamaican memory.[57] Yet from the point of view of Jamaican food history, the breadfruit was simply the most spectacular example in terms of cost and persistence. Rather than symbolizing the beginning of an imperial enterprise to transform the Jamaican landscape, the breadfruit effectively marked its closure.

ACKEE

The scientific name of the ackee is *Blighia sapida*. However, although named to honour Bligh of the breadfruit, it was not Bligh who brought the ackee to Jamaica. The earliest identified reference to ackee occurs in the *Hortus Eastensis*, the catalogue prepared by the botanist Arthur Broughton of the "exotic plants" growing in Hinton East's botanic garden near Gordon Town at the time of East's death in 1792. In that listing Broughton gave no scientific name and simply called the plant "The Akee". He sourced it to Dr. Thomas Clarke in 1778, meaning that this was the year in which Clarke had given it to East. Tantalizingly, Broughton added: "This plant was brought here in a slave ship from the coast of Africa, and now grows very luxuriant, producing every year large quantities of fruit." He noted also that "several gentlemen are encouraging the propagation of it".[58]

All of this points to recent activity and suggests that the ackee did not grow in Jamaica until perhaps the 1770s. Exactly why, how and when the plant came to the island remains to be established. It was not a practical food for voyagers and, unlike the yam and coco, was an improbable candidate for self-conscious transfer by slave traders. It is more likely that the seed was carried as a curiosity, selected for the beauty of the tree, its flowers and its unique fruit.

Several writers have argued that the seed was carried by an enslaved person. Perhaps the first to suggest this, and the most specific, was Oscar Plummer of Kingston, who in 1915 stated that "the ackee was brought to Jamaica in 1777 by an African slave boy, who cherished a seed as a plaything on his long voyage. The boy was bought and carried to St Thomas in the East where he planted the seed on his Master's property. The first dish of ackee was eaten in 1780." Plummer's claim to such precise knowledge must be viewed in the context of his objective to defend "our wholesome and delicious ackee" and particularly to support his theory that vomiting sickness had existed in Jamaica long before the arrival of the ackee and that the ackee was not, therefore, its source. In the 1970s, one writer noted that "it is believed that seeds were brought to the island by African slaves", and another claimed the "handsome and glossy" black seeds of the ackee were "brought by slaves who wore them as hope".[59] Although documentary evidence has not been found to justify these claims, an argument for the role of African agency is plausible and carries more weight in the case of the ackee than it does for the root crops.

Broughton was correct in thinking the ackee an undescribed genus, and it was a Jamaican example of the plant, rather than one from its native African soil, that did eventually provide the scientific model. When Bligh arrived in Jamaica with the breadfruit in 1793, the Assembly put together a collection of both wild and economic plants growing in the island to send to Kew. Broughton was one of the local botanists given the task of assembling the several hundred containers of rooted plants and samples of seeds. Most of these were indigenous to Jamaica, but some exotics were also included. The ackee was one of these. It travelled on the *Providence* to England in 1793, as a rooted plant. The list prepared by Broughton identified it as "Akea Africana". A Kew botanist, Charles Konig, eventually provided the scientific description in 1806 and gave it the name *Blighia sapida* because Bligh (who took up the position of governor of New South Wales in that year) had brought it from Jamaica. The minor term *sapida* refers to the savoury taste of the ackee.[60] Why the honour of receiving Bligh's name was singled out for the ackee is unclear, though appropriate enough given his temperament and the ackee's duplicity.

The ackee tree grows eight to fifteen metres tall, with a crown of glossy green leaves, and is valued for its ornamental qualities (Figure 5.6). It grows best in low-lying and intermediate zones, and though it does not fruit well above five hundred metres, it tolerates drought and succeeds on most soils, even stony ones. It flowers twice a year, occasionally more often, the fragrant blooms developing into pear-shaped fruit. When ripe, the fruit is red or a yellow-tinged red and splits open to reveal three fleshy yellow arils, each with a shiny round black seed at its end. It is the aril that is eaten.[61]

The terms "ripe" and "fit" have particular significance for the ackee. The fruit can be poisonous at certain stages of development, and Jamaicans believe it must be allowed to open naturally on the tree in order to avoid its toxicity. Ackees picked before this stage are not ripe. For a long time this relationship was not fully understood. When in 1877 a child living on Elletson Road in Kingston died soon after "eating the ackee in its raw

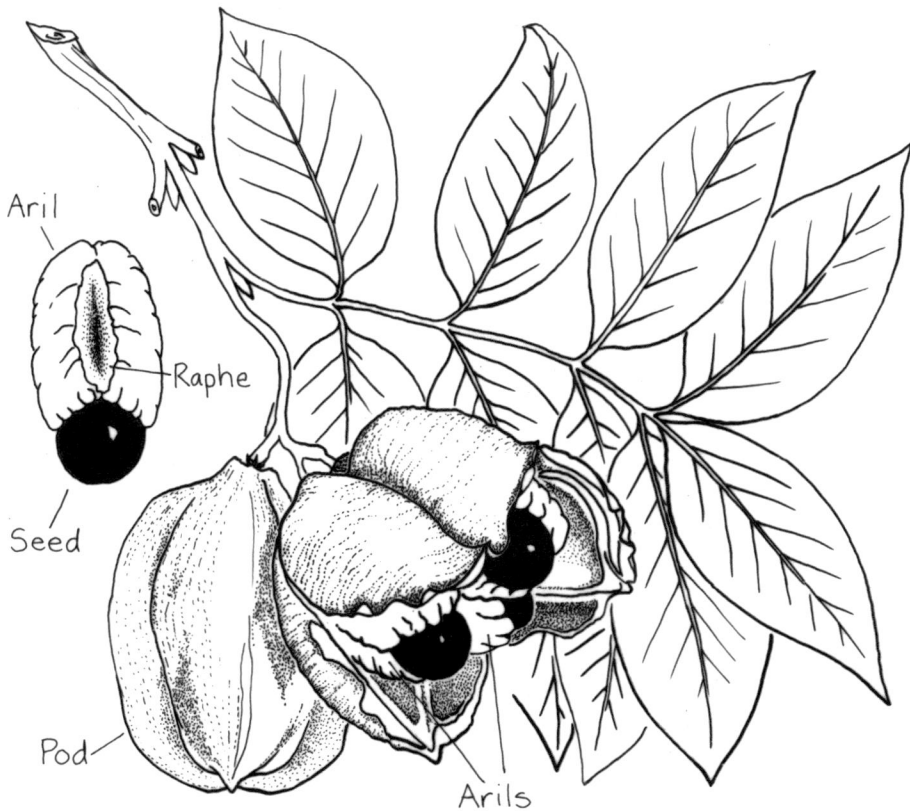

Figure 5.6 Ackee fruit

state, and before it had come to perfection", it was proposed "to hold a coroner's inquest, when, perhaps, positive evidence will be given as to whether the ackee is poisonous or not". In the 1880s cases were reported of people dying less than twenty minutes after eating "unripe" fruit instead of "waiting for it to ripen and burst". Although the "vomiting sickness" and its association with the eating of ackee was first noticed around 1880, it did not come to prominence until 1914, and debate on the role of the ackee continued much longer. In 1917 there were calls for ackee trees to be cut down, and again in 1940 it seemed necessary to reassure people that "fears that Government intends to destroy all ackee trees are not well founded".[62]

Chemical analysis eventually established that the toxicity of the ackee, found in both immature and over-mature fruit, stems from the presence of an amino acid, hypoglycin A. Isolated from the fruit, hypoglycin A may interfere with the oxidation of fatty acids, leading to a depletion of carbohydrates and to hypoglycemia, which in turn inhibits hydrogen delivery and damages nerve cells, causing seizures. There may also be damage to the liver. Intoxication results in severe vomiting and coma, and even, in extreme cases – among the malnourished – death. The mechanism is still not fully understood, but the source of the poison is probably the bitter red fibrous paper-like raphe that joins the aril to the seed.[63]

In light of these alarming possibilities and experiences, the difficult question remains why Jamaicans have been so enthusiastic about the ackee. As demonstrated by their unwillingness to try other foods thought hazardous, it is clear that Jamaicans are not inveterate risk-takers. Their enthusiasm for the fruit was far from inevitable. Perhaps the ackee can be accommodated within a general model of conservative taste, and it did not have to endure the initial close scrutiny and rejection suffered by the breadfruit, but Jamaicans remain unique in their embrace of the fruit. Even in West Africa the fruit has no particular presence, though it is not regarded as threatening.

As a native of Africa, the ackee was familiar to core contingents of enslaved people, and in Jamaica the tree and its fruit have never had any name other than their African derivation, the Kru a-kee.[64] Distinctively associating it with their homelands, the enslaved may have played an active role in the plant's dissemination within Jamaica. Whereas former slave village sites contain only the occasional breadfruit tree, some of these abandoned settlements are indicated by large groves of ackee trees. The ackee was self-propagating, the seeds dispersed into fences and other niches, and allowed to grow there because of the ornamental beauty of the tree. For these reasons, it is easy to argue for an early acceptance of the ackee within Jamaica.

Rejection, on the other hand, was always a possibility. In the eastern Caribbean the ackee suffered a long-term dismissal much more decisive than that resulting from the initial trials of the breadfruit. In those islands, despite their similar histories and demographic origins, the ackee is virtually never seen or eaten, and the name ackee has been appropriated to the innoxious fruit Jamaicans call "guinep". Aversion to the ackee outside Jamaica is associated with the fruit's reputation as poisonous. Canned ackee began to be exported to North America in 1955, but the United States placed an alert on the entry of ackee in the 1970s; this restriction became a ban in 1993, and was not lifted until 2000.[65]

Since the late nineteenth century, botanists and cookbook-writers have been eager to reassure consumers about the edibility of the ackee. Although the mechanisms were poorly understood, it was generally recognized that the problem lay not in the mode of the fruit's preparation but in the stage of its ripeness. Sullivan, in 1893, said that ackees were "a delicate tree vegetable, and, if carefully prepared for table, are most enjoyable; but if eaten before the fruit opens on the tree, or if *forced-ripe*, or musty, or over-ripe, a more unsafe edible could not be found". Similarly, the botanist C.D. Adams said in 1971, "The arils of ripe ackees, lightly boiled in water that is then discarded, are perfectly safe for normally well-nourished people to eat." Even at the end of the twentieth century, cookbooks produced outside Jamaica often emphasized the perils of the ackee, saying both unripe and overripe fruit had arils that caused the deadly "Jamaica Poisoning".[66]

By itself, *raw or boiled, the taste of ackee has been described as "mild" or even* "bland". Ancient African references compare the ackee's taste to banana and its appearance to quince. Titford, who knew nothing of the fruit's hazards, said in 1811 that the arils had the consistency of beef fat and tasted "exactly like marrow", and that either parboiled or fried, the fruit was "the richest and most delicate of vegetables". Modern commentators often make a comparison with scrambled eggs , though this seems to have more to do with colour, look and texture than with taste. Ackee has also been attributed a "slightly nutty flavour and silky texture", and compared to avocado. Occasionally, a distinction is made between the "butter ackee" and the "cheese ackee", the former being softer and richer in flavour, and the latter firmer, paler and preferred by canners.[67]

In Jamaica, ackee is rarely eaten fresh from the tree or by itself. Some modern observers claim the ackee is never eaten raw, but John Rashford's studies show that raw ackee can form an "opportunistic snack" eaten in small quantities.[68] West Africans much more often eat the ackee raw from the tree, but also have it in soup, fried in oil or roasted as a sweetmeat. Lunan claimed to know that "the inhabitants of Guinea" gently boiled the arils, which were "served at table alone or mixed with broth or pottage". In Jamaica, ackee is most often prepared by boiling or parboiling the arils, separated from pods, seeds and raphe. Further cooking follows several different methods but almost always involves combination with other ingredients that counterpoint its essential mildness. An exception is fried ackee. Matthew Gregory Lewis, the Gothic novelist and absentee proprietor, visiting his Westmoreland plantations in 1816, observed, "The achie fruit is a kind of vegetable, which generally is fried in butter; many people, I am told, are fond of it, but I could find no merit in it." Marianne North claimed to have eaten at King's House in 1872 "fried 'ackee' mango-stew". Sullivan said ackees were "excellent" boiled, fried or curried, and gave a recipe for a soup, the ackees mashed smooth; this was seasoned, along with thyme and scallion, and boiled with fresh beef and "a small piece of salt pork or salt beef to make it tasty". Sullivan also proposed "ackee pudding", made with sugar, milk, nutmeg and cloves.[69]

In 1940 "ackees cooked with rice" was said to have "always been a favourite Jamaica dish". Roasted ackee has been reported but seems to have been rare in the twentieth century, as does ackee soup, though recipes survive from the 1950s. Ackee can also be stuffed into breadfruit, mixed with callaloo, eaten with liver or kidney, or used in rundown (with mackerel, cooked in coconut milk). Less traditional ways of using boiled ackee emerged in the late twentieth century, including ackee quiche, ackee soufflé, ackee croquettes, ackee au gratin, ackee jerk pork style, corned beef and ackee casserole, and "Captain Bligh's Puree of Ackee Soup" (using noodle soup stock). Ackees also went well with callaloo, liver, kidney or Vienna sausage. An ackee salad, meatless and fishless but including cheese, was created in the 1990s. Ackee ice cream remains an exotic experiment.[70]

The one way of cooking ackee that is truly popular in Jamaica is ackee and saltfish, which has often been called Jamaica's "national dish". Certainly it is still a national favourite, especially at breakfast. However, ackee and saltfish began its life as "saltfish and ackee", and the role reversal suggested by this change in name is a significant part of its history. The earliest known references to "saltfish and ackee" occur quite late. In 1889, F.S. Sanguinetti referred to "the well known compound dish of salt-fish and akee" in which saltfish was the "main ingredient". The first example identified from the *Gleaner* comes from 1893, in the "introductory" stanzas of a poem, "The Spanish Town Gala Days", by an unknown author, comparing Jamaica's Fair with that at Chicago. In the course of this imperial paean, mention was made of "breakfast of saltfish and ackee". Sullivan's *Jamaica Cookery Book* appeared the same year, and she declared in it, "Salt fish is often mixed with ackees, and forms one of the popular Jamaica luncheon or breakfast dishes". Sullivan also referred to "salt fish fritters made either with seasoning and eggs, or with ackees instead of eggs". Her recipe for "saltfish and ackees" called for one pound (454 grams) of saltfish, the fruit of twelve ackee pods, lard, butter and black pepper. The saltfish was to be soaked overnight, then "put on in cold water to boil, otherwise it hardens: throw off the first water and put it on again to boil". The ackees were picked free of "all red inside, which is dangerous". After twenty minutes' boiling, the ackees were added to the saltfish,which was cut in small pieces, along with lard, butter and pepper. Sullivan noted that "some prefer the saltfish and ackees mashed together and the melted lard and butter poured over the top".[71]

At the beginning of the twentieth century, saltfish and ackee was called "a native dainty", and was a regular dish on the planter's breakfast table. Among the poor the balance began to shift towards the ackee because although the ackee could generally be got free, saltfish had become "distinctly expensive".[72] In 1915, Government Bacteriologist Dr Scott observed that whereas "in Kingston 'salt fish and ackee' is a favourite dish with many", in rural Jamaica the "'salt fish' may not be fish at all". He cited the district medical officer's contention that many of the country people were "in the habit of adding salt to the ackees and boiling it and then [adding] it to their food calling it 'salt fish'". Thus, "when they say they had yam, banana, and salt fish for breakfast, the salt fish they refer to is salted ackee". Shortages of saltfish during World War I similarly inhibited the making of the dish. A 1918 report on the produce market at, appropriately, Linstead, noted, "Ackees have started to ripen, but the palatable dish of salt fish and ackee is missing from the table up to now, due to the scarcity of the fish." At nearby Glengoffe, "The ackee is coming in which will to a small extent relieve the situation; but ackees needs [sic] salt fish, and that's what we can't get." A resident of Annotto Bay expressed the same sentiment, saying, "ackees without [salt] fish are like mustard without beef".[73] In 1920 H.G. De Lisser said a favourite dish was "saltfish with ackees, and a liberal supply of coconut oil", and in 1933 he called "salt fish and ackee" a dish "dear to the heart of every true Jamaican". As late as the 1950s, recipes maintained the proportion of saltfish to ackee recommended by Sullivan and continued to call the dish "saltfish and ackee".[74]

The earliest identified use of "ackee and saltfish", as opposed to "saltfish and ackee", comes from 1930. Even those who persisted in calling the dish "saltfish and ackee" generally agreed by the time of Independence that the saltfish "need only be used for flavour", though some retained the proportions proposed by Sullivan. Modern cooks double the proportion of ackee and do everything they can to avoid mashing the ackees, to keep the soft arils as whole as possible in order to enhance the look of the dish. Onion, tomato, scallion and fried bacon are commonly included, and recipes occasionally call for thyme, country pepper or even ketchup. Appropriate accompaniments are boiled green bananas, bammy, roast breadfruit, boiled or fried dumplings, and avocado pear.[75]

By the end of the twentieth century, ackee and saltfish had found its way into edible containers, filling pastry shells, patties and pies, and was served at cocktail parties. But the scarcity and high price of saltfish, rising steadily through the 1980s, meant the ackee often had to perform on its own or with new companions. A reduction in the price of saltfish in May 1986 was greeted with enthusiasm, because "we can de-bunk one of the myths that was going the rounds and gaining ground because it was sponsored by officialdom – that it is the ackee that is the most important part of the national dish". Only Jamaicans had "taken this fruit seriously and elevated it from table decoration to gourmet's delight", it was said, but the ackee was short on nutritional value and needed a protein food to make it serve as a main meal, hence "ackee needs saltfish". In 1988 cooks were looking for substitutes, combining ackee with salted grey snapper, salted Banga Mary, red herring or mackerel, or abandoning fish altogether and trying salted meats such as corned beef or corned pork. In 1991 it was said, "the palates of many Jamaicans may not be able to savour the national dish again as it may cost them dearly to do so". Vegetarian cookbooks could happily identify ackees as "part of the national dish of Jamaica" without mention of saltfish and offer recipes for dishes such as "ackee heritage" made with textured vegetable protein.[76]

When and how was the "famous gastronomic marriage" of ackee and saltfish consecrated? The combination of a fruit from West Africa with salted fish from the North

Atlantic might seem improbable, but it followed some well-established general princi-ples. The enslaved people of Jamaica had learned to add small amounts of salted meat and fish to their "soup" of vegetables and ground provisions in order to make it palatable and to eke out the meagre allowances they received from their masters. These bits of salted meat and fish came to be known as "saalting", the fundamental complement to "food". Adding saltfish to ackee might seem a natural choice. When the practice began is harder to tell, though the components were in place by the 1780s. Parry in 1954 called saltfish and ackee Jamaica's "most characteristic dish" and dated it to the time of the ackee's introduction but offered no citations. Similarly, Rashford refers to "the lowly ackee and saltfish from the days of forced labor" but identifies no reference earlier than 1912.[77] Sanguinetti's initial reference, in 1889, suggests only that the dish was already well established. For the moment, it seems possible to conclude only that the dish was created sometime between 1780 and 1880.

Against the argument that ackee and saltfish was a creation of the poor, during slavery, is the basic fact that it was a fried dish, requiring oil or butter. It was the planter class that had access to these, and we have seen that as early as 1810 the planters enjoyed ackee fried in butter. Eating saltfish in plentiful quantities, fried in oil or butter, was also a privilege of the planter class. The high proportion of saltfish in Sullivan's recipe certainly does not suggest an association with poverty. The enslaved consumed much more pickled herring than they did salted cod, as we will see in chapter 8, and herring and ackee seem never to have been combined. Indeed, no explicit reference to enslaved people eating ackee in any form has been found. The planters' tables were set with dishes of various sorts, and they loaded their plates with dollops of all and sundry. It is easy to imagine separate serving dishes of ackees fried in butter and of saltfish fried in butter, and the saltfish and the ackee ending up side by side on an eater's plate and spilling into one another. This blending is a common experience when we eat, but it does not lead naturally to the cooking of ingredients as a single dish.[78] Saltfish and ackee may well have been a creation of the planter's kitchen rather than of the slave village or a rich person's version of a dish born in hardship.

AVOCADO

At the time of the Spanish Conquest, the avocado, *Persea americana*, was spread widely through Mexico and Central and South America but not found in the Caribbean. The avocado had been an important food, especially for the Mexicans, since about 9000 BP (before the present time), sometimes collected wild, sometimes cultivated in groves. It was from the Aztecs that the Spanish adopted the name *ahuacacuauhitl*, or "testicle tree", a reference perhaps both to the dangling fruit with its large seed and to its supposed aphrodisiac qualities. This was reduced to *aguacate* and became, in English, *avocado*, "allicada" or "alligator pear". Modern Jamaicans commonly say simply "pear", rarely needing to distinguish it from other pear-like fruit.[79]

The domesticated avocado, writes Jonathan Sauer, is "a compilospecies descended from various wild progenitors that were taken into cultivation independently but have since coalesced into a single breeding population". Domestication has selected for quality and for larger fruit. Dispersal was assisted by the largeness of the seed, which enables it to store enough food to survive a relatively long time and to wait on the ground for a gap to open in the forest canopy. This characteristic allowed the tree to spread rapidly through the Caribbean islands after the Conquest, and the avocado must have reached Jamaica early in the sixteenth century. The Spanish took an early liking to the avocado, but global approval was a slow process and the taste for the fruit was limited until the twentieth century, when improved cultivars were planted.[80] For a long period, the avocado (eaten with saalting) was more a poor person's food than a luxury.

The avocado tree is an evergreen, growing to twenty metres. Its fruits vary considerably in colour, shape and size, the largest weighing more than a kilogram. A single tree can bear hundreds of fruit, some too high to be easily harvested with a pole. Bruising occurs in high winds, and a hurricane can harvest an entire crop instantly. When mature, the flesh surrounding the single large seed is commonly described as "buttery" in consistency and is yellow, except near the skin, where it turns greenish. The flesh comes away easily from the skin when fully ripe, and separates from the thin membrane that encloses the seed. The Reverend John Lindsay illustrated this quite clearly in 1770, along with a rather curious drawing of the tree (Plate 6). Compared to other fruits, the avocado has a high protein content and a low proportion of carbohydrates. And whereas most fruits contain little oil, the avocado is 5 to 25 per cent fat. It shares some of these characteristics with the coconut and the olive but heads the list for the combination of proteins, minerals and fat. Traditionally, the avocado season was limited to the months August, September and October, but by the 1980s out-of-season varieties such as Lulu, Collinson and Winslowson, ripening between December and February, became popular, though Simmonds remained the most common variety.[81] Few groves were planted for commercial exploitation and most trees appeared in gardens only adventitiously.

Avocado is one of the few fruits that must be eaten raw, because it becomes rancid when cooked. The English learned this from the Spanish colonists and they in turn followed the practice of the Taino. William Hughes said in 1672 that the "Spanish pear" was common in Jamaica, and he thought it "one of the most rare and most pleasant fruits in that island". Extolling its virtues, he said, "It nourisheth and strengtheneth the body, corroborating the vital spirits, and procuring lust exceedingly: the pulp being taken out and macerated in some convenient thing, and eaten with a little vinegar and pepper, or several other ways, is very delicious meat." Barham, writing in the early eighteenth century, said the ripe fruit was eaten with pepper and salt, or mixed with lemon juice and sugar. He also claimed some people boiled the fruit and had it with salt beef. Long, in the later eighteenth century, distinguished green and red (dark purple?) "species", the latter preferred for its "firmer, better-tasted flesh". According to Long, the avocado was "in universal esteem" and "generally eaten with sugar and lime juice, or pepper and salt". Lunan similarly thought the avocado "so rich and mild that most people make use of some spice or pungent substance to give it poignancy", achieving this by using "wine, sugar, lime-juice, but mostly pepper and salt". The pulp, said Long, "has a delicate rich flavour, and is extremely nourishing". Referring to the fats and digestible oil in the pulp, some called the avocado "vegetable marrow" or "real vegetable marrow". John Stewart, in 1823, said that the "avagato pear" was bitter until ripe, then "so rich and luscious, but without any degree of sweetness, that it has, appropriately enough, been styled the vegetable marrow of the western world".[82]

Avocado was a "favourite food" of enslaved people in Jamaica in the eighteenth century. Indeed, Long claimed the fruit was often "the sole support of many of the lazier, who have neglected to stock their grounds with other provisions". He also identified an earlier harvest season than is the modern pattern, saying the fruit was "in perfection from May to September". The weeks before August were the period of immaturity. Long noted that "the Negroes are sometimes apt to eat it immediately after the May rains, or when it is crude and watery, in which state it occasions fluxes and diarrhœas". This identifies the avocado as a food of the hungry. Lunan, however, said that when the fruit ripened, from August to October, "with a little salt, and one or two plantains, they afford a hearty meal to the negroes, and are introduced at every table, being by many considered a great luxury". The avocado was not mentioned among the trees of the gardens and grounds of the enslaved and was apparently more common in wild woodland where it thrived and was harvested.[83]

Early in the nineteenth century, avocado was sometimes spread on bread or toast in place of butter. This practice was generally associated with naval officers, giving the fruit the names "midshipman's butter" and "subaltern's butter" – hence the "butter pear". Sullivan, in 1893, said avocado was "chiefly eaten at breakfast or luncheon with pepper and salt". A dessert was also made, by mashing the pulp with sugar, nutmeg and sherry, but this went out of fashion in the twentieth century.[84] Few twentieth-century recipes called for more than combining the fruit with vegetable salads, and most often it was consumed without modification. Creaming the pulp into a dip or spread was limited to cocktail parties and other entertaining. Stuffed avocado, avocado soup and avocado soufflé never caught on, but avocado ice cream was more successful.[85] Most cooks and consumers knew avocado was best in its natural state, wonderfully complementing ackee and saltfish, breadfruit and bammy.

MANGO

All of the fruits considered thus far – plantain, banana, breadfruit, ackee and avocado – have been largely associated with the carbohydrates and with the vegetable component of diet, and consumed in dishes enjoyed for savoury rather than sweet flavours. Only at certain stages of their maturity, when the sugars outweighed the starches, have they been appreciated as sweets and desserts. They are, in fact, unusual as fruits, lacking the typical sweetness and juiciness. Most of the fruits that follow in this chapter have been valued above all for their sugars and used only occasionally as substitutes for the starchy staples. Many were indigenous to Jamaica or the region, rarely arriving as offshoots of voyaging or economic botany. Of the few that were introduced, most came late to the island. None of them became a staple, but some did play important roles in Jamaican food history – none more so than the mango.

The mango tree, *Mangifera indica*, was domesticated in India around 4000 BP, and the virtues of its fruit have been extolled for almost as long. Some Hindus believe the mango tree to be a form of the creator of all creatures, Prajapathi, and Buddhists regarded it as sacred because it was in a mango grove that the Buddha took his rest. The tree has a dense spreading canopy with many potential fruiting points, and a mature tree can bear four to six hundred fruit in a season. The harvest generally extends from May to July but, because the cropping season varies from place to place, mangoes can be purchased – at a price – throughout the year. Warm, low sites with limited rainfall provide the best growing conditions, and the tree thrives up to one thousand metres above sea level. In commercial production, eight tonnes per hectare is normal. Trees can remain productive for up to a century but tend to bear poorly some years.[86]

Lal Behari Singh, in 1960, identified mango as "decidedly the most popular fruit among millions of people in the Orient, particularly in India, where it is considered to be the choicest of all indigenous fruits". Jamaicans share this enthusiasm. As early as 1811, Titford could declare the mango "a fine fruit" with "a yellow, juicy pulp, of a delicious sweet taste, and, if not stringy, reckoned one of the best fruits" (Plate 2 and Figure 5.7). By the 1890s the mango was "the common food of the common people

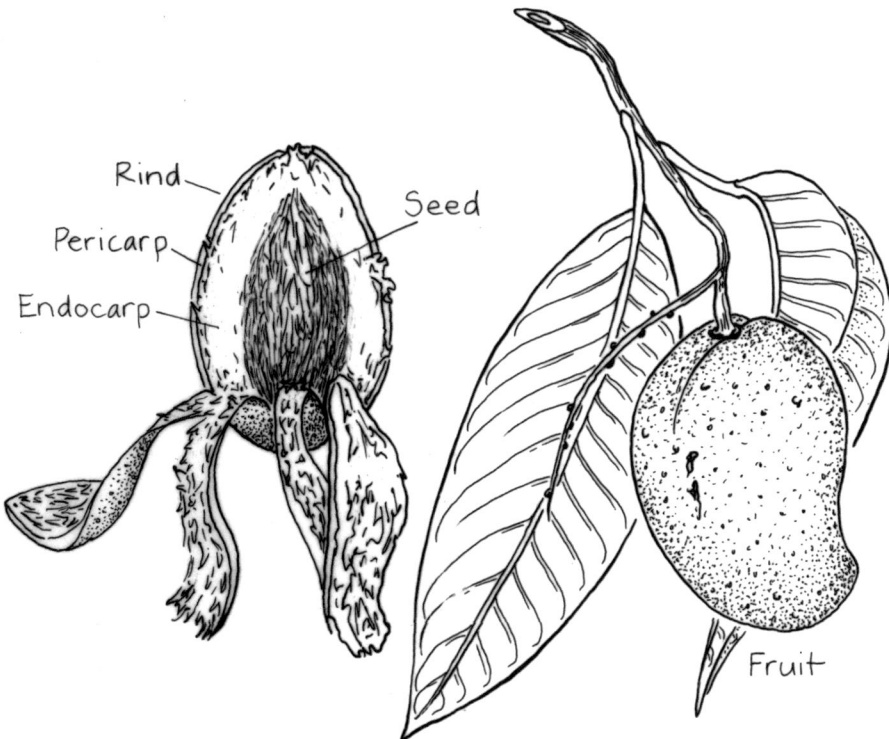

Figure 5.7 Mango fruit

and the prized dessert of the better classes". It was Jamaica's most popular fruit in the 1930s, and in 1992, with prices sky high, the mango was still "perhaps the favourite fruit among most Jamaicans".[87]

In spite of its superior taste, the mango was slow to reach Jamaica. It had the disadvantage of not being a useful voyaging food and, more important, the seed had a limited range of viability. The Portuguese had brought it to Brazil by the beginning of the eighteenth century, and from there it was moved on to Barbados in 1742. It has often been stated that the mango came to Jamaica in a French ship sailing from Mauritius to St Domingue that was captured by Lord Rodney's squadron in 1782. These seedlings were indeed important, but they were not in fact the first. More than a decade earlier, in 1769, Thistlewood recorded news that the mango was being introduced to Jamaica, and he himself planted seeds in his garden in 1773, though they failed to grow. In 1779 he saw a mango tree growing, almost a metre tall, in Westmoreland. The seedlings taken from the French were cultivated in East's garden, and Bligh brought more mango trees, from Timor, on his second breadfruit voyage. When he visited the botanical garden at Bath in 1793, Bligh remarked that "the mango grew luxuriantly, and these are plentiful all over the island".[88]

By 1814 Lunan could declare that the mango had "now become one of the commonest fruit trees in Jamaica, in a great number of its varieties". Soon after it could be said that "mangoes are become so common, and are so plentiful in the season of bearing, that the hogs are fed with them". The tree quickly became part of the gardens of the enslaved. Joseph Sturge and Thomas Harvey, in 1837, said the mango had "spread with great rapidity, and is now found in every part of the island; the fruit, which it produces in very great abundance, is dessert for the whites and food for the negros, as well as for cattle, horses, and hogs". Philip Henry Gosse, in 1845, said that the mango "grows almost everywhere, at least around every homestead, gentle or simple". In modern Jamaica, "the ubiquitous mango" occurs throughout the landscape, including urban zones, though it is less common on the north coast. As Singh observed, the mango has "established itself so well in Jamaica that it looks almost indigenous to that island".[89]

The seedlings taken from the French in 1782 carried identification numbers, and these numbers were left intact with the trees in East's garden. This proved a wise decision: the mango takes four to five years to bear and is highly heterozygous, meaning that every seedling is potentially a new variety. Some of the numbered trees never gained other names; in 1837 James Macfadyen could report that the most esteemed mangoes in Jamaica were "Number 11" and "Number 32". By the 1870s, Number 11 stood alone at the peak of quality. It remains popular today, and is often referred to simply as "Number". Other names recorded by Macfadyen include carrot mango, papaw mango, yellow mango, green mango, tie-tie mango, plum mango, parrot mango, turpentine mango, finger mango and dwarf mango.[90]

In 1869 grafted varieties were introduced to Jamaica from India, via Kew, and in 1884 more came from the botanic gardens of Martinique. The "East Indian" variety came relatively late to Jamaica, the first fruit ripening in the island in 1880 at Hope. These mangoes were declared "in bulk and shape very similar to the 'yam' mango", with a distinctive pleasant flavour and a "rosy, comely exterior"; "the rind is exceedingly thick, and the edible part is firm, but not stringy". However, although "superior to many varieties of Jamaica mango, they do not . . . in any way approach our Number Eleven – the mango par excellence". Because they were sweet and seemed likely to be able to keep, they were thought suited to the week-long journey to New York markets, which had already been pioneered by other, more fragile mangoes.[91]

Sullivan agreed that Number 11 was the best table mango, but she recognized a "great variety" of mangoes, including common, golden, yam, beef, East Indian, hairy, black, kidney and plummy. She believed some people preferred the commoner sorts, while others did not like mangoes at all. In 1938 the most common types were the hairy mango and the stringy, along with the Number 11, black, yam, beef, sugar, turpentine and robin mangoes, while the "aristocracy" were the East Indian and Bombay. The proliferation of varieties continued into the twentieth century, with subtle variations of shape, colour, appearance, taste, smell and texture. Prominent in Jamaica today are the East Indian, Bombay, Lucea, St Julian (Julie), Hayden and Tommy Atkins, and new names are constantly being added.

The preferred mangoes are sweet and luscious. Inferior versions can be stringy and watery, with a hint of turpentine, like the hairy or common mango. It was the objective of selection to replace these with larger, better eating fruit, but taste could always be traded against availability and cost. In 1985 the preferred varieties on the local market were St Julian, East Indian and Bombay. In Kingston in 1992, the hierarchy of value placed East Indian, Nelson and Governor at the top, selling for $80 a dozen, Hayden for $50 to $60, St Julian for $40, Number 11 for $20, common hairy mangoes for $10 to $20 and black mangoes (greenskins) for $6. In the country the more common types at least were still for the asking or picking.[92]

Although the Jamaican mango is an introduced species, one indigenous tree has occasionally been included among the class: *Grias cauliflora*, a slender tree with few branches, growing to fifteen metres. Generally, it is known as "anchovy" or "anchovy pear", but it was called by Long in 1774 "anchovy pear, or West India mango, calophylum". He described it as a "beautiful tree" common in the mountains and in "low moist bottoms". The fruit was about the size and shape of an alligator's egg, and russet brown. Long said that "when pickled, it exactly resembles the East India mango, and by some conjectured to be the same, or at least to have the nearest affinity to it".[93]

A ripe mango is best eaten fresh, the juice running over hands and face. The green mango requires more labour, and is used to make pickles and preserves. Green mangoes have also been stewed to make tarts, fools (with nutmeg and milk), jellies (boiled up with cloves, cinnamon and sugar), chutneys, puddings and dumplings. In 1938 a mango sandwich was served by the Myrtle Bank Hotel, made of thin slices of "green mango well salted with tomato, cucumber, and a tiny slice of red pepper" on brown bread and eaten with baked black crab.[94] The refrigerator made possible more recipes using the ripe fruit, and stewed mangoes became less popular after about 1945. Mango jelly was made with gelatin and evaporated milk, and mango bread (using eggs, coconut, cinnamon and lots of sugar and oil) proved a great advance on banana bread. Cookbook writers persisted with mango fool but, having access to the refrigerator, now used fresh ripe fruit prepared in a blender with cream, vanilla and icing sugar.[95] The freezer enabled mango ice creams. Chutneys remained popular, using either green or ripe mango, and so did jams made from "slightly under-ripe" fruit. "Mango cheese", made from firm ripe Number 11s boiled with sugar, could be kept in airtight tins for "a long time". Fruit punches often included fresh mango, and commercial producers canned both sliced fruit and juice or "nectar". On the other hand, Jamaicans did not follow the Indians in making mango curry, nor did they preserve the pulp by drying or make the kernels into flour for bread.[96]

JACKFRUIT

A relative of the breadfruit, the jackfruit (*Artocarpus heterophyllus*, sometimes called *A. integrifolia*) is another native of India. The plant came to Jamaica with Rodney in 1782 and was listed as the Indian Jaca Tree in the *Hortus Eastensis*. The tree grows to fifteen metres and its fruit are the largest of all those cultivated, weighing up to twenty-five kilograms. Unusually, the fruit bear on the trunk and old branches of the tree, with a horny pericarp and a very strong, unpleasant smell (Figure 5.8). Titford thought the smell of the fruit "so powerful that some persons cannot bear it in a house". Although

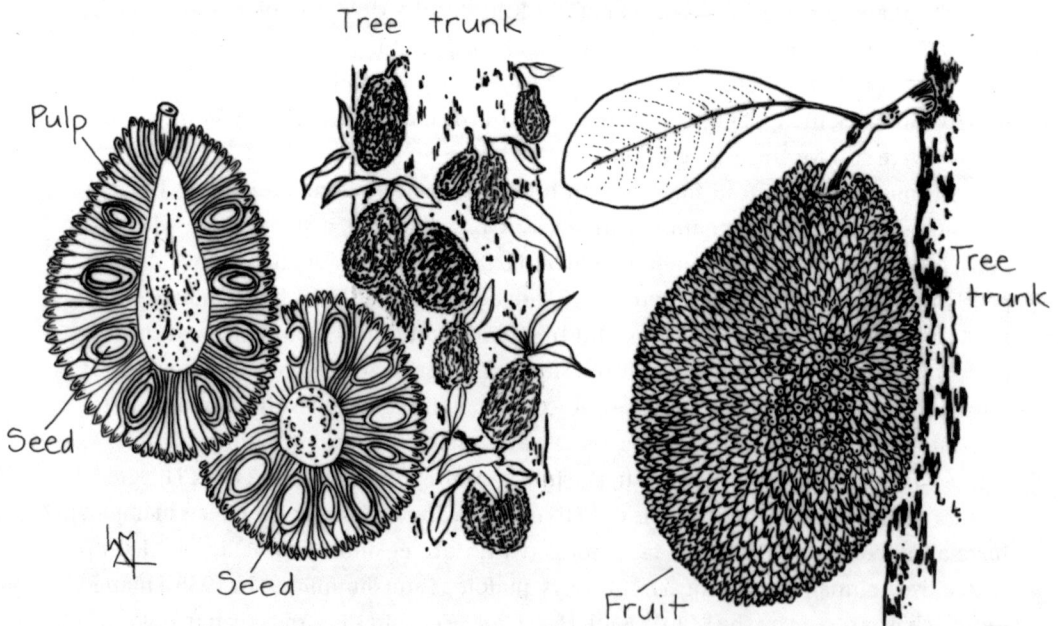

Figure 5.8 Jackfruit on tree trunk and in section

most of the white pulp was "tasteless", the numerous seeds were "surrounded by an orange-coloured pulp, about half an inch thick, of a very rich, sweet taste, which, after being washed in salt and water, is preferred by many to all the fruits in the island". Roasted, the seeds resembled chestnuts.[97]

The fruit is eaten raw, salted or cooked, but Jamaican recipes are rare. Modern cooks sometimes use the seeds as "beans", seasoned and stewed with pepper. The immature pulp serves as a vegetable in curries, and it may also be used to make puddings or parboiled and baked to make a bread. A recipe for "jackfruit whack" was thought to be "born out of a desperate effort to make a meal out of the only ingredients available at the moment". In this recipe, the seeds from an almost-rotting jackfruit were boiled, then pounded in a mortar and cooked with coconut milk and seasonings to create a mass similar to turn cornmeal. When the mixture consolidated, it could be cut into slices.

The jackfruit is less popular in Jamaica than in South Asia, where it sometimes forms a standard item of diet in season.[98] Apart from the unpleasant smell, Jamaicans say it can be unlucky to travel with a whole jackfruit – you will puncture a tyre.

COCONUT

Although the coconut, *Cocos nucifera*, was widely dispersed across the Indo-Pacific region in geological time, aided by the colonizing qualities of drifting nuts stranded on tropical beaches, it reached the Caribbean islands only after Columbus. Exactly when the first trees grew in Jamaica is uncertain. The earliest known introduction to the Caribbean was to Puerto Rico in 1582, and Sauer has argued that "coconut planting spread slowly and was of slight economic importance through the eighteenth century". He notes only that "a few coconuts from unspecified sources" were planted in Jamaica in the seventeenth century and that Bligh brought more from Tahiti in 1793.[99] This, however, seems counter to a good deal of contemporary testimony. For example, Hughes said the "cocus, or coco-nut-tree" was commonly planted on Jamaican plantations, Browne thought the "cocco-nut tree" common, and Long found the "cocoa-nut tree . . . planted in most parts of the island, both for its beauty and productions". Stewart, in 1823, said the coconut grew "in great luxuriance, and abounds in every part of the island". Trees grew in the gardens of the enslaved. Some plantations had groves, the oil being extracted and used to light the works during crop; the nuts were "occasionally distributed among the slaves as an article of food".[100] This suggests a more rapid and substantial rate of adoption than that proposed by Sauer.

Large-scale commercial cultivation of coconuts began in Jamaica in the 1860s, and by the end of the nineteenth century, coconuts grew alongside bananas to supply a major export market. As with the banana, trade increased local availability. Hurricanes and lethal yellowing (a disease first noticed in the 1870s) depleted plantations, and dwarf varieties resistant to wind and to lethal yellowing were developed. By the 1970s coconut production had become heavily concentrated on large farms. Jamaica Talls were seriously affected by lethal yellowing and Malaysian Dwarfs dominated the market.

Exocarp
Mesocarp
Endocarp

Solid
endosperm

Liquid endosperm

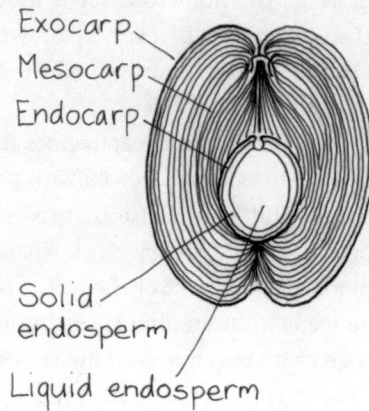

Figure 5.9 Coconut: longitudinal section

At the beginning of the twenty-first century, the disease attacked again, and hardly any of the graceful tall palms remained to be seen. Production fell from 3.5 million nuts in 1997 to 312,000 in 2004.[101]

The coconut tree or palm has multiple uses, food being but just one. Eighteenth-century writers regularly declared that "it furnishes meat, drink, physic, cloathing, lodging, and fuel". As a food, the fruit offered new resources at each stage of development and ripening. Bunched at the top of the tree, within the crown of leaves, the fruit is first green, then changes from yellow to orange to red as it matures. It consists of an outer skin, or exocarp, surrounding a fibrous layer, or mesocarp (the husk), and a hard shell, or endocarp (the nut). Within the shell, the white endosperm, or kernel, is covered by a thin brown coat; when the fruit is mature, its interior cavity is filled with liquid (Figure 5.9). Reaching maturity is a slow process, taking twelve or thirteen months.[102] Lindsay produced a splendid drawing of the development of the coconut in 1767, in addition to his image of the palm sketched the year before (Plates 7–8).

The liquid inside the unripe nut makes a cooling drink, slightly acid. Edmund Hickeringill, writing in 1661, thought "the milky juice . . . a most ambrosian dainty, very diuretick, and proper pharmacy for nephritick distempers". Hughes declared "the wine, or liquor within, quencheth thirst, refrigerateth the spirits", and Long found it "one of the pleasantest drinks in America".[103] Since the early nineteenth century, the liquid has been known as "coconut water". (Occasionally it was called "coconut milk", but this usage lapsed.) The young coconut, or "water coconut", is drunk when its sugar content is at its maximum, the sugar providing the only nutritional benefit. To obtain the water, the top of the fruit is cut off with a sharp machete, slicing through husk, shell and kernel to create a small opening to drink from. The next stage of development is the "jelly coconut", or simply "jelly", referring to the thin gelatinous layer (the endosperm) formed inside the nut (the endocarp) that can be scooped out and eaten with a spoon.

The spoon is cut from the side of the husk, after the water has been drunk and the fruit split in half. The earliest citation for the term "jelly coconut" comes from 1834. Sullivan suggested using the jelly to make a "cocoanut water ice", by freezing the jelly of young coconuts together with sweetened coconut water. A "cocoanut curry" was made by boiling the jelly of a very young coconut with cinnamon, and adding curry powder.[104] By the early twentieth century, specialist sellers of water and jelly coconuts set up at road junctions or roamed the streets of towns in carts loaded with fruit. Towards the end of the century it was complained that the growth of the market for fresh young coconut reduced the supply of mature nuts for use in the production of copra and oil. A market developed for bottled and plastic-bagged coconut water for those unhappy with dealing with the nut.

When the liquid in the cavity reduces or dries up and the white flesh (the endosperm) hardens, the nut can be removed from its husk and broken open, and the creamy meat separated. Grated, the meat can be used to make a variety of confections, the best known being grater cake, drops, gizada and busta backbone, or tooloom. These names were adopted in the early twentieth century. Originally, grater cake was made by mixing grated coconut with unrefined or new wet sugar, but it is now often made with white sugar. Coconut drops, or "cut cake", are made by boiling small pieces of chopped coconut meat in spiced brown sugar and dropping lumps of the mixture onto a surface to form rough cakes. Gizadas, or "sweet cakes", are made from grated coconut mixed with brown sugar, coconut water, nutmeg, cinnamon and beaten egg, baked in pastry shells. These open tartlets are also known as "pinch-me-round", in reference to the shaping of the shells. H.G. De Lisser, in 1932, described the "geezada" as "made of grated, stewed coconut, baked in a round crust with a corrugated edge". It was sold in schooltime, in the 1890s, for a gill (three farthings).[105]

Browne had said as early as 1756 that "the kernel is frequently rasped, and made into fritters and small cakes", but he offered no particular names for the products. Sullivan gave simple recipes for coconut cakes and biscuits, and De Lisser similarly distinguished coconut biscuits and grater cake from the gizada. Small round cakes called "totoes" were made from flour, brown sugar and grated coconut. Modern versions added cinnamon, nutmeg, pimento, vanilla, butter, beaten egg and milk. By the 1990s the toto was rarely produced by commercial bakers, though it was sought after.[106]

The etymology of *toto* (or *tuoto*) is uncertain. Cassidy and Le Page point to equally plausible possible origins in Fante and Spanish. *Gizada* seems more definitively Spanish, and *grater cake* French (derived from *grater brute* or *brut*, meaning "crude and unrefined"). Whether the etymology is useful in deciding how and when these items were introduced to Jamaica (or created there) is even less certain. Grater cake requires the least technology – not even an oven – and gizada the most. It may be that these three related confections emerged from different sectors of society more or less simultaneously, as perhaps happened for ackee and saltfish, producing variations on a theme controlled by the availability of tools and materials. Recent additions to the tradition include even more refined products, such as coconut macaroons, but also coarser versions, like coconut bread, coconut buns, coconut muffins and coconut rock cakes.

Grated coconut meat can be turned into coconut milk or coconut cream. This is achieved by pouring water over the grated meat and squeezing out a thick white liquid. Sullivan proposed "cocoanut soup", adding coconut milk in the final stages of boiling up fresh beef, with salt pork or beef, cocos, scallion and thyme. Of "ricey cocoa", made with rice, coconut cream, nutmeg, cinnamon, rosewater and sugar, she said "the people often eat this for breakfast". There were also coconut pudding, coconut custard, coconut blancmange, and coconut and tapioca pudding. "Cocoanut ice cream" was made by grating four coconuts and squeezing out the juice, to yield a pint (568 millilitres) of cream, which was mixed with a similar volume of cow's milk and sweetened with sugar before freezing. Sullivan explained that "it must be rather sweet, as freezing makes it require a little extra sweetness", though she gave no advice on what she thought an appropriate quantity, simply directing, "sugar to taste".[107]

Coconut milk serves an important role as the base ingredient for a series of substantial dishes, including curries, rundown, and rice and peas. Rundown, or "run-dung", occasionally appears in modern cookbooks as "coconut rundown" or "coconut rundown sauce". Cassidy and Le Page described rundown as "a kind of sauce made by boiling coconut down till it becomes like custard (but stops short of becoming oil)". Alternative names were round-the-road and flabob, or flombob. The name and its method of preparation suggest a connection with Indonesian rendang, but how this might have come about is unknown. The earliest citations in the *Dictionary of Jamaican English* are from the 1940s, in the forms "rung-dung" and "rundung". The earliest references found in the *Gleaner* are to "shad rundown" and "mackerel rundown", in 1963, with "coconut rundown, known as 'dip and fall back'", appearing in 1964 and "rundung" in 1979. Recipes from before Independence are hard to find. Most recipes, overall, begin with grated coconut, processed to make coconut milk, and it is this milk that is boiled rapidly "until it is reduced to something resembling curdled custard and oil". At this stage, salt or pickled fish is added (shad and herring in earlier times, most often mackerel in the late twentieth century), the fish having been first soaked and the fins, side bones and heads removed. When the fish is cooked, seasonings are put into the pot: Scotch bonnet peppers, garlic, scallion, thyme and tomato. Sometimes green bananas are cooked in the sauce. Vegetarian versions emerged in the later twentieth century, as, for example, a "vegetable rundown" made with sweet potato, green banana and chocho, or alternatively eggplant or Congo peas rundown.[108]

Down to the middle of the twentieth century, it was common for a dish of rundown to form a communal bowl into which boiled or roasted "bread-kind" was dipped: coco, yam and plantain, as well as breadfruit and banana. The association with these starchy staples persists, though the communal bowl is much less common. Rundown is the most important example of the combination of sauce with bread-kind, the larger category having a variety of names referring to the actions involved in eating: "dip-and-fall-back", "dip-and-come-back" and "dip-and-shake-off". Other, earlier suggestive names include "assistant" and "breadfruit remedy". The origin of the combination of foods surrounding rundown appears strongly African in its fundamentals.

On the other hand, in parts of Jamaica during the 1950s the common name for rundown was "pakassa", a sauce with etymological roots in Hindi but widely known in rural Jamaican communities. The difference between rundown and pakassa is that the latter includes flour and butter and is coloured with anatto. Pakassa is also commonly vegetarian, though one 1950s recipe for "banana pakassa" includes saltfish and pig's tail. It is hard to tell whether pakassa was influential in the development of rundown or whether rundown existed before Indian indenture: the earliest citations for both words given in the *Dictionary of Jamaican English* are from the 1940s. The ready availability of coconuts by the late eighteenth century suggests the possibility of a much earlier date for the origins of some such dish, but the absence of explicit references demands caution. In the 1980s, pakassa was made by colouring coconut milk with anatto, then cooking it down to a custard or oil. Next, a seasoned paste was made using flour, black pepper, scallion, thyme and perhaps country pepper, and stirred into the sauce until it bubbled up, allowing the flour to cook for a few minutes. The sauce was poured over boiled food, such as yam and coco.[109] More recent versions see the food cooked in the same pot as the sauce.

When dried, coconut meat becomes "copra", the raw material for cooking oil, margarine, soap and other products. Copra's good storage properties meant that it was often exported in this state for processing. Another process, in which the coconut meat is first pared then dried, makes dessicated coconut. This was first produced in England in the 1880s and became common where the fresh fruit is not readily available, but rarely seen in Jamaica. Coconut oil was sometimes imported (Figure 5.10). In the period after records commence, in the 1820s, coconut oil arrived in small quantities between 1830 and 1860. In 1880 a Kingston merchant offered "400 gallons best foreign pressed cocoanut oil of very heavy body, and of superior quality".[110] It then disappeared, to return in larger amounts after 1945, and imports peaked, per capita, in the 1970s. Even when imports seemed to disappear, small shipments trickled through. Local production of coconuts peaked in 1980, but production of refined coconut cooking oil is harder to chart, and copra was used to manufacture soap and animal feeds as well as for edible fats and oils. Coconut oil competed with both animal fats and alternative imported cooking oils. Cotton seed oil dominated from 1895 to 1930, and after 1965, soya bean oil. By 1950 Jamaica was thought to be producing enough cooking oil, margarine and lard to be almost self-sufficient.

In 1975 only 20 per cent of the coconut crop was consumed fresh, but ten years later fewer than 10 per cent of Jamaica's coconuts were being processed into copra, making it necessary to import soya beans to produce cooking oil. Deliveries to the copra factories were low because growers found it "hard to refuse the higher price being paid by the jelly man, the higgler and the oil boiler". Coconut oil came to have a

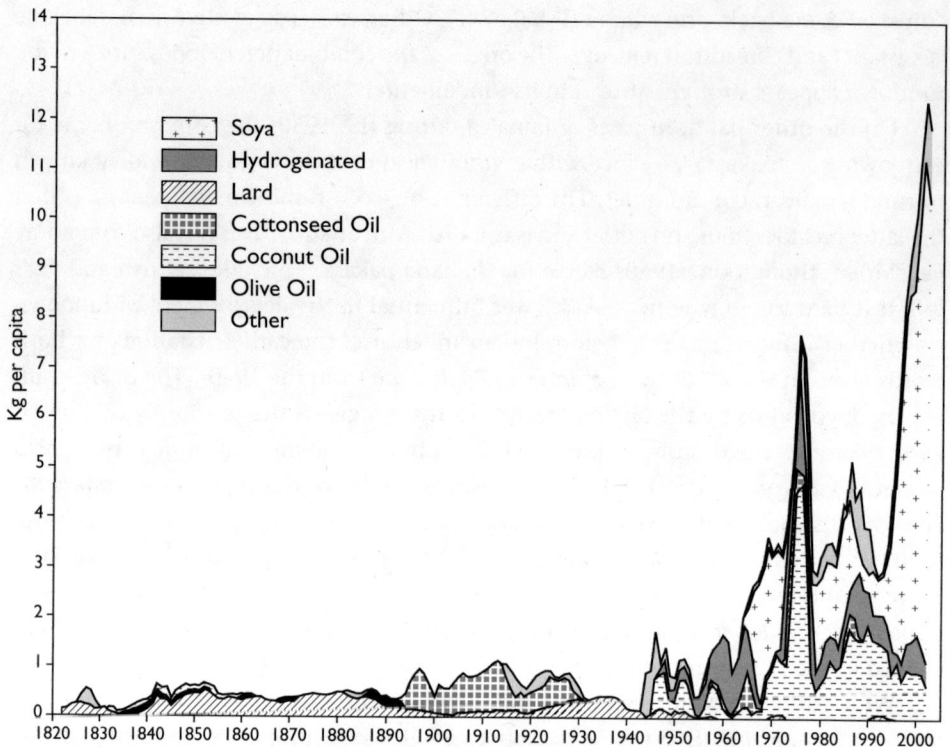

Figure 5.10 Coconut and other edible oils, imports per capita, 1822–2004. Source: Appendix 1.

negative image because, unlike the unsaturated vegetable oils, it was "pure fat and loaded with calories". In the 1990s it was assessed more positively, and if not quite "good for you" it was at least not viewed as an unhealthy food. Consumers were told "coconut oil neither lowers nor raises blood cholesterol levels". Although rich in saturated fat, it was argued, "the unique structure of the fat in coconut oil, being of a medium chain length, may be of benefit to the body". This meant that it was easily digested and left little toxic residue.[111]

Although the coconut was never a substantial element of the Jamaican diet, it came to be one of the most common ingredients in a wide range of dishes, giving flavour and body to basics such as rice and peas, pakassa and rundown. Taking the names of recipes as an index, coconut proved itself an easy winner in Sullivan's cookbook of 1893 (6 per cent of the total) and slipped only slightly, to second place after chicken, in Donaldson's 1993 book (5 per cent). In various forms and various roles, it appeared frequently in many other dishes.

OIL PALM, MACCAFAT, DATE

The oil palm, *Elaeis guineensis*, came to Jamaica from West Africa in the seventeenth century. Its fruit is a drupe, the oily outer pulp, or mesocarp, being the part most used;

it covers an inner hard-shelled nut which contains the palm kernel. According to Long, the "palm-tree, or oily palm", was "not so frequent in Jamaica as it deserves, being chiefly cultivated by the Negroes only". He found that the nut, when roasted, "tastes very much like the outside fat of roasted mutton". The oil was produced by boiling the nuts in water and straining out the oily substance. Long said, "The Negroes are fond of this oil, which sometimes makes an ingredient in their food; but they oftener apply it by way of embrocation, for strains, or to discuss rheumatic aches, for which purposes it is very efficacious." Titford talked of "abbays, (*Elaeis guineensis*)", the fruit of "a species of palm, called oily palm, which produces palm oil". The fruit had "a fibrous, yellow, oily pulp over the stone, and when boiled are pleasant and wholesome".[112]

Palm oil entered world trade as a significant commodity only after 1850, being used for a variety of products, not all of them edible. It was favoured because, like coconut oil, it melted rapidly at a temperature a little lower than that of the human body but *was hard and brittle when solid. Margarine and compound cooking fats from palm oil* remained important in the late twentieth century. Palm oil was commonly consumed in Jamaica, though rarely as a product of the island. It was never grown there as a plantation crop, though the palm itself naturalized.[113] Palm wine similarly failed to become a significant drink in Jamaica, for reasons that are less than obvious.

The endemic and common maccafat (palm) tree, *Acrocomia spinosa*, also produces oil-bearing fruit. Named for its thorny stem, maccafat is related to – and was sometimes confused with – *E. guineensis*. Browne, for example, said that its product was "not unlike, or inferior to, the real palm-oil". The yellowish fruit encloses its nut in an edible gummy pulp, which is no longer popular. De Lisser, recalling in 1932 the fruits available in the late nineteenth century, particularly in schoolyards, said "makkafat was sometimes a drug on the fruit market".[114]

The date tree or palm, *Phoenix dactylifera*, was tried in gardens in the eighteenth century, with apparent success, but is now said not to produce edible fruit in Jamaica. Although dates were, long before 1400, one of the most important fruits of West Africa, the palms grew best in the marginal desert oases and were traded to the coastal zone.[115] Most of the dates eaten in Jamaica were imported.

WATERMELON, MUSKMELON

The melons belong to the family Cucurbitaceae, one of the most important in the food systems of the tropics and closely integrated into human cultures. The Cucurbitaceae consist of many species, characterized by watery fruit growing on straggly vines, climbing or prostrate, often with rough leaves. The fruit of the prostrate species are sometimes large, among the largest in the plant kingdom, and all of them vary considerably in size, shape and colour. The origins of these diverse species are divided roughly equally between Old and New World sites. For Jamaica, the most important of the indigenous cucurbits are chocho, cerasee, pumpkin and squash, which will be discussed later in the chapter.

Red-fleshed watermelons, *Citrullus vulgaris*, are a native of tropical Africa and have been cultivated in the Nile Valley for at least four thousand years. Some are round, others oval or ellipsoidal; they are shaded from white to dark green, and weigh up to twenty kilograms. A large proportion of the fruit is edible. In Jamaica, the vine thrived and the fruit grew to "monstrous" size. It was not, however, always praised for taste. Long, for example, declared the watermelon "more recommended by its good effect in cooling the blood, than by its flavour, which much resembles that of water, slightly sweetened with sugar". Following Hughes's warnings, Long cautioned that all of the melons and cucumbers, but particularly the watermelon, should be eaten with "circumspection" because they tended to induce colics, fluxes, "a foul stomach" and even worms. The solution, he advised, was to eat them sparingly, with sugar, Madeira wine, lime juice, or pepper and salt.[116]

When the absentee planter Matthew Gregory Lewis tasted a watermelon at Black River in 1815, he declared,

> I never met with a worse article in my life; the pulp is of a faint greenish yellow, stained here and there with spots of moist red, so that it looks exactly as if the servant in slicing it had cut his finger, and suffered it to bleed over the fruit. Then the seeds, being of a dark purple, present the happiest imitation of drops of clotted gore; and altogether (prejudiced as I was by its appearance), when I had put a single bit into my mouth, it has such a kind of Shylocky taste of raw flesh about it (not that I recollect having ever eaten a bit of raw flesh itself), that I sent away my plate, and was perfectly satisfied as to the merits of the fruit.[117]

In spite of this lack of enthusiasm, the watermelon became a favourite fruit in Jamaica, eaten fresh in thick, cool slices. Sullivan even found a use for the white pith close to the rind, stewing it with sugar, cinnamon and rosewater. The stewed melon could be used to fill a pastry tart. St Elizabeth is now recognized as a major producer, but competition comes from imported, foreign fruit.[118]

The muskmelon and cantaloupe, *Cucumis melo*, belong to the squash family and are therefore close relatives of the cucumber. A "large and polymorphous species", these plants probably had their origins in Africa but came to Jamaica via Europe. Long observed that the several varieties of melon cultivated in Jamaica grew much larger than in Europe and thrived with little attention. Of them all, he considered cantaloupe "by far the richest, finest flavoured, and dissolves in the mouth".[119] However, the orange-fleshed muskmelon and cantaloupe have only a small place in modern Jamaican agriculture. It is the watermelon that is sold in quantities from the backs of laden trucks.

CUCUMBER, GHERKIN, GOURD

The cucumber, *Cucumis sativus*, is generally considered indigenous to South Asia, particularly India. Cultivation was common in Jamaica by the early eighteenth century, and the "cooling fruit" was "generally esteemed", served as a salad. Sometimes it was used

Plate 9
Egg plant, by Rev. John Lindsay, 1768. Bristol Museum and Art Gallery.

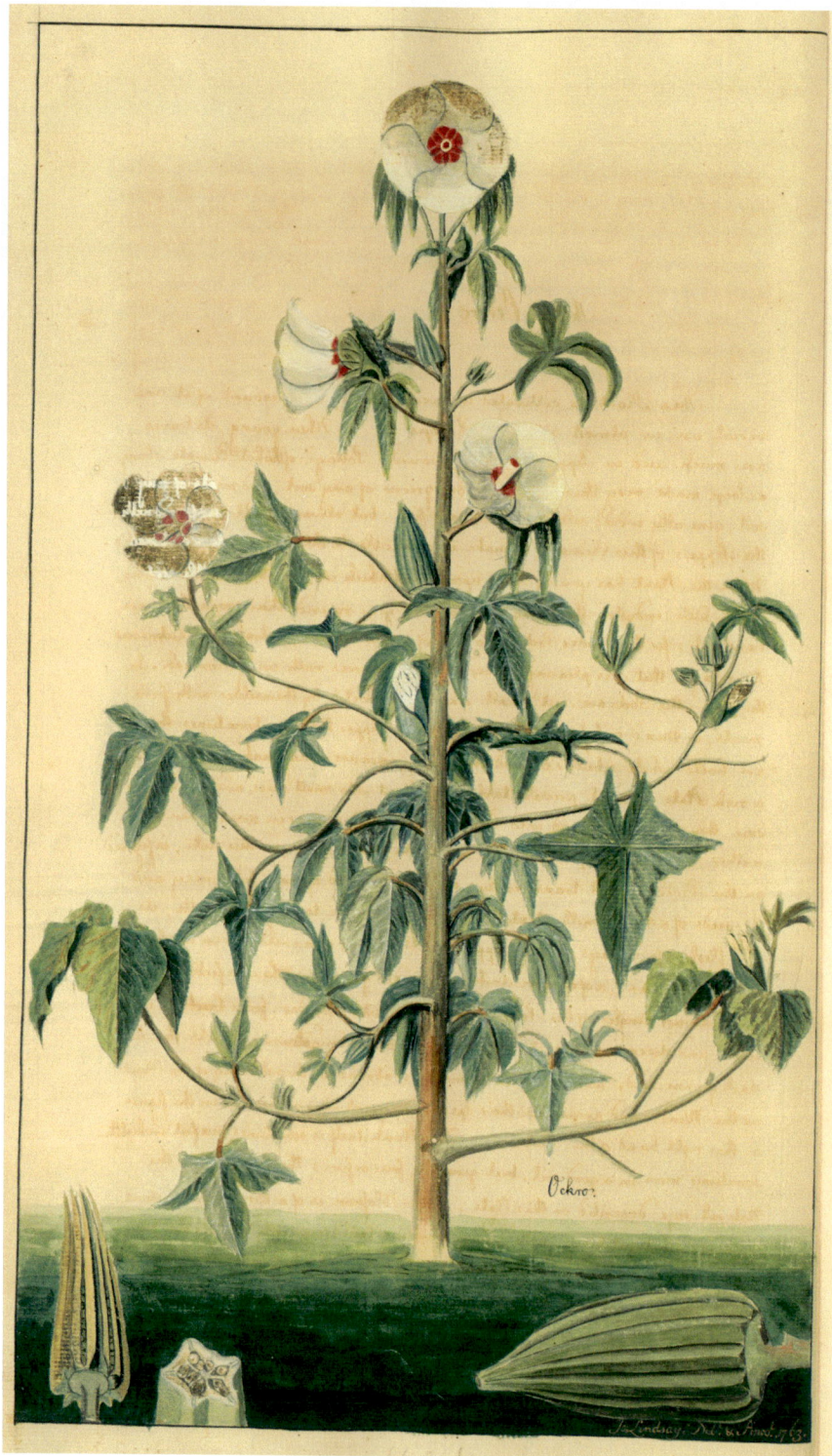

Plate 10

Okra, by Rev. John Lindsay, 1763. Bristol Museum and Art Gallery.

The Pomegranate.

Jos Lindsay delt pinxt pbl

Plate 11
Pomegranate, by Rev. John Lindsay, 1762. Bristol Museum and Art Gallery.

Plate 12

Pineapple, by Rev. John Lindsay, 1767. Bristol Museum and Art Gallery.

Plate 13
Pawpaw tree, by Rev. John Lindsay, 1766. Bristol Museum and Art Gallery.

Plate 14

Pawpaw fruit, by Rev. John Lindsay, 1766. Bristol Museum and Art Gallery.

Plate 15
Cashew, by Rev. John Lindsay, 1768. Bristol Museum and Art Gallery.

Plate 16
Granadilla, by Rev. John Lindsay, 1761. Bristol Museum and Art Gallery.

as a condiment with oil and pepper.[120] These uses persisted to the present, and cucumber is now also sometimes juiced.

In addition to the common cucumber, Jamaica has a "small wild cucumber" with a prickly rind, identified by Titford as *C. anguria*. Most writers regarded it as native to Jamaica but the plant was later described as the West India gherkin, with origins in Africa rather than the Americas. The species had travelled to Jamaica in the slave trade, being established in the island by the early seventeenth century and mutating to create a non-bitter cultigen that was a variant of a wild African bitter species. The plant grew luxuriantly in Jamaica. Thus, by the eighteenth century, it was easily thought indigenous.[121]

The fruit of *C. anguria* is smaller than that of *C. sativus*, only about six centimetres long. It is covered with curved prickles, ellipsoid and almost round in cross-section, the rind turning lemon yellow when ripe. It made good pickles, said Lunan, and was "frequently used with other herbs in soups, and proves a very agreeable ingredient". In 1880 a Kingston company sought supplies of "wild cucumbers" for preserving. Sullivan, not many years later, offered a recipe for boiled wild cucumbers, using the young fruit, served with butter and pepper or smothered by white sauce. She also proposed a "savory" in which boiled wild cucumbers were placed on anchovy toast, and hot coconut cream poured over the lot.[122] Although the wild cucumber remains locally common, often growing adventitiously in rough places, it has disappeared from the catalogue of edibles.

According to Long, the "slender-wandering gourd, or sweet gourd" (apparently the cucurbit, *Lagenaria vulgaris*, or bottle gourd, a native of Africa) was cultivated in Jamaica, its fruit boiled and made into puddings or eaten with salted meat.[123] This too seems to have disappeared from the repertoire.

EGGPLANT

Modern Jamaicans use the names "eggplant" and "garden egg" to refer to *Solanum melongena*, a small short-lived shrub grown for its edible purple fruit, known in the eastern Caribbean as "melongene" and in some parts of the world as "aubergine". A native of South Asia, the plant had reached interior West Africa by 1400, but not the coastal zone. In Asia, it was linked to brinjal and hence to callaloo, apparently leading to some of the early terms used in Jamaica. Browne and Long called it "brownjolly, valinghanna, or mad apple (*Solanum pomiferum*)". These names, however, had little currency in Jamaica, and Lindsay in 1768 identified the plant as "vegitable egg". He thought it less useful than ornamental, and therefore worthy of a picture (Plate 9), but added that "when young they are sometimes eat (and mostly by the Hebrew Nation) by boiling them several times in salt and water, and when mash'd and a little butter added to the plate, eats (as some fancy) something resembling an artichoak". Long, who believed the plant had been introduced to Jamaica by Jews, similarly noted that the ripe fruit, "sliced, pickled for a few hours, and boiled to a tenderness, are used instead of greens". Some people parboiled them, removed the skin and fried them in oil or butter.[124]

Titford correctly classified the "egg fruit or mad apple" as *S. melongena*, noting that it was "called in India, Branjaw, in Jamaica, Garden Egg and Valanghanna, Brown Jolly or Bolangena". Parboiled, sliced and fried, it tasted, he claimed, like fried eggs. Lunan said the fruit was "often introduced at table both boiled and dressed as turnips, as well as fried, and either way is an agreeable food, and accounted to be aphrodisiac". Sullivan gave recipes for "garden eggs" fried and stuffed.[125] The link with India remained strong, the eggplant being cultivated for market by East Indians in the early twentieth century. The fruit was common in the market, but ideas on how to prepare it were limited, particularly compared to the many variations found in Asia and the Middle East, and the eggplant was hardly ever found in twentieth-century Jamaican cookbooks.

OKRA

The okra, *Abelmoschus esculentus*, is a native of tropical Africa but now widely spread. An annual, the shrub can grow as tall as two metres, with attractive flowers, and bears green finger-like pods up to ten centimetres in length. Lindsay produced a picture of the "ockro" in 1763, probably impressed more by the beauty of the plant's flowers than by its fruit (Plate 10). The plant, he said, was "cultivated in every garden, on account of it[s] universal use in almost all sorts of soops". The leaves of the young plant were added to pepperpots, said Lindsay, as remains common in West Africa today, where they are also cooked as spinach. Lindsay declared the tender pods "so full of a restorative, nutritive, and lubricous mucilage, that it is pleasing to every palate and agrees with every stomach. In this use, the pods are cut small and either boild by themselves with fresh meats, or mix'd . . . with greens in the pepper pots. Sometimes, they are boiled whole, and butter'd, and in this appearance, they make a much loved and rich plate at most private tables. If cut into small slices, and dryd in the sun, they may be reduced into powder, which will answer in soops when dry wether may burn up the plant."[126] Other eighteenth-century writers said much the same, emphasizing the role of okra as "a great strengthener, and a mighty ingredient in their Sunday pepper-pots", and as "very cooling, emollient, and of great nourishment".[127]

Peter Marsden claimed in 1788 that the "ocro" was "the favourite vegetable" of the enslaved people of Jamaica, and common in their gardens. It was "best and most tender when the size of a large walnut; if older, they are stringy, and the seed is red". Marsden emphasized the role of the okra's "glutinous pulp" in pepperpot. Others said the enslaved made broths "in which ochros, cocos, and ceracee predominates either in quantity, or in the flavour by which they are distinguished; the general name for each kind of spoon meat, being pot". Lunan claimed okra to be "the chief vegetable in West-India pepper-pots, and renders them very palateable, rich, and nourishing", and praised their "rich mucilaginous flavour and quality". Okra pie was another possibility.[128]

In 1828 the fictional Marly said, "Okra pepper-pot is a favourite dish with all creoles, and those long-colonized, and may be called the Currie of the West Indies." He described pepperpot as a "soup" made from "the land crabs which abound in the island, thickened with vegetables, especially with a very small pea denominated by the negroes, okra, a kind of what is called squashies, and highly seasoned with the long pepper of the island". Sullivan offered a recipe for "ochro soup", made with Indian kale or callaloo, salt beef and a little salt pork, tomato, scallion and thyme, adding that some "black crabs boiled and added to the soup make it excellent". More unusual was her suggestion that the seeds, removed from their pods, might be boiled, mixed with onion and tomato, seasoned and served on buttered toast. Sullivan also suggested drying okra, slicing the pods crossways and leaving them in the sun a few days – but the ultimate destination was still a soup. This method followed West African practice, in which the fruits were sometimes "sliced, sun-dried, ground to a powder, and then stored until needed".[129] Few of these recipes are used by modern Jamaican cooks, and the fruit is most often served steamed, particularly as an accompaniment to steamed fish, almost as a decoration rather than a fundamental ingredient. Some find it unacceptably slimy.

CITRUS

The genus *Citrus* is native to a wide region of Southeast Asia, stretching from India to China to the Philippines. Ancient domestication did much to modify its genetics and distribution, producing a large number of hybrids and cultivars as well as true species. From the Asian homeland, plants spread east and west at different rates. Thus the sour orange, *C. aurantium*, reached the Mediterranean around the time of Christ, and Spain by the tenth century, whereas the sweet orange, *C. sinensis*, found its way to Spain and the Canary Islands only in the later fifteenth century. Columbus took seeds of both these hybrids to the Caribbean. In Jamaica, the sour orange came to be known as Seville orange, while the sweet orange was generally called "common orange" or simply "orange" rather than Valencia.

Columbus also carried seeds of the lime (*C. aurantifolia*), the citron (*C. medica*) and probably the lemon (*C. limon*). The citron, now uncommon, had its origins in the foothills of the Himalayas. The tree is small and its fruit large, with an uneven but smooth rind that is thick and difficult to peel. The flesh yields its juice reluctantly and may be either sweet or acidic. The citron is important as a parent of other citrus varieties. The shaddock, *C. grandis*, probably originated in southern China and reached Jamaica well after Columbus, in the seventeenth century. The lemon is now thought to be an ancient hybrid of citron, lime and probably shaddock, from the Punjab region of South Asia. It had already spread throughout the Mediterranean before Columbus brought it to the Caribbean. Although originating in Malaysia, what is called the "West Indian lime" is often known as the "true lime"; it has a small round fruit with a thin pungent rind and highly acid juice.[130] The mandarin, *C. reticulata*, spread much more slowly outside Asia, though orchards were established in the West Indies during the nineteenth century. Jamaicans distinguish between mandarin and tangerine, the former being a smaller and tighter fruit, though botanically they are one (Figure 5.11).

Ortanique

Ugli

Grapefruit

Orange

Tangerine

Citron

Shaddock

Lime

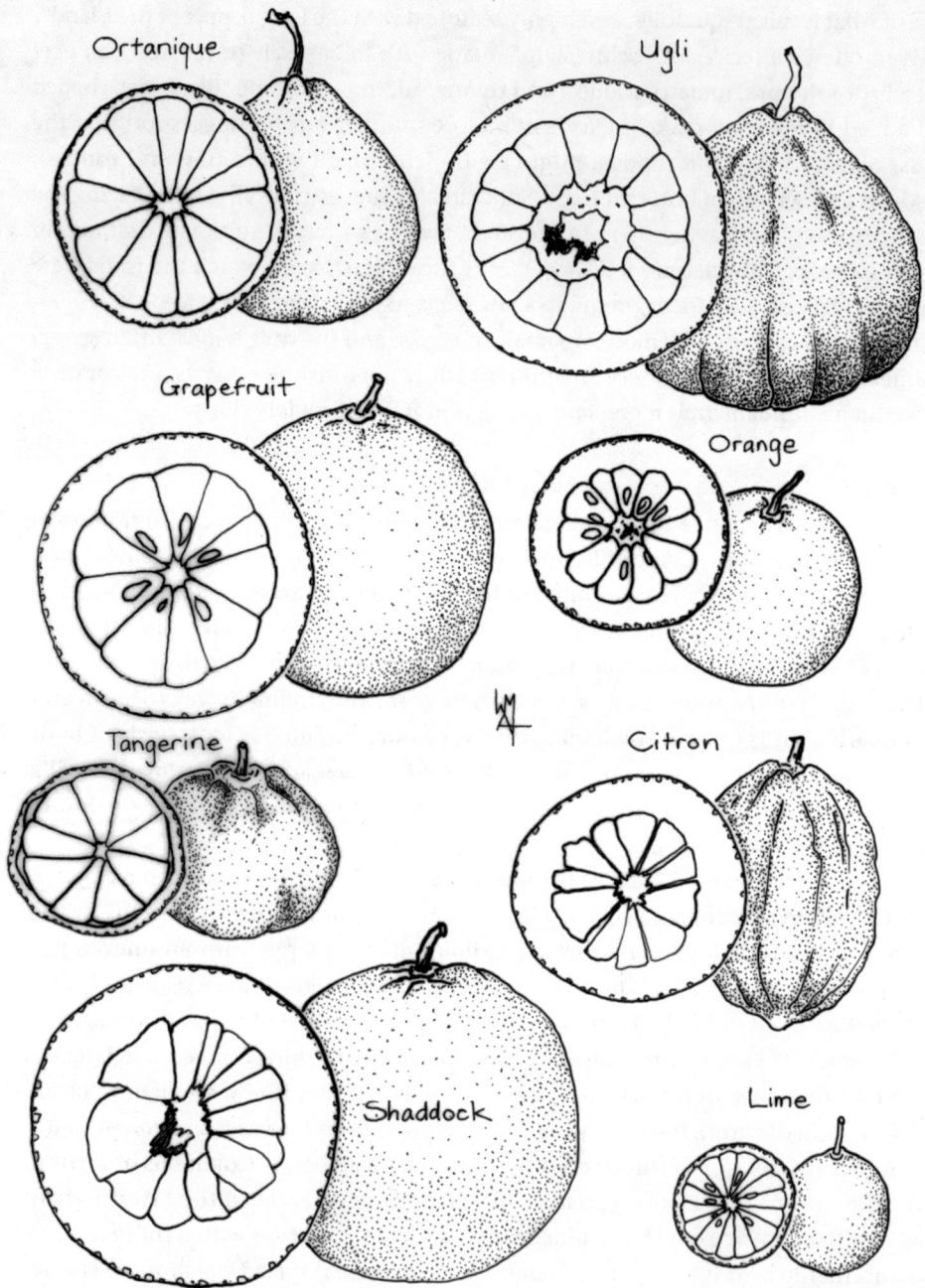

Figure 5.11 Citrus fruit varieties

The grapefruit, *C. paradisi*, is a hybrid between sweet orange and shaddock that occurred first in Barbados and second in Jamaica. The earliest recorded use of the word "grapefruit" occurred in Jamaica but reflected the confusion that led to the fruit being first known as "Barbadoes grapefruit". By the early nineteenth century it was sometimes called "grape or cluster fruit".[131] Mutations produced pink and red varieties of grapefruit, which were introduced to Jamaica in the twentieth century.

Jamaica produced its own unique hybrids, notably the ortanique and the ugli. The ortanique is a natural hybrid of sweet orange and tangerine; it was discovered in Jamaica around 1920. The tree is large and grows vigorously, and is highly productive. The fruit, when grown in Jamaica, has a thin skin and few seeds, with tender pulp, and as much as 60 per cent of it can be extracted as juice. The flavour is "extremely sweet but well balanced with acidity and has a strong, rich aroma", lacking any trace of bitterness. Propagation of the ortanique was begun in 1933 by Charles P. Jackson of Chellaston, Mandeville. In 1946, Jackson declared himself both the "originator of the variety and [its] namer". The name is a synthesis of *o*range, *tangerine* and un*ique.*[132]

The earliest *Gleaner* references to the ortanique date from March 1941, when the fruit were generally called "ortanique tangelos". Lawson Bros, in Kingston, offered for sale "Ortanique Tangelos in packed boxes". This terminology indicates confusion, because whereas the ortanique brought together orange and tangerine, the true tangelo combined grapefruit and tangerine. The tangelo, so-named, was developed in the United States in 1918, by the Bureau of Plant Industry, "through a cross between the tangerine orange and the grapefruit or pomelo". It was said to resemble more closely the orange than any of its parents, with little acidity. The Temple orange, a little-known orange-tangerine hybrid, was found growing wild in Jamaica much earlier, in 1896, and was propagated in Florida beginning in 1919, but remained insignificant outside Florida. By 1943, when ortanique plants first became available commercially in Jamaica, they were more appropriately called "ortanique oranges". Kingston traders offered "Jamaica's finest table oranges, the delicious Ortanique variety", held in cold storage for freshness. An advertisement for land at Constant Spring, St Andrew, in 1946 boasted "about 100 budded fruit trees, just on two years old, many of them bearing", and "every variety of citrus to be found in Jamaica, including Valencia, Surprise Navel, Ortanique and Parson Brown Oranges, Marsh Seedless and Pink Grapefruit, Tangelos, Tangerines, Uglis, Tahitian and Common Limes".[133]

Although the ugli is "of somewhat uncertain parentage", it is almost certainly a tangelo, bringing together grapefruit and tangerine. The fruit is often larger than a grapefruit and its peel uneven, rough and thick. The core is large and open, and the segments small but tender, sweet and very juicy, without any bitterness. It was found growing wild in 1914, some accounts say near Brown's Town, others Trout Hall. Exports to the United Kingdom began in 1938. Some objected to the name, preferring "Jamaica Lovely", but "ugli" it remained. In May the English press told readers, "The ugli (pronounced 'oogly') is the new fruit from Jamaica which became popular after it was recently introduced to the Queen at the British Industries Fair." Other new fruits entering the metropolitan market included the lychee from South Africa (praised by the king), the kumquat from China, and purple plums from Australia, though no method had been found to carry the Malayan rambutan.[134] The ugli remains a fruit nearly unique to Jamaica. When grown elsewhere it tends to acidity and lacks the Jamaican sweetness.

By the end of the twentieth century, new methods of hybridization were being applied aggressively to citrus varieties, creating hundreds of intergeneric types.[135] Many of these crosses were developed to produce seedless varieties while retaining flavour, juice content and thin skins, all characteristics appreciated by consumers. The combinations and permutations are almost endless, but the earlier hybrids remain dominant.

All citrus trees are hardy. They quickly established themselves in the Jamaican vegetation, escaping from cultivation to form wild groves. In some Caribbean islands they proved a plague in grazing land, but in sixteenth-century Jamaica they provided fodder for feral cattle and pigs. The prickly limbs of the shrubby citrus trees discouraged climbing animals, but the tempting fruit attracted low-browsing cattle and created a carpet of food on the ground. Following the Conquest, English observers regularly remarked upon the abundance of orange and lime trees in Jamaica, though they sometimes called the lime "a bastard lemon". The lime tree was common in the woods in the late seventeenth century, the lemon not so common. By 1739, Leslie said, Jamaica could "boast of the finest orange and lemon-trees, in great plenty". With the establishment of plantations and pens, lime trees became a common form of hedge, or "beautiful and strong fence", the trees growing as high as five metres. Other citrus trees were rarely planted to make living fences but frequently sprung up in them as a result of natural dispersal. The gardens of both the enslaved and the planters came to include orange, shaddock and lime.[136]

Jamaicans were not slow to make claims for the superiority of their oranges. As early as 1740, it was said that the sweet oranges of Jamaica were "finer in their kinds than those of Europe". Long looked at South Carolina, which was already exporting oranges in the 1770s, and wondered why Jamaica could not do the same. Fruit grown on the North American mainland could not compete in quality, and as for the mother country, Long observed, "the finest China orange [*C. sinensis*] I ever ate in England, was not comparable to the worst I have tasted in Jamaica". This perception persisted. Macfadyen felt confident in saying in 1837 that Jamaica-grown oranges were the best in the world, characterized by their sweetness and "richness of flavour". Even the acerbic Englishman James Anthony Froude, travelling in Jamaica in 1887, conceded that "the worst orange I ate in Jamaica was better than the best I ever ate in Europe". Froude took the Jamaicans to task for failing to graft and improve the culture of their trees but concluded that "so favourable is the soil and climate that the oranges of Jamaica are prized above all others which are sold in the American market". Export of Jamaica's oranges to New York had begun in the 1870s.[137]

The shaddock too was considered worthy of trade. In 1740, it was claimed that the island's shaddocks were "not so good as their oranges", though some people preferred them. Long said of the shaddock, "it is surely some satisfaction to possess so favourite a fruit in its most perfect and delicious state, whether for consumption within the island, or for exportation". Titford described the shaddock as "a fine fruit, roundish, about six inches in diameter, having a yellow, spotted rind, of a pungent, aromatic flavour. The pulp within is red or flesh colour, separated into divisions, and is granulated in the form of pegs or wedges, containing a sweet, aromatic, subacid juice, highly grateful and cooling." Lunan thought the shaddock had "a much milder sweet taste than any other of the orange kind". Modern assessments claim the flavour of the juice varies from acidic to insipid. Shaddocks hybridize easily, resulting in a large number of distinctive varieties.[138]

The value of lime and lemon juice in preventing scurvy at sea was well known by the seventeenth century, creating the basis of an export market. Hughes said lime juice quenched thirst and corrected "feverish distempers" but was also "exceedingly much in esteem in America for the making of punch; a drink which most there use, to be merry withal; and the chiefest liquor they make use of to entertain strangers and friends". Mixed with rum, the juice was used to make shrub, a common liquor of the period. In the 1890s there were attempts to use "a lime condensing apparatus" to produce lime juice for export. Sullivan gave a recipe for a frozen lime ice.[139] Commercial production of drinks based on citrus proved successful in the late twentieth century, notably the grapefruit-based drink Ting.

Large-scale production of citrus for export developed slowly, regardless of the supposed perfection of the Jamaican fruit. Oranges entered the trade only when steamer service to the United States became viable in the 1880s, following on the emergence of the banana industry, and competition from Florida hindered progress into the 1930s. Oranges dominated exports from the beginning, while some other citrus varieties, notably the shaddock and citron, faded from memory. The agricultural census of 1943 found that 63 per cent of Jamaica's farms had orange trees, 30 per cent had grapefruit and 27 per cent had limes. Exports took up a significant part of these crops, mostly in the form of canned fruit and juices.[140] By the 1990s, oranges, ugli and ortaniques dominated, far ahead of grapefruit, while limes had disappeared from the lists.

Citrus, like the coconut, was never a fundamental of diet, yet it has played a prominent role in Jamaican food culture. By the late twentieth century, the orange was indeed said to be the most common food of all, and the "citrus favourite". Strings of tangerines and mandarins dangled temptingly from roadside stalls on narrow highways or were pushed up to train windows. These were easily peeled with the fingers and eaten fresh. The feel of a fat tangerine in the hand and the peeling of its skin was a sensuous experience, thought John Hearne, the juice "thin, cool and sweetly astringent". Oranges, dominating the roadsides of Bog Walk, were sold singly, peeled in such a way that the pericarp remained intact; cut in half, the orange was sucked dry. Fruit in quantity was increasingly sold in plastic bags, to be taken home and juiced. Grapefruit "hearts" and juice were canned beginning in the late 1930s but were directed at export markets. From the 1970s, refrigerated or preserved "box juice" became common. These drinks continued the tradition of "orangeade" and "the juice of a common orange and a Seville orange mixed, which is very refreshing" that was established by the eighteenth century.[141]

In Sullivan's cookbook, sweet oranges appeared in the titles of three puddings and custards, two cakes, "matrimony" (described below), an ice and a wine. Seville oranges are used in a pudding, a biscuit, a jelly, "buttered orange juice" and a wine (mixed with sweet orange). The "seville-sweet" or bittersweet orange made another custard, and the citron a preserve. Limes gave names to a pickle, an ice, a jelly and two drinks. Lemon made just a cake, the fruit of the lemon being regarded by Jamaicans as insipid and inferior to that of the lime. Sullivan also included in her *Jamaica Cookery Book* "orange biscuits or little cakes, from receipt of 1809". To make these, whole Seville oranges were boiled in two or three pans of water until the bitterness was gone. Next, the oranges were cut in half and the pulp and juice removed. The skins were beaten in a mortar until fine, mixed with an equal weight of double refined sugar and sifted. Once the mixture had formed a paste, it was spread thinly and dried, then cut into pieces. These could be stored in a box between layers of paper, served for dessert or carried in the pocket on journeys. Sullivan also offered directions for the preparation of shaddock and forbidden fruit (a juicy member of the "'orange-shaddock' tribe") to be eaten at table using two forks. Titford had said that forbidden fruit resembled orange and shaddock, falling between these two in size and having "a sweet aromatic flavour" (Plate 2).[142]

Donaldson, writing one hundred years after Sullivan, made no mention of shaddock or citron or forbidden fruit, and made no use of Seville oranges. She did, on the other hand, offer two recipes for tangerine – a wine and a liqueur. Drinks were prominent among her recipes: she used sweet oranges and limes to make squashes, syrups, liqueurs, lemonade and limeade. Donaldson's recipe for "grapefruit delight" required simply grapefruit segments mixed with "enough condensed milk to sweeten", chilled and sprinkled with nutmeg. Donaldson included an orange ice cream and an ice-box pie but no puddings and just one cake. She did, however, introduce orange to chicken and duck ("canard à l'orange"). The pattern in Donaldson was typical of the period; if anything, she gave more attention to citrus than most.[143]

TAMARIND

The tamarind tree, *Tamarindus indica*, is probably a native of Africa but is now widely naturalized and cultivated throughout the tropics. By the eighteenth century it was common in the savannas of Jamaica, growing as tall as sixteen metres or even higher, with an immense trunk (Plate 1). Its fruit, or pods, reached maturity at different times in different parts of the island, generally being gathered between June and August. They were harvested fully ripe, at which time they broke open easily (Figure 5.12). Once removed from the hard shell, the fruit was packed in casks and covered with first-copper-boiling sugar syrup. Alternatively, said Long, a "more elegant method" was to

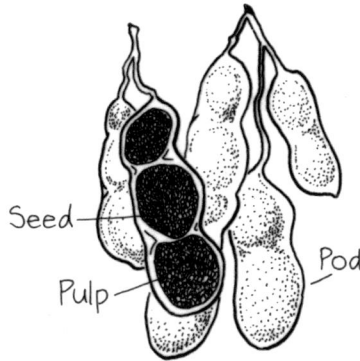

Figure 5.12 Tamarind pods

cover the tamarind "with sugar well clarified with eggs, till a clear transparent syrup is formed, which gives the fruit a much pleasanter flavour". He emphasized the medical uses of tamarind, mentioning only in passing that it was "frequently made an ingredient in punch, especially at sea, and never fails to open the body". Governor Nugent had "tamarind drink" in 1802, before dinner. Sullivan stewed green tamarinds, simmering them with cinnamon and "light brown or albion sugar".[144] In the twentieth century, tamarind was eaten most often fresh or formed into small balls, the pulp rolled together with sugar.

SORREL

The sorrel of Jamaica, *Hibiscus sabdariffa*, is unrelated to other plants of the same name except in the sense that "sorrel" indicates sourness. A native of the Old World tropics, *H. sabdariffa* probably came to Jamaica from Africa, and as early as 1750 it was called "Jamaica sorrel" in order to distinguish it from other plants that shared the label. In Jamaica, its best-known product is a drink commonly called "sorrel" and closely associated with Christmas celebrations, but it is also used to make jams, jellies and marmalades. These use the fruit of the sorrel plant, a shrubby annual growing to 1.5 metres, planted in August and reaching maturity in December or January. The parts of the fruit used are the succulent calyces, or sepals, that swell and become fleshy as the fruit matures, after the petals of the flower have fallen off, and surround the seed (Figure 5.13).

The drink was first noted by Sloane in 1707, but he thought it unwholesome because it turned sour within twenty-four hours. Other observers recognized that there were two types of sorrel, the red and the white, both of which were used, and that "sorrel cool-drink" could be made from either fresh or dried calyces. Some said citron was added to the mix. Long distinguished the red from the white variety but believed both were "cultivated in most gardens". To make sorrel drink, he said, "take the capsules or flower-leaves which are most juicy, and, adding twice their weight of double-refined sugar, put

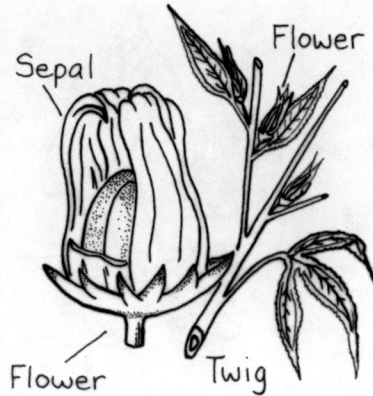

Figure 5.13 Sorrel flower

them without any water into a glass vessel, and place it in a sand-heat [surrounding the vessel with hot sand]; the digestion is carried on with a moderate heat, till the leaves are all dissolved, which soon happens, as they are soft and succulent".[145]

Modern recipes are based on steeping in boiling water. Clark, for example, recommended in 1945 steeping for twenty-four hours with ginger, orange peel and cloves. Ginger became the essential additive, with rum or wine an optional preservative; later writers sometimes also added pimento and rice grains to begin fermentation.

By the late twentieth century, sorrel had become a cookbook standard. As well as making the drink, sorrel was stewed for use in tarts, jams and jellies. In the 1980s, "reggae dot muffins" were made by adding to the muffin mixture sorrel stewed with sugar and ginger. The Best Food Idea for 1997 was awarded to sorrel chutney.[146] All of these uses of Jamaica sorrel had their roots firmly in the eighteenth century.

NATURALIZED APPLES AND PLUMS

A number of minor contributors to the range of fruit grown and consumed in Jamaica have their origins elsewhere but have come to seem a natural part of the creole landscape and food culture. Several of these are called, often interchangeably, "apples" and "plums", a usage derived from European comparators. For example, the "apple banana", smaller than the usual banana and with a delicate flavour, is used as a dessert fruit. The "apple mango" is so named for its shape. Neither is an apple: the terminology is not always helpful and can create further confusion.

Common in modern Jamaica is the otaheite apple, *Syzygium malaccense*, introduced by Bligh in 1793 and now growing wild as well as cultivated. Known outside Jamaica as "pomerac" or "Malay apple", the tree is universally thought beautiful, reaching twenty metres, with dense foliage and bright red flowers. It fruits twice a year, from February to March and again from June to July. The fruit is red- or pink-skinned, with crisp white flesh and a somewhat floury texture reminiscent of an apple, though some kinds are

Figure 5.14 Otaheite apple

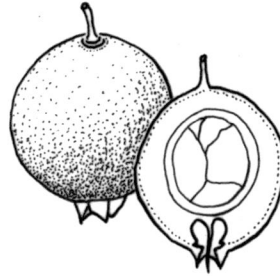

Figure 5.15 Roseapple

shaped more like a pear (Figure 5.14). All have a single large seed. In the past, some people have found the taste astringent and recommended stewing with half the fruit's weight in sugar. Modern Jamaicans generally eat the otaheite apple fresh and uncooked or made into a drink with ginger and sugar.[147]

Roseapple, *Syzygium jambos*, a native of the Indo-Malaysian and Pacific regions, is naturalized and grows wild in moist areas of Jamaica at elevations of up to one thousand metres, especially along streams. The tree grows to eighteen metres in height, with dense green foliage, and it fruits sporadically through the year. Its fruit is spherical, three to six centimetres in diameter and yellow, with a single large seed (Figure 5.15). Although often described as "insipid", it is generally eaten raw and only occasionally sweetened by making it into a preserve. Titford said the fruit "smells exactly like a rose, and the taste is much the same, with a faint sweetness".[148]

Other apples of the *Syzygium* genus include *S. cumini*, known in Jamaica as "jambolan" or "Java plum" (Figure 5.16). Although highly regarded in other countries and said to be "naturalized in Jamaica" by the 1860s, the tree is now uncommon and its fruit is rarely mentioned in modern cookbooks. Sullivan called the fruit "jamblangs" and described them as "large long narrow very dark blue black". She said they were "not very common but very much liked when they can be had". The fruit was "nice" eaten raw and "excellent" as a preserve.[149] The jambolan is often confused with the jimbling and bimbling, which Sullivan described separately. In his systematic botanical catalogue, Dennis Adams associated the jimbling with *Phyllanthus acidus* but offered as alternative common names "short jimbelin", "cheramina" and "Otaheite gooseberry". The last of these identifies the jimbling as another of the plants brought to Jamaica by Bligh in 1793, collected in Timor and perhaps ultimately from Brazil. It is rare in Jamaica and occurs most often in cultivation. The small, yellow fruit is very acid. Modern Jamaicans have called the jimbling "sour as hell" and only good stewed with lots of sugar. Confusingly, Sullivan described the jimbling as "blueish black . . . very stainy to the taste but fresh

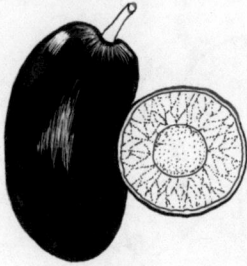

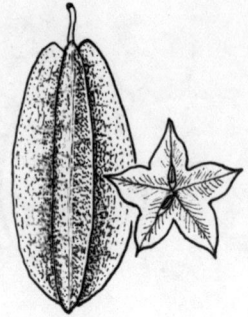

Figure 5.16 Jambolan   Figure 5.17 Bilimbi   Figure 5.18 Carambola

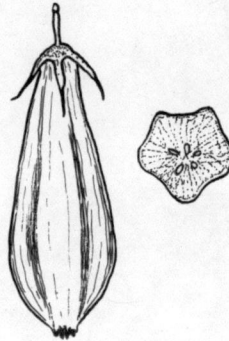

and juicy". She called the bimbling a "sort of berry, very acid indeed", and said that it was generally used as a preserve but needed to be soaked first in salt and water and cooked with "an immense amount of sugar". Adams does not include bimbling in his catalogue, but Cassidy and Le Page connect the bimbling plum with *Averrhoa bilimbi*, which Adams in turn relates to bilimbi and long jumbelin (Figure 5.17). Lunan claimed that the bilimbi came to Jamaica on the *Providence* in 1793, its fruit valued as a preserve or pickle.[150] However named, these fruits are not to be found in modern cookbooks or on the stalls of roadside vendors. Their sweeter relative, carambola, or star fruit (*Averrhoa carambola*), originally from Malaysia, is much more common (Figure 5.18).

Jew or June plum, *Spondias dulcis*, was reportedly introduced first to Jamaica in 1782 and again in 1793, probably from Tahiti. The "June" is a relatively recent alternative, and the names are now generally elided. The tree is cultivated and its yellow-green, duck-egg-sized fruits are readily available from vendors in town and country. Fibrous spines attached to the seed leave troublesome strings between the teeth when the fruit is eaten raw, so most often the flesh is cut away and processed into juices, wines, jams and pickles, or eaten stewed (Figure 5.19). Sullivan made no mention of the fruit, but it appeared regularly in cookbooks after 1970, most often called the June plum.[151]

Coolie plum, *Ziziphus mauritiana*, known also in Jamaica as "crab apple" and "jujube", is elsewhere called "Indian jujube" (Figure 5.20). Although this suggests that the tree came late to Jamaica, along with Indian indentured labourers in the later nineteenth century, the coolie plum was in fact widely distributed in West Africa before 1400 and used there for its fresh fruit and "flour".[152] In Jamaica, the plant is fully naturalized in the dry lowlands and quickly forms thickets in waste places. The acrid scent of flower and fruit hangs heavily on the air from September to December. Although the small brownish orange fruit is tart, it is eaten on the run, especially by children, much as "almonds" are stoned from their trees (*Terminalia catappa*) and the pods broken open. In the 1950s, coolie plums were eaten in quantity when in season, along with mangoes and guavas, but no recipes for their preparation and cooking have been found. Unlike the "Jew" of Jew plum, "coolie" remains firmly in currency.

Figure 5.19 June plum   Figure 5.20 Coolie plum

The pomegranate tree, *Punica granatum*, introduced by the Spanish from its Mediterranean home, grew abundantly in Jamaica by the middle of the seventeenth century. Lindsay said the larger variety of the tree produced fruit the inside of which could be separated and "put in large saucers, as part of our deserts". This, he said, gave "the appearance of a parcel of large granates and rubys thrown together on a dish", while the fruit's "delicious curran[t]-like taste and sharpness, is also by many very much coveted". Lindsay carefully illustrated the tree and fruit in 1762, though without revealing its insides (Plate 11). Titford said the pulp that surrounded the seeds of the pomegranate was "of a fine cooling nature" and tasted "of mixed acid and sweet".[153] Although its fruit could be made into drinks, wine and syrups (such as "grenadine"), its use in Jamaica seems to have been mostly ornamental.

FOREIGN FRUIT

Alongside the fruit of naturalized introduced plants, Jamaica has long imported certain varieties, either because the conditions for local cultivation have not existed or because the local product has not been able to compete with the foreign. Most of the imports have been natives of temperate climates. Their availability has varied considerably over time, with increased supplies following on innovations in processing and transportation technologies. Other fruits have struggled to establish a foothold in the island's agricultural system.

In his 1774 *History*, Long provided a list of "European and North American herbs, roots, and fruits, cultivated in this island, where, from their free vegetation, they may be considered as naturalized productions". The fruits included in this list were in fact few: apple, grape, mulberry Carolina, mulberry Virginia, peach, quince and strawberry. Only the first four of these also appeared in Long's general list of "dissert fruits" (in which the "apple" became the "apple of Europe"), and they were swamped by the tropical bounty. Although he claimed naturalization for these European and North American fruits, his notes on particular plants generally emphasized their ability to grow rather than their fruiting qualities. Thus, he said, mulberries thrive "but do not bear fruit when planted in the low-lands". Peaches "seldom fructify, nor does the fruit attain to any tolerable size; but it has all the fine flavour peculiar to it". John Stewart claimed in 1823 that "none of the European fruits arrive at perfection here, except grapes". James Phillippo thought the only exceptions to this general failure were "the apple and the strawberry, and these are degenerated both in size and flavour".[154]

Long's "apple of Europe" was generally called an "English apple" by the late nineteenth century, and was swamped in the twentieth by the "American apple". It was the rarity of these imported fruit before 1850 that made it easy for Jamaicans to happily apply the label "apple" to fruits lacking any botanical association with the various domesticated *Malus* species of the temperate world. Actual apple trees did struggle for existence in the cooler uplands of Jamaica in the eighteenth century but became woody and bore little fruit.[155] Few of their fruits reached the local markets. Sullivan did say, in 1893, that "English apples" were brought to town by the "mountain people", but they were small and acid. However, the good storing qualities of apples grown in temperate zones enabled trade, and the apples eaten by Jamaicans in all periods were almost all imported, whether fresh, dried or canned. In 1873 Charles Rampini saw higglers in Kingston with heaps of "rosy apples which the ice-ship had just brought over from America", but apple was more likely to come from imported tins. American apples arrived in quantity in the twentieth century, to peak in 1972, when they were banned. They reappeared in the early 1990s and soon became plentiful in markets and supermarkets, finding a place alongside the indigenous fruit of country roadside stalls.[156]

Peaches (*Prunus persica*) achieved popularity in Jamaica only after they became available in cans, beginning in the 1870s. Fresh and dried imports were always slight, regardless of technological possibilities. The peach tree did prosper somewhat better than the apple and the fruit continues to be harvested from trees growing in the hills above Kingston. These peaches are generally small and hard, good only for stewing but well flavoured. By the 1970s fresh local peaches could be purchased in supermarkets. Other species of *Prunus*, such as sweet cherry, plum, apricot and nectarine, reached Jamaica only in cans, preserved in syrup or, in the late twentieth century, fresh. The same applied to pears (*Pyrus communis* and *P. pyrifolia*). Titford had said definitively that "neither apples nor pears, (*Pyrus*) will grow in Jamaica". Long did claim that the quince (*Cydonia vulgaris*) prospered in the mountains and "bear[s] in as great perfection as in most parts of England",[157] but it never entered the diet and was neither grown locally nor imported, in any form.

Strawberries (*Fragaria* spp.) were much more successful. The first plants introduced to Jamaica were wild species that produced abundant fruit of "great perfection" in the early eighteenth century. The cultivated plant arose from a chance hybridization of two American species in France around 1750; the controlled creation of the modern commercial cultivars did not begin until the nineteenth century. In the 1870s, a Kingston higgler might offer "a little saucerful of Alpine strawberries, brought down that morning from the Newcastle hills". These competed with imported "preserved strawberries" packed in tins. In 1890 a daily special at Gardner's in Kingston was "Jamaica strawberries and custard cream", and another was "Jamaica strawberries fresh from the hills" or "Jamaica strawberries in ice cream". Sullivan offered a recipe for "English apples and wood strawberries", meaning "wild ones". She did note that "at Newcastle and at other high places in the hills the cultivated ones bear and grow to a fair size".[158] This was Sullivan's only recipe using "European" fruits, though the fruits were in fact the local product. She was unusual in offering even one. Modern Jamaican cookbooks ignore them completely.

Strawberries trickled (and occasionally briefly flooded) into local markets throughout the twentieth century, supplemented by imported canned fruit and jams.[159] Availability received a major boost in the 1970s, when Jamaica began to produce strawberries for export. Cultivation was concentrated in the uplands of Trelawny rather than the hills of St Andrew. As with bananas and pawpaws, "reject" fruit found its way into supermarkets at relatively low prices, those strawberries generally too large or oddly shaped to satisfy foreign consumers. But the strawberry remained absent from Jamaican cookbooks and from most tables, the fruit still being perceived as too foreign.

Raspberries fell into the same basket, occasionally grown in the hills but strictly exotic. Local blackberries also sometimes found their way to market. Sullivan noticed this but offered no "Jamaica" versions, saying they could be "prepared in accordance with receipts given in English books". Earlier in the nineteenth century, Lunan had reported the "blackberry bramble" common on ruinate, making "an excellent tart". Titford said explicitly that "neither the European currant nor gooseberry will grow in Jamaica".[160] Jamaican consumers were most likely to encounter all of these in cans, jams or imported prepared pastries.

The grapes eaten by Jamaicans similarly came most often from imported jars, bottles, cans or packets, whether fresh, preserved, dried as currants and raisins, or fermented as wine. When white grapes were imported by ship from New York in 1900, they were considered a delicacy.[161] Grapevines have, however, been grown with some success in Jamaica, and agriculturists persist in promoting the crop. The plant is said to thrive in the warm lowlands of the south coast, but commercial plantings have been rare. The European or wine grape, *Vitis vinifera*, was brought to the Caribbean by Columbus, but by the 1680s there were few vines remaining and it was thought "impossible to make wine without great quantities and great labour". It mattered little: although grapes had reached West Africa much earlier, they were not important in the diet.[162] In 1740 it was said Jamaica had "very good grapes; but they pull them before they are ripe; they only use them for eating". Long considered the red and white grapes of Jamaica more fleshy and less watery than the French fruit, but believed they "might doubtless produce a fine mellow wine, if cultivated in any sufficient extent, and by persons of competent skill". In addition to the European grape, there was the "Jamaica grape-vine" or "wild grape", *V. tiliifolia* (the water withe, discussed in the previous chapter), which produced "a large quantity of small, black grapes, of a rough taste, which would undoubtedly make an excellent red wine, under proper management". Lunan contended that Jamaica could use *V. vinifera* to make "as rich and mellow a wine, as in any part of the world", but when the Jamaican brewers Desnoes and Geddes started making wine in 1974, they used imported concentrates.[163]

In the long term, the most important wine imported into Jamaica was Madeira. Sloane said that Madeira wine was second only to water in the 1680s as a common drink in Jamaica, coming in both red and white varieties. It was regarded as "a cheap, simple table wine", but by the end of the eighteenth century, argues David Hancock, Madeira had been transformed by commercial initiative into "an expensive, exotic, status-laden, and highly-processed wine" made from unblended stock and fortified with brandy. The addition of brandy was designed to reduce the sweetness of the wine, but the planters of the West Indies demanded instead "dark, sweet wines" with less brandy, and sometimes specifically ordered "a quarter cask of red must [new wine or the unfermented juice as pressed from the grape] and another of brandy along with a pipe of unfortified wine so that it could be colored and strengthened to taste". In the early nineteenth century, a Morant Bay merchant advertised "old Madeira wine, of excellent quality" in pipes, hogsheads and quarter casks. Another had "pipes of best Madeira wine, which have been twelve months in the island, Sheffield and Young brand", and another, "Old London Particular Madeira wine, of the approved brand of Scott and Co.". In Kingston, William Hull offered "Madeira wine of the first quality", which, as proof of purity, he sold in casks "sealed black with his initials W.H.".[164] This early branding of product was soon to be applied to Jamaican rum, which had long since become the more popular drink.

PINEAPPLE

All of the fruits considered thus far were introduced or imported species, brought to Jamaica from the Old World, Asia and the Pacific, but most became so completely naturalized to Jamaica that they seem to belong in the vegetated landscape. Within that landscape, they joined indigenous plants and plants, such as the pineapple, brought to Jamaica from other regions of the neotropics by the first people.

The pineapple, *Ananas comosus*, derives its English name from the fruit's supposed resemblance to the cone of a pine tree. Jamaicans often call it "sweet pine" or simply "pine". It is a cultigen, separated from its wild, seedy progenitors, native to eastern South America and prehistorically selected for quality and size. Domestication produced a seedless fruit and vegetative propagation. The offshoots remain viable for weeks or months, thus facilitating dispersal. The pineapple spread through the Caribbean as a cultivated plant, following the movement of the first people. Pineapples were grown by the Taino "planted in rows like in a vineyard".[165]

A. comosus is a bromeliad. This enables it to channel rainwater to its root, but unlike most of its family, it lives on the ground rather than in trees. It requires relatively little water but can tolerate heavy rainfall so long as the drainage is good. In Jamaica, it has prospered best on brick mould soils, on the tops of raised ridges. Ripening is slow, taking up to a year or more, but can be induced to enable a year-round harvest. Commercial farming can produce yields of forty tonnes per hectare, but in Jamaica most pineapple cultivation is actually by small farmers. The pineapple could have, but never did, become a major agricultural export. The canning of whole pineapples began in the 1880s, but in the long term much of the canned product was sold in the domestic market.[166]

Modern Jamaican farmers producing for canning factories grow two varieties, the Cayenne ("Smooth Cayenne") and Red Spanish ("Cowboy"). It is the Cayenne, a clone virtually equivalent to the ancient domesticated cultivar, that dominates world production. The Cayenne variety originated in French Guiana and reached Jamaica only in 1870 via France, England and Florida. Other varieties grown in Jamaica in the 1980s included Queen, Abacaxi, Sugar Loaf or China, and Ripley. The last was attributed to a John Ripley, in 1764, and was known as "Ripley Pine" by the 1780s. Ripley had three hectares in pines in 1764 on his plantation near the site of the future August Town in St Andrew; and a later map identifies an area called "Ripley Pinery".[167] Earlier, in the 1740s, only three varieties were recognized, "the cabbage, the orange, and the sugar-loaf", the last being "the best esteem'd". Lindsay illustrated four distinctly different-shaped types in 1767 (Plate 12). The Sugar Loaf was sometimes called the "pyramidical", and a smaller green or yellow version the "Montserrat". A "smooth-leaved, or king pine" was distinguished from the "queen pine" and from the "bog-walk pine", which was compressed in form, with a green or yellow coat and white flesh, and "not so sweet or agreeable". The Sugar Loaf is still regarded as the "best eating variety". By 1890 Jamaica produced both "wild and cultivated pines . . . , bearing apples of varying flavor and juiciness, from the 'bastard' to the Ripley pine", the latter highly regarded. As happened elsewhere, once the pineapple became an item of export it took the name of its own place, so that the "Jamaica pineapple" eventually gained currency to stand beside the "Jamaica banana"; nonetheless, partly because the pineapple lacked the banana's visibility in overseas markets, its reputation was less.[168] This is curious, as the banana was long thought vastly inferior to the pineapple.

A 1657 English description declared the "pyne" of Jamaica "the best that ever was eat". Sloane found the pineapple used as dessert, "either raw, or when not yet ripe, candied, and is accounted the most delicious fruit these places, or the world affords, having the flavour of rasberries, strawberries, etc.". For himself, Sloane thought the pineapple "not to be so extremely pleasant, but too sower, setting the teeth on edge very speedily". In 1740 it was said that the pineapple of Jamaica, grown in both gardens and grounds, tasted "far richer" than that produced in the hothouses of England. Some claimed it tasted "of all sorts of fruit". In Europe, elaborate efforts were made to grow pineapples using glasshouses and furnaces because, declared one English writer in 1759, the fruit earned "the highest estimation . . . of all the vegetable productions intended for alimental food, with which the bounteous God of Nature hath supplied mankind".[169]

Jamaicans agree that the pineapple is "best eaten fresh". It has most often been consumed this way, either peeled with the eyes removed in spiral patterns or simply sliced into wedges with the skin intact. It was almost always a common and cheap item of street trade, or was harvested from the wild, only in the later twentieth century beginning to become more expensive. Today, sliced fresh pineapple is sold in plastic bags by sidewalk vendors.[170]

Fruit salads, which entered American and British cookbooks only after 1850 and which remained wrapped in quotation marks until about 1900, generally had pineapple as their base ingredient. Sullivan offered two versions, the first made from sliced pineapple, banana and orange, strewn with sugar, and a second, elaborate recipe that included pineapple, mango, naseberry, orange, banana, musk melon, watermelon, grated coconut, brandy, and curaçao or mareschino, iced. In this second fruit salad, some of the fruit was juiced and all of it was cut into a variety of shapes. The idea of the fruit salad seems to have evolved from the earlier "dish of fruit" that was often a centrepiece on wealthier English (and perhaps planter) tables, in which a whole pineapple crowned the pieces of fruit that had been formed into a small hill. Mrs Beeton recommended only this version in her classic guide of 1861, without any mention of fruit salad. Sullivan similarly recommended that the fruit salad should be piled up high, the juices poured over the lot rather than allowing them to soak in the modern manner. She also proposed an "ice" made with fresh pineapple, mashed and bruised in a mortar, frozen together with lime juice, sugar and water.[171]

As well as being eaten fresh, by itself or combined with other fruits, the pineapple provided the basis for a variety of drinks. Long claimed pineapple made "a very pleasant wine . . . sometimes mixed in cisterns that contain the liquor for rum, in order to communicate a more agreeable zest". In the late nineteenth century, a cool drink might consist of "Moselle and seltzer, flavoured with slices of pine-apple, and lumps of ice". Sullivan's recipe for "pine drink" used a whole fruit, sugar and water, and a bit of chewstick and ginger, guaranteeing that it would effervesce within a day after bottling.[172] More recent versions often use the peels, boiled up with sugar, cloves and dried orange peel, and diluted with water.

By the 1750s, the fruit was being used to make "pine tarts". Lewis, in 1816, served them on his Westmoreland plantation, saying "pine-apples make the best tarts that I ever tasted". Sullivan gave recipes for two ways of stewing (using "a full, but not ripe, black pine, or one of the common sort") and one for a jam (to be eaten with rice and coconut cream or made into tarts or a snow). Twentieth-century offerings included a stodgy steamed pudding, a cheese or fudge, and a milk sherbet (to be frozen in a refrigerator).[173] After Independence came the very popular pineapple upside-down cake, as well as pineapple gingerbread, frozen pineapple and coconut, pineapple fantasy (using Jamaica rum and Jamaica rum cream), pineapple surprise (a juice), pineapple delight (using rum and ice cream), fruit salad, soufflé, fritters, liqueur, chutney and chicken (stewed with seasonings, sauces and a small pineapple). Pineapple was also an essential in sweet-and-sour cookery, and was used as a dried fruit. Some of this pineapple came out of cans, but the fresh fruit remained the most desired.

PAWPAW

Jamaicans "wrongly" use the names "pawpaw" or "papaw" to refer to *Carica papaya*, though the word "papaya" has been partially adopted in recent years, particularly through the influence of the export trade. The pawpaw tree is a fast-growing evergreen herb, rising to as much as ten metres, but generally beginning to bear when only six months old and just two metres tall. Although varying considerably in size and shape, the fruit is typically globular and hollow, showing its relationship to the melon and pumpkin family. Descriptions of the flavour of pawpaw vary by variety, but it is generally said to be "sweet with strong fruity notes", which is not particularly helpful. The chemical compounds contributing to this perception are shared with a number of other tropical fruit, including guava, passion fruit, pineapple and soursop. Although the genus is native to Mesoamerica, most accounts argue that the tree did not reach the Caribbean islands, including Jamaica, until carried there by the Spanish in the early sixteenth century. By the eighteenth century, the "papaw tree" grew wild in many parts of Jamaica and was easily propagated from the seed.[174]

Lindsay, in 1766, produced finely detailed images of the "papaw tree" and its fruit, flower and seeds, dissected to show the vital stages of development (Plates 13–14). The grove of trees he depicted was of the taller variety, reaching seven metres, the large fruit hanging pendulously from the trunk. Lindsay saw the fruit as "a very choice and ready support" to the enslaved and to the "poor planter" but also "used at the tables of the best sort of people". However, he noted, "alas, when green and unripe, the fruit (as well as every part of the tree) is full of a milky corrosive juice" causing "distempers in the bowels" among those who ate them before ripe. Some people made "a rich and fragrant sweet meat" from the blossom, while others pickled the young fruit. When the fruit was ripe but still retained its "green colour and crispness", he said, some "have the rinds thinly chipp'd off, and served up in delicate tarts", or it might be "boil'd and used under boild meats and are much superior to either the carrot or turnep". Further, "if apple sawses are wanted, this makes so excellent a substitute, when well boild and mashed into a thin pulp and disguised with a little mixture of cinnamon and sharpened with a little lime juice, that the best European judges have been frequently deceived". In this state, the pawpaw could produce a substitute apple pie. When the fruit was riper, showing yellow in its colour, it was "fit to eat as a melon". It had to be prepared, said Lindsay, by scoring the skin and putting the "papaw" in the sun so the corrosive juices could drain or evaporate. In this state, "the pulp is by many esteem'd in a desert preferable to a musk melon, and it is then so cold and so void of its hot corrosive qualities, that the seeds are prudently eaten by many, being of a hot mustard-like nature, to prevent any disagreeable effects, as the hot rind of the cucumber when young is an antedote to the coolness of its inward juices". Fully ripe, the pawpaw took on a "deep redish yellow", Lindsay observed, "but when use'd for the table it has more of the green: and when cut melon ways, it also displays a hollow middle, beset with round seeds hanging by a yellow substance".[175]

Other eighteenth-century commentators said that when green, the fruit could be boiled like a squash or mixed with lime juice and sugar to make an "apple-sauce" to be eaten with geese or pork. Thistlewood served dinners in 1768 and 1771 that included "quarter of roast pork with paw paw sauce". He did not give his recipe for pawpaw sauce, but modern cookbooks offer "paw paw glaze" for baked ham, made from mashed pawpaw, orange juice and sugar, boiled to a light syrup. When the fruit was ripe and yellow, eighteenth-century cooks made a vinegar from the juice, said to be "not acider than some old cyder".[176]

Surprisingly, what is not clear is whether in the eighteenth century the ripe pawpaw was eaten raw and fresh. Lindsay recommended elaborate preparation, in order to avoid the corrosive juices. Browne was vague, saying only that "the fruit, when ripe, has a pleasant sweetish taste, and is much liked by many people". Long, however, said clearly that "the rounder fruit when ripe is boiled, and eaten with any kind of flesh meat, and is looked upon as perfectly wholesome; but eaten raw, it contains an acrid juice, very injurious to the intestines". He found proof of the hazard in his observation that "so penetrating is this fluid in the green unripe fruit, that, boiled with the hardest salt meat, it will render it perfectly soft and tender". Similarly, although John Dovaston recognized in the 1770s that the "papaw" made "excellent sweet meats", its greatest merit was that "the juice of the fruit being rubb'd upon a spit, will intenerate [tenderize] kill'd fowls". This was "a circumstance of great consequence in a climate where the heat renders whatever meats are attempted to be made tender by keeping, unfit for culinary purposes". Further, said Dovaston, when "boiled with salted beef it renders it easy of digestion".[177]

By the early nineteenth century, if not before, the fresh, raw, ripe fruit had gained favour. Lunan said that when ripe, pawpaw was eaten with pepper, sugar and salt. By the 1890s, Sullivan could write without mention of the boiling of pawpaw and declare that it was "cut and eaten like musk-melon only without the addition of sugar, pepper and salt". She added, however, that although "extremely sweet", the pawpaw was "not always a favourite fruit". Hyatt Verrill, in 1931, repeated the observation that the pawpaw "may be eaten plain, with salt, with salt and pepper or with sugar – depending upon one's personal taste". Some people never came to enjoy it, he said, and for others it was an acquired taste.[178]

In modern times the pawpaw has been eaten fresh and ripe, much like the mango or the avocado. In 1938 the pawpaw of Jamaica could be declared "the best in the world". Mary Gaunt, at Negril in 1932, enjoyed "paw-paw jam", saying it was "the most attractive jam it has ever been my good fortune to eat". Cookbooks of the later twentieth century offered recipes for pawpaw pie, crêpes, ice cream, sherbet and punch. Green pawpaw could replace ackee to make "paw paw and salt fish", the unripe fruit boiled along with the cod. Although the green fruit required boiling to tenderness before baking, stuffed "semi-ripe paw-paws" could go straight into the oven, filled with seasoned minced beef.[179] In spite of this elaboration of uses of the pawpaw, only the fruit seems ever to have been eaten in Jamaica, whereas in other parts of the world where the plant has been introduced, the flowers are also consumed.

Commercial production of pawpaw for export began only in the 1980s. Before then, the varieties grown in Jamaica were "outlandish types" used for processing and the local fresh fruit market. Solo cultivars, small and neatly shaped, were introduced in 1983. Their fruit was quickly accepted by Jamaican consumers, but the amount available to them depended on export surpluses, so local supply varied erratically. Processed pawpaw was used to make chutneys and nectars, or was candied for the local baking and confectionery industries. Some complained that the local market became driven by export tastes, the new small varieties lacking the aesthetic appeal of "those large luscious pawpaws, from which one could cut a generous curving slice, which was so attractive to look at, and equally delicious to taste".[180]

SUSUMBER

Unlike the fruits discussed thus far, susumber (*Solanum torvum*) is indigenous to Jamaica, having found its own way without the aid of human beings. However, neither susumber nor any other of the indigenous fruit-producing plants became staples of the Jamaican diet. Their indigeneity inserted them into the natural vegetation, and their abundance there meant active cultivation was rare for most of Jamaica's history. Only a handful are produced for export and often they do not travel well. Most are eaten fresh and uncooked, with little culinary preparation.

A small thorny bush, susumber grows in Jamaica both wild and in cultivation. It is also known as "gully bean" because of its typical sites of growth. It bears in abundance a bitter berry about one centimetre in diameter that has a refreshing sourish taste when eaten immature but that is sometimes poisonous (Figure 5.21). Adams identifies only *S. torvum* as susumber, whereas Cassidy and Le Page extend the class to *S. mammosum* (to which Adams attributes the common name "bachelor's pear"); Lunan listed two varieties.[181]

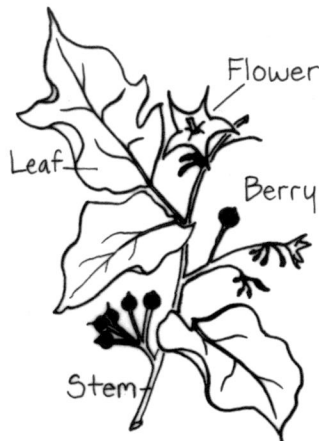

Figure 5.21 Susumber

Susumber is best known as substitute for ackee with saltfish. Sullivan offered a recipe for "salt fish and susumbers", cautioning, "one must be careful to choose the right kind of susumber as there are two sorts". She recommended using young berries, which gave the dish "a bitterish taste highly appreciated by the natives, but not palatable to everybody". Beckwith claimed that "salt cod cooked with the fruit of the ackee or with its substitute, the sosuma berry, is a favorite breakfast dish even upon the tables of the whites". In the 1930s, susumber was declared one of the most widely used vegetables in Jamaica. By the 1980s it could be termed "genuine 'roots' relish", because "its useage in Jamaican diet was once restricted to peasants too poor to buy meats and fish, so they used the berries" to stretch a meal.[182]

Modern cookbooks refer to the possibility of combining susumber berries with saltfish but provide no recipes. The occasional writer has proposed other dishes, such as "sussumber soup" (using eight dozen berries) and "sussumber pies" (using salt pork and saltfish). In 1986 the *Gleaner* challenged readers to introduce susumber to the cocktail circuit, and provided a recipe in which bright green, slightly soft berries were boiled with saltfish and crushed together, then fried with onion and scallion to make a paste that could be stored in a refrigerator and served on crackers or together with a lunch or dinner meal. By the 1990s, susumber was being combined with ackee and callaloo, and thought "very delicious in mackerel rundown". The leaves are boiled up to make a tea.[183]

SWEETSOP, SOURSOP, CUSTARD APPLE, CHERIMOYA

These four indigenous fruits belong to the *Annona* family. The sweetsop, or "sugar apple" (*A. squamosa*), is a roundish fruit, about the size of an apple, with a lumpy green skin enclosing a smooth white pulp and more than a dozen smooth hard seeds that equal the pulp in volume (Figure 5.22). The soursop, *A. muricata*, is larger, up to thirty centimetres long and weighing up to two kilograms, with a smoother skin (Figure 5.23). Its pulp is similar to that of the sweetsop, "white, cottony and slightly grainy in texture", but more acrid ("sour") and embedding a smaller proportion of seeds. It has a "unique and pleasant flavour" and "exotic fruit character", with fatty notes, derived largely from volatile esters. Custard apple, *A. reticulata*, is closer to the sweetsop, with a yellowish, grainy pulp, but a little larger and smoother (Figure 5.24). It is occasionally called "bullock's heart", "bullock's heart apple" or, like the sweetsop, "sugar apple". The fruit of the cherimoya, *A. cherimola*, is up to twenty centimetres long, with a whitish pulp (Figure 5.25). Verrill said the flavour of the cherimoya was "next to impossible to describe" but that the fruit needed to be eaten "fully ripe". It has been compared to vanilla ice cream but slightly acid.[184] The cherimoya is less common than its three close relatives, thriving only between one and two thousand metres' elevation, recalling its origins in the South American highlands. With the exception of the soursop, all of these prefer dry situations. The trees are shrubby and grow only to about six metres, so can be planted densely. The sweetsop bears between April and July, the others August to November.

Rind
Seed
Pulp

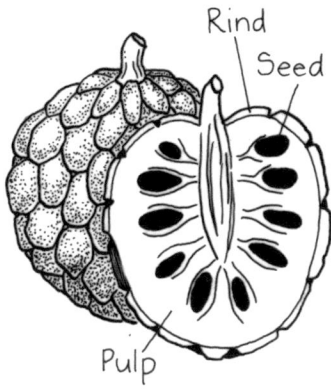

Figure 5.22 Sweetsop

Figure 5.23 Soursop

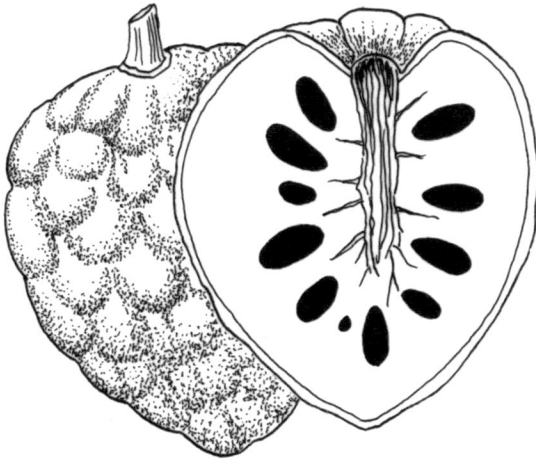

Figure 5.24 Custard apple

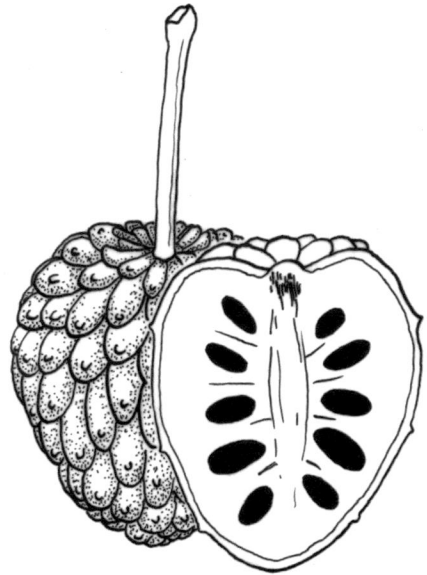

Figure 5.25 Cherimoya

Descriptions of gardens and grounds during slavery generally fail to notice the presence of sweetsop, soursop, custard apple or cherimoya. Dovaston said the soursop was "wholesome but seldom admitted to the tables of the elegant", suggesting an association with the poor. Opinion on the fruit was divided. While Titford considered the pulp of the soursop "white, juicy, soft, and of a sweet and acid taste mixed", he admitted that the fruit was "considered grateful and cooling by some, and by others compared to cotton dipped in vinegar". He himself found the sweetsop luscious and sweet, but declared the custard apple "frequently watery and without flavour". Lunan said in 1814 that the cherimoya was "esteemed a delicate fruit" and that the custard apple was "much esteemed by some people". The cherimoya, said Macfadyen, fell somewhere between the sweetsop and the custard apple, and was "one of the most delicious of the kind; there being a slight agreeable acidity mingled with a luscious sweetness". He found the custard apple to be common on the Liguanea Plain but rarely brought to market. It was "rather luscious to the taste". Gosse described the custard apple as "a custard inclosed in a rough skin bag, most lusciously sweet".[185]

Sullivan praised the custard apple over the "others of the same tribe", saying it had been called "the Jamaica Ice Cream". She thought it "most delicate", with a "rich creamy flavour". It required no sugar and was to be eaten with a spoon, like the sweetsop and cherimoya, "removing the seeds first" – a difficult operation. Moderns spit out the seeds as they eat and often forgo the spoon. Sullivan recommended soursop ice cream, a dish that has survived very well. She also suggested that soursop could be made into a drink, with sugar to sweeten; this juice or "punch" also remains popular. In the 1870s, cherimoya tart was regarded as a delicacy.[186] Otherwise, these fruits are eaten fresh and untransformed.

MAMMEE APPLE, MAMMEE SAPOTA, NASEBERRY

Mammee apple, *Mammea americana*, fruits on a large tree, up to eighteen metres in height, between June and August (Plate 1). The fruit is the size of a large grapefruit, with a hard skin and one to four large seeds in a yellow pulp (Figure 5.26). The ripe fruit is "perfectly luscious", tasting like an apricot, declared Long in 1774. Dovaston similarly thought that eaten raw, the "mammey" had "an apricot quality", and added that it was made into "exquisite" sweetmeats and "the best West India cordials". Titford said the mammee apple had a firm, yellow pulp, "of a peculiar flavour and sweetness, preferred by some to all other fruits". Never common to begin with, by the twentieth century it was rare, hardly mentioned in cookbooks. One reason for the rarity of the tree is that it takes almost fifty years to bear; it was a common saying that "they who plant the stone or seed of these trees, never live long enough to eat of their fruit".[187]

Mammee apple has often been confused with mammee sapota (*Pouteria sapota*), the fruit of which contained a darkish red, soft pulp with a sweet taste. It is eaten raw and sometimes called "natural marmalade" or "American marmalade". Barham called it "luscious eating".[188]

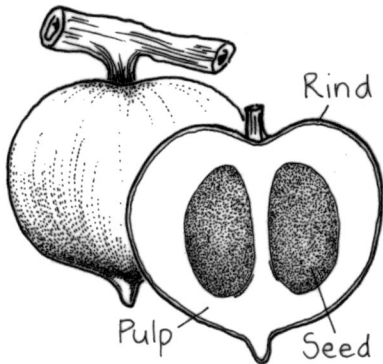

Figure 5.26 Mammee apple

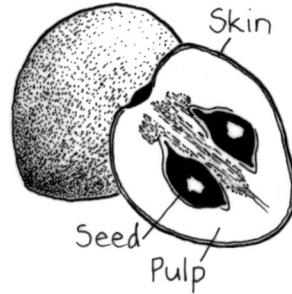

Figure 5.27 Naseberry

These two – mammee apple and mammee sapota – have also been confused with naseberry (*Manilkara zapota*), at first called "sapodilla" in Jamaica and still so named in most of the Caribbean. All three are indigenous to the American tropics. The naseberry has come to be the most popular of the group, sold in dishes from roadside stalls and frequently assessed "one of the best of all fruits". As early as 1657, an English writer said the "nispero" was "esteemed the best fruit in the Indies by the Spaniards".[189] Its golden brown flesh is contained in a smooth skin, and the fruit is ovoid or heart-shaped and up to six centimetres long (Figure 5.27). The tree stands up to fifteen metres and fruits year-round. Scattered broadly through the landscape, sometimes wild, sometimes cultivated, it grows best at altitudes below five hundred metres and is most common in the eastern and southern parishes. The naseberry seems not to have featured in the gardens of the enslaved but was probably collected from the wild.

Sullivan distinguished the naseberry from the "sapadilla", saying the latter was "very luscious" and identifying it as "a very large kind of naseberry". She said that the naseberry itself was "by many people very highly appreciated" and known as the "Jamaica Medlar", thus identifying the Spanish etymology of the transition from *sapodilla* to *naseberry*. The medlar is an ancient Old World apple that looks more like a plum and is famous for the fact that it is not edible until it has passed ripeness and entered decay. Lunan said that picked tree-ripe, the naseberry was "so acerb as to draw the mouth together, and cannot be eaten until some days till rotten as medlars". Others compared the taste to that of "a mellow ripe bergamot pear". Sullivan thought the naseberry very sweet, and recommended eating skin as well as flesh. Verrill said, "Within the brown and uninviting skin of the naseberry is a pale greenish or straw-colored pulp that, to my mind and the minds of many others, is the nearest thing to nectar that ever grew on trees." The naseberry could never be really overripe, he argued, and was actually "at its best when, to the uninitiated, it would appear to be rotten, when it is about ready to fall apart of its own weight".[190] The fruit must be picked by hand, as the green and the ripe naseberry appear very similar. Picked too early, the fruit is slow to ripen and never particularly palatable. Picked too late, it becomes soft and mushy. Storage is difficult, refrigeration unfriendly to the fruit's flavour.

GUAVA

Another indigenous fruit of Jamaica with broad popularity is guava, *Psidium guajava*, now grown throughout the tropics. Sometimes eaten fresh, especially by children, guava is also commonly stewed or processed into purée, paste, jelly, jam or "cheese". Hughes claimed in 1672 that the "goavo" was, when fully ripe, "by reason of a pretty picquancy it hath, very grateful [pleasing, refreshing] in taste; cooling and refreshing, and may safely be eaten, as other fruit, with moderation". By 1740 it was said that "guavers" were stewed like quinces or made into guava preserve or marmalade. Guava jelly was first so called early in the nineteenth century. Lunan observed that the marmalade was made from the rind, "and from the whole fruit a very fine jelly". Sullivan offered a recipe for stewed guava, to be eaten cold with milk, custard or coconut cream, or used to make guava pudding (which could alternatively be made with guava jelly).[191] Guava cheese remains popular, but the jelly has become the most famous product.

The shrubby, scraggly guava tree tolerates a wide range of soil and rainfall conditions, growing wild where other plants fail, but is sensitive to low temperatures and hence rare above 1,500 metres. Leslie saw them in 1739 as part of the "great plenty" of uncultivated fruits in Jamaica: "On the way-sides you may pick the star-apple, the guava, the citron, the mamme, and others." Wild guava are of poor quality and output; to harvest big juicy fruit it is necessary to select superior seedlings.[192] The fruit are about the size of a small orange, the trees flowering and fruiting sporadically throughout the year (Figure 5.28). Good bearing is established by the fourth year. Fruit flies are a pest, and a mass of worms can be hidden beneath an unblemished skin, so that biting into the fresh fruit is hazardous.

GUINEP

The fruit of the indigenous guinep tree, *Melicoccus bijugatus*, is always eaten ripe, fresh and uncooked. Guineps are small and round, with a green skin that separates easily from

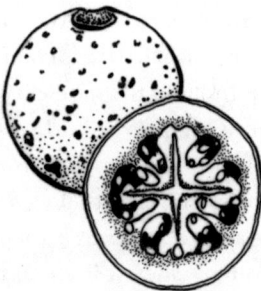

Figure 5.28 Guava

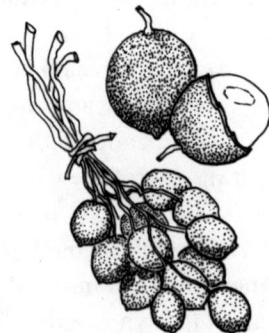

Figure 5.29 Guinep

the pulp when bitten into, like a lychee (Figure 5.29). The seed is large, about half the volume of the fruit. Lunan said the seed was "covered with a deliciously sweet-acid gelatinous substance, like the yolk of an egg . . . and is very agreeable to the taste". Normally, the seed is thrown away, but Sullivan claimed that when roasted, they were "somewhat similar to chestnuts".[193] Discard of the seeds by perambulatory consumers led to the tree's wide dispersal. Guinep trees, growing to sixteen metres in height, are now common along roadsides and in secondary woodland. Although contemporary accounts do not include the tree among those growing in the gardens and grounds of the enslaved, it does grow freely on abandoned plantation village sites. Today, the fruit is eaten opportunistically or as a snack when and where available. During the fruiting season, from May to December, guinep is sold in bunches by hawkers in town and country.

CHERRIES, PLUMS

Other indigenous fruits eaten on the run include varieties of "cherries" and "plums". The wild cherry, *Malphigia glabra*, is a shrub or tree bearing small (cherry-sized) fruit throughout the year. It is common in rough and rocky places, including thickets and pastures. The acerola cherry, *Malpighia punicifolia*, on the other hand, is rare in the wild but common in cultivation, generally growing only in shrubby form (Figure 5.30). Known also as "garden cherry", "Barbados cherry" and "West Indian cherry", the fruit is larger than that of the wild cherry and yellow or red when ripe, with a high vitamin C content. The "sweet fruity notes" of acerola are traced to volatile esters, similar to compounds found in passion fruit. As well as being eaten fresh from the tree – with an eye out for worms – acerola cherry is often juiced and made into jams and ice cream. In the eighteenth century it made "very agreeable tarts, and excellent jellies". Commercial planting has been attempted.[194]

Of the indigenous plums, some that were eaten in the eighteenth century are no longer commonly consumed. The damson plum or wild star apple, *Chrysophyllum oliviforme*, is a small tree common in scattered thickets growing on limestone. The fruit is "full of milk" and when ripe "sweet, gelatinous, with an agreeable clamminess, and is very much esteemed". The fruit of the coco plum, *Chrysobalanus icaco*, is larger, up to three centimetres in diameter, and turns from green to purple to black as it ripens. The fruit has often been described as insipid, but the nut with its large kernel was said to have a "delicious flavour" that overcame the pulp, eaten raw or preserved in sugar. The nut was considered a delicacy; it was offered preserved as a gift for friends overseas and as a souvenir for tourists by the 1880s. Long said the Spanish plum (*Spondias purpurea*, identified by Adams as "Jamaican plum") was "tolerably pleasant", and it has remained in use. Maiden plum, *Comocladia pinnatifolia*, native to Hispaniola and possibly introduced to Jamaica, is "eatable, though not inviting".[195] It is fairly common in woods growing on limestone. None of these appear in cookbooks.

Hogplum, *Spondias mombin*, an unlikely sounding candidate, is occasionally awarded a jelly recipe using its coarse fruit, and is sometimes seen for sale (Figure 5.31). The fruit

Figure 5.30 Acerola cherry

Figure 5.31 Hog plum

grows on a large shade tree common along roadsides and in field margins. Titford said the yellow hogplum had "a sweetish taste and mealy, not much esteemed by the whites".[196]

BREADNUT, COBNUT

An even bigger shade tree, buttressed and reaching thirty metres, is the indigenous breadnut, *Brosimum alicastrum* (Figure 5.32). In 1740, the ripe seed was assessed as "sweet and luscious", and as handy: "When green, if hurricanes happen to blow down their plantane walks, supply their place as food." Browne found the breadnut common in St James and St Elizabeth, making up one-third of the woods there. Often found growing in old fences and flourishing in woods on limestone, it remains common in the western parishes. According to Browne, "the fruit, boiled with salt-fish, pork, beef, or pickle, has been frequently the support of the negroes and poorer sort of white people, in times of scarcity; and proved a wholesome and not unpleasant food: when roasted, they eat something like our European chesnuts". The tree, however, fruits only sporadically, so the food security it could offer was limited. Lunan advocated planting the breadnut tree primarily as a source of timber for puncheon staves, but also as "a rich resource in times of scarcity, or famine, as food for the negroes". On one large property in St Elizabeth, the enslaved people were fed breadnuts from July to September. Others noted that, during slavery, "the kernels of the fruit afford an equally substantial diet to the negroes", without confining its use to hard times.[197] Sullivan thought that the roasted nuts were floury and "as delicious as chestnuts". They could be "served in the same way in a folded napkin at dessert". In the twentieth century, references to the breadnut were confined to the use of the evergreen leaves as fodder for cows and horses, particularly during drought.[198]

Less well known is the cobnut (*Omphalea triandra*), a tree growing to fifteen metres, and also known as "pig", "hog" or "pop nut". Lunan declared that, roasted, the cobnut was better-tasting than any chestnut. He thought the tree "might easily

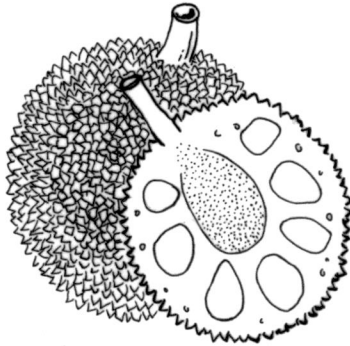

Figure 5.32 Breadnut

be cultivated from the seeds along intervals, or interspersed among pastures, to which they would not only prove ornamental, but useful, by furnishing abundance of their fruit, and affording an agreeable shade to cattle and other live stock".[199] The cobnut is a Jamaican endemic.

CASHEW

The cashew or cashewnut tree, *Anacardium occidentale*, grows to ten metres in height, with wide-spreading branches. Because it is hardy and drought-resistant, it can produce on soils too poor or too dry for many other crops, but it yields best on well-watered, well-drained sites. Indigenous to tropical America, the cashew was common throughout Jamaica in the eighteenth and nineteenth centuries, except in the high mountains; it thrived on the dry open plains. The tree flowers from January through June and fruits from May through August. From the flower, two edible parts develop, both of which are eaten. Attached to the tree is a pear-shaped "apple" six to ten centimetres long, and from this a kidney-shaped drupe extends a further three centimetres. It is the drupe that holds the nut (the true fruit) that has become an important article of commerce (Figure 5.33). The aromatic "cashew apple", the receptacle for the nut, actually appears after the nut and is a pseudo-fruit. It has a complex aroma.[200]

In 1768, Lindsay produced a fine composite picture showing a cashew tree in fruit, with one man climbing and another waiting below with a basket, as well as the flower and fruit at different stages of development and a cross-section of the nut and its kernel (Plate 15). Lindsay's contemporaries described the cashew as "a very juicy fruit", but sometimes added that although sweet and juicy, it left an astringent, acid sensation on the tongue. The fruit could be stewed or baked to make a kind of marmalade, "a very excellent preserve", put into rum or sliced to make "the beverage, known, in the country, by the name of cashew-punch". The juice produced "very good wine" and, said Macfadyen in 1837, "a spirit not inferior to rum or brandy, possessed of diuretic

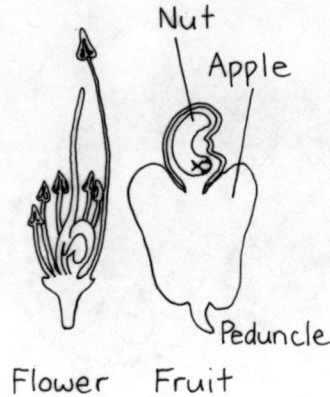

Figure 5.33 Cashew nut and apple

properties, may be obtained by distillation". Sullivan gave a recipe for stewed cashews, the seeds extracted and the fruit boiled pound for pound with sugar and some cinnamon and spices, the juice coming down to the consistency of treacle. Although tart and acidic, the apple is rich in vitamin C and is still stewed and used to make candied preserves, wines and cordials.[201]

The cashew nut is rich in oil and protein. Most often, fallen nuts are collected, sun-dried for several days to reduce the skin-blistering oil in the shell, roasted and cracked open by hand to extract the seed or kernel. The kernel of the nut, said Titford, "when green, is delicate as a walnut, and is also eaten roasted when ripe". At that stage of ripeness, it was full of "sweet milky juice" and could be used in puddings or ground with cacao to make "an excellent chocolate". The roasted kernel was said to be good for the memory, so that a preparation made from it was known as *confection des sages*.[202] Sullivan recommended roasting and salting, but later writers preferred pounding the roasted kernels to make a sauce, crushing them to stuff green pawpaw or pumpkin, and sprinkling them on this and that. In the 1980s it was said that few Jamaicans included cashews in their cooking, though they were high in protein and gave "fine flavour to meat dishes, fruit salads and certain baked products". Recipes were offered for chicken with cashews, a nutty fruit cup for dessert and peanut cookies with a whole cashew sunk in the top.[203] Most Jamaicans now know cashew mainly as the roasted, salted nut commonly sold in small plastic bags along roadsides, especially on the south side of the island.

STAR APPLE

A regular in the modern Jamaican cookbook is the star apple (*Chrysophyllum cainito*), partly because of the beauty of the tree and its fruit, but more obviously because it is the base ingredient of the dish "matrimony". Cassidy, in 1961, called matrimony "perhaps the best known" of Jamaica's fruit desserts. The star apple is an evergreen indigenous to the Greater Antilles; the tree grows to twenty metres, with leaves that are a glossy green on their upper sides and golden underneath (Plate 1). It is common along the sides of fields and tracks. From November to March, it produces globe-shaped fruit

Figure 5.34 Star apple fruit

five to eight centimetres in diameter, with a rich purple or light green glossy skin that contains a sticky latex (Figure 5.34). The pulpy flesh is a soft purple-white, sweet-flavoured, juicy and jelly-like.[204] The seeds and surrounding pulp create, when sliced across, the fruit's eponymous star .

Matrimony has been described as a "most sensuously smooth dessert", appreciated for its "texture and taste". A simple recipe for matrimony, published in the 1957 *Farmer's Food Manual*, used three star apples, two oranges, two teaspoons of sugar and four table-spoons of cream. The pulp of the star apples was scooped out and combined with sections from the peeled oranges, mixed with the cream and sugar, and chilled. In the 1960s matrimony was sometimes served with whipped cream. Jill Roberts proposed, in 1987, four star apples, three oranges, 150 millilitres of cream or evaporated milk, a tablespoon of condensed milk, and another of white rum. Others have used only star apples, oranges, condensed milk and nutmeg.[205]

How did "matrimony" get its name, in an island long known for its low marriage rate? Sullivan did not use the name in 1893, but she did offer a recipe for "oranges and star apples" and noted that the dish was "called 'strawberries and cream'". However, although Sullivan mentioned cream, there was nothing milky in her recipe to match the modern versions. Her method involved scooping the pulp of star apples into a tumbler, squeezing orange juice over it, adding a little sugar, nutmeg and sherry, and mixing it all together. This recipe was known much earlier; Titford, in 1811, said of the star apple's pulp that it was "of a rich, clammy, sweet taste, and mixed with orange juice, resembles strawberries and cream".[206] For Titford and Sullivan, the creaminess of the dish was supplied by the pulp of the star apple itself.

The earliest reference to matrimony in the *Dictionary of Jamaican English* is from 1920, and the first uses in the *Gleaner* also come from the 1920s, when it described "a delicious concoction . . . made up of the juice of the orange with the pulp of the star apple to which is added ice, sugar, nutmeg, sometimes milk, and what not". The *Oxford English Dictionary* offers *matrimony* as a broader slang term for the "mixture of two comestibles or beverages", generally an "injudicious" combination, with a first citation from 1813. It also refers to a Jamaican example published in 1893, found in the autobiography of English traveller Marianne North, who visited Jamaica in 1871 and 1872. North found the ripe star apple "filled with blancmange flavoured with black currants". While in the hills above Port Antonio, she recalled, with friends of her landlady, a brown woman, "gave us glasses of 'matrimony', a delicious compound made of star-apple, sugar and the juice of Seville oranges, like strawberry cream". This was close to Sullivan's recipe, with a tarter taste than the modern, creamy version. As late as 1946, matrimony could be described as simply star apple "mixed with sour orange". Thus the creamy version, with its sweetened condensed milk, seems to have become dominant only after about 1950, taking away some of the bite of the earlier notion of injudicious partnership and pandering to the Jamaican taste for sweetness. In spite of its regular appearance in cookbooks, by the 1990s it was said that matrimony, formerly a much-loved after-Sunday-dinner sweet beverage, had become obsolete and was unknown to the young.[207]

GRANADILLA, SWEET-CUP, GOLDEN APPLE, PASSION FRUIT

The role of fences and field margins in nurturing fruit trees is an important theme, the trees sometimes selected for their merits as living fencing materials and other times simply finding shade and protection from molestation. This applies to naturalized trees and shrubs as much as to indigenous fruits, but the latter have generally been the ones most in need of secure niches in which to survive and prosper. Over these fences and marginal barriers, full of large as well as small trees, climbing and twining vines have produced yet another layer of potential food resources. Of the latter, the *Passifloraceae* family has contributed most. Granadilla (*P. ligularis*), sweet-cup (*P. maliformis*), golden apple (*P. laurifolia*) and passion fruit (*P. edulis*) are the leading members, all of them indigenous and having their roots in South America, and varying only in size and taste. Contained within a tough skin, their pulp and seeds form a sweet mass, mostly eaten fresh, but occasionally, in more recent times, made into a drink or, in the past, mixed with nutmeg and sherry.[208]

Lindsay said the granadilla was a favourite vine, cultivated for its foliage, aroma and "agreeable fruit". His illustration, drawn in 1761, showed it in flower and in fruit, rambling over a wooden frame, and with a fruit cut to expose its seeds and pulp (Plate 16). He explained that the fruit had a thick rind, "forming a large hollow or opening in which is contained a quantity of an agreeable cooling jelly". Some thought the pulp of the granadilla "the greatest dainty in the fruit kind; while others form its thick pulpy rind into tarts, pies, in imitation of the English apple". Lindsay thought "the sweet and the tart . . . very equally joined together", but said some people added grated sugar to the fruit if the jelly was not fully ripe. Some commentators noted that when the vine died it left "an excellent yam at its root", but how this was cooked is unknown. [209]

Lewis, writing in 1816, was even more effusive, saying the granadilla had "the most singular and exquisite flavour, perhaps", of all the fruit of Jamaica. It had to be "suffered to hang till it is dead ripe, when it is scarcely any thing except juice and seeds, which can only be eaten with a spoon". In this state it needed sugar, said Lewis, though "the acid is truly delicious" and the fruit combined "the different tastes of almost all other fruits, and has, at the same time, a very strong flavour of wine". The English traveller North said that the "granadilla passion-flower" was "most delicious, and almost more than one person can eat at a time". She observed, "Jamaica people scoop out all the seeds and juice, and stir it up in a large tumbler with ice and sugar, and nothing can be better for late breakfast." Sir Sibbald David Scott, at Newcastle in 1876, had "a refreshing drink of granadilla seed (like those in the inside of a melon or passion-flower) mixed up with sherry". Sullivan recommended stewing the outer pulp of the peeled fruit, to make tarts and fritters. It could be purchased as a preserve, for Christmas gifts.[210]

Perhaps because they came to be considered too seedy, too short on substance, however sweet they were, these formerly appreciated fruits, most notably the granadilla, were broadly neglected or forgotten in the twentieth century, hardly ever gaining a place in cookbooks – not even as a supplementary ingredient – and scarce in the market.

TOMATO

Jamaica has a close association with the tomato, and it is indeed probable that it was in Jamaica that the fruit was first known as "tomato", a corruption of the Aztec *tomatl* and the Spanish *tomate*. English-language speakers had called the fruit "love apple" until Sloane found what he called the "tomato berry" growing wild around Spanish Town. Barham noted that some people talked of "tomatoes", but he attributed the term "love-apples" to the Spanish, who were said to believe the tomato to be an aphrodisiac and who used the fruit in sauces and gravies "because the juice, as they say, is as good as any gravy, and so by its richness warms the blood". Only in the second half of the eighteenth century did "tomato" begin to become common.[211]

If the word *tomato* originated in Jamaica, the plant itself, *Lycopersicon esculentum*, occurs wild in various parts of tropical America and evolved from the cherry tomato. It was probably domesticated in Mexico, the straggling wild plant trained to grow into a tall bush or vine up to two metres, supported by a stake and bearing many fruit. Exactly how the tomato reached Jamaica is uncertain, but it was probably from the Caribbean that it was introduced to North America in the late eighteenth century. The fruit is a fleshy berry, varied in colour and shape. Long said of the "tomato" that "these berries are very large, compressed at both ends, and deeply furrowed all over the sides, filled with a pulpy juice".[212] The taste of the tomato depends on the interaction of sugars, acids and volatiles. The fruit contains tomatine, an alkaloid that can be toxic to humans but decreases as the fruit ripens, and it may have been the eating of unripe tomato that gave it an early reputation as poisonous among North Americans and Europeans.

Down to the early twentieth century, fresh tomato seems to have been relatively rare in Jamaica. Thus it could be claimed in 1938 that, previously, "tomatoes were rated among the luxuries of life: most people only served them on the family table on high days and holidays". Canned "fresh" tomatoes were imported, and "American tomatoes" could be bought in Kingston even in the depths of the Depression. Shortly before the labour disturbances of 1938, "crates, barrows and baskets of tomatoes" were hawked on the streets for one penny per pound (454 grams), and the fruit was being "made into chutneys, jams and jellies, butters and marmalades, and used as a filling for tarts and pies".[213] Local production increased to supply the market, but in the 1990s free trade agreements encouraged further imports of fresh tomatoes and, as one Clarendon farmer complained, "the foreign tomato was mostly bigger and prettier than the local, so the housewife dem just go for the prettier thing". Others bemoaned the demise of "those glorious oxheart tomatoes", the "large juicy, incomparably flavoured tomatoes [that] could be thickly sliced to serve about four people". The oxheart was replaced by the "salad" tomato and later, around 1970, by the "plummy", only to return to the market in the middle of the 1990s.[214] As is well known, improvement of the tomato produced a fruit smoother, rounder and more resistant to damage by handling, but also one generally considered inferior in taste (Figure 5.35).

Modern Jamaicans often use the word "salad" as a synonym for tomato. Consumption of the fruit fresh ripe and raw is no doubt the most ancient way of eating tomato, either bitten into whole in the wild or sliced in circular cross-sections, as is more common now. Recipes for the cooking of tomatoes were rare before the later nineteenth century; when it came to cooking, the fruit was seen only as an appropriate ingredient to give colour and flavour to gravies, sauces and soups, or to fry with eggs. Sullivan, however, gave two recipes for stewed "tree-tomato", the skin scalded and removed, and the fruit boiled up with plenty of sugar. Another possibility was "tree-tomato dolce", made by steaming ripe fruit (with the pulp and seeds removed), rubbing them through a sieve and adding an equal weight of sugar. Sullivan also proposed a "sweet pickle of green tomatoes".[215]

Tomato sauce (ketchup) became a commercial product in the second half of the nineteenth century, initially using fruit rejected for canning. A small number of American companies, led by Heinz, quickly came to dominate, though homemade versions persisted. Tomato sauce had the great advantage of keeping well without refrigeration.

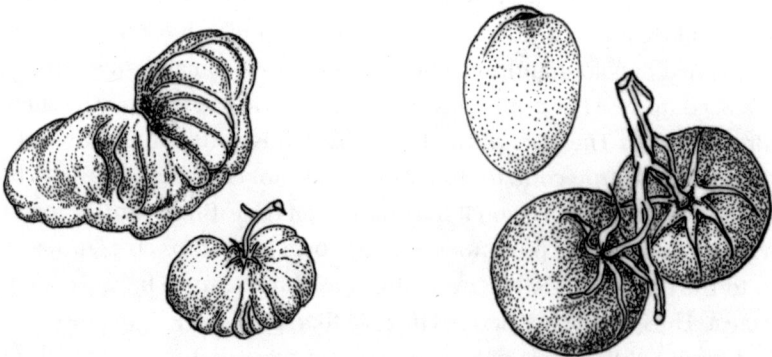

Figure 5.35 Tomato varieties: ancient, oxheart, salad and plummy

It also seemed to supply an elemental splash of redness that served as a "blood substitute" while at the same time satisfying a supposed universal taste for the sweet, combined with a tangy saltiness.[216] This was a combination that seemed well suited to the Jamaican palate, and ketchup became an item of import. Local manufacturers did their best to compete but were most successful when they followed the Jamaican taste for spice and pepper, reduced the proportion of tomato, and created varieties such as Pickapeppa and less refined pepper sauces.

CHOCHO, CERASEE

The chocho is a cucurbit, but indigenous rather than introduced and unusual in the structure of its fruit. The chocho vine, *Sechium edule*, is a native of tropical America that was cultivated by the Taino. A vigorous climber, the chocho grew best in "the cooler mountains, where the vines are always observed to run and spread very much". Occasionally, down to the twentieth century, Jamaicans call chocho "chota". This relates to the Spanish *chayote*, itself probably a corruption of the Aztec *chayotl*, and points to the Central American origin of the plant.[217] Elsewhere the chocho has been called, among other names, "choko" and "christophene". Unlike most cucurbits, such as the pumpkin or gourd, the pear-shaped fruit of the chocho contains a single flat seed within the centre of its whitish flesh (Figure 5.36). Rich in sugars and starch, the fruit also stores well, lasting six weeks or more. Even more highly prized were the seeds, which were roasted, and it is possible that the cucurbits were first domesticated for their seeds rather than their flesh.[218]

The people who came after the Taino, having a wider range of choice, sometimes looked down on the chocho, considering it a humble, essentially tasteless and watery fruit. Browne, for example, thought the chocho "too insipid to be much liked", though he said it was "sometimes boiled, and served up at table by way of green, in which state it is generally looked upon as wholesome and refreshing". Long was more positive but noted that the fruit was used to fatten hogs, generally a bad omen for appreciation as human food. It was, he thought, "much improved by lime juice, by salt, or spicy ingredients".[219]

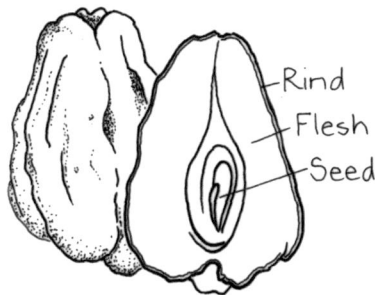

Figure 5.36 Chocho

Chocho's reputation as a substitute for the English or American apple stretches back to the eighteenth century. Lunan believed that "mixed with lime juice it is a good succedaneum [substitute] for apple sauce". Further, he said, "the seeds, or hearts, are very good if taken out after the fruit is boiled and fried with butter". He also found a use for the root of the old vine, saying it was "something like a yam, and on being boiled or roasted, is farinaceous and wholesome". Sullivan too suggested that the seeds could be boiled tender, and served on toast with anchovy and a white sauce. Her recipe for "cho-cho savory" saw the boiled fruit cut in fingers and placed on anchovy toast, and very hot coconut cream poured over the lot.[220]

In 1880 the Jamaica Manufacturing Company advertised for "chotas", offering fair prices for "sound and freshly picked" fruit. Sullivan promoted the chocho as a "very useful vegetable", saying "the natives are very partial to it, it being, as they say, 'so cooling'". It was used in soups, stews, puddings and tarts, but also good simply boiled and served with butter or a white sauce, or mashed with butter and black pepper. By boiling the fruit with cloves and cinnamon or mixing it with sugar, nutmeg and lime juice, puddings acquired "the *apple taste*".[221]

By the 1980s the humble chocho had become moderately expensive but was called "Jamaica's most versatile plant", substituting for the then-banned American apples in apple pie or flavoured to imitate pear halves, and making "lunch for the toothless". Another possibility was "spicy chocho sauce", made by stirring and heating grated chocho and milk into a roux, and, when the roux had thickened, adding minced garlic, onion or scallion, tomatoes and parsley, and seasoning with salt and pepper. This sauce could be poured over baked savoury dishes. The fruit could also be stuffed with seasoned bully beef and baked in the oven. Although some still contended that the chocho was "flavourless", cooks were encouraged to bake and pickle it as well as using it to replace expensive apples and strawberries in pies and tarts.[222]

Another important indigenous climber amidst the mass of vines and bushes covering fences, walls and bushes was cerasee (*Momordica charantia*), a cucurbit common throughout the tropics. In Jamaica, its fruit was always valued primarily as a herbal tea rather than a food. The orange-yellow fruit is rich in vitamin C and can be used as a vegetable or in pickles and curries, and the shoots and young leaves can be cooked as spinach. Salt is added to reduce the bitterness of the taste. Cerasee tea, on the other hand, made from the aerial parts of the plant, is valued for exactly this bitterness. Lindsay in the 1760s called cerasee a "vegitable" and mentioned only the use of the green leaves in pottages, with a bitter but not unpleasant taste. His beautiful image of the fruit was produced in 1768 (Plate 17). Later writers often wondered at its popularity, but by the 1990s it was said that "many persons are now using the green cerasee as a vegetable, cooked with meat or fish".[223]

PUMPKIN, SQUASH

Pumpkins, squashes, marrows and gourds present a botanical puzzle as complex as the intertwined vines of a vegetable patch, all of them spreading out from their origins in

Mexico and other Central American areas. *Cucurbita pepo* exists in Jamaica as "field pumpkin", "ornamental gourd" and "vegetable marrow", but is known elsewhere as "winter" or "summer squash". *C. maxima* is described by Adams as "Melon Pumpkin (English), Autumn and Winter Squash (American)" and by others as including "Winter Squash, Turban Squash, Marrow, Pumpkin". *C. moschata* is a pie pumpkin, sometimes confused with the winter squash or pumpkin, *C. mixta*.[224]

In eighteenth- and nineteenth-century Jamaica, pumpkin was "much cultivated as an article of food, boiled, or made into a pie", and its "fruit" was declared "in universal esteem at every table". By the twentieth century, the pumpkin was less often thought of as a fruit and more often as a vegetable, suggesting it was good only for savoury dishes. Jamaicans were said to prefer "deeply yellow varieties" because these had superior iron content to those with "pale yellow flesh". It was also commonly believed that the iron was concentrated in the skin, so soups were cooked with the skin on and it was removed before serving. Pumpkin was a vital element in "Saturday soup", along with fresh beef bone, carrot, turnip, chocho, okra, yellow yam, scallion and Scotch bonnet pepper. This soup was called traditional but was actually relatively modern. Sullivan's 1893 recipe for pumpkin soup consisted mostly of pumpkin, boiled with some fresh soup meat, black pepper and thyme, and "if liked a small bit of salt pork or salt beef, or else salt to taste". This "particularly palatable" soup was to be served strained and "curried". One hundred years later, an unusual "country-style pumpkin soup" described by Ralph Jacobs used Vienna sausages in place of beef or chicken. It depended on a "powdery dry" pumpkin, puréed and cooked with garlic, scallion, thyme and pimento until the pumpkin was dissolved and the liquid thick. Irish potato was added and cooked until nearly tender, then a packet of chicken noodle soup mix and, when everything else was done, the sausages, sliced into small sections.[225]

Sullivan said that "a favourite dish among the natives" was pumpkin and rice, made by boiling a large piece of pumpkin with rice, then mixing it with chopped scallion, tomatoes, pepper, butter and some diced salt pork. The "natives", she reported, preferred to boil their pumpkin in large "junks" with a dash of black pepper over it, rather than the "more refined way" – mashed with butter, salt and pepper, and shaped in a dish. Pumpkin could also be made into fritters or sweet tarts, a pie or a pudding, she said. Not much had changed by the end of the twentieth century, when it was said pumpkin could be creamed, baked or cooked with rice, made into a salad or a pie with soaked fruits, as well as making the traditional soup.[226]

Unlike the ubiquitous pumpkin, squash is not much heard of in Jamaican food history, though in the eighteenth century it was said to be common, eaten boiled.[227]

CALABASH

The common calabash tree of Jamaica, *Crescentia cujete*, grows to about ten metres and bears its round gourd-shaped fruit on trunk and branches (Plate 2). Browne and more recent writers have claimed that the pulp of the fruit was sometimes eaten as a vegetable or made into a pickle. Long said that the "Negroes" not only used the fruit of the calabash tree to make utensils, but also steeped its seeds in water to make "a tart, cooling beverage". John Rashford casts doubt on this pattern of reported consumption, contending that the "fetid odour and . . . unsavoury taste" of calabash pulp and seeds made it unattractive, as indeed Browne conceded. Sullivan did give a recipe for "calabash pickle", advising the use of young calabashes, as small as possible. These were cut in two and set in "strong salt and water" for a day, then steeped in vinegar boiled with pimento.[228]

PIMENTO

Pimento, known also as "allspice" and "Jamaica pepper", is said to combine the flavours of clove, cinnamon, nutmeg, juniper and pepper, offering an unequalled flavouring for many foods. The tree that produces the berries is a member of the Myrtaceae family, closely related to the bay and to cloves. There is a rare wild pimento, *Pimenta jamaicensis*, but the tree that bears the pimento or allspice used as food is *P. dioica*. An evergreen, *P. dioica* grows to fifteen metres, with a shiny, pale brown bark and dark green leaves that are sometimes used to make pimento-leaf oil. Flowering occurs at widely different seasons in different regions of Jamaica, the berry taking three or more months to mature, depending on weather conditions. These conditions also affect the time of harvest and the quantity of berries produced. The fruit is a drupe, similar to a cherry but smaller, with a round berry about five millimetres in diameter (Figure 5.37). The berry contains pulp and two seeds separated by a thin membrane. It is harvested when mature, but in a "green" state, before ripening. Harvesting has generally been done by simply tearing off the fruited twigs and branches, the berries dried on a barbecue for about ten days. Properly cured, the dried berries darken and shrink, the seeds rattling. This gives them a long storage life, increasing their value as a spice by enabling both use over the year and transport over long distances in trade.[229]

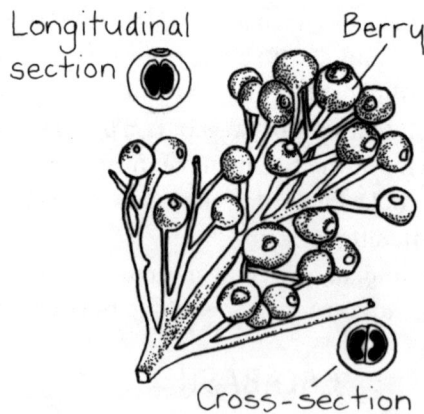

Figure 5.37 Pimento

The Spanish found the pimento tree growing in Jamaica when they first came to the island, and its name derives from the Spanish *pimienta*, or "pepper". The fruit was used by the Taino. The tree also occurred in Cuba and Mexico, but it appears that Jamaica is the only place in which pimento has been produced continuously since the beginning of the sixteenth century. Although the plant has been dispersed widely around the world, in no other place does it bear as plentifully or possess the particular quality it achieves in the special niches it occupies in the Jamaican environment. Indeed, for many years, Jamaica was the sole significant commercial producer of pimento, hence its special association with the island.[230]

The pimento was called "Jamaica pepper" as early as the 1670s. An even earlier description, from 1657, began its list of Jamaican fruits with the pimento, calling it "pepper smelling like cloves". Richard Blome thought pimento "very aromatical, and of a curious gousto [flavour], having the mixt taste of divers spices" but more particularly "the exact taste both of cinnamon and cloves". Long said pimento was "deservedly esteemed the most temperate, mild, and innocent, of all the common spices, and fit to come into more general use, instead of the Eastern commodities of this kind, which it far surpasses, by promoting digestion, attenuating strong humours, moderately warming and fortifying the stomach, expelling wind, and doing other friendly offices to the bowels". Stewart, on the other hand, claimed that the enslaved people never used pimento in their food, preferring "native pepper".[231]

In modern cookery, pimento is thrown whole into many dishes, to provide flavour. Some people chew and swallow the cooked berries, but most push them to the side of the plate. In 1987 the Jamaica Pimento Association produced a booklet of recipes to promote the berry's ability to "convert tasteless and unpalatable foods into delightful flavours and therefore, give satisfaction to human needs". Addressing in particular the market outside Jamaica, the booklet recommended pimento for flavouring fish, poultry, beef, ham, hamburgers, sausages, soups, stews, sauces, gravies, pickles and marinades, as well as cakes and desserts. The fruit remains fundamental to the liqueur called "pimento dram".[232]

ANATTO

The pods of the once-common shrubby tree *Bixa orellana* contain, when ripe, dark orange-red berries. The berries' waxy coating was used for colouring food and drinks. A native of the region from Mexico to Brazil, the tree probably came to Jamaica with the Taino. At the beginning of the eighteenth century, anatto was being used most often as a dye and as a medicine, but it was also added to chocolate, sauces, broths and soups, giving "a saffron colour, and a pleasant taste". The berries were steeped in hot water until the coating, or "red *farina*", could easily be washed off by hand and allowed to settle. The sediment was dried in the shade and rolled into balls or cakes, which, when perfectly dry and firm, were ready for market. The powder was said to be "cooling" and "cordial". Anatto had lost favour as a dye by the middle of the eighteenth century, and it increasingly coloured only foods, including butter and cheese. More distinctively Jamaican applications include the use of anatto to colour and flavour dishes such as patties and pakassa.[233]

PEPPER

Species of *Capsicum* were among the first plants cultivated in the Americas, including the West Indies, before the coming of Europeans. The wild relatives of these cultivated plants were broadly distributed, and it is most probable that they were domesticated independently in different places. Whereas wild peppers bear small, red, pungent fruit in various shapes, sticking up erect and easily removed by the birds that dispersed the seed, Amerindian domestication and selection produced plants with larger fruit, pendant rather than erect, and less easily removed by birds.[234] Peppers played a vital role in the food culture of the Taino, who appreciated them for their pungency. The heat of hot peppers comes from the alkaloid capsaicin, which contributes both to complex vanilla-like flavours and fragrance and to a burning sensation, by acting on the pain receptors of mouth and throat. After Columbus, peppers quickly became widely dispersed around the world; their origin in the Americas was often forgotten as the plants became naturalized and easily out-competed indigenous pungent rivals.

In English, capsicums of any variety were known in the late seventeenth century as "cod-pepper", and thus clearly distinguished from "Jamaica pepper", or pimento. Hughes distinguished two types of "red pepper-tree or bush", one growing to 1.5 metres and the other smaller, as well as a "sweet-scented pepper", which was hot but not biting and was often used to perfume chocolate. As many as twenty varieties of "capsicum peppers" were named in the eighteenth century, generally on the basis of differences in shape and colour. The most common of these were bell pepper, bird pepper, bonnet pepper, cherry pepper, coral pepper, finger pepper, goat pepper, hen pepper, olive pepper and red pepper. Those mentioned less often were Barbary pepper, fat pork pepper, forked pepper, great pepper, nipple pepper, pigeon pepper, Negro pepper, purple or sore-throat pepper and ram's-horn pepper. Individual commentators identified smaller numbers and regarded some of the names as synonyms. Collectively, the capsicums were sometimes called "Indian peppers". In the nineteenth century, they were more often called "Guinea peppers", suggesting a link with Africa rather than their true hearth of domestication.[235] By the end of the century, the term "country pepper" had become common, initially relating the peppers to the island and their indigeneity but over time referring more specifically to rurality and to those peppers defined as characteristically hot and spicy. Some of the names attributed to peppers before 1850 were short-lived or survived on the margins of the language, many of them used to characterize the shape of the fruit. Guinea pepper, cherry pepper, finger pepper and coral pepper were all known in the markets of twentieth-century Jamaica but otherwise not much mentioned. The hottest peppers gained names such as devil pepper, devil-damnation pepper, devil-hell pepper and red-devil pepper.

Plate 17
Cerasee, by Rev. John Lindsay, 1768. Bristol Museum and Art Gallery.

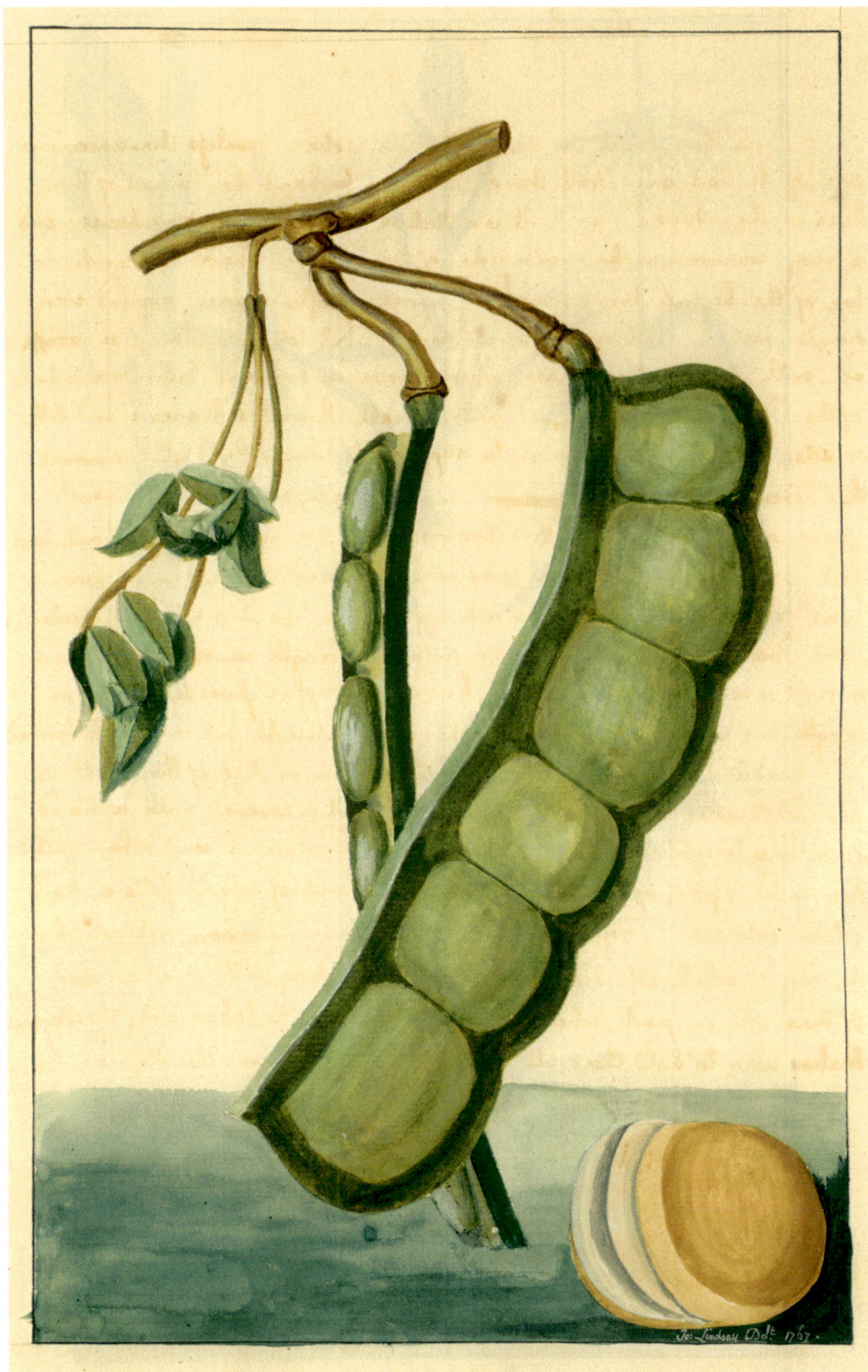

Plate 24

Cacoon, by Rev. John Lindsay, 1767. Bristol Museum and Art Gallery.

Modern Jamaicans came to apply the name "capsicum" narrowly to the bell or "sweet" pepper, *C. annum*. This is the largest of the capsicums, named for its bell-like shape, but it "can hardly be termed a spice" and was thus called "capsicum" to distinguish it from the pungent *C. frutescens*, commonly known as "chillies" or country pepper. In eighteenth-century Jamaica, the bell pepper was sometimes sent to Europe as a pickle, a product thought to aid digestion. The pickling process was quite elaborate. The pods were gathered while still tender and, before they reached full size, were slit open to remove the seeds then soaked for two or three days in salty water. Next they were drained and placed in bottles, and had boiling vinegar poured over them. The sealed bottles were left to stand for two months, after which they were "boiled in vinegar, to make them green". Capsicum is used to make paprika, a dried, ground product valued for its colouring qualities more than its flavour and exported largely by Spain and Hungary. The sweet pepper was not appreciated by Jamaican people generally in the making of soups and pepperpots. As early as 1740 it was observed that "the bell-pepper is red when ripe; the Negroes will not use it, because it is not hot enough for them".[236]

Lindsay identified ten "Indean peppers" in 1767 – bell, Negro, goat, bonnet, bird, hen, cherry, fat pork, and finger or coral pepper – but illustrated only six of these (with the bell pepper on a separate sheet), to accompany his image of an unidentified bush (Plates 18–19). Curiously, he described "Negroe Pepper" as "the most universally admired; and is even by the curious dry'd in the sun and beat into a powder, in which shape it is sent to Europe, under the name of Cayan or Kaian pepper, and there, much valued in all rich sauces, especially fish".[237] Lindsay is the only person known to have used this name, and it is not clear where it fits with other identifications.

References to bird pepper, *C. baccatum* or *C. frutescens*, run from the seventeenth century to the present. The plant is a low shrub, with small and narrow fruits rarely more than three centimetres long, green and yellow when immature but tending to red when mature; it has small yellow seeds and is "extremely pungent". The bird pepper, named for the attraction it holds for birds, grows wild throughout the Caribbean, though it is often cultivated. Lindsay said that, because of its size, it was "more easily swallow'd by the small birds" and thus seeded widely, "to be found in the wilds of the wood as well as under the care of the gardner". In a fence or supported by other shrubs, the bird pepper bush might grow to almost two metres, he said, and it produced "the favourite peppers of some more delicate stomachs: who love not the heat of the hen nor the rank flavour of the goat peppers". Browne described bird pepper as "an agreeable seasoning with those sorts of food that require a gentle stimulus to promote the inner digestion", something he thought valuable in warm countries where "a more free and constant perspiration seldom fails to produce a weakness and languor in the bowels". Long claimed that bird pepper was "gathered when ripe, dried in the sun, pounded, and mixed with salt, and kept, close-stopped in bottles". This was known as "cayan-butter" and used in spicing soups and turtle. Sullivan's recipe for pepperpot called for a handful of bird peppers, but they became less popular during the twentieth century and were associated particularly with the cooking of (East) Indians in Jamaica.[238]

Bonnet pepper, named for its tam-o'-shanter shape and commonly known by the middle of the nineteenth century as Scotch bonnet, was eventually recognized as a distinct species, *C. chinense*. It is closely related to the bird pepper but distinguished by the characteristic branching of its stalks, or pedicels, as well as by the shape of its fruit (Figure 5.38). *C. chinense* is now the most commonly cultivated and most highly esteemed of the peppers in the Caribbean region, described in flavour science as bearing "extremely pungent" fruit of variable size and colour. The plant is small, generally growing to less than a metre, while the one- to twelve-centimetre-long fruits vary "from spherical to elongate, smooth or variously wrinkled and when mature may be red, pink, orange, yellow or brown. The seed margins are usually wavy and are rarely smooth." By 2002 the Scotch bonnet was recognized as one of Jamaica's continuing competitive non-traditional export crops.[239] It can be eaten raw with a meal, boiled in a pot of soup (taking care the pepper does not burst and removing it carefully before serving), cooked in rice and peas or used to make seasonings for meat, including jerk. The seeds are regarded as their most potent element and are generally extracted or otherwise not eaten. A Scotch bonnet may be held down with a fork while it is being sliced, to prevent the scorching juice from being moved from finger to the eye or some other sensitive body part.

Goat pepper was named for its smell. Lindsay noted that "although it has a rankness in its flavour full as strong and perfectly similar to that of a he-goat, very disagreeable to some, especially strangers, yet it so gains upon the taste and stomach as to become the greatest favourite of many: who will eat them with a little salt and bread, by way of salad". It was also appreciated for its "beautiful shining yellow colour". The cherry pepper, according to Lindsay, was more an ornamental plant, "being but little made

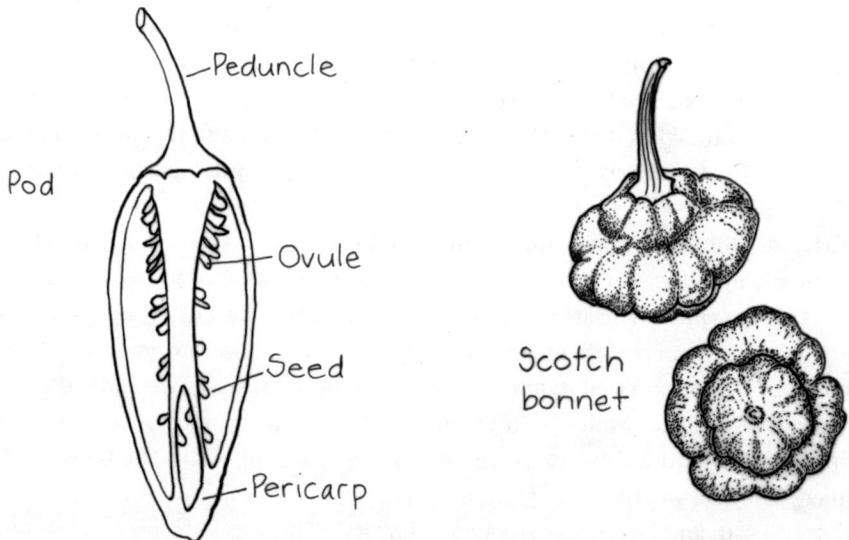

Figure 5.38 Peppers: Scotch bonnet and pod in longitudinal section

use of – tho I know not for what reason, as it is not only a fleshy fruit, but full as hot and poignant as the Negroe pepper – and I think full as delicate to the palate". What he called "fat pork pepper" differed from the cherry pepper only in shape, getting its name from "the fleshyness of the pulp".[240]

Peppers, Long said, were "used liberally in the West-Indies, gathered fresh from the bush". Long rightly considered them useful "to assist digestion, promote the tonic motion of the bowels, invigorate the blood, and correct the flatulency of vegetable aliments". In order to "provoke the most languid appetite", he recommended a mixture called "man-dram", made from sliced cucumbers, scallion or onions, lime juice and Madeira wine, "with a few pods of bird or bonnet-pepper, well-mashed, and mixed with the liquor". Sullivan's recipe for "pickled peppers" used "one dozen ripe, one dozen green, also some salmon coloured if possible, and cherry peppers if they can be had". The peppers (except for the cherry peppers) were sliced, and steeped in boiling vinegar with some pimento seeds. Her recipe for "poor man's sauce" was made from ripe peppers, shallots and mustard seed, boiled down in pork or herring pickle, with onions and vinegar added when the sauce had cooled.[241]

One unique Jamaican product that has gained international status is Pickapeppa Sauce, made at Shooter's Hill in Manchester since 1921. To make the sauce, "red peppers are prepared by removing their stems and all natural ingredients – onions, raisins, mangoes, tomatoes, tamarinds, vinegar and twenty one spices – are cooked in copper pots for four hours". Once cooked, the mixture is poured into wooden casks to ferment, then aged for at least one and up to four years. The details of the recipe remain "a well-guarded family secret that has been passed down through the family over the 75 years of its existence". Other versions included "Pepper Getchup", advertised in 1946 as "Jamaica's most popular sauce condiment".[242]

Jamaicans also used black pepper, the berry of the climbing vine *Piper nigrum*, native to southern India. White pepper – the dried fruit with the mesocarp removed, rather than the whole berry – is less important in Jamaican cookery, and both black and white pepper have to compete with the many indigenous peppers. The essential oils from the berries and leaves of *P. nigrum* are "pleasant, aromatic piney with medicinal odour" and are used in perfumes as well as for flavouring food.[243] Black pepper was one of the first articles of trade between the East and Europe, and most of the black pepper used in Jamaica has been imported. Efforts were made following shortages at the end of World War II to establish the plant in Jamaica, and experimental plantings were made. But black pepper remains an uncommon commercial crop throughout the Americas, the only significant traders being Guatemala and Honduras.[244]

CACTUS, SEASIDE GRAPE, MANCHINEEL

Though the burning sensation associated with the eating of country pepper might be at least temporarily painful, the flavours of the fruit have proved sufficient to outweigh this and have enabled peppers to occupy a central place in Jamaican taste. The ackee too is esteemed in spite of its well-known potential hazards, the attractions of the fruit balancing out the risk. At the same time, other potential foods, such as mushrooms, are feared in the face of lesser probabilities of hazard; and some fruit was eaten only rarely and largely disappeared from the Jamaican repertoire – for good reasons. Considering a sample of these helps raise some larger questions about the nature of choice.

Least offensive of the foods in this category were the cacti. They presented a variety of hazards, some of them easily avoided but others more sinister. For example, Lindsay noticed, in the 1760s, that the fruit of the prickly pear (*Opuntia tuna*), a common plant in Jamaican pastures, was "very agreeable to the teast". However, he warned,

> in eating of it, besides the sharp pointed bristles that appear to the eye in the outside, the stranger will do well to take care least like the Tree of Knowledge, he learns both Good and Evel: for immediately under the rind, where the hollow socket in the top draws to a point (i.e. under the bottom of the socket) lies concealed a sort of sharp pointed star-like figure, hard, and tho' so small, that a greedy eater may with the gummy pap pass it unheeded from the tongue, yet may meet with obstruction in the throat.[245]

Later, in the 1840s, Gosse was tempted by "the plumpness and rich blooming colour" of opuntia fruit but quickly found his lips "full of the spines, which are detached from their base with the slightest force, and left sticking in the flesh; yet the pulp and juice, both of which were of the richest crimson hue, were pleasantly sweet-acid, though somewhat insipid, and full of stony seeds".[246]

Lindsay also observed in the pastures varieties of "the dildo pear tree or small erect Indean fig". This plant, *Cereus gracilis*, bore a shiny, pale yellow fruit, easily picked by felling the whole tree or lopping its arms off. Lindsay thought the fruit had an agreeable taste and noted that "they become in scarce seasons of the years a principle part of the food of the poorer sort of Negroes", but he believed they could not be "any way very wholesome eaten in great quantities; being in their nature of too binding a quality". Lindsay contrasted this plant with the "large erect Indean fig or dildo", *Cereus peruvianus*, which bore a smaller fruit on a larger plant, the fruit appearing high on the plant. Although the fruit had a pleasant taste, he said, "they are not endeed much eaten by the slaves: but it is because they are difficult to come at; and their weight and prickles makes them dangerous to fall them". He also noticed "the triangular leav'd Indean fig commonly called the strawberry pear", *C. triangularis*, which hung from trees, suckering onto the branches. He produced a picture of this as well as of several other varieties of cactus (Plate 20). The fruit of *C. triangularis* was sweet-tasting, said Lindsay, and "a dainty amongst children – and greedily eat by all the Negroes when they are to be found".[247] In more recent times, cacti are less likely to be eaten than to be used for medical or cosmetic purposes.

The seaside grape, or sea grape (*Coccoloba uvifera*), is, as its name suggests, common near beaches. It is a shrubby tree bearing fleshy fruit that dangles in bunches like European grapes and becomes purple when ripe. The ripe fruit are edible and are sometimes used for jellies. In the early eighteenth century, Barham said of the "sea-grape" or "mangrove-grape" that "until they are thoroughly ripe there is no eating of them, they are so rough and restringent, curing fluxes; and when ever so ripe, they have a stipticity [*sic*] and roughness upon the tongue, and binding". Titford similarly declared it "a pleasant acid grape with a purplish skin, but so highly astringent as to render it dangerous to eat them".[248]

As a fruit considered poisonous, manchineel offers an interesting example of processes of selection and rejection. The manchineel tree, *Hippomane mancinella*, grows to twenty metres, yielding a copious milky, sticky sap and bearing yellow fruit three centimetres in diameter. It is common throughout the Caribbean and, like the seaside grape, its typical location is coastal. European sailors shipwrecked or coming ashore encountered the manchineel immediately and were seduced by its fruit, which they took to be a kind of crab apple. Many tales were told of their dying in agony on eating the fruit of the tree. Long paid much attention to the manchineel in his 1774 *History* but concluded that the stories told of the dire effects of the fruit were "certainly to be classed amongst vulgar errors". These "romantic tales" had been repeated so often that "the credibility of their relations, thus built upon a series of such frail authorities, has at length been received as authentic and indisputable". Long produced his own examples of people who had tasted fruit, bark, leaf and sap, all without ill effect, and concluded that "when green, the juice of the fruit is disagreeable from its acrimony, and when ripe, for its insipidity". He expressed no surprise that people who consumed numbers of the green fruit suffered pain, but thought the ripe fruit safe "unless perhaps in very weak and delicate habits". Thus he dismissed the tales as fictions even while he thought they might "have their use, as cautionary to straggling sailors, and others, against smarting for the rash indulgence of a liquorish appetite upon every occasion; for they are too prompt to eat of any fruit that falls in their way". Modern medicine has been less dismissive, and caution remains valid. Contact with the toxic latex is proven to damage the eyes, while the fruit possesses a separate toxic principle.[249]

CHAPTER 6

SEEDS

For many plants, the single most important objective is the production and dispersal of viable seed. The consequence is that seeds tend to contain the greatest concentrations of nutritional material and therefore play a large role in human food history and in conceptions of civilization. Seed crushed or cooked for human and animal food is, however, not functional for the reproduction of the plant, so the attractiveness of a fruit designed to assist dispersal needs to stop short of the modification of the seed. This helps explain the conundrum noticed earlier, that when fruits are eaten, the seeds are rarely eaten as well unless they consist of small, hard seeds that pass intact through the digestive system, like the seeds of the passion fruit, which some eaters attempt to spit out rather than swallow. Other seeds become attractive as human food only when modified and, unlike the edibility that helps define a fruit, are hardly ever eaten raw. Like the roots, almost every one of the seeds discussed in this chapter is eaten only after cooking of some sort.

Botanically, as discussed in the previous chapter, the seeds of flowering plants are enclosed by the fruit. The seed itself is the mature ovule, made up of a seed coat, or testa, endosperm and embryo. The testa is derived from the maternal tissue, and in many plants becomes extremely tough. The endosperm is the seed's food store, often rich in carbohydrates and proteins, and for some important plants, such as the cereals, it remains the main part of the seed at maturity. The embryo contains all the elements of the new plant; some mature seeds, such as peas, are almost all embryo. These elements remain viable while the seed is in its dormant, dehydrated state, awaiting germination. As human food and as agricultural plants, these characteristics are very important, enabling storage and delayed processing.[1]

The structure, shape, size and abundance of seeds vary dramatically from species to species, as do the ways in which they become human food. Indeed, W.J. Titford devoted a full page to the variety of seeds encountered in Jamaica in his 1811 *Hortus Botanicus Americanus* (Plate 21). Abundant small seeds enable broad dispersal, whereas large seeds have the benefit of larger stores of nutrients available for germination. Some seeds are so small and diffused that people eat them along with the ripe fruit. Large seeds, such as the seed of the mango, are almost impossible to swallow and digest, and are rarely milled to produce food.[2] Those species most important to humans – and the focus of agriculture – are generally plants that produce large numbers of smallish seeds with strong nutritional qualities derived from the storage of food in the endosperm and other parts of the seed. Cereals and legumes dominate the field, though Jamaica is also famous for its coffee and cocoa, which are less often thought of as the products of seeds. Cereal grains are the seeds of grasses, anatomically similar but varying in size and shape, used only when in dormancy and suited to milling to varying grades of fineness. Legumes may be used as food at varying stages of ripeness and dormancy, some of them containing large amounts of protein and oil, like the peanut and the soybean, and others containing much less protein and significant carbohydrate, like peas and beans. The seeds of legumes grow within fruit pods, sometimes on vines, sometimes on low bushes. They are less valued than the cereals because they have nutritional deficiencies, are sometimes toxic and cause flatulence.[3]

The cereals are easily the most important of the seeds in human food history. Although many species of plants are edible and occasionally eaten, the three leading cereals – wheat, rice and corn – account for more than 50 per cent of the plant food consumed around the world. Even in the tropics, ten times as much land is now planted in cereals as is planted in alternative carbohydrate staple crops such as roots and bananas.[4] This dependence on cereals is, for Jamaica, a relatively recent phenomenon. As staple foods, the cereals were for centuries in competition with the root crops, and in Jamaica the roots remained in the ascendancy down to the nineteenth century. One explanation for the shift towards the cereals is found in the superior nutrition they deliver, but this had to be weighed against taste and economics. In part, the superiority of the cereals was discovered by consumers themselves, but much of the impetus came from nutritionists and from government policymakers concerned to ensure a healthy labouring population that would be less of a burden on state budgets.

Cereals generally have higher nutritive value than roots, as measured in units of weight. Cereals also tend to have a high calorie content and significant protein, B vitamins and minerals. Some of these characteristics are present only in the whole or lightly milled state, and losses from milling are different for different cereals. Rice suffers most by milling, losing a substantial proportion of its vitamins and minerals. The starchy roots and fruits often give better calorie returns than grains by area planted. Cassava yields about seven times the weight per hectare achieved by corn, six times that of wheat, and five times that of rice. The root crops perform much less well in terms of protein yields per hectare, and poorly in terms of protein quality. But the greatest advantage of the cereals is their short cropping period. In view of these findings, it has been argued since the 1960s that replacement of roots by cereals is nutritionally advantageous.[5]

In addition to their nutritional value, cereals have a number of practical, mechanical advantages, both as dry whole grains and as flour, that make them free-flowing and almost fluid. Stripped of their husks, their seeds are more or less completely free of the unwanted accessory matter, particularly skins and adherent earth, that cling to roots and add to the cost of transportation and to the waste produced in peeling and cleaning. Whole grains and flour can be stored and transported efficiently in containers of various convenient sizes, more cheaply than bulky, odd-shaped roots. Cereal grains and flour also have better storage qualities that enabled shipment over long distances. Further, the great geographical expansion of grain-growing that marked the European colonization of temperate lands in the nineteenth century made available vast stocks of grain for international trade, reducing the real cost. Improved transportation technologies similarly reduced the price of grain and flour, and the development of bulk shipment after World War II meant that grain could be transferred efficiently from ship to silo and mill. The ability to treat cereal grains this way depended on their hardness and on their free-flowing characteristics. Roots could not be treated so roughly and entered international trade only as fragile goods, packed carefully in boxes and carried by air to market. The resulting relative cheapness of cereals made the shift away from roots attractive both to the mercantile class and to the poor. Taste followed cost.

In the kitchen, cereal grains and flour can be used in whatever quantity required, without leaving a raw wound of the sort that oozed at the end of a sliced yam. Precise measurements can be made, and if too much is poured out, it is possible to recover. Because relatively small quantities are required, grains and flour can be stored in small spaces and cooked in small pots, making moderate demands on fuel. Convenience is another important factor: rice, flour and cornmeal have increasingly been sold in sealed packages, ready to cook. All these features became particularly influential in Jamaica in the twentieth century. In 1918, when war made local resources seem more vital, it was observed that agricultural shows had formerly encouraged the "household arts" but that these were "gradually falling into disuse through the increasing easiness of getting shop flour, mostly imported, such as wheat flour, cornmeal and rice and packets and preparations of wheat, oats, rice and barley". These were all cheaper and more reliable than local meals and flours made by hard labour from breadfruit, banana and sweet potato.[6] As well as the difference in price, roots and fruits lacked the mechanical and chemical qualities that made cereal grains so attractive. This comparative advantage was largely a product of developments in the nineteenth and twentieth centuries. Before 1800, seeds were much less successful in their competition with the roots.

CORN

Jamaicans follow American practice in using the word "corn" to mean maize (*Zea mays*). Within the island, "maize" was only occasionally more important historically. The English, on the other hand, frequently used "corn" to refer collectively to grains or cereals, and more specifically to wheat. Richard Blome, in 1672, referred to "Indian Maiz, or wheat", and William Hughes observed that "wheat of America, or maiz", grew on most plantations in the hotter parts of Jamaica. Hans Sloane, at the beginning of the eighteenth century, called it "Indian corn or maiz". This continued as a common formula, though Patrick Browne talked in 1756 of "great corn or maize" and Edward Long, in 1774, of "great corn, or Indian maize".[7]

To call maize "Indian corn" is to point to the origins of the crop in the Americas. The plant is a native, known to have been growing in Mesoamerica by at least 10,000 BP and to have been domesticated, probably in what is now Mexico, by 6000 BP. The domesticated species diffused slowly and probably was not cultivated by the Taino in Jamaica before AD 1000. Columbus certainly found it growing in the Greater Antilles. He carried the seed to Spain, and from there the plant became widely established, eventually becoming one of the world's largest cereal crops. The global spread of maize sometimes led to confusion over the true origins of the domesticated plant. Even the generally well-informed Long speculated that maize "was probably brought from Guiney". Perhaps the error arose from his observation that corn was important in provisioning slave ships. Maize had spread early to West Africa and prospered as a cash crop in the seventeenth and eighteenth centuries for this purpose.[8]

Like sugar cane, *Zea mays* is a tall grass with a thick stem. It can grow to five metres high, with large drooping leaves and a number of "ears", varying from three to sixty centimetres in length, that bear unusually large seeds. The Reverend John Lindsay illustrated the plant and the ear in 1766 (Plate 22). *Zea mays* is the only known species, with no wild or uncultivated forms, but there are more than three hundred "races" with many cultivars and lineages, hence the great range of shapes and sizes. Only the seeds, carried on a cob enclosed by a tough husk, are important in human food systems. Immature, the ears can be eaten as a vegetable. It is the hard grain that is most used, because of its good storage qualities and the wide range of possible styles of preparation.[9] The grains are classified into different types, from popcorn to sweet corn, depending largely on their proportions of starch and sugars, but the most important in human consumption are flint corn and dent corn. Although grains are arranged differently, the germ is the main source of oil, vitamins and minerals, whereas the endosperm contains oil, protein and the dominant carbohydrate (Figure 6.1).

Zea mays was the only significant cereal crop for the Taino in Jamaica, but it never rivalled cassava or sweet potato as a source of food. In the long term, following the settlement of Europeans and Africans in the island, this balance was overturned, with corn becoming vastly more important than cassava. Returns to labour are greater for corn,

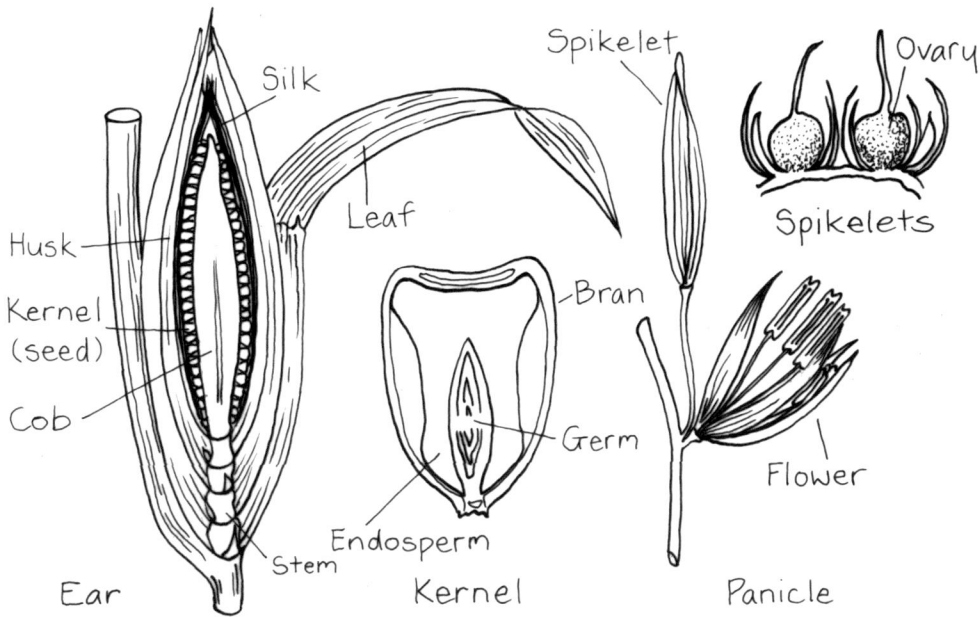

Figure 6.1 Corn cob and seed

and eating the product is much safer. Why did the Tainos prefer bitter cassava to sweet corn? One reason is that corn requires fertile soil, which was generally found at some distance from the coastal settlement sites preferred by the Taino, whereas cassava tolerates less favourable conditions. Corn is also a seasonal crop, and its storage, other than in the husk in the field, could not compete with the long-lasting cassava. The preparation of bitter cassava was a time-consuming operation, but corn – ground to make meal, for example – was also demanding on labour. For the Taino, the security offered by cassava was most important, and it was, in any case, the crop they knew best from their journeying through tropical America. The outcome was that corn had only a small role in Taino horticulture.[10]

Another difference between the Taino and the European colonizers of Jamaica was that the Taino lacked domesticated animals that might be significant intermediate consumers of corn. When the Spanish brought cattle to Jamaica, they turned the animals onto the fields of corn and created pastures. The English planted corn between the canes on sugar plantations and harvested the corn first, but this practice was criticized for impoverishing the soil and reducing sugar yields. As a result, planters sometimes grew corn separately, specifically to feed small stock for the tables of the white people, or occasionally for children or sick enslaved people. By the early eighteenth century, corn was also frequently planted in provision grounds. Although corn was by this time grown widely throughout Jamaica, it soon became clear to the planters that it yielded best and grew the largest grain on rich soils with good rain. The result was competition between cane and corn, a battle that corn had little hope of winning during slavery. Corn was usually planted a little before the rainy seasons, and many expected two crops in a year. Long calculated that each seed could produce three stalks and each stalk three ears, providing a return of about two thousand to one.[11]

Because of the plantation economy's preoccupation with sugar, the cultivation of corn moved forward only slowly, and in the eighteenth century Jamaica imported substantial quantities of corn from North America. Critics said the island in fact produced enough to cover its needs but failed to move it around the island efficiently. Long described the corn imported from North America as "chiefly of the white, large, flat grain". The latter sold cheaper but was "reckoned far inferior in substance and goodness to the Jamaica product". Some of this imported corn was given to enslaved people as rations in the eighteenth century, particularly when other provisions were short. The extension of corn cultivation in case of scarcity was advocated, though not at the expense of sugar production.[12]

Corn imports increased strongly after slavery, in the 1840s and 1850s, and again between 1885 and 1910 (Figure 6.2). Internal trade also developed, with the peasant sector extending cultivation as part of a mixed agriculture. By the 1870s, "country corn" was being shipped by boat from Black River to Kingston. In 1920 the Montego Bay Cornmeal Factory, established during World War I, offered "our new crop native cornmeal, quality fine and pure". During World War II the slogan "Eat More Cornmeal" was part of a plan to reduce the need for shipping. The government built a cornmeal factory at Kingston Pen, the products of which were "palatable and acceptable" but came into competition with the surplus of bananas and ground provisions. The factory soon supplied the island's demand, and imports temporarily ceased. Larger producers took an interest, but down to the middle of the twentieth century little effort was made to select the best seed for replanting. Much of the corn grown in Jamaica was red-grained and of mixed origin, producing hard unattractive cobs. It was relegated to marginal land because of low yields and low prices. As early as 1914 individual attempts were made to "improve the corn production of the country by hybridising, developing and improving the varieties of American corn with our hardy native grown corn".[13]

The development of systematic research, beginning in 1940, led to the isolation of yellow segment from the popular Jamaica Red Corn and to the planting of higher-yielding tropical hybrids. Fertilizer, insecticide and herbicide were applied to crops to boost output. By 1950 Jamaica was almost self-sufficient. Hybridization experiments begun in 1964 also served to increase yields dramatically. Yet in spite of these achievements, imports of corn and cornmeal easily outstripped local production in the 1960s, and local farmers, large and small, were reluctant to commit much of their land to what proved a relatively unprofitable crop.[14]

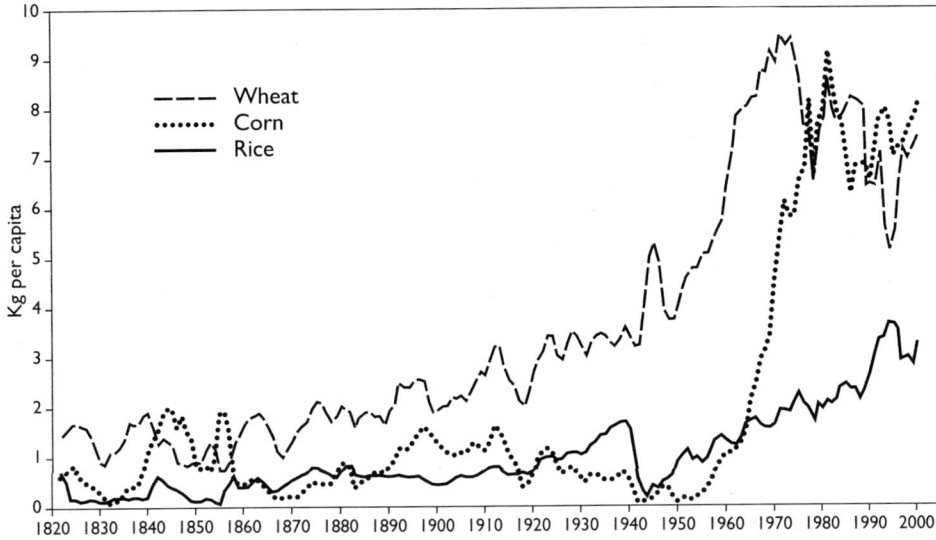

Figure 6.2 Corn, rice and wheat imports per capita, 1822–2004. Source: Appendix 1.

Imports of corn and cornmeal climbed dramatically between 1960 and 1980, then levelled off at a per capita rate almost ten times higher than at the beginning of the period. Imported cornmeal now dominated the market: local production of corn and cornmeal fell from 17 per cent of total consumption at the time of Independence to a mere 0.5 per cent by the beginning of the twenty-first century. A large proportion of the increased import of corn was destined for feedlots and barns, to fatten mammals and birds – above all the chicken.[15] Thus corn entered the food chain at several points without necessarily being appreciated for its inherent qualities.

Corn can be prepared in a variety of ways, the range reflecting its use at different stages of maturity (Figure 6.3). The fresh whole ear can be boiled or roasted. The grains can be ground or pounded, and boiled, baked or fried. Corn can also be fermented. Fresh corn, boiled or roasted, has long been enjoyed. The whole ear prepared this way is in Jamaica called simply "a corn". Speaking about the late seventeenth century, Sloane had observed, "Indian corn or maiz, either tosted or boil'd, is fed on by the slaves, especially the young ears of it, before ripe, are rosted under the coals and eaten; this is thought by them very delicious, and call'd mutton". Similarly, in 1774 John Dovaston noted that "the Negroes when its just ripe, roast the ears of corn or rather parch them; of which they eat". Corn on the cob remains an important food, best known as a street food, boiled in vast pots or drums along the rural roadside and served with a wedge of dry coconut, wrapped in its husk, or roasted.[16]

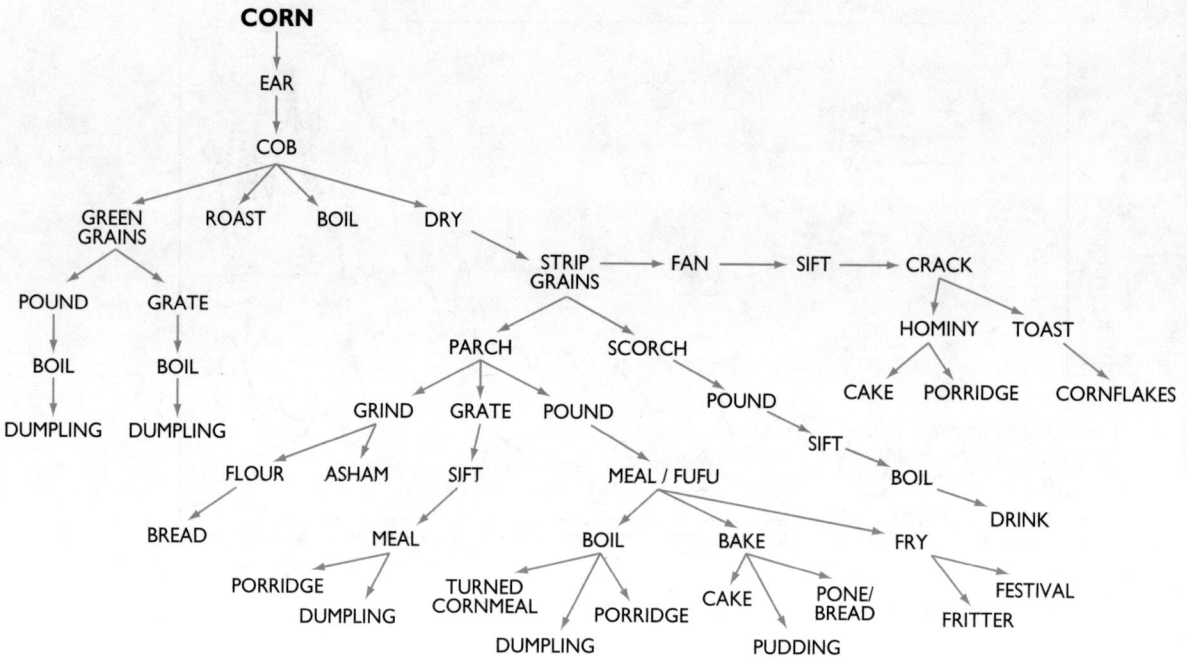

Figure 6.3 Corn: processing flow chart

Another traveller's food is asham, described from the eighteenth century, though without its Twi-derived name. In 1774 Long said, "The Negroes parch and grind it [corn] into powder, sometimes mixing a little sugar with it", using it as a "dainty" for long journeys. Martha Beckwith, in the 1920s, described "Brown George" as parched dry corn beaten fine in a mortar and eaten with sugar and salt. The modern version of this is asham, sold by street vendors in small sealed plastic bags containing about fifteen grams each.[17]

Beginning in the seventeenth century, corn pounded in a wooden mortar was often made into "puddings". One of these was described by Charles Leslie in 1739: the "Negroes" took "callilu, which is the top of a small root, and boil it with beat maiz or Indian corn, (which they call fu fu), herring, salt fish, and red pepper, and when 'tis ready, eat it as we [the English] do broth". The puddings made from pounded corn gained more specific names in the nineteenth century. By 1893 Caroline Sullivan could propose "cornmeal pudding", using one cup of cornmeal to half a cup of "English flour", baked in a pie dish.[18]

Ground into a flour, corn could be used to make bread, but this was never much appreciated. William Hughes complained that the corn of Jamaica was "naturally very dry, and nourisheth very little", and the bread made from it "very dry and hard" and difficult to digest. Long similarly found that corn did not "make a good bread by itself";

it produced a heavy dough that fermented poorly and had to be substantially supplemented by wheat flour. Corn seems largely to have disappeared from commercially baked bread in the nineteenth century but emerged again in the hardship of World War I. In 1918, bakers were required to use 15 per cent cornmeal in wheat-flour loaves. This "war bread" was not liked, and many people baked their own loaves instead, or turned to water crackers and roast yam, or simply did without. War bread came more quickly in World War II and bakers were required to use a proportion of "wholemeal", meaning meal made from the whole corn, including the eye and skin. This bread was declared off-white and nutty, acceptable only as a wartime sacrifice. When the order was rescinded in 1942, because the corn crop was much reduced, it was said that "at first bakeries obeyed the order, but latterly cornmeal had almost entirely disappeared from bread, except in the case of a few bakers who adopted the expedient of attaching a small cornmeal loaf to each wheat-flour loaf".[19]

Homemade cornmeal pone and corn bread proved more successful, with recipes appearing in cookbooks of the late twentieth century. The pone was made by mixing sieved cornmeal and wheat flour with sugar, coconut milk, nutmeg, vanilla and rum, and baking the resulting batter sprinkled with some raisins. When the pone was half-done, a mixture of coconut milk, sugar and butter could be poured on top, and the pone put back to bake until golden brown. The bread might use baking powder, salt, eggs, corn oil and milk. A richer version added pumpkin, used brown rather than granulated sugar and sprinkled more brown sugar with cinnamon and chopped nuts on top before baking. These pones and breads were not far from what Sullivan had called "cornmeal cake", made from cornmeal, a smaller proportion of "English flour", eggs, butter, sugar and milk. The modern versions are more often served as a cake than a bread, the term "bread" coming into favour for this baked product only after war bread was long forgotten. An "ital burger" is a small round corn bread filled with ackees cooked in coconut milk, and seasoned with green ganja, pepper and scallion.[20]

Sullivan gave recipes for cornmeal dumplings and cornmeal fritters, the dumplings boiled and the fritters fried. Her dumplings used cornmeal and wheat flour in equal quantities, mixed with salt, pepper and water to make a thick paste, which was "thrown by spoonfuls or rolled into balls into boiling water to harden". Some later writers followed Sullivan and even, during World War II, used no wheat flour at all in their cornmeal dumplings. Beckwith observed in the 1920s that the peasantry made dumplings "by breaking the young ears before they are quite dry in the field and mixing the grated meal with white flour". Green corn dumplings, close to Beckwith's version, using freshly grated corn from the cob, mixed with flour and boiled, made an occasional appearance into the 1980s.[21]

When homemade cornmeal became rare in the later twentieth century, dumplings of hand-grated corn were replaced by commercial products. The best known of these is "festival", created at the newly popular Hellshire beaches that became accessible to

Kingston in the 1970s with the building of a causeway, and named for the Jamaica Festival of Arts and Culture that marked annual Independence celebrations. This "festival" is a cornmeal dumpling, using both cornmeal and white flour, with baking powder and sugar, mixed and formed into a lozenge and fried in deep hot oil to produce a golden crisp crust (Figure 6.10). The cornmeal used comes from commercially milled packets. The new elements that set festival apart from Sullivan's cornmeal dumpling were the sweet taste derived from the sugar and frying rather than boiling. Both of these elements appealed to modern taste. However, when a Festival Mix was launched by Jamaica Flour Mills in 1991, the company attributed the invention to a Braeton fisherman, said it was "inspired by a combination of the Indian roti and the Jamaican Johnny Cake" and told customers, "if you thought you had to go to Hellshire to get the real taste of festival, think again". Some Hellshire vendors agreed with this story, but others attributed the invention to Oratius Thompson, a Naggo Head beachside cook who claimed that he had created and named the product in 1975, and that his recipe was unique. Hellshire vendors thought the commercial mix inferior and lacking respect for their intellectual property: "All dem a do none a dem can ketch fi we Festival."[22]

Sullivan's recipe for "turned cornmeal" is the earliest Jamaican example identified, apparently a close relative or descendant of the earlier cornmeal pudding. To make turned cornmeal, a pint (568 millilitres) of cornmeal was mixed with water and stirred over a fire. Once it achieved a stiff consistency, scallion, tomatoes, butter, lard, salt, fresh or black pepper, and diced salt pork were added. By 1941 turned cornmeal was no longer "the favourite dish it used to be", though "very palatable" and "highly nutritious". But as a wartime expedient, housewives were encouraged to try "modern turned cornmeal". This was made by mixing cornmeal in salted boiling water and adding raisins, margarine and butter, then cooking "as usual". Divided up, each part was shaken in a bowl until it was shaped like a ball. It could be served with "a float of honey". Later versions of turned cornmeal added coconut milk, saltfish, okra, onion, sweet pepper and hot pepper. Vegetarian cooks towards the end of the twentieth century accepted these additions, threw in some garlic and rejected the meat and fish.[23]

In 1985 "turn meal" was declared "the finest Jamaican one-pot meal". By then, the recipe could include the milk of a coconut, onion, thyme, black pepper, sweet pepper, margarine and tomato. Sometimes it was called "turn pudding", or even "'turned' corn cou-cou", which used okra. This last recipe sounds much like what Beckwith called "funga", a mixture of cornmeal and flour boiled in a pot with okra. In 1990 it was said that "turn cornmeal is getting popular again – glorified". Renamed "golden cheese spoon bread", it was made with cheese and beaten eggs instead of salt meat, and served with melted butter poured over the top. Another version used all of these old and new ingredients, along with canned corn from the cob to supplement the cornmeal.[24]

Cornmeal is equally well known for its porridge, sweetened with condensed milk and sugar and spiced with nutmeg and cinnamon. Some versions, following ital principles, use fresh cow's milk rather than condensed and raw cane sugar rather than granulated. It can also be made without cow's milk or with coconut milk, and salt and vanilla may be added. Cornmeal porridge is descended from what Sullivan called "cornmeal pap", a dish of boiled cornmeal with milk, sugar and nutmeg which she thought much loved by the "natives", who ate it for breakfast.[25]

The old methods of grating cornmeal were time-consuming and required much effort. The dried corns had to be passed through a grater several times, then sieved and sifted. The coarser products of the process were good for cornmeal porridge, but the finer grains needed for dumplings required repeated grating. Down to the 1950s, some cookbooks offered only the harder methods, without making them seem too arduous. One recipe for "corn porridge" simply called on the cook to "grate a few nearly-dry cobs and pass through a fairly fine sieve". This porridge was distinguished from "hominy porridge", made with "hominy corn" or the "dry or nearly dry grains of maize from which the skin or bran has been stripped . . . then lightly cracked".[26] Hominy corn was made by "soaking, drying, fanning, sifting, sieving and other tedious processes". Sullivan, as early as the 1890s, encouraged cooks to buy it ready-made. The porridge was made by soaking hominy corn in salted water, then simmering until the corn was softened. The now-tender corn was minced coarse and simmered in cow's milk and coconut milk with some cinnamon stick or leaves. After about an hour's cooking, the porridge could be sweetened. Condensed milk became the preferred sweetener by the 1950s. As well as the porridge, Sullivan recommended "hominy cakes", made by boiling hominy corn until very thick, letting it cool and cutting slices to be fried in lard for breakfast. Early in the twentieth century, corn also joined wheat in providing the raw materials for industrialized "breakfast cereals"; before long, cornflakes had become the most characteristic of all these products. Kellogg's Toasted Corn Flakes were first advertised in Jamaica in 1911, along with Quaker Corn Flakes and Puffed Rice.[27]

An uncommon use of corn was for pseudo-coffee. Dried grains were scorched in a large pot until almost burnt, then pounded in a mortar and sifted. The fine dark powder that passed through the sieve was used to brew a hot drink "not easily distinguished from coffee in colour, aroma and taste".[28]

GUINEA CORN

The transition from human food to animal-fattening food was more complete for Guinea corn (*Sorghum bicolor*) than for *Zea mays*. First cultivated in East Africa by 6000 BP, the seed reached Jamaica through the slave trade, and it remains an important staple subsistence crop for human food in much of the interior savanna zone of West Africa, as well as in Asia. Often it has been the leading cereal, though in some areas second to millet. In West Africa it is used to make porridge and cakes, fermented and unfermented dumplings, and beer.[29] In the Americas generally, in contrast, sorghum is now used only as animal food. Historically, it has been considered a hardship or famine food, to be replaced by its three major rivals when possible, yet globally today it is the fourth most valuable cereal crop, after rice, wheat and maize.

Guinea corn is less demanding than corn. It can be grown on relatively saline soils in sites affected by drought. As John Stewart noted in 1823, "in some districts on the south side [of Jamaica] the slaves are chiefly subsisted on this grain, which is peculiarly calculated to endure the two greatest disadvantages to vegetable productions, poverty of soil and drought".[30] The plant has considerable genetic and morphological variation, partly as a consequence of its adaptation to widely different environments, but the single species *S. bicolor* comprehends all of the domesticated sorghums cultivated for their grain. Often the plant retains a weedy habit. In the field, Guinea corn looks much like corn but is marked by its distinctive seed heads. The seed also is similar to that of corn but somewhat smaller and more spherical (Figure 6.4). A typical plant carries up to two thousand seeds, roughly the same as corn.

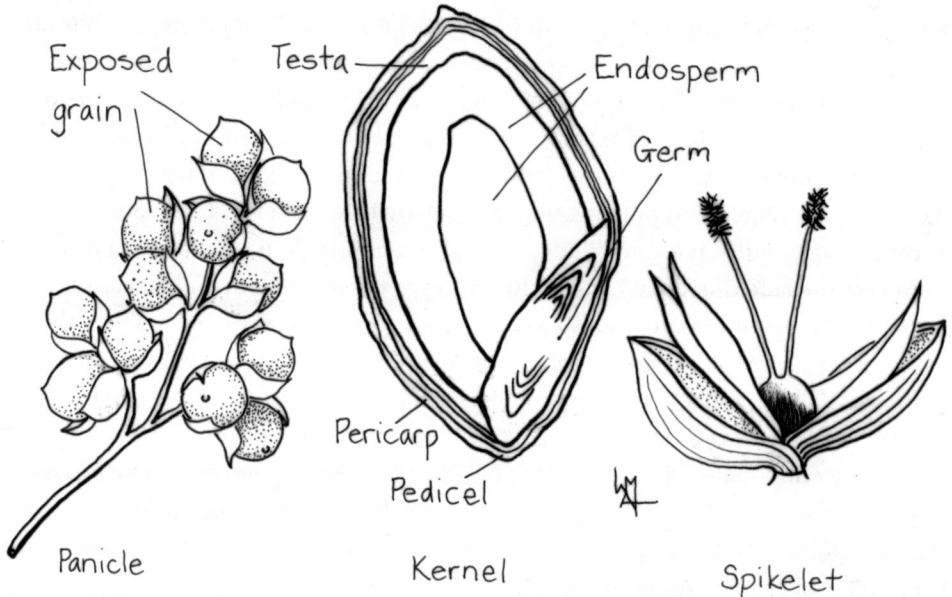

Figure 6.4 Guinea corn seed

In Jamaica in 1766, Lindsay found Guinea corn interesting enough to deserve illustration (Plate 23). The plant was common in the agricultural landscape. Ten years earlier, Browne had said that Guinea corn was often planted in the provision grounds of plantation slaves. This suggests that it was favoured, as a crop known from Africa, but it was cultivated on plantation lands as well in certain regions of the island. At the end of the eighteenth century, Simon Taylor considered the Guinea corn crop vital to St Catherine, St Dorothy, Vere and lower Clarendon, because "that is what their Negroes have chiefly to exist on". Cynric Williams, in the 1820s, found Guinea corn most important in Vere, where drought made the plantain unreliable. There planters sowed the seed during the October rains and gathered the harvest in February, storing the grain in "immense barns" for at least a year's supply.[31]

A penkeeper in western Jamaica claimed, in the 1820s, that Guinea corn yielded "the finest flour in the world". Long had earlier stated that the grain made "a fine, white flour, very nourishing, and constitutes a principal part of the food of the Negroes". Lunan thought the flour could keep for years if properly stored. In southern Clarendon in the early nineteenth century, the grain was issued in rations and, "when freed from the husk, and pounded in a wooden mortar, it produces a meal as white as snow, which is formed into a kind of bread, and small delicious cakes". From this region came "an abundance of fat pork, and excellent poultry of all sorts, which are carried for sale to Spanish Town and Kingston", all fattened on Guinea corn.[32]

Sloane said that in the 1680s Guinea corn was eaten like rice "and tasts as well, and is as nourishing". There are, however, few surviving descriptions of the foods made from Guinea corn, and it must be assumed that the grain was prepared in much the same way as corn. The most precise reference known is from 1788, when Peter Marsden said that "Guinea corn, when ground, makes tolerable cakes, which are almost as thin as a wafer".[33] The lack of specific items in the documentary record does not mean that Guinea corn was poorly regarded; a rare song of the enslaved people of Jamaica, collected in the late eighteenth century, suggests the opposite:

Guinea Corn, I long to see you
Guinea Corn, I long to plant you
Guinea Corn, I long to mould you
Guinea Corn, I long to weed you
Guinea Corn, I long to hoe you
Guinea Corn, I long to top you
Guinea Corn, I long to cut you
Guinea Corn, I long to dry you
Guinea Corn, I long to beat you
Guinea Corn, I long to trash you
Guinea Corn, I long to parch you
Guinea Corn, I long to grind you
Guinea Corn, I long to turn you
Guinea Corn, I long to eat you[34]

The song's conclusion points to an emphatic appreciation of Guinea corn as a food, perhaps as a version of turned meal, though the deliberate enumeration of the many tasks of cultivation and preparation equally suggests the tedious character of the labour.

After slavery, little was heard of Guinea corn as a human food. The flour, however, remained available down to the 1870s, when, for example, the Kingston Corn and Feed Mills advertised that it daily ground "Country cornmeal – corn grits – Guinea corn meal –

Guinea corn grits – Rice flour – Plantain flour". But animal-feed products already dominated, sold both in and out of the husk, and the flour was soon forgotten. Cookbooks never provided recipes. A few suggestions that Guinea corn could be human food did survive: in World War II, "a local sorghum product" called "Victory Rice" was said to be popular with schoolchildren, and in the 1950s there were calls for the development of "dwarf guinea corn" for human consumption.[35] But only small areas were cultivated, and by the 1990s sorghum became an article of importation.

Why did Guinea corn cease to be a human foodstuff in Jamaica? Although of African origin, it was effectively replaced by "Indian" corn and, ironically, it was East Indians who came to be the major cultivators in Jamaica in the early twentieth century.[36] Guinea corn is not so easily digested (unless fermented, as it is in Africa), and it suffers from bird damage. In the long term, in the Americas generally, the market has come to be determined by demand for animal feeds. Pigeons, poultry and pigs early established themselves as major consumers of Guinea corn, pushing up its price relative to the increasingly cheap rice and wheat.

RICE

By the 1970s rice was rightly called one of Jamaica's "staple foods".[37] Like corn, almost all of it was imported, and the decline in local production was even more dramatic. At Independence, 21 per cent of the island's rice consumption came from local fields; by the beginning of the twenty-first century, hardly a grain. In the long term, per capita imports of rice increased more slowly than those of corn, largely because most of the rice was human food whereas much of the corn went to feed animals (Figure 6.2).

Why did Jamaica grow so little rice? During the period of slavery, rice consumption was relatively low, but even when it became much greater, local cultivation still supplied only a small proportion of demand. Indeed, rice consumption might have been higher in the eighteenth century than it was if local supplies had existed. Rice seems rarely to have been given as a staple ration during slavery, except in times of hardship when other provisions were in short supply. It was typically allocated only to the sick, to "new Negroes", to house slaves and to the young and needy.[38] Neither was it prominent on the tables of the planters.

Thus it is necessary to ask not only why the planters failed to make rice a commodity produced by enslaved labour, but also why the enslaved did not cultivate rice in their provision grounds, and why after slavery the peasantry failed to show enthusiasm for the crop. Many potential sites suited to rice agriculture exist in Jamaica, but they were planted in other crops. Jamaican planters, unlike their counterparts in South Carolina and Georgia, never saw rice as a competitive, profitable export crop, but they similarly ignored it as a potential food crop for enslaved people, preferring to plant other cereals, such as sorghum and maize. There seems to be no evidence to suggest that rice was ever planted in provision grounds. Indeed, apart from corn, cereals were almost completely missing.

The absence of Asian rice, *Oryza sativa*, from Jamaican agriculture until the arrival of the East Indians in the later nineteenth century might seem to be simply a cultural question, but African rice, *Oryza glaberrima*, had long been an important indigenous subsistence crop in much of West Africa. Elsewhere in the Americas, rice cultivation depended on enslaved labourers drawn from the rice-growing regions of Africa. Indeed, it has been argued that it was the knowledge and skills of the enslaved Africans that made possible the development of rice-growing by English and French planters in the seventeenth century, and that the enslaved people were active agents in this process. Rice was also important in South America, in a zone stretching from Brazil to Suriname; oral tradition attributes the introduction of rice there to an African woman who hid grains in her hair. Certainly African rice was one of the foods loaded on ships in the slave trade.[39]

Alongside the role of enslaved people in the development of rice as a plantation crop, it has also been argued, notably by Judith A. Carney, that provision-ground agriculture created potential "sites for establishing African dietary staples in the Americas". Carney sees rice as having played an important role in these gardens and grounds. But the absence of rice from Jamaica's flourishing provision-ground system, one of the best known in the Americas, remains puzzling. Carney contends that "in the Jamaican sugarcane economy, slaves attempted to grow rice as a provision crop", but "their efforts to maintain a dietary favourite were frustrated by hand milling, which burdened their exhausted bodies". Sloane provided a possible explanation: "Rice is here planted by some Negros in their own plantations, and thrives well, but because it requires much beating, and a particular art to separate the grain from the husk, 'tis thought too troublesome for its price, and so neglected by most planters." While this was an argument more about the profitability of applying enslaved plantation labour to the crop than about the relative insignificance of rice in the provision-ground economy, Sloane also said that rice was neglected because "the use of it may be supplied by other grains, more easily cultivated and made fit for use by less labour".[40]

Experiments and advocacy continued through the eighteenth century. Barham, who recognized that rice grew well in Africa, planted some in "a moist parcel of ground" in about 1720 and found that this land "bore an extraordinary quantity of grain". Long thought it should be cultivated only where fields could be flooded, but he identified a series of such niches scattered around the island in "moist bottoms between the mountains" and in the marshy grounds of Ferry, St Thomas-in-the-East, Black River and Negril. These places he thought "naturally adapted" to rice "if it should be thought worthwhile to cultivate it, as an additional supply of food for the Negroes". He hinted, though, that few planters were knowledgeable about the crop, including the correct seasons for planting. In 1751 a critic of trade with the North American colonies noted that much rice was imported and stated simply, "Rice we may have of our own growth." After the American Revolution, "prime East-India rice", "East India rice, of the best quality", was increasingly imported, replacing the North American trade, while local cultivation was still not encouraged.[41]

Complaints of neglect continued in the nineteenth century. Titford proposed bringing the "mountain rice" of the East Indies to Jamaica, where it could be cultivated on the dry uplands, but it was the coming of the indentured Indians, rather than the seeds, that created change. By 1890 it could be said that rice cultivation was "extending a great deal" in Westmoreland, and was of "excellent quality". One gentleman said, "the white rice was the prettiest he had ever seen" and that the supply could not meet the demand for it. He also reported that it was grown "principally" by indentured East Indians and commonly known as "coolie rice". This was a term applied also to some rice imported from India, sold in the markets in competition with "native brown and white rice", "Ballam rice" (a cheap variety), "white table rice" and "best table rice". Indentured people cultivated the crop in their "spare time" on low-lying lands not wanted for other crops. Rather like corn and Guinea corn, the local rice was sold unhulled (left in the husk) and was often used to fatten livestock.[42]

The steady increase in rice consumption that marked the twentieth century was interrupted only by World War II (Figure 6.2). The grain's success was based largely on economics, though it came to be strongly preferred to alternative grains and roots. By the 1980s, the poor were reduced to eating rice "with gravy or a vegetable sauce for their main meal". Increases in the cost of living made many families dependent on rice: it was easy to prepare and, unlike roots and tubers, suffered little wastage, and it could accompany almost any meal. Efforts to increase local production, with government support, were attempted in the 1970s, but apart from an unsustained peak in 1984, domestic output continued to shrink. In 1989 rice was promoted by merchants as "the perfect food for our time – praised by cooking experts for its versatility, praised by nutritionists as a healthful source of energizing complex carbohydrates". Eaters could enjoy rice dishes "without the guilt of having forbidden calories". Rice was "your most useful food" because it was "economical, delicious, nutritious, versatile, easy to prepare, and bland enough to pair with almost any other food to the advantage of both". Now identified as an "American" crop, Jamaicans were offered recipes such as Charleston rice, rice spoon bread and rice Waldorf salad (perhaps using "cho-cho soaked in apple juice" in place of apples).[43]

Rice grains come in a variety of types, from long (with grains longer than 6.6 millimetres and a thousand-grain weight of 15 to 20 grams) to short (less than 5.5 millimetres long and 20 to 24 grams), with a medium grade in between. By the late twentieth century, when rice ruled, Jamaicans had come to prefer their grains white (with the bran and germ removed), fluffy, unbroken and generally clearly separated (Figure 6.5). Although unmilled and "brown" rice have nutritional advantages, they were not broadly appreciated. Nor did Jamaicans have any great liking for parboiled rice, produced by soaking and steaming before milling, which retained more of its nutrients than milled rice but was often unattractive to consumers in colour, flavour and taste.[44]

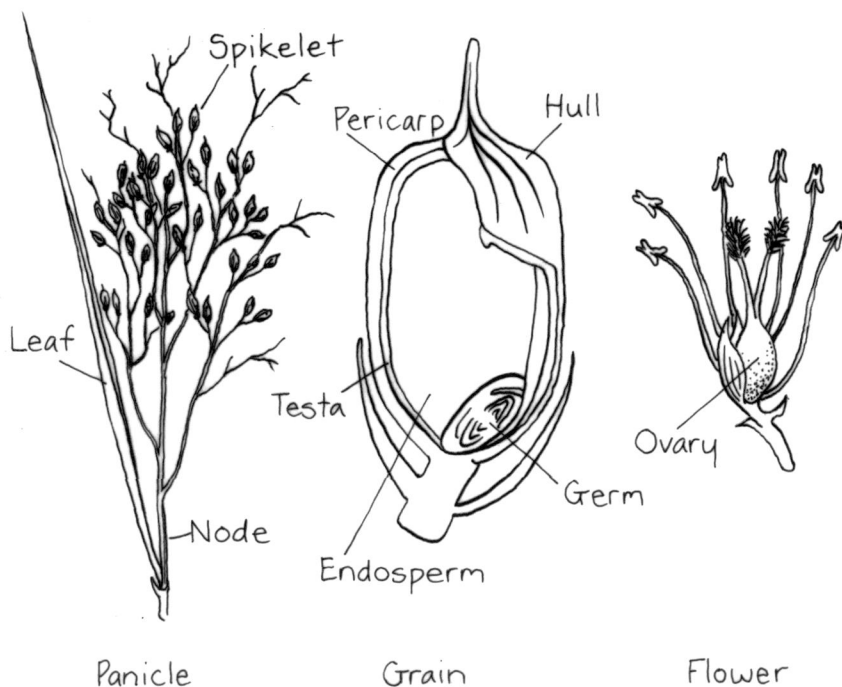

Figure 6.5 Rice grain

Methods of preparing rice dishes are limited. Most often the rice is simply steamed and combined with some other food that supplies the "Jamaican" taste element. Cookbooks, other than those produced by the traders and promoters of rice, have little to offer in rice cookery. The one great exception is rice and peas, mentioned in chapter 1 as a candidate for the status of national dish, and to be discussed fully later in this chapter among the peas and beans. It is a dish that combines two seeds, and unusual in that respect.

WHEAT

For each of the seeds discussed thus far – corn, Guinea corn and rice – a central question has been why they have been cultivated much less in Jamaica than they might have been. Corn was Amerindian, and Guinea corn and rice were well known from Africa, but local cultivation declined and effectively disappeared at the same time as the consumption of corn and rice increased substantially. The gap had to be filled by imports. By comparison with these seeds, the story of wheat seems simple. Rather than appealing to economics and taste, agroecological factors supply a straightforward answer. Wheat has a relatively wide climatic range, but in the tropics appropriate sites occur only in small patches, generally in elevated places like Mexico or unusually dry regions of Egypt and India. Jamaica was always going to be an importer. Apart from a few quickly abandoned experiments by the Spanish, Jamaicans therefore came to know wheat as a grain rather than a plant, and most often (unlike rice and corn) simply as a flour.

The wheat grain is a little larger and rounder than a rice grain, and is elongated with a furrow running from end to end. Its outer coat of bran is made up of several layers of fibre (Figure 6.6). Beneath the bran is the aleurone layer, which is particularly important to nutrition, containing large cells rich in protein, vitamins and minerals. The endosperm stores the food of the germ or embryo, and it is this portion (roughly 80 per cent of the grain) that is made into flour. Most of the endosperm is starch, but it also contains protein and water-insoluble gluten essential to producing bread dough. Flour is made by grinding the grains and removing unwanted components, which can be used in a variety of other foods. The flour itself can be produced in different grades and qualities, depending on taste, demand, technology and the character of the grains. Further, wheat flour is classified in terms of strength, a concept not applied to other cereals. A "strong" flour made from hard wheat with a high gluten content enables relatively great expansion of bread dough and the baking of a well-structured large loaf with a well-piled top. Strong flour is more expensive than the weaker classifications. Medium-strength flour is softer and its gluten stretches more readily. This is the flour most often used in modern bread-baking, the gluten supplying the elasticity that enables the dough to make a light-textured, risen loaf by retaining bubbles of carbon dioxide produced by fermentation with yeast. Soft wheat flour, with relatively little gluten, makes poor bread but is good for cakes, pastries and biscuits.[45]

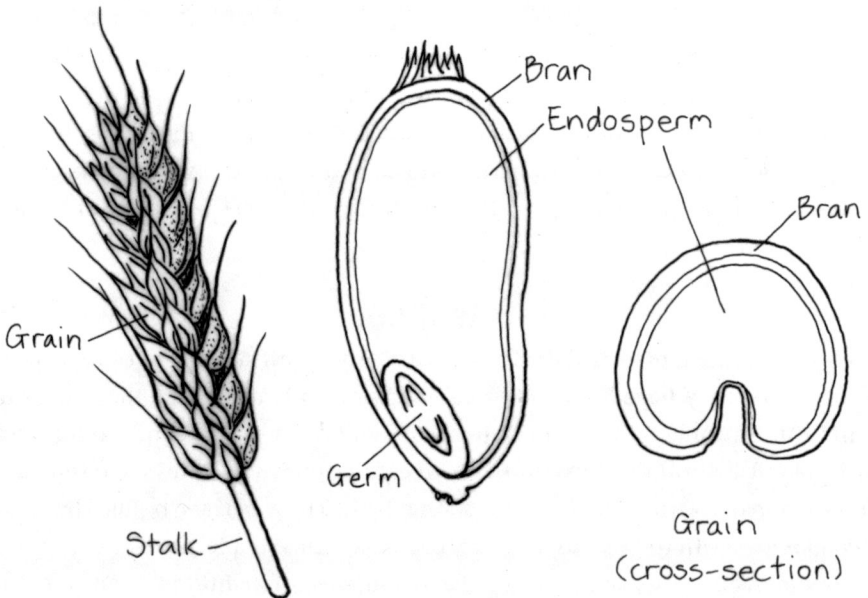

Figure 6.6 Wheat grain

Until 1968 Jamaica had no flour mills, and imported wheat products reached the island most often as flour rather than grain. Before the American Revolution, most of this flour came from North America, and was Jamaica's most substantial import from those colonies, worth close to one-quarter of the total value of their trade. Critics sometimes argued that Jamaica would have been better off if it had brought its flour from England, but the trade with the northern colonies was part of a larger imperial economy. After the Revolution, Jamaicans complained of being denied the flour of New York and the rice of South Carolina, saying Canadian flour was no substitute. One reason for this, said the planters, was that "flour in particular will not keep in the West Indies, and requires a constant supply by as short a voyage as possible: Even in the short voyage from England it frequently grows sour".[46] Improved storage solved some of these problems, and in the long run Canadian and US wheats and flours remained in competition for the Jamaican market.

Although wheat flour was already important to Jamaica's trade with North America in the eighteenth century, consumption was limited because flour was only occasionally included among the rations given to enslaved people. As a food, wheat flour was less useful to poor people than the other cereals because flour required more complex, expensive technology. Whereas corn, Guinea corn and rice were most often cooked by boiling or roasting, wheat flour was generally appreciated baked or fried. To make effective use of wheat flour, large ovens were need, and this led to the early rise of commercial bakeries capable of baking bread and pastries. When the official statistics commenced in the 1820s, per capita imports of wheat exceeded both corn and rice, and they continued to do so down to 1980 (Figure 6.2). The level of imports remained relatively flat throughout the nineteenth century and increased dramatically only after World War II before reaching a peak in the early 1970s and then levelling off. This pattern reflected a growing acceptance of bread in the twentieth century, the development of large-scale baking corporations capable of supplying every corner of the island and, to a lesser extent, an extension of the range of baked products.

For most of the eighteenth and nineteenth centuries, wheat flour was essentially generic, imported in barrels. Later in the nineteenth century, cloth bags and small packages began to enter the market, some of the flour branded and some of it modified. Self-raising flour was first advertised in Jamaica in 1866, described as "an invaluable article for producing in a few moments by the addition of cold water only without yeast or salt, the most nutritious and wholesome bread". Varieties of flour imported in the 1890s included "superfine", "No. 2", "shop", "baking" and "pearl", along with brand names like Knickerbocker and Rip Van Winkle. Washburn-Crosby's Gold Medal Flour, offering "uniform success in baking" and "more loaves to the barrel", came in bags by 1920. Various brands of Canadian and American "bakers' flour" were offered, as well as "counter grade flour", "shop grade flour", "medium grade counter flour" and Aunt Jemima pancake flour.[47]

By the middle of the twentieth century, the basic distinction in flours was between "baking flour" (or "American baking flour") and "counter flour". In 1949 the baking trade used the more expensive baking flour at a ratio of 6:1 counter flour in a single loaf but asked permission to use equal quantities in bread, so "bakers would be able to sell a bigger loaf for the same price, and bigger cakes, and more pastry also". Dr W.E. McCulloch, the medical nutritionist, not only bemoaned the quality of the wheat flour imported into Jamaica, saying some called it "the dregs of the mills", but also argued that "some of our bread is of such appalling quality because of . . . the uncontrolled method of mixing the so-called 'sour' or 'hard' dough". He also complained that the "craze for a whiter flour" had led to the use of chemical bleaches, particularly in the United States, and to other "nutritional absurdities". Whole wheat flour would be better, he believed, but was hard to store in the tropics. The solution, he argued in 1955, was to import the grain and mill it in Jamaica, both to produce a high-quality baking flour and to have the benefit of the bran and the germ as livestock feeds.[48]

In response to these concerns, Jamaica Flour Mills Limited was incorporated in 1964. The company began trading four years later, producing bakery flour from its own mill on Kingston Harbour. This was Jamaica's first flour mill, with its own pier and silos for the storage of imported wheat. Agreements were made with the American company Pillsbury and other overseas companies for training, technical assistance and the use of trademarks. The mill used steel rollers to grind the grains, an innovation that had generally replaced millstones by the end of the nineteenth century. The introduction of this system reduced the cost of production and permitted the best possible separation of the endosperm as flour without contamination from bran or germ, and thus produced more consistent, finer, whiter flour.[49]

In the 1950s, before the establishment of Jamaica Flour Mills, about one-half of the flour imported had come from Canada, and in the early 1960s "high protein hard wheat" bread flour came from Australia. The new mill's link with Pillsbury shifted supply towards the United States and to soft rather than hard wheat. The mill produced named brands for its distributors: Caribbean Maid for Lascelles, Caribbean Flour for Musson, Bakers Choice for Grace and Northern King for Geddes Grant. Flour for household use was produced beginning in 1971, but it was only in the early 1980s, when the capacity of the plant was substantially expanded, that the mill had the capacity to satisfy household demand. The expansion also enabled a more diversified output, including products such as Quik 'N Easy packaged cake, muffin, pancake and waffle mixes.[50]

In 1992 Pillsbury divested its interest in Jamaica Flour Mills, and the company assumed responsibility for purchasing its own wheat rather than doing its purchasing through the government agency, the Jamaica Commodity Trading Company. The mills sold bakery flour and the slightly cheaper counter flour in forty-five-kilogram bags, and bulk wheat middlings by the tonne.[51] Some flour continued to be imported, particularly counter flour made from soft wheat, shipped in bulk rather than packaged and branded.

When the price of wheat flour was increased early in 1995, consumer groups called for a boycott, but many voices recognized that bread (with rice) was a staple that could not easily be replaced by tubers or green banana. Earlier, in 1988, it had been acknowledged that Jamaicans could not be weaned from the product, however high the price might rise. As Aimee Webster contended, "White wheat is the foundation of the Jamaican table – rich, poor, and middle-income." She bemoaned the lost skills of making flour from cassava, coco and green banana, the decline of cornmeal and the lost "diversity of splendid foods made with these flours". Corn pone, "that succulent slightly cinnamon scented slab" with the "satisfying flavour, texture and nut taste", had somehow "given way to white wheat biscuits called 'fresh crackers'". Webster asked, "Did Jamaicans slip into white wheat preference by accident? Or were Jamaicans directly encouraged to consume imported flour products because imported flour yields import duties? That reaped from flour is one of the government's largest tax sources." Others complained of a lack of nationalism. In 1986 a Spanish Town letter-writer complained that advertisements shown on government-controlled television depicted banana and callaloo as "a dull, colourless, painful ordeal for breakfast, causing long faces and grimaces instead of smiles . . . , contrasted with 'nice and easy muffins' which bring radiant smiles, and hungry anxious hands stretching across the colourful breakfast table to reach for another". In a country that did not grow wheat, this was cause to "cry shame": Jamaicans should be producing more of what they ate rather than falling for "foreign tastes".[52]

To counter nationalist nostalgia, bread made from wheat flour had on its side economy, convenience and, in particularly favourable circumstances, taste. There were also ways of baking with flour that were distinctively "Jamaican" and that led eventually to the creation of products recognized as worthy of carriage to the diaspora.

In its simplest form, bread is made by kneading flour and water with some salt, and baking. When flour is mixed with water, the gluten forms a three-dimensional water-insoluble protein network; the dough requires mechanical work, the kneading, to give it structure. Leavening – the use of yeast as a raising agent – was an ancient innovation that increased the palatability of bread. Little changed in the technology of bread-making until the nineteenth century, when machines were first applied to the mixing of dough and to the loading and unloading of ovens, leading ultimately to computerized control and continuous process. Economies of scale, slicing and wrapping machines, and the use of motor vehicles to transport the product all began in the 1930s as ways to expand the potential market for a bakery's bread, releasing it from a retail trade tied to the shopfront of the bakery. The commercial bakery producing bread for a geographically dispersed market became viable and effectively ended household bread-baking, only marginally moderated by the use of bread-making machines in a sprinkling of kitchens in the late twentieth century; it also, though less definitively, led to the end of the village baker. Varieties of bread became increasingly "national" and less individual.

In the early eighteenth century, according to Leslie, every Jamaican creole household had an oven; the people, he said, "bake as they find occasion". But this bread was made without yeast, he claimed, "and their loaves are so bad that few chuse to eat them". In the nineteenth century, home baking was made easier by baking powder and self-raising flour, both first imported in 1866, which made bread and pastry "light and easy of digestion". Sullivan recommended using baking powder for scones in 1893, but "soda" for her "home-made bread" and "breakfast rolls".[53] A brick oven in the yard of a household remained a common sight into the twentieth century, though after about 1950 most of them were on the way to becoming archaeological artefacts.

The bread sold by bakeries was controlled by weight rather than price, from the seventeenth century to the 1940s. Prices did not go up: instead the breads got smaller and lighter. In July 1839 there were complaints from Montego Bay that the five-penny loaf had shrunk to 12 ounces (340 grams). By October it was down to 9 ounces: "Already a sparrow could hop with a loaf under each wing, and no great exertion either: we suppose we shall soon see the very ants and cockrotches making light of their burden." Hence the "penny breads" and "half-penny" loaves made by Kingston bakeries in the 1890s, and penny bread came to name a particular type of bread, similar to a modern dinner roll. In 1947 the government decided "not to increase the price of the standard 3d loaf, but to reduce it by an ounce in weight" to 5.5 ounces (155 grams). The price of "sandwich loaves" was increased because the technology did not easily permit a reduction in weight and size.[54] Jamaicans soon became used to increases in the price of bread, protesting loudly only occasionally.

The most distinctive bread made in Jamaica is "hard dough", a dense, heavy, large white loaf, of the variety disparaged by McCulloch in the 1950s (Figure 6.7). The earliest known references to hard-dough bread come from the years before World War I, but by then it was already well established as a favourite. Claude McKay claimed that the rural people of Jamaica were not easily shifted from their "cheap and wholesome tropical breadkind to a general consumption of cheap white bread", and when they did eat white bread, they "preferred the well-kneaded compact loaf, like Spanish bread, to the light and loose steam bread". In 1912 a Texan miller visiting Jamaica commented that almost the only bread he had seen in the island was "a hard dough bread that cannot readily assimilate, and that enters the stomach with the same effect as if you swallowed leaden pellets". The problems, he said, were lack of flavour, the toughness of the texture and the overfermentation of the protein. Jamaican bakers continued to produce hard dough because "the public demands that class of bread" rather than the lighter "steam" bread. Some bakers referred to "the ordinary hard dough texture bread".[55] The popularity of hard dough persisted, and bakers – some claiming against their better judgement – kept

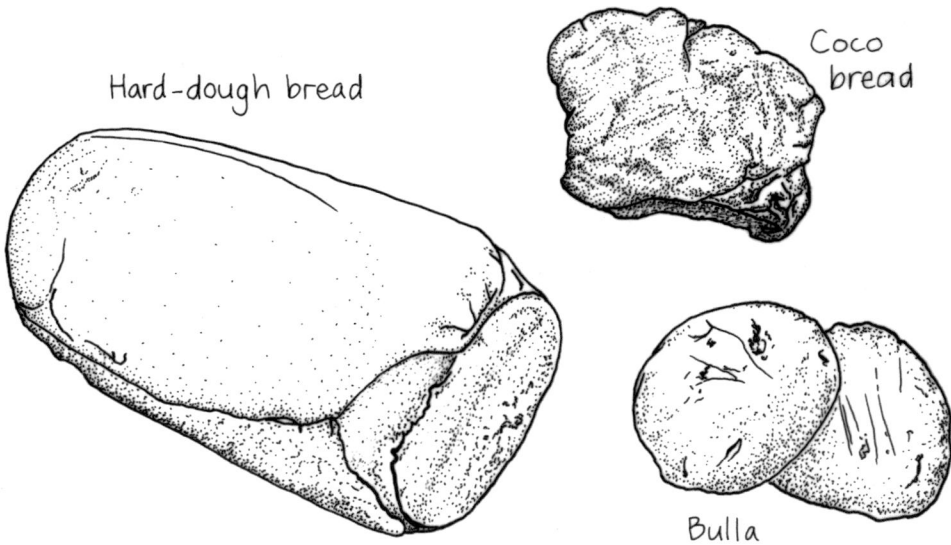

Figure 6.7 Hard-dough bread, coco bread and bulla

on producing it. By the late twentieth century, hard dough, or "hardo", had become a noun, identifying a particular bread rather than simply the description of a quality.

"Steam bread" derived its name from the method of baking, using a brick oven heated by steam pipes raised to high, even temperatures to bake the bread an attractive golden brown. The steamed oven keeps the surface of the dough moist, postponing the formation of a brown crust while allowing the loaf to reach its maximum volume. Thus the steam bread of Jamaica was a product much like the round-topped, cracked-crust, soft-centred breads typical of contemporary North America and Britain. Even the smaller towns had "steam bakeries" in the later nineteenth century, using "continuous heat steam ovens". As early as 1912 what they produced could be called "old time steam bread". It was advertised as malted and scientifically fermented, with a nut-like aroma, and delivering "a maximum of nourishment and a minimum of starch"; these were "advantages not enjoyed by hard dough bread". It was this loaf that was to become sliced bread, a neat block wrapped in paper or plastic. By 1950, lighter sliced loaves became known as "sandwich" bread, "bursting with its fine flavour and oven-freshness".[56]

Another important transition was the driving out of brown bread by white. In England, the shift from brown to white bread began in the middle of the eighteenth century and was complete by the later nineteenth century, the demand for ever-whiter bread strongly correlated with purity and palatability. This was considered a "significant change in public taste", as white bread moved from being a luxury of the rich to the most basic of fare. White bread held this position in Britain even in the face of arguments in favour of the nutritional advantages of wholemeal and "natural" breads, beginning in the 1890s.[57] In Kingston, both white and brown bread were baked, but brown bread was still being imported in 1900. In 1914 it was said that Jamaicans preferred white bread but that brown was better. In 1918 M.H. Segree of Savanna la Mar explained that brown bread was made with "whole wheat which is locally known as 'Graham Flour' and does not keep well" because the bran and germ decomposed rapidly in dough and attacked the gluten that enabled bread made from wheaten flour to form a "light, spongy, well-risen loaf". Whole wheat inevitably produced a "heavy, sodden indigestible bread" even when excessively baked to make a thicker crust, whereas white bread was "more healthily made, and will be free from acidity when whole meal and dark breads are sour and unwholesome". For most people, said Segree, brown bread was "nauseous, frequently causing flatulency".[58]

In the 1920s much was written in favour of brown or whole wheat bread as a source of vitamins. The nutrition-advocacy magazine *Jamaica Public Health* claimed that it was "doubtful if real whole wheat bread is made in the Colony; most of the brown bread is made from white flour with a mixture of 50 per cent or more of whole wheat flour, while some of it may be made of white flour mixed with bran". The real problem with bread in Jamaica was its price and a lack of hygiene, and Jamaica's bakeries were criticized because the bread they produced "does not have a pleasant taste". Because bread was sold by weight, said *Jamaica Public Health*, Jamaicans preferred loaves that were "compact and with very small air cells, evidently believing that more bread is obtained for a given amount of money if the bread is practically solid". The magazine promoted the modern notion that bread should be elastic and resume its shape if squeezed, and that it should be wrapped in paper at the bakery. Some of the leading bakeries were already wrapping bread by machine, in paper waxed on both sides; the heat of the bread sealed the paper and made paste and paste brush redundant. One bakery said it would wrap all of its bread if loaves could be made rectangular, but "some people, however, for reasons known only to themselves, demand and will accept no bread other than long drawn-out loaves with pointed ends".[59]

Jamaica had had commercial bakeries since the seventeenth century, but their flour was often stale and most firms were short-lived. Bakeries established after the abolition of slavery had greater longevity, partly because of the greatly expanded market for their products. Some of them survived into the twentieth century. The Kingston Mills bakery, founded about 1840, operated until World War I and claimed to be "the principal bread-making establishment of the island" since 1860. One of the largest bakeries in the later twentieth century was National Continental Corporation, established in 1952 by Karl and Larry Hendrickson, sons of Reginald Hendrickson, who had operated the National Bakery in Mandeville. NCC was the first "modern" Jamaican bakery, producing sliced bread, but it also baked traditional hard dough and buns using Reginald Hendrickson's methods. A bakers' association was established by 1960 and grew to a peak of one hundred members, representing 90 per cent of the baking industry. The number of bakeries declined, but by 2000 Jamaicans could purchase a greater variety of breads than ever before, including pita or Syrian bread, oat bran breads and bagels.[60]

Before fresh-baked bread was readily available in Jamaica, bread and biscuit had often been imported. Coarse, hard "ship-bisket, either brown or white", came to Jamaica beginning in the seventeenth century. Ship biscuits continued to be eaten, and even produced in Jamaican bakeries, down to the 1920s.[61] Another variety of hard, dry biscuit was the water cracker, American in origin and first advertised in Jamaica in 1869. In 1873 these were new to the Englishman Rampini, who reported eating in Kingston "a small biscuit called 'crackers' soaked in butter". When the Jamaica Biscuit Company commenced operation in 1911, it began with water crackers and employed an American biscuit maker, John Crook. By 1920 it was advertising "Jamaica Water Crackers", and encouraging subscribers to "cultivate the latest habit by having them for breakfast, lunch, or dinner". More delicate were "butter crackers".[62] Some ate "soaked biscuits" or "crackers boiled in slightly salted water, drained, buttered lavishly, and served to those who like the delicacy but needed a good digestion if they would suffer no after-discomfort". Excelsior Biscuits – delicious, fresh, crisp, nourishing – became popular as Excelsior Water Crackers, prime candidates for any Jamaican's grip going northward (Figure 6.8). Another crisp, dry type was the Crisco biscuit, made in Jamaica by the 1920s, using the first vegetable shortening, Crisco, which had been developed in 1911 using hydrogenated cottonseed oil. Saltines also emerged in this period, as a tea biscuit.[63]

By 1920 the Jamaica Biscuit Company's products included sweet, salt and whole wheat biscuits, as well as biscuits suitable for tea, jelly, cheese and soup. Among the sweet biscuits were 5 O'clock Tea, Honey Girls, Orange Crisp and Ginger Snap, and the "latest products" of 1920: Victory Biscuit, Malt Biscuit, Contingent Biscuit and Osbourne Biscuit. In 1938 there were Chocolate Cream, Picnic Cream, Mustafa Cake (a short

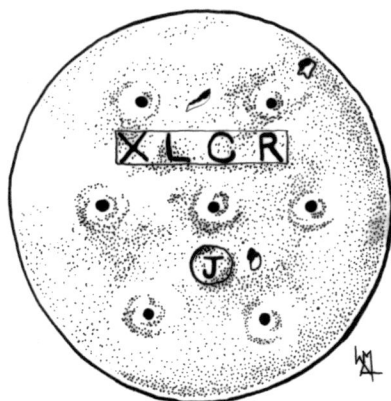

Figure 6.8 Excelsior Water Cracker

bread), Mocha and Marie, all "carefully put up in convenient packs". Other biscuits "made in Jamaica by Jamaicans for Jamaicans" around 1920 included arrowroot, Albert, creams and saltines. As well as the locally made biscuits, there were imports. Even during the Depression of the 1930s, Huntley and Palmers English Cakes and tins of their biscuits, "the Best Biscuits in the World", were on sale in Kingston at Christmas time. The Jamaica Biscuit Company had little local competition until the National Baking Company entered the market in the 1950s. In 1972 the Jamaica Biscuit Company was acquired by Carreras and new biscuit lines were introduced, using modern machinery and techniques learned from Canadian manufacturers. The Excelsior Water Cracker retained its character and was proclaimed "the country's most famous brand name ever". In 2005 a cinnamon flavour was introduced.[64]

Jamaica produced some distinctive cakes using wheat flour, generally distinguished by their form rather than their ingredients. Claude McKay described some of these special shapes as baked in rural Jamaica, at the beginning of the twentieth century, for auction at tea meetings: flowers, fruit, letters, birds, cats, a village gate, and the crown for the queen of the tea meeting. One cake that disappeared, perhaps by the 1920s, was the "blanket", made from two flat, triangle-shaped pieces of sponge cake with jam in between. In 1938 Zora Hurston saw many-layered elaborate cakes in St Mary, baked for a wedding and carried on the heads of dancers.[65]

Somewhere between cake, bun and gingerbread was the bulla (Figure 6.7). Spelled "buller" down to about 1940, and also known as "cartman's hymn-book", the bulla emerged in the late nineteenth century. A flat round cake, up to ten centimetres in diameter, it was made from a cheap grade of soft wheat flour, wet sugar, soda and water, and flavoured with ginger. It was dark brown and sometimes had a hole in the centre. The earliest identified reference in the *Gleaner* occurred in 1920, when a Mrs Louise Brown opened a cake depot on Orange Street in Kingston offering "well flavoured bullers and fine cakes of various kinds". H.G. De Lisser wrote about the bulla nostalgically in 1932, referring to "the era of thirty or forty years ago, to the older Jamaica, the Jamaica that is rapidly vanishing". When he was a boy, he said, "the Butterdough or Buller" was the only cake he and his fellows claimed to dislike, thinking it something indulged in only by the lower classes, though he came to see this as hypocrisy. One bulla was sufficient to satisfy any normal appetite, he said, and it remained, in 1932, "the cheapest of edibles". It was sometimes "made small" and served at the Myrtle Bank hotel with a French name. De Lisser wondered about the etymology of "buller", thinking it came perhaps from a baker's surname, but others playfully traced it to the time of Henry VIII and the "Papal Bulla".[66]

By the 1960s, refined versions of the bulla were using additional ingredients, such as baking powder, butter, salt, cinnamon, nutmeg, ground ginger, pimento, orange peel and vanilla to increase the spiciness. Eaten with salted butter or avocado, even the "humble bulla" became appreciated, enjoyed by schoolchildren, who called, "Three cheers, bulla and pear, come fi yu share." But other baked products competed strongly after Independence and the bulla retreated to country bakeries and shops. It re-emerged in the 1980s as a product of the larger bakeries, in new shapes and sizes, sometimes square rather than round.[67]

These changes in the bulla meant that by the 1990s it was increasingly confused with the toto. Like the bulla, the toto or tuoto or "toe-toe bulla" appears to be a twentieth-century invention, though smaller, at about seven centimetres in diameter, and sometimes square. Made with flour, brown sugar and shredded coconut, the toto, was "puffed with baking powder and soda and flavoured with coconut milk". By the end of the twentieth century, it was hard to find, as were soda cakes – flour cakes "made with plenty bicarbonate of soda and light brown sugar" and with lots of flour rubbed on top before baking. More completely lost was "sugar dash" or "mess-around", which was even larger and thicker than the bulla, made with golden brown sugar and with plenty of sugar sprinkled on top before baking. It may have been named in the 1920s, when the mess-around was a popular dance step, or alternatively so labelled simply because it required much stirring. Another form of sugar dash that failed to survive was roly-poly, "flavoured with plenty of vanilla, oblong in shape folded like a crust and the centre doubled with jam".[68]

Emerging in citations at the same time as the bulla, in the 1940s, was "jackass corn", a hard, crisp biscuit or cake, said to get its name from the sound made when it was eaten, suggesting the sound of a donkey eating corn. Jackass corn contained no corn but was made from wheat flour, baking soda, sugar, nutmeg, salt, shredded coconut and water. The dough was rolled out and cut into rectangles and baked, the biscuits hardening as they cooled. Recipes appeared into the 1990s.[69]

Closely related was "coco bread", described in the 1950s as a baked dumpling made by pounding flour dough flat and folding it over before baking (Figure 6.7). It appears to be a late arrival, with the origin of its name wrapped in mystery, and recipes are hard to find. Yeast was dissolved in sugar and water, mixed with warm milk, salt and beaten egg, then plain flour added to make the dough. This was kneaded for perhaps ten minutes and left to rise for an hour. Pieces of the dough were rolled out, brushed with melted butter and folded over twice, then baked to a golden brown. It is now a common lunchtime food, buttered or filled with bully beef.[70]

Another close relative of these distinctive breads and cakes was the "Jamaican bun" or "Jamaican Easter bun", a rectangular loaf, moist and heavy, with lots of fruit and a light brown colour. In the late twentieth century, this bun was often referred to as traditional, but the origins of the bun and of the tradition may not be so distant. Before the installation of the Jamaican bun, Jamaicans followed the tradition of baking hot cross buns at Easter time. These buns were made round to represent the full moon, and the cross with which they were decorated symbolized the four quarters. In 1870 "hot cross buns" were advertised to be available at 5:30 a.m. on Good Friday from a Kingston bakery on Luke Lane, located "opposite the English and German Synagogue". The ingredients are not known but may have been more spicy than the modern bland version. The Phoenix Bakery offered in 1880 "hot X buns" to "those who like a real good northside hot spiced bun". These were the only variety of buns offered by bakeries down to the 1950s. In 1957 the *Farmer's Food Manual* offered only a recipe for "hot cross buns" made from flour, sugar, yeast, milk, shortening, currants, mixed ground spice, egg and salt. The dough was shaped into "round buns", a cross marked on top with melted sugar, and the buns baked.[71]

Although hot cross buns continued to be baked in small quantities, they came to be little favoured in Jamaica and by the 1960s had been displaced by the crossless loaf-shaped spice bun. Thus Leila Brandon's cookbook of 1963 ignored the hot cross bun and included only a recipe for "Easter spiced bun", without giving it a "Jamaican" label. She combined milk and water, poured the liquid over butter, sugar, salt, cinnamon and mixed spice in a bowl, and added an egg. Flour was sieved in and stirred. Dissolved yeast was added to the mixture, along with crystallized cherries, raisins and citron, all chopped. The dough was allowed to double in bulk, and kneaded twice with additional flour. Shaped into "loaves", it was left to rise and double once more. Finally, the dough was turned into loaf tins and baked until the buns left the sides of the tins and felt springy. There is little in this recipe to suggest evolution from the hot cross bun. On the other hand, seeing the Jamaican Easter bun as both "unique" and "part of our rich English heritage" remains valid. Norma Benghiat has argued that "spiced fruit buns were the original Good Friday hot cross buns which became very popular during Tudor days in England". Further, she says, such buns continue to be made in England at Easter, and "some of the Yorkshire buns are identical to our Easter buns". Certainly Jamaican bakers produced "spiced buns" by the early twentieth century without any connection with Easter, and offered them along with sugar buns and related cakes and breads.[72]

The style of bun represented by Brandon's recipe of 1963 was subject to only minor modification. Thirty years later, Enid Donaldson's cookbook gave no fewer than four different recipes for "Easter spice bun", one made with baking soda, the others with baking powder, yeast and stout. Stout became a common addition, used not only to give flavour but also to provide the much desired moistness. Some cooks included dried pawpaw among the fruits and recommended adding a little extra water to the batter before baking at a low temperature. Others claimed the best buns used eggs and stout but no yeast. When Jamaica Flour Mills published a recipe for a traditional "rich, moist, fruity, Easter bun" in 1995, it began by soaking raisins, currants and mixed peel in stout, then blended this with "all purpose" flour, baking powder, mixed spice, cinnamon, melted margarine, eggs, honey and browning (a colouring agent, either artificial or produced from brown sugar). This bun was glazed with a "bun wash" made of sugar and water boiled to a thick syrup. Others added honey to the glaze, and by 2003 soya milk became a potential ingredient. A "Rasta Bun and Cheese" was made with grated coconut, butter, sugar, coconut milk, nutmeg, flour and ginger powder, and served with soya cheese.[73]

Most of the Easter buns consumed in Jamaica have been the products of commercial bakeries, using yeast and their own secret combinations of spices. Beginning in the 1980s, it was complained that Jamaica's Easter buns had become "tasteless shadows of their former selves". Demand was heavy, overseas as well as locally, and shortages occurred. Jamaicans abroad tried to replicate the bun where they settled, "yet they never succeed entirely in reproducing either the appearance or flavour of the Easter bun baked in Jamaica". The reason for this failure was perhaps the "absence of tropical temperature and the conditioning of dried fruits which are nowadays made from processed chocho, granadilla, pineapple and pawpaw".[74] In Jamaica, consumers complained most of dry bun and sparse fruit.

The regular companion of bun is cheese, specifically the processed variety known as "tin cheese". By 1990 it could be claimed that the two had been put together for "many years" as a Lenten custom to balance the denial of flesh-eating. In 1928, for example, stores offered "Easter cheese" (Cheddar, Dutch and Kraft) along with "Easter buns". The "Jamaican bun" served with cheese came to be regarded as "a wonderful compromise for people who had given up desserts for the Lenten period between Ash Wednesday and the day of Ascension". Cheese-makers could tell consumers, "a truly Jamaican Easter begins with bun and cheese. Spicy buns chock-full with raisins and cherries and topped with chunks of delicious cheese, are all a part of the Jamaican Easter tradition." The popularity of the Jamaican "Easter" bun quickly made it available all year round, eaten with cheese and without butter.[75]

Almost as popular as the Easter bun was Jamaican Christmas pudding, which took the place of the Christmas cake and Christmas pudding as made in Britain and other places, and was sometimes referred to as a "rich fruit cake". The distinguishing features of the Jamaican Christmas "pudding" were that it acted as both cake and pudding (the same mixture making a "cake" if baked differently and perhaps iced) and that was always served cold, with a moistness that pointed to its origins in fruits (raisins, currants, prunes, cherries, mixed peel) soaked in wine and rum, with grated nutmeg and ground cinnamon or perhaps mixed spice. The soaking process began at least a month before the making of the pudding. Flour and breadcrumbs made up the bulk of the pudding, sieved with baking powder and salt, but the strained fruits were to be prominent, the whole flavoured by port wine, sherry and the liquid from the soaked fruits, mixed with vanilla and almond flavouring. The pudding was given a dark colour by using browning, either bought in a shop or made from dark sugar or granulated sugar and coffee, added along with eggs to the creamed butter and sugar. Covered and set in a pan of boiling water, a pudding was the result; left open in the oven, it produced a cake. As soon as it came out of the oven, sherry or rum was poured over it, further regular doses were given until the pudding or cake was served, and pudding might also be had with a rum butter.[76]

In contrast to the rich, moist, fruity Jamaican Easter bun and Christmas pudding were varieties of buns promoted for their nutritional values. In 2005 a bran bun was created by HTB (Hannah Town Bakery), spicy and shaped like an Easter bun but delivering lots of fibre and promoted as "not too sweet" and as healthy, offering "bun without guilt". More importantly, as part of the Schools Feeding Programme that commenced in 1973, students were provided with subsidized milk, and to this was added first a spice cake, then a spice bun, and from 1982 a "fortified nutri-bun" baked by Nutrition Products, a government enterprise. Some complained that this contributed to the dominance of wheat flour products at the expense of equally healthy home-grown alternatives.[77]

Another favourite baked wheat-flour pastry product of the twentieth century is the Jamaican patty. Pastry dough is rolled out into a circle, a scoop of spiced, seasoned filling placed on one side, the pastry folded over to make a semicircle and its edges sealed, and the patty baked in an oven (Figure 6.9). The most common filling is minced beef. Some have traced the patty to the island's English heritage, and more specifically to the Cornish pasty. Others have found strong similarities between the Jamaican patty and the South American empanada, though the latter is distinguished by the inclusion of cumin, raisins, nuts and olives.[78] Yet it has come to be regarded as a uniquely Jamaican product.

The basic concept for the patty can be found in eighteenth-century English cookery, but the filling, or forcemeat, was as likely to be made of veal, chicken, turkey, fish, oyster or lobster, and the finished patty was small and delicate. The patty began life in England as a food of the rich, using large quantities of meat and requiring an oven for baking. Rather than a complete lunch or snack, these early patties were sometimes simply used as "garnish" to surround large dishes on a table. Hannah Glasse, in 1747, had a recipe for "petit patties for garnishing of dishes", the pastry just an inch deep and filled with seasoned veal, beef, bacon, oysters, or suet and mushrooms, depending on the main dish. Richard Briggs followed closely in his American 1792 recipe for "force-meat patties", to be made in "little tin patty pans, about the size of a tea cup, but not so deep" (Figure 6.9). Briggs's pastry was "a rich puff-paste" formed like a little pie, the cover rubbed with egg yolk and baked to "a fine gold colour". Briggs offered another method of shaping the patty pastry, much closer to modern practice, in which the puff pastry was rolled into a small circle, turned over the contents and sealed "like an apple puff". This was not baked but fried quickly to "a fine brown" in a pan of "boiling hot hogs-lard".[79] The modern Jamaican patty draws on these English and American methods and combines elements from the two styles described by Briggs at the end of the eighteenth century.

Throughout most of the nineteenth century, patties baked in Jamaica continued the tradition of small pies stuffed with meat. Sullivan offered a recipe in 1893 for "salt fish patties" made in "patty-pans lined with pastry", covered and baked. Here the filling was made from saltfish stewed with scallion, tomato, pepper, parsley, herbs and butter, with "a little sauce and nutmeg".[80] Sullivan's patties were made in a pan which came with its own holes, producing small discs rather than the folded-over, semi-circular

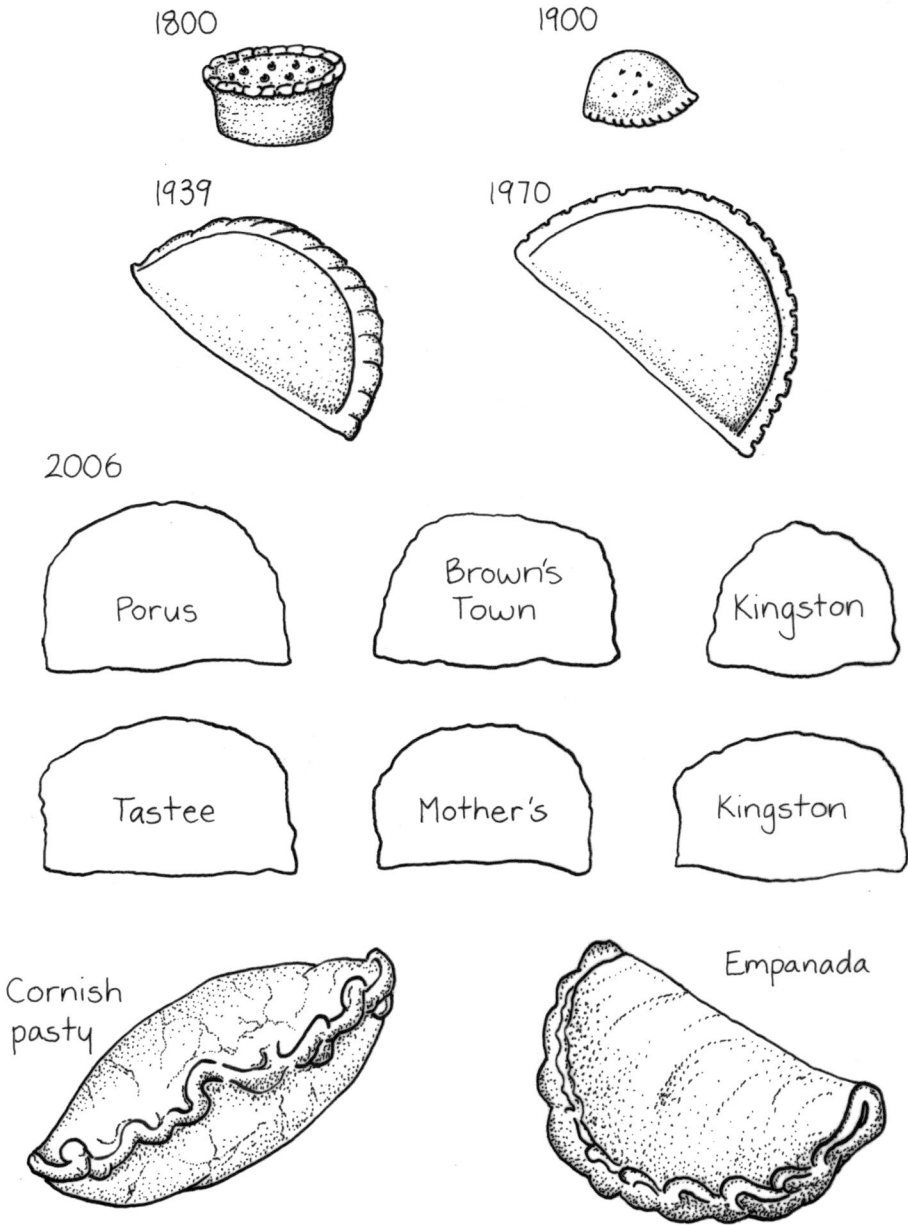

1800

1900

1939

1970

2006

Porus

Brown's Town

Kingston

Tastee

Mother's

Kingston

Cornish pasty

Empanada

Figure 6.9 Evolution of the patty. The six outlines for 2006 are based on tracings of actual patties, drawn to scale.

patty that became a trademark of the Jamaican version. Her use of saltfish as the filling also seems not to connect with the monopoly held by beef by the early twentieth century. The modern patty initially retained a strong connection with entertaining and this, together with the costly technology of baking, suggests that its twentieth-century evolution may have occurred in the kitchens of the better-off rather than in the yards of the poor.

The earliest identified reference in the *Gleaner* to "beef patties" came in 1927, when they were included in lunches offered to patrons at Sabina Park cricket matches. Individual beef patties cost three pence. The first reference in the *Gleaner* to "a 3d. pattie" was in 1926. From 1927, Kingston bakeries and restaurants began regularly to advertise "hot patties made daily", often specifying that these were "beef patties". The first known image of a patty in its modern shape appeared in an advertisement published in 1939 (Figure 6.9). Some versions of this advertisement identified the patty as "a delicious meat pie". In 1932, De Lisser, looking back to his boyhood in the 1890s, recalled "hot patties" sold for a quattie (a penny half-penny) and "each containing as it seemed to us then, about two pounds of meat, and with a flaky crust that melted in our mouths but stuck in our stomachs".[81]

Cold patties were never appreciated. By 1940 patties had begun to be kept warm in "a receptacle shaped like a cash register which is heated by electricity". Street sellers faced greater challenges in keeping their fare warm, but handcarts pushed around Kingston offered "curried patties" among other things – the food of the working class. In the 1950s, a vendor of patties was sometimes called a "ball-pan man", taking his name from the earlier street seller of meatballs and similar foods from a box or pan.[82]

Beef patties were at first made with fresh meat, but during World War II the fresh meat came to be supplemented with canned bully beef. Patties were advertised as "milk crust patties" and "crispy". The "original Jamaican patty crust" used beef suet, but short-crust pastry was often substituted.[83] The pastry had to be flaky and lightly browned, with a hint of anatto. Popular brands of the late 1940s included Bartley's Patties, sold at four pence, with the slogan "Lawd dem nice", and Briggs' Patties, produced by Briggs' Pastry Shop in Cross Roads and also sold by Times Store on King Street. Better known was Bruce's, which evolved from the "uptown" (Cross Roads) club established in 1945 by Wilfred Augustus "Massa" Prendergast, a St Mary–born planter and race-horse owner. By 1961 Bruce's Patties were advertised as "fresh-hourly" and "famous in Jamaica".[84] Large bakeries also began to enter the patty market. Webster's on Old Hope Road stopped baking bread in 1955 to concentrate on cakes, patties and pastries. Similarly, Tastee, established by baker Vincent Chang at Cross Roads in 1966, at first made only biscuits, sweets and buns, but quickly turned to the patty, using "fresh, home-grown beef, highly seasoned", and opened the first Tastee outlet on Church Street in 1969. A number of chains were established, specializing in the sale of patties baked on the spot.[85] Indeed, the patty was the only food product to have its own shops.

By the 1990s the patty could be declared "Jamaica's favourite fast food". Tastee was the biggest seller at the beginning of the decade but faced new rivals. Mother's, established in 1981, soon claimed to be the island's largest local fast food chain, selling both meat and vegetable patties as well as hot dogs, hamburgers, chicken and roast beef sandwiches, fries, pastries, donuts, gizzadas, cakes, ice cream, sundaes, milkshakes and popcorn. In 1987 another new brand, Juici Beef Patties, entered the Kingston market from its earlier bases in May Pen, Santa Cruz, Christiana and Old Harbour, and quickly established a widespread chain.[86] The patty gradually shifted from its semicircular shape to approximate a larger rectangle, thus minimizing the proportion of wasted pastry, and the shape was increasingly standardized by the use of specialized machines (Figure 6.9).

Beef was not the only filling for the modern patty. Chicken patties appeared as early as 1944, and from the 1970s alternatives included callaloo, peas, mixed vegetables, chicken, lobster, shrimp, and ackee (crushed) with saltfish. The "beef" patty filling of the 1970s was not, in any case, exclusively beef, but consisted of minced beef and pork, cubes of Irish potato, onion or scallion, sometimes turnips, breadcrumbs and seasonings (garlic, thyme, salt, black pepper, pimento and Scotch bonnet pepper); it could even be said that no one was "really quite certain about just what goes into an authentic Jamaican patty".[87]

The patty was sometimes eaten stuffed into yet another baked pastry product, the coco bread or cruss (crust). Charles Hyatt recalled cruss in 1989, saying it was "the dough leave over when yuh mekkin' patty an the meat finish. Them roll it an fold it over few times and then cut it into four inch pieces an bake it. Nice!" Barbara Gloudon also remembered cruss fondly as "a crisp fold of pastry shaped to nestle the patty in its warm embrace, sold from a 'patty pan' a two-tiered tin box equipped with hot coals to heat the precious contents".[88]

Patty-, bun- and bread-making came to be dominated by commercial bakeries largely because of the cost of the technology required to produce quality products in quantity, and this in turn made them the dominant users of wheat flour. For the poor and the rural peasantry, these baked products were of no great concern, at least down to World War I. In times of hardship, when the root crops failed, the peasantry might buy barrels of wheat flour and bags of cornmeal but, as McKay noticed, the people rarely used it for "the common baked bread". Rather, they turned it into "dumplings, johnnycake, corn pone, corn cake, puddings, porridges". Loaf bread was, for the peasantry, "a delicacy" reserved for Sundays or weddings. When a change from the regular "food" crops was desired, they turned to rice rather than to wheat.[89] The idea that bread was something special to Sundays persisted down to the middle of the century; it required purchase of a cooked food from a shop. Dumpling and porridge, on the other hand, could be boiled more cheaply, using simple tools, or, with somewhat greater investment, fried.

Boiled wheat-flour dumplings came in various shapes and sizes (Figure 6.10). The smallest was the "spinner", made by rubbing the two hands together with a small amount of dough in between; the largest was commonly known as "belly-bottom concrete" or "cartwheel dumpling", flattened out to form a large disc. The resulting dumplings, regardless of size, were a flour product tighter and heavier than hard-dough bread but cheap and palatable, taking on flavour from the soup or stew in which it was boiled – and big enough to choke to death on if it stuck in the throat. Once bread became common, the cartwheel dumpling was thought "old-fashioned". In the 1950s, the "cow-tongue" dumpling was rolled like a spinner, flattened, and grooved to resemble the tongue of a cow. All of these dumplings could be made from just flour and water. A 1970s recipe for "soft dumplings" combined flour, baking powder, skimmed milk powder and salt, mixed with water and cooking oil. This dough was dropped from a spoon or formed in the hand to make small round balls, to boil in a large pan of water. Cooks were advised not to flatten these. Cheese dumplings were prepared by the same method, adding grated cheese, omitting the salt and making the oil optional. By the 1980s, the "most popular" were the "rounded, slightly flattened flour dumplings with the thumb imprint in the centres". It was this style of dumpling that went into soups and stews or were boiled in salted water to accompany meat dishes. All of these forms of dumpling were essentially plain – not filled with other ingredients – but they were joined by steamed Chinese dumplings or buns, *char shau pao* stuffed with roast pork.[90]

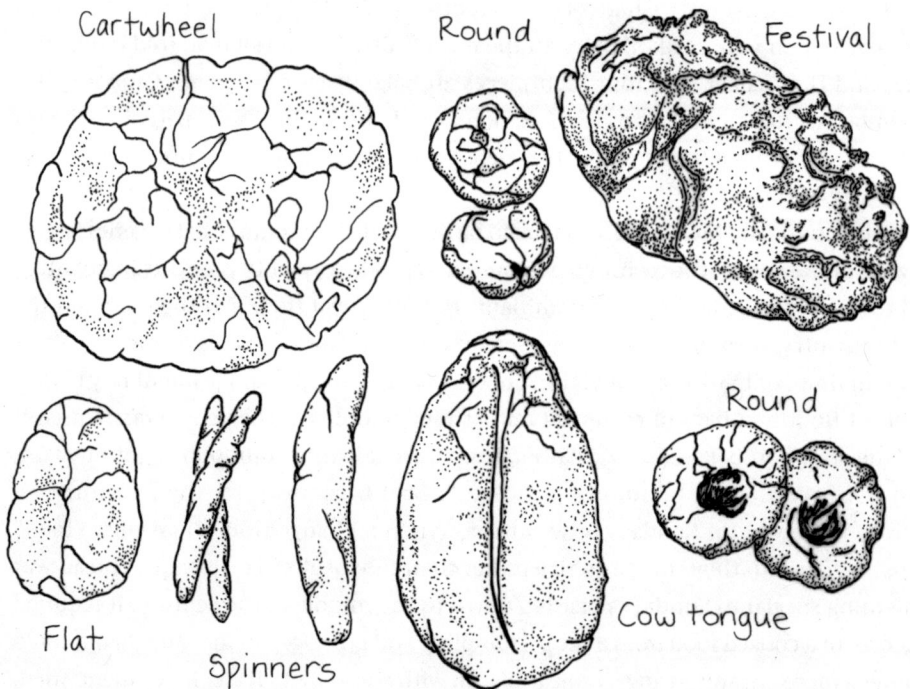

Figure 6.10 Dumplings: spinner, cartwheel, cow tongue, round, flat, festival

The toasted or fried version of the dumpling was often called a "johnnycake". Sullivan gave a recipe for "Johnny or journey cakes" made from flour dough cut into rounds and baked on a gridiron. When cooked, these were opened, buttered, and closed again. She had "seen these fried; but they are, in that case, not opened but served intact". In 1922 De Lisser referred to "little cakes of flour, brown and crisp, split in two and richly buttered" but did not say how they were cooked. Frying seems to have become popular only after World War II. A recipe from the 1970s recommended making "fried johnny cakes" by mixing flour, skimmed milk powder, salt, baking powder, margarine and water to form a dough, shaping the dumplings "as desired" and frying them in hot fat until golden brown. Alternatively, additional water could be added and the mixture dropped from a spoon.[91] Cornmeal was not an ingredient in this version but it soon entered, as in festival.

Pasta is perhaps the ultimate example of the malleability of flour dough, enabled by its gluten, and made from the paste wheat (*Triticum durum*) rather than the modern bread wheat (*T. aestivum*). It reached Jamaica in various forms and shapes and sizes. By 1913 Kingston grocers could offer canned spaghetti from the Heinz "57 varieties" range, and later added ravioli and other shapes and sizes. The first reference to macaroni came in 1927 when a Kingston restaurant offered macaroni and cheese, a dish that was to become a popular home-baked dish later in the century. When they came in cans, most of these early pasta products were combined with tomato sauce and meatballs, and advertised as "Italian dishes". Dried vermicelli, long and thin, became common in grocery shops. By the 1950s Italian cookery was associated with pizza pies and pizza pie mix, a baked rather than a boiled dough, but the first specialist "pizza parlour" was not established until 1982, in New Kingston. In 2005 Pizza Hut offered a "pizza patty", promoted as "the pizza that locks the flavour inside". It looked like a patty, with a sprinkling of herbs baked on top and a cheesy filling. Pasta and pizza became increasingly popular, particularly among the young and the travelled, and pizza shops were some of the first to home-deliver cooked food. Long before the Italians, the Chinese had created and become great lovers of wheat-flour pasta, and some of their particular products, such as noodles, entered the Jamaican food system through Chinese restaurants and through the gradual diffusion of Chinese styles of home-cooking in the later twentieth century, though noodles became known best in chicken noodle soup, introduced to Jamaica in 1945. Wheat was not the only grain used to make pasta, in either China or Italy, but it was the first and the most important, and it was the peculiar mechanical qualities of the grain's gluten that enabled its transformation into plastic art.[92]

Breakfast cereals, which were first considered a class of food in the late nineteenth century, contrasted strongly with the transformation of wheat grains symbolized by pasta. They sought to identify with the natural grain, though broken and roasted in various ways. Crushed wheat was available in Jamaica by 1876, and Cream of Wheat by 1903. In 1928 a Kingston bakery offered "wholewheat porridge flour". These wheat products faced stiff competition from corn. Another competitor was oats, notably Quaker Oats, imported by 1897 for porridge-making. By the 1980s, oats also served as a base ingredient of the drink Magnum Force, blended with peanuts, condensed milk, sugar, plantain, ripe banana, nutmeg and water.[93]

More generic was the "grape nut", which reached Jamaica in 1901. A 1918 advertisement proclaimed its virtues as a food for children, saying, "its sweet, nut-like flavour appeals to the growing child's appetite, and its wholesome composition of wheat, barley and other grains makes it a 'builder' of the highest type". Grape nuts were quickly marketed for their "distinctive blend of whole wheat and malted barley which is so substantially nutritious and so good in flavour".[94] By the end of the twentieth century, they appeared most often as an ingredient in ice cream and were rarely recognized as a wheat product.

Finally, wheat formed the base ingredient of some vegetarian products intended as substitutes for meat. An important Jamaican producer of such items was WESTICO Foods, based at West Indies College in Mandeville, a Seventh-Day Adventist institution. For example, WESTICO's Loma Linda Vegetable Steak, introduced in 1990, was "meatless protein which is free of animal fat and cholesterol", made from "wheat protein, soy oil, dry yeast, soy protein, soy flour and onion powder".[95]

PEAS, BEANS

The distinction between a pea and a bean is arbitrary, and Jamaicans commonly call "peas" what other people call "beans". All of these seeds belong to a large family, the members of which are popularly known as "legumes" or "pulses" and which are some of the world's most important food plants. Unlike the cereal grains, which come from grasses with their seeds enclosed in husks, the legumes are flowering plants with fruit pods that contain the seeds. When green and immature, the entire pod is eaten, as in snow peas or string beans, along with some of the fresh shoots, leaves and sprouts (the germinated seeds). Other peas and beans are removed from their pods for cooking, while still green and soft or when dry and hard. Most of the legumes are good sources of protein and carbohydrates, and some yield edible oil, though toxins may also be present that necessitate special preparation. As early as the seventeenth century, some of Jamaica's peas, such as the horse-eye bean, were reputed to cause death if eaten. Many of them had problems of digestibility.[96]

Sorting out the many varieties of legumes cultivated and consumed in Jamaica, and relating the colourfully descriptive common names to the correct scientific names, is often a puzzle (Figure 6.11). Writing about the late seventeenth century, Sloane declared the legumes a very numerous tribe in Jamaica "and of great use to the inhabitants, who feed much on the kinds of beans, pease, or phaseoli".[97] The best approach is to begin with the scientific names.

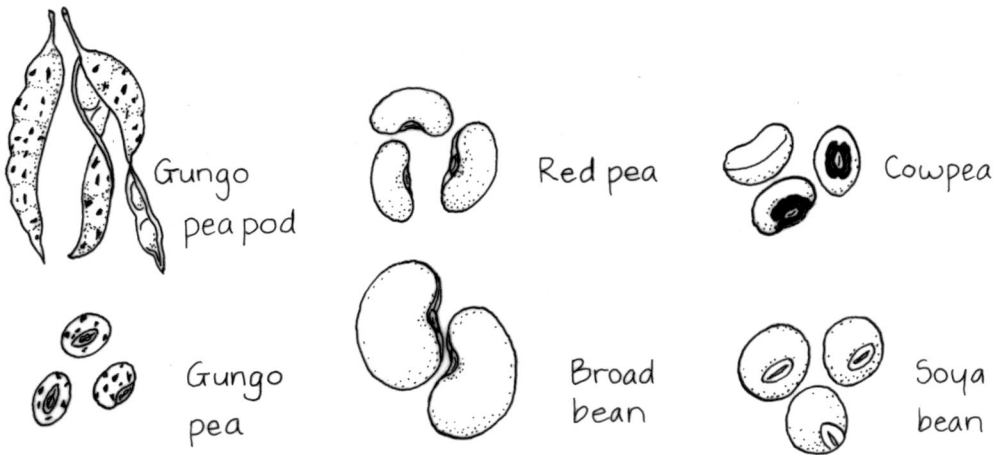

Figure 6.11 Beans and peas

Cajanus cajan is the pea most closely associated with Jamaica. Although it has literally scores of names, the best known in Jamaica are gungo or gungu pea, Congo pea, Angola pea, pigeon pea, no-eye pea, seven-year pea or (confusingly and apparently exclusive to Jamaica) red pea. Thus, in the early eighteenth century, Barham referred to "the great Angola red pease". Hughes, in 1672, had talked only of the "seven year pease", so named because it required planting only every seventh year. Lunan reported in 1814 that because the "pigeon or Angola pea" bore at the end of the year, it was "therefore sometimes called in Jamaica the *Christmas pea*". Gungo was not recorded until the 1860s. By the 1980s, when gungo was hailed as a "great favourite", esteemed for its flavour and texture, three varieties were recognized: "the black or brown skinned, the striped skinned which might well be a hybrid, and the green skinned". The black was associated with Clarendon and considered the richest-tasting, while the tender green variety was concentrated in St Elizabeth and the striped variety widely distributed.[98]

C. cajan is probably a native of South Asia and perhaps tropical Africa, but is now widespread in the tropics and subtropics. A shrub, growing to three metres in height, it has whitish green stalks, yellow flowers, and small green leaves. The leaves and immature pods can be eaten as a vegetable, but this seems uncommon in Jamaica. The peas are greyish when dried, and often speckled. During slavery, the bushes were sometimes used as fences, and gungo was generally common in provision grounds, where it was valued because it was a perennial, was happy in even the most parched sites and needed little care in cultivation. The peas were eaten both green and dried, the latter often needing long boiling to make them soft.[99]

Phaseolus vulgaris is the true red pea, also commonly called kidney bean or, less often, French bean. Although less characteristically Jamaican than gungo, the red pea is a native of the Americas and is the "common bean" of the region, domesticated in Mexico by 7000 BP. By the middle of the twentieth century, it was easily the most popular pea in Jamaica. The plant came in many forms, from vine to bush, and its pods in shades from green to purple. One large variety was known as "cockstone", so named for its supposed resemblance to the testicle of a cock, with great variation in shape, size and colour. Immature, the pods can be eaten as string beans; when dried, they are used in soups and combined with rice. Red peas are the typical bean of baked beans in tomato sauce. By the 1990s, Donaldson could reasonably claim that in Jamaica, "red peas or kidney beans, whether stewed in soup, or cooked with rice and coconut milk, are the most used and best liked of the legumes".[100]

Early English writers often referred to red peas as "calavances". Hughes described "calavanc, or calavances", as peas growing on a low-branched plant with long pods like kidney beans, and said some people called them Indian peas. He considered them "very good food", causing less trouble with wind than most peas. The colonists in Jamaica, said Hughes, "when [the peas] are green, they boil and butter them, and so do sometimes when they are dry; or else they boil and eat them with pork, or wild hog". Barham grouped calavances with the *phaseoli*, and said the pods contained "a small white pea, resembling the kidney", that was "very good and sweet, green or dry, and easy of digestion; and therefore proper for a hot climate". Browne called *P. vulgaris* "calavances, or red pease", and Long called them "calavances, or red bean".[101]

P. lunatus is best known in Jamaica as "broad bean", but is also referred to as "lima bean", "sugar bean" and "great bean". Sloane, who called it "the great bean", thought it came to Jamaica from Africa, but it is in fact a native of tropical America. It grows on an annual or short-lived perennial twining plant, rising to two metres and climbing on poles or other plants. The beans or seeds are contained in large pods about fifteen millimetres long that follow flowering and are often whitish. Sloane said the broad bean was "planted in most gardens, and provision plantations" and eaten when green in December. James Macfadyen in 1837, believed the lima bean to be "justly considered as among the most delicate of the pulse tribe cultivated in Jamaica". *P. lunatus* was unusual among the peas and beans in being recognized as toxic by the middle of the twentieth century, with a cyanide principle similar to that found in cassava but generally overcome by correct cooking (boiling and crushing).[102]

Lablab purpureus is known as "bonavist bean" or "banner bean". Probably a native of Africa, this perennial is now widely cultivated throughout the tropical world. Hughes described "bonniviss" peas as growing on a tall plant, running up, and flourishing all year, "having blows, kids, green pease and ripe, growing on them at one and the same time". He thought these peas harder to digest than calavances, being "a little windy", and therefore generally eaten with hot pepper. Browne said bonavist was "cultivated by most of the inhabitants in the country parts of Jamaica; for it thrived better than any of the other species; and the seeds are generally reckoned very wholesome and palatable". It grew in dry spots, spreading extensively over nearby bushes and rocks. By the early twentieth century, bonavist was often called "bannabis". McKay's 1912 poem "Me Bannabees" praised the pea and extolled its virtues compared to gungo and cockstone. A proverb intended to instill the virtue of patience ran, "Time neber too long fe Bannabis bear bean".[103]

Vigna sinensis – cowpea or black-eye pea – was domesticated in Central Africa and spread to West Africa by about AD 900. This bean is not the same as the American bean that is now broadly popular.[104]

Canavalia ensiformis, known in Jamaica as "horse bean", "overlook bean" or "jack bean", is a climbing or bushy plant bearing pods with perfectly white kidney-shaped seeds, and is grown as a cover crop. Sloane, at the end of the seventeenth century, said the seeds were "counted good food, though their greatest use is to fatten hogs", whereas Barham declared the horse bean "venomous, and not to be eaten". Macfadyen found no current use, except that the "Negroes" planted them on the margins of provision grounds, on the superstition that the overlook serves as "watchman" and "from some dreaded power ascribed to it, protects the provisions from plunder".[105] Modern accounts do mention the occasional use of the horse bean as food.

Glycine max, or soya bean, has been declared the best of the legumes, because it is the only plant food to contain a complete protein. It has become the most widely consumed legume in the world. A traditional food of East Asia, the soya bean was first promoted in Jamaica during World War II, as a general substitute; the freshly picked beans were used to make "stewed green soya bean", and the dry beans were boiled or were made into cakes. They soon drifted out of sight, though soy sauce, made from the fermented bean, entered through Chinese-style cooking. By the 1980s, tofu, or "bean curd", processed from soya bean, was available in health food shops and Chinese delicatessens and advocated as a source of plant protein in many dishes.[106]

Soy became more common after 1990, as a highly processed product, generally imported. Soya milk is made by boiling the bean, strained, and the curds used with salt to make tofu and soy cheese. Soy came to partially replace local products such as coconut, aloe vera, cocoa and banana, appealing particularly to those many Jamaicans who are lactose intolerant. Dried, chilled, canned and long-life versions of the milk became popular. The Lasoy brand (in regular, lite and milk-free versions) was strongly promoted by the food group Lasco as a base ingredient of creamy soups and baked meat dishes. Soya milk was also promoted by nutritionists as a "creamy, luscious drink" and as a major ingredient in dishes prepared specially for people living with HIV/AIDS. But there were limits to its utility: "the intolerance of soy milk to heat will never give you a good cup of Blue Mountain coffee". Its Chinese and vegetarian roots remained prominent into the twenty-first century, with little evidence of absorption into the creole tradition. Tofu in particular is regarded as bland, leading to attempts to spice it up, as in "jerk tofu".[107]

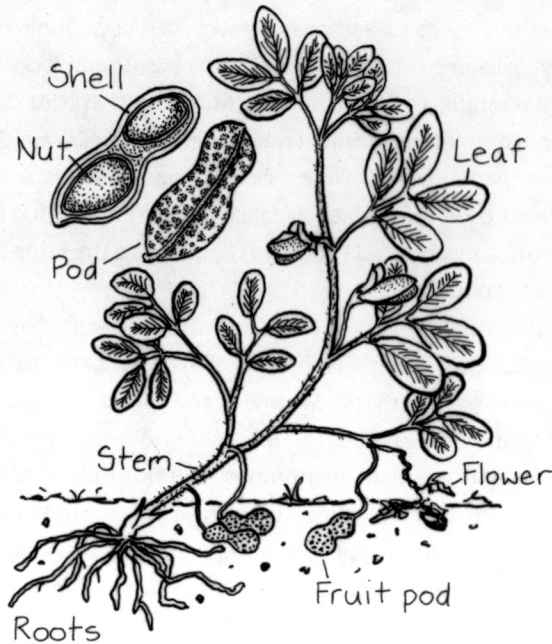

Figure 6.12 Peanut plant, fruit and nut

Arachis hypogaea is commonly known as "peanut" or "groundnut" but is in fact no more a nut than are the grape nuts crushed from wheat grains. Occasionally, it has been called a tuber, because the "nut" is an underground product, but the plant that bears it is a legume that pushes its flower stems into the ground after flowering and pollination, where the fruit pods develop (Figure 6.12). Although *A. hypogaea* is indigenous to South America, it was diffused to Africa, where it prospered alongside native grounduts. In the 1680s Sloane was told that enslaved people on ships from Africa were fed "pindals, or Indian earth-nuts, a sort of pea or bean producing its pods under ground". Browne called peanuts "pindar's or ground-nuts". He believed the seeds were "frequently imported to Jamaica, in the ships from Africa; and sometimes cultivated there [in Jamaica], though it is but very rarely, and in very small quantities".[108]

Leaving aside the seasonal prices attached to gungo, the most expensive of the legumes in Jamaica's markets was generally the red pea, followed by gungo, black-eye pea and cowpea. Prices were sometimes driven down by imports, as in the 1930s, when cheap Chilean red peas were admitted. Similarly, in 1985 there were complaints that imported red peas were on the market in spite of a bumper local harvest (Figure 6.13). Even in the eighteenth century, planters had imported barrels of "whole pease" and "bean kernels" as common food, and *Pisum sativum*, the common garden pea of England, was sometimes grown in the mountains – using imported seed.[109] Some of the peas

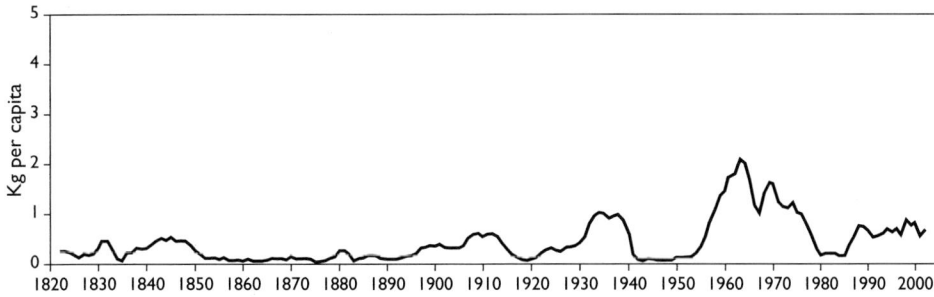

Figure 6.13 Imports of peas and beans per capita, 1822–2004. Source: Appendix 1.

were not produced in sufficient quantity to meet demand and black-eye peas and red kidney beans were being imported from the United States by the late 1870s. Canned baked beans arrived in the island by 1881. By 1900 they were joined by canned peas and stringless beans. Recipes using them appeared in the 1940s, to create dishes such as "combination baked-bean casserole", made with layers of Heinz oven-baked baked beans with pork, tomato sauce and Heinz oven-baked red kidney beans, each layer having some Heinz tomato ketchup spread over it, and slices of bacon laid on top. In the 1970s a ginger peas bun was proposed, along with "African" bread and cake, all of these recipes using puréed "African red peas" along with wheat flour.[110]

Peas contribute vital ingredients to three important Jamaican dishes: rice and peas, stew peas and rice, and (gungo) pea soup. These are all one- or two-pot dishes, boiled or stewed, and are not dependent on cooking oil. All three seem good candidates for having originated in the cooking pots of the poor, perhaps in the eighteenth century. The soup is straightforward enough; all the ingredients are boiled together in a single pot from the beginning. In the case of rice and peas, the popular eastern Caribbean version of the dish has retained the reverse title "peas and rice" and has most often been prepared in two separate pots and served separately. As with the evolution of ackee and saltfish (reversed from "saltfish and ackee"), it is possible to conceive the Jamaican dish rice and peas beginning with these two separate servings in a plate or bowl spilling together, the seasoned peas flavouring the rice, and eventually cooked together in a single pot, to enhance the flavours and save on tools and energy. Stew peas and rice, on the other hand, has not been reduced to fewer than two separate pots. Everything together in one pot would produce a slushy rice, and the point of the combination is to have the gravy of the stew peas melting over and embracing the dry, separate white rice grains.

To make rice and peas, a cup of red peas is simmered in a pot with the milk of a medium-sized coconut and a clove of garlic. Dried peas might first be soaked overnight. When the peas are tender but have not begun to break up, two stalks of scallion are added, along with some thyme, salt, black pepper, three cups of rice and enough water to boil the rice fully. A little salt pork might also be added at this stage. The dish is finished when the rice is soft but not sticky, and flavoured with the seasoning, with the peas well distributed and whole.[111] Rice and peas can be eaten as a meal in itself but is typically served with some meat and vegetables.

References to rice and peas begin later than might be expected for a dish so strongly identified with Jamaica. Sullivan gave no recipe in 1893. The first four citations identified in the *Gleaner* occurred between 1872 and 1904, all of them in court cases. Three of these were trials for murder or attempted murder (ground glass in the meal) but all of the accused were acquitted. The food was never thought to be directly responsible, though a doctor testified regarding a woman who had died of heart failure in a fight that "he would have found sufficient cause of death in the enormous meal of rice and peas which she had taken". In these cases, "rice and peas" and "peas and rice" were used interchangeably.[112] Yet in 1900 rice and peas was already regarded as an institution, essential at least to every Sunday dinner of the Kingston poor. The dish was declared "a very great food in Jamaica" and "a food equal to a diet of meat". By the 1930s it was readily available and could be called a "favourite" food.[113] When De Lisser visited Jigger-Foot Market in early 1938, he got from a vendor for one and a half pence "a fair quantity of rice and peas, some stewed meat, and a little bit of stewed vegetable stuff in a tin plate". De Lisser was "cut to the quick" to hear that some people "scorn the dish known as rice-and-peas, the food by which so many of us swear and which has even been described as Jamaica's Coat of Arms". In the 1990s, it could still be said "rice and peas is easily the best liked dish in Jamaica, called the coat of arms", but no longer reserved for Sunday – in some households, indeed, it was served throughout the week.[114]

In the 1930s, the peas used were commonly red peas, black-eye peas or gungo peas, but by the 1990s red kidney beans were the norm, with green gungo, in season, and dried gungo less often. As well as the natural evolution of rice and peas suggested earlier, it is also plausible to look for the origins of the Jamaican version of the dish in migrant movement from Jamaica to the Hispanic Caribbean in the later nineteenth century. Beans and rice are a prominent part of the cooking of Latin America. In the Spanish-speaking Americas, the original dish was generally called red beans and rice, though an earlier version was black beans and rice, which seems not to have travelled to Jamaica. De Lisser recognized the existence in 1938 of "various forms" of the dish throughout the tropical Americas, seeing a unity between pea and bean. The same year, a Kingston restaurant offered "arroz con pallo [*sic*]".[115] Related dishes are jambalaya and paella, and the Indian dish pillau.

Where rice and peas directly combined the two seeds, a less immediate association was created in stew peas and rice. The first mention of "stew peas and rice" in the *Gleaner* occurred only in 1946, offered by the new restaurant opened at Bartley's Silver City Club. The more refined "stewed peas with rice" dated from 1941, as a restaurant dish, and "stewed peas (salt beef), rice, dumplings" was given as a school lunch no earlier than 1938. All of these dates seem late. It is equally surprising that the earliest cookbook

Plate 25
Coffee, by Rev. John Lindsay, c. 1770. Bristol Museum and Art Gallery.

Plate 26
Squid, by Rev. John Lindsay, 1767–69. Bristol Museum and Art Gallery.

Plate 27
Octopus, by Rev. John Lindsay, c. 1770. Bristol Museum and Art Gallery.

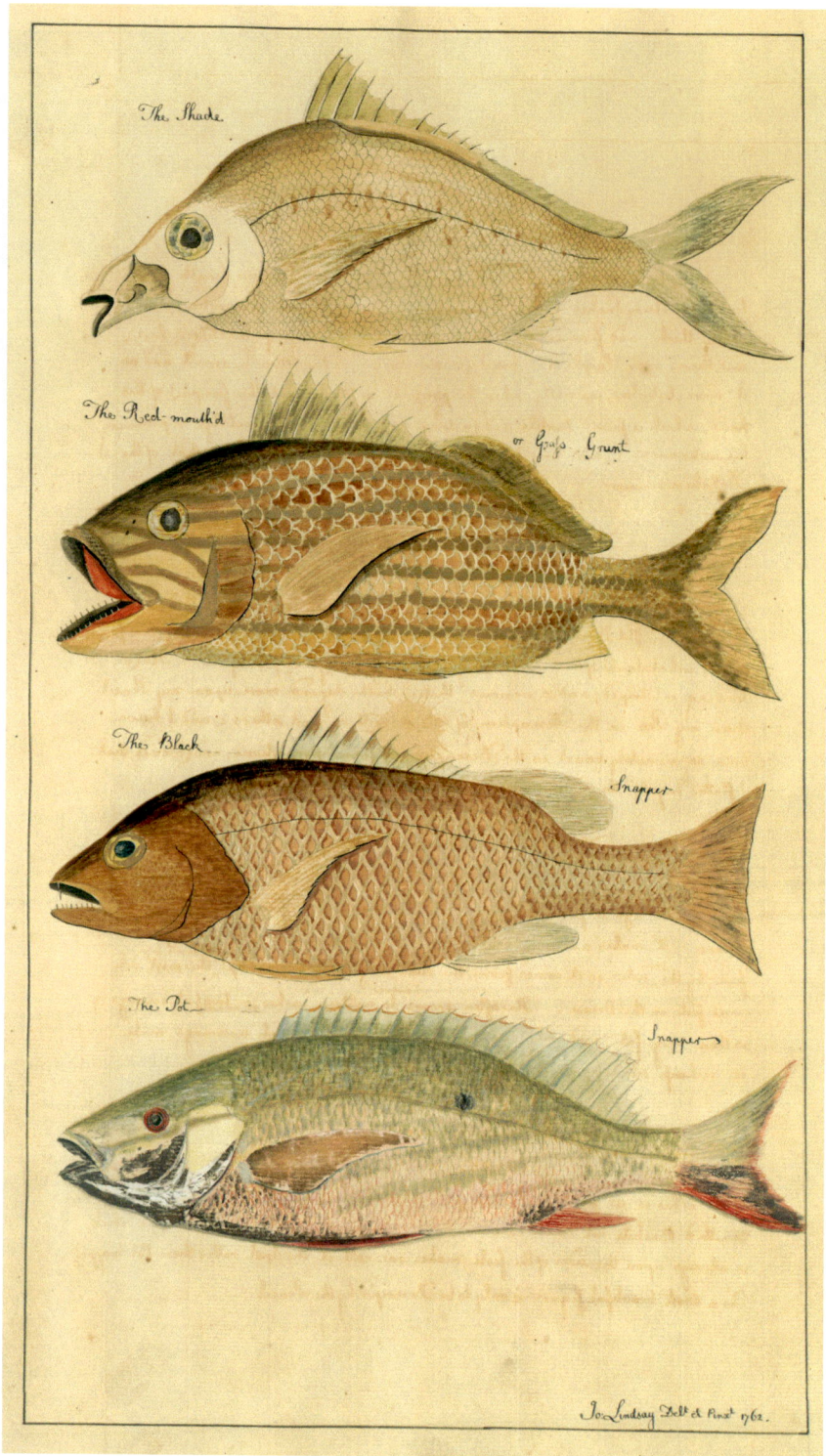

Plate 30
Shad, grunt, snapper, by Rev. John Lindsay, 1762. Bristol Museum and Art Gallery.

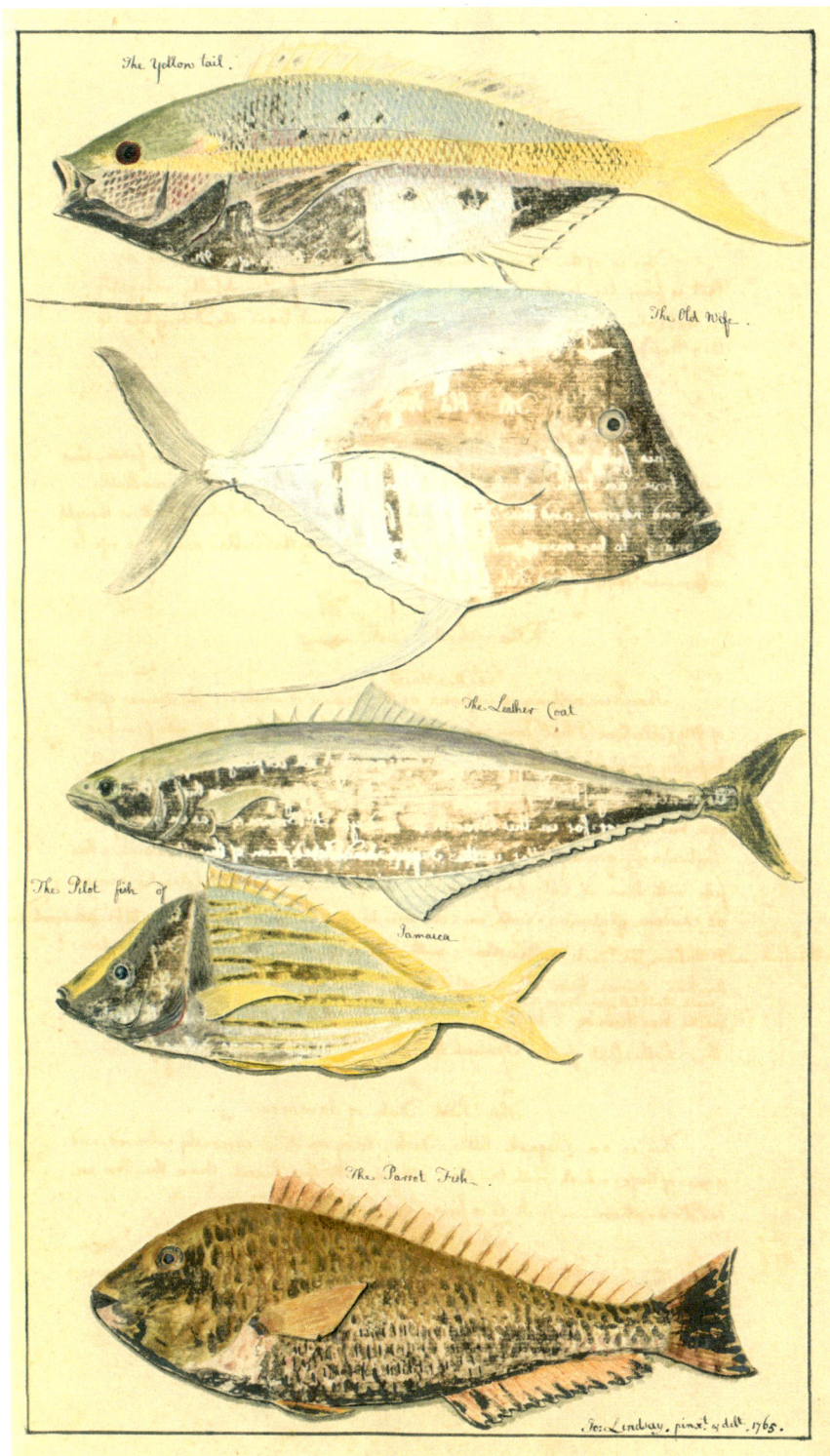

The Yellow tail.

The Old Wife. 1765.

The Leather Coat

The Pilot fish of

Jamaica

The Parrot Fish.

Jos.¹ Lindsay. pinx.¹ & delt. 1765.

Plate 31
Yellowtail, oldwife, leather coat, pilot fish, parrot fish, by Rev. John Lindsay, 1765. Bristol Museum and Art Gallery.

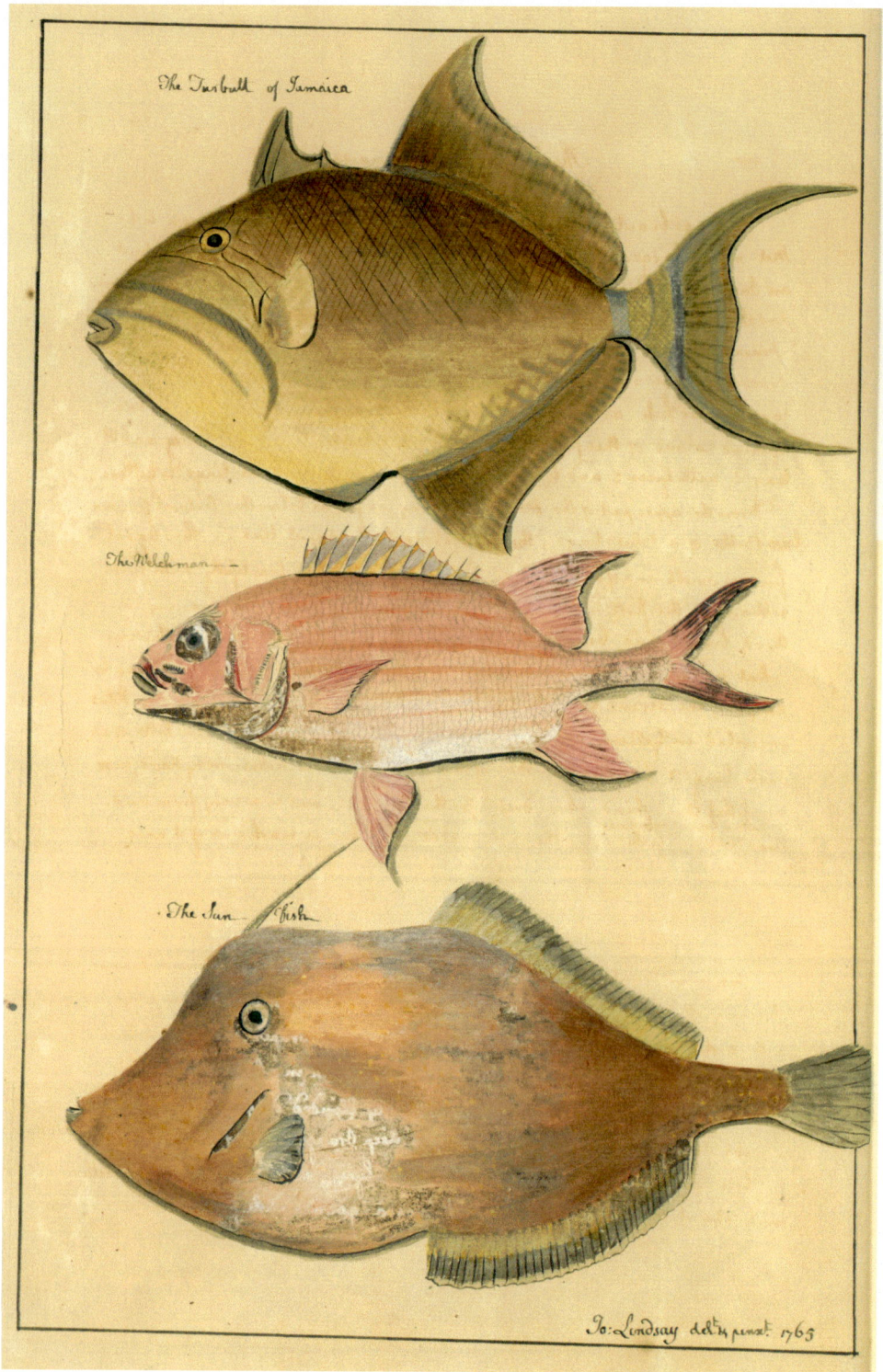

The Turbutt of Jamaica

The Welchman

The Sun Fish

Jo: Lindsay del & pinxt 1765

Plate 32
Turbot, welchman, sunfish, by Rev. John Lindsay, 1765. Bristol Museum and Art Gallery.

recipe identified is from 1970, the stew peas combining red peas, pig's tail, salt beef, fresh beef and butter, with onion, ketchup, thyme, black pepper and water, slow-boiled until the peas were soft, then seasoned and cooked further with spinner dumplings. The rice was cooked separately, the two elements being brought together finally on the plate, the rich gravy of the stew peas suffusing the grains of the rice.[116]

Was stew peas and rice a Jamaican invention, perhaps beginning with the poor and only slowly finding its way into the cookbooks? Or was it, possibly like rice and peas, introduced from some other place? The national dish of Brazil, *feijoada completa*, has much in common with it in terms of ingredients and is served with steamed rice. It is a more elaborate dish than stew peas, prepared for parties with a larger array of meats, and served separately from the beans, the whole sprinkled with *farofa* or toasted cassava flour; yet it has been described as "a mixture of meat and beans that is a sophisticated version of the workingman's humble daily fare". This dish comes from Bahia, the sugar-producing region of Brazil, and seems to have emerged in the nineteenth century. By the 1930s the combination of (white) rice and (black) beans in *feijoada* was seen as a symbol of Brazil's "racial democracy".[117] Yet while the concept behind stew peas, and rice and peas for that matter, is Latin American, the roots may be traced to Africa, and the Jamaican versions proved sufficiently individual to stand on their own.

Only occasionally in Jamaica has stew peas been described without being associated with rice. In the late 1980s, when some of the ingredients became expensive, it was suggested that the meat could be replaced by (imported) tripe and cooked with MSG as well as local seasonings. More extreme was the suggestion that the salt meat could be replaced by chicken neck and back to make a "stew peas for all classes of cooks and diners". Vegetarian versions of "stew pigeon peas" dispensed with meat and introduced pumpkin and gluten or "vegemeat" but retained the salt. Perhaps because of these hardship alternatives, by the 1990s stew peas and rice, properly made with red peas and salt pig's tail, was sometimes called "the best dish made in Jamaica".[118]

Soups made from peas used a variety of types. Sullivan gave recipes for both red and white peas soups, and proposed also a soup made with "green fresh sugar beans". She observed that the "natives" did not strain their peas soups but consumed them "boiled with yam, coco and dumplings [made with equal parts of flour and cornmeal] and often with a remarkable concoction called 'foo-foo' which consists of yam or coco boiled and beaten and then added to the soup". The result, she said, was "a decidedly substantial repast". By the 1970s, alternatives were soups made with black-eye peas, cowpeas or split peas, combined with pig's tail, carrot, pumpkin, Irish potatoes and flour dumplings. Red peas soup similarly used also yam or coco or sweet potato, stewing beef or soup meat, pepper, thyme, salt and perhaps some pig's tail and spinners.[119]

Gungo pea soup was already a rural favourite by the early twentieth century, and by the end of the century, green gungo soup came to be declared the "top ranking" peas recipe, because it retained the "full bodied" characteristic flavour of the peas. The reason for this, cooks were told in 1986, was that "the distinct flavour of gungo combines best with salted meats – salt pork, salt beef, ham, corn beef and corn pork, bacon, sausage". As a result, gungo pea soup made a substantial dish. In the 1930s, a "soup lunch" bought in the Kingston markets consisted of "gungo peas soup" with pieces of yam, salt beef, fresh meat and small dumpling. Gungo pea soup made in St Elizabeth was particularly dense because of the addition of cassava, its quality judged according to the rule that "spoon mus' tanup".[120]

One authentic recipe, published in 1991, used green gungo and began with the task of searching the peas for foreign matter. The peas were brought to boil in a large pot, along with a quantity of navel stew, from the end of a banana stem. Once the pot came to a boil, okra, scallion, onion, garlic, country pepper and pimento were added, along with ham skin, ham bones and any available bones from roast meat and poultry, and cooked for an hour and a half, when the peas would be soft. After this, the bones could be scraped of their meat and discarded. A cup of leftover macaroni and cheese was added, with marjoram, thyme, parsley, MSG, tomato paste and salt. Next, some of the peas were taken out, pulped, returned to the mixture and further cooked. Peeled coco, yellow yam and Irish potato went into the pot. When the yam was soft, some cornmeal dumplings were added and cooked until done. Finally, the ham skin was removed and sliced into strips, returned to the pot along with the meat, and the navel stew removed and sliced into equal sections.[121]

All of the dishes using peas mentioned thus far have been savoury. The one legume used for sweets and snacks was the peanut. In the eighteenth century, peanuts were eaten only "raw, roasted, or boiled". Lunan, however, believed that "when roasted, ground, and boiled, they make a good substitute for chocolate". Sullivan said "pindars" could be bought raw or roasted and were much liked when eaten with salt. In 1957, when the nutritional benefits of the peanut were being promoted in Jamaica, the *Farmer's Food Manual* offered thirty-five recipes using peanuts, though few of them had any obviously Jamaican component. In the 1980s it was said that few Jamaicans included peanuts in their cooking, although peanuts were high in protein and gave "fine flavour to meat dishes, fruit salads and certain baked products". Recipes were offered for chicken with peanuts, a nutty fruit cup for dessert, and nut cookies.[122] By 2005, "peanut rice" was on offer, along with peanut porridge and peanut punch. Roasted and salted, peanuts long continued as a street food sold from specially designed handcarts, and the nuts were incorporated into a toffee stick.

WANGLA

Wangla, *Sesamum orientale*, is a small climbing plant related to sesame, *S. indicum*, and was formerly exploited in Jamaica for its oily seeds. In 1774, Long referred to "vanglo, wongala, or oil-plant", saying there were two species of the plant. The seeds were often used in broths and, in the East, made into an oil. Long said, "The Negroes grind the seeds between two stones, parch them, and mix with other ingredients. The Jews use the oil in cakes, instead of butter. In Æthipoia and Ægypt it is used for the same purposes as we do the olive oil." He advocated production, arguing that the oil "might, with the greatest propriety, be admitted into general domestic use, in the room of that abominable rancid butter imported hither from Europe". It would serve equally well as a substitute for imported olive oil, "generally rancid before it arrives, and fitter for perukes [wigs] than salads".[123]

By the late nineteenth century, wangla seeds were being traded by the bagful, but "wangla" then shifted its meaning from the seed to a sugar cake made with the seeds. Sullivan, discussing the use of "pindars", said, "The natives make a sugar cake with the nuts [peanuts] thrown in, as they also do with cashewnuts, and a bean called 'wangla'." By the middle of the twentieth century, wangla seed had generally been replaced by peanuts, though the sugar cake or candy might retain the name "wangla". The only sweets offered by the "Candy Seller" of Louise Bennett's poem were pindacake and wangla, along with peppermint. By the 1960s, "wangla" was defined as a sugar cake made with sesame seeds, sitting alongside the "pindar-cake", which in turn transformed into the peanut-toffee stick or peanut brittle.[124]

CACOON

The cacoon, *Entada gigas*, is a parasitic climbing vine producing very large fruit pods, each pod up to two metres in length, each containing about ten hard round beans three to five centimetres in diameter. A native plant, it is generally found on trees near the margins of the wet forests or along riverbanks. Lindsay drew it in 1767 (Plate 24). He said the plant grew well in the cooler mountains – as, for example, upper Clarendon – and he called it the "purse cacoon", because when dry the pod could be split down the middle and "the Negroes make use [of it], to hold their little cash". Lindsay made no mention of the use of the seeds for food, but Maroons certainly collected the dried kernels of the beans and ate them roasted, pounded, salted and softened or stewed, added to soup or pounded to make a drink. The cacoon was poisonous, however, and had to be carefully prepared to remove the toxin. Barham, in the early eighteenth century, said the kernel was "very bitter, and vomits and purges strongly".[125] According to Colonel C.L.G. Harris, writing in 1967,

> In the preparation of the cacoon they were thrown into a fire and when a popping sound was given off they were removed and burst open. The kernels were then removed, sliced into strips of about a quarter of an inch in width, and thereafter properly wrapped in the leaves of a giant fern known locally as ferril macca, and placed in running water for three or four days. They were then taken out, boiled, and eaten with great relish. Indeed a dish of soup made from janga, thatch-head [mountain cabbage or palm heart], cacoon and cocoes is a delicacy one does not readily forget.[126]

VANILLA

Vanilla is the fruit of an orchid, *Vanilla fragrans*, and is widely used as a flavouring and spice, in ice cream, chocolate, cakes, drinks and confectionery. The fruit, commonly called "vanilla bean", is harvested before fully ripe and fermented and cured to produce a liquid extract. Vanilla is valued for its fragrance as well as its flavour (closely related to the flavour associated with Jamaican country pepper), and is used in perfumes as well as food. The fragrance derives from the aromatic compound vanillin, first isolated in the 1850s; to some extent synthetic products have now displaced the natural.[127]

The vanilla plant is indigenous to Central America, a wild climber in the forests. It was used by the Aztecs, who called it *tlilxochitl*, in blending chocolate. Exactly when and how it reached Jamaica is uncertain. In eighteenth-century Jamaica vanilla grew wild, as a climbing vine, particularly on the north coast, but could be propagated from seed or cuttings planted along walls or at the feet of trees. Pods up to fifteen centimetres long dangled from the vines, turning from green to yellow to brown as they ripened (Figure 6.14). Neither the flowers nor the fruit gave any hint of their fragrant aroma; the beans remained essentially tasteless until sweated and dried for several months in order to force the development of vanillin. The pods were harvested before fully ripe, left to ferment, then dried, rubbed with oil and flattened with the hand.

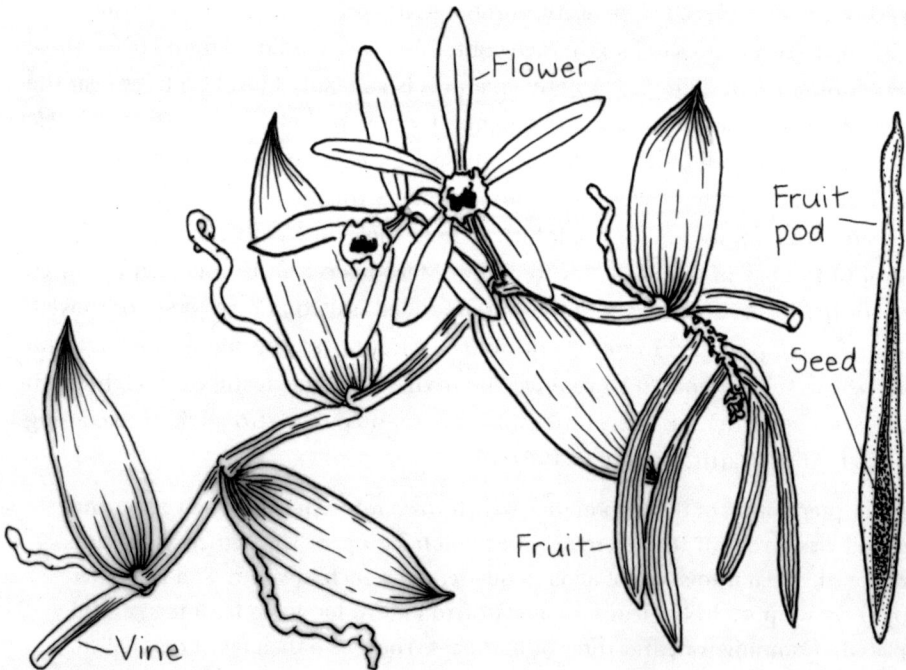

Figure 6.14 Vanilla

Long, writing in the eighteenth century, thought vanilla good for the stomach but believed it was rarely used medicinally. The Spanish and the French mixed vanilla in chocolate "to give it a delicate smell and agreeable flavour". Jamaica never became a major producer or exporter, and much of the vanilla used to flavour Jamaican puddings and cakes arrived as bottled essence – sometimes the genuine natural product, sometimes, openly or not, artificial. It remained expensive to the end of the nineteenth century. Sullivan suggested it for just one dish, her boiled chocho pudding, and even then she said only that it might be "flavoured with either lime-peel, essence of lemon or vanilla".[128] By the end of the twentieth century, however, Jamaican cooks were using it plentifully. Vanilla appears in more than twenty of the recipes in Donaldson's cookbook.

NUTMEG

The nutmeg tree, *Myristica fragrans*, is unusual in that it produces *two* spices: both nutmeg (the oval kernel of the seed) and mace (the dried aril that encases the single seed within the fruit). The tree is slow-growing, taking over ten years to achieve maturity, but it then yields about two thousand nuts annually. Fruits are fully ripe when the pericarp splits to reveal the mace-enclosed testa (Figure 6.15). The mace consists of narrow flaps, attached to the seed only at its base but enclosing the shell tightly. After being removed with a knife, the mace is dried, turns orange and takes on its characteristic aroma. The

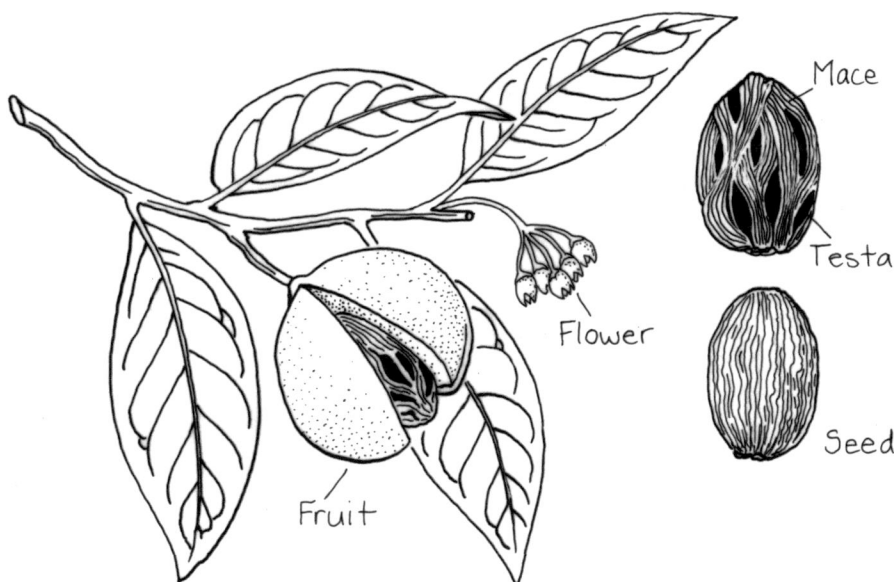

Figure 6.15 Nutmeg

nutmegs are also dried, until the seed rattles in the testa. When the shell is cracked, the nut is removed and grated to flavour cakes and drinks. The more expensive mace is used in savoury dishes, pickles and ketchups. Nutmeg is also used as medicine, and it has long been known that excessive doses can produce intoxication. Both the seed and the arils have narcotic properties.[129]

The nutmeg tree is indigenous to the Moluccas (in Indonesia), and the spice was already being traded to the West in the Middle Ages. Although there were occasional claims of an "American nutmeg" growing in the island, mace was imported into Jamaica in the eighteenth century: the true nutmeg tree was not planted in the West Indies until the next century. The major producers are now Indonesia and Grenada, where the tree was introduced in 1843.[130] In Jamaica, nutmeg eventually became a common though minor crop.

COFFEE

The culture of cultivating and brewing coffee is quite recent. The plant, *Coffea arabica*, originated in Ethiopia, but trade in coffee berries collected from wild trees began only in the sixteenth century, and until 1700 planting was confined to small areas of the Middle East (Plate 25). The beverage rapidly became popular in Islamic societies, which were denied alcohol, and equally quickly spread into Christian Europe, where it competed successfully with tea and cocoa as well as with wine and beer. The roasting and making of coffee was unknown in England until the middle of the seventeenth century, but coffee-houses quickly became popular and were first licensed in 1663. Their development, and the new demand for coffee, occurred along with the English colonization of Jamaica, and the coffee-houses, much frequented by merchants and absentee West Indian planters, became important places for the exchange of information. Tea displaced coffee in the British scene in the eighteenth century, but as a result of tariff-driven price differences rather than of changing tastes.[131]

The earliest known reference to a coffee-house in Jamaica comes from Kingston, in the early 1730s. The coffee brewed there was probably imported rather than locally grown. The first coffee trees had been introduced to Jamaica from Martinique only in 1728, and exports did not commence until 1737. Although the tree was said to grow "luxuriantly in all the inland parts of Jamaica", the product suffered by its "want of flavour, or having a disagreeable one". But beginning in the 1780s, new plants and the planting of different areas led to a great boom in coffee production, for export. Output peaked in 1814, when Jamaica exported fifteen thousand tonnes – a remarkable 30 per cent of world trade – but output fell away rapidly and never regained that high level. As well as the impressive quantity of this output, Lunan could claim in 1814 that the quality of Jamaica's coffee was equal to the best Arabian.[132]

Botanically, the fruit or berry of the coffee tree is really a drupe. The berries take eight to ten months to mature, turning cherry red as they ripen and darkening as they

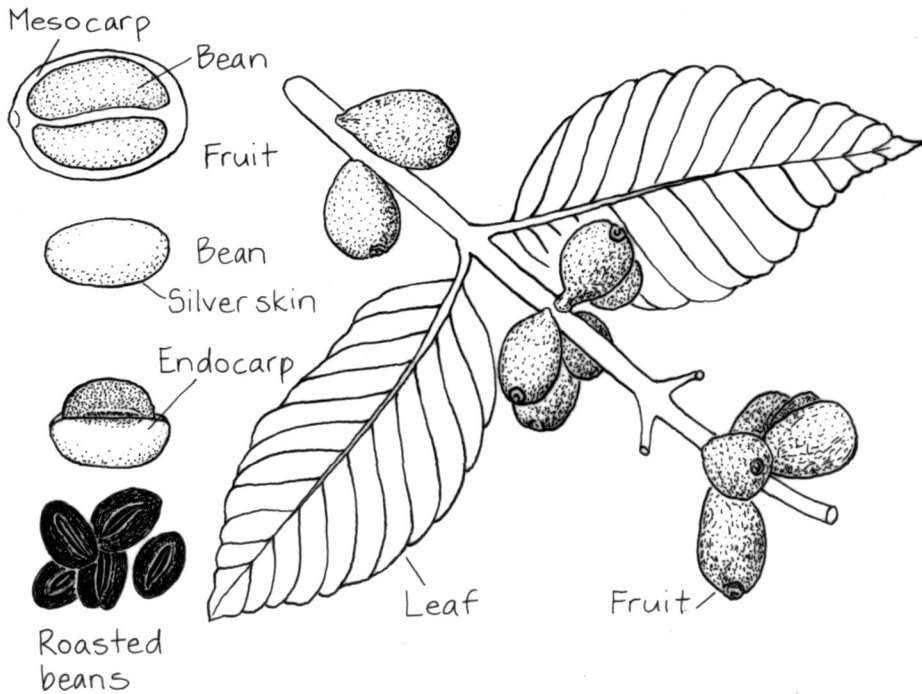

Figure 6.16 Coffee fruit and bean

dry. Inside the skin, the pulp (mesocarp) normally contains two seeds (beans) covered by a thin membrane called the "silver skin" and by a tough parchment (endocarp; Figure 6.16). Trees take four or five years to come to full bearing but, once established, flowering and fruiting may continue throughout the year, and they can bear for up to thirty-five years. In some parts of the world, but not in Jamaica, the pulp rather than the bean is dried and used. The leaves of the tree are also sometimes boiled to make "tea", but this seems not to have happened in Jamaica.[133] The pulp can be removed from the beans by fermentation in water followed by drying, leaving the parchment in place, or by initial drying and the mechanical hulling of pulp and parchment. One great advantage of the coffee bean is that it improves with age, enabling benefits from storage and long-distance trade. Roasting, the next stage of processing, can thus be delayed until the beans reach their market. It is roasting that gives coffee its unique aroma. After roasting, deterioration begins. The same applies to grinding, especially for fine-ground coffee – hence the attraction of the kitchen coffee-mill, ready to grind the morning's brew.

The most important factor for determining the quality of cultivated coffee is the environment, particularly the microclimate. Jamaican coffee was early divided into two main types: highland and lowland. The most famous of Jamaican coffees, Blue Mountain, is produced in the core of the highland zone that extends above five hundred metres in elevation, while lowland coffees are grown between three hundred and five hundred metres. Because Blue Mountain attracts the highest prices, most of the product has always been exported, and even the lesser varieties are generally used to create a cash income rather than being consumed by the producer. By the 1880s, "Blue Mountain coffee" was a named, "branded" commodity clearly associated with Jamaica, and assessed the finest on the market. As early as 1900, "the Blue Mountain variety" could be called "perhaps, the finest coffee grown in the world". That reputation persisted: in 1987, *Playboy* magazine declared Blue Mountain "the best coffee in the world", and at the end of the twentieth century it was the world's most expensive.[134]

High prices reflect both objective characteristics and subjective perceptions and preferences, as well as the pressure of limited supply. In the 1890s, "every grain" of the Blue Mountain coffee crop was exported to England, where it was thought to possess "peculiar qualities for blending". None of it was brewed in Jamaica. By the 1990s as much as 85 per cent of the coffee went to Japan, with the balance divided between the United States (10 per cent) and Europe (5 per cent). In 2001 Jamaican coffee was described as "distinctive because of 'appearance' (big, bold, bluish green beans) and taste – aromatic, mild acidity, clean (no extraneous taste or smell), sweetish and good body". The best crops, said another writer, produced "a cup that is an exquisite balance of nutty aroma; bright, but not overwhelming acidity; delicate sweetness; and a clean but nectar-like finish".[135] It was so good that hardly any of Jamaica's best coffee was drunk by Jamaicans in Jamaica.

The aroma of roasted and brewed *C. arabica* contains about nine hundred volatile chemical compounds, but fewer than twenty of these are responsible for its typical sweetish/caramel, roasty/sulphurous, earthy, smoky, buttery and green odour notes. These odours come not only from the inherent natural properties of the coffee bean, but also from the mode of processing, particularly thermally generated flavours. Green coffee beans lack the colour and aroma characteristic of roasted, ground and brewed coffee. Roasting causes a drastic transformation of the chemical composition of the beans, with changes in characteristics directly affected by the quantity of heat transferred. Coffee oil makes up about 10 per cent of the volume of roasted beans; it is this oil that carries the aroma. The staleness of roasted ground coffee that has been stored too long is perceived as a sweet but unpleasant aroma which reflects the oxidization of the attractive volatiles, whereas change in the acid constituents produces a rather bland tone.[136]

The quality of coffee depends very much on its post-harvest treatment. During slavery, much labour was devoted to the drying and pulping of the berries, using both manual and milling technologies. Most of Jamaica's coffee was produced by large plantations, though the house gardens of enslaved workers did occasionally include coffee trees, producing either for household consumption or for sale in local markets. After the abolition of slavery, coffee had certain advantages as a smallholder's crop.[137] The genetic uniformity of the plant enables high-quality propagation of unselected seedlings without breeding or grafting, and the plant is resilient. Further, small quantities of beans can be processed simply, by drying the berries in the sun and taking off the pulp in a mortar, and raw beans can be stored for long periods. Problems occur with dry curing in places with humid, cloudy weather, like that found in the Blue Mountains. In order to avoid loss, it was necessary to separate the beans from the fresh cherry and to dry the beans as quickly as possible. Mechanical pulpers were invented and eventually perfected in 1854, when James Meacock of Kingston patented his machine. This method became known as "West Indies" or "wet" preparation. The cherries were pulped immediately after picking; the skins were then discarded, and the pulped mass rapidly fermented until the mucilage could be removed, and then it was washed, producing parchment coffee that needed five rather than fifteen days of sun-drying.[138] Only in the second half of the twentieth century did large-scale pulperies begin to command the market and assert control over quality, working under the Coffee Industry Board, which was set up in 1950.

Coffee does contain useful nutrients, but it is rarely consumed as a solid food. Above all it is appreciated for its stimulatory effects and sensory pleasure. These derive from the alkaloid caffeine, found not only in the beans but also in the pulp and leaves of the plant. Similar alkaloids occur in the leaves of tea and in the cocoa bean. Adulteration has been a problem, as in the mixing of chicory into ground coffee feared in Jamaica in the 1880s and 1890s. In the late nineteenth century, controversy developed, outside Jamaica, over the effects of caffeine and the status of coffee as a drug. This led to the invention of "decaffeinated" coffee, patented in 1906. "Instant" coffee followed, in the form of refined coffee crystals, first made by an American in 1910. Little of this was advertised in Jamaica until the 1950s, and Jamaica did not begin production of instant coffee until 1963.[139] In recent times, the coffee used in baking cakes and biscuits has generally been instant.

Jamaican cookbooks pay little attention to coffee in any form. Typically, Sullivan gave no instructions for the brewing of coffee and only in the second edition of her cookbook offered a token recipe for coffee cake, which included in its ingredients a "cupful of coffee ready boiled and very strong". Donaldson not only omitted coffee from her otherwise comprehensive A–Z of Jamaican foods, but also omitted coffee from her recipe for "coffee cake", telling her readers, "Some people expect coffee in coffee cake, but this crispy, crunchy coffee cake is an excellent 'go-with' for a steaming cup of Blue Mountain coffee."[140] Like Sullivan, Donaldson gave no directions how best to make that cup.

It is perhaps surprising that Jamaica, the home of one of the world's most esteemed coffees, never elaborated the uses of coffee in cooking, never highly valued roasting and blending skills, and never developed ritualized consumption. In part, this was determined by the high price of Blue Mountain, which meant that few of the premium beans were consumed in the island. Apart from the early coffee-houses, Jamaica saw few attempts to establish commercial sites of consumption, with only a handful of "coffee bars" when they became popular internationally at the beginning of the twenty-first century. The notion that the brewing of coffee requires no explanation reflects the extent to which coffee had become a common commodity, consumed even by the poor, in cheap forms, increasingly overwhelmed by the addition of sweetened condensed milk.[141] Coffee was thus accommodated within the broader range of "tea", specifically "coffee-tea".

In 1985 the Coffee Industry Board promoted a Coffee Brewing Week, "carrying the message of how to properly prepare coffee to bring out the best quality and the exotic aroma of this beverage". This was not designed out of a desire to change local habits, however: the target audience was the food and beverage managers of the island's hotels. Demonstrators explained the three ways of preparing coffee, by drawing, by percolating and by the drip method of brewing. Drawing was seen as "the old-time method", in which "ground coffee is placed in a muslin bag and boiling water poured into the bag with the coffee, the water passing through both coffee and bag into a container". This produced a pure brew. Lunan had recommended making it one-third stronger than usual, adding as much boiling milk as water while it was still on the fire, letting it settle, then drinking it with or without cream, and adding very little sugar. For the drip method, described in 1922 as a way to make breakfast coffee, berries could be "toasted and ground the night before, and the essence distilled by an all-night dripping through a cafetiere. A little of this essence of coffee put in a cup, followed by a cupful of boiling cow's milk drawn that morning from the cow, made a delicious beverage."[142]

In an unusually detailed treatment of the subject, Phyllis Clark's 1945 *West Indian Cookery* advised readers to use freshly roasted and ground beans, stored if necessary in an air-tight container. The coffee could be made, said Clark, "using a jug, a saucepan, an ordinary percolator or a 'drip' percolator". Whatever the equipment, her recipe always included a pinch of salt. To make coffee in a jug or pan, Clark recommended first putting in the coffee and salt, then pouring on boiling water to infuse for ten to fifteen minutes. Next the pan was heated to boiling point. Clark warned against long or fast boiling, which made the coffee bitter. A dash of cold water was thrown into the boiling pot to settle the grounds, and the coffee strained through a piece of muslin or flannel into a warmed coffee pot. The coffee was to be served with boiled milk and sugar. To make iced coffee, condensed milk or a mixture of milk and egg might replace the boiled milk.[143]

Whereas recent Jamaican cookbooks are largely silent on how best to brew a cup of coffee, they do occasionally tell how to make Irish coffee, using rum and whiskey. Reversing the proportions, coffee can also be consumed as a flavouring in alcoholic drinks. Perhaps the most famous of Jamaica's rum liqueurs, Tia Maria, was made with "the subtle taste of exquisite Blue Mountain coffee", following a secret formula. Production began in 1947, but the company was taken over by a United States distiller in 1964, and although Tia Maria became an international best-seller, it was "not a great favourite with the average Jamaican".[144]

KOLANUT

Coffee sometimes suffered by being rolled together with other caffeine-containing beverages. Most obviously, the first caffeinated soft drink, Coca-Cola, was initially sold as a tonic or patent medicine and faced the courts, accused of introducing potentially harmful substances. The "Coca" of the name came from coca wine, a drink derived from the leaves of the South American coca plant, as was cocaine. The "Cola" was taken from a tonic, popular in late-nineteenth-century Britain, made from the caffeine-rich kolanut of Africa and promoted as a wholesome food. When combined in 1886 to produce Coca-Cola, the drink, like coffee, was advertised as a brain food. In 1911 the Coca-Cola Company was taken to court by the United States government, accused of adding caffeine – a harmful ingredient – to its product. Coca-Cola won the case merely on technical grounds, and caffeine continued to be branded as a poison by antagonists. The impact of these efforts on Jamaican consumption patterns was slight, however, and coffee and Coca-Cola both proved popular drinks throughout the twentieth century. Coca-Cola, delivering "tingling good taste", was first bottled in Jamaica in 1941. The local brewers Desnoes and Geddes began bottling Pepsi-Cola in 1947.[145]

The kolanut tree, *Cola acuminata*, grew in Jamaica by the seventeenth century, and was known then as "bissy nut" or "bissy tree". The nut is a bitter seed the size of a chestnut, grows like cocoa in wrinkled pods, generally without endosperm, and is yellow when ripe (Figure 6.17). The tree had been brought from its native West Africa, where chewing the nuts as a stimulant had long been popular, and even the basis of a trade between the tropical forest and the interior savanna. Sloane said the nuts were both eaten and used to cure belly pains. Around 1740 it was said that the "besse or Negroe fruit" was much loved by the people but rare. Long listed it among the "dissert fruits" of Jamaica. Later writers thought of bissy as a stimulating and medicinal drink.[146]

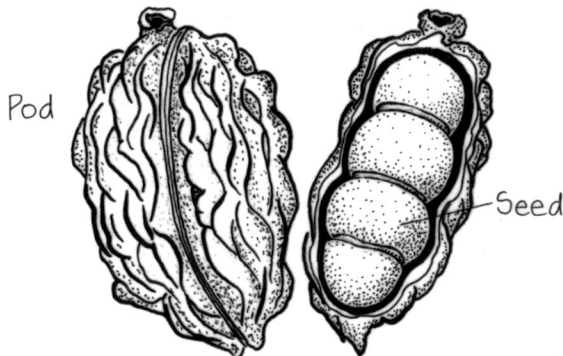

Figure 6.17 Kolanut pod and seed

In 1898 "rum and kola" was described as "another of the greatly prized drinks of the island, and there is a tradition that this beverage is a lineal descendant of the ambrosia served the gods and go[d]desses in their Olympian [t]ravels". When Edwin Charley established the St Catherine Aerated Water Factory and Brewery in 1900, among its leading products were Kola Champagne, Kola Tonic, Kola (Dry), Kola Stomachic Bitters and Kola Wine, along with Barm Beer, Iron Brew and ginger ale. The Montego Bay Aerated Water Company offered a similar range, including Kola Champagne, Kola Tonic, Kolazone, Kola Bitters and Iron Brew, and emphasized that all its kola products contained "the active principle of kola nut". The "barm" in Barm Beer, a drink described as "cool" with an "excellent flavour", was a froth of yeast formed on malt liquors while fermenting. Charley's brews competed with imported kola wines, the latter prepared from "kola nut and pure Angostura bark" and regularly advertised as assisting digestion and being "refreshing, nutritious, and invigorating" and "good for blood, bone, brain". The Englishman Alfred Leader said in 1907 that the better-off in Jamaica drank "kola, a non-intoxicant aerated water, made from the kola nut, with a few other native products added"; it was drunk iced. When Desnoes and Geddes introduced Dandy Shandy, a "unique Jamaican drink", in 1991, it came in three flavours: Ginger, Lemonade and Kola Champagne.[147]

COCOA

An important difference between cocoa and coffee was that cocoa could be taken through several processes of modification. It could be used to make both a beverage (sometimes called "cocoa", sometimes "chocolate") and a solid food (chocolate). In Jamaica, the plant that produces cocoa is still sometimes called a "chocolate tree", a usage now little known elsewhere.[148] This terminology served originally to distinguish cocoa from coco and coconut, the confusion noted in chapter 3, caused in early Jamaican history by calling the seeds of the cocoa tree "cocoa-nuts" or "chocolate-nuts" (Plate 2). Further, on the modern world linguistic map, some writers hold firmly to "cocoa" to mean both the tree and its fruit, while others equally stubbornly use the botanically correct "cacao".

Theobroma cacao belongs to the same family as the kolanut and is therefore another good source of caffeine. It is an evergreen tree, growing to eight metres and unusual in flowering and fruiting from the trunk and the older branches. The fruit pods each contain twenty to sixty seeds (or "beans") enclosed in a sweet sticky pulp (Figure 6.18). The pods turn orange or red when ripe; the main harvest in Jamaica occurs from September to December, with a minor harvest in March to June. Trees can bear for up to fifty years, though they take three to four years to produce their first crop. After plucking, the pods are split open and the seeds removed from the pulp. Next the seeds are "cured" by being heaped up to ferment for several days and spread to dry in the sun for about a week. Fermentation and drying are essential to removing the pulp and dampening the bitter taste of the beans, thus creating the typical "cocoa" flavour. As

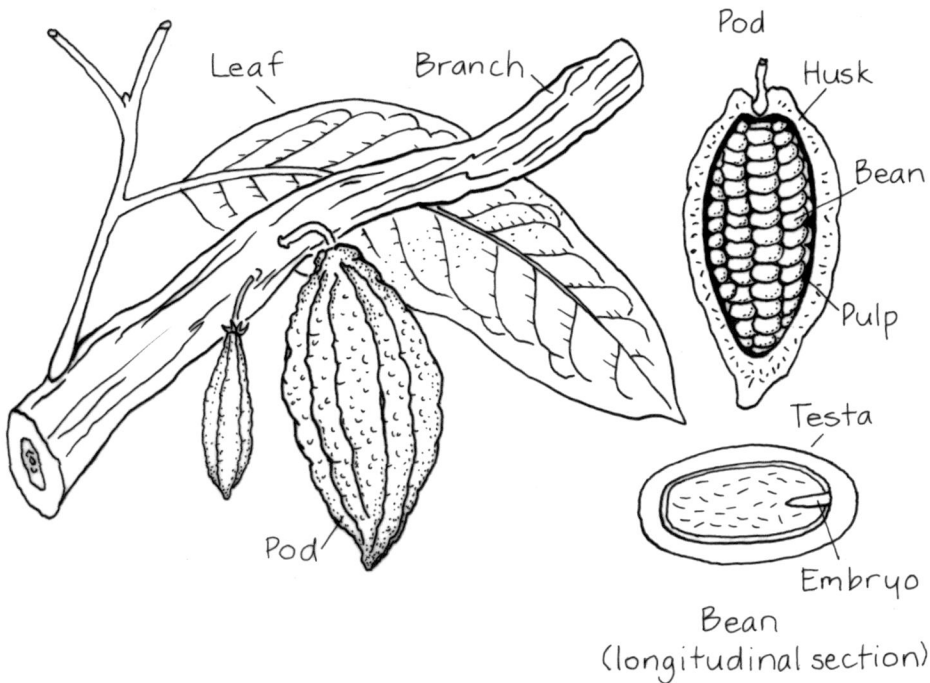

Figure 6.18 Cocoa pod and bean

with coffee, the flavour of cocoa (and chocolate) comes from its fermentation and heat treatment during processing as well as from its inherent qualities.[149]

Although the evolutionary origins of the cocoa tree were in the Amazon, the major zone of agricultural domestication was tropical Mexico and Central America, and it was there that chocolate-making had its birthplace.[150] The Maya prized cocoa as a beverage and elaborated many recipes. The Spanish conquistadors quickly exploited the cultivation and trade in cocoa but were slower to appreciate the taste, because the original Mesoamerican beverages were bitter. The introduction of sugar cane enabled sweeter versions and, particularly after cinnamon was added, the Spanish soon developed a passion for the drink.

Cocoa was not indigenous to Jamaica but was planted by the Spanish in the early sixteenth century for colonial and European markets. The smallness of the labour force initially limited output. By the time of the English conquest, however, "cacoa-walks" were common, covering up to five hectares and "orderly set". Early English colonization was directed towards expansion of cocoa production, and the island experienced a brief boom around 1670. Cocoa was often thought to be an aphrodisiac. Henry Stubbe, writing in 1662, upheld this opinion, and declared chocolate a wonderful thing, since "it alone may supply all food and physick". Chocolate-houses appeared in Europe in the middle of the seventeenth century, even earlier than coffee-houses. Sloane promoted his own brand of "milk chocolate", recommended as a drink "for its lightness on the stomach and its great use in all consumptive cases".[151]

By the beginning of the eighteenth century, Jamaican cocoa was being displaced by sugar and was sidelined as a plantation crop. The collapse of cocoa production was accelerated by a wilting disease and by the unwillingness of planters to wait on the trees' coming to bearing. Unlike coffee, cocoa was not included in lists of plants grown in the gardens and grounds of the enslaved, but trees survived in the wild and some of this fruit was collected. Dovaston reported in 1774 that "the Negroes make hard rolls of chocolate, which is much richer than what is made in England". The English, he said, mixed the cocoa with flour and used "fatt, and gravys" to make it cohere, which was "not very cleanly or wholesome". In Jamaica, he reported,

> The method the Negroes use is to beat the nuts after having gently warm'd them thro' (not roasted them) over a fire in a pan, and then in a stone mortar, under which is placed a gentle charcoal fire, to keep the stone warm and to cause the oyl in the nuts to flow, they are beat as fine as butter with a wooden pestle, the more they are beat the more they go into a past[e], and the finer and better the chocolate is. This pulp is by them made into rolls for use; and in England they mix loaf sugar with the past to a certain sweetness and then cast it in moulds, with or without a mixture of venella in which form we buy it.[152]

After the abolition of slavery, cocoa became established as a minor cash crop for smallholders and as a source of household-processed food. It was thought of as easy to produce, in spite of varied hazards, and easy to market. By 1890 Kingston had a "steam chocolate factory", offering packets wholesale and retail. A Cocoa Industry Board, set up in 1957, worked to improve quality by establishing central fermentaries. These turned out a high-grade fine, or flavour, cocoa that fetched premium prices, but production remained small, and indeed declined to barely exceed one thousand tonnes of beans by the end of the twentieth century.[153]

Further processing of cocoa generally takes place in temperate countries, the major markets, where the beans are transformed into chocolate, cocoa powder and cocoa butter. The beans are first roasted, to bring out further flavour, then ground and pressed. The fat extracted by pressing, called cocoa butter, makes up more than half the weight, while the remaining dry material is the cocoa powder. High-fat powders are used for beverages, low-fat powders for flavourings. Cocoa butter is a valuable commodity because it has good storage qualities and does not develop free fatty acids, yet it melts at body temperature and is easily digested. Chocolate is made by grinding roasted beans into a mass and mixing this with extra cocoa butter and, generally, sugar. The ground beans are too stiff to be moulded, hence the need for additional cocoa butter. Most commercially produced chocolate now also contains a significant amount of milk solids.[154]

The general trend throughout the twentieth century was towards standardization and towards reduced differentiation and hierarchy of origins, partly because of the increased demand for cocoa butter but also because of technological changes which made possible the modification of colour and aroma. Working in the opposite direction, and in Jamaica's favour, was a growing desire to regain a lost diversity of supplies and a new interest in the "historical" origins of different cocoas. Around 1900, fine or flavour cocoa accounted for roughly one-half of world production, but by 2000 this proportion had fallen to a mere 4 per cent. The International Cocoa Organization today recognizes only eight countries as exclusive producers of fine or flavour cocoa, and all but one of these (Samoa) is in the West Indies, including Jamaica. Thus Jamaican cocoa is one of the sought-after names in the premium cocoa world at the beginning of the twenty-first century. Particularly sought is high-quality single-origin cocoa (generally grown on the criollo or trinitario tree) rather than bulk or "ordinary" beans (grown on the forastero tree).[155]

Consumption of cocoa in Jamaica and elsewhere long focused on the beverage and shifted only in the second half of the twentieth century towards the solid food. At first, the Mayan recipes were influential, but experimentation led to the addition of ingredients such as corn, peppers, anatto, vanilla and a range of flowers, seeds and roots. Hughes claimed the "native Indians" had rejected these additives, "desiring rather to preserve their healths, then to gratifie and please their palats, until the Spaniards coming amongst them, made several mixtures and compounds; which instead of making the former better (as they supposed) have made it much worse". The English in Jamaica followed this bad practice, mixing the cocoa paste with anatto, peppers and sugar, and beating the mass into lumps, balls and cakes. Stubbe offered recipes for "'common Chocolata' and for 'Chocolata-Royal', using the mild spices of Jamaica, for people to drink in health". He prepared chocolate for Charles II, doubling the usual proportion of cocoa kernel. However, said Hughes, "in Jamaica there is a sort of chocolate made up of only the paste of the cacao itself, in rowls or lumps of a pound or two, or three pound together, the better for keeping good; which the people there account most ordinary, by reason they bestow not so much pains as to grinde it into the smallest particles; and being but grossly made up, they grate it very fine, immediately before they use it for drinks".[156]

The best-known method for making a drink of chocolate at the end of the seventeenth century began by grating the lumps on a fine tin grater. In a separate pot, cassava bread, in quantity equal to the cocoa, was added to water and brought to a boil. The grated cocoa was added, and after boiling for fifteen minutes, the whole was removed from the heat and poured into "some handsome large dish or bason; and after they have sweetened it a little with sugar, being all together, and sitting down round about it like good fellows, every one dips in his calabash, or some other dish, supping it off very hot". A second way was to add red pepper, sweet pepper or vanilla, to make it more a compound. Some people boiled milk and water, added grated chocolate and cassava, then sweetened the drink. It could also be made with milk, a little water, beaten eggs and cocoa, and drunk frothing up. Maroons, hunters and other travellers used "balls or lozenges finely made up with cacao, and some of the fore-mentioned ingredients besides, and as much sugar as will sufficiently sweeten it: and when they have an inclination to make use of those tablets or lozenges, they only dissolve them in water, froth it, or stir it well, and so drink it off". Or a ball of cocoa and anatto could be grated thin, mixed with finely beaten ship biscuit, added to boiling water and milk, sweetened with sugar, and supped "very hot, without frothing". Chocolate, Hughes concluded, was a "most excellent nectar".[157]

These methods were refined and modified in the eighteenth and nineteenth centuries, only sometimes using milk. By the time of Sullivan's cookbook, the instructions were simpler. "Jamaica chocolate" was made by parching cocoa beans, pinching off the outer skin and beating the beans to a fine powder in a mortar. When hardened, the powder was pounded with spices, sugar and perhaps a little milk, and rolled into balls. Sullivan thought "half a ball makes a cup of good chocolate when grated and mixed very smooth". Imported cocoa preparations soon became available for the better-off. Rowntree's Elect Cocoa, packed in tins in England, was first advertised in Jamaica in 1898 as "in every respect a true food – nourishing, stimulating, digestible, and, in addition, supremely delicious". Only half a teaspoonful was needed to make a breakfast cup. The drink was more closely associated with the Jamaican poor than with the rich.[158]

Beckwith's 1920s ethnography described cocoa-making as part of peasant life. The process she described involved "cracking off the outer pod, parching the beans (thirty or more in a pod) over the fire, cleaning off the skin, and then pounding the white kernels in a mortar until they 'begin to fat', that is, to exude oil". Next the paste was "rolled into a ball or stick with the hand and set in the sun to dry", flavoured with nutmeg or cinnamon, and sweetened with cane juice. In the 1930s, the chocolate of the peasantry was sometimes mixed hot with coconut milk and wet sugar, but rarely with cow's milk. Clark, in 1945, recommended using either a stick of "cocoa or chocolate sold in the market" or a heaped teaspoon of "cocoa powder". This was added to boiling water and boiled two to three minutes, with sugar "if necessary". Clark feared most people skipped the boiling stage, so that the starch in the cocoa remained raw, causing indigestion. After the boiling, boiled or condensed milk was added: the greater the proportion of milk to water, "the better the cocoa". While coffee and tea were both "mild stimulants", said Clark, she advocated cocoa, because "as well as being stimulating [it] is a true food". Its starch and fat made cocoa "a good drink for children or people doing hard work".[159] "Cocoa-tea" belongs to the same family of Jamaican beverages as coffee-tea and tea-tea, and in recent times all of these drinks have been assimilated by the addition of sweetened condensed milk as well as sugar.

Solid chocolate, as a food rather than as an ingredient for a beverage, became popular only in the later nineteenth century, when new technologies were applied to the extraction of cocoa butter, creating both an "instant" cocoa powder and smooth, refined chocolate bars using powdered milk to produce new versions of milk chocolate. Refined varieties of chocolate were imported until in 1969 Cadbury Brothers Limited, in conjunction with Jamaica Food Products Limited, began production of a range of Cadbury and Fry cocoa and chocolate lines using local raw materials. (Jamaica Food Products Limited had been incorporated earlier, in 1966, and established a factory at Highgate, St Mary, in the centre of the cocoa-growing region.) Consumption of chocolate confectionery in Jamaica averaged only two hundred grams per year, and substantial expansion of the market was predicted. But not all went well, and in 1977 Cadbury was replaced by a locally owned enterprise, Highgate Foods Limited. The new company began by producing bulk cocoa and by 1987 added quality chocolate confectionery, drinking chocolate, breakfast cocoa, instant drink mixes and a gelatin dessert, and served both a local and export market. In 1992 Highgate was the largest maker of chocolate and cocoa products in the Caribbean.[160]

Cocoa and chocolate were both used in cooking in the twentieth century. Clark's recipe for "chocolate buns" used cocoa powder, while her chocolate fudge and chocolate icing used either and her "chocolate sauce for ice-creams" used only "plain chocolate" or "flaked breakfast chocolate". Other twentieth-century cookbooks recommended the use of chocolate, cocoa or both in cakes and puddings, but provided few recipes. By the 1970s, boxed chocolate cake mixes were popular. Occasionally it was suggested that Milo, a commercial brand of prepared "cocoa tea", might be substituted in cake recipes, in the same way as instant coffee was.[161]

In modern times, the consumption of chocolate is frequently framed as sinful, and Jamaica has its share of "chocoholics", a long way from the botanical name of the chocolate tree, literally "food for the gods".

PART 2: ANIMALS

CHAPTER 7

MOLLUSCS, CRUSTACEANS, INSECTS, REPTILES

In deciding what to eat, the distinction between plant and animal food is a fundamental one, leading in the case of vegetarianism to a complete or partial avoidance of animal materials. Although strict versions of vegetarianism are difficult to practise, because the environment is rich in animals, the attempt can be made. Animals are distinguished by their dependence for their nutrition on the ingestion of organic materials formed in nature and by their inability to construct those materials from inorganic chemicals, as plants do. Thus human beings, like other animals, obtain their food by eating whole organisms or decomposing organic matter. Some animal species are herbivores and others carnivores (as indeed are a few plants), while still others, including humans, are omnivorous. For human beings generally, choices about which animals to eat and which to reject are complicated. These decisions are guided not only by cost, nutrition and taste, but also by aesthetic and ethical considerations.

Historically, Jamaicans have not often been strict vegetarians. They have, however, chosen quite selectively from the vast range of potential food offered by the animal kingdom. Just as the range of plants used as staple foods, particularly the cereal grains, was dramatically narrowed over time, so too was the diversity of animals reduced to a small number of major contributors. This process occurred alongside expansion of the species found in Jamaica, resulting from the introduction of domesticated animals, and alongside trade in animal food. In broad terms, the narrowing of the range of animals used as food was particularly focused on avoiding species commonly assigned to the lower branches of animal life. Often the change was viewed by European people as a shift away from African and Taino practices and as evidence of the growth of Judeo-Christian religion. Thus missionaries sometimes found proof of growing faith and moral upliftment after the abolition of slavery in the disappearance of the "savage custom of impaling and eating reptiles and unclean animals".[1] Although the supposed decline in the eating of such animals is not always borne out by contemporary evidence, and although some animals and parts of animals have risen and fallen with fashion, it is broadly true that the foods obtained from these sources have become relatively uncommon in the Jamaican diet or seen as unattractive, though with some significant exceptions.

The animals discussed in this chapter fall largely into the categories that are commonly thought unattractive as food. Several of them were once consumed by Jamaicans but are no longer on the menu. Others were once considered delicacies but suffered depletion by over-exploitation and disappeared from the repertoire. Some remain highly favoured. Almost all of them can be placed among the creepy crawlies, physically unattractive if not actually ugly, and broadly feared. Zoologically, however, the animals lumped together in this way come from diverse branches of the evolutionary tree and are related inconsistently with the fish, birds and mammals of the following chapters.

The reptiles, identified by the Christian missionaries as the least appropriate of animal foods, are actually the closest to the mammals and humankind. Lizards, snakes, alligators and turtles are all vertebrates but lack warm blood and body insulation. This helps explain why, in Jamaica, the turtle came to be included among the fish rather than the reptiles, even though it had dry skin and laid eggs with shells. Farthest away are the molluscs (conches, oysters, octopuses and squid) belonging to the phylum Mollusca and characterized by their muscular feet, their visceral mass containing most of the internal organs, and, often, their limy shells or mantles. (A phylum is a major classificatory division of the animal, or plant, kingdom that can be successively divided into class, order, family, genus and species.) The crustaceans (shrimp, crab, lobster, jonga) might seem to have much in common with the molluscs, because of their shells and aquatic habit, but they were in fact members of the phylum Arthropoda, which also included the insects (macaca, honeybee), all of them possessing segmented bodies, jointed appendages and hard exoskeleton. Finally, of the animals included in this chapter, the sea egg is the only one with its own phylum, Echinodermata, having more in common with the fish, birds and mammals than with the marine molluscs and crustaceans. The fish (Pisces), birds (Aves) and mammals (Mammalia) are not distinct phyla, but are rather classes within the phylum Chordata, which also includes the class Reptilia. All of these – the major sources of animal food consumed by humans – belong to the subphylum Vertebrata and are distinguished by (among other things) their backbones.[2]

Although they are something of a mixed bag, with the exception of the reptiles all of the animals in this chapter are invertebrates. None of them are warm-blooded, and most are defended and held together by tough shells. As well as these distinguishing characteristics, they shared many basic features with other animals, as potential human food. A vital difference between animals and plants, of course, is that animals are mobile and therefore less easily farmed than plants. Animals are only occasionally domesticated and raised within agricultural or industrial conditions. Most animals remain effectively wild and have to be hunted and caught, meaning that they are less often selected for particular characteristics or genetically modified. Another significant difference between plants and animals is that whereas particular, limited parts of plants are typically chosen for food, once an animal enters the human food system it is likely to be consumed whole or to have a number of its parts used. A mango tree yields only fruit, but a cow yields edible food from almost every part of its body, as well as milk. Thus the chapters on plants have been organized according to parts (roots, fruits and so on) while the following chapters deal with animals and groups of animals as a whole. Reasons for this difference between plant and animal use are the cost of producing animal food and the high proportion of edible matter found in the many soft tissues in animals compared to the hard materials of the stems and roots of plants. "Meat" consists of muscle fibres and connective tissues, and its "toughness" varies with the amount of connective tissue associated with the fibres and blood vessels. Small muscles tend to be relatively tough because they include substantial proportions of connective tissue, whereas larger muscles are more tender, especially if they include distributed fat. In birds and mammals, the upper body generally has more fat and tender flesh than the legs. These contrasts help explain the unattractiveness of some of the animals discussed in this chapter.

CONCH, OYSTER, OCTOPUS, SQUID

Modern Jamaicans are not particularly fond of molluscs as food. Several of them are even thought repulsive. Ancient Jamaicans, on the other hand, with a much more limited range of animals to choose from as potential food sources, depended quite heavily on molluscs for their diet. The shells of marine molluscs are prominent in the middens of the Taino, their presence magnified by the high ratio of shell to meat. The big advantage of molluscs for the Taino was that these creatures were generally found in shallow water close to shore, on intertidal rocks, and often were slow-moving and easily gathered. Douglas Armstrong has argued, based on his excavations at the coastal sugar plantation Drax Hall, that molluscs were eaten only occasionally during slavery but became more important after 1838.[3]

Among the simpler marine molluscs, some have a single shell while others, known as bivalves, have two shells hinged together. The most important of the single-shell molluscs are the queen or pink conch, *Strombus gigas* (Figure 7.1), and the whelk, *Cittarium pica*, with its characteristic spiral horn-like shell. The Taino consumed the conch in large quantities. Armstrong found the whelk to be the most common species in remains from the period of slavery, with smaller varieties of shellfish increasing in the larger catches of the post-slavery period. All of these were collected from shallow waters close to shore. Modern Jamaicans have not shared the Tainos' enthusiasm for the meat of the conch. It is better known for its shell, which is sold as a tourist curio. Only small catches were delivered by divers to local markets down to the 1980s. Conch soup was one of the late-night "Jamaican delicacies" sold on the street in Montego Bay, along

Figure 7.1 Conch shell

with roast yam and saltfish, but the meat was considered "rubbery" and did not enter mainstream diets. Conch fritters are sometimes mentioned, but their provenance seems to lie outside Jamaica.[4]

In 1989 a commercial queen conch industry was established, supplying an export market from the resources of the Pedro Cays and Pedro Bank (Figure 2.1). The fishery developed rapidly and by 1992 was the largest producer in the Caribbean. Concerns were expressed for its sustainability, however, because the sedentary queen conch is found close to shore and is easily overfished by free diving. In 1999 the fishery was described as "the last remaining large queen conch resource in the world", but the industry was unregulated, putting the stock at risk. Cooperation between the fishers and government, along with a recognition that short-term exploitation was not in the interest of any of the parties, led to regulation and protection under an Endangered Species Act but equally jeopardized the export industry and the potential use of conch as a domestic food.[5]

The most important of the bivalves in Jamaica are oysters and mussels. Mussels are not popular, though occasional recipes (as, for example, "Solomon Gundy mussels") appear in cookbooks. In Jamaican waters, oysters sometimes attached themselves to the roots of mangroves, giving rise to jokes about the "oyster-tree". William Hughes said in 1672 that these were plentiful on the Liguanea side of Kingston Harbour, "where the islanders often carry their friends to be merry, and eat oysters, and that they may gather them off the trees themselves". Edward Long identified the mangrove oyster as indigenous, saying it was smaller than the European oyster but "extremely delicate, and not at all inferior to the Colchester". (Colchester, in Essex, was the home of the renowned Pyfleet oyster, taken from estuaries running over clay.) Long thought the English bank oyster found in Jamaica was descended from imports but had degenerated. Charles Rampini had oysters from the mangrove trees of Port Royal in 1873. Twenty years later, Caroline Sullivan distinguished between a "round" oyster, eaten raw, and a "flat", or cooking, oyster. The latter she thought best prepared as scallops or patties.[6]

These local oysters had to compete with imports, first of all in cans, then, after about 1900, on the shell. These were among the "English and American delicacies" beyond the reach of the common people. Even when a project was initiated in the 1970s to improve the culture of mangrove oysters on the St Thomas coastline, most went to hotels. The oysters raised from these beds were a "larger, tastier and more aesthetically pleasing product" and were declared "a fine delicacy". Consumers were encouraged to try oyster fritters, scrambled eggs with oysters, sandwiches and omelettes. Oyster punch was popular, because "many Jamaican men feel that oyster increases and sustains their sexual prowess", but even these attractions found only a limited market.[7]

More complex than the single-shell marine molluscs and the bivalves are the cephalopods, characterized by tentacles attached to their heads. Here the most important are octopus (*Octopus vulgaris*) and squid (*Sepioteuthis sepioidea*). In some reef zones the squid is the dominant fauna. Both octopus and squid were illustrated by the Reverend John Lindsay in the 1760s, without comment (Plates 26–27). They may have been important in the diets of the ancient Taino but, because they lacked substantial external shells, they left no hard archaeological evidence. They were also more difficult to catch than the barely mobile shelled molluscs. Modern Jamaican cookbooks generally ignore squid. They do occasionally offer recipes for "sea puss" or octopus, as something to be stewed, but it is generally regarded as an unattractive creature and is uncommon on Jamaican tables. Jamaicans are not alone in finding the cephalopods repulsive: outside the Mediterranean and East Asia, all of them are unusual in food systems. Within the Caribbean, fishermen are more likely to use squid as bait than to eat them, squid being the natural food of fishes such as grouper and snapper.[8]

The molluscs of Jamaica live mostly in the sea. However, one small edible freshwater snail, *Neritina virginea*, known as "busu" in the parish of Portland, is used in soup. It has also been called a mussel and a whelk. As noted in chapter 1, busu has become the symbol of a food festival.

SHRIMP, CRAB, LOBSTER, JONGA

Like the molluscs, crustaceans are mainly marine or aquatic creatures. Along with insects, spiders and scorpions, the crustaceans belong to the arthropods, the group of segmented invertebrates characterized by their jointed legs and by a hard exterior skeleton that can be shed and replaced. Many of them are too small to be considered potential human food. Most are edible, and in spite of the fact that they are omnivorous and eat the corpses of other aquatic animals, the meat of crustaceans is considered of fine quality, worth the effort of extracting from hard shells. The most favoured are shrimp, crab and lobster.

Jamaicans follow American practice in lumping prawns with shrimps regardless of size. Shrimps belong to the order Decapoda Crustacea, or ten-footed crustaceans. The best-known Jamaican species come from the St Elizabeth wetlands. Attempts to produce shrimp in commercial freshwater ponds were made in the 1960s (using imported species) and again in the 1980s, but failed. Writers from the eighteenth century to the present have praised Jamaican shrimps. Patrick Browne in 1756 said shrimps were common and grew up to ten centimetres long, being "chiefly used in sauces, though many of the people eat them alone, especially when boiled with salt". "Pepper shrimp", prepared with Scotch bonnet and bird pepper, became a specialty of Middle Quarters in the twentieth century, a dozen or so sold in a small paper bag to appeal to travellers.[9] Like some small fish, these shrimp were cooked whole and served with head, shell and feet, and the consumer was left to make the decisions about what to discard and what to eat.

Crabs have also sometimes been served whole or in their own shells and occasionally eaten whole. Browne observed that oyster-crabs were small and tender, and found in the shells of mangrove oysters, "and such as eat the oysters, do not think them a bit the worse for being accompanied with some of these crabs, which they swallow with the fish". On the other hand, the mangrove crab, common in low and marshy lands close to the sea, was "often used by the negroes, but said to be sometimes poisonous; which is attributed to their feeding upon the bark of the mangeneel [manchineel] tree, growing chiefly in such places". Long too said the "mangrove or white crab" was "chiefly eaten by the Negroes".[10]

More important have been the land crabs, and of these it is the black crab, *Gecarcinus ruricola*, sometimes called the "mountain-crab", that has been most highly regarded (Figure 1.1). Many writers, beginning in the eighteenth century, have described the crab's habits and praised its taste. The black crab lives mostly on dry land, at some distance from the sea, but comes down once a year to wash off its spawn, between December and May. It was in spawn that the crabs were "prized as one of the greatest luxuries of the country". They came out at night to feed, said John Stewart, "at which time the negroes, with torches, catch them". According to Browne, "When the black crab is fat and in a perfect state, it surpasses every thing of the sort, in flavour and delicacy; and frequently joins a little of the bitter with its native richness, which renders it not only the more agreeable in general, but makes it sit extremely easy upon the stomach." By the early nineteenth century, it could be claimed all "creoles" agreed with Bryan Edwards that mountain crabs were "the most savory and delicious morsels in nature" and even "the greatest delicacy in the world". Dolf Wyllarde, in 1909, said, "He who has not tasted the land crab of the country has not known all the joys of the epicure." By the 1960s, however, it could be complained that "baked black crabs, a great delicacy, seem to have disappeared from our menus" or had become expensive. In spite of this scarcity, recipes continue to appear in cookbooks.[11]

In the eighteenth century, black crabs were "frequently boiled and served up whole; but are commonly stewed when served up at the more sumptuous tables". Marly said in 1828 that "creole epicures" preferred their pepperpot soup made from land crabs, "but when these animals are awanting, they supply their place with salt fish or salt meat, and sometimes even with fresh meat". Sullivan recommended boiling or baking black crabs, and adding them to soup. Walter Jekyll, in 1904, thought the "black land-crab . . . a much-esteemed delicacy", made scarce by the introduction of the mongoose. In 1938 "baked black crabs" were on the menu of the City Lunch Room, Tower Street, Kingston.[12]

Inferior varieties of land crabs were found on the south side of the island. Although of lesser quality, said James Phillippo, "during the rainy season they swarm, and afford abundant food for the poorer classes of both town and country. By some creole families they are kept for months in barrels, or some other place of security, and, being fed with corn and the refuse of vegetables, are almost as great a delicacy as the mountain species." In the twentieth century, land crabs were generally not further distinguished, probably reflecting the scarcity of the black crab, and it becomes difficult to be sure which varieties were being exploited. In Kingston, a long-lasting "crab corner" became established in the 1950s on what became Heroes Circle, and in the 1990s live crabs purchased at Coronation Market were cooked in large pots over coal fires, the water seasoned with salt, scallion, thyme and pimento, and the dish served with roast yellow yam. When Enid Donaldson offered a recipe for crab backs in 1993, she referred to people going out to hunt for "land crabs" in the May rains, and she recommended baking the shells filled with a mixture of crab meat, bread soaked in milk, bread crumbs, onion, pepper and salt, and butter.[13]

The "lobster" of Jamaica is not a true lobster but rather a marine crayfish. The species most commonly eaten by humans is the Caribbean spiny lobster, *Panulirus argus* (Figure 7.2). It inhabits the island's reefs, where it feeds on molluscs, starfish, sea urchins, small crustaceans and algae, using its massive mandibles to crush them all. Browne thought the "horny lobster or great cray-fish" was common in Jamaica's harbours, sometimes growing to a large size, and that it was "much used by all sorts of people". Sullivan gave a recipe for lobster soup, adding the pounded meat of a boiled lobster to a stock made from fish, seasoning it, and enriching it with milk, butter and nutmeg. She also proposed roasted and baked lobster, lobster cutlets (the meat diced and shaped like a cutlet) and lobster croquettes.[14]

In the 1950s the spiny lobster was regarded as "a genuine delicacy". But export to the United States began, and the majority of the catch went overseas. As a result, the lobster population became seriously depleted. In 1975 it was made illegal to catch "berried" female lobsters – with eggs – or lobsters less than seven centimetres' carapace length, but this law was shown little respect. Beginning in 1988 the catching of the spiny lobster was prohibited during the breeding season, from April to June. Still, demand for the "delicacy" remained high, particularly in the hotel sector. In 1990, "vast quantities of spawning and under-sized lobsters were still being harvested from the banks and cays around Jamaica's coast", and there had been "no reduction in the volume of the delicacy being served in restaurants, hotels and other eateries" along the north coast. Some restaurants and beach vendors continued to sell lobster, in spite of visits from the Fisheries Division of the Ministry of Agriculture. Poachers came from other places, such as the Dominican Republic, to fish on the banks.[15]

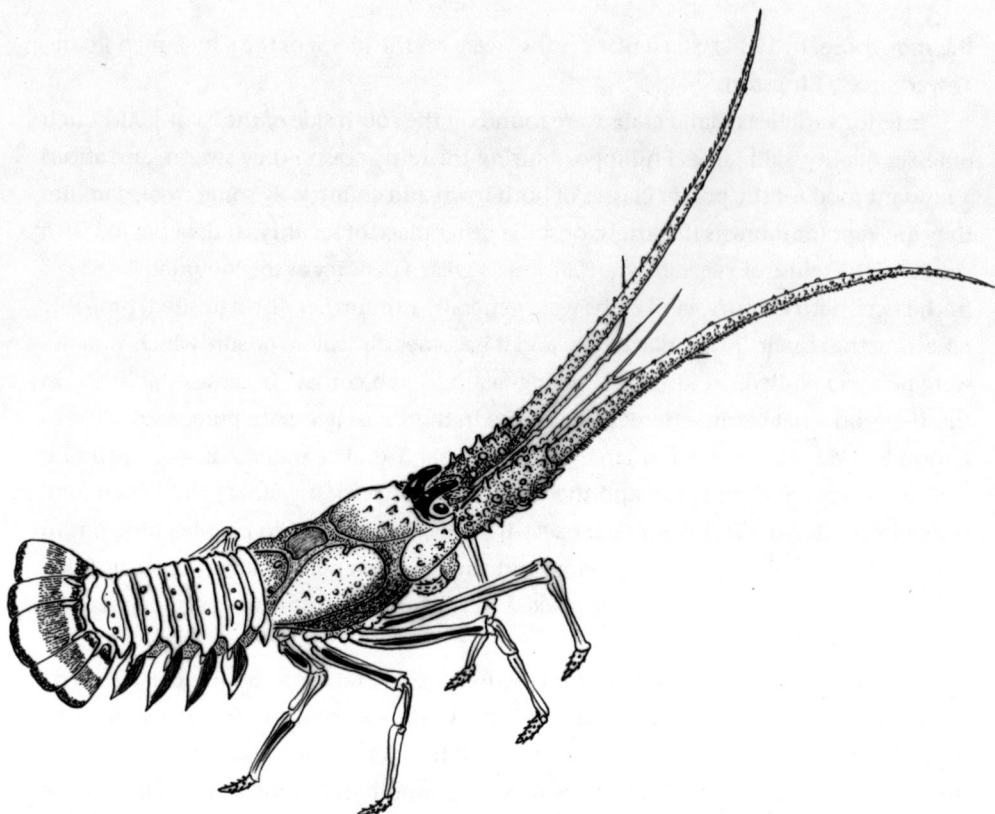

Figure 7.2 Spiny lobster

Sullivan had a recipe for "jonga soup", explaining that jongas were "a kind of small cray-fish which are often found in our mountain rivers". They could be cooked like lobster, as stew, fricassee or curry, or made into soup. Earlier, Browne had said the "river cray-fish" was used in soups and stews. In the twentieth century they remained popular, frequently called "janga" and declared "excellent" boiled, stewed or in soup.[16]

SEA EGG

Although commonly associated with the molluscs and crustaceans of the reefs and inner shore, the sea egg, or sea urchin (*Diadema antillarum*), is strictly an Echinoderm, a distinct phylum related more closely to fish (Pisces) than to molluscs or crustaceans. It is almost spherical or egg-shaped, with a rigid shell-like skin, or test, bearing many long movable spines, as well as five double rows of tube feet, an unusual mouth (an extraordinary apparatus known as "Aristotle's lantern"), and anus on the top of its shell (Figure 7.3). Attached to the inner side of the test are five gonads. The sea egg uses its feet and spines to move around the rocks and mud of the seashore, feeding on seaweed or dead animal matter, and passing mud and sand through its long digestive tract. Sea eggs play a key

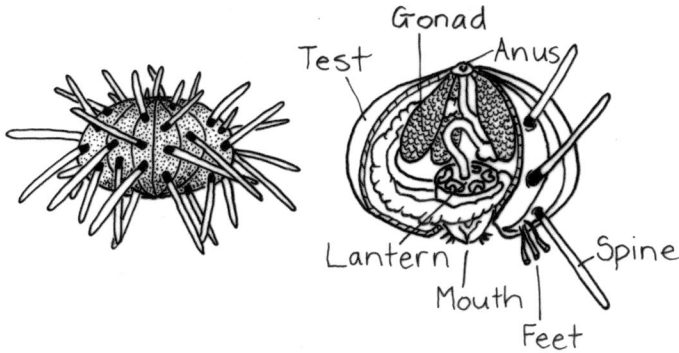

Figure 7.3 Sea egg anatomy

role in controlling the health of coral reef systems: when they were struck by disease in the 1980s there were dire consequences for Jamaican reefs.[17]

The abundance of *D. antillarum* is sometimes attributed to overfishing and the disturbance of reef ecology, but it appears that the species was already abundant around Jamaica long before humans reached the island. In the late seventeenth century, Sloane "found them in great numbers" on the reefs off Port Royal and the cays, saying the deep purple sea egg had long prickles that were "very rough and considered poisonous". (Modern studies show some species but not *D. antillarum* to be poisonous).[18]

In the nineteenth century, visiting Barbadians sometimes wondered why Jamaicans had not made the sea egg "an article of diet". They swore that "this fish is second to none, and, save the oyster, is not equalled". In 1893 the *Gleaner* published directions on the preparation of the sea egg: "Break the sea eggs open and wash the insides of the shells thoroughly with sea water, just shaking them in the water, you will then see pieces of creamy coloured substance adhering to the insides of the shells. Remove these, the edible portion carefully." They could be fried with salt, pepper and onion, or steamed.[19] During World War II, when food supplies were under stress and Jamaicans were searching for alternatives, J.W. Graham wrote "to invite the attention of our local epicures and gourmets to a delicacy which is popular in some of the other West Indian Islands, but has not, as far as I know, been exploited here". He pointed out that the shallow coastal waters of Jamaica, particularly on the north side, "simply teem with what are locally known as 'sea-eggs'". The black variety was spiny and a painful hazard to swimmers, but the white variety had no sharp spines and "during the spawning season they carry five layers of roe [the gonads] placed at intervals around the inside of the 'shell'". Graham had eaten sea eggs in Barbados, around 1900. They were easily cooked: "Plunge the sea-egg into boiling water for a few minutes and then carefully break the shell and with a spoon remove the layers of roe and treat it just as one would do cod roe from a tin."

The flavour was like that of black crab, "and a dozen of them would provide a substantial dish for the breakfast table". Purported "Jamaican" cookbooks occasionally include recipes for "sea urchin (sea eggs)", but these recipes seem to have been imported from the Bahamas.[20]

MACACA

Although insects are the most common animal species in the natural world, modern Jamaicans, like most Western peoples, generally consider the eating of these invertebrates repulsive. The eating of insects has typically been associated with "primitive" hunter-gatherer societies, in some of which the seasonal and occasional consumption of grasshoppers, caterpillars, crickets, beetles, moths, flies, termites and ants formed a significant part of the diet and an important source of sugar and fats. In practical terms, although insects can deliver substantial amounts of protein, they are typically small animals that need to be collected in large numbers, making them economic only when abundant and easily harvested. A further disadvantage is that insect abundance is often seasonal, limiting the value of the resource, though storage in dried and roasted form for later use in breads or soups is common. Few insects are poisonous, but many can sting or fly quickly, and others bury themselves in fortified nests, making their capture challenging. To exploit them as human food, it is therefore wise to capture insects while larvae or soft-bodied, before they have put on their body armour and while they are still rich in protein and energy.[21]

The Taino, with few land animals available, reportedly stored dried and salted stocks of locusts, grasshoppers and crickets, and also traded in these insects. These, together with beetle grubs, wild bees, caterpillars and moths, were part of the diet, just as they were throughout most of the Americas before the European invasions. European people at the time of Columbus were less likely to eat insects, but Africans brought to Jamaica in the slave trade were common consumers of caterpillars, palmworms, termites, locusts and other insects.[22]

According to F.S. Bodenheimer, in his 1951 classic work on insects as human food, "the most famous insect resources of the West Indies were a number of beetle grubs, which were soon adopted as a rare delicacy by the new immigrant Europeans as well as Negroes". The most desirable of these was the larva of the fallow-deer beetle, *Stenodontes (Prionus) damicornis*, a grub as thick as a little finger and growing up to ten centimetres long. Bodenheimer claimed this grub was "considered by epicures as one of the great delicacies of the New World". His account depended heavily on the natural histories of Sloane and Browne. Sloane had said the Taino appreciated these grubs, cooking them in soups and stews, and that enslaved Africans in Jamaica roasted them over a fire. Browne described the "Macacca Beetle" as the largest fly-like insect in Jamaica, breeding in the decayed trunks of dead trees, and said "their large caterpillars, commonly called Macaccas" were "studiously sought for by some people, who think them a very great delicacy". Lindsay illustrated the "macacca beetle" in the 1760s, saying it was "produced from a large, soft, shiney, white caterpillar, which breeds in rotten trees of a soft and spungy contexture", but he contested Browne's claims about its eating qualities. Although Lindsay admitted, "I am told that they are eat as a rarity and dainty" and acknowledged that they were "certainly very fat, tender, and must be delicious", he declared that "after seeing the loathsome looking animal, I fancy no other stomach than that of a French and Spaniard, can look upon them as a delicacy". Certainly, said Lindsay, after almost ten years in Jamaica, "I have never known one of them brought to a table; or (notwith-standing of their great plenty) have been ever preferr'd even by the poorer sort to a junck of salt beef." A few years later, Long observed that the silk cotton tree when decayed "becomes a nest for the macaca beetle; whose caterpillar, gutted, and fried, is esteemed by many persons one of the greatest delicacies in the world".[23]

The etymology of *macaca* is uncertain but probably relates to an African word for beetle. In Jamaica, the word gradually came to be used generically for any kind of grub. Rampini said "macoco beetles" were "a delicacy as dear to the negro as the snail or frog to a Frenchman". In the 1920s some still regarded "the macaca grub as a delicacy" but others already considered it an experimental food, not to be repeated. In 1938 one writer reported that "there is a species of grub which spends its larva days in rotten wood – the peasantry call it ma-ca-ca, which is a delicacy in some parts of the island". By 1955, however, macaca was described as a "2-inch white worm from rotten wood; ugly, fatty-like; not eaten any more".[24]

HONEYBEE

Eaters of honey rarely think of it as an insect product. Honey is in fact the mixture of nectar and saliva produced by social, domestic bees (*Apis mellifica*), nicely exposing the supposed repulsiveness of insects as a hypocritical attitude. Honey is the highest-quality food item available in nature in terms of calories per measure of mass, and is enthusi-astically consumed without apparent concern for its constituents.[25]

Before cane sugar came to dominate the market for sweeteners, beginning in the sixteenth century, Europeans depended heavily on honey. European honeybees were introduced to Jamaica from England and, by the eighteenth century, formed a large population in the woods. Some planters had apiaries. Jamaican honey, according to Long, was "aromatic, delicious, and, like the Minorcan, always in a fluid state". There was also a "wild bee" that produced a "most delicious honey", and Long thought these deserved to be taken into apiaries to protect them from predators. Nests of wild bees were sometimes found in the Cockpits by Maroons on the hunt, who ate the "dripping honeycombs" on the spot.[26]

Sullivan asserted "the flavour of Jamaica honey is very delicate". According to Martha Beckwith, logwood produced the best honey, in February – "clear amber and white" and superior to the "dark mango honey" of April and later. The "water-pale logwood honey" remained popular throughout the twentieth century. In the 1930s, a planter's breakfast might include "a great slice of Jamaican honeycomb dripping with honey . . . with a knife on a large dish". However, the eating of honey was relatively uncommon. During World War II, some called on the government to encourage "the daily Honey Eating Habit" as a "national movement in this Colony", seeing honey as both food and medicine.[27]

Continuing the promotion, the 1957 *Farmer's Food Manual* included a surprisingly extensive chapter on "honey in dietary", offering nineteen recipes for breads, eight for desserts and five for candies, though few of these contained "Jamaican" elements. The manual explained that honey was "a natural, unrefined food" with a high energy-producing value, because it contained 75 to 80 per cent sugars, and that these were more easily digested than cane or beet sugars. The principal components of honey are the simple sugars levulose (41 per cent) and dextrose (34 per cent), water (18 per cent), sucrose (2 per cent), and dextrins and gums (2 per cent). According to the *Farmer's Food Manual*, levulose can be called "the queen of sugars", because it is "almost twice as sweet as cane sugar, and besides its sweetness, it carries to the human senses something that might almost be called a flavour". Levulose is hard to find in a pure state but is common in fruits. It dissolves easily in water and rarely crystallizes. Dextrose, on the other hand, is only half as sweet as cane sugar and crystallizes easily in solution. Honey granulates because it contains almost twice as much dextrose as water. The manual went on to promote honey as a potential (minor) source of vitamins and minerals and as a suitable food for infants and growing children.[28]

By 2005 Jamaica had an estimated 1,500 bee farmers. Their apiaries are damaged by hurricanes and attacked by mites, and the nutritional value of honey remains a subject of public debate, but in spite of these obstacles, much of Jamaica's honey is exported and "pure Jamaican honey" is marketed to tourists.[29]

LIZARD, SNAKE

Reptiles rarely appear on modern Jamaican menus and their often endangered status has little to do with their being hunted for food. Modern Jamaicans generally find reptiles of all sorts repulsive and sometimes threatening. The thought of eating lizard is unattractive, in spite of their abundance and availability – lizards seem very comfortable and unthreatened in people's homes, including their kitchens.

Jamaica has twenty-four species of indigenous lizards, twenty of them endemic, and they are to be seen everywhere. None are poisonous. The island's largest lizard, the Jamaican iguana, *Cyclura collei*, is now found only in the Hellshire Hills. It was hunted and eaten by the Taino. When the first Spanish and English settlers in Jamaica faced inadequate food supplies, they ate iguanas as well as snakes. An English writer of the late seventeenth century said the "guanaes" were "small, and of the shape of an allegator", but "the flesh is sweet and tender". Similarly, Sloane thought the "gwana" was common in Jamaica and "very fat and good meat".[30] Lindsay illustrated the iguana but said nothing of its use as food (Plate 28). There seems little evidence of the iguana being eaten by Africans in Jamaica during the eighteenth century.

By the early nineteenth century, English attitudes were changing. Maria Nugent in 1804 recorded that her husband, the governor, played a trick on a visitor, an army quartermaster, "by ordering an extraordinary fricassée for dinner, of which the Colonel ate twice, and highly commended it. It passed for chicken, but was really a guana". The next morning, when the joke was revealed, it was found the dish "had perfectly agreed with those that ate it", and Nugent noted that "indeed, it is considered not only a wholesome dish, but a great delicacy, by many creoles; but the sight of it, while living, is disgusting, as it is covered with scales, and looks frightful altogether". In the 1960s, Philip Wright claimed that "the Jamaican guana continued to be of use until recent years, when it became extinct". Although the iguana is not in fact extinct, it is an endangered species, but one threatened more by loss of habitat than by modern cooking pots. There has been no attempt to farm iguana in Jamaica as practised in Central America. There is little evidence that other, smaller lizards were ever an important part of the post-Columbian diet, though lizards of various sizes remain abundant and had been eaten in Africa.[31]

Five or six species of snake have been recorded for Jamaica, none of them poisonous. Some are now extinct, and all are rare. Sloane said snakes were eaten by the "Indians and Negros", and a contemporary writer claimed the snakes of Jamaica had been "eaten by the Indians as regaloes", meaning as a feast or a choice food. In some areas of West Africa, snake had long been an item of food, and early English settlers had no problem with it.[32]

In the middle of the eighteenth century, the yellow snake, or Jamaican boa (*Epicrates subflavus*), was still common in rural Jamaica. Browne, who said it grew to six metres, asserted, "Many of the negroes eat these reptiles, and look upon them as a rich and delicate food; but they generally preserve the fat, which is considered as a good resolutive." Long said that Africans in Jamaica sometimes made the yellow snake "a favourite part of their food, whenever they can catch it. They extract the fat from it by boiling, and use it instead of butter; but it is said to render them scabby". Reports of its being eaten end in the middle of the nineteenth century, and the population was much reduced by the mongoose. The yellow snake survives in remote habitats, particularly the Cockpit Country, feeding on rats, birds, lizards and frogs, though growing no longer than three metres, half the length claimed by Browne.[33]

ALLIGATOR

The "alligator" of Jamaica is in truth a crocodile, but the difference matters little. A writer in the 1680s claimed "in many rivers and ponds of Jamaica there's vast numbers of crocodiles, or allegators, that is an amphibious creature, and breeds of an egg, hatch'd by the sun in the sand"; however, "their flesh is not good, they are voracious, and live on fowls and beasts that they catch by surprise, but seldom or never hurt a man". Another writer of the 1680s contended that the young alligator was eatable. Long believed in 1774 that the alligator had been eaten by the Taino, and opined, "Nothing, I venture to think, but their ill looks has saved these animals from being a favourite article of food among the Negroes; but, if this prejudice should happen to wear off, their numbers in Jamaica would be considerably lessened in the course of a few years." Crocodiles were in fact hunted and eaten in West Africa, though declared unclean by Muslims.[34]

William Beckford, writing in 1790, included the alligator among the "disgusting" members of the animal kingdom, along with snakes and lizards and sharks. Other planters were more willing to experiment. When an alligator was killed at the mill of George's Plain in 1816, Matthew Gregory Lewis had a steak cut off and broiled with pepper and salt. Eaten with an onion sauce, he declared it "by no means to be despised; but the consistence of the meat was disagreeable, being as tough as a piece of eel-skin". Perhaps the alligator was old. He was encouraged by the enslaved people on his Cornwall Estate not to eat the alligator, because they thought it poisonous. Lewis said, "The eggs are said to be very palatable; nor have the negroes who live near morasses, the same objection with those of Cornwall to eating the flesh", though the gall was indeed a dangerous poison. Earlier, Long had noted that the alligator laid many eggs, which were "far from being disgustful; but, when boiled hard, are as relishing as the eggs of a duck or a goose". Although he had not himself eaten alligator, Long had "no doubt but that the flesh of a middle-sized one is as relishing as a turtle", and had been assured of this by a man who had bravely made the experiment.[35]

TURTLE

The Caribbean is the home of the sea turtle, but of the five indigenous species, only the green turtle, *Chelonia mydas*, has been important historically as human food. All of the turtles are reptiles, belonging to the order Chelonia and distinguished by the bony plates that protect their bodies; the "tortoise" is just one family among this order. The logger-head turtle, *Caretta caretta*, is not of commercial importance. The hawksbill turtle, *Thallasochelys imbricata*, was better known for its shell than for its flesh, which was considered not only dry but also "very strong and unsavoury", "coarse and fishy".[36]

These assessments changed somewhat over time. The depletion of the Jamaican and Caymanian breeding rookeries meant that both the hawksbill and the loggerhead came to be considered edible, though inferior to the green turtle. Still, by the 1870s, it was said that though "fisher-folk" consumed the inferior species, only the green turtle was commonly sold as food. The depletion of the breeding rookeries occurred on a large scale but took time because of the great abundance of the original population. It has been estimated that the rookery at Grand Cayman had a population of 6.5 million in 1492, but it had collapsed by the end of the eighteenth century. The Jamaican green turtle rookery was smaller but nonetheless substantial. However, by the 1990s "only a few hundred animals" survived around Jamaica. Their numbers were so diminished

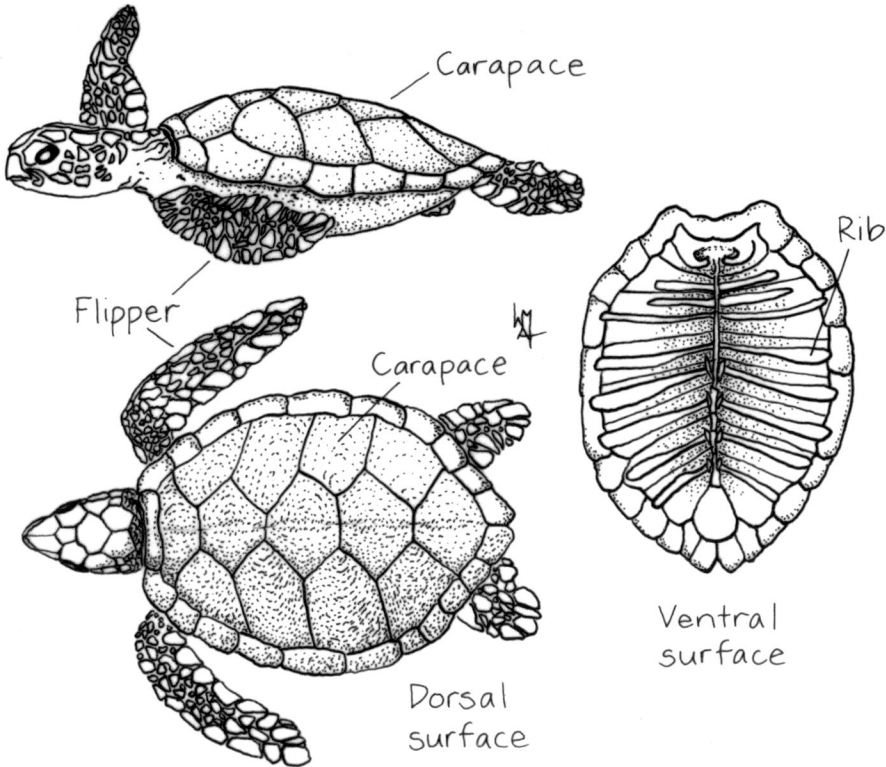

Figure 7.4 Green turtle

that "the cultural and social significance of these creatures, if not the culinary appeal, is all but gone".[37]

The green turtle "is almost unique in being an air-breathing, migratory marine herbivore". Typically, it has a carapace one metre long, olive green to brown or almost black, and smooth, with the laminae closely knit rather than overlapping (Figure 7.4). It weighs up to three hundred kilograms and can live to fifteen years, generally preferring the shallow water inside reefs, shoals and lagoons where marine grasses and algae provide plentiful food. Breeding takes place in late summer, the eggs laid in a shallow hole dug in a sandy area then covered over. An average 120 eggs are laid at a time, and each turtle may lay on more than five nights. The eggs are spherical, about forty millimetres in diameter, with a parchment-like shell. While laying, which takes about two hours, the female is "indifferent to disturbances".[38]

This pattern of behaviour, with other habits, made the green turtle vulnerable to hunters. Turtles swimming in clear water close to the surface to feed on the submarine grasses were easily caught with nets and other means. The green turtle grazed in large herds. On shore, they were easily immobilized by being turned on their backs (Plate

29). The nesting season created even greater opportunities: females attempting to lay could be turned over and their eggs easily collected.

Turtle eggs remain soft even when cooked and the contents are sucked out through a small hole. The green turtle itself was largely taken for its meat, the flesh making up about 40 per cent of the entire body weight, including muscles and flippers. The flesh is covered by a layer of gelatinous fat, which is also found under the surface of the exoskeleton. This fat is valued for soup-making. The greenish dorsal fat and flipper fat are called "calipash", while the yellowish fat from the ventral surface of the body is called "calipee". The cartilage of the carapace is also said to make "excellent soup".[39]

For the coastal Taino, the green turtle was "by far and away the major source of animal protein", claimed David Watts. The eggs were nutritious, and "almost all parts of this animal could be eaten: in addition to the main, savoury meat, pieces of the front and rear shoulder were particularly sought after, as also were the cartilaginous substances lining the upper shell, the intestines, lungs, liver, and even immature unlaid eggs". Taino exploitation was significant, and archaeological evidence suggests that it was sufficiently substantial to have had an impact on the population before Europeans reached the Caribbean. Sea and river turtles were also important in the diet of coastal peoples of West Africa before European intrusion, and in some cases were the principal food.[40]

By the late seventeenth century, much of the green turtle eaten in Jamaica was being brought from the Cayman Islands. One 1680s writer noted that "tortoise are taken much on this coast, but chiefly at the island Cay Manos, 30 leagues to the west of this island, whither the vessels go May, June, and July to load of their flesh that they may pickle in bulk, and take them in that season, when they come on shore to lay their eggs". Sloane declared green turtle "very good victuals". Forty Port Royal sloops were engaged in bringing turtles from the Cayman Islands and the cays south of Cuba; the turtles were kept in pens in the sea and killed when needed. But the resource was already stressed, and in 1681 conservation legislation was enacted that called for fines or lashes for "any person whatsoever that shall destroy any turtle nests, or take away any of the eggs thereof, upon any bay or place within this island, where the turtle shall lay".[41]

Compared to other reptiles, the turtle was long considered a great delicacy, and it was the subject of some of the earliest culinary elaboration and recipe-making. Blome observed in 1672 that the flesh of the green turtle was "reputed the wholsomest and best provision in all the West-Indies". Similarly, Thomas Trapham, in 1679, said the turtle ranked at the head of all the "fish" available in Jamaica, "gratifying the curious palate with extraordinary delicacy, exceeding that of marrow and fatness in any other creature I know of". Most of the turtle's meat was like tender white veal, he said, while the "callapee", or belly, vied with venison when baked. Another contemporary said that "the belly, which they call the callope of the turtle, pepper'd and salted, or roasted and baked, is an excellent dish". The remainder of the flesh, made into a broth, was pronounced "good and nourishing . . . , especially if some of the eggs are mixt with it".

Sloane said "the female with egg is reckoned the best", and that whereas "the callepee, or under part of the brest or belly, bak'd, is reckon'd the best piece, the liver and fat are counted delicacies". These distinctions became a part of the market pricing structure. A 1693 law stipulated that no "cutter-up of turtle" could require purchasers to take head, feet and innards along with the defined quarters, joints or pieces by weight.[42]

At the beginning of the eighteenth century, Edward Ward could say of the (white) Jamaican settlers that "the chiefest of their provisions is sea-turtle, or toad in a shell, stew'd in its own gravy; its lean is as white as a green-sickness girl, its fat of a calves-turd colour". Even in the middle of the century, the green turtle remained common along the coast of Jamaica and was sold "like beef, in all the markets". Although turtle meat was "tough and gristly" when old, the meat of the young turtle was "exquisitely pleasant" and "in the highest repute", making "a great dish baked with forc'd meat balls". The turtle was prepared in "a plainer manner" in Jamaica than in England, with less sauce or seasoning.[43]

Eighteenth-century English and North American cookbooks regularly included directions on how to prepare turtle, and these were often the most elaborate of all the recipes presented in those books. Indeed, they were more elaborate than the recipes for any other Jamaican or West Indian dish, before or since. Thus Susannah Carter's directions "to dress a turtle" occupied four full pages of her 1772 English cookbook. Richard Briggs's recipe for how "to dress a turtle the West-India way", in his *New Art of Cookery*, published in Philadelphia in 1792, can serve as representative: [44]

> As turtles are of various sizes, from one pound to eight or nine hundred weight, I shall confine my directions to one of about fifty or sixty pounds, bigger or less in proportion. Kill your turtle the night before you intend to dress it, which you must proceed to do in the following manner. Tie it by its hind fins with a cord sufficient to hold it, then cut off the head and hang it up to bleed all night; in the morning cut the callipee, which is the belly, round, and raise it up, cut as much of the white meat to it as you conveniently can, throw it into spring water and salt for half an hour, cut the fins off and scald them with the head, and take the scales off, cut all the white part out, and throw it into spring water (the guts and lungs must be taken out, but be careful you do not break the gall) wash the lungs and heart well, and slit the guts and maw all through with a penknife, wash them well in warm water, scrape all the inside skin off, and boil them tender in two gallons of water; (you had better throw the liver away, seldom any person eats it, and it always makes your turtle look black) then take and saw the back shell about two inches deep all round, and scald it, and take off the shell; in the mean time make a good veal stock in the following manner. Take a knuckle of veal and two neat's feet cut in small pieces, and put them on, with three gallons of water, a bundle of sweet herbs, four onions, a quarter of an ounce of cloves and mace, and when it boils skim it well, boil it for three hours and strain it off; cut all the white meat from the bones, save out about two pounds, and cut it in pieces as big as an egg, put a quarter of a pound of butter at the bottom of a stew-pan, put in the white meat, set it over a slow fire, and sweat it gently till you find

it tender; put the lungs and the part of the back shell into a stew-pan, and cover them with the veal-stock, with six shallots, two onions, a little basil, sweet marjorum, winter savory, thyme, and parsley, all chopped fine, a quarter of an ounce of cloves and mace, and twelve corns of all-spice beat fine, and stew it till tender; take it out of this liquor, and strain it off; put the fins on in the same manner as the lungs, and stew them till tender; take them out of the liquor and strain it off, put half a pound of butter into a stew-pan, melt it, and put three spoonsful of flour in, stir it well till it is smooth, and by degrees pour in the liquor that came from the lungs and white meat, and stir it well till it boils, put in a bottle of Madeira, and season it with Cayan pepper and salt pretty high; cut your lungs and the part of the back shell in pieces, with the two hind fins cut in three pieces each, and the white meat put in; stew it fifteen minutes, put a stiff paste all round the edge of the backshell, which is called the calipash, and ornament it with leaves, &c. cut out of the paste to your fancy, season the shell with Cayan pepper and salt, put in these ingredients, with the juice of two lemons, some force-meat and egg balls, and bake it two hours; raise the white meat of the belly shell, which is called the callipee, and stuff it with forcemeat, then notch it across at the top, and season it with beaten spice, basil, marjorum, winter savory, and thyme, chopped fine, and some little bits of butter here and there on it, some Cayan pepper and salt, put a paste round the rim, and bake it three hours; put the bones and the two pounds of white meat on, with some of the stock and a quart of water, with a bundle of sweet herbs, some cloves and mace, and stew it till you find the soup is good: strain it off then put it in a soup-pot, thicken it with flour and butter about as thick as cream, season it with Cayan pepper and salt, and put in half a pint of Madeira, boil it gently for about fifteen minutes, and skim it well; put some butter into a stew-pan and melt it, with a spoonful of flour, stir it till it is smooth, then by degrees pour in the liquor the fins were stewed in; stir till it boils, season it with Cayan pepper and salt, half a pint of Madeira, and the juice of a lemon, put in the two fore-fins, and stew them fifteen minutes, with some force-meat and egg-balls; put a little butter into another stew-pan, and a spoonful of flour, stir it till it is smooth, and by degrees pour in a pint and a half of hock, stir it till it boils, put the guts and maw, cut in pieces about three inches long, into it, and stew it for fifteen minutes; season it with Cayan pepper and salt, mix the yolks of three eggs with a pint of cream, and grate some nutmeg in, put it in, and keep it stirring till it is ready to boil; then take it off, keep it shaking, and squeeze in a lemon; have your calipash, callipee, soup, fins, and fricasee, all hot together, and dish them up hot in the following manner, your soup in a tureen in the middle.

Callipash

Fricasee   Soup   Fins

Callipee

When you send the calipash and callipee to bake, you should put them in a tin dripping pan, and put bricks underneath to keep them steady, that the liquor may not spill.[45]

If all of this was not enough, Briggs offered an alternative method, for a small turtle, recommending that everything be cut up and baked in tureens. This approached Carter's recipe, in which the flesh from the different parts of the turtle were mixed together, in layers, before baking. The West Indian way was to maintain the separation of parts and to introduce the soup. The well-known plagiarist Hannah Glasse had noted, in 1747, that "in the West Indies they generally souse the fins, and eat them cold, omit the liver, and only send to the table the callepy, and soop".[46]

Although turtle was much less common by the end of the nineteenth century, the dishes made from it remained at the centre of the culinary tradition. Thus Rampini, writing in 1873, found that, as a food, turtle was "in high repute all over the West Indies", with turtle steaks, stewed fins, liver, tripe and eggs all regarded as delicacies. The very first recipe in Sullivan's *Jamaican Cookery Book* was for turtle soup. She began with "turtle stew meat" rather than a whole turtle, but the method was complicated enough. Turtle soups, said Sullivan, could be "prepared in many way, some preferring it thin, others thick". Her particular preference was to have it "nice and thick like cream". Sullivan offered four more turtle recipes in the section of the book devoted to "fish": fried crumbed cutlets, fried meatballs made from salt beef minced with the turtle, steaks in gravy, and stew made from the tougher turtle meat. By 1905 it could be said that "turtle soup was something for Christmas and tourists", but Beckwith soon after observed that "turtle-spearing is still carried on at night in the marshes of the Black River by setting fire to the long grass and driving the turtles to take refuge in the water", and she thought turtle soup one of the "common delicacies on the creole table". Phyllis Clark's 1945 cookbook offered "creole turtle soup" made with turtle fin.[47]

The export of live and dried turtle from Jamaica effectively ended in the 1940s. The catching of turtles was prohibited in the nesting months, from April to September; the eggs could not be collected and no turtles could be taken from beaches. As in the early eighteenth century, a high proportion of the turtles sold in Jamaica were taken by Cayman Islanders working the cays and few came from Jamaica's own coastal waters. Live turtles had been sent on board ships to Europe beginning in the seventeenth century, but the "barbarity" and heavy mortality of the live trade had long been denounced. When a Turtle and Preserve Manufacturing Company was established on Hanover Street in Kingston in the 1870s, it produced "the various preparations of the most luxurious of all animal food preserved in cans for keeping and for exportation", but it also sold locally fresh turtle steaks, soup and sausages.[48]

Efforts to breed, hatch and "cultivate" sea turtles have not been successful. In 1982 Jamaica legislated complete protection of all species of sea turtles under the Wildlife Protection Act, but the turtles found nesting increasingly difficult on the island's disrupted beaches. The slaughter of turtles for steak and soup has continued, and turtle is still considered a delicacy. Recent cookbooks have occasionally included recipes for turtle soup or stew, using turtle meat, and supermarkets and restaurants have advertised turtle soup and meat. One cookbook, published in the United States in 1992, claimed that "in Florida you'd be jailed for killing a turtle for food, but in Jamaica, the Bahamas, and the Cayman Islands, they're local delicacies". Conservationists, meanwhile, struggled to "save the few remaining sea turtles coming into Jamaican waters", and a recovery plan has been put in place.[49]

In addition to the sea turtles, Jamaica exploited the terrapin, a freshwater or tidewater turtle of the family Emydidae that was once common in the lagoons and morasses of Jamaica and that has occasionally been highly valued. Sloane said that "land-turtles are counted more delicate food than those of the sea, though smaller", and Browne said the terrapin was "often served up at gentlemen's tables in that island, and looked upon as delicate wholesome food by many people". Beckford, in 1790, found that "the land turtle of Jamaica are among the principal delicacies of the island; and there are but few people who have resided there long, who do not give them a decided preference". He praised their fatness and said that "when large the females are often full of eggs; and when they are in perfection, it is difficult to conceive any viand more rich and nutritive". Philip Henry Gosse observed pond turtles (*Emys decussata*) in Westmoreland, and noted, "The flesh of these animals is esteemed superior even to that of the famed Green Turtle, by those who have abundant opportunities for judging of both; hence many are caught for the table."[50]

Sullivan offered a recipe for "land turtle or terrapin" using a whole animal. She began, "Cut off the head, and open the back. Remove the flesh from the inside and take away the bones, and also get what meat you can from the legs." The meat was diced and combined with salt pork and salt beef, then mixed with tomatoes, scallion, herbs, black pepper, cinnamon, nutmeg, sauce, butter, lime juice and sherry, and finally returned to the turtle's back, covered with bread crumbs and baked. These turtles had little meat, said Sullivan, so that it took two turtles to fill one shell. The terrapin was also made into soup.[51]

CHAPTER 8

FISH

Jamaicans have, over the long term, been large consumers of fish. In the 1950s, for example, they ate, per capita, almost four times as much fish as did Europeans and North Americans. Local waters never supplied more than one-quarter of that consumption, however. The greater part was sourced from the North Atlantic, particularly the abundant fishing banks that stretched from Cape Cod to Labrador.[1] The foundation of this system was built in the seventeenth century, as a means of provisioning the enslaved African people who laboured on the sugar plantations of the English. The result was an emphasis on fish above all other forms of animal protein and an emphasis on imported, preserved varieties. Most of the fish eaten was saltwater fish, preserved in salt.

Whereas consumption of many foods increased over the long term, as already noticed in the case of cereal grains, oils and onions, per capita imports of fish have declined steadily since the end of slavery. The decline in imports was not balanced by any substantial increase in the local catch; the lowest level was reached as early as 1915 (Figure 8.1). The decline in fish consumption was quite different to the reductions discussed in the previous chapter, though the depletion of the stock was parallel and often closely related. At least some of the reptiles, molluscs and crustaceans that had an important place in the diet before the twentieth century, and especially in the diet of the Taino, ultimately disappeared from the Jamaican repertoire because they came to be seen as unattractive as food and perhaps repulsive. But few fish were removed from the list of edible foods: the decline in consumption reflected the depletion of the fish population and changes in taste and relative cost. Other animals became increasingly important as sources of protein, notably chicken, cow, pig and goat. Yet the significance of this one bird and these three mammals became established only after 1950, roughly fifty years after fish had bottomed out.

Within this general trend, the composition of fish consumption changed quite radically. In the centuries before the trends shown in Figure 8.1 commenced, the Taino

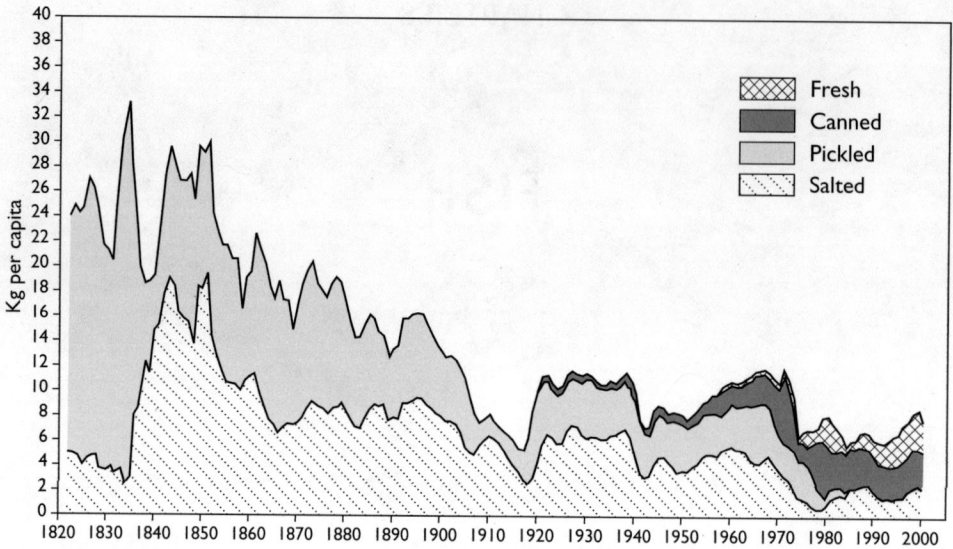

Figure 8.1 Imports of fish per capita, 1822–2000. Source: Appendix 1.

necessarily focused exclusively on local fresh fish, but from the late seventeenth century to the end of slavery, imported cured fish dominated. Enslaved people were given as rations mostly pickled fish, preserved in barrels of brine. Five times as much pickled fish was imported as saltfish, and a good proportion of the latter was eaten by the free people. The end of slavery meant a rapid shift away from pickled to salted fish, which had always been preferred, and by 1910 three times as much saltfish was imported as pickled. The proportion shifted somewhat erratically thereafter, but by 1985 pickled varieties ceased to be statistically significant. They were replaced by canned fish, beginning in 1920 but substantially only after 1960. With ackee plentiful and saltfish scarce in the later 1960s, it was correctly predicted that "fish-hungry Jamaicans" would increase demand for higher-quality canned product. Fresh fish (iced and frozen) was imported in the 1930s but was not important until after 1975. By 2000, salted, canned and fresh fish were imported in roughly equal proportions. Wherever their fish came from, consumers were wary of freshness, continuing to wash fish in plenty of lime juice, dry it and season it with salt and pepper.[2]

Whether local or imported, fresh or cured, the fish used as human food have generally been taken from the wild. They have never been domesticated in the way the birds and mammals used by humans have been selected and modified. Most fish are taken from their natural habitats, though some have been "farmed" in enclosed ponds. Dependence on the natural rhythms and migrations of fish populations necessarily means variations in seasonal supply and availability. Hook and net are relatively unselective, compared to the farming of birds and mammals, so that fish from a wide variety of species enter the human food system. Modern fishers employ sophisticated technologies to identify and catch oceanic fish, but before about 1950 most of these tools were not available and fishing was much more unpredictable. Without access to freezing, fishers had to find other ways of preserving their catch in order to get it to distant markets in a palatable state. Modern technologies also enable fishers to exploit distant stocks of pelagic fish (those living near the ocean surfaces) and to reach the benthic varieties that live on the sea floor. Yet the efficiency of these modern technologies has resulted in depleted fisheries and often in short supply to traditional markets. Historically, overfishing was much less common and drastic. There seemed to exist an inexhaustible resource of fresh and saltwater species.

Early English descriptions of Jamaica portrayed an abundance of aquatic resources in pond, stream, estuary and sea. Richard Blome observed in 1687 that "Jamaica very much abounds both in its rivers, bays, roads, and creeks, with great variety of excellent fish, the great abundance whereof very much contributes to the feeding of the inhabitants, and others who frequent the island". The "vast variety" of the fish meant that "it would be too tedious to repeat their names, were they known or remembered". Hans Sloane said he knew of no place on earth with "greater plenty of fresh water and sea fishes, than in the island and on the coast of Jamaica". The same was true in the eighteenth century: Edward Long listed thirty-nine varieties of fish, saying these were a mere sample of the richness of the seas around Jamaica.[3]

In spite of this plenty, there were early fears of overfishing of local resources. In 1711 the Assembly attempted to regulate fishing, by prohibiting the use of "evil and ill-disposed methods of destroying the fish in and about this island", such as the "poisoning or intoxication" of fish, the setting of fishpots in streams and the building of weirs across them. Only those who owned land could set pots on the sides of the streams that belonged to them, except in parts of the parish of Vere, where even this was prohibited. The 1711 law regulated the mesh of nets, prohibiting those with less than "one inch and a quarter between knot and knot", excepting shrimp nets, which were limited in total length. In spite of these regulations, by the end of the eighteenth century the inshore and reef fisheries of Jamaica were already overexploited, and alternative technologies, such as longline fishing and trawling, were always inappropriate to the environment. Locally caught fish accounted for little more than 10 per cent of the total fish consumed in the island. Later legislation, such as the 1885 Birds and Fish Protection Law, similarly sought to prohibit the use of poisons, intoxicants and dynamite for catching fish, limited mesh sizes and applied closed seasons.[4]

In the period of slavery, many plantations employed a specialist fisherman to catch fish, crab and turtle from streams, morasses, ponds and the sea. These men produced only enough to supply the greedy tables of the planters and rarely contributed to the cooking pots of the enslaved. Maria Nugent, in 1802, noticed a plantation fishpond emptied by drought but heard from the gardener that "as soon as the rainy season began, he would fill the pool immediately, by sending negroes to the mountains in the night, with lanterns, and they could fetch abundance". Cynric Williams, near Montego Bay in 1823, described ten or twelve enslaved men belonging to a pen hauling the seine at a beach near daylight, catching "goggle-eyed jacks, yellow tails, baracootas, silver oldwives, trunk fish, and others with no less barbarous names". In the 1840s fishermen used line, seine and pots. Philip Henry Gosse thought the seine was the fisherman's most efficient tool, netting those fish which would not unwarily enter a pot or be tempted by a bait, but the net also caught many fish termed "rubbish" by the local fishermen, "being of no esteem in the market". By the 1920s, fishing was done using pots, nets, spears and towing lines. Later, dynamite was sometimes deployed, helping to destroy both juvenile fish and the coral reefs which nourished them. Some fishermen added chlorine to their armoury, to blind freshwater fish.[5]

Why not cure and salt local fish? During the period of slavery, when fish were relatively abundant, a small amount of the catch was so treated. Appropriate methods were known from both Europe and Africa, but the labour of the enslaved people of Jamaica was worth more to their masters when applied to production for export. The time available to the enslaved was too short to enable them to carry out the necessary processes, as was also the case with cassava and yam. Imported saltfish was cheap. The labour factor changed after 1838, but not the cost factor. Curing did continue on a local scale, but it was harder to start a competitive industry.[6]

In 1880 the Jamaica Institute offered prizes for "the best specimen of fish from island waters, preserved by dry process, in boxes or barrels, weighing not less than 100 lbs net, and certified to have been put up six weeks previous". Prizes were also offered for "wet process" product. Ten years later, the government made a grant to a company that planned to cure fish for the local market, using boracic acid. The idea came up again in 1917 when imported food was short. There was "no great art in curing fish"; it was already done by "the fishermen at Alligator Pond, Pedro and elsewhere, and corned fish is vended in the interior parts regularly". Further short-lived projects were tried. In 1933 Caribbean Fisheries Inc. was founded to attempt deep-sea fishing, using Kingston as the fleet's home port and curing some of the fish taken "on the same principle as is done in Newfoundland". In the 1960s cod and pollack were imported fresh and salted in Jamaica, and in 1987 grey snapper and Banga Mary ("bangga" was derived from West African words for a small fish) were similarly imported and salted locally, but neither of these enterprises was sustained.[7]

If local salting could not easily compete with imports, why not an industrial approach to the supply of fresh fish? As Algernon Aspinall observed in 1912, "it may seem an anomalous state of affairs that though the waters surrounding the West Indian islands teem with fish, quantities of salt fish should be imported into the West Indies every year". However, attempts to develop a local industrial fishery failed. In 1870 a "fish company" was proposed for Falmouth, to supply fresh fish cheaply, but this came to nothing. In 1898 operations were commenced by a British-based Caribbean Sea

Fisheries Development Syndicate, with inducements from the Legislative Council of Jamaica, and in 1900 the Kingston Fishery Company advertised fish at three pence per pound (454 grams). Trawling proved a failure because of coral growths and a lack of bottom fish. The use of smaller-scale fishpots and short-lines was advocated. More successful than these attempts at industrial-scale fishing were local initiatives to deliver fresh fish to the interior of the island. In 1918 fresh fish was "rushed from Alligator Pond to Mandeville" by runners, using a "system of marketing that is not done in any other part of the island" and that was said to deserve emulation.[8]

Organized exploitation of Jamaica's fishery, through the establishment of cooperatives, the granting of credit and the upgrading of technologies, began in 1955. The use of outboard motors opened up the shelf, while ferry boats plied between Kingston and the cays to purchase fish from resident fishers (Figure 2.1). Production from the inshore fishery peaked around 1960 at ten thousand tonnes annually, the south coast proving the most productive zone. But the number of boats employed in the offshore fishery, working the shelf and banks, declined after 1980. Nonetheless, at the end of the twentieth century there were still more than ten thousand registered fishers operating from island landing sites. Some lived long-term on the Pedro and Morant cays, selling their catches to "fish carriers", who travelled to the cays to collect the fish and supplied the fishers with food, fuel and other equipment. The fish carriers returned to Greenwich Farm fishing village, in Kingston, and sold the fish to vendors who came from across the island. In the 1990s the fish carriers complained increasingly that the fish were small and that the fishers mixed the good (doctor, snapper, Welshman and turbot) with the bad (Caesar, shiny head parrot and small red belly parrot). By 2001 territorial disputes had erupted, with boats from Honduras and Colombia coming to sell directly on Jamaican beaches and undercutting prices, while the island's supermarkets were almost exclusively stocked from imported sources, including from Guyana, Honduras and Mexico.[9]

What were the fish most commonly eaten by Jamaicans? It is clear that availability and price were important factors, balanced against taste preferences. In the 1960s the chief varieties of saltwater fish were kingfish, snapper, jack, mackerel, whiting, bonito and tuna, and of freshwater fish, tarpon, snook, jewfish, African perch and mullet. Novlet Jones, in 1977, listed the main families of fish caught and sold in Jamaican waters as jack, grouper, snapper, doctorfish, parrotfish, porgy and turbot. Donaldson considered "Jamaica's best loved fish" in 1993 to be salted fish (cod), kingfish, sprats, snapper, blue marlin, pickled mackerel and pickled shad, adding the "fish" conch, lobster, crab and shrimp. And in 2001, the most common fresh fish in the market were Banga Mary, red trout, grey and red snapper, and kingfish.[10] These varied listings are sufficient to demonstrate differences over even the most recent decades – and also differences in perception and reporting.

In earlier centuries, local and imported varieties were significantly different, with a much greater emphasis on the qualities of local freshwater fish. The mountain mullet, for example, mentioned in chapter 1 as one of the true delicacies of Jamaican food, features in none of the twentieth-century listings and is today little known.

MOUNTAIN MULLET

The mountain mullet, *Agonostomus monticola*, was long extolled as Jamaica's best freshwater fish (Figure 1.1). Relatively common in the many short, steep streams in the eastern end of the island, it has rarely swum in the lower reaches or estuarine waters except, apparently, to spawn in summer. The fish grow to 20 centimetres and weigh up to 160 grams, but swim in small schools that include many smaller individuals. Larger fish were reported in the nineteenth century, with "green fat and yellow fat, just like a turtle". They feed heavily on insects but also eat freshwater prawns (jonga), plant matter and algae.[11]

Sloane declared that the "fresh-water mullet" was "very good and delicious food, being extremely fat and savory". Long said it was "justly reputed one of the most delicious fish in the universe", and noted that in season, "the female bears roe nearly as big as her body". Nugent ate mountain mullet in 1802 while travelling in Clarendon, and thought it "very small, but excellent" and a "marrow-like little fish". Matthew Gregory Lewis, who complained in 1816 that the endless variety of fish found in Jamaica was more a "variety of names than of flavour", excepted the mountain mullet, which was, he said, "almost the best fish that I ever tasted". Others agreed, including Gosse, who found mullet in the "holes and basins" of small rivers near Bluefields, saying some grew to forty-five centimetres. They might be caught with the hook, especially one baited with avocado pear, and were "often taken by hand; the negroes plunging their arm into the holes beneath the bank, and feeling for the fish". The mullet was both beautiful and "one of the most highly esteemed fishes for the table".[12]

Charles Rampini said in 1873 that the "little mountain mullet" deserved its reputation "as the delicatest fish that swims in Jamaica rivers". He believed it was best eaten as soon it was taken from the stream, when, "wrapped in plantain leaves, or better still in note-paper, and lightly heated on a gridiron over a clear wood fire, it forms, in Brillat Savarin's phrase, a veritable *bocca di Cardinale*". Caroline Sullivan also praised the mountain mullet for its "excellent flavour" and, like Rampini, recommended "rolling them in buttered paper and frying them, sending them to table in the paper; but they can of course be fried plain or boiled if preferred". But by the 1980s, Norma Benghiat could say only that it was "best grilled over charcoal, though rarely seen for sale".[13]

Although closed seasons were introduced by the early twentieth century, it was complained that these were set for inappropriate dates, so that the Hope River from Gordon Town to Papine no longer had large mountain mullet while fish could be bought in October "filled with roe, ready to be deposited". In the 1940s the Angling Association issued calls for conservation, because the mountain mullet was being taken regularly in "vast numbers" by nets, fishpots and dams. Extinction was predicted but did not occur.[14]

TILAPIA, MUDFISH

Although the idea was suggested as early as the 1890s, commercial farming of freshwater fish in inland ponds was not attempted in Jamaica until the 1950s. The first fish tried was the African perch, or Mozambique tilapia (*Oreochromis mossambica*), which was introduced to swamps, rice fields and tanks. The tilapia is a prolific breeder, rapidly producing a vast number of fish. This creates its own problem, as the fish multiply so rapidly that in confined ponds they become overcrowded and reach maturity before they are big enough to eat. A full-grown tilapia can reach one kilogram, whereas the stunted fish matures at just eighty grams (Figure 8.2). Further, because they are aggressively carnivorous, it is difficult to keep any other species of fish with them. Thus early experiments failed, until species were bred composed almost entirely of males.[15]

Initially, African perch "ran into a problem with consumer acceptance" because of the dark colour of its flesh and its muddy taste. Recipes from the early 1970s recommended using it in salads ("mumby salad") or fried in breadcrumbs ("Ala-Afro"). In 1978 the silver or Nile tilapia, *O. nilotica*, was introduced from the United States, and this proved more acceptable in colour and in having a fleshier body. The African perch was phased out. Red-skinned hybrids began to be produced on a large scale in commercial pond-fisheries and "found great acceptance on the market". Although there were

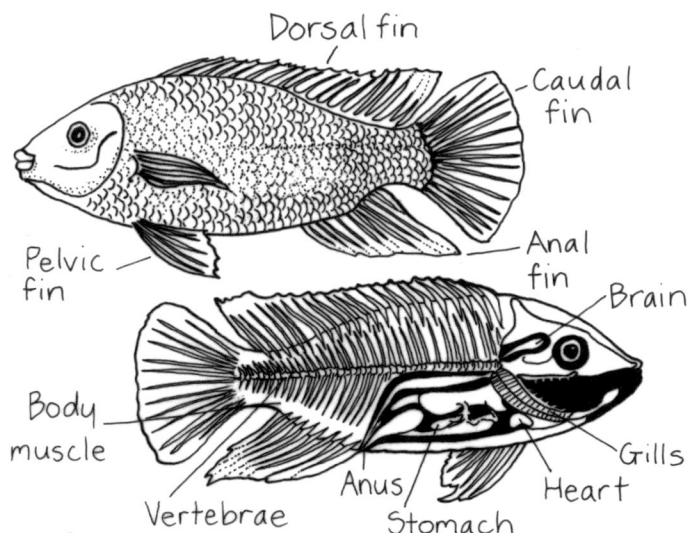

Figure 8.2 Tilapia anatomy

problems with off flavours resulting from various environmental causes, giving a musty-earthy or muddy taste that was not attractive, consumers gradually became accustomed to it and appreciated the cheapness of the fish.[16] By 1990 one-third of the fish produced locally was freshwater, and output of pond tilapia reached 4,200 tonnes in 1997. There was enough to enable exports. Recipes for the fish were not common, but in 2005 "herb-stuffed tilapia in banana leaf", produced by Longville Park Farms, won a prize in the Best New Food Item category at the *Jamaica Observer* Table Talk Food Awards. Some commentators nevertheless continued to call pond fish "tasteless" compared with the "real fish" that came from the sea.[17]

Unrelated was the indigenous mudfish, a highly praised freshwater fish in the eighteenth century. Precise identification is unfortunately impossible because of the broad application of the name. Patrick Browne, writing in 1756, said the "mud-fish" was common in the rivers and creeks of Jamaica and thought it "the most delicate fish I have yet known, when in full perfection". Thomas Thistlewood hooked some in the Cabarita River in 1761, along with drummers and tarpons, and later served "stewed mudfish, and pickled crabs". But the mudfish dropped out of sight in the nineteenth century, or perhaps took on new names.[18]

CALIPEVER, SNOOK, OLDWIFE

The "real fish" that swam in salt water included some well-regarded species that divided their time between sea and stream. Many of these spent most of the year in marine waters, swimming upriver only to spawn, in the manner of the salmon. Perhaps as a result of this behaviour, these are often compared to the salmon as food fishes. One of the best known in Jamaican waters is calipever, *Mugil liza*, "a large sea and river mullet".[19] In the eighteenth century, Browne, the Reverend John Lindsay and Long thought the calipever was merely a larger species of the sea mullet, swimming in the deeper ocean. Browne said it grew to about sixty centimetres and was "looked upon as a very delicate fish". Lindsay, who drew many images of fishes, claimed that the "Calapaver" or "Mullet of the Sea" was "esteem'd by some, of whom I am one, as the best fish of this kind, in these seas". Its flesh was firm, and "fleak'd like the salmon and when boild and eat with fennel sauce, gives one a pretty good idea of that fish". A further advantage, noted Lindsay, of "the mullet too (of all the large, oblong, tumid form'd fish) is that we have in greatest plenty all the year round". Calipever came near to shore around November and were then at their most plentiful, with a roe similar to salmon roe.[20]

In the nineteenth century, John Stewart asserted that the "calapavor" was "almost equal to the salmon" in "richness and flavour". Sullivan went further, saying the "cale-peaver" was "sometimes called the Salmon of Jamaica". It was "a very rich, delicately flavoured fish", most common "in the vicinity of Spanish Town". She recommended that it be boiled slowly, served with butter and parsley and with some fresh lime squeezed over the dish.[21] The fish was a regular in the markets, and in 1906 "calipever roes" could

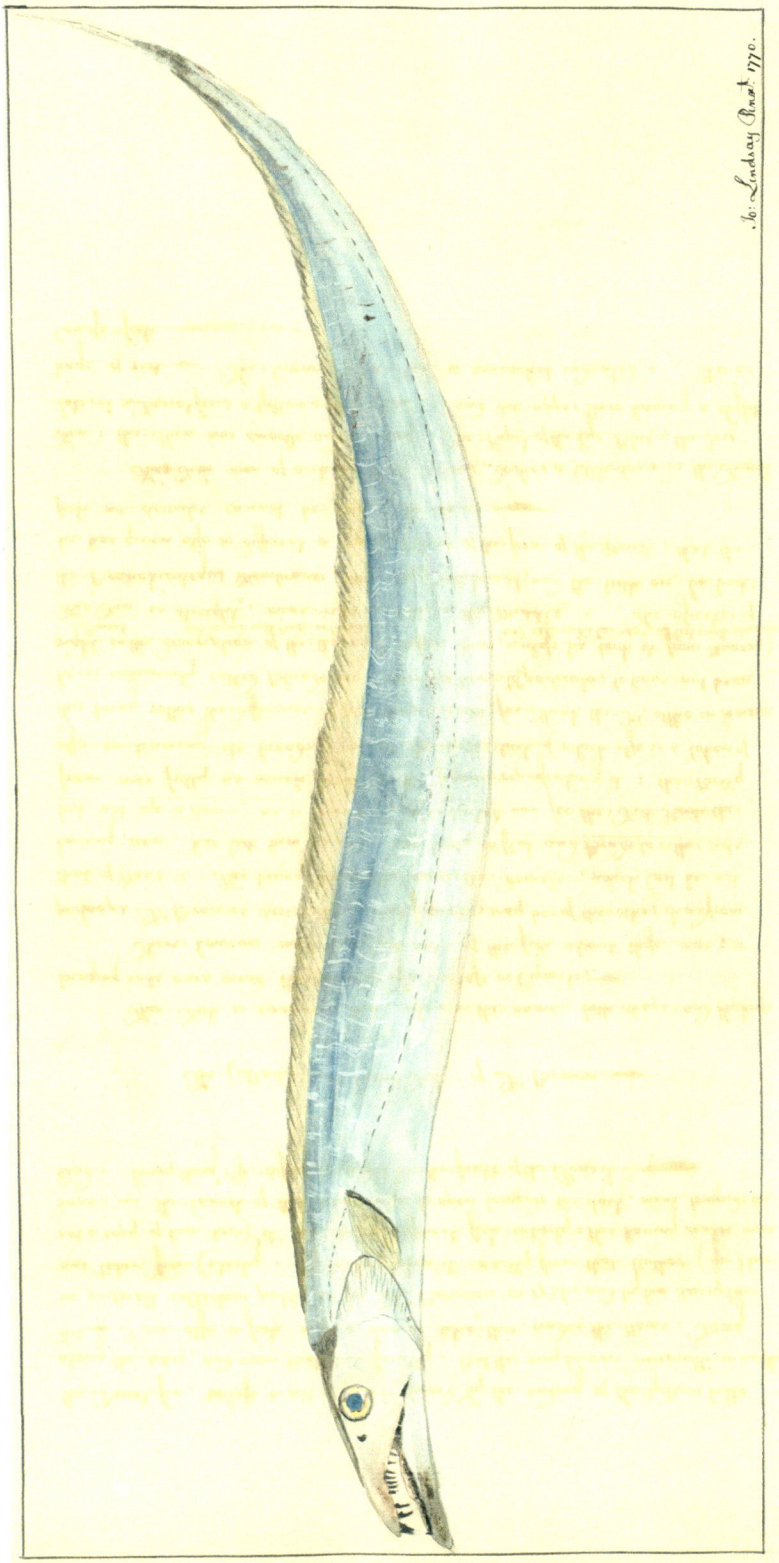

Plate 33

Cutlassfish, by Rev. John Lindsay, 1770. Bristol Museum and Art Gallery.

Plate 40

Monk seal, by Rev. John Lindsay, c. 1770. Bristol Museum and Art Gallery.

be had at the Commercial Bar and Billiard Rooms on Harbour Street, along with imported oysters and other fish. Milk River was well stocked, and into the 1950s "calipeiver mullet" hid in the caves of Gut River, Clarendon. But supply was already short, and this encouraged fraud. In May 1943, for example – out of season – it was reported that "it is the practice of certain fish vendors to buy young barracuda, cut off the head, scale it and retail it as Calipever". People had taken ill as a result of eating the barracuda, and the health authorities advised "not to purchase any fish which has been scaled prior to their seeing it, nor to buy any fish for the present which is stated to be Calipever".[22] Occasional recipes for "calapeeva (found in Jamaican rivers)" appeared in cookbooks down to the 1980s, the fish sometimes still called "Jamaica salmon".

The true Atlantic and Pacific salmon first came to Jamaica as "fresh fish" in cans, beginning in the 1860s, or as smoked salmon, included among the imported "English and American delicacies" that were beyond the reach of the common people.[23]

The snook, *Centropomus undecimalis*, inhabits warm, shallow seas from Florida to Brazil, and sometimes leaves the sea to swim in brackish waters or to travel far up freshwater streams. It typically reaches about two kilograms in weight, though it can grow much larger. Snook, a predator, feeds on shrimps, crabs and smaller fish. Once abundant, it is now considered a game fish. Browne thought the snook one of the best species in the Americas, eating "very much like a full grown cod-fish". Thistlewood noted in 1774, "My Negroes now get great quantities of snooks, tarpons, mudfish, etc., the morasses being full of new water." In 1763 he had given a dinner that included "stewed snook and ketchup sauce", along with various game birds. Sullivan, however, offered no recipes specifically for snook, and although it swam in some of the island's streams into the middle of the twentieth century, the fish has since been absent from cookbooks.[24]

Another American marine fish that runs up freshwater streams to spawn was oldwife, or alewife (*Alosa pseudoharengus*), a relative of the herring. It also resembles the shad but is smaller, reaching a maximum thirty centimetres (Plates 30–31). In Jamaica, "oldwife" has been its most common name, but it has also been called "nigger-fish", "old wench", "tobacco fish" and "turbot", this last referring to species of triggerfishes and filefishes rather than to the European turbot or flounder. Lindsay said in 1765 that "the old wife" came in different sizes but was "thought by many to be one of our greatest dainties upon the table and gives rise to a common saying *good fish but bad flesh*". Another fish was variously identified as "The Angel Fish; Portuguise; or Old Wife Fish". Lindsay thought it "tolerably good for the table", though thin, and noted that "to dress it some take off the skin, which is so tough and rough that the Negroes use it to scoure plates dishes &c. in the kitchen".[25]

Pickled, oldwife was one of the fish given to enslaved people, along with herring, and both were generally disliked. It continued to be imported, and as late as 1890 "No. 1 alewives" were on sale in Kingston. Sullivan described the "old wife" as "a queer flat fish". She recommended frying it in egg and breadcrumbs and serving with butter and parsley.[26] It vanished from the Jamaican culinary tradition in the twentieth century, perhaps because it was both ugly and too long associated with pickling.

ANCHOVY, SNAPPER, GRUNT, GROUPER, JEWFISH

Common in tropical waters, the striped anchovy, *Anchoa hepsetus*, is a small, weak, silvery fish, rarely growing to more than ten centimetres, that swims in large schools close to shore. It inhabits the coastal zone of Jamaica, neither venturing into the open sea, where it might be eaten by predators, nor swimming up streams. Browne said the "anchovie or small silver fish" was common in the harbours of Jamaica and, though small, "extremely delicate, and in great esteem with most lovers of fish". In Jamaica, he said, anchovies were "generally served up fried; and when well pickled are no ways inferior to those of the name in Europe". Today, the anchovy is generally filleted and salted or made into a paste, but is most likely to reach Jamaica in a bottle.[27]

Snapper inhabit warm seas around the world and make up a large family of fishes, with more than 250 species, many so similar that they are not easily distinguished. Globally, red snapper (*Lutjanus campechanus*) is the most important commercial species. Red snapper swims about 50 metres deep, in coastal waters stretching from the Gulf of Mexico to Brazil. Its typical weight is about 2 kilograms, though larger and smaller fish are frequently taken. A recipe for "Jamaica red snapper" from the 1960s called for a fish not less than 500 grams. In the deep waters of Jamaica's shelf, snappers were the most important of the commercial fishes taken by hook and line in the 1960s, particularly the silk or silver snapper (*L. vivanus*), which is also red but with a yellow tail, the blackfin (*L. buccanella*) and the black snapper (*Apsilus dentatus*). The yellowtail snapper (*Ocyurus chrysurus*), also popular in the 1960s, is generally taken at night from shallow waters.[28]

Since the eighteenth century, snapper has been well regarded in Jamaica. Browne listed several species, saying they were "all highly esteemed" and "reckoned superior to most of our European fishes, both in delicacy and richness". In 1762 Lindsay distinguished the "black snapper" and the "pot or spot snapper". He thought the former rare but characterized by its "delicacy", and said that "if thrown upon a fire, by the sea side as it comes from the net, ungutted, it is perhaps when of a small size the most delicious fish in the ocean". When the black snapper grew to fifty centimetres, it was "very fat, and only drest in barbecue, where high seasonings make its richness set easy on the stomach". Lindsay called the pot or spot snapper "a pretty common tho delicate and middling sized fish"; it was regularly caught in "pots or small mouth'd baskets let down into the seas", and, he added, "the remarkable black spot which is always upon the sides of the fish, makes me call it the Spot rather than Pot Snapper". Lindsay also called the yellowtail a very good fish of "the snapper kind" (Plates 30–31). Gosse, at Bluefields in 1845, gave a fuller list: "The most esteemed fishes for the table, and the most common, are the Snappers, Yellow-tails, Silks and Hinds (various species of *Serranina*, or Marine Perches), and the Grunts and Squirrels (species of *Sciaenadae*)."[29]

Grunts (*Haemulon* sp.), which often swim with snapper, are distinguished by the shape and structure of their fins, as well as by the sound they make by grinding their teeth – the source of their name. There are many species of grunts, inhabiting warm waters around the world, most of them bottom-feeders. They were broadly scattered around the coast of Jamaica, and regarded as small but good eating. Lindsay referred only to the "red mouth'd, or grass grunt" (Plate 30). This species was, he said, "esteemed by many an excellent fish; and commonly call'd about the towns, Old Harbour Mutton, because it forms the principal part of the food of the poorer inhabitants of that port being there caught in such great plenty".[30]

Sullivan offered no recipes for either snapper or grunt. Donaldson, in 1993, on the other hand, said snapper was the best-known fish to Jamaicans, widely believed to be the fish used by Jesus to feed the five thousand. It was eaten fried, steamed, escoveitched (as described below under mackerel), baked, roasted or jerked. She gave recipes for these methods, though without particularly associating them with the snapper. She did not mention the grunt, but rolled the snapper with the butterfish and the parrot.[31]

Grouper belongs to the sea basses, and is common along rocky shores and reefs. In the Caribbean the best-known species is the red grouper, *Epinephelus morio*, which averages under five kilograms but may reach four times this weight and grow to one hundred centimetres. Large groupers were taken in Jamaican shallow waters near the crest of the reef into the 1960s, including the Nassau grouper (*E. striatus*) and the yellowfin grouper (*Mycteroperca venenosa*). Lindsay thought the "blue grooper" was rare but "a good eating fish".[32]

The jewfish, *Epinephelus itajara*, is a giant among the sea basses. It averages 10 kilograms, but weights up to 50 kilograms are not uncommon, and records reach around 350 kilograms. The jewfish is at home in the Caribbean but spreads as far as Florida and Panama. It typically lives in a deep hole, often close to shore. Modern writers say the flesh has a strong but not objectionable flavour: the smaller the fish, the better the taste. Thomas Trapham, in 1679, said the jewfish had "well relished flesh" while "his fat eyes and brains exercise the palate with an unusual taste of a most singular marrow, the whole skin is well moistened with such fat, and renders it most nourishing and restaurative". One writer in 1740 said "the jew-fish is the most valued for its richness, altho' its skin looks like an old toad". Long thought those under five kilograms were best, the larger ones possessing "a disagreeable rankness, not to be subdued by all the arts of cookery".[33]

By the late nineteenth century, the jewfish was sometimes called "junefish", following the same path as the transition from "Jew plum" to "June plum". Sullivan described the "June fish" as "cottony" and recommended stewing it in "a rich brown sauce with onions, tomatoes, and herbs, and a wineglass of port wine added towards the end of the cooking and thickened with a little flour". She cautiously suggested that "a little fresh pepper makes an agreeable addition, but very little". The fish continued to be celebrated for its size, reputedly "often" weighing between 150 and 180 kilograms, and was said to eat like cowfoot. One "monster" junefish caught by a fisherman in 1890 and sent to the Montego Bay market measured 2 metres long and weighed just 90 kilograms – without the intestine. Its flesh was said to look like pork. The jewfish was sometimes used at the end of the nineteenth century as an example to demonstrate that the waters around Jamaica "swarm[ed] with some of the best food fish in the world" and might form the foundation of an industry that could help displace imported fish. The idea came up again in the 1940s, when substitutes for imported codfish were sought, but when fishermen happened to land "Jew or June fish" weighing more than 150 kilograms, they had difficulty disposing of it, "due to its bulk and the limited time at their disposal before it spoils".[34] Occasional catches were reported during the twentieth century, but jewfish and junefish disappeared from kitchens and cookbooks.

PARROT, GOAT, DOCTOR, MACCABACK, WELCHMAN

Swimming within Jamaica's reefs, these and other fish found nourishment and relative security. The offshore cays and the reefs, which surround much of the coastline, supported a bounty of diverse species. The destruction of this system and the modern dominance of small fishes and invertebrates is often taken as a model of the disastrous impact of overexploitation, though the components of the collapse are in fact complex. In particular, the early removal of the large herbivores and carnivores, such as manatee, green turtle and monk seal, which had previously churned up the seagrass beds on the reefs, transformed the food chain. The small fish that replaced the megavertebrates could not perform this role, though some tried hard.[35]

Parrotfish are so called because their teeth are fused into a beak. This enables them to nibble small organisms attached to a reef and to dig out those inside. There are about one hundred species, all of them brightly coloured, with large scales and thick bodies. One of the most common species in Caribbean reefs is the multicoloured rainbow parrotfish, *Scarus guacamaia*, which averages about thirty centimetres in length but may grow up to a metre long and weigh up to ten kilograms. Browne said the "parrot-fish" was common throughout the Americas but was "not so much esteemed in Jamaica". Lindsay, in the 1760s, however, said "the parrot fish" was rare, though he agreed "it is a very soft fish and indifferent eating" (Plate 31).[36]

Goatfish also live near tropical reefs, distinguished by their long, goat-like chin whiskers, which are used to probe the bottom for crustaceans and other invertebrates. There are about fifty species, generally pinkish in colour, and growing to fifteen to twenty centimetres. By the 1970s it was said that goatfish was "a favourite of many persons" but not readily available because it was caught only by handline.[37]

What were the favoured ways of cooking small to medium-sized fishes such as goat and parrotfish? Sullivan, at the end of the nineteenth century, recommended baking almost any kind of fresh fish, stuffing it like chicken, with butter or salt pork on top.

Frying became popular in the later twentieth century, but this too was relatively costly. For the poor, steaming was a more practical use of resources, but it produced a rather bland result. Increasingly preferred was the method known as "brown stew". Sullivan had recommended adding a brown gravy to broiled kingfish and stewing junefish in a brown sauce, thickened with flour. In 1900 London kosher restaurants offered both "brown-stewed" and "white-stewed" fish dishes, the former "a strong rich sauce", including treacle, gingerbread and onion.[38] How these dishes might have fed into the Jamaican version of brown stew is uncertain.

Brown-stewing is the steaming of fish, in an open or covered pan over a fire or stove, along with rich seasonings. These were methods that could be applied to any fish, but the best varieties for brown-stewing were small and brightly coloured, such as goatfish, parrotfish and butterfish. Much of the appeal of the dish was in the sight of "the whole fish surrounded by delicious sauce" as well as the "retention of character-istic flavour within the unsliced body of the fish". The fish was first rubbed with salt, black pepper, scallion and garlic, sprinkled with vinegar and allowed to rest for an hour, perhaps in the sun, to dry. The fish was then floured, fried brown and steamed until tender. Next, a sauce made of water, ketchup, Worcestershire sauce, margarine and pimento was poured over the fish, which was allowed to simmer and absorb some of the liquid. Many believed country pepper was an essential ingredient, some ate brown-stew fish with dumplings and others preferred rice. In the 1980s "fastidious oldtimers" complained that brown stew had lost its "ruddy colour and distinctive flavour of yesterday" because cooks had stopped using anatto, which was by no means properly substituted by tomato ketchup or brown sugar.[39]

Another way of cooking small reef fishes was in "fish tea", a favourite Jamaican food of the twentieth century. This used a variety of fish, but some of the most favoured were doctorfish, maccaback and welchman. In the 1990s these three were among the cheapest of the so-called trash fish, along with sprat, snit and turbot. Some fish were placed in this class simply because they were small, but others, notably the sprat, were mostly enjoyed fried until crisp.[40]

The doctorfish, *Acanthurus chirurgus*, belongs to the "surgeonfishes", so called because they have a knifelike spine that they can raise and use as a weapon when disturbed. They swim in small groups and, like parrotfish, feed by using their teeth to scrape animal and plant life off reefs. They grow to about twenty-five centimetres. Lindsay said the doctor was thin, never more than three centimetres thick, but "a very good eating fish".[41]

In Jamaican usage, maccaback (*Gerres rhombeus*) is a small sea fish with sharp spines or "macca" on its dorsal fin. This is technically a variety of shad, and it is sometimes called "maccaback shad" to distinguish it from the maccaback doctor, a blue doctorfish with a similarly spiny dorsal fin. As well as its use in fish tea, a 1960s recipe for maccaback and green bananas called for steaming the fish together with the banana, cooking it until the flesh left the bones.[42]

Jamaicans apply the names "welchman", "welshman", "wenchman" and "wensham" to squirrelfishes of the family Holocentridae that inhabit the coral reefs. They are brightly coloured but generally red, and wary and hard to catch, staying close to the bottom. The most common species in the Caribbean rarely grow to more than thirty centimetres and average only about five hundred grams in weight. Lindsay considered the "Welchman" a beautiful little fish, and "a good fish for the table" (Plate 32).[43]

In the eighteenth century, other fish "of no esteem" and considered suitable only for the making of "broth" included the whiskered "Cat Fish of Jamaica" and "The Ten Pounder", which was "not only dry and course, but very full of small troublesome bones". Fish tea was made by boiling up bones and head, fins and tail, along with seasonings, such as scallion, thyme, pimento and country pepper. Because Jamaicans like to eat fish head (including the eyes), it was not always put into the soup pot, and sometimes the fillet went in before the head. Beginning in the eighteenth century, Jamaicans used both fish kettles and tea kettles, which no doubt led to the dish's being known as "fish tea". The term was slow to emerge; the first citation in the *Gleaner* is from 1930, when Fish Tea was the name of a race horse. References to the serving of fish tea with rum punch, became common only in the 1950s.[44] F.G. Cassidy and R.B. Le Page provide no earlier citations. Sullivan gave no recipes, nor did she offer any recipes specifically for the "refuse" types of fish that came to fill the pot in the twentieth century, though versions no doubt existed long before her time.

A thicker soup, less obviously a "tea", could be made from whole small fish, including shad, turbot and grunt, along with yam, green bananas, dumplings and vegetables such as okra, carrot, Irish potato, chocho and pumpkin. Sometimes different types of fish were associated with distinct fish tea recipes. For example, maccaback could be boiled with salt, tomatoes, onion and black pepper until the flesh began to disintegrate. The fish tea was strained, scraping as much as possible of the flesh through the sieve, more water was added and it was brought again to the boil. Maccaback soup was sometimes served by hotels in the 1960s. Doctorfish was boiled with lime juice, salt, scallion, ginger, butter and black pepper, the flesh picked from the bones and returned to the tea. A soup made from maccaback and doctorfish, green banana, okra, cabbage, onion, callaloo and seasonings was thought to be an aphrodisiac, though this quality was commonly attributed to the "gumption" supplied by the okra rather than to the fish.[45]

BUTTERFISH, BARRACUDA, CUTLASS, JACK, MARLIN, DOLPHIN, SHARK, TRUNKFISH

The butterfish and its allies swam in the deeper waters of the Caribbean, beyond the protection of the reefs, though they might wander closer to shore from time to time. Generally they took some trouble to catch, and were regarded as worthwhile only in their larger sizes. Butterfish are almost round, with a blunt snout and weak teeth. The Atlantic butterfish, *Peprilus triacanthus*, averages twenty centimetres in length, and several other species also reach sizes sufficiently large for commercial exploitation as human food. The red or yellow butterfish, *Cephalopholis fulva*, was one of the most common commercial fishes of Jamaica in the 1960s, when it was caught by handline near the reef tops and on the banks.[46]

Barracuda (*Sphyraena* sp.) are known for their teeth. Widely distributed in the warmer waters of the world, they vary considerably in size and weight. On top of their reputation for tearing bodies to bloody shreds, the barracuda is feared as food because it is thought to be poisonous. Sloane noticed the fish on sale in Jamaican markets but warned that it was poisonous in some seasons and places. He believed that it was always poisonous when it had fed on "venomous food". Similarly Stewart, in the early nineteenth century, thought the "baracoota" dangerous to eat when it had fed on "some poisonous substance in the ocean, of the nature of copperas". To avoid this hazard, "a silver spoon is put into the vessel in which the fish is boiled; if it comes out of a dusky greenish colour the fish is unsound; if not, it may be safely ate".[47]

In 1917, deaths in Westmoreland were attributed to the eating of poisonous fish, and the Central Board of Health was asked to prohibit the consumption of barracuda. The board declined to interfere, and some said it was more a matter of fish feeding on smaller poisonous fish or on decomposing food than something specific to the barracuda. Mary Gaunt reported in 1932 that many Jamaicans thought the "barracouta" poisonous and refused to eat it, and she recounted a story of East Indian immigrants feasting, without ill effect, on barracuda that had been refused by both black and white Jamaicans. In the 1960s A.L. Carnegie observed that poisoning was particularly associated with barracuda in Jamaica, and sometimes attributed also to jack, snapper and catfish, but that it occurred in "only a very small proportion of each species". The source of the toxin remained unknown. People were urged never to eat the viscera of the barracuda and to avoid those weighing more than a kilogram. However, ichthyologist David K. Caldwell dismissed these claims, saying that "all fishes obtained commercially were eaten at all seasons of the year and nowhere on either coast did I find any reference to poisoning from this source".[48]

The Atlantic cutlassfish, *Trichiurus lepturus*, takes its name from the machete, for both its long, thin, flat shape and its shiny, silvery smooth appearance. It can grow to almost 150 centimetres, with head and teeth resembling the barracuda's. The cutlass swims swiftly, generally staying close to the bottom; in Jamaican waters it is most common around Kingston. Lindsay said the "cutlash or sword fish" was "exceeding thin" and "a course fish" (Plate 33). The cutlassfish and the swordfish (*Xiphias gladius*), are, however, distinct species, the latter's bill making up as much as one-third of its four- to five-metre length. Another very thin fish, less than two centimetres thick, was "The Sun Fish or Bahama Unicorn" with a "tough, rough, and course" skin. Lindsay said, "It is not thought a fish fit to be eat.".[49]

The cutlassfish is caught off the southern coast of Jamaica. Sullivan described the "cutlas" as "a long ribbony fish" with small bones on the side that needed to be removed before cooking. It made very good cutlets, said Sullivan, but a better way to use it was in fish cakes or fish pie, "and they would do excellently for Kedgeree, a mixture of boiled rice, picked fish, mustard, butter and curry powder".[50] It is interesting that she felt it necessary to explain kedgeree to her Jamaican readers. The dish was already in Mrs Beeton and had travelled around the British colonial world from India. Modern Jamaican cooks have most often used cutlassfish for frying.

The jacks belong to the Carangidae family, made up of more than two hundred species widely distributed around the world and most abundant in inshore waters. They include the leather jackets and pilotfish that sometimes entered the Jamaican food system, all of them swift and smooth-scaled. The jacks were common in Jamaican waters and a popular species in the 1960s and 1970s, but of erratic distribution and supply. The largest of all, the greater amber-jacks (*Seriola dumerili*) grew to two metres long and weighed up to seventy kilograms, though they were taken by handlines.[51] In the nineteenth century, large catches were reported from Montego Bay, and from Savanna la Mar one hundred years later. Some varieties resemble mackerel, and canned "jack mackerel" (indicating a jack rather than a true mackerel) became common in Jamaica in the later twentieth century. In 2003 Lasco promoted "Lasco Mackerel Run Down", using its own brand of canned jack mackerel, along with its coconut cream powder, tomato ketchup and white cane vinegar, with generic onion, thyme, lime and pimento.[52]

Blue marlin appeared in Jamaican cookbooks only in the later twentieth century, recognized from game-fishing tournaments held at Port Antonio. The fish weighed up to seventy kilograms and were occasionally caught by local fishermen. The steaks were good for grilling, while smoked marlin was said to rival smoked salmon. Donaldson called blue marlin "a welcome addition to our Jamaican menu".[53]

Dolphin became a popular luxury flesh only in the later twentieth century, at the same time as it was recognized as an unusually intelligent animal – in fact a mammal – and became the subject of ethical conservation. In the eighteenth century, Browne had described dolphin as "too dry a fish to be esteemed; and is seldome used unless when young and tender". Lindsay merely illustrated the dolphin, without a label (Plate 34). Gosse reported herds in Kingston harbour in the 1840s but said the fishermen left them alone because they believed the dolphins reduced the numbers of sharks by eating their young. When taken up in a seine by chance, he said, dolphins were an unwanted catch, because "they are altogether unmarketable prizes". Shark was eaten more often.[54]

Finally, of the fish swimming in deep waters, the trunkfish or boxfish (*Lactophrys quadricornis*) has a hard outer covering of tightly fused scales, creating an armour so rigid that it can barely wiggle and necessarily swims only slowly. It is, not surprisingly, easily caught. By the 1950s "trunk fish" had come to be used broadly by fishermen to describe any of the fish of the family Ostraciidae, though local variations included "scuttle", "buck-buck", "cunny-buck", "cow-fish", "horney-money" and "chonk-fish", some of these names referencing eighteenth-century usage. In the 1760s, Lindsay put together "The Cone Fish: or Cunny Fish of Sloane" and "The Triangular Fish of Hughes; and Trunck Fish of Brown". Some called it the "coney fish" because of its shape, with a hard shell or skin and a thin flesh adhering to the shell, like a turtle (Plate 35). It was "seasoned in the same manner as a turtle when dress'd *a la* Calapee and baked in the oven". Lindsay thought its "taste and look in the flesh is like that of the white of a dunghill fowl". Only the liver was eaten from the innards, this being "very large and perhaps the richest, mellowest and most restoring morsel to a weak person that can well be met with". Sloane and others declared the liver poisonous, but Lindsay claimed to have eaten it without intoxication. He admitted, though, to never eating the head and said the tail was never eaten either.[55]

HERRING

The fish considered thus far have been those taken from Jamaican streams or the warm waters surrounding the island. However, some of the fish best known in Jamaica came from much farther away, most of them from the cold waters of the North Atlantic, and reached the island in various states of preservation (Figure 8.3). The most important of these have been herring, shad, mackerel, kingfish, sardine and, above all, cod.

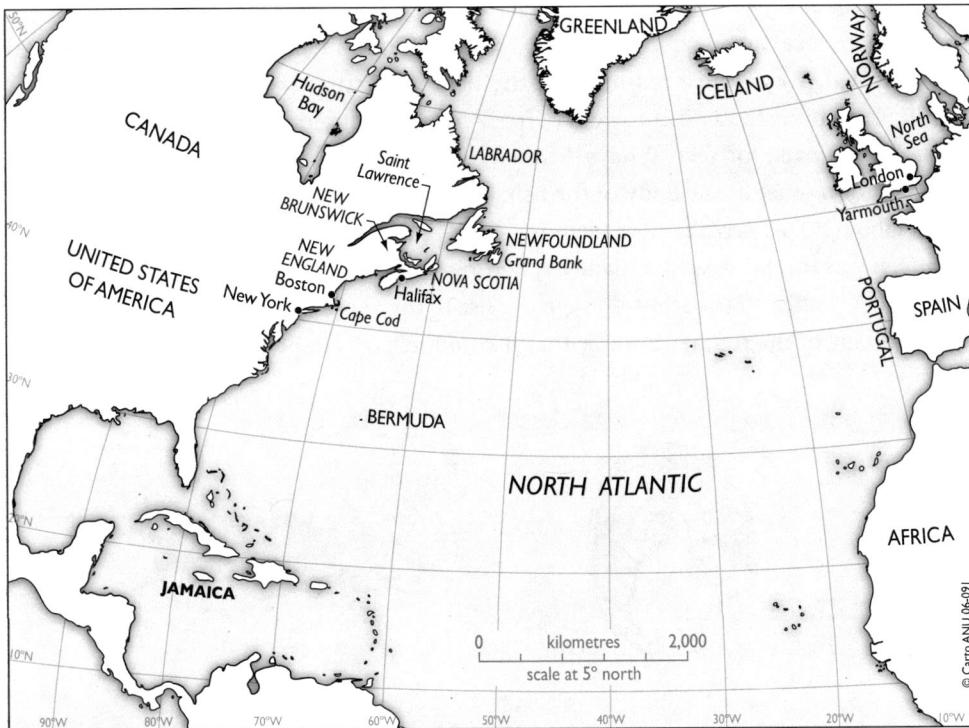

Figure 8.3 Atlantic fishery grounds

An oily fish, rich in protein, minerals, omega-3 fatty acids and vitamins, the herring is now promoted for its health benefits. For most of its long history, though, the herring was regarded as a food of the poor, eaten out of simple necessity rather than selected by choice. It was hated because it is bony and unpalatable when fresh and smelly when pickled. In spite of this, the herring became a staple of the British and of other Northern Europeans in the Middle Ages, eaten fried, grilled or baked but not steamed or poached.[56] Until recent times, the herring's reputation was not much better in Jamaica.

The herring proper, *Clupea harengus*, is a small, silvery fish, rarely growing longer than thirty centimetres or weighing more than two kilograms (Figure 8.4). It swims in huge schools made up of billions of individuals that move into shallower water to spawn. By the end of their first year of life, herrings reach about twelve centimetres and are known commercially as "sardines". They achieve their final size and are ready to spawn in their fourth year, when they are called "fats" because they have begun to store the fat that makes them oily. The herring is related to the sprat (*Clupea sprattus*), which when immature may be sold as an "anchovy" and which never grows to more than half the size of a herring.[57]

The Dutch dominated the seventeenth-century herring fishery, but during the eighteenth century a strong Scottish industry emerged, encouraged by bounties on exports and by tax-free salt. The Scottish industry produced both "red herring", or fish salted ungutted, and "white herring", which was gutted before being laid in salt. Modern Jamaicans take care to remove the "guts" from herring and sardine, whether it be canned or pickled. To produce red herring, the fish was first soaked in brine (with added saltpetre), hung to dry in a current of fresh air for twenty-four or forty-eight hours, and heavily smoked for several days. The success of the curing process depended on the proportion of fat in the body of the fish. Those herring with the maximum amount of fat (about 20 per cent) tend to be mushy when salted, but too little fat is also problematic. It was this process that made red herring the strongest-tasting – sufficient to put a hunter's hound off the scent, thus giving rise to the expression "red herring". The great advantage of the red herring was that it could remain edible for six months or more,

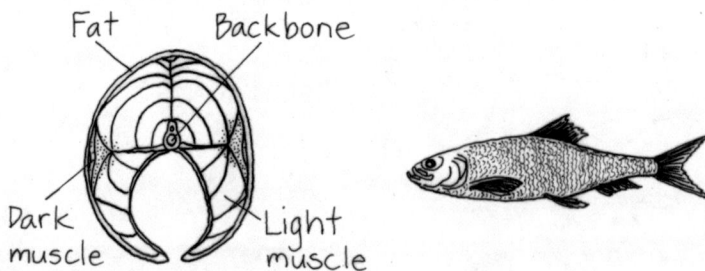

Figure 8.4 Herring fish and cross-section

so that supplies could be brought in just twice a year.[58] When barrelled in salt for export, however, the pickled fish often became soggy and eventually rotten.

In Jamaica, the herring – specifically, the red herring – was the most common fish allocated to enslaved people. Thistlewood generally issued as rations herrings (or their close equivalent, "jumpers") and shad. Stewart said enslaved people were given seven or eight herrings by their masters each week, but that this was "a food which most of them, who can afford better, despise; and they accordingly sell them in the markets, and purchase salted pork, of which they are exceedingly fond".[59] Herring continued to be imported after the abolition of slavery, in spite of the distaste for it. By the 1870s, small herrings were being canned and marketed as "sardines", the fish being first decapitated, gutted and put into salt, sometimes with mustard and other spices to offer a range of tastes. In 1890 Jamaica imported "smoked herring", "split herrings" and "R.S. [round and split] herrings". In 1900, shoppers could purchase tins of "fresh herrings" as well as of herrings in shrimp sauce, herrings and mustard, herrings in tomato sauce, Yarmouth bloaters (steeped in salt), kippered herrings and smoked herrings in boxes.[60]

Sullivan, in 1893, offered a recipe named simply "salt herrings", made by soaking and boiling the salted fish (changing the water to prevent it from being "too salt"), and served with melted butter and parsley, slices of fresh pepper, fried onions and tomatoes. An alternative was to put some red herring in a soup plate and pour "Jamaica strong rum" over it, then set fire to the rum; the fish was cooked when the fire went out. By 1939, it was said that those who moved on to a "daintier and choicer diet" left herrings behind.[61]

After 1945 the North Sea herring fishery was rapidly depleted, and by the 1970s it had come close to collapse. It was closed for some years but reopened in 1981, after which the stock remained relatively strong. Much of the herring was taken as a by-catch. Only a small proportion went to human consumption, the larger part being processed into fish meal or pig food, or even used in the generation of electricity. Herrings continued to reach Jamaica in tomato sauce, canned, and when cooked with vegetables served as an occasional substitute for "the heavy meats". It remains a relatively cheap fish, and its rejection has been far from total. In the 1990s the "popular salt-ting red herring" was readily available in Jamaica, used as a "delightful accompaniment to the green bananas or breadfruit or the St Vincent or yellow yam", and, properly seasoned, it "could be a big hit with the entire family". One Rastafarian cook used red herring not as a relish but as the basis of a dish in which the fish was singed with white rum and stewed with tomato, onion, soy sauce, barbecue sauce and black pepper, and eaten with dumplings, boiled green banana and yam.[62]

A unique way of using pickled red herring is in the dish Solomon Gundy, now often considered a Jamaican specialty. Recent recipes and commercial versions of Solomon Gundy take as their ingredients red herring, country peppers, pimento, onion, oil and vinegar. These are blended to a paste – sometimes described as a "fish paste" – containing a lot of salt. The paste is generally spread on crackers, but it can also be used to coat grilled fish or in pasta.[63] Earlier versions were often quite different. Sullivan made "salma-gundy" with soaked, shredded red herring, in a sauce of vinegar and oil, and served it "with slices of onion, tomatoes and fresh pepper over it". In his 1899 guide to London restaurants, Lieutenant-Colonel Nathaniel Newnham-Davis said of his visit to a kosher Jewish restaurant that "the *hors-d'oeuvre*, Solomon Gundy, which had a strange sound to me, was a form of pickled herring, excellently appetising". It was offered as an alter-native to smoked salmon. The earliest identified reference in the *Gleaner* is from 1918, when "Kingston's latest up-to-date restaurant", The Cabin on Harbour Street, included in its menu just two "special Jamaica dishes" – "escovitch fish" and Solomon Gundy – at sixpence each. At this price, it seems unlikely that this Solomon Gundy was simply the modern paste. A recipe from the 1960s added pickled mackerel and shad to the herring, and directed that the fish be mixed with chopped Scotch bonnet pepper, onion and scallion. This was placed on a dish, salad oil was trickled over the fish, and boiled vinegar and pimento seeds were poured over the lot. This was left to stand outside the refrigerator overnight before use.[64]

Where did Jamaica's Solomon Gundy come from? Cassidy and Le Page have an entry for Solomon Gundy but simply refer readers to "the dish salmagundi" and to the *Oxford English Dictionary*. More recent accounts claim that salmagundi was "a traditional British salad", popular in the seventeenth and eighteenth centuries. Recipes occasion-ally call it "Solomon-a-Gundy", following the rhyme "Solomon-a-Gundy, born on a Monday, christened on a Tuesday, married on a Wednesday, took ill on a Thursday, worse on a Friday, died on a Saturday, buried on a Sunday, that is the end of . . . you know who." A 1999 cookbook mistakenly called it "Solomon Grundy" and rejected the link with salmagundi, arguing that the dish "clearly harks back to the days of the British when pickled herring was sent from home for consumption by the colonists. Solomon Grundy is a character in a British nursery rhyme".[65]

Sometimes "salmagundy" is traced to France in the reign of Louis XIV. In 1788 *The Times* of London reviewed a new pantomime calling it "a most miserable hash of old matter in respect to scenery and taste; a *Selon-mon-gout* to suit the distressed fable of the theatre – but not as *John Bull* has corrupted the word, a *Solomon-gundy* that will please everybody". The following year, *The Times* referred to the mix of social classes at a dinner, probably a royal or political one, as "that kind of mixture which the French call Selon-mon-gout, and which John Bull has corrupted into Solomon-gundy – Onions and ortolans, anchovies and red-herrings, neck of beef and pheasant".[66] Literally, *selon-mon-gout* means "according to my taste" or, more freely translated, "as I like it".

Even earlier, in 1747, Glasse had given three recipes for "salamongundy" and another for "salamangundy", spellings close to the Jamaican version. These were all elaborate constructions built with lettuce, anchovies, eggs, lemon, parsley and onion, with salad oil poured over. Only the third and fourth versions included pickled herring.

Briggs offered a recipe in 1792 which was part fish, part fowl, part other meats and vegetables, called "salamungundy". The vital element was variety of colour and form, and, said Briggs, "the more different colours you have, the better it looks, as it is more fancy than otherwise, which must direct you". Briggs started his recipe with herring, but more or less by chance, it seems. The herring was boned and chopped fine, and the same process was applied to chicken breast, chicken legs, hard-boiled egg whites and yolks, parsley and ham, all elements kept separate. Once they were ready, said Briggs, "turn a small China dish bottom uppermost in another China dish, just to fit it, then take a tea-spoon and lay every thing separate in shapes", starting perhaps with "a shape of parsley, then of herrings, then of eggs, and so on till you have covered your dish, and all your ingredients are used". The edge of the dish might be garnished with curled parsley or flowers.[67]

The transformation of Solomon Gundy from these elaborate eighteenth-century versions to the modern paste of Jamaica remains difficult to trace in detail, but continuity there certainly was. Probably, the modern Jamaican variety appealed to the salty taste of a poorer constituency, for whom chicken long remained a luxury and fussy decoration no priority.

SHAD

The American shad, *Alosa sapidissima*, belongs to the herrings; lengths of up to 45 centimetres and weights that top 5 kilograms make it the largest of the family. The average weight, however, is nearer to 1.5 kilograms. In 1762 Lindsay described the shad as "a very common fish all over the American seas", 25 to 35 centimetres long, reddish grey in colour, with large eyes and a small mouth, and a tail "as handsomely forked as that of the dolphin" (Plate 30). The flesh of the shad, he said, was "moderately thick and firm". The original distribution of the shad stretched down the Atlantic Coast from the St Lawrence to Florida, but the shad was also introduced to the Pacific Coast, in the late nineteenth century. Like herring, shad run up tributary streams to spawn. Once abundant, its numbers have been much diminished by overfishing and pollution. Fresh shad is now considered a delicacy, and its roe are highly prized.[68]

Donaldson said in 1993 that pickled shad was not as popular as pickled mackerel because it was bony, but it was "still, however, a favourite of many", and "usually cooked with its garnish as a package in quailed, green banana leaves, tied with the bark of the banana, and boiled". Sullivan had earlier offered an interesting recipe for "shad paste", as a substitute for anchovy. This was made from salt shad, which was indeed "very salt". The preparation of the paste was "tiresome and tedious, but the result is good and it is of great use in the country where fresh meat is not plentiful and perhaps only the inevitable fresh salmon to be had in the way of tinned meats". To make it, the shad was scalded and cooled, and every bone removed. The fish was then mixed with butter, nutmeg, black pepper, cinnamon and cayenne, pounded to a smooth paste in a mortar and kept in a jar.[69] This was not unlike the modern Solomon Gundy, though Sullivan carefully distinguished the recipe from that preparation of red herring.

MACKEREL, KINGFISH

Mackerels and tuna belong to the family Scombridae, generally schooling fishes of the open seas characterized by their streamlined shape and distributed between some seventy-five species. Atlantic mackerel, *Scomber scombrus*, common off the New England coast, averages less than five hundred grams, though heavier specimens are often caught. It is a predator, feeding on herrings, pilchards, shrimps and crustaceans. Spanish mackerel, *Scomberomorus maculatus*, swims in warm waters on both sides of the Atlantic, in both inshore and offshore zones. It averages about one kilogram – twice the size of the Atlantic mackerel – and is more closely related to the kingfish, or "king mackerel" (*Scomberomorus cavalla*), which averages about five kilograms. The kingfish is common in Caribbean waters during spring, migrating from the open seas into the Gulf of Mexico.[70]

Atlantic mackerel first came to Jamaica as saltfish. Sloane, writing in the 1680s, said, "Salt mackerel are here a great provision, especially for Negroes, who covet them extreamly in pepper-pots, or oglios, etc." Sullivan's two recipes for mackerel used the salted variety. Her first, called simply "salt mackerel", was made by soaking and boiling the fish and serving it with butter sauce, lime, tomatoes and fresh peppers. The second recipe, "salt mackerel cutlets", involved soaking and boiling the fish, cutting it into slices, dipping them in egg and breadcrumbs, and frying them in lard. By the 1880s, "fresh mackerel" was imported in tins.[71]

Frozen mackerel entered Jamaica in the late twentieth century. From 1968 to 1987 a government-owned company, Jamaica Frozen Foods, imported it from Canada and Norway and pickled it for the local market. This product was displaced by imported pickled mackerel, which came at a cheaper price. Canned mackerel remained popular, however, fried up with plummy tomatoes, okra, Irish potato and seasonings. Fried "mackerel balls" were made from canned fish, breadcrumbs, egg, scallion, garlic, salt, black pepper and Scotch bonnet pepper. In 1985, recipes combined pickled mackerel with ackee, chocho and cabbage, or exalted it to mackerel quiche Lorraine (baked in a pie shell with beaten eggs) or pickled mackerel à la king (in a creamy sauce).[72] By the early twenty-first century, mackerel was sometimes conflated with the jacks, or "jack mackerel". Salt or pickled mackerel is an ideal fish for the Jamaican specialty "rundown", described in chapter 5, and increasingly it was also proposed that this could be made from jack mackerel.

Spanish mackerel was sometimes considered inferior to Atlantic mackerel. Lindsay said in the 1760s that although the "Spanish Mackarell" grew to fifty centimetres, it was "in no great repute, being a dry course fish" (Plate 36). Browne, on the other hand, contended that Spanish mackerel and kingfish were "both hard, dry eating, but answer extremely well coveeched; and when dressed in that manner, are very agreeable to most over-heated palates". In 1893, Sullivan said the kingfish was "a much esteemed fish, and is good cooked in any way". She recommended three alternatives: it could be boiled and served with butter and parsley or with oyster or anchovy sauce; cut in thick steaks and broiled with onions and covered with a rich brown gravy; or stuffed with breadcrumbs and oysters, and served with a tomato sauce. In 1946 kingfish was rated above the "humble sprats and snappers". It had the advantage of coming with few bones, especially when purchased as cutlets.[73]

Fresh mackerel and kingfish were popular fishes for the preparation of escoveitch, though the dish could also be made from other firm fish such as snapper. The concept comes from the Spanish *escabeche*, meaning pickled fish; the modern spelling is a corrected form of the earlier "caveach" or "scaveech". In 1756 Browne explained that "to coveech a fish, it must be cut into juncks, fried with onions and oil; and afterwards potted with vinegar, a little pepper or cloves, fryed onions, and some oil". A recipe in the 1957 *Farmer's Food Manual* called for fillets or slices of fish, seasoned with salt and pepper and fried in oil, laid out in a shallow dish. Vinegar and pimento were boiled and poured over the fish, with onion rings and sliced green and "ripe" peppers. This was left for twelve hours, turned occasionally, and served cold. Later recipes followed these principles quite closely, though decoration with fancy-cut chocho and carrot also became more common. In the 1990s, Donaldson justly claimed that escoveitch was "very popular" in Jamaica and could be made from "nearly any fish that swims in our waters".[74]

SARDINE

As already noted, small herrings are sometimes marketed as "sardines", and became popular canned fish in the 1870s. The true sardine family, however, includes the Spanish sardine (*Sardinella anchovia*), several other almost indistinguishable Atlantic varieties, and the Pacific sardine (*Sardinops sagax*), which has been prolific historically. Canned sardines reached Jamaica early, beginning in 1867 (Figure 8.5). Quality quickly improved

Figure 8.5 Canned sardines

but prices declined, so that sardine came to be seen as a food of the poor. By the 1980s, with its price supported by the government, the canned sardine became "the most economical and easily prepared savory in Jamaica today". Recipes appeared encouraging its use in escoveitch, as well as in rissoles and sandwiches and as cocktail servings.[75] The better-off could buy them by the case. After 2000, sardines in oil and spring water were joined by canned sardines in "jerk sauce".

COD

The Atlantic cod, *Gadus morhua*, is a large fish, from forty-five to ninety centimetres in length and averaging nine kilograms (Figure 8.6). A high proportion of its mass is suitable for human consumption. It is both voracious and omnivorous, swimming with its mouth open, ready to swallow whatever comes its way, the head making up one-quarter of its length. The cod is prized for the whiteness of its flesh, rich and gelatinous without being fatty like salmon or herring. Until recent times, the cod was a dominant fish on the cold-water continental shelves of the North Atlantic, swimming in schools and appearing inshore annually, when it fed on shoals of smaller fish. The cod matures in two to eight years, enters the fishery at about four and lives for up to fifty years.[76]

The cod of the North Atlantic entered trade in the Middle Ages in a variety of modes of preservation. Norwegians dried it without salt for export to the Baltic, cod becoming so common there that it was called generically "stockfish". The English, with only limited access to salt, developed a well-dried lightly salted product that came to be known simply as "saltfish". To make this salted dried cod, the fish was split along the underside so that it could be laid flat, the head, offal and most of the backbone being discarded. After washing, the flattened fish were lightly salted and heaped in layers, then spread out to dry in the sun. Once thoroughly dried, the saltfish could be stored

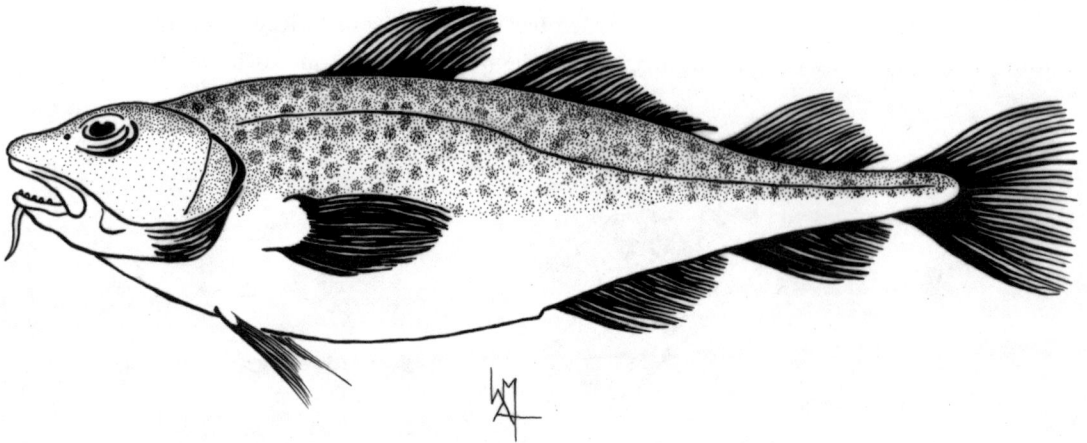

Figure 8.6 Atlantic cod

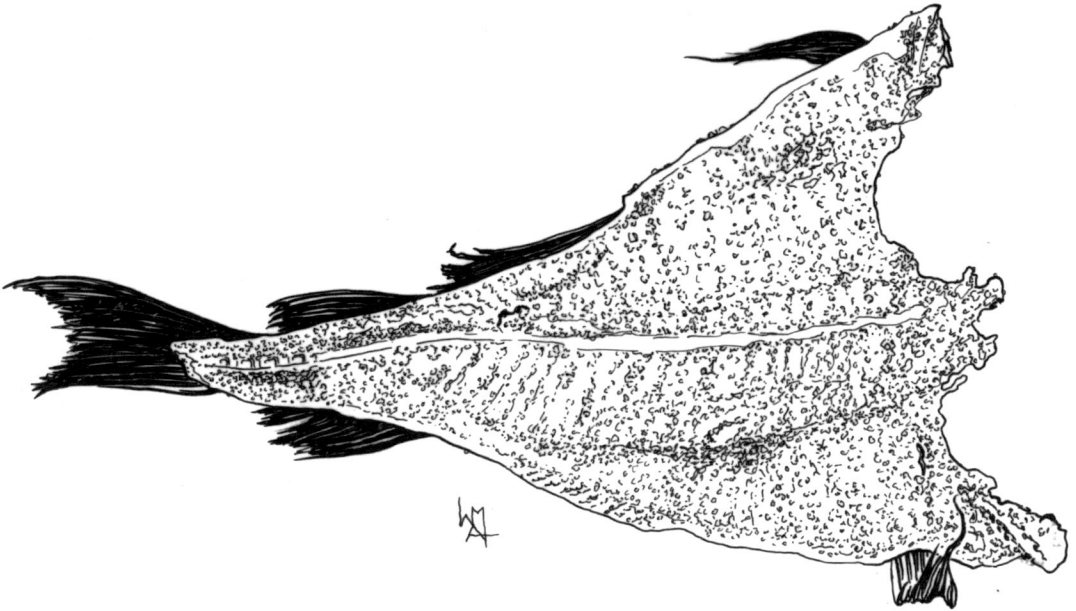

Figure 8.7 Salted cod

for years, and because it was stiff and flat, the fish could also be tied into bundles and easily transported (Figure 8.7). In this respect it had a great advantage over the alternative method of preservation, pickling, which required cumbersome and potentially leaky barrels. Slices of cod could be cut or torn off, making the saltfish almost currency. Further, dried cod has almost no fat and is 80 per cent protein.[77]

The cod is widespread in the North Atlantic, but it was the great stocks of fish surrounding Newfoundland and its banks, discovered by Europeans in the fifteenth century, that became the basis of the international industry (Figure 8.3). Down to the American Revolution, most of the saltfish imported into Jamaica and the British West Indies came from the New England colonies. Salt cod or stockfish was also one of the foods carried on ships in the slave trade from Africa and fed to enslaved people. The West Indies became an important market particularly because the planters happily purchased as rations for their slaves the "refuse saltfish" that was unsaleable elsewhere. Some of this was improperly cured, with too much or too little salt, and some of it was simply ragged and misshapen. Imperfect curing resulted from careless splitting and heading, and from poor drying conditions of temperature and breeze. It also occurred when the fishermen did not let the pickle drain off the fish in order to obtain a heavier fish with a white, salty coat. Contemporary white observers regularly remarked the preference of the enslaved for putrid fish, but most often they had no choice.[78]

After the American Revolution, Newfoundland and Nova Scotia emerged as the major suppliers of the West Indies, with Jamaica taking the largest quantity. Imports of saltfish increased dramatically after the abolition of slavery and remained high until about 1860, when they entered a long-term gradual decline to reach a minimum at the end of the 1970s. In 1980 per capita imports of salted fish were only one-twentieth what they had been at the peak of 1850 (Figure 8.1). In the early nineteenth century, the West Indian colonies continued to be a market for the cheapest varieties, permitting the fisheries to dump surplus product. By the 1890s, codfish was sometimes distinguished as "P.S. [Prime Shore] codfish" or "Newfoundland codfish", but generally came simply as "codfish". The West Indian market remained important well into the twentieth century, and in 1930 Jamaica took as much as one-quarter of all the saltfish exported from Newfoundland (which became a province of Canada only in 1949).[79]

The dramatic leap in saltfish imports after abolition, and the parallel decline in pickled fish, reflected preferences established during slavery. According to Stewart, the enslaved people of Jamaica got "about eight pounds of salted cod-fish once or twice a-year: this food is more a favourite with them than the herrings, for no reason that can be imagined, but because the former is a greater rarity than the latter". The preference was rooted in appearance and flavour rather than mere whim, and appreciation of salt cod spread widely among the creole population. Thus Sullivan could say in 1893 that "in Jamaica there is hardly a more popular dish among the natives and often among the upper classes than the despised salt fish, eaten at home [in England] not from choice, but as a sort of penitential dish". She claimed it was "the almost daily, and certainly the favourite food of the people generally; and cooked, as they cook it, it cannot fail to please the most fastidious". Similarly, in 1907 Leader said, "The negro is not the only consumer of the salt fish (dried cod and haddock from Canada) . . . since it appears sometimes upon the tables of the well-to-do and in the hotels, and is, when thoroughly soaked and served with akees, an appetizing, if not particularly digestible dish." Sullivan offered fourteen recipes for saltfish, never explicitly mentioning cod but distinguishing only three recipes as being made from other fish – two from salt mackerel and one from salt herring – the remainder being generic saltfish.[80] "Saltfish" and "codfish" came to be almost synonymous.

As early as 1920, saltfish was declared "a luxury" whereas it "used to be the food of the poor". By the 1930s the relative nutritional value of cod was acknowledged for its valuable protein, whereas salt herring and mackerel were seen as merely savoury. In 1940, facing pressure to reduce imports, saltfish was compared negatively with home-grown chicken in terms of food value and nutrition. The high price of saltfish also led to various kinds of fraud. Some sellers soaked it in water to increase its weight, and others attempted to pass off fish other than Atlantic cod as the genuine article. In 1948 there were complaints that the quality of "the people's staple savoury", the cod, had declined, the fish now "all skin, bones and tail".[81]

After World War II, other forces gathered on the supply side that were to have a much more dramatic impact on the use and appreciation of codfish. The cod stocks that had seemed inexhaustible came under severe pressure. Foreign fleets entered the industry, resulting in the so-called cod wars between the North Atlantic fishing nations. The catch peaked at 800,000 tonnes in the 1960s and then declined, until in the 1970s Canada imposed quotas that reserved much of the catch for Canadians. Catches increased through the 1980s, but the stock was severely depleted: 99 per cent of the fishable biomass disappeared between 1962 and 1992. In 1992 Canada responded to "the ecological disaster of the century" with a moratorium that officially closed the fishery. Even with no fishing, the stock is unlikely to be restored before 2025.[82]

In Jamaica, the 1992 fishery closure was tracked closely, as supply tightened and prices skyrocketed. The removal of a government subsidy further affected prices. Fish had come from Norway as well as Canada, but production fell in all of the fisheries, and growing North American demand for fresh cod fillets in the late 1980s increased the pressure in the international market. The Norwegians marketed their fish as "a product of pure nature, which follows a special method of preservation which maintains that the product is low in fat, rich in minerals such as iodine, iron and calcium, and vitamins, including the important vitamin B". They recommended that their salted codfish be prepared for cooking by removing the skin, cutting the fish into small pieces, soaking in water for a day or two, parboiling, and removing the bones. Such lengthy soaking of the saltfish was effective in removing the salt taste, but it was an approach contrary to the Jamaican taste, which relished the salt. Recipes for cooking saltfish the Norwegian way seem not to have been published in Jamaica, though the *Gleaner* did offer Spanish, Portuguese and Italian styles. Some thought that cooks found the preparation of saltfish (the soaking, stripping and flaking) a chore, and in 1986 canned prepared saltfish was experimented with in Canada and exported to the Caribbean but with little success, primarily because the product lacked the raw saltiness of the dry variety. Similarly, Jamaicans were impatient with the advice that "if salted fish are soaked and cooked in milk, they become much sweeter than when soaked in water".[83]

In September 1991, immediately before the closure of the Newfoundland fishery, saltfish was declared "one of the more expensive meatkinds" in Jamaica. The Norwegian Fish Exporters Association began an advertising campaign touting it as "value for money with its many diverse ways of preparation and bridging of gaps while providing essential nutrients such as protein". They encouraged consumers to continue buying because saltfish was "a part of our unique national culture and culinary style". The price jumped 50 per cent in October 1991. In November a Port Maria letter-writer observed that saltfish had become the food of the rich: "One word I got to say to saltfish, 'it was nice knowing you. I can't eat you any more, so, good bye saltfish, you are not for us the poor any more.'"[84] By late 1993, saltfish was, pound for pound, three times the price of chicken, leading Jamaicans to "bemoan the absence of that once inexpensive staple, Canadian codfish". Saltfish became scarce at any price, though in the late 1990s it was available from higglers in the "bend down" (sidewalk) markets. In spite of the scarcity and the high price, cookbooks of the 1990s continued to give codfish a central place, as "a native necessity" for several dishes. A small piece could go a long way, Jamaicans were told – a far cry from the heaps of buttered codfish that blended with the little piles of ackee a century before to create the putative national dish.[85] The notion that codfish could be made to serve a savoury purpose in small quantities was effectively a return to the culinary choices of the eighteenth century. By the late twentieth century, with free salt cheap and available in quantity – indeed in unhealthy large doses in many processed and prepared foods – the role of codfish was now essentially different.

More broadly within the Caribbean, the most common saltfish dish is often said to be "saltfish and rice". Sullivan included a recipe for "salt fish and rice" in her *Jamaica Cookery Book*, saying it was "a favourite native dish". It was made by boiling together about half a pound of saltfish to a pint (568 millilitres) of rice, with a piece of salt pork and a little butter. In Jamaica, this dish was overtaken by ackee and saltfish. In the 1990s, street cooks sold yellow yam and saltfish roasted in a blazing fire, flaked and mixed in a dutchy with onion, pepper, tomato, scallion and oil. Earlier, when codfish was cheap and plentiful – even in 1942 – it was appreciated "swimming in a bath of 'nuff cokenat ile'". The better-off breakfasted on "broiled saltfish swimming in butter".[86]

Salt cod was also the basis of "stamp-and-go", now known as crisp-fried fritters. These existed by the 1870s at least. Sullivan, in 1893, located them in her chapter on cakes and biscuits, in the section dealing with cornmeal. She described them as "rough cakes" made with cornmeal and flour, saltfish, butter and lard, and lots of fresh country pepper, sold at "way-side shops" and eaten with a slice of bread. Sullivan said "stamp and go" could either be boiled as a kind of dumpling or fried. The boiled variety disappeared. Stamp-and-go paste was moulded in the hands before cooking, while another variety of saltfish fritter, known as aachi, was dropped from the spoon. In her chapter on saltfish, Sullivan gave three distinct recipes for "salt fish fritters", with added ingredients such as eggs, rice, ackees, tomatoes, scallion and parsley. By the middle of the twentieth century, codfish fritters were known also as "flitters" or "flaa-flaa", emphasizing the flour that was their major component, and later they were sometimes called "flatters", in reference to their being pressed flat in the pan. Sullivan's other generic recipes included fried saltfish (with onions, tomato and pepper), saltfish twice-laid (baked with mashed potatoes or yam, and lard, scallion, parsley, pepper, tomatoes, and herbs, combined with eggs), curried saltfish, saltfish and susumbers (described in chapter 5), shredded saltfish (fried in lard with scallion, tomatoes and pepper) and saltfish patties (described in chapter 6).[87]

Cod also reached Jamaica in the form of cod liver oil, long given to children for its purgative qualities and taken as a remedy for coughs, colds and bronchitis. Waterbury's, in 1918, claimed their "tasteless, odourless" cod liver oil was "as pleasant as honey".[88] Probably few of those compelled to swallow it connected cod liver oil with the fish that gave the taste to codfish and ackee.

CHAPTER 9

BIRDS

Jamaica has 252 resident bird species. Slightly fewer than half of these are permanent residents, while the others are seasonally migrant or casual. Of the permanent residents, only 24 species are endemic, meaning that they both are unique to Jamaica and possess a unique genetic composition. And of the indigenous birds that are permanent residents, just 4 were introduced by humans and now live naturally in the wild. Few of the indigenous birds were ever domesticated, even as pets. As with fish, most of those that were eaten were hunted or trapped.[1] Overall, only a small proportion of the resident bird species were ever used as human food.

In the long run, only one bird – the introduced, domesticated chicken – proved important in the food system of Jamaica. It is not included among the resident species because it was not naturalized, never becoming feral or living naturally in the wild. The chicken has been in Jamaica five hundred years but remains confined to the domesticated niche. Guides to the avifauna of Jamaica therefore almost universally ignore the chicken, even when they are designed as guides to "the commoner birds of the island, those which are to be seen without trouble in the ordinary course of the day".[2] Today, chickens are vastly more numerous than ever before, but in truth they are not commonly seen because they are now hidden in large sheds.

The chicken had several advantages as a food bird, though it took a long time for these to become truly apparent. Domesticated for many centuries before it came to Jamaica, the chicken was effectively flightless and was selected for its capacity to produce eggs and flesh. Unlike the wild indigenous birds of Jamaica, it could easily be run to ground, needing to be fenced out of vegetable gardens rather than having to be fenced in. Its eggs were moderately large and plentiful, and could be efficiently collected from easily located habitual nests. The chicken's body has a high proportion of edible flesh relative to bone and tendon, and almost every part of it can be eaten.

By contrast, many of the indigenous birds of Jamaica were hard to catch. The seasonal visitors not only were of limited availability but were high-flyers, often with relatively small proportions of edible flesh and fat. Many of the permanent residents were similarly equipped to fly, darting from flower to flower and eluding their natural predators. To exploit them as human food often necessitated elaborate cages. And some of the birds were simply too small to be worth much effort. The hummingbird is the supreme example of these qualities, and apparently never eaten, not so much because of its beauty but because it was just too hard to catch. At the other extreme, the John crow, *Cathartes aura*, was big and fat but unattractive because it fed on carrion. Similarly, the docile cattle egret, *Bubulcus ibis*, which had found its way from Southeast Asia to Jamaica by 1953 as part of a global colonization and which became numerous and easy to target, did not enter the food system. It was seen to feed on the ticks and other small insects of cattle, and indeed was often called the "tick bird", though most of its food actually came from insects, slugs and frogs disturbed by moving cattle.[3]

The local birds that did reach Jamaican tables, such as the Muscovy duck, were often highly esteemed, but they could not compete with the introduced, domesticated varieties. The Taino lacked these domesticates entirely and seem to have made relatively little use of birds as food, though as with fish, crustaceans and reptiles, the bird population remained abundant until European colonization. The indigenous birds were then subjected to a broad-scale onslaught and new species were quickly introduced by the Spanish. In the later seventeenth century, however, English observers continued to be struck by the abundance of bird life in the island, both introduced and local wild varieties. Richard Blome, for example, said Jamaica had "great store of tame hens, turkies, some geese and ducks, but of wild fowl such plenty, that it is almost incredible, viz. ducks, teal, wigeon, geese, turkies, pigeons, Guinea hens, plover, flemingo's, snipes, parots, paracheto's, with abundance more, whose names are not yet known".[4]

Because the onslaught was so heavy, even the planter-dominated Assembly quickly felt obliged to regulate the hunting and trapping of birds, including them in the 1711 Act that dealt with fishing. There was self-interest, of course, the planters seeking to preserve for themselves the sport of game shooting and the delights of the table. The 1711 Act attempted to regulate "fowling", and particularly directed its attention at those who used "evil and ill-disposed methods of destroying . . . the pigeons at an unseasonable time of year". It prohibited the killing of "wild pigeons, young or old, within the parishes of St. Catherine and St. John" and on "the several islands or quays belonging to this island". A century later, John Stewart claimed that shooting for sport was largely confined to game birds such as wild pigeons, ducks and teal, quail, coots, snipes, plover and ortolans. He contended, indeed, that there were no game laws and that "this indiscriminate license has diminished the number of species of the indigenous game, and would in time probably destroy the whole, were it not for the rugged and difficult retreats which the country affords them". Philip Henry Gosse approved the repeal of the "oppressive" 1711 law after the abolition of slavery.[5]

Some species disappeared early. The migratory red flamingo, *Phoenicopterus ruber*, was drawn by the Reverend John Lindsay in the 1760s, but had ceased to be common by 1800 (Plate 37). The flesh of this beautiful bird was regarded as tough, but the settlers had skinned and boiled them, the orange-coloured fat of the bird giving the broth "a very agreeable and rich appearance". Some species, such as hopping dick, were reduced by the mongoose, which was introduced in the late nineteenth century, but at the same time other species were thought to have become more numerous. Yet the concern remained: in the early twentieth century, it was feared that the "annual slaughter" of birds by armed sportsmen, as well as the mongoose's depredations on nests for eggs, would quickly bring the extinction of the blue dove, quail and wild guineafowl. The blue pigeon, ringtail and baldpate were already rarely seen, it was said in 1914. Martha Beckwith observed in 1929 that "the Negroes sometimes vary their diet by bird-trapping, and many valuable birds of the pigeon tribe have been almost exterminated by the practice. The ringdove was in old days a famous table delicacy, and today the whitewing, pea dove, baldpate, whitebelly, 'hopping Dick,' quail, and partridge are the chief birds hunted."[6] Some of the traps used were complex, but most consisted simply of a noose, a cage propped up by a small stick that dropped over birds when they pecked at seed scattered underneath and troubled the support.

At the end of the twentieth century, the bird-shooting season ran from August to January, with shooting allowed on Saturday morning, Saturday afternoon and Sunday morning, and the bag limited to fifteen birds per shoot. Guns, slingshots and catapults were used to hunt, the latter mostly bringing down birds that fed on fruit and berries, such as the goolie banana katie, picherry goldfringe or mark head, hopping dick, woodpecker John Chewit, ground doves, blue quit and pea dove. The gun was more likely to kill doves such as baldpates, blue pigeons, pea doves mountain witch, partridge white belly and white wing. The pigeons ate fruit and berries, the doves grain. There were many ways of preparing "a traditional 'bird-feed' of white-wing, baldpate, wild duck and other Jamaican game birds". After their feathers were removed, the birds were washed with lime or vinegar water, split in half down the backbone, rubbed with salt and marinated in garlic, onion and oil. According to Enid Donaldson, birds shot with the catapult were usually "fried or barbecued and eaten hot off the coals". Other birds were browned in hot oil, then stewed until tender, the doves cooking faster than the pigeons. Even small birds might be stuffed. [7]

PIGEON, DOVE

Pigeons and doves belong to a single family, the Columbidae, with "pigeon" the most common general term for them all. In many parts of the world, including Jamaica, they

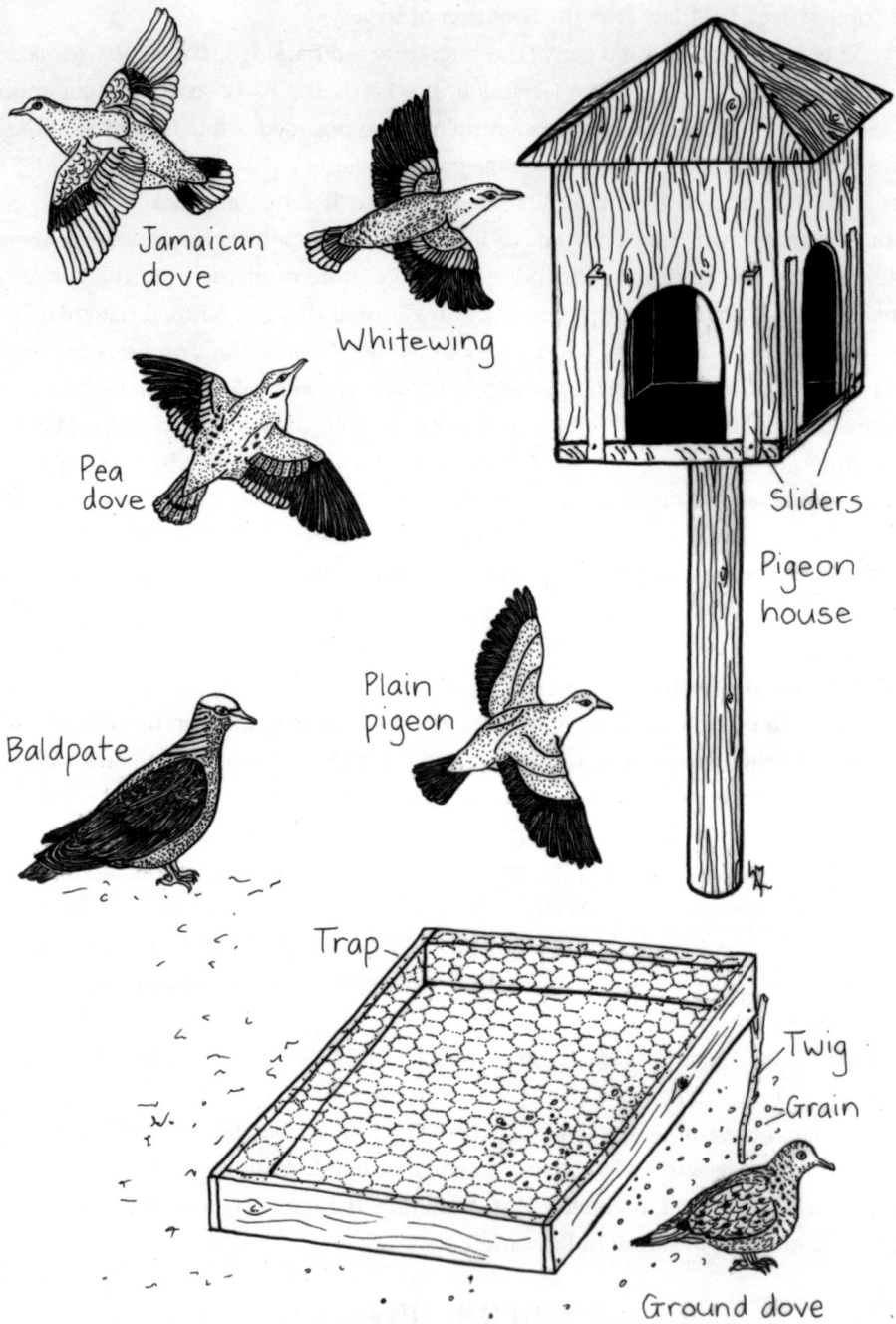

Figure 9.1 Pigeons and doves, pigeon house and trap

have been perhaps surprisingly successful and numerous. Although they live in trees – at least for nesting, roosting and refuge – they are often to be seen on the ground pecking away at seeds and fruit (Figure 9.1). The success of the pigeons has been achieved in spite of their apparent vulnerability of habit, their lack of strong defences against predators and their plumpness and edibility. As noted above, Beckwith focused her account of trapping and depletion on the "pigeon tribe", but somehow they have survived. They are not as docile as they look, and they have come to live happily in settlement niches, exploiting a wide range of resources and spaces. Their main advantage is that, although they have clutches of only one or two eggs at a time, those offspring have short incubation and fledgling periods. Thus the pigeons cope well with relatively heavy losses.[8] This ability to recuperate, together with their relatively high ratio of edible flesh to total weight, has made the pigeons some of the most popular of the common game birds of Jamaica. Those with really large proportions of fat have achieved even greater esteem.

As noted in chapter 1, the ringtail pigeon was once regarded as one of Jamaica's supreme delicacies, along with the black land crab and the mountain mullet. Indeed, Gosse could claim in 1847 that "of the three superlative delicacies of which the natives of Jamaica boast, the Ring-tail holds the undisputed pre-eminence". The birds were hunted and shot in the interior and carried to the major towns, where they were "eagerly purchased for the table; though, as the distance which they are carried usually prevents their arrival on the day they are killed, they are almost invariably deplumed and drawn, and the inside strongly peppered before they are sent to market". The ringtail was esteemed "for the richness, the delicacy, and the tenderness of his flesh", said Gosse. From September to November, the bird was "a mass of luscious fat, and his plump and well-enveloped flesh acquires for him a superiority over that of all his tribe". Edward Long had said much the same in the 1770s, observing that the ringtail was "esteemed one of the principal dainties by the epicures of the island; it is often so turgid with fat, as to burst on falling to the ground after it is shot". Matthew Gregory Lewis in 1816 said the ringtail pigeon "has been allowed to rank with the most exquisite of the winged species, by epicures of such distinction, that their opinion, in matters of this nature, almost carries with it the weight of a law".[9]

The ringtail pigeon, *Columba caribaea*, is an endemic species, inhabiting the forests of the mountainous interior and descending lower in winter. Named for the black band across its tail, it is largish for a pigeon, growing to forty centimetres in length (Figure 1.1). William Beckford claimed in the late eighteenth century that it was hard to take because its "excessive fatness" rendered it inactive and it rarely declared itself by cooing. Gosse described in detail the hunting of the ringtail, which he said was done by "Negro fowlers" who moved soundlessly through the dense mountain forests where the bird was most common. Maroons were among the most common hunters. Although the ringtail remains common in some locations, illegal hunting and the removal of its forest habitat is a threat to survival. By the 1990s it was a protected species.[10]

Gosse also praised the plain pigeon, *Columba inornata*, which had a similar habit to the ringtail and was its rival in "delicacy and flavour" and was "but little less in request". The plain pigeon is paler than most, with a reddish brown tinge on its wings and breast, and only slightly smaller than the ringtail. It is now relatively rare and localized, living mostly in forest and scrublands, its numbers varying with the seasonal availability of fruit.[11]

The white-crowned pigeon, or baldpate (*Columba leucocephala*), remains relatively common. It was formerly found most often in the logwood and pimento groves of livestock pens and in coastal mangroves. It fed on pimento and other berries and was shot during the breeding season, when it was less wary. In September and October, according to Gosse, baldpate were "in fine condition, often exceedingly fat and juicy, and of exquisite flavour". He compared them to other pigeons, saying the baldpate had dark red flesh, whereas "that of the Mountain Witch is whiter than a chicken's; the former the more juicy, the latter tender, but dry; both are delicious in flavour". Of the baldpate, Long said, "in the season they are fat and well-tasted, but afterwards their flesh acquires the bitterness of gall, and it is not eatable; this is ascribed to their feeding on the seeds of the red mangrove".[12]

Recipes for baldpate were much more common than for the ringtail and other pigeons, and appeared in cookbooks down to the end of the twentieth century. Cooks were sometimes given detailed directions on how to pluck and draw the birds. Even though small, baldpate could be grilled, baked, stuffed and roasted, or fricasseed, two birds to a person. These methods were applied to pigeons generally. In the eighteenth century, the planters most often ate them boiled or broiled. In her 1893 *Jamaica Cookery Book*, Caroline Sullivan offered little help beyond a general reference to "birds on toast", though she did give prices for "wild birds" such as ground doves and Guinea birds.[13]

Perhaps the most common of the pigeons of Jamaica is the ground dove, *Columbina passerina*. It is widely distributed, particularly in the plains and the hilly areas bordering clearings and forest edges. It habitually walks on the ground, as its name suggests, or sits in shrubs and trees. A small bird, it can grow to fifteen centimetres. Gosse said it was numerous all year and was frequently caught near water.[14]

Another common pigeon is the pea dove, *Zenaida aurita*. About twice as big as the ground dove, it is distributed even more broadly across the island, being common in the mountains as well as at sea level. It often inhabits gardens and grounds. Patrick Browne said in 1756 that the "pea-dove, ground-dove" and their relatives were "very rich and delicate meat". Birds from the interior woods were eaten only by the wealthy, because they were "the produce of the fowlers labours", said Browne, whereas "such as resort to the lower lands are very common in the markets, being generally taken in large baskets, and the work of every negro that pleases to toil for them". Gosse thought the pea dove had "white and juicy" flesh and "when in good condition" was "in general estimation".[15]

Gosse singled out the whitewing, *Zenaida asiatica*, as unusual among the doves in being gregarious. It fed on seeds found on the ground and also on berries, fruits and Guinea corn, and became plentiful in pastures early in the year when the physic nut was ripening and the oranges came in. It was "very easily shot, as they walk about on the ground". Gosse also noted that whitewings were "taken very readily in springes, and in traps called *calambans*, baited with orange seeds". The calamban or, more usually, calaban was a box-like wicker trap. Because the whitewing was so easily trapped, said Gosse, "they are a good deal eaten, though seldom fat, and rather subject to be bitter". The whitewing grows to thirty centimetres in length, with a large patch of white on its wings and a touch of white on the tip of its tail. It is generally coastal in habit, found in gardens, wood and scrubland, and mangroves. Recipes for whitewing appeared into the 1980s, roasted and served with a creamy sauce.[16]

The whitebelly, *Leptotila jamaicensis*, is a plump, middle-sized ground-dwelling dove, also known as "Jamaican dove". It feeds largely on seeds picked up on the ground, generally keeping hidden under bushes and shrubs in semi-arid areas but easily caught in traps. Gosse said, "Its flesh is generally esteemed; it is white, juicy, and well-flavoured, without being liable to bitterness."[17]

However easy it might have been to trap pigeons, the planters of the eighteenth century also used pigeon houses to seduce the birds to a convenient location – close to the kitchen – where a regular supply could be ensured (Figure 9.1). John Dovaston advised in 1774 that in order to cope with the demands of plantation hospitality, it was useful to have a good supply of pigeons, drawn from "a dovecote builded for to breed in". Lewis described a "pigeon-house" in 1817, set on a pole and big enough for a man to enter. Holes in the walls were fitted with sliders so that pigeons that had flown into the house could be locked in, and people entered the house through its bottom by climbing a ladder. Corn was placed inside for these "domestic pigeons". Pigeon houses are occasionally still seen in rural Jamaica, and recipes, including pigeon pie, pigeon with cabbage and pigeon with pineapple, continue to appear in cookbooks.[18] In these ways, the pigeon served many of the purposes that would become the province of the chicken in the twentieth century.

PARROT

When Maria Nugent saw "a flight of parrots" in 1802, she made a note in her journal that "the negroes eat them, and some people make soup of them". Other observers, before and after, similarly claimed that parrots were "largely consumed by the negroes of the mountain districts, who say they resemble pigeon in flavour". Gosse, however, described the habits of the endemic black-billed parrot, *Amazona agilis*, and the yellow-billed parrot, *A. collaria*, without mention of their being eaten.[19] Once widespread and common, the parrot's numbers declined along with the retreat of natural forests. They remain relatively numerous only in some of the moist forests, notably the Cockpit

Country and the John Crow Mountains. Some were poached for the local pet trade and sold as cage birds but, in the twentieth century, they seem not to have been eaten.[20]

JAMAICAN CROW

Similarly, eighteenth-century commentators reported the eating of the "Javaline Crow", whereas Gosse said of the jabbering crow, *Corvus jamaicensis*, that "the flesh is not eaten". But he did confess that "having curiosity to taste it, I had one broiled. The flesh of the breast was well-tasted and juicy, but so dark, tough, and coarse-grained, that I should readily have mistaken it for *beef*." Perhaps the jabbering or "Jamaican" crow was bracketed with the carrion, but it was in fact omnivorous, eating ripening soursops and pimento berries, plantains and bananas, as well as foraging for small amphibians, crabs, grubs, lizards and eggs. Gosse thought the bird deserved its name because it sounded like "half-a dozen Welshmen quarrelling" but noted that "the negroes" interpreted the jabbering as "Walk fast, crab! do buckra work. – Cuttacoo [a woven hand-basket] better than wallet."[21]

PETCHARY

The petchary belongs to the tyrant flycatchers, a family of land birds represented in Jamaica by eight breeding species, making it the most common bird after pigeons. Both permanent-resident and migratory varieties may be found. Of the latter, the best known is the grey kingbird or petchary, *Tyrannus dominicensis*, a medium-sized bird, growing to about twenty-five centimetres, with a heavy beak and slightly forked tail. Richard Hill, in 1845, described great flocks of the grey petchary arriving in September, particularly to the coastal savannas and pastures and nearby cattle pens. Hill said, "They do not appear among us many days before they become exceedingly fat: then they are eagerly sought after by the sportsman, who follows the flocks to their favourite haunts, and slaughters them by dozens." Modern reports say that the grey petchary's range stretches from North America to the rimland of the Caribbean, and that it is a "permanent resident" from Hispaniola east and south to the northern mainland of South America. It is common in gardens and grounds, in open woods and among coastal mangroves.[22]

The non-migratory common petchary, *Tyrannus caudifasciatus*, is generally known in Jamaica as the loggerhead (Figure 9.2). It was common in the nineteenth century and before, feeding on the swarms of insects around fruit and timber trees. In September, like the grey petchary, said Gosse, common petcharies became "a mere mass of fat, and are at this time in much request for the table". He was told that the birds reached this fatness by "feeding on the honey-bees, which then resort in great numbers to the magnif-icent bloom-spike of the cabbage-palm". Recalling the 1870s, an engineer compared the petchary to the ortolan, and called it "a gastronomic delicacy". By the 1950s, when bee-keepers were trying hard to promote honey, the petchary was often regarded as a pest, and "our gunmen ever eager and ready to kill anything wearing feathers have

Figure 9.2 Petchary

taken the law into their own hands and have made it the mass victim of organized shooting parties and thereafter returned to their homes to pies and other dishes made with these much maligned and extremely useful birds".[23]

ORTOLAN, TEAL, SNIPE

The exclusively seasonal migrant species came to Jamaica in large numbers each year, mostly from the continental north but also from Cuba. The migrations began in early October, and most of these birds are gone by March. Some bred in the island and remained all year, in reduced numbers. All of them were considered game by Jamaica's "sportsmen". In 1774 Long listed a numerous variety of these "birds of passage", saying they arrived in "prodigious flocks". He began with the ortolan or "butter bird", known in South Carolina as the "rice bird", which grew "exceedingly fat in Jamaica, in the season, and are esteemed by connoisseurs not inferior to the true ortolan". The ortolan fed on Guinea grass seeds in the pastures of the pens and, said Stewart, were "much esteemed by the lovers of good eating, being thought little inferior to the French ortolan, so highly prized in the London market". Gosse observed in the 1840s that the "butter-bird" arrived from the United States in October in "vast numbers", settling on the Guinea grass in flocks of five hundred and more, and feeding on the seeds. The bird was "a bonne bouche" – only "a mouthful, but a luscious and delightful one".[24]

Long also praised the wild ducks and teal, saying they had a "fishy" taste when they first got to Jamaica but, "after being some time in the country, they grow exceedingly fat and delicious". Lindsay illustrated several varieties of wild duck (Plate 38). Stewart added to the list crane, white galding (a variety of heron), plover and snipe. The snipe was "beautiful and delicious" and common in the wetlands from November to April. Thomas Thistlewood, earlier, gave one dinner that included "roast squab, a roast teal, roast coot and roast snipe", and at another had "fryed ortolans". Recipes for "teal (wild duck)", roasted and served with a sauce made from oranges, rum and cloves, were occasionally included in cookbooks right into the 1980s.[25] Yet overall, the migrant birds came in smaller flocks during the twentieth century and ceased to be a significant seasonal resource.

TERN, NODDY

Jamaicans refer to most species of seabirds collectively as "boobies", though it is not the masked booby (*Sula dactylatra*) or the brown booby (*S. leucogaster*), nesting in the Morant and Pedro Cays off the coast to the south of the island, that enters the human food system. "Booby eggs" are, rather, the eggs of the sooty tern (*Sterna fuscata*) and the brown noddy (*Anous stolidus*), which visit the cays in summer. These two birds grow to about forty centimetres in length and spend most of their time far offshore. They are distinguished chiefly by their coloration, the sooty tern also by its deeply forked tail.[26] Gosse grouped together various terns and gannets as "egg-birds", saying they were of commercial significance because their eggs "form an object of profitable adventure to the crews of numerous small vessels, fitted out in the spring from Kingston and other ports". These boats went mainly to the Morant and Pedro Cays, a hundred kilometres south of Kingston, where tens of thousands of "sea-fowl" collected to nest. Few birds came as close to the island as Lime Cay. At the end of the nineteenth century, "enormous" numbers of eggs were still being taken from the distant cays, individual sloops carrying fifty to sixty thousand eggs. The first arrivals, in late April, were eagerly sought after and quickly sold.[27]

The sooty tern contributed the larger proportion of the harvest, laying eggs about the size of those of a modern chicken, with a bright orange-red yolk rather than the pale yellow of the noddy. Buckets of booby eggs, "pale brown with purplish-brown mottles", were offered for sale in Kingston in the 1920s and 1930s. Vendors roamed the streets selling the eggs, boiled and raw, which were "a favorite breakfast dish with a bit of salt which the vendor also carries in her basket". Beckwith thought they tasted "a little like a duck's egg". Others said the eggs had a "salt and fishy taste". By the end of the 1960s, the harvest had dwindled to about 250,000 eggs annually, from the Pedro Cays and the Morant Cays together, and by the early 1980s the resource was "virtually exhausted".[28] They became a subject only for nostalgia.

PELICAN, PEACOCK

The pelican, *Pelecanus occidentalis*, is a common bird in the calmer coastal waters of Jamaica, with a wingspan of two metres or more and equipped with a long beak for fishing at sea. Gosse reported that fishers sometimes caught it, and that "the flesh is eaten by some of the negroes, notwithstanding its insupportable fishy odour; to overcome which in some degree, they bury it for some hours in the sand of the beach, after which they subject it to three or four boilings before it is eaten".[29]

In 1801 Nugent recorded a supper served at a grand ball in Spanish Town, given by the Council in her honour: "One dish I will never forget; it was a roasted peacock, placed before me, with all the feathers of the tail stuck in, and spread so naturally, that I expected every minute to see him strut out of the dish."[30]

GOOSE, DUCK, TURKEY

Roasted goose was more acceptable on the planter's table. At a dinner in 1770, Thistlewood served a "fine roast goose and paw-paw sauce, stewed giblets, . . . a roast coot and two roast plovers", and the following year "goose and paw-paw sauce", this time along with "roast whistling duck". Domesticated geese, turkeys and ducks were commonly raised on eighteenth-century plantations for the planter and his guests. These birds were raised in pens and fed on seed. Gosse said black-billed whistling ducks, *Dendrocygna arborea*, were lovers of Guinea corn and attacked the crops en masse but were given away by their whistle, so that the young were often taken and "brought up in the poultry yard with the tame ducks, either pinioned, or sufficiently subdued by kindness to be allowed liberty". These semi-domesticated ducks served also to attract their wild relations, creating easy targets for shooters. Down to the middle of the nineteenth century, the wetlands around Spanish Town and Old Harbour Bay provided a plentiful supply of ducks to the town markets, the great flocks being attacked by shooters in boats.[31]

Geese were sometimes said to be rare in Jamaica. This was remarked as early as the 1680s. Stewart said in 1823 that Jamaica raised all kinds of poultry, "excepting geese and the common duck, neither of which, with all the care that can be bestowed on them, multiply to such a degree as to render them profitable to their owners". On the other hand, the indigenous Muscovy duck, *Cairina moschata*, was "as hardy and prolific here as the common duck is in England". Even in the 1980s, Benghiat could observe that "a nicely roasted duck is not often encountered". Many Jamaicans came to think of duck as a "Chinese dish".

Turkeys did somewhat better in the long run. Beginning in the 1980s turkey necks and wings were imported, described as "meaty, high protein" items, good for currying and stewing, though they were also sometimes defined as dumped products and not subject to duty.[32]

GUINEAFOWL, CLUCKING HEN

The guineafowl, *Numida meleagris*, was domesticated in northern Africa about 4000 BP but became common in urban West Africa (Guinea) only about 1500 BP, at the same time as the domestic chicken, *Gallus gallus*.[33] It is terrestrial, growing to about fifty centimetres in length, with a characteristic body shape and speckled feathers, and is valued for both its eggs and its flesh (Plate 39). The guineafowl lays large numbers of eggs, and raises many young at a time. In some of the West Indian islands the bird became feral. In Jamaica it ran wild in the nineteenth century, attacking provision grounds, but it is now found only in pens and houseyards.[34]

Gosse reported in the 1840s that some people considered guineafowl to be as good-tasting as pheasant, but commented that "though savoury, and in high request for the table, the Guinea-fowl sometimes acquires an insufferably rank odour, from feeding on the fetid *Petiveria alliacea*; and is then uneatable". This was the common plant "Guinea hen weed" or "strong man's weed", which gave off a heavy garlicky odour when broken. Recipes for guineafowl are few. Sullivan merely included "roasted guinea fowl" in her list of "meals for a small family". Guinea hen or guineafowl appeared in the occasional cookbook into the 1980s, including "African style" (stewed with tomatoes and sweet potatoes). But guineafowl was by then no longer common and rarely sold in the markets. Its flavour was thought gamey, somewhere between chicken and pheasant.[35]

Stewart described the "Guinea fowl" as "a wild and wandering sort of bird, that will not be confined to the discipline of a poultry-house". Eggs had to be searched for in odd places, and "placed under a clucking hen, who hatches and rears the young strangers". The clucking hen, *Aramus guarauna*, lived on water snails in the riverine wetlands and was "looked upon as the best wild-fowl of the country". Gosse reported that the clucking hen became fat enough towards the end of the year to be "esteemed fit for the table", either fricasseed or roasted, in the same way as guineafowl, and he himself thought the taste excellent.[36] Neither clucking hen nor guineafowl ever became common or popular.

CHICKEN

By the 1980s, chicken could be declared the favourite meat of Jamaicans, perhaps even their favourite food. It could then be claimed that "there is probably not a single Jamaican consumer who would, all things being equal, choose anything – perhaps even beef – over chicken". In 2005, confidence in the truth of the claim was even stronger, and it was possible to declare that "chicken is the number one protein consumed, so much so that in some circles it is referred to as the 'national meat'".[37]

The high status of the chicken in the Jamaican food hierarchy is a relatively recent phenomenon, no more than fifty years old. Before 1950, the diverse indigenous and migratory birds discussed above contributed to the diet but often only in a selective and seasonal fashion, because they were generally expensive or difficult to catch. All birds suffered in competition with fish and the meat of mammals that were more appropriate to salting and pickling. Birds needed to be eaten fresh, and dissection of birds into smaller parts depended on freezing in order to be traded long-distance. These developments worked themselves out in distinct ways in Jamaica but they paralleled change in many other parts of the world.

The chicken is a domesticated bird, descended from the red junglefowl, *Gallus gallus*, whose original habitat stretched from eastern India to Java. The red junglefowl grows to forty-five centimetres in length, the rooster carrying dramatic plumage, with a long bushy tail and prominent red wattles and head comb, and the hen brownish with less splendid plumage. Domestication of the chicken (sometimes distinguished as *Gallus domesticus*) began about 8000 BP and was complete by 5000 BP. The original domestication probably occurred in Thailand. It spread around the world at varied rates, reaching Europe by 3000 BP and West Africa by about 1500 BP, though the chicken generally remained a small bird and was often confined to elite households.[38]

Domestication resulted in a series of physical and behavioural modifications, all designed to make the chicken a more useful bird for food, but also for symbolic and decorative purposes and as a fighting cock. The process was advanced by hybridization and artificial selection, producing distinct breeds for the production of meat and for the laying of eggs. Modern broilers, bred for their ability to efficiently convert feed into body mass, weigh four times as much as the red junglefowl, and hybrid layers produce eggs twice as heavy. Intensive selection based on quantitative genetic methods has been pursued for fifty years, with continuous increments to production traits, making chicken-breeding "one of the most remarkable examples of directed evolution". These changes have become much better understood in recent years. *G. gallus* was the first bird, and the first farmed animal, to have its genome sequenced, with the draft of the sequence published in 2004. From a genetic point of view, the chicken is important in providing a bridge across the evolutionary gap between mammals and other vertebrates. From the point of view of the chicken as a human food, this new knowledge is likely to mean even greater modification of physical and behavioural characteristics, keeping the chicken at the centre of meat production.[39]

Before the twentieth century, the chicken was rarely even called "chicken". The more common generic terms were "fowl", "dunghill fowl" and "poultry". Down to 1950 most Jamaican chickens were permitted to scratch about in houseyards, finding what they could to peck at and relishing the scraps and occasional grain that might come from the hands of their keepers. In this system, the dunghill fowl was both typical and symbolic. At the same time, it was argued as early as the 1680s that the "hens, turkeys, and ducks" of Jamaica "bred better, and are better flesh than in England". Along with guineafowl, turkey and duck, it was the "dunghill cock" that supplied the planter's table in the eighteenth century, "especially in the country parts, where they cannot be so well supplied with butchers meat". Enslaved people often raised "a few poultry, and other stock", but these, said Browne, were generally sold in the public markets "to enable them to purchase some decent as well as necessary cloaths for their wives and themselves". Similarly, Stewart said the enslaved "cannot afford to indulge themselves with a fowl or a duck, except upon particular occasions".[40]

Few specialized chicken farms existed in Jamaica before 1900. In 1896, Airy View "poultry farm" of St Mary advertised eggs and birds for sale – "pure bred Plymouth Rocks" – but it was not until the twentieth century that notice began to be taken of more scientific methods of breeding and husbandry. Generally, chickens simply continued to scratch for insects, with unpredictable results – the meat sometimes good, sometimes bad. In the 1930s, because of this uncertainty, the larger hotels imported frozen poultry. Often in the 1940s chickens reached market only after a long life of laying eggs, when they were no longer young "but to use the common Kingston derisive expression, 'old fowl'". The most common breeds were the Plymouth Rock, Leghorn, Black Minorca, Orpington and Wyandotte, with many peel-neck fowl.[41]

In 1952 Chapman complained that "although there are a few people who raise poultry on modern scientific lines, chickens and turkeys are often thin and scraggy and the fat tender capon is practically unknown". Change was on the way. By the early 1940s, a Kingston company was encouraging the use of "scientifically balanced" Purina Poultry Chows, with mixes specifically for chicks, layers and broilers. The company also sold "Sunstrain triple-tested chicks", saying, "Our sturdy, thrifty Purina embryo-fed chicks are free from disease and bred for high production." The 1950s saw more dramatic changes. Whereas in 1950 "the broiler was an almost unknown form of meatstuff locally", used only by hotels and imported, by 1960 it was common.[42]

Chicken became an industrialized product, raised in quantity on factory lines. This was a global change, in which Jamaica shared, that made chicken relatively cheap and increasingly common and popular. By the middle of the 1980s, two major Jamaican companies, Jamaica Broilers and Caribbean Broilers, were producing large quantities of chicken meat, though still not enough to meet demand. In 1990 Jamaica Broilers advertised "The Best Dressed Chicken" as "the best meat buy, pound for pound", being the most versatile and having the lowest fat content. Chicken meat was one-third the price of fillet steak, oxtail, pork fillet and kingfish, and more expensive only than pork trotters. By 1993 it was true that "Jamaicans now eat more chicken by far than any other form of meat or poultry – or fish for that matter". Jamaica had become "a country of chicken-eaters". With saltfish three times as expensive as chicken, "the Jamaican consumer has little choice", and the producers were able to increase prices without significantly depressing demand. Chicken had become "by far the most popular meat in Jamaica, comprising 60 per cent of meat in the Jamaican diet".[43]

The Jamaican chicken increased dramatically in weight after Independence, moving from 1 kilogram on average to 1.5 kilograms by 2005. Over the same period, the chicken population increased from less than 2 million to more than 12 million birds. The increasing size of the birds, and their increasing numbers, contributed to the vast increase in chicken-meat production in the island, exceeding 80,000 tonnes in 2005 – almost four times the weight of local beef, mutton and pork combined. From just 1 kilogram per capita per annum when the official record begins in 1955, consumption increased to 43 kilograms per capita by 2000 (Figure 9.3). As noted in the previous chapter, the spectacular increase in chicken consumption in Jamaica effectively replaced the dominant role played by fish before the Morant Bay Rebellion. Worldwide, by the year 2000, chicken meat had almost overtaken beef consumption, but in Jamaica this transition happened earlier.

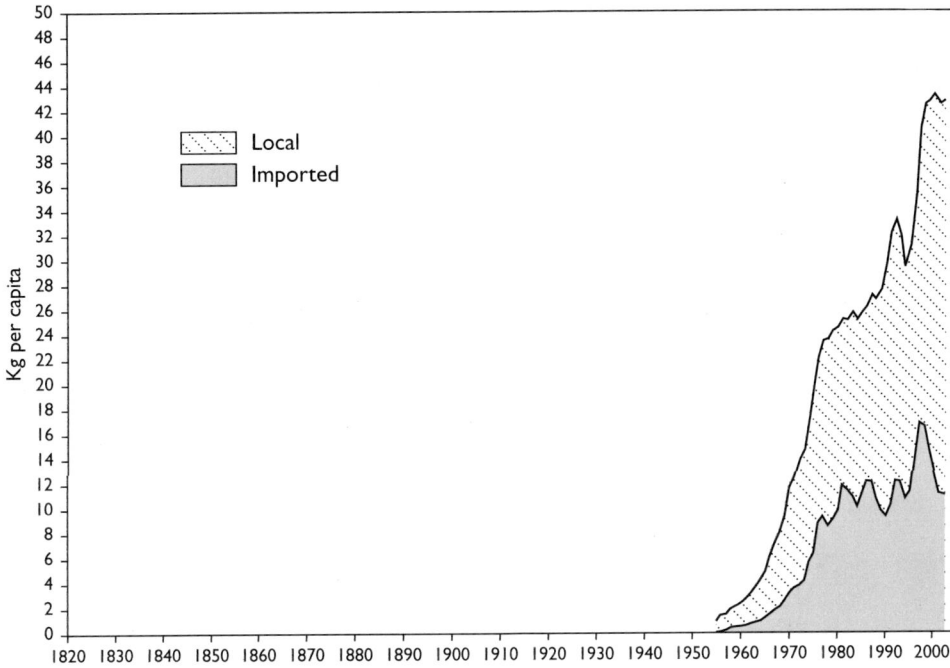

Figure 9.3 Local production and imports of poultry per capita, 1955–2004. Source: Appendix 1.

In the early 1990s Jamaicans, like many people around the world, were also being told about free-range chickens and their advantages over the modern caged varieties that "lacked the flavour and texture of the chicken of old". However, the free-range variety was thought to lack some of the fat that gave flavour, and enthusiasm for the chicken's return to freedom was muted.[44]

A number of technologies came together to make the modern industrial chicken viable. For the consumer, refrigeration was the most important of these, because it meant that whole chickens and, increasingly, dissected chickens could be stored safely. Previously, when chicken was a relative rarity for most Jamaicans, the bird was raised in the yard or purchased live and kept alive until the morning it would be killed, plucked and gutted by a member of the household. There was, therefore, an incentive to use every part possible one way or another. Refrigeration meant that the chicken could be separated into parts and sold to separate customers, creating a hierarchy of cost and taste (Figure 9.4). The chicken was commodified, translated into its anatomical components and made into a meat-producing creature. The gap between the human eater of chicken and the living bird became wider and wider as the killing and plucking of chickens was removed from the household. At the same time, it could be claimed that the method of slaughter – by a quick, clean cut at the neck and hanging by the feet to drain the blood – was "kosher", introduced to Jamaica by Sephardic Jews. By the early 1960s, supermarkets

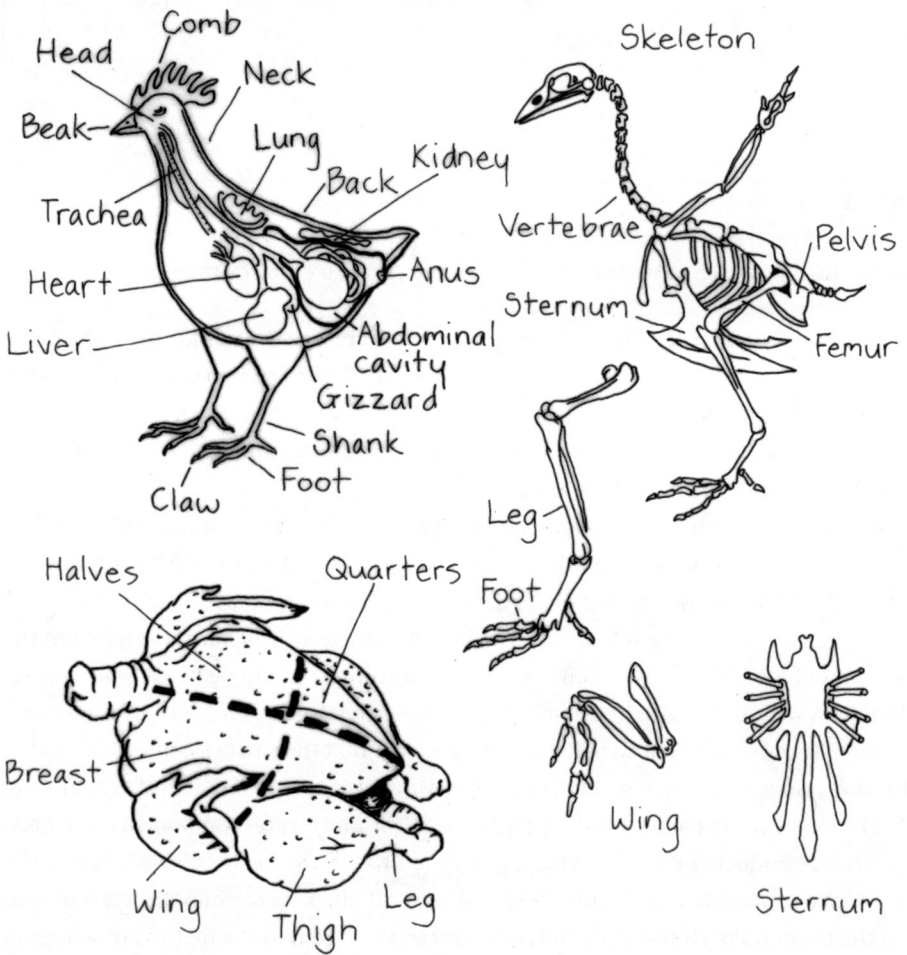

Figure 9.4 Chicken breeds and anatomy

sold "cut-up chickens" and "chicken feet" separately. "Chicken neck and back" soon became a popular cheap purchase, though 50 per cent of its weight was regarded as waste. Previously, the "trimmings" (neck, feet, liver, heart, kidney and gizzard) were often used only to make stock for gravies and soups.[45] By the 1970s, "whole" chickens packed in plastic bags and refrigerated in supermarkets had the neck, liver, heart and kidney wrapped in paper and stuffed into the abdominal cavity, but came without head and feet.

In the 1980s, there were complaints that supermarkets had begun to sell "chicken parts" at inflated prices. In 1985, when the price of chicken meat increased sharply, consumers began "searching supermarket freezers for the more economic chicken necks and backs to add the taste of chicken to whatever it is that we prepare for our families". Necks and backs were stewed or cooked in soup, as well as curried and chopped into smaller pieces and steamed in rice. Consumers were even encouraged to cut up whole chickens, leaving the back intact after jointing the legs, thighs, wings and breast. Chicken carcass or ribcage became known as "chicken chassis". The problem with the chicken back, however, was that it contained much skin, fat and bone. Cooks were told how to extract the maximum meat by cutting off these elements, boiling the carcass and picking out the meat from the bone for use in fritters, macaroni or soup. At the same time, processors offered specialized "packaged parts" (breasts, boneless breasts, wings, legs and thighs, drumsticks, halves and quarters), so that the consumer could "pick up an economical pack of just the parts you need".[46] In this way, the parts were disconnected from the body of the chicken and packed generically.

In 1988, immediately following Hurricane Gilbert, the destruction of broiler farms and processing plants and, often, the lack of availability of refrigeration, led to the sale of "live fully-grown chickens". For many middle-class consumers, this proved problematic: they and their helpers had become unaccustomed to the killing and dressing of chicken, and cookbooks no longer offered much guidance. Down to the 1950s, the reverse had been true, with more attention directed to the dressing of the fowl than to its cooking. Thus, although in 1945 Phyllis Clark did not tell her readers how to kill the chicken, she began her recipes for these cooking methods saying, "pluck and singe the bird". For roast chicken she recommended using a "young fowl" but said, "if the bird is not very young pour hot water over it before plucking to loosen feathers and kill lice". Clearly, this was a fowl that had spent some time scratching around in yards. For boiled fowl, Clark said, "an old fowl can be made tender by careful boiling". After plucking and singeing, the next step for the cook was to cut off the chicken's head (it had probably been strangled) and to "make a long slit at back of neck, loosen skin and cut off neck close to body leaving skin on the bird. Cut round vent to free entrails, remove gullet, crop, windpipe, and all internal organs. Cut out oil sack above tail." The cook washed and dried the bird, and rubbed it with lime and salt. The feet were still attached, so it was necessary to "break legs above spur, twist and draw out sinews". The cavity was stuffed and the skin at the neck folded over. Legs and wings were tied closely to the body of the bird. Slices of fat bacon were placed on the breast, and the chicken was rested on a grid in a dripping pan and basted frequently while baking in a hot oven. Finally, the breast was browned by removing the bacon, sprinkling with flour and basting. Clark recommended serving the roast chicken with bacon rolls, gravy and bread sauce. The 1957 *Farmer's Food Manual* followed much the same principles as Clark, instructing the cook first how "to draw [disembowel] a fowl or chicken", but without explaining the method of killing and cutting off the head during the process. To truss the bird for roasting, it was necessary to "cut off the toes at the first joint" and "draw the sinews".[47]

Descriptions of the methods of drawing and dressing whole chicken disappeared after 1960, at which time removal of the bones began to become popular. In this method, the cook began with a dressed whole chicken, without having to cope with feathers and entrails. Boning was intended to preserve the look of the chicken as a bird, in contrast to the packaged, dissected parts. The objective was to keep the skin intact, and the new cook was encouraged not to "despair if the chicken looks wrecked without the bones; the stuffing takes the place of the bones and the chicken can be reshaped almost perfectly". By the 1990s, when packaged parts were the order of the day and reshaping a complete bird was no longer a common objective, cooks were more likely to be instructed "how to debone a chicken leg" than a whole chicken.[48]

Down to the middle of the twentieth century, chicken was most often boiled. Sullivan mentioned nothing more than "boiled fowl" and "boiled chickens". Much earlier, in the 1760s, Lindsay had advocated the use of green pawpaw to tenderize meat, saying, "a little of the water in which a little of this papaw is boild, poured down the throat of an old foul or one but newly killd, before you put it to the fire will make the one eat like a chicken, and the other as if kill'd the night before". But once the modern, young tender-fleshed chicken was available, roasting quickly replaced boiling as the favourite cooking method. Cooks at the beginning of the 1970s who found this "a bore" were encouraged to marinade chicken halves before roasting, with the additional option of serving the halves "lightly sewn together across back to give impression of whole chickens".[49]

An elaboration on boiled fowl was fricasseed chicken, a cooking style that remained a favourite in Jamaica into the 1990s. In the 1950s, this was made by jointing the bird, frying in fat or oil, then making it into a stew with tomatoes and onions, and sometimes curry powder. Donaldson claimed in 1993 that fricassee was "the most popular way of cooking chicken in Jamaica". It meant, she said, "really braising chicken, with as many additions as there are cooks", with lots of gravy and served with rice and peas. Her recipe used a whole chicken cut up, seasoned with salt, sugar, black pepper, garlic, scallion and thyme, and lightly browned. Chicken stock was added to the frying pan, along with Pickapeppa sauce and ketchup, Irish potato, carrot, chocho and onion, and brought down to gravy. The minimum seasonings were salt, black pepper, garlic powder, soy sauce and cooking oil, and with these the result might be "just as delectable and succulent" as more complex methods.[50] The result was closely akin to the brown stew that became popular for fresh fish.

Jerk chicken emerged in the 1970s, the chicken most often split in half and grilled and chopped into smaller pieces for customers. By the 1990s it could be claimed that "most persons feel jerk chicken is now preferred to jerk pork". Jerk chicken is essentially a version of grilling and barbecue, but it was joined by drum chicken, in which the cooking takes place in a longitudinally split oil drum on a metal stand. Glowing coals placed in the bottom half of the drum provide radiant heat, while closing the lid or upper half confines the smoke. The result is closer to roasting in an oven than to cooking on a barbecue, the meat succulent rather than partially charred. This is specific to chicken, having no equivalent for other meats such as pork. Drum chicken became known as "pan chicken", the meat broiled or grilled with seasonings. In 2005 Caribbean Broilers had held the first "pan chicken championships", with "over $2 million in cash and prizes". Jerk chicken also found its way into new forms. Tinned jerk sausage was marketed, made from chicken, pork, water, salt, pimento, pepper, onion, scallion and spices. In such sausages the provenance of the chicken meat remained undeclared.[51]

By the 1980s, popular taste had shifted from roast to fried chicken, preferably cooked in deep fat or – particularly at home, where the cost of the oil was a factor – coated with a well-seasoned batter and oven-baked. This was not something unique to Jamaica but rather represented part of chicken's global conquest, beginning with fried chicken as prepared in the American South and promoted by fast food outlets. As early as 1938 the Glass Bucket Club in Kingston offered "fried chicken Southern style".[52] Recipes for "chicken Maryland" (joints coated with breadcrumbs and braised) were published into the 1990s, and it was claimed that "nearly everyone enjoys Southern Fried Chicken or Roasted Chicken". The Americanness of the dish was further emphasized in the combination "Southern fried chicken and gravy with USA rice". Global criticism of fast foods led to changes, marked particularly by the avoidance of "fried" dishes and the promotion of healthy salad vegetables. In 2005, in Jamaica as elsewhere around the world, McDonald's restaurants were promoting a new product: "deluxe chicken salads", constructed from sliced, warm, grilled or crispy chicken breast in a plate surrounded by lettuce, tomato, carrot and cucumber.[53]

In spite of these strong American influences, some authentic Jamaican methods of cooking chicken, in addition to the application of jerk, did emerge. For example, "chicken Retreat Content" got its name from the tiny village of Retreat Content in St Mary, which "achieved fame by giving its name to this type of chicken stew which is known all over the island". To make this dish, a partly cooked whole chicken was cut into serving-sized pieces and put in a large saucepan with chicken stock or a can of chicken soup, sweet corn cobs cut into slices, onion, chives, parsley, thyme, salt and country pepper. The pot was brought to the boil, then simmered until the onion was tender, when cooked or canned string beans were added with slices of partly cooked potatoes, more liquid was added and simmered, and the dish finished with a dash of Tabasco or Worcester-shire sauce. This dish had its devotees, but even locally it struggled to compete with fried chicken. On the other hand, when commercial fried chicken was introduced by Kentucky Fried Chicken, attempts were made to give the food a Jamaican flavour. In 1994 it was even claimed that "when KFC developed its unique blend of spices for its chicken in 1940, all the spices came from Jamaica". In 2000 Kentucky Fried Chicken introduced "hot and spicy chicken . . . blazing with flavour".[54] This made fried chicken seem an indigenous Jamaican creation rather than an imperial imposition.

Fried chicken depended on the chicken being cut up into relatively small parts, so that the seasoning could coat it fully and the heat could penetrate to the bone. By the 1990s, consumers buying three or more chickens at a time were being encouraged to cut them into parts and put legs, wings, breast, liver and gizzard in separate packages for storage, "so as to vary the presentation at the table", by baking or frying the legs, currying wings, using breast in fried rice or chop suey or stir-fry, and serving liver and gizzard with boiled bananas for breakfast or preparing "chicken livers en brioche" (baked on skewers with bacon, salt and pepper) as a hot snack. Another option was sweet and sour chicken gizzards. Parts also proved popular for currying, though whole chickens were jointed for the same purpose. A peculiarly Jamaican version was "run-down curried chicken", in which a method normally associated with fish was used to transform the curry by adding coconut cream and shredded coconut to make a custard. Parts might also be added to packaged dehydrated soup mixes, notably "cock soup mix". Commer-cial packaged seasonings were advertised with fried chicken particularly in mind. In 2005 varieties included "ginger, garlic and pimento seasoning mix" and "cock flavour seasoning mix".[55]

The dissection of the chicken into its parts naturally created a hierarchy. Indeed chicken "parts" came specifically to mean those elements rejected or discarded by the better-off: the bony, scraggy, fatty parts left for the poor. When these were imported from the United States in the 1990s, the trade was decried by Jamaican chicken producers as dumping. Chicken back was often seen as a last resort, when whole chicken became scarce and expensive. Nutritionists called for the ending of importation of "chicken foot, neck, back" because these contained few nutrients. Others made wider moral arguments, complaining that the "exploding demand for imported chicken back" demonstrated "not just emptiness of pocket, but also poverty of spirit, absence of self-esteem and a glaring lack of industry".[56]

In 1985 it was said that in Jamaica, "chicken feet have been popularly used in soups since comparatively recent times and more so with citizens of west Kingston and west-Central Kingston. Some of these persons even use chicken feet in stew peas to substi-tute meats: such as, beef, salt-beef and pigs tail." In the 1990s, "stew chicken foot with red peas" was a favourite dish sold by street kitchens. "Fowl foot soup", also known as "steppers soup", remained popular, the feet having been stripped of their outer skin.

In 2005, chicken foot soup mix could be bought in supermarkets, in a pack containing two raw chicken feet and a selection of vegetables. An upmarket version of chicken foot soup might be called a "suey mein", using vegetables and Chinese sauces. Chicken feet were also curried. Chicken wings, on the other hand, sometimes found their way into more upmarket dishes – served at cocktail parties marinated in rum, Pickapeppa sauce, ginger and garlic, barbecued or fried. For home cooking, the final joint or tip of the wing was regarded as inferior, with little flesh, and was sometimes removed for separate treatment.[57]

Finally, it is clear that for a long period of Jamaican history, chickens were appreciated more for their eggs than for their meat, the birds being allowed to grow old and tough in the service of egg-laying. Hen eggs could be eaten raw but were often thought unattractive in this way, and the hazard of random laying sites meant the eggs might not be discovered until they approached the rotten, foul-smelling stage. Although most of an egg is composed of water, it also offers a high nutritional return in protein, minerals and vitamins. The shell of the egg surrounds membranes that contain the white, or albumen, and the white in turn is made up of three distinct layers that enclose the protein-rich yolk (Figure 9.5).

The role of eggs in the Jamaican diet is not as clear as it might be. For example, what happened to the eggs laid in the gardens of the enslaved? References to their consumption are hard to find, the archaeological evidence is not helpful and the technologies available for cooking eggs were limited. Probably, most of the eggs were sold in the local markets or carried to the doors of the privileged, who owned ovens and frying pans. In West Africa, before Columbus, references are similarly absent; there the eggs were apparently kept for hatching. Sullivan offered few recipes based on eggs in 1893, and even in her recommended breakfast menus included them only for Tuesdays, when she proposed "eggs poached on callilu, or on Indian kale", and Saturdays, in "omelettes of oysters or fish".[58]

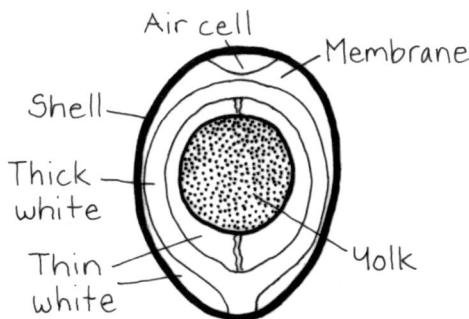

Figure 9.5 Hen egg section

Down to World War II, Jamaica was not self-sufficient in eggs, but by 1959 imports of eggs had been almost entirely replaced by local production. Imports did, nonetheless, increase gradually, both absolutely and as a proportion of consumption, so that by 2000 they contributed more than one-third of the total. Local production of eggs increased fivefold between Independence and the peak year, 1987, but then declined again. In 2005 Jamaica was producing 132 million eggs annually.[59]

Egg nog was a traditional Christmas morning drink in Jamaica. A recipe published in 1940 called for one dozen eggs, two quarts of rich milk, a bottle (a fifth) of rum and a cup of sugar or syrup, to make enough for twelve people. The egg whites and yolks were separated and the whites beaten with the sugar. In a separate bowl, the yolks were beaten with the milk and the rum stirred in. Next, the whites were poured slowly into the bowl while stirring slowly, some grated nutmeg was sprinkled on top and the bowl was placed in an ice box to chill. Later recipes, sometimes called "egg punch", used fewer eggs. In 2005 an "egg-nergiser" drink was unveiled, in which egg was "blended with carrot juice, oats, cow's milk, sugar, rum (optional), nutmeg and a dash of angostura bitters".[60]

The spectacular rise of the chicken, followed less dramatically by the egg, was marked by the inauguration in 2004 of a Jamaica Chicken Festival. Its objectives were educational and culinary, and particularly directed at the island's many chicken farmers. In 2005, when the festival shifted from St Ann to Clarendon, visitors were offered "chicken foot cuisine, gizzards, patties, soups, fast food, Indian, Chinese, stewed, sautéed and more", under the general theme "From Gourmet to Roots". Commercial booths offered chicken and banana fritters, fried chicken wings, chicken salad in regular and barbecue versions, spicy chicken nuggets, chicken foot soup, "run-d-boat chicken" (a Grace product) and curried chicken. There was a master chef cooking competition, a competition for "the best Pan Chicken man in the island" and a competition for the best amateur recipes using chicken and eggs, as well as for Saturday soup and chicken foot soup.[61]

CHAPTER 10

MAMMALS

Before the arrival of Europeans, Jamaica had few land mammals, all of them small: coney, rice rat and about twenty-three species of bats. Swimming in the coastal waters were two much larger mammals, the manatee and the monk seal. None of these animals were ever domesticated or important in the food system of Jamaica. Even the Taino made little use of them. With the exception of the bats, all of these are now either extinct or endangered.[1]

In the long term, even though the cost of introducing new varieties was low, the range of mammals commonly used as human food in Jamaica remained narrow. Just three – cow, pig and goat – account for the greater part of the food contribution of mammals. Of these, the cow, because it provides milk as well as meat, is most important overall. Yet this limited range rivalled the ultimate dominance of the chicken among the birds and the earlier predominance of cod and herring among the fish. Rather than expanding, the list of mammals became shorter. Mammals eaten in former times, such as camel, rat, cat and dog, came to seem improbable sources of food and were not replaced by new animals. Thus in 1938 it could be readily agreed that "today, of course, no one would think of eating cane-piece rats or snakes", even though this had been practised in the seventeenth and eighteenth centuries.[2] In addition to these broadly accepted social prohibitions, substantial religious groups within Jamaica have come to place taboos on particular "unclean" mammals, such as the pig. Some of these taboos are ancient and well known to Jamaicans from the Old Testament, but they are increasingly influential in the twentieth century among Rastafarians, Seventh-Day Adventists and Jehovah's Witnesses, and they also overlap with Muslim prohibitions.

As well as wondering why so few mammals have come to dominate, it is necessary also to ask why potential alternatives have not been exploited more widely or have not been tried at all. The introduction of species from around the world has been relatively easy in recent centuries, but few have come to Jamaica and of these even fewer have been eaten. For example, why not eat the mongoose, *Herpestes auropunctatus*? It was introduced from India to control infestations of rats in cane and corn pieces, and did a good job. Perhaps the mongoose was not considered a candidate for the cooking pot partly because it served these useful purposes, but more importantly because it was a carnivore and known to eat reptiles and other unclean, unattractive animals. The possibility was raised in 1938, when a writer asked who would be bold enough to add fricasseed mongoose to the Jamaican bill of fare, saying it was "a far cleaner animal than some of those that we guzzle without a blush".[3] The rejection of the mongoose as food parallels the case of the cattle egret. Overall, in Jamaica as elsewhere, people find it easier to add mammals to the prohibited list than to start eating new ones.

Whereas Jamaicans rejected the majority of mammals as potential human food, the few they did admit were eaten with enthusiasm. What were the advantages of cow, goat and pig as sources of food? Perhaps the principal attraction was that, compared to *most fish and all birds, these three mammals were relatively large, with a high propor*tion of edible flesh and soft tissue. The cow and, to a lesser extent, the goat also supplied substantial quantities of milk. They had been domesticated for millennia, selected not only for their qualities as suppliers of milk and meat, but also, in the case of cattle, for their ability to perform agricultural work. Thus they came to Jamaica as domesticated animals, and, apart from some short periods and in small numbers, rarely became wild or feral.

These animals were raised on farms rather than hunted. The coexistence of wild animals and farming created tensions, and depredations by wild and feral creatures led both to attempts to exterminate them and to more controlled hunting. Thus, in 1681, the Assembly enacted that only planters and landholders could hunt with gangs of dogs, and that no one could do so "within four miles of any crawl or settlement" except on their own land or with the permission of the owner. Further, no person could "set any snare or engine in any place whatsoever, his planted ground only excepted". The objective of this law was to protect the livestock of the planter class, in a land still rarely fenced.[4]

Although the number of important domesticated mammals worldwide might seem small, they in fact form a much larger proportion of the total mammal population than birds, fish or any other animal group. Mammals were the first animals to be domesticated: the domestication of cow, pig and goat, as well as sheep, was complete by 8000 BP, when the domestication of the chicken was just beginning and long before guineafowl, duck, rabbit, pigeon and turkey were brought into the fold.[5]

Of the few large mammals that have been domesticated, the most important, for Jamaica and the world at large, is the cow (*Bos Taurus* and *Bos indicus*). The choice of these large ungulate (hoofed) mammals for domestication can be explained by their gregariousness, their low fear reactions (particularly to humans), the precocity of their young and the ease with which their largely herbivorous feeding needs can be supplied by humans. Thus, the initial choice of large mammals for domestication depended very much on their social relation to humans rather than on whether their flesh was regarded as good-tasting. The large mammals that have not been domesticated are more likely to have great agility, eat meat and show aggressive behaviour, or to be reluctant to breed in captivity and to have long birth spacing and few young. Thus leopard, antelope and rhinoceros, for example, were not good candidates for domestication. This does not mean that their flesh lacks potential as human food, and indeed it has been argued that the domestication of more animals is the best way of maintaining diversity. Domestication typically increases the ratio of edible meat to tough muscle fibres and connective tissue, and the ratio of fat to meat, but the proportions vary from animal to animal and between breeds of cattle, pigs, sheep and goats.[6]

Cattle had an unusual place in the animal economy of Jamaica because they were long valued more for their capacity to perform work than for their meat and milk. Most of the animals eaten by humans in Jamaica were not also made to work, and those that worked (like camels, horses and donkeys) were not universally regarded as good to eat. In the plantation economy of Jamaica, cattle were multipurpose animals, made to supply milk and meat, skins and glue, as well as perform agricultural work. Part of this capacity was matched to the life cycle of the cow and reflected the large investment made in the animal. It also had to do with simple size and strength.

Potential competitors were the buffalo and the camel, both important in other parts of the tropical world. The Asian water buffalo, *Bubalus bubalis*, produces milk that is richer than that of the cow, but gives less per lactation and cannot be milked in the absence of her calf. The cow, by contrast, can produce as much as three thousand litres per lactation, depending on the quality of her feed. Although the water buffalo belongs to the same family, it cannot cross-breed with cattle. Its meat is considered stronger or gamier than beef. The buffalo was never introduced to Jamaica and remains largely confined to Asia and northeastern Africa. The camel was tried in Jamaica in the eighteenth century, apparently as a working animal rather than for its meat or milk. In Africa, camels have long been used for transport and traction as well as for milk and meat, but they are generally regarded as better suited to the hardship conditions of arid and desert areas than to the wet tropics. Another competitor was the horse. Together with the donkey and their progeny the mule, the horse was sometimes used to power sugar mills but rarely, it seems, to haul cane carts. Cattle were better for both of these tasks. On top of that, the flesh of the horse was not favoured by the English or the Africans of Jamaica, and the milk of the donkey was drunk only occasionally. In the 1770s Long proposed the importation of llamas, or "Peruvian sheep", as beasts of burden, to be fattened for meat when "past labour", but nothing came of this dream.[7]

Goat, pig and sheep were marginal to the plantation economy of Jamaica and never effective competitors with the cow. Even for the peasantry, the smaller mammals served only as sources of meat and, occasionally, milk. Thus down to the early twentieth century, so long as domesticated large mammals were regarded as more important for their capacity to pull ploughs, haul carts and power mills than for their milk or meat, the cow reigned supreme. Although the cow is now valued for its meat and milk and rarely used to perform labour, it was that capacity that selected it for plantation dominance. Within the context of the plantation economy of Jamaica, goats, pigs and sheep were relatively unprofitable luxuries, good only for their meat and, occasionally, milk and skins. Elsewhere, sheep might be valued for their wool, but the wool of tropical Jamaica's sheep dangled like tangled dreadlocks and was recognized early on by both Spanish and English as of little value. The skins of the island's goats were of better quality but remained relatively unimportant in the economy. Goat and sheep did have advantages, particularly their willingness to accept feed rejected by cattle, their hardiness, their high reproduction rates and their relatively low cost to the farmer. Still, sheep's milk was rarely consumed in Jamaica and that of the goat was always less popular than cow's milk.

Of the mammals to be discussed in this chapter, the most important are the cow, pig and goat, followed by the sheep, all of them European introductions and still important in the Jamaican food system. The flesh of the mammals in this group is typically referred to as something other than the name of the animal, by taking the French terms: beef (*boeuf*, "cow"), pork (*porc*, "pig") and mutton (both goat and sheep – *mouton*). The other mammals kept their names as animals when killed for their meat, as did birds and fish. A second group is made up of introduced mammals that were eaten from time to time but that are now rarely used as human food: camel, horse and donkey, cat, dog and rat. Rabbit is an uncommon food in Jamaica, but not as unusual as this last group. Three indigenous mammals – coney, manatee and monk seal – conclude the chapter, none of them any longer significant as human food. What all of these animals have in common – what characterizes them as mammals – is body hair (as opposed to the feathers of birds and the scales of fish), their birth as whole beings (rather than hatched) and the mammary glands of mothers that supply milk to feed their young. Humans, *Homo sapiens*, with their relatively large brains, are no different in this regard, and their first food is normally milk secreted by their mother's breasts.

HUMAN

The consumption of human milk is universal. Most children depend totally or partially on their mother's milk for the first months of life, both for nourishment and for protection from disease. Human milk has important characteristics that mean it cannot easily be substituted by alternative foods, including the milk of other mammals. It contains less protein, calcium and phosphate than any other milk, and the highest concentration of lactose. It also has more carbohydrate and about the same amount of fat as the milk of cow or goat. This is important because the newborn child is unable to cope with large amounts of protein and mineral material.[8]

Although the mammary glands of different female mammals have much in common in terms of development and structure, the human breast does not store large amounts of milk but rather secretes it in response to hormonal stimulation, the milk entering a system of ducts connected to the nipple. The milk is ejected by means of the "let down" reflex, responding to signals from the child. Most breastfeeding mothers suckle their babies but may, alternatively, express the milk into a cup or bottle.[9]

Modern Jamaican mothers breastfeed their babies for significantly shorter periods than do African mothers. In the past, the length of breastfeeding in Jamaica was longer, more like that typical of Africa. During slavery, breastfeeding among the enslaved population continued for about two years, with extension in some cases to three. This pattern reflected African practice, in which continued breastfeeding was directed at the preservation of the life of the young child and associated with taboos on sexual intercourse before weaning.[10] However, breastfeeding did not always commence immediately. Following traditional West African practice, mothers in the eighteenth century often first bathed their newborns in water in which herbs had been boiled, then force-fed water and herbs to cleanse the stomach. Breast milk was not given immediately the child cried after birth because this early milk was thought bitter and dangerous. The mother's milk could be withheld for up to four days while it was tested for purity. Some elements of these practices survived in the long term, but not, apparently, the initial withholding of the breast or the feeding of herbs.[11]

The length of breastfeeding in Jamaica declined during the nineteenth century. By about 1920 Jamaican infants were generally weaned at nine months, and breastfeeding rarely continued longer than eighteen months. It was in the 1920s that the decline in the period of breastfeeding began to be seen as a problem, and it was argued that children should receive at least some breast milk for the first six months of life. In the 1950s, a survey found most children in the poorer class were "completely breast fed for from seven to nine months, although longer periods are more common in country districts". Frequency declined over the months, as breastfeeding came to be supplemented by "cornmeal porridge and sugar, mixed with a little sweetened condensed milk".[12] By the 1970s, weaning was commonly complete by six months and few children were fully breastfed beyond four weeks. This long-term decline in breastfeeding rates matched the experience of many other countries, where scientific ideas and commercial alternatives worked against traditional practices and women's rights. In particular, the introduction and promotion of infant formula made breastfeeding problematic.[13]

The 1970s saw much activity to restore breastfeeding as "the biological option". The Ministry of Health mounted a campaign, "The Breast is Best", and Jamaican mothers were told, "breast milk is the best food for your baby in the first months of his life". It was "the perfect food . . . nourishing, pure and protective". To prepare for breastfeeding, pregnant women were encouraged to eat "a good mixture of foods" and a little more than usual, to massage their breasts and nipples, and to squeeze colostrum from the breasts every day from the seventh month. The baby was to be put to the breast as soon as possible after birth; the natural colostrum produced at first would be followed in about three days by "real milk". Colostrum contains abundant nutrients in a sweet mixture that benefits the child. After about the third day, the milk becomes thinner but maintains its sweet lactose taste. Mothers were told they should "breastfeed for at least six months, and after that for as long as you want", and that "baby needs no food other than breast milk for the first four to six months of life".[14]

By the beginning of the twenty-first century, when breastfeeding was clearly understood to protect against sickness as well as provide nutrition, almost all Jamaican mothers initiated breastfeeding but only about 50 per cent practised exclusive breastfeeding for the first six weeks. At four months only about one-quarter breastfed exclusively. Few breastfed for a whole year.[15]

In view of these supposed failures and inequalities, why has there not developed a trade in human milk? One fundamental reason is that human milk is understood as a direct and intimate transfer from mother to child, and it is commonly believed that drinking the milk of other mothers might be dangerous. Other reasons are the psychological mechanisms of secretion – though these can be stimulated artificially – and the limited storage capacity of the human breast. The result is that most Jamaican children have drunk only the milk of their own mothers. In the eighteenth century, however, it was common for the children of the white planter class to be suckled by black wet nurses, a practice which continued until the 1930s.[16]

Breastfeeding was rarely discussed in Jamaican cookbooks, though Clark, in 1945, included a section in her chapter on "feeding babies". She considered breastfeeding ideal, so long as the mother was "healthy and clean in her habits", but did not say how long she thought it should go on. Clark also discussed alternative sources of milk for the baby, including tinned milk, and said this was to be preferred whenever there was doubt about the purity of fresh milk. As to sweetened condensed milk, Clark said this contained "more sugar than baby really needs, but some people recommend it because it keeps better than unsweetened evaporated milk". In the 1940s, Nestlé's Sweetened Condensed Milk, Lactogen, Nestlé's Powdered Full Cream Milk and Nestlé's Milk Food were all being advertised as substitutes for breast milk. The 1957 *Farmer's Food Manual*, in a chapter devoted to milk and cheese, declared that milk was the most important food and, indeed, "the one food we have which Nature intended as food". However, although the manual noted that milk was the essential food of young children, it said little about human milk and devoted its attention to the milk of cow and goat.[17]

Milk has been the only human food consumed by Jamaicans and, as everywhere else in the world, it has been a food strictly for infants, never for adults. Profound cultural taboos consider the notion of using human milk to make butter, cheese or ice cream as something akin to cannibalism. Although some societies may have eaten human meat as food in normal times, cannibalism has always been extremely rare and the evidence is broadly contested. There is nothing to suggest it was practised by the peoples of Jamaica, though the Taino were said to attribute it to their feared competitors the Caribs, from whose name the word "cannibal" derives. The Englishman Edmund Hickeringill inserted some verse into his 1661 *Jamaica Viewed* with primary citations both for "barbacu'd" human flesh and for its consumers, the "*Caribs*, or *Cannibals*".[18] In modern "civilized" societies, eating people has long been taboo, and battlefield carnage is not seen as a source of meat. Genocide is more acceptable than cannibalism, and captives are worth more alive than dead, as payers of tribute or potential forced labourers. In the case of Jamaica, the "total" power that slave masters possessed over the bodies of enslaved people, including murder, did not extend to cannibalism. Although the masters claimed to understand enslaved African people as inferior beings – even distinct species – and counted them among the plantation livestock, slaves were not potential meat. This taboo existed long before the colonization of the island, and its functionality remained intact. In any case, the available domesticated mammals were vastly more efficient at turning green plants into flesh.

COW

The first cattle of Jamaica were introduced by the Spanish. These animals were of the "European" variety, *Bos taurus*, first domesticated in the Middle East but also represented by ancient breeds in Africa. Cattle had reached West Africa by 6000 BP, coming perhaps from an indigenous domestication in northeastern Africa and arriving earlier than sheep and goat. Only towards the end of the nineteenth century was the hump-backed Asian or Zebu variety, *Bos indicus*, introduced and interbred. The milk potential of *Bos indicus* is lower, but the variety was brought to Jamaica particularly to improve the stock of draft animals, being relatively heat-tolerant and resistant to the diseases of the tropics.[19]

After 1900, Jamaica played a leading role in the breeding of improved tropical cattle and sought to produce hardier animals with increased productivity of milk, shorter calving periods and superior meat-producing qualities. Common breeds of butchers' cattle included all the English varieties, such as Shorthorn, Hereford, Devon, Aberdeen-Angus and Suffolk, while most of the dairy cows were Jersey. Beginning in 1911, the cross-breeding of Jersey and Sahiwal (India's leading dairy cow) led to the development of the Jamaica Hope, bred chiefly to produce milk (Figure 10.1). By 1950 all the important genetic factors were present in the Jamaica Hope and it was recognized as "one of the most productive milking breeds in the tropical world".[20] Attention turned after World War II to Red Polls. The 1960s saw increased use of Holstein-Friesian cattle for milking, the males and culled females entering the beef market. The leading beef breeds at the time were Jamaica Red Poll, Jamaica Black and Jamaica Brahman. Opinions varied on the standard of the meat, some saying it was "good quality" while others contended that even cattle specially bred and fed for beef had a poor reputation, and the meat was called tasteless, inconsistent or simply shoe leather. Criticism was applied even to the beef coming from feedlots that became increasingly common from the 1970s.[21]

The size of the Jamaican cattle herd is difficult to estimate for the centuries before 1900. When the English took Jamaica in 1655, they found "great store of wild cattel". This feral population was quickly reduced, being exploited for hides as well as for meat. In the eighteenth century, the ratio of livestock to people was high, but the cattle were used in plantation work rather than exploited for their milk or meat. The herd peaked at about 200,000 in 1820 but suffered long-term decline until returning to the same size in the 1930s. By the end of the 1960s numbers had grown to 250,000 and peaked again at 460,000 in 1992 before declining once more. Slaughter rates increased

Jamaica Hope

Jamaica Brahman

Jamaica Red

Jamaica Black

Stomach

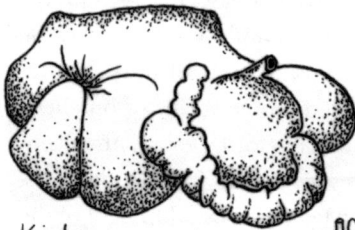

Foot

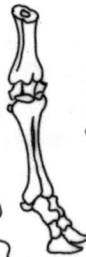

Muscles

Kidney

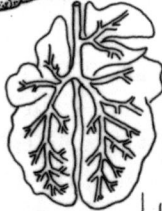

Lungs

Fat   Blood vessel

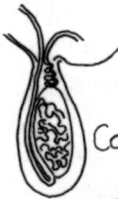

Cod

Muscle

Muscle fibre   Tendon

Tongue

Head

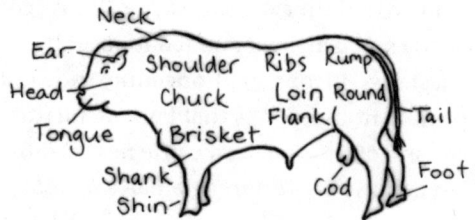

Neck

Ear   Shoulder   Ribs   Rump
Head   Chuck   Loin   Round
Tongue   Brisket   Flank   Tail
    Shank   Cod   Foot
    Shin

Figure 10.1 Cow breeds and anatomy

throughout the twentieth century, especially in the 1950s, as more of the herd were sent to the beef market rather than to the field.[22]

The size of the milking herd is even harder to estimate, particularly because of the multiple uses of cattle. It is equally difficult to assess the output of milk and butter. Beginning in the seventeenth century, a small number of plantations had their own dairies where cream and butter were made, but most plantations probably simply milked a cow or two for daily use, without bothering to separate the cream or to make butter. Edward Ward claimed in 1700 that milk was plentiful in Jamaica but cream scarce and locally made butter impossible to find. It was sometimes complained that the cows gave little milk and this was "often poor and waterish". But by the early twentieth century, with the breeding of the Jamaica Hope barely begun, it was argued that "the milk of the Jamaica cow compares favourably with that of imported animals", and the "fat of milk" higher than in temperate countries.[23]

Cow's milk, like all milk, is mostly water. The next most important component is lactose, which accounts for about 5 per cent by weight, and fat and protein at roughly 4 per cent each. Milk is colloidal, meaning that the sugar, salts and other proteins effectively float independently. This characteristic is important to the potentials for processing, as can be seen when milk curdles or when the cream rises to the top. When the cream is removed, the result is skimmed milk, with a lower fat content. More important for the Jamaican food system in the long run was the development of "concentrated liquid milk", in both its evaporated and condensed forms, and dried powdered milk. These processes, invented in the nineteenth century, meant that milk products could be imported and simultaneously gave it a greatly extended useful life.

Both evaporated and condensed milk are made by boiling milk at a low temperature in a vacuum, so that most of the water is driven off. To make evaporated milk, the resulting thick liquid is sterilized by exposure to heat. Condensed milk is not sterilized but is preserved by mixing it with sugar. The distinctive tastes of evaporated and condensed milk result from these different treatments. Both evaporated and condensed milk were first sold in metal cans, as was thick cream, and the innovations in processing depended on the invention of effective canning. Evaporated milk lasted no longer than fresh milk once the can was opened, but it could be mixed with an equal quantity of water for household use. A further invention, based on technological developments of the early twentieth century, enabled the emergence of a powdered dried-milk industry. Powdered milk, made by spraying skimmed milk into a drum filled with hot air, acquires a somewhat unpleasant taste because the flavour is altered by oxidation and the heat applied. All of these products could be marketed over long distances, because of their keeping qualities, in contrast to localized markets for fresh milk.

Not much is known of the drinking of fresh milk in Jamaica before the twentieth century. In some societies, milk has never been part of the adult diet and has been regarded with disgust, as in East Asia and Southeast Asia. But most of the African, Indian and European peoples of Jamaica came from agro-pastoral societies with experience drinking animal milk, including the milk of the cow. For most Indians, the "sacred cow" was indeed recognized primarily as a giver of milk, and Tadeusz Lewicki argues that milk was "a widely popular drink" in West Africa before 1400, taken from cow, camel, goat and sheep, though used more often sour than fresh. John Dovaston in 1774 said herdsmen on Jamaican plantations had to be vigilant because "Negroes are very apt to milk the cows at night which robs the calf of its milk".[24] This suggests a continued enthusiasm.

Cow's milk became the centre of attention in the 1920s when it was promoted by nutritionists as "the most nearly perfect food". *Jamaica Public Health* described milk in 1928 as "our most important food", containing all the elements needed to build the body and easily digested. Two years later the magazine declared milk "a perfect food for children and if used with fruits, leafy vegetables, and cereals it becomes a perfect food for all ages". The problem was that Jamaica lacked "an adequate supply of fresh milk *produced under sanitary conditions which would enable it to be used in its fresh state*". Pasteurization was advocated, but "prolonged boiling, such as is carried out at many Jamaica homes, is not necessary to destroy any disease germs which may be in the milk, and such boiling certainly decreases the value of the milk as a food". Many boiled it, for fear of tuberculosis.[25]

By 1933 there were seven dairies in Kingston, twenty-two milk shops, twelve people selling liquid milk from their residences, forty-nine street vendors and eighty-one vehicles used to distribute bottled milk within the city. Milk came to Kingston by the early train from Kendal, Old Harbour, Bushy Park, Spanish Town, Ewarton and Bog Walk. Each week an inspector went to the railway station to test every can of milk. The standard was considered very high. Much of the product was, however, unprocessed raw milk, sold from open cans by vendors on the streets. A study concluded in 1955 that efforts towards pasteurization remained largely ineffective and that "milk reaching the retail market in Kingston is grossly contaminated and often unsafe for consumption without boiling by the housewife". In spite of these hazards, milk was a popular street drink. For a different market, Ovaltine was promoted by the 1930s as ensuring "sleep that is completely refreshing and restorative" or, mixed in a tumbler of cold milk with an egg and shaken, "a creamy delicious drink, wonderfully invigorating on a hot day". Roots versions included Yeast Punch, made of milk, yeast, egg, sugar, rosewater or vanilla, and cinnamon or nutmeg, left to ferment overnight and frothed up before serving. This brew, along with fresh milk and ginger, was the popular street drink of the 1930s, before it was overtaken by cheap aerated sweet drinks in bottles.[26]

In modern Jamaica, most fluid milk is pasteurized, whole or reconstituted. Cremo milk, for example, was promoted in 1968 as "homogenized, pasteurized and intensified with vitamins, minerals and proteins". Sold in cartons, "cool, farm-fresh cow's milk [was] the 'in' drink". When the Schools Feeding Programme commenced in 1973, it began by distributing subsidized milk in half-pint boxes, but by 1985 there was a shift to plastic pouches, filled with Nuff brand whole milk. Supermarkets and shops sold milk in relatively large containers and also tried plastic bags, but problems with spoilage (and leakage) persisted. Smaller cartons (generally pints) were sold by street vendors, operating from stands, bikes or pushcarts, and consumed on the street.[27]

Fresh cow's milk was always a local product, never imported. As a fluid drink, its most direct competitor was powdered, dried milk, but the rivalry did not become intense until the 1980s. The advantages of dried milk were that it could be stored and used in small quantities, without refrigeration, and could be diluted in whatever proportion the household could best afford. Early versions of dried milk had not been successful because they used unskimmed milk to produce powdered whole milk that had a bad taste. To overcome this disadvantage, it was generally combined with other materials. This gave rise to products such as malted milk, first promoted in Jamaica in 1889 as an ideal food for infants, invalids, travellers and the aged, being "prepared from very pure fresh cow's milk, combined with the extract of selected wheat and malted barley in a *dry powdered form*". This "*perfect substitute for mother's milk*" *was marketed in 1900* as Horlick's Malted Milk, a food specially for infants and nursing mothers.[28]

Dried skimmed milk gained rapidly in importance as an import between 1950 and 1975, at which point it levelled off and declined (Figure 10.2). Deregulation of the market for milk solids in 1985 had an impact, but in the following year a locally produced powder, Readi-Milk, was introduced in small packets. The government attempted to limit the effects of cheap imported, subsidized milk solids by controlling prices, requiring that all milk sold in quart-size or larger containers be 100 per cent whole milk and restricting the retail sale of powdered milk to small packets. But in spite of these efforts, the Jamaican dairy industry suffered much pain, both as a direct result of competition with the imported powder and because of competition between newly established local milk companies, including Cremo, Dairy Farmers, Shaw Park Dairies and the short-lived Cornwall Dairies. Much of the fresh milk sold by shops spoiled quickly and came to be left on the shelves, alongside growing acceptance of powdered and "long life" or UHT (ultra high temperature) milk.[29]

By the early 1990s Jamaica was importing more than 80 per cent of its dairy products, in skimmed milk powder, cheese, butter and butter oil. Although local full-cream milk was promoted, skimmed milk powder was also recommended as a "nutritious substitute" with the advantages of cheapness and long shelf life, and "being readily convertible to full cream milk by adding water and butter, margarine or oil". Increases in the price of "boxed" fresh liquid milk and the problem of spoilage led to widespread adoption of powdered milk. Efforts to promote the natural, local product continued, in spite of these difficulties. Thus in 1990 Cremo introduced a new boxed product: "2% low fat cow's milk", homogenized, pasteurized and enriched with vitamins A and D. "Nature's best made better", it was rich in protein and calcium, with "no milk powder added, so you taste the flavour of fresh milk but with less fat". Ultimately, the switch to powdered milk affected not only the fresh product, but also tinned evaporated and condensed milks, and children grew to prefer the taste through familiarity. Jamaican dairies

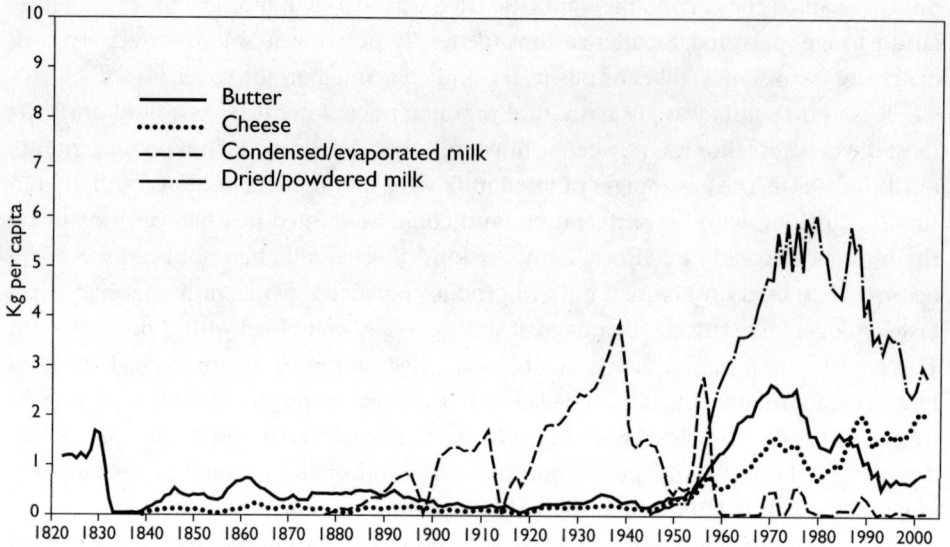

Figure 10.2 Imports of dairy products per capita, 1822–2005. Source: Appendix 1.

produced powdered milk but faced overwhelming competition from skimmed milk powder dumped by the European Union.[30]

On top of these difficulties of competition and substitution, the message of nutritionists in Jamaica and elsewhere had shifted massively by the 1990s, from advocacy of milk as the perfect food to warning of the hazards of cow's milk, particularly for the lactase-deficient, and including advice that "whole milk should be used if at all, in moderation after reaching adult life". The news was perhaps worse for Jamaicans than other peoples, because deficiency in the enzyme lactase (which breaks down the milk sugar or lactose components in milk) is reportedly common among those of African descent, though not as common as in the non-milk-drinking cultures of East Asia. Lactose-intolerant people are unable to digest milk, and suffer gas, flatulence, cramps and diarrhoea when they drink too much, effects well recognized by Jamaicans. Thus the human consumption of the milk of animals came to be considered both unnecessary and unnatural, and even actually harmful. In 2006 a proposal was brought before the Parliament of Jamaica calling for milk to be declared not fit for human consumption.[31]

Before the mixed messages of twentieth-century nutritionists, and before competition from powdered milk, the Jamaican dairy industry had to confront the earlier versions of processed milk in its condensed and evaporated forms (Figure 10.2). Rather than attempting to replicate pure, fresh cow's milk, the condensed and evaporated versions were fundamentally transformed products, as intended by their technologies of processing. Developments in condensing technology in the 1850s led to the establishment in 1865 of the Anglo-Swiss Condensed Milk Company, and tinned milk appeared in Jamaica the same year, a month after the Morant Bay Rebellion. Other brands, such as Borden's, quickly entered the market. Condensed milk was relatively expensive at first: Anglo-Swiss condensed milk sold for nine pence a tin in Jamaica in 1880. Anglo-Swiss declared its product "pure" and "superior in quality, more economical in use, and of a rich creamy colour, in contrast with the chalky appearance of so many condensed milks in the world. It is therefore invaluable infant's food and for all purposes when genuine milk is required." In 1880 a Kingston merchant advertised that he had received a case of Nestlé's Milk Food for Infants, saying it needed "neither milk nor sugar in its preparation it is simply made by boiling with water". He also had a case of Savory and Moore's Food for Infants, "the most preferred substitute for Mothers Milk".[32]

Condensed milk was greeted with enthusiasm in Jamaica, finding there a natural home, especially once prices began to fall. By 1890 some held the view that "it is too late to begin to develop our milk resources, because condensed milk now occupies the field, and that article at 6d a tin is so cheap, and it serves so many purposes that at 6d a quart penkeepers need not hope to effect large sales". If Jamaica was "really a milk country", though, it might make its own condensed milk and perhaps have enough to export. This idea took fifty years to come to fruition. In the meantime, a variety of tinned milks were imported. In 1900, Ideal Milk was advertised as "a perfect substitute for fresh milk", being sterilized rather than sweetened, and enriched with 20 per cent cream. Nestlé's Swiss Milk claimed to be the richest in cream and "an absolutely pure article retaining all the nutritive qualities of fresh milk". Milkmaid declared itself the world's leading seller, delivering full cream.[33]

In 1914 it was claimed that tropical cow's milk was less rich in butterfat than that of the cold-climate cow and that Jamaican milk had to be boiled to be made safe to drink. Thus, "it is therefore quite obvious that tropical milk should not be used when a good condensed milk may be had". But dependence on imported milk made consumers vulnerable, and during World War I the urban poor found it hard to afford milk for their children, at "nearly a shilling a tin". By the early 1930s, there were renewed calls for Jamaica to establish its own condensery. A representative of Messrs Henri Nestle and Company came to Jamaica in 1933 and inspected the potential supply regions in the middle and western parishes, but the amount of raw milk that could be guaranteed by contract proved insufficient, and the decision to establish a condensery was postponed. Nutritionists sometimes opposed the objective. Two months before the labour disturbances of 1938, Dr W.E. McCulloch argued that the government should rather seek to increase the supply of fresh, clean milk and to reduce the use of imported evaporated milk by gradually cutting the entry quota, with "condensed sweetened milk being the first to be quoted out of existence".[34]

Others defended condensed milk, and in the long run their view was to hold sway. In 1938 W.E.O. Turvill responded to McCulloch, saying that because sweetened condensed milk was not sterilized but simply condensed in a vacuum at a low temperature, it preserved the vitamins A, B and C, and had been "widely used for infant feeding for many years with success". Only a few of Jamaica's dairies were capable of preventing the contamination of their fresh milk, so "sweetened condensed milk is a godsend to the community". Even if fresh milk were freely available, it was argued the poor had no way of keeping it, because "they cannot afford ice boxes and must consume it at once or run the risk of it going sour". Sweetened condensed milk, on the other hand, could last for "many days". McCulloch saw a problem for "food habits": "By using a highly sweetened milk we continue to educate the children of this island to develop a taste for a sweetened milk, and they form a definite dislike to fresh cow's milk." He complained that sweetened condensed milk was 16 per cent sugar, and indeed the proportion was often substantially higher, with up to 45 per cent in "ordinary refined sugar" in the 1930s. By the 1990s it reached as much as 60 per cent. The sugar helped to preserve the milk, even after opening, when the evaporated variety deteriorated.[35]

Jamaica did eventually make its own condensed milk. The Bybrook Condensery, operated by the Jamaica Milk Products Company Limited, opened for business at Bog Walk in 1940 and was soon supplying one-third of the island's demand, under the brands Nestlé's, Betty, Dairy Queen and Schoolboy. In 1941 Bybrook was making eight thousand cases of condensed milk each month, and importing another three thousand from Canada.[36] By the 1950s, much milk was being processed and a small proportion of the condensed milk that was made was exported. It was now accepted that "condensed milk is not regarded as a very good substitute for fresh milk for all purposes, because of the large amount of sugar it contains, nevertheless, it is widely used in Jamaica". The big attraction was that the milk could keep without refrigeration for several days after the tin had been opened, preferably stored in a clean glass bottle. Expansion of the Bybrook plant began in 1961. For the following decades, local output ruled the market, using both fresh and powdered milk, and catered to local taste. Only occasionally were consumers encouraged to make their own, using skimmed milk powder. Even Rastafarians sometimes allowed the use of sweetened evaporated milk, though only as a substitute when coconut milk was unobtainable, the latter being "more Ital".[37]

Deregulation of the trade in milk solids in 1985 had significant implications for production. Imported condensed milk, first from Holland, appeared in supermarkets and competed with local condensed milk. Jamaica Milk Products was required by law to collect and process the milk of local dairy farmers. Nestlé's brand condensed milk was made from this fresh milk (together with imported milk solids – skimmed milk powder and butterfat), and defined as full cream, while the company's Betty brand was half cream. But Jamaican taste had been firmly established, and in the early 1990s there were complaints that condensed milk was not as thick as in former days and that it took more spoonfuls to sweeten a cup of tea. When a new plant was built at Bog Walk in 1991, changes were made to increase the viscosity of its condensed milk in order to satisfy this taste. The condensed milk was produced from fresh milk (or a combination with milk powder) and butterfat combined with sugar, in a 30:40 ratio.[38]

By 1988 a corporate recipe book could confidently declare that "Nestle Sweetened Condensed Milk is truly a part of the daily lives of just about every Jamaican household". It was used to sweeten tea and coffee, in Milo and other cold beverages, and for so many other things that it was "a can of magic". As Enid Donaldson opined in 1993, "Jamaicans have developed a taste for sweetened condensed milk and use it instead of sugar wherever milk and sugar can be used". Earlier, in 1938 Kenneth Pringle, an Englishman travelling in the Blue Mountains, had observed that Jamaicans liked tea made into "a sweet-sick mulch . . . with condensed milk and sugar". A contemporary advertisement for Nestlé's Sweetened Condensed Milk promoted its use as a childrens' party treat, "spread nice and thick on thin slices of bread". This was "milk at its creamiest, milk at its cleanest, milk at its safest and best". During World War II, condensed milk was called "the staple article of diet for our babies".[39]

Although sweetened condensed milk came to contain more sugar than milk, it remained a fluid "milk", as did evaporated milk and skimmed milk powder. More fundamentally transformed by-products of cow's milk were butter, cheese and ice cream. Butter and cheese were imported over a long period, whereas ice cream, a relatively recent invention, was generally produced locally. Before refrigeration, the long-distance transport of these commodities often meant poor quality.

In 1774, Edward Long disparaged the "abominable rancid butter imported hither from Europe". As noted in chapter 6, he encouraged Jamaicans to use wangla oil in place of imported butter and olive oil. "Nothing but the grossest prejudice, in favour of old habits", he wrote, "can influence the inhabitants to persevere in the importation of that unwholesome, nauseous stuff, and to swallow it every day with their food, when they may supply themselves with so fine, nourishing, and wholesome an oil, as the sesamum, for an ingredient in their pastry". Long returned to this theme in 1784, after American independence had interrupted trade, saying, "The Irish butter which comes to the West Indies between the months of April and October, is generally liquefied into a rancid oil, more disgusting, if possible, than blubber; which none of mankind, except the Esquimaux savages, would swallow by choice."[40]

Imported salted butter proved too salty for some tastes and, down to the end of the nineteenth century, was washed in water with a squeeze of lime juice or in milk. Canning created new possibilities, but how to store the butter once the tin was opened remained a problem; cans neither displaced other kinds of containers nor survived as a long-term solution. In the 1880s, Irish butter came "specially prepared for hot climates in hermetically closed tins of all sizes, in small kegs, and firkins". Butter also came in glass bottles. Demand for fresh butter increased after 1900 and improved creameries were built, but down to the 1930s these were unable to fully supply the market. Penkeepers complained of the increasing import of New Zealand butter, but this quickly came to dominate, driving out Canadian butter.[41] Per capita, consumption of imported butter peaked around 1970 (Figure 10.2).

Locally made butter also had to compete with an increasing number of butter substitutes. In 1939 there were advertisements for Daisy Butterine, a "new, wholesome, nourishing bread spread, always so fresh and sweet" and "chockfull of health-giving vitamins". It "put pep into your step". Margarine was by then common, some of it produced in Jamaica. It was claimed later that "when margarine was imported it was salted especially to satisfy the Jamaican taste". Margarine had begun to enter the island in the early twentieth century, but the supply was interrupted by World War I. In 1920 margarine in tins was again imported to "pre-war standards", the Omnibus brand being "prepared specially for the West Indian market".[42] There was a distinct Jamaican taste (salty) when it came to butter just as there was a Jamaican taste (sweet) in condensed milk. The same applied to cheese, even though it too was rarely manufactured in Jamaica from Jamaican ingredients.

In spite of a failure to produce cheese locally from local milk, and despite the island's long dependence on imports, a "Jamaican cheese" did eventually emerge. This was a processed cheese, created in the 1980s from mostly imported materials. Previously, the market had been dominated by English varieties such as Cheddar, Cheshire and Gloucester, and by American cheese.[43] When Dairy Industries (Jamaica) Limited brought Irish experts to the island in 1985, the initial objective was to develop "natural cheeses" (feta and cheddar) using the milk of Jamaican cows and goats. Samples were produced and sold, but the enterprise did not prosper. So Dairy Industries – a company jointly owned by the New Zealand Dairy Board and Jamaican wholesalers – set about creating a cheese to their own recipe. By 1986 Jamaicans had their "very own cheese", its firm texture that of a processed cheese, and much in demand by Jamaicans overseas.[44]

In 1988 Dairy Industries imported butter and cheese in bulk from New Zealand and, to a lesser extent, from the United States. Most of the imported cheese was processed and packed into 5-pound (2.3-kilogram) tins. Much advertising was undertaken to promote the consumption of cheese, a *Jamaican Cheese Cookbook* published, and an annual Cheese Month instituted. Consumption increased steadily to reach 2 kilograms per capita per annum by 2005 (Figure 10.2).

Jamaica's "tin cheese" was popular in the island and equally sought after by Jamaicans abroad. Its capacity to survive outside refrigeration was an important element of this popularity, proved, for example, immediately after Hurricane Gilbert in 1988, but its salty taste was also appreciated, along with the rich orange colour.[45] This was the cheese of (Jamaican) bun and cheese: "Every bun have him cheese, every hoe have him stick a bush."

Jamaican ice cream was less successful in developing a unique Jamaican taste. An invention of the seventeenth and eighteenth centuries, ice cream long remained confined to exclusive caterers and dependent on a ready supply of industrial ice to make it a viable product in the tropics. It was first sold in 1866 at the Family Grocery on King Street, in Kingston, established "after the style of similar houses in the United States", with an upstairs "ice cream and refreshment saloon" for families. The Family Grocery also served cakes, calf feet jelly and iced syrups but no intoxicating drinks. By 1869 freezers were available that could make ice cream in ten minutes, but it remained uncommon until Kingston got its first ice factory.[46] Soon after, in 1873, Charles Rampini saw men at night in Kingston "with little glass models of houses brilliantly illuminated on their heads", selling ice cream, "a luxury which, strange to say, is to be got in this burning land at no other hour of the day". In 1890 ice cream was the leading attraction at Gardner's Luncheon and Refreshment Room in Kingston, and Señor Juan Rondon opened an Ice Cream Palace, with a machine capable of freezing one hundred quarts per hour to make "ices of every conceivable description". In 1900 a Kingston firm of confectioners made "ices" from "pure cows milk, fresh every morning".[47]

In 1938 the "fudgicle" was advertised as a "new delicious ice cream on a stick", being sold by roving vendors as well as at the Dixie Doodle Luncheonette, where another innovation, the "banana smoothee", could also be obtained. Previously a luxury, by 1940 ice cream was "eaten by everyone" and "a prime favourite". The advent of the domestic refrigerator made possible simple versions of ice-cream making – particularly after 1945, when "ready mixes" came on the market – and these ice creams were sometimes mixed with fresh or canned fruit. Some families persisted with the hand-turned ice-cream churn down to Independence. After 1950, "Fudgie" the ice-cream seller *roamed the streets on a bicycle or a motorbike, selling ice-cream cake, fudge, nutty buddy, zooper dooper and scoops*, but by the 1980s he faced increasing competition from ice-cream parlours and outlets in malls and centres of entertainment, including Devon House, with its many fruity flavours. Supermarkets sold pans of ice cream, often made from skimmed milk powder. Some flavours were novelties, but others persisted over the long term. Cremo offered rum and raisin as early as 1942, as well as chocolate, cherry and grapenut, and, less resiliently, custard and pineapple. In 1991 Cremo introduced a new line of frozen snacks, including "chocolate caramel fudge, fruit flavoured icicle, twin flavoured ice-cream, ice-cream sandwich, and nut covered ice-cream cone". Some of these matched long-standing favourites, while others foreshadowed competition from multinationals. Häagen-Dazs and Baskin-Robbins – "the world's largest ice-cream franchise" – established themselves in Jamaica in 2005 and brought to the island "exotic flavours" such as Macadamia Brittle and Belgian Chocolate. The following year, Devon House released "stout ice cream".[48]

Whereas milk and its by-products came from the living, lactating, calf-bearing cow, the other food uses of cattle involved slaughter. In Jamaica the flesh of the cow is commonly called "beef", though some lesser parts of the animal are subsumed under older terms that refer directly to the animal, as in "cow head", "cowfoot", "cowskin" or "ox skin", and "cow tail" or "oxtail". A few parts fall ambiguously between these two classes, notably the tongue and the liver, for which "beef", "cow", "bullock" and "ox" (this last, strictly, the castrated adult male) may be interchangeable labels. Apart from the contents of the intestines, the large bones and teeth, and the hair, almost all parts of the cow were thought to be edible and were used in some way (Figure 10.1). This was one of the attractions of the cow as a food animal for humans, its large size and high monetary value being matched by the maximum extraction of edible skeletal muscle tissue.

A full-grown cow weighs as much as five or six men, which was true even when cattle were smaller and less determinedly bred for their meat. To kill and butcher so large an animal requires an equal or larger number of strong men and substantial technologies. In 1961 the average weight of animals killed in Jamaica for beef and veal was 194 kilograms; by 2005 this had increased to 223 kilograms. A three- or four-year-old steer weighs twice as much. The result is that the killing of cattle has almost always been a formal and structured process, something beyond the capacity of the typical household or cook. Beginning in the seventeenth century, many of Jamaica's livestock pens had their own butcheries, even when they lacked dairies and creameries. Once a cow was penned, it could be shot, its throat cut and its body hauled up to bleed. Small settlers and farmers occasionally had facilities, but by the later nineteenth century the slaughter of cattle had shifted largely to public abattoirs and public markets. Well into the twentieth century, some of the animals slaughtered for meat were not inspected by officials for disease and healthiness, and were sold instead around the countryside to "the unsuspecting peasant".[49]

In Kingston, public slaughterhouses were established relatively early. But it was complained in 1914, for example, that in spite of improvements in recent years, carcasses (strictly, the portion left after removal of head, feet, hide, tail and viscera) were put on sale in the markets and butcher's shops of Kingston at 6 a.m., the animals having been slaughtered only three hours before – insufficient time for the blood heat and watery matter to drain off. It was argued that slaughter should take place the night before so that the carcasses could be hung for twelve hours before sale. In 1918 an order was issued requiring Jamaicans slaughtering cattle, sheep, goats and pigs for public sale to obtain a written licence from an inspector of police.[50]

Refrigeration made possible the more effective storage of slaughtered animals, stretching supply to better match demand. In 1918 the West India Cold Storage plant in Kingston was remodelled and "arranged for the constant supply of the very best in beef, mutton, pork, veal, fish and poultry that can be secured in this island". The beef was to come from finest imported strains, reared on the leading pens. In 1933 a cold storage plant was erected in Kingston by the Moneague Butchery.[51]

Freezing technologies had a larger impact, making possible the import of fresh meat slaughtered in other countries. Down to World War I, imports of frozen beef remained small, most from Canada. But in the early 1930s, during the Depression, supply exceeded demand. Imports had increased rapidly, making it "almost impossible for penkeepers to dispose of butchers' stock". With large numbers of fat stock on their hands, penkeepers were forced "to employ men to kill some of their steers weekly, and send the meat to market, to be sold at threepence per lb.", bringing them into competition with the butchers who usually purchased animals from them. Penkeepers complained that for fresh beef, there was "always the competition of the salted fishes upon which the Jamaicans have been reared for the last two hundred and fifty years" and for which they retained a strong taste. There was, however, the hope that cheaper beef could change the pattern of demand. The Saturday glut of beef that followed from the tradi-tional killing of cows on Fridays meant the availability of cheap bones, contributing to the dominance of "Saturday soup" on Jamaican tables. This tradition remains strong in spite of changes in the availability of beef and bones.[52]

By the 1980s, large-scale processing plants had become more common, some of them operated by the owners of feedlots. For example, Content Agricultural Products took over a plant formerly operated by Garo in Bog Walk. Cattle were transported to the plant by truck, rested overnight, then were led through a race to a pen where they were shot in the skull with a stunning pistol. The animals were hoisted by the hind legs and bled to death (within five minutes) by severing the large blood vessels of the throat, without cutting the windpipe or spinal column. The head was cut off, the carcass skinned and the viscera, heart, liver, kidney, tongue, suet, lungs, intestines, stomach and feet removed. The carcass was split vertically using an electric saw, the halves washed and trimmed, and the spinal column removed. The hanging halves of the carcass, as well as the parts removed, were inspected by a government official for authorization as fit *for human consumption. The sides of beef were then hung from rails in a cool room* for up to three weeks, awaiting delivery. In the 1990s, only licensed butchers could kill large animals for human consumption, and they had to have "a suitable slaughtering place as prescribed by the Public Health Department". All parts of the slaughtered animal, including head, skin and internal organs, had to be inspected and declared fit before they left the slaughter place, and they were inspected again on reaching market. Fears have recently emerged regarding the safety of beef, resulting directly from a resurgence of so-called mad cow disease, first diagnosed in the United Kingdom in 1986 and problematically associated with bovine spongiform encephalosis and Creutzfeldt-Jakob disease. Sales of local beef were down about one-third in early 2001 and levels of imported bully beef also declined. Jamaican consumers were assured that the local herd was free of disease, but the following year a Jamaican (formerly resident in the United Kingdom) was identified as the first US victim of mad cow disease.[53]

Special methods of slaughter, such as those following kosher and halal rules, seem to have been rarely practised in Jamaica. Down to the early twentieth century, however, the Jewish community in Kingston had a *shochet*, or ritual slaughterer, and kosher meat was sold at the Victoria Market. But most of the kosher beef, sausage and smoked tongue available in the island was imported, and sold along with kosher butter, kosher cheese and matzos. In the later twentieth century, less was imported and the Jewish community of Jamaica came to be fairly relaxed about the meats they ate.[54]

What was different about the Jamaican butcher, said Caroline Sullivan in her 1893 cookbook, was that all cuts were sold at a standard price, the bone included along with the flesh. Thus as much as half of a parcel of meat might be made up of "'weigh-meat' or large pieces of bone". This was a long-standing complaint. A 1681 law setting the maximum prices that could be charged for beef, as well as for mutton and pork, stipulated that the meat was to be weighed "without the head, entrails, or feet", and that the suet could not be sold at a premium. In 1693 the law was amended to define and distinguish more precisely the parts of slaughtered animals. Prices were set for breast and loin of veal (from the young cow), but still separated the total weight from the "head, entrails, or feet". It also stipulated that "any meat brought to market, and offered, after cut up, to be sold for veal, weighing above twenty-five pounds the quarter, shall be adjudged beef". These distinctions remained important in the long term, determining both price and methods of cooking (Figure 10.1). Thus, 250 years after these laws, when the government set maximum retail prices for beef in 1946 for the Kingston Corporate Area, the animal was classified as follows: fillet (3 shillings per pound [454 grams]); liver (1 shilling 9 pence per pound); tongue (1 shilling 3 pence per pound); sirloin (including undercut), rib roast and rump (1 shilling 2 pence per pound); round, shoulder, leg o'loin, kidney (1 shilling per pound); short ribs, tail, suet and back steak (8 pence per pound); brisket, navel, chuck steak, flank, chuck skin, neck, cross ribs and heart (7 pence per pound); shins (5 pence per pound); feet (1 shilling 6 pence each); and "part of fifth quarter" (head, four feet, stomach, intestines and two ears, 18 shillings).[55]

The term "fifth quarter" first appears in Jamaican texts in the 1930s, in association with the butchering of pigs. It derives from American English, where the hide and tallow of a slaughtered animal were called the fifth quarter by the early nineteenth century. In some cases, the fifth quarter meant the parts of the animal the butcher could dispose of to his own benefit. In English usage from the 1860s, a cow "cut up in the London manner" was classified into five qualities, the fifth class including hock and shin. The phrase fell out of common use in the United States after about 1950, but the English sometimes still adopted it to cover all varieties of "offal". It survived better in Jamaica. Occasionally it was replaced by "pickings", meaning, in the late 1930s, "the odds and ends of the cow, such as bits of the entrails or tripe preserved in such a manner as to become hard and capable of being kept for sometime, parts of the feet, the ears, and so forth, all these tied into a bundle and hawked about the streets at a very insignificant price". By the 1980s the "delicacies" tripe, cow tail and cowfoot were sometimes grouped as the "fifth quarter", without the head and ears.[56]

The relative scarcity of favoured parts from the fifth quarter resulted not only from demand, but also from their natural small proportion to the total weight of a cow. Each cow has only one tongue and one tail, but the weight of beef muscle tissue can be as much as four hundred kilograms, with the result that parts were expensive rather than cheap. There was also the basis for an import trade, the parts favoured by Jamaicans often being far less popular in North America, and desired by Jamaicans rather than simply classified as cheap rejects, like chicken neck and back. In response, butchers sometimes practised their own rationing systems. In the 1960s, when there were about fifteen beef butchers at the Santa Cruz market, "liver and kidneys, trotters and tripe and the popular cow's feet and tails" were "reserved as a special treat for the regular buyers of beef or for those whose meat bill surpasses a certain amount". In the long run, this favouritism was corrected by the market, and the prices of parts increased to come much closer to, or even exceed, the prices of fleshy beef cuts. By the early 1980s, beef prices by weight were highest for oxtail, along with sirloin and T-bone steak ($4.90 per pound), followed in descending order by broad steak, pot roast, chuck steak, shoulder steak, rib steak, shin, stew, cowfoot ($3.30) and soup ($1.40). In the 1990s, cowfoot was imported at a price competitive pound for pound with other meats and little cheaper than the local product. It could be combined with peas, beans or vegetables, or served with rice and peas or yam or any other of the starches. Street kitchens sold "cow head, foot, or skin" just a little more cheaply than stew beef.[57]

Jamaican inclusions changed over time, and the "lesser" parts of the cow were not necessarily spurned by the better-off. On Christmas Eve 1778, Thomas Thistlewood shot a cow and gave his slaves "the head, liver, lights and guts for their supper", and on Christmas Day about 1.6 kilograms each of the flesh and bone, as well as taking some for himself to corn, "as it was good meat". Thistlewood did not mention the tongue or the tail; these more highly valued parts he probably kept for himself. On another occasion, he noted that he had eaten at Sunday dinner "roasted bullock's tongue, very good". *Recipes for cow brains, however, were rare.*[58]

Fresh ox tongue remained a long-term favourite but was matched by preserved, imported products. In the late nineteenth century, Kingston merchants offered a choice of large smoked ox tongues, boneless preserved (cooked) ox tongues, boneless ox tongues in jelly, boneless pickled (cooked) ox tongues, "lunch tongues" and "devilled tongues", all of these imported. As well as tongues, merchants imported ox cheeks and calf's head, calves' feet jelly in assorted flavours and jars of tripe, to appeal to upper-class tastes. Down to the late twentieth century, householders pickled fresh tongues for their own use, but increasingly the tongue was purchased pickled, then boiled and eaten either cold or hot, with a sauce. Enid Donaldson gave a recipe for "pickled cow tongue", the tongue being placed in a brine made of water, brown sugar, saltpetre and salt for three or four days, then boiled, set in a mould and served cold. Oxtail similarly held a high place among the hierarchy of cow parts. The appreciation of oxtail stewed down with beans matched the enjoyment of stew peas, which depended on the pickled tails of pigs.[59]

Liver, kidney, tripe and lights (or "lite") were the main components of cow "guts", the lights coming from the lungs. In 1992 a recipe for "macaroni and lite" was promoted as a wonderful way to stretch a meat dish: the lights were curried until tender, a sufficient sauce was made, and the cooked macaroni added at the very end. "Jamaican-style lite hash" combined the meat with mashed Irish potatoes. Beef liver was not much liked in the 1980s, because of its dark bloody look and its flavour, but it became relatively cheap, imported, the only challenge being overcooking.[60] Kidneys were regarded similarly.

Tripe comes from the first and second divisions of the stomach of the cow (or other ruminant). It could be bought cheaply, in small amounts, and by the late nineteenth century tins of tripe and onions were being imported. Martha Beckwith claimed tripe was "a favorite relish of the people". In 1970 it was promoted as the main ingredient of "freedom dinner", a type of risotto with beans, onion, country pepper, black pepper, curry powder, coconut milk and chicken stock. Canned sweet green beans were suggested as an alternative to broad beans and butter beans in the 1990s.[61] As with many of the dishes prepared from the fifth quarter, appreciation tended to extremes, but none of the elements from the guts were thought positively unhealthy.

Cowfoot came lower in the order and by the 1980s was under attack for its supposed lack of nutritional qualities. Ardent defenders of cowfoot (or "calf's feet") declared that it contained protein and was rich in calcium and phosphorus, and that like tripe it was easily digestible. The criticism encouraged the publication of a substantial number of recipes. Norma Benghiat, in 1985, gave a recipe for cowfoot and broad beans, reducing the foot to a rich gravy and removing the bones. She considered this a "delicious dish" best served with rice, plantain and avocado, and also gave a recipe for cowfoot jelly, "made from the gelatinous stock produced from the boiling of the cow's foot for the preparation of cowfoot and beans". The excess liquid was strained, mixed with sugar, nutmeg, rum, milk and strawberry syrup, then refrigerated to make "a light, delicate jelly". A recipe for "stew cow foot" took meat and skimmings reserved after boiling for three hours, combined it with hot water, black pepper, onion, scallion, thyme, pimento, salt, tomatoes, country pepper and garlic, and boiled this for another hour; cracker crumbs and sliced cucumbers were added to the pot, and it was simmered to produce a rich gravy. An alternative method was to curry the meat, with or without vegetables, peas and dumplings. "Brown stew cow foot" was for those who found it too time-consuming to separate the meat from the bones. In this recipe, the cowfoot was boiled for an hour, the liquid skimmed and the water thrown away. Fresh water was poured on the cowfoot, the fat skimmings returned to the pot, salt added, and the whole cooked until the meat was soft. A gravy was made using the remaining liquid, with onion, marjoram, celery, thyme, black pepper, browning and broad beans, simmering until finished. One 1998 cookbook offered a similar recipe for "cow foot stew", in which butter beans were used and the cowfoot never left the pot during the cooking. A 1988 recipe made "cow heel soup" by boiling the cowfoot, removing the meat from the bone, simmering with onion, celery and root vegetables, and finally adding pumpkin, parsley, lime juice and grated nutmeg. Sugar beans, breadfruit, yam, dasheen and dumplings could replace pumpkin, and MSG, peppers and pimento could be added.[62]

Cowskin was criticized even earlier – and more severely – than cowfoot. In the 1970s it was claimed that cowskin delivered only poor-quality protein. Most people placed it at the bottom of the scale of edible parts of the cow, its only serious rival being cow cod, or testicle, which, used in cow cod soup, remained a favourite though many thought it repulsive. In spite of the criticism directed at it, cowskin too was recognized as a favourite Jamaican food and by the 1980s was gaining in popularity. This "growing dependence" was considered unfortunate, because cowskin contained "nothing nutritious to recommend it". The other problem was that cowskin, although admittedly a local product, needed long cooking and "a good deal of onions and pepper and other seasoning before it begins to take on flavour, and it needs beans to make it worthwhile, nutritionally speaking". Cowskin had the advantage of being relatively cheap, advertised at $3.20 per pound in 1986, compared with cowfoot ($3.90) and shoulder steak ($6.50).[63]

In 1992 a notice published in the *Gleaner* and the *Star* declared, "Of all the countries in the world Jamaica is the only known place where cow skin is eaten abundantly. Cow skins have no nutritional or medicinal value whatsoever. Cow skins are treated with harmful chemicals, like insecticide, which may cause cancer and later death." Callers to the *Gleaner* "complained that cow skin was what poor people could afford and should not be denigrated". Sadie Campbell of the Caribbean Food and Nutrition Institute reported that "the meat primarily produces gelatin, a type of protein which the body utilises poorly" and had no useful minerals or vitamins. It was claimed that Jamaicans chose to eat cowskin because it was cheap, swelled when cooked, and was "tasty", especially when combined with beans, vegetables or dumplings – though it was essentially true that they were unusual in doing so. Although it might lack nutritional value, cowskin was much esteemed when cooked in gungo soup, with coconut milk, dumplings, yam, sweet potato, corned meat, country pepper, scallion and thyme. The cowskin soup sold by street vendors was made from the skin along with cowfoot, bone, water, salt, seasoning, flour dumplings and pieces of yam.[64]

In 1823 Cynric Willams described "a famous mess" of cowskin served in calabashes to young children on an estate, made of "cow or ox hide (the hair of which is first singed off) boiled to a jelly, with yams, cocos, ochro, and other vegetables". A 1970 recipe for cowskin soup used 900 grams of skin, cut into small squares and washed, and boiled with two cups of peas, pig's tail and salt beef, until the peas were cooked. Three pegs of breadfruit were added, along with seasoning made up of scallion, ketchup, onion, black pepper and salt to taste, and it was simmered for a further thirty minutes. Other recipes used yellow yam, coco or Irish potato rather than breadfruit. A 1990 recipe for "red peas and cow skin" began by cooking the skin and peas until nearly tender, when yellow yam, coco, flour dumplings, coconut cream, thyme, scallion and pepper were added, and the whole simmered a further thirty minutes.[65] This recipe was similar to that for cowskin soup as well as to stew peas.

Overall, Jamaicans have devoted more attention to how to cook the fifth quarter of the cow than they have to the fleshy cuts of beef, and even the names of the major cuts have been less familiar. For example, veal, the meat of young calves, became uncommon in the eighteenth century and remained so into the twentieth century. It was argued in the late eighteenth century that the planters preferred a riper age of meat, but the origins of this supposed preference probably have to do with the role of cattle as working animals within the plantation economy. Full-grown animals were too valuable for traction to permit the killing of calves. The notion of a standard price for cow meat (including bone) also discouraged the separation of potentially more expensive cuts. Butchers complained in 1942 that they had to charge a fixed price even for "special cuts" of boneless beef, including "sirloin with fillet, rib roast chimed, leg-o-loin". Although some of the pens produced a top-class "filet steak", it was argued into the 1950s that "the system of marketing in the cities makes it difficult for the buyer to choose the best beef and the very bad methods of butchering make it almost impossible to obtain the best cuts".[66]

How was beef, the fleshy muscle tissue, cooked in Jamaica? Sullivan began her section on "meat" by explaining that she had included no "methods of dressing beef, sheep-mutton, pork or poultry" and implying that Jamaica had nothing to offer that might not be found in a regular English cookbook. Less sympathetic was Esther Chapman, who in 1951 warned English and American people thinking of living in Jamaica that the local cook "will not know how to cook beef". In Jamaica, said Chapman, it was customary to pierce a joint and stuff it with herbs, then rub it with salt and pepper and onion or scallion, and roast it "until all the juices have been successfully destroyed and it resembles a dark greyish-brown mound of leather". This Jamaican preference for well-cooked meats has sometimes been traced to the dominant role of parts in cooking: oxtail, cowfoot, tripe and skin all required many hours on the fire, and it has therefore been argued that "this preference [for well-done meats] goes back to the days of slavery when the slaves ate what was called the 'fifth quarter'". In the 1990s it could be contended that "today, many persons say their favourite is still oxtail etc., but many local restaurants and canteens say the demand is so great, butchers cannot keep up with the orders and it has pushed the price sky high". The preference for well-cooked, well-seasoned meat extends to the freshest, most tender of beef. Modern Jamaican cooks commonly choose to marinate meats overnight, leaving them "to soak in the liquid derived from fresh herbs and spices". Soy or Pickapeppa sauce, garlic and salt are rubbed into the exterior, and the meat may be stuffed with a mixture of garlic, onion, scallion, salt, ginger, Scotch bonnet and black pepper. Oil is applied to lean and dry meats, acid juices to tough joints.[67]

Another reason for desiring well-cooked, well-seasoned beef – and for the complementary fear of bloody rare steaks – can be found in the difficulty of preparing meat in the era before refrigeration. Thus Sloane, who praised Jamaica's beef as "well tasted, and good", observed that "they cannot keep beef past some few days, and that salted, otherwise in three or four hours 'tis ready to corrupt". After the establishment of the plantation economy, and with the general use of cattle for work, beef was more often declared "tough and lean, scarce fit for any thing but soups", though it might be "sweet and savoury" so long as "the animal be not too old and over-wrought".[68]

Most Jamaican meals including fresh beef have used only small amounts. The piece of beef (or pork or mutton) was often set on top a pile of rice, with a sauce of gravy and vegetables, and in consequence the meat was referred to as "the watchman". Writing in 1930, recalling Kingston race meetings of the 1870s, A. Bain Alves described the poorest of the people asking food sellers, "'Please for a quattie rice and peas with a good lively watchman.' The old mother would dip a long iron spoon into a huge yauba pot of rice and peas and put it into a small pudding pan, she would then take her iron spoon and mould up the rice and peas into a small hill on top of that she would put a piece of salt pork that was called the watchman, or look-out. She would then throw over all two spoonfuls of flour sauce."[69] The use of such small amounts applied equally to fresh and pickled beef. In the twentieth century, the expense of beef was solved by mincing the flesh into a mass from which small quantities could be separated and cooked with seasoning or, more often, mixed with a large proportion of other materials to stretch it into a more substantial item. For the manufacturer, there was the opportunity to use scraggly and small off-cuts and to reduce everything to a homogeneous texture and colour. The process could be applied in a variety of ways, for both fresh and corned beef.

By the second half of the twentieth century, the favourite way of eating beef was as spiced mince in a patty, and these tasty pastries became big business. As noted in chapter 6, the Jamaican "patty" was sometimes in terminological difficulty, foreign countries using the word to mean a formed circle of minced beef, such as the filling of a hamburger. The hamburger, however, made only limited inroads in the Jamaican market, unable to overcome the strong defence put up by the patty. The home of the hamburger is Hamburg in Germany, and the hamburger was first, in the 1880s, known as "Hamburg steak". The hamburger as a bun with minced beef in between is a later invention, taking the same name. When a Kingston restaurant offered "hamburgher steak" in 1938, it was eaten with rice and peas. Hamburgers and hot dogs, common-place in the United States by World War I, could be bought in Kingston by the outbreak of World War II, but the hot dog (and particularly the shiny metal machine used to keep frankfurters warm) remained closely associated with Americans visiting the island. The hamburger also followed the American model, using minced beef, but with the idea also that a "burger" could be made from ingredients other than beef, such as the "bean burger" (made of cooked dried beans, cornflakes, onion, egg, ketchup, salt and pepper) described in 1945.[70]

When the American fast food chain Burger King opened its first Jamaican outlet, in Ocho Rios in 1985, it offered three varieties of hamburger. These were the Whopper, a "hefty" double cheeseburger and a "big 'n beefy" bacon double cheeseburger. To make the Whopper, an advertisement explained, "we start with sizzling hot flamed-broiled beef. We add fresh tomato, crispy lettuce, crunchy onion and other tasty fixin's." Burger King's customers could also choose chicken sandwich or the Whaler (a fish filet in a bun). In 1997 Mother's launched a "jerk burger", contending that Jamaicans needed "to give greater value to our culinary skills". The company expected it to be "a big seller, as the taste is familiar to Jamaican consumers". When McDonald's was criticized for not using local beef, Burger King proclaimed it used "100% Jamaican beef", from Content, calling it "the best hamburger meat".[71]

Whereas fresh beef was almost always a relatively expensive option in Jamaica, the salted version was more common and competed directly with saltfish and pickled or fresh fifth quarter. Before the twentieth century, salt beef came mostly in chunks or cuts, rather than minced. In either form, the attraction of salt beef was both the ability to use small amounts for (salt) flavour and its keeping qualities. In the seventeenth century, wild cattle were hunted and jerked or cured as dried meat. In the eighteenth century, salt beef was eaten more often than fresh beef by enslaved people, who used money earned in the markets to purchase small amounts. Most of the salted and pickled beef was imported, much of it from Ireland, and it was sometimes "exceeding coarse". Thistlewood and other planters corned beef with salt, after pressing out the blood, using methods known from England.[72] In the late nineteenth century there were efforts to replace imports with local enterprise. In 1880, for example, Fullerswood Park Butchery advertised its "superior cured beef unsurpassed by the finest American or English, put up in kegs containing 50 lbs and upward and delivered on the wharf at Black River at 6d per lb". A few months later, the Jamaica Institute offered prizes for the best locally salted beef and pork. The 1930s saw efforts to establish a plant in Kingston for the curing and canning of "wet salted beef and pork products", but this was abandoned because of a shortage of cattle. Occasionally, in the 1960s, recipes were offered for home-made "Jamaica corned beef", but these were useful only to those who could afford large cuts of meat.[73]

Corned beef or "bully beef", made by combining roughly minced cooked beef with salt, water, sugar and sodium nitrate, began to arrive in cans at the end of the nineteenth century, often termed "English bully beef". At first, the cans were large – up to three kilograms – and some bully beef continued to come in barrels down to the early twentieth century. The cans got smaller and more affordable – and more popular – by the 1930s.[74] In the 1980s bully beef was declared "surely the most popular and most inexpensive source of protein available to us in the land of high prices". This popularity related to the small-scale packaging, somewhat like the popularity of condensed milk, but the salt taste was equally important. Cold bully beef mixed with onion, tomato sauce and country pepper made a prime filling for hard-dough bread sandwiches. Cooked, it was most often hashed and fried in a pan with seasonings. Other ways of using bully beef were promoted, from curried beef to beef stew, beef pie, and beef and macaroni. More adventurous ideas, proposed by Grace in 1989, included corned beef and chocho, corned beef and ackee, corn and bully beef all-in-one and corned beef quiche. An advertisement for a brand of Brazilian corned beef included a recipe for "Delite Shepherd's Pie" and "Saucy Delite Corned Beef Fritters". In 2003 Lasco corned beef was promoted as the basis of a stew, a pie, a curry, meat balls, a macaroni dish and "corned beef pyramids".[75]

While the taste of beef was less than distinctive for Jamaicans, the notion of reducing it to little more than a flavouring agent persisted into the twentieth century. Products such as Oxo cubes were used to add "delicious beefy flavour" and make meals "much more tasty and appetizing", or to prepare a "stimulating, beefy drink". A 1938 advertisement claimed that Bovril, a similar product, "'steers' you to health". Consumers were encouraged to "add a little Bovril to soups, stews, curries and all savoury dishes" to get full flavour and nourishment, and to be "stronger, fitter and more cheerful".[76]

Another product of the cow was gelatin, the basis of jellies and glues, made by boiling down ligaments, bones and skin into a yellowish, odourless, almost tasteless organic substance that becomes brittle and granular when dry. Gelatin was used to make "jellied bouillon" by blending it with Oxo cubes and boiling water, seasoning with salt and pepper, and allowing it to set with some parsley or a steamed egg in a soup cup. Gelatin was also used, in the 1930s, to make moulded jellied vegetable salads, with condensed soup in jelly and additions such as chicken, eggs, cooked carrots and green peas. These moulds lost popularity, though a new recipe of the 1980s promoted shrimp aspic, made with Lushus lemon-flavoured jelly and with flaked shrimp, orange juice, diced tomatoes, and pepper or mint jelly folded in. When chilled and firm, the aspic was spooned into avocado halves and decorated with parsley and a wedge of lime.[77]

Gelatin became better known as the basis of sweet foods. In 1991 it was recalled nostalgically that "many years ago it was fashionable for women higglers to trod the streets of Kingston peddling cow foot jelly". The favourite flavours were lemon and strawberry, the jelly packed on ice in large shut pans. This local delicacy was supplanted by packaged jelly crystals, beginning in the 1930s. Jell-O brand quickly became a generic term for gelatin in Jamaica. Jell-O was recommended as an accompaniment to afternoon teas. A "supper salad ring" was made by adding salted grapefruit to dissolved Jell-O, chilled until firm, then unmoulded and the centre of the ring filled with tinned tuna, garnished with celery leaves and served with mayonnaise. In 1938 Royal Quick Setting Gelatin, one of Jell-O's competitors, was promoted for use in desserts such as "mango aurora", made simply with Royal Strawberry Gelatin, water and fresh mango.[78]

After World War II, "jello" recipes remained common but were almost always sweet rather than savoury. Most recipes now recommended the mixing of the variously flavoured packaged jelly crystals with hot water (sometimes together with fruit juices or vinegar) and combining with fresh fruit (such as banana or strawberry) or tinned fruit (such as peach, pineapple or fruit salad). These chilled dishes were given names such as "melody fruit cup" and "autumn delight".[79] "Jello" remained a popular dessert for the rest of the twentieth century. Its origins in the cow and the fifth quarter were rarely remembered.

PIG

All domesticated pigs are descended from a wild ancestor, *Sus scrofa*, a native of North Africa. Unlike the cow, the pig was always raised for its meat, and its domestication and breeding were specifically directed at improving the yield and quality of flesh. Pigs reached parts of West-Central Africa before Europeans, but they disappeared from some of those places following the rise of Islam, and they were not always part of the diet of people carried to Jamaica in the slave trade.[80] The Portuguese did, however, introduce pigs to some coastal areas of West Africa.

The pigs brought to Jamaica as food animals by the Spanish quickly joined cattle in becoming feral. When the English took the island, they found an "abundance" of wild pigs. Edmund Hickeringill, writing in 1661, said they were "fat and large" and thrived on fallen fruit. With the animals raised in a "crawle" and fed on corn, claimed Richard Blome, the flesh of the pigs was "far better tasted, more nourishing, and much easier to be digested, than those of Europe; which is the reason why it is so much eaten in this, and indeed all the other islands throughout all the West Indies". Similarly,

Edward Ward said in 1700 that the Jamaican settlers "value themselves greatly upon the sweetness of their pork, which is indeed lushious, but as flabby as the flesh of one just risen from a flux".[81]

Later in the eighteenth century, Charles Leslie declared the meat of Jamaica's pigs "so sweet and delicate, that nothing can equal it". Edward Long particularly praised the "firm, fat flesh" of pigs fed with corn, and declared that "the pork of corn-fed hogs is esteemed the finest in the world for flavour and goodness". He distinguished the wild hog, English hog and Guinea hog, saying, "the tame sorts are very profitable stock to the settler or planter, as they multiply fast, and are kept or fattened with very little trouble". Dovaston believed "the kind generally used, are a dwarf mixture between the wild hog, and the English, which causes the flesh of them to be much sweeter than the English hog". They needed to be penned to keep them out of the canes, said Dovaston, and "their being penned up in a well littered stye, and fed with grass, corn, sugar, offale and the refuse of the kitchen made into wash, will afford you the best kind of muck for your land; besides they fatten up for pork much sooner and better". In the nineteenth century, Jamaica's pigs were declared "far superior in sweetness and delicacy to the British, or North American pork, and can hardly be excelled by any in the world". Wild pigs became relatively uncommon and hunting was restricted largely to the Maroons, who brought some of the meat to market.[82]

Down to Independence, Jamaica's pigs were raised by "small settlers and agricultural labourers, who keep a few head either in a stye or tied by a leg in a small yard". Most were heavily interbred dark-coloured types, the Berkshire being popular (Figure 10.3). The pigs were typically scavengers, fed on surplus food plants and household waste, coco heads and hogmeat vines, and small amounts of compound feeds made from coconut oil, meal and rice bran. Traders travelled around the countryside buying pigs and selling to butchers. Most of the meat produced was sold as fresh pork. Attempts to cure bacon and ham wilted in the face of imports. Large quantities of salted pork and lard were also imported. Local pork was less often praised, and sometimes described as "apt to be very fatty and without much lean flesh". Esther Chapman warned the English visitor that "if you are accustomed to the delicious white loins of, say, Lincolnshire pork, you had better not challenge comparison".[83]

The 1960s saw the establishment of a modern pig industry, paralleling developments in cattle and poultry. Large White, Landrace, Hampshire and Duroc breeds were introduced, and feedlots became the common site of production, using branded compounded feeds prepared in Jamaica from ingredients largely imported from the United States, along with a small amount of local material such as wheat middlings, molasses and coconut oil meal. Marketing was through specialized processing plants, though most of the meat was still sold as fresh pork or entered the jerk pork trade.[84] Small-scale production continued, both in rural and urban areas. Pigs killed for meat increased substantially in weight, from an average of forty kilograms in 1961 to an

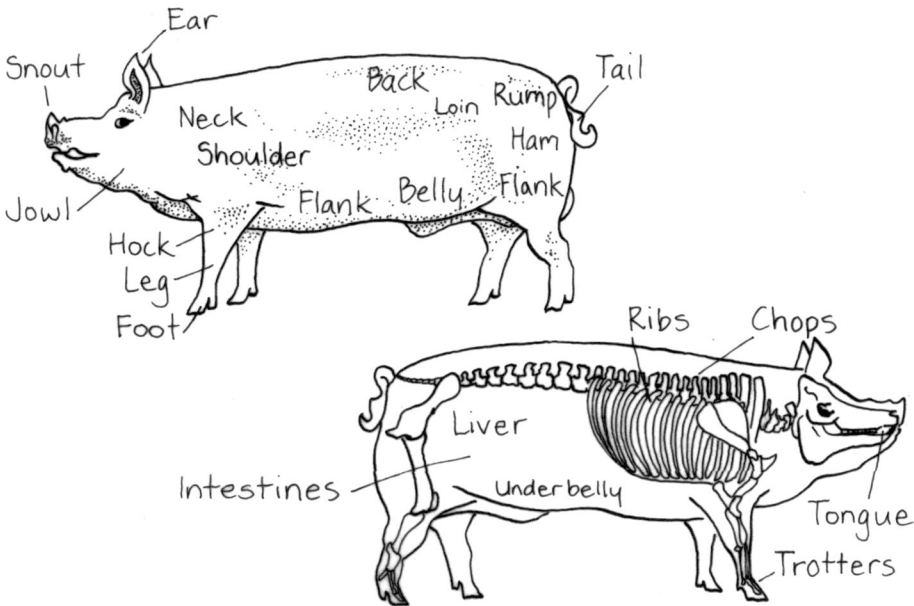

Figure 10.3 Pig anatomy

average of sixty-one kilograms by 2005, a much larger rate of increase than achieved for cattle and equivalent to the increased weight of the chicken over the same period.

Jamaica is closely associated with the development of pig cookery, notably barbecue and jerk. Although "barbecue" is said to be a Taino word, the roasting of animal food by the Taino was in fact limited by the lack of large land animals. It was with the Spanish and their herds of cattle and pigs that roasting came into prominence, and it continued with the English. By 1740, one writer said of Jamaica, "Their pork exceeds that of Europe, and a barbicu of a porker (or, as it is call'd there, a shoot) is a planter's grand entertainment." A wild hog provided "the most delicate barbecue, and the joy and festivity of a feast of that kind is scarce to be equalled in any part of the world". By 1774 Long could claim, "The fame of our Jamaica *barbecue* and brawn is so well established, that it would answer no purpose to reiterate their praises, except to tantalize the reader."[85] By "brawn" Long meant the smoked flesh of the wild boar, rather than the potted and jellied versions that came to dominate after the eighteenth century.

As noted in chapter 1, "barbecue" was used in Jamaica to mean both a method of cooking and a plastered platform on which berries, such as coffee and pimento, could be dried. The word could be applied equally to the structure on which pig meat was cooked. Modern definitions of barbecue as a cooking method emphasize the roasting or broiling of whole animals or parts of them, sometimes stuffed and basted, over a smoky fire. But technologies of barbecue have changed, so what exactly was the method of barbecue in the eighteenth and nineteenth centuries? Close to the modern under-standing of the term, the English traveller Sir Sibbald David Scott stated in 1876, "Barbecue is, I find, a term used in the West Indies for dressing a hog whole, by splitting it to the backbone and laying it upon a large gridiron, raised about two feet above a charcoal fire, with which it is also surrounded." Here the emphasis was on cooking by radiation for immediate consumption. Earlier, in the 1820s, John Stewart had empha-sized the smoke and its aroma, in describing "what is called a *barbecue*, (considered as a great delicacy here, being the hog's flesh smoked with a certain odiferous wood, which communicates to it a peculiar flavour)". Somewhat different again was Matthew Gregory Lewis's account of serving "barbecued pig" to some local gentlemen visiting for dinner; he declared it one of "the best and richest dishes that I have ever tasted". The pig was "dressed in the true maroon fashion, being placed on a barbecue (a frame of wicker-work, through whose interstices the steam can ascend), filled with peppers and spices of the highest flavour, *wrapt in plantain leaves, and then buried in a hole filled with hot* stones, by whose vapour it is baked, no particle of the juice being thus suffered to evaporate". On the other hand, Richard Briggs's 1792 American cookbook offered a recipe for "barbicued pig" that had no Jamaican overtones apart from the use of pimento, and Briggs even thought it acceptable to broil or roast the pig in an oven.[86]

Jerk was closely associated with barbecue, but both the meaning of the word and the process changed. By the early nineteenth century, a distinction was made between "barbecued hog" and "jerked hog".[87] Initially, and down to the middle of the nine-teenth century, "jerking" most often meant smoking and drying to produce a cured meat. This is similar to what is elsewhere called "jerky". The method of jerking practised in Jamaica today, in contrast, does not depend on drying and is not intended as a method of preserving the meat. Smoke is still part of the process, but it is now the seasoning that matters most, and it is this association that makes jerk transportable and even appropriate to the modern urban kitchen.

Early accounts sometimes suggest a simpler process of salting and sun-drying. Sloane, writing of the late seventeenth century, claimed that in this process wild hogs were "cut open, the bones taken out, and the flesh is gash'd on the inside into the skin, fill'd with salt and expos'd to the sun, which is call'd jirking". This meat, said Sloane, was "brought home to their masters by the hunters, and eats much as bacon, if broil'd on coals". According to William Beckford, "the negroes smoak and dry this animal [the pig], from whence the pieces thus smoaked, obtain the appellation of *jirked hog*; and it is, when thus cured, a very savoury and a pleasing relish". This variety of jerk declined: by the 1870s it was believed that "importations of American bacon have driven out of the market the 'jerked hog' of the Maroon".[88] It was quickly replaced by the modern variety, though no doubt there was a period of transition in which the two styles overlapped with one another, and with the barbecue.

Mountain travellers of the late nineteenth century talked of the "very highly flavoured jerked pork". Many continued to refer to jerk as a method of smoke-drying and generally also salting. Herbert Thomas observed the process on his expeditions into the mountains in the 1880s. It began with the construction of

> a gridiron of green sticks about two feet from the ground. This is called about the Blue Mountain a 'patta,' while among the Maroons, and in the Cuna-Cuna district it is known as a 'caban' – a word that has a distinctly Spanish flavour. Underneath this a fire is kindled, into which the carcase is first thrust in order to singe the hair, which is then easily scraped off with a knife. This done, the animal is disembowelled, split open down the back, the bones extracted, and the carcase laid skin downwards upon the sticks and subjected to a slow grilling during which it is plentifully sprinkled with black pepper and salt. This process lasts from six to eight or nine hours, according to the size of the animal. The adding of pimento leaves, or those of the pepper elder to the fire imparts an improved flavour to the meat, which, when properly done, is as gamey and toothsome a dish as a hungry man can desire.[89]

Another account, published in 1893, claimed that jerking involved "a slow grilling over a wood fire, among the embers of which aromatic leaves are cast, while powdered pimento seed and salt are sprinkled upon the meat". This was watched through the night, and when three or four hogs had been prepared, they were carried down from the mountains to the markets. The meat fetched a good price (nine pence or a shilling per pound), and "when properly done it is a most toothsome morsel, and perfectly clean and wholesome, as the food of these wild hogs consists entirely of roots, berries and fruit, and their drink of the purest water". Alan Quartermain defined "jerk" in 1895 simply as "wild hog flesh smoke-cured".[90]

The technology of jerk changed after about 1900. The major change was a shift from the raised platform to cooking nearer ground level. This could be achieved in at least two ways. Among the Maroons, the process continued with a raised platform that was lowered after the fire was reduced to coals. The deboned and gashed meat was rubbed with ground salt, bird peppers and Scotch bonnet peppers, wild cinnamon, pimento and other seasonings. An alternative method was to dig a pit in soil or sand, make a fire in the base and reduce it to glowing coals (Figure 10.4). A rack constructed from green sticks or, increasingly, wire mesh or a metal grate was placed level with the ground, the sticks or grate extending across the pit or set down into it. The latter arrangement was most common when the pit became permanent rather than part of a temporary bush camp, in the Maroon style. The advantage of setting the rack below ground level was that a metal sheet – often galvanized roof metal – could be placed over the whole to contain the heat and smoke. As a result, the meat came closer to the glowing coals and the transfer of radiant heat was more efficient than in the original platform arrangement. In the earlier method, slow cooking at a low temperature was achieved, but much of the smoke was dissipated and blown away. The more permanent versions became known as "jerk pits", and were covered from sun and rain by open-sided shelters.[91]

For most of the twentieth century, jerked pork was considered a specialty of Portland, particularly Boston. In 1964 a recipe entered in the Culinary Arts Finals was titled

Figure 10.4 Jerk technologies

"Boston jerk pork", but the cook was merely instructed to "get" some jerk pork and add this to steamed vegetables. However, "jerk pork men" did sell at Kingston race meetings, at least by the 1930s and probably much earlier, offering "a quattie jerk pork, with bread and mustard". The idea of preparing jerk pork in a domestic kitchen was unknown and impractical. The focus remained on the cooking of a whole pig, its belly cavity rubbed with a mixture of "blood, pepper, pimento seeds, scallion, minced onions and salt", on a stand or "pata" of green pimento sticks over a coal fire. In 1977 the Chelsea Jerk Centre was established in Kingston, and this proved influential in encouraging the spread of jerk pits in the city. The "secret" of jerking was said by some to lie in the process of smoking, while others attributed it to the use of pimento wood or the seasonings employed. Pimento wood became scarce, and by the 1990s the seasoned meat was cooked on grills over hot coals and covered with zinc sheets. No oil was used. Pork took about five hours to jerk.[92]

These commercial developments brought jerk into the mainstream of cooking methods, practised in town as well as in remote rural settings. Gas and electric grills were now used to cook versions of jerk in private homes. These were quicker methods than the earlier open-air versions, closer to high-heat barbecuing than to slow smoking. Rather than a way to preserve the meat, jerk pork became a fast food. By the end of the twentieth century, "jerk" referred more often to the seasoning than to the cooking technology. Bottled or powdered "jerk seasoning" of various brands was marketed without necessarily claiming appropriateness for any particular meat. In 1993 Busha Browne's Walkerswood Jerk Seasoning was described as a "hot, spicy seasoning paste" that would give a barbecue "the most pungent flavour and an absolutely irresistible aroma". Cooks were encouraged to try producing jerked pork at home: pork chops were rubbed with prepared seasoning and oil, lightly salted and left to marinate for several hours, then cooked for ten minutes each side. Boston asserted its priority, establishing in 2000 the Boston Jerk Festival, and by 2005 bottled Boston Jerk Seasoning competed with other, longer-established brands.[93]

Jerk and barbecue were not the only cooking methods used for the pig. Closely related was roasting, particularly of suckling pigs, served whole. Berrisford Clarke, a Lambs River, Westmoreland, specialist pig-roaster with his own brick oven, explained the process in 1996: "First you kill the pig, scrape it and remove the belly. Mash up the *bones in the back, then scald it in a big copper pot with pepper and salt. You then take* it out and let it drain. Then I season it up stuff it with rice or irish potato or banana. . . . You now put it in a oven to roast."[94]

The fifth quarter of the pig was also highly regarded. Until recent times, jerk and barbecue were chiefly the pleasures of the wealthy and of Maroon hunters. In these methods of cookery, and in roasting, it is the whole hog that is generally used, including the more expensive fleshy parts of the animal. Even the Maroons, hunting in the woods, sometimes discarded the fifth quarter as too difficult. Here the expression "living high on the hog" makes sense, indicating the capacity to purchase and consume the meat from the upper part of the body and to reject the trotters and underbelly. Where an individual could afford to purchase an entire pig – even a small one for a special occasion – all of the parts might be given prominence in a meal, but those who could afford only parts were more likely to end up with the least fleshy cuts. Legislation in the 1680s and 1690s stipulated that pigs (like cattle) should be sold by weight but separating the "head, entrails, or feet". In 1946 the government set maximum retail prices for pork, in Kingston, as follows: shoulders, chops, legs, liver (ten pence per pound), stew and lard (eight pence), and head and trotters (seven pence). Outside Kingston, all cuts and lard were sold for a standard eight pence per pound.[95] As in the case of the cow, the choices did not always fall out simply, so that for some head and feet were sought after delicacies.

The head of the pig was sometimes used to make jellied brawn, but was more often stewed. Thistlewood served at a 1768 dinner, among other things, "stewed hog's head", "fried liver" and a "quarter of roast pork with paw paw sauce". Recipes for "pig's head stew" still appeared in newspapers in the 1980s, as a "down-to-earth, rib-sticking" dish ideal for serving the throng on Labour Day.[96] The tail, pickled, is a vital ingredient of stew peas.

Pig's feet (trotters) were made into soup or stewed, and occasionally curried. Jamaicans rarely referred to or made souse – pig's feet and head, pickled in salt and vinegar with limes, peppers and cucumber – though recipes attributed to Barbados or

Antigua were sometimes offered in newspapers and cookbooks from the 1950s to the 1980s.[97] Similarly, black pudding, or blood sausage, was much less popular in Jamaica than in the eastern Caribbean.

More often, the fifth quarter of pig was used pickled, and much of this was imported from overseas. Occasionally, local efforts were made to preserve by pickling rather than jerking or smoking. Dovaston in 1774 said,

> The offal of a hog that is killed in the woods, such as the head feet and intestines; should be sent home; and plunged in a vatt, of well prepared brine made of salt, and salt peter, which will keep good for several days, and become nicely corned. A planters house therefore should always have a good brine vatt, well supply'd with brine that is made by dissolving one part of sea salt, three parts of common salt and a 32nd part of salt petre. . . . The longer this pickle is kept adding now and then more salt of the different kinds to it as it requires, and by sometimes boiling of the same up, to evaporate any moisture it might have imbibed, it will serve many years and be better, for keeping, and be always ready for preventing meat that is more than you can use from spoiling, in that hot climate, where meat so soon taints as to be rendered putrid in a few hours after killing, if not used, or prevented.[98]

Pickled pig's tongues had some vogue: in the late nineteenth century, Jamaica imported tinned pig's tongues, pig's jowls, boneless pig's feet and jellied brawn. In 1933 the Community Store advertised "delicacies fine enough to tempt a stoic", including Wilson's Certified Boneless Pork Feet packed in a glass jar.[99]

Apart from this relatively small-scale importation of canned pork products, salt pork and pickled pork established itself as a desired meat as early as the eighteenth century. A large part of the attraction, as for saltfish and salt beef, was not the meat but the salt. Browne noticed that enslaved people used money earned in the markets to purchase small amounts of salt pork, and Stewart observed, "Strange as it may appear, the Irish pickled pork is sold to the negroes by the small retail dealers in provisions, at nearly double the price of the fresh pork of the country." This he explained by "the fondness of the negroes for whatever is highly-seasoned and calculated to give a zest to their vegetable broths". By the 1890s, pickled meat imported in barrels included "clear pork", "clear back pork" and "heavy mess pork". Down to the 1970s, barrels stood in the corners of country shops, the customer pushing her arm down into the brine to fish around for an acceptable piece of pork. By the 1990s, corned pork and pickled pork were less commonly available but could still be found in some of the meatshops of Kingston and Montego Bay, along with pig's tail and salt beef.[100]

Ham and bacon had the advantage of dryness, which meant they did not need to be packed in barrels of brine. In the eighteenth century they were imported from North America and England; most of the hams were eaten by the planters but occasionally given to enslaved people. By the late nineteenth century, they were being imported both whole and sliced in tins, and were particularly directed at the Christmas market.[101]

Only in the later twentieth century were hams produced locally, by Grace and other food processors.

The changing role of cured, salted products in Jamaican food history had significance for levels of importation and consumption of the meat of different mammals (Figure 10.5). Taking the mammals overall, cured product had a monopoly of imports down to 1920 when canned "fresh" meat began to make an impact. Fresh (frozen and chilled) meat competed from 1950 but became really significant only after Independence. Cured meat remained important well beyond Independence and hit low levels only after 1980. This resilience reflected the role of pig products in imports in the long term, beginning with pickled pork and moving to ham and bacon, to be overtaken by the cow only when bully beef and fresh beef became popular (Figure 10.6). Although imports of pig meat increased somewhat after 1980, this was not enough to balance the decline in local production or to hold off the strong competition from cow and, above all, chicken.

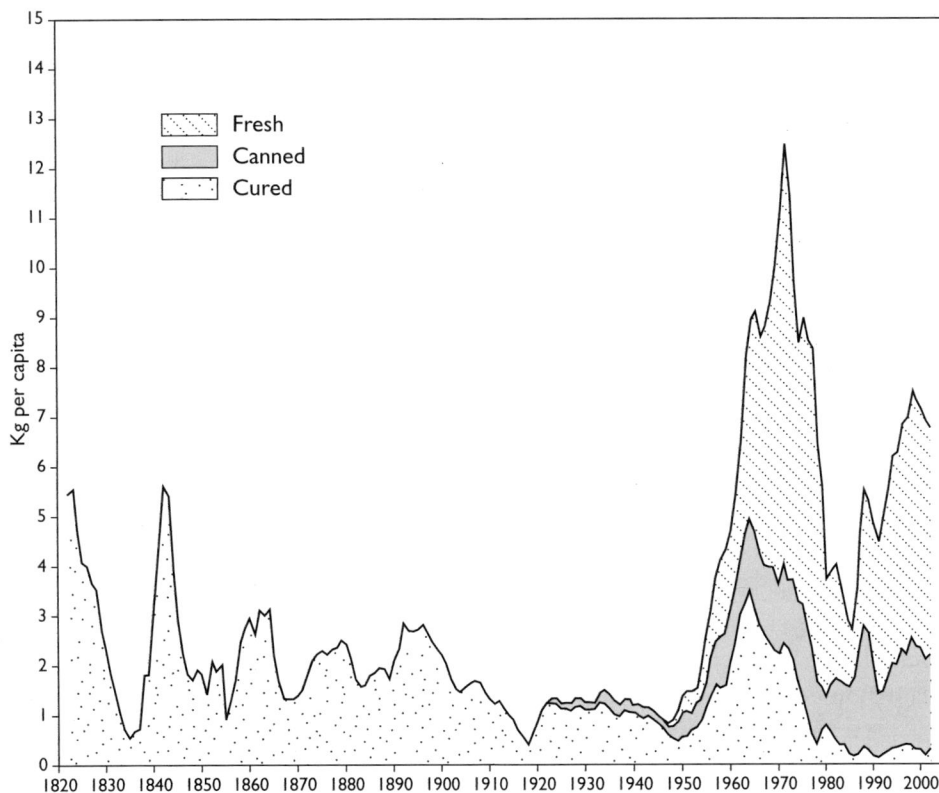

Figure 10.5 Imported meat of mammals (cured, canned, fresh) per capita, 1822–2005. Source: Appendix 1.

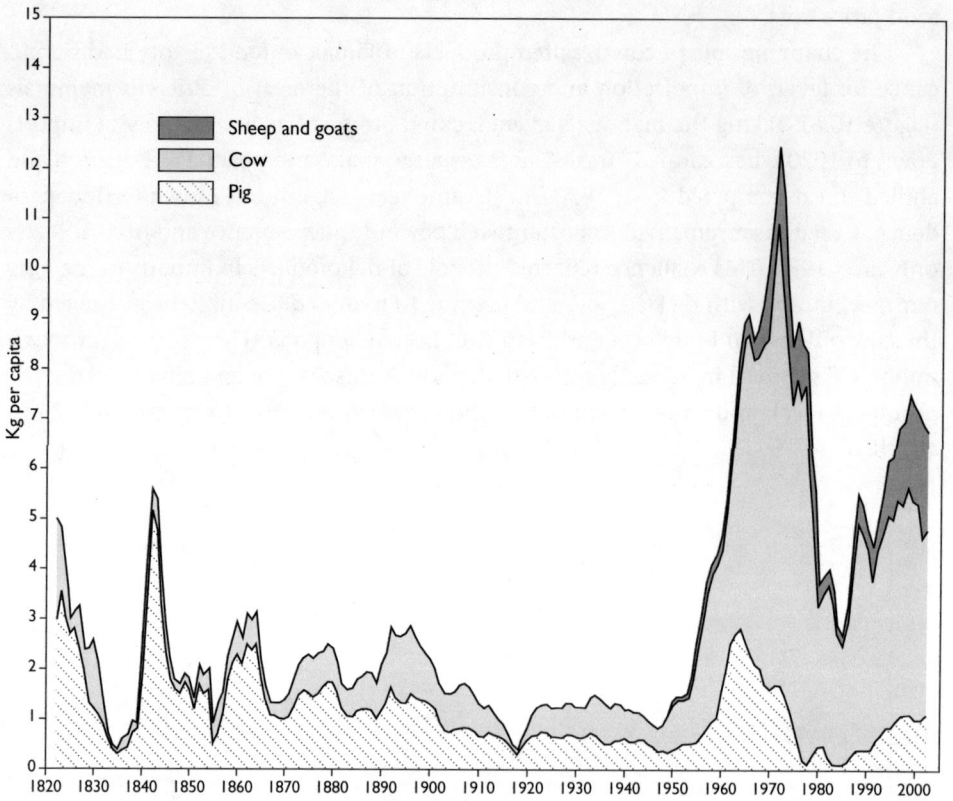

Figure 10.6 Imported meat of mammals (pig, cow, sheep and goat) per capita, 1822–2005.
Source: Appendix 1.

In 2005 Jamaica's pig population was estimated at 85,000, but it was in decline, and substantially less than the 128,000 of 1961. Part of this decline was cyclical. Numbers had increased fairly steadily after Independence, to peak at 230,000 in 1985, then declined in the face of imports. In any case, the island's pig population was consistently smaller than that of cattle, and the ratio of pigs to cows also declined, from 1:2 in 1961 to 1:5 in 2005. It is not possible to estimate ratios for the period before 1900, but the multiple uses of the cow meant that it always had a more prominent position in the plantation economy and, because of this, in the food system. In any case, both cow and pig were easily overtaken by chicken. At Independence, the weight of local beef easily exceeded the total of pig, goat and chicken combined, and pig exceeded chicken. By 2005, the total production of pig came to only 7 per cent that of chicken, and beef to only 18 per cent. This pattern contrasted with world production levels, which pig led, followed by chicken, cow, sheep, turkey and goat.

GOAT

Comparison with goat, *Capra hircus*, raises some interesting questions. In 1961, when Jamaica's goat population was 580,000, there were more goats than all the cows, pigs and sheep combined. But the number of goats declined fairly rapidly after Independence, to a low of 300,000 by the middle of the 1970s, recovering to 440,000 by the end of the 1980s. Only occasionally did the number of goats in the island fall below the number of cows. It was the goat, used only for its meat and sometimes also for its milk, that was most characteristic of Jamaica's food mammals, a status it had achieved as early as the late nineteenth century. Thus Sullivan, in 1893, devoted a good deal of attention to "goat mutton", seeing it as central to Jamaican "native" meat cookery, and indeed, every one of the recipes in her section on "meat" was for goat. As already noticed, she had no interest in anything to do with cow, pig or sheep.[102]

At the end of the twentieth century, Jamaicans were declared "among the world's foremost eaters of goat's flesh". Demand exceeded local production by a wide margin, and much goat meat was imported, most of it from New Zealand, at cheaper prices than the local product (Figure 10.6). The two breeds of goat most popular in Jamaica were the Anglo-Nubian and the Saanen. The Anglo-Nubian was in Jamaica at least by 1907; the Saanen, valued more for its milk than its meat, was introduced from the United States in 1929, followed by the Alpine in 1945. All of these interbred with the creole goats derived from the earliest introductions by the Spanish (Figure 10.7). Regular efforts were made to improve the strain. Pedigree Anglo-Nubian goats were introduced from the United Kingdom in 1992 for breeding, and in 1996 Boer goats were brought in to increase the availability of meat.[103]

Unlike cows and pigs, goats have rarely been closely farmed or subjected to feedlot systems, and rather than increasing, their average weight has actually fallen slightly, from twelve kilograms in 1961 to eleven in 2005. Goats carry a smaller proportion of fat than cows, pigs or sheep, making them less attractive as meat animals. The number of goats killed for meat declined quite heavily between Independence and 2005. At Independence, the total weight of local goat meat on the market was 72 per cent that of local pig meat and 75 per cent that of chicken, making it a strong rival, but by 2005 these quantities had dipped to 28 per cent for pig and a mere 2 per cent for chicken.

Blome said in the 1680s that Jamaica had "great plenty of goats, which thrive and increase there exceedingly, the country being found very fit for them". Although wild goats persisted in the Hellshire Hills and on Goat Island into the 1840s, they were rarely seen and generally kept away, and were kept away, from the plantations. By the 1730s goat owners were being fined if they allowed their animals to trespass. During slavery, goats were barely tolerated on the sugar estates, and even where enslaved people were allowed to possess cows, pigs and poultry, there is little to suggest this tolerance extended to goats. After 1838, however, goats rapidly became popular among the peasantry, and by the early twentieth century, goat-raising was "almost entirely in the hands of the small settlers".[104]

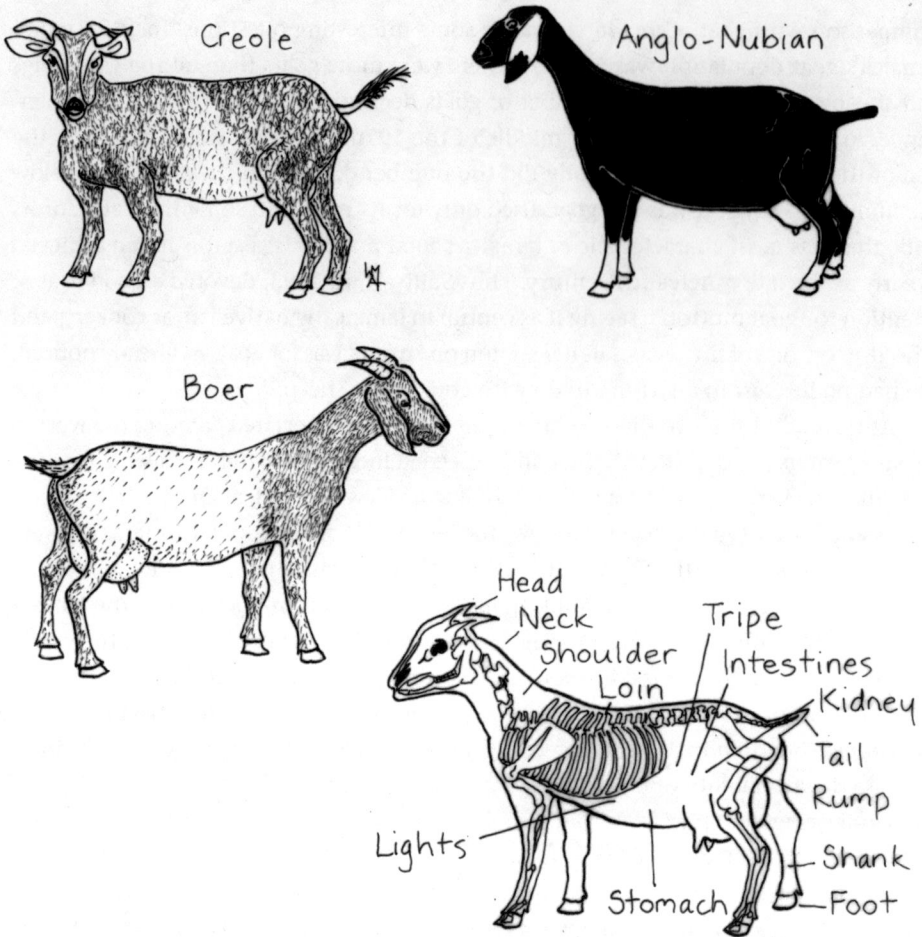

Figure 10.7 Goat breeds and anatomy

Goats are more efficient converters of feed to meat than are cows, with a shorter gestation period and more multiple births. They produce milk and meat more quickly and more cheaply. Smallholders also appreciated goats for their small size, which made them relatively cheap and meant that slaughter, butchering and sale were easier. Further, the goat was happy feeding from a variety of forage and commonly browsed the steepest slopes. For the small farmer, goat had the added advantage of selling for higher prices than pig, and was competitive with sheep and cow for most cuts. While the government in 1946 set prices according to the parts of the cow, pig and sheep, "goat mutton" was sold at a single price (one shilling per pound in Kingston, ten pence in the country).[105] For the purchaser (or a group of purchasers), a slaughtered whole goat was affordable even when the price by weight was high, because the animal was relatively small.

One reason for the relatively high price of goat was that it became popular for festive occasions, when it was served curried and as a soup. References to "curry goat" became common in the 1930s, but the origins of the dish go back further and are generally traced to the East Indian community. The *Dictionary of Jamaican English*, in its 1967 first edition, included citations from the 1940s and assertions that "coolie bring it in". Curry probably became most closely associated with goat meat in Jamaica because goat was the most commonly eaten mammal in India, after the sheep. Jamaicans strongly associated curry with goat well into the twentieth century. In the 1940s the dish was sometimes called "Indian curried goat" or even "real Indian curry goat". An article introducing "Indian cooking", published in 1964, observed that "many folk believe that only goat can be curried" and pointed out that pork, beef and fish, as well as breadfruit, pumpkin and ground provisions, could all be made with this "spice combination". Although Sullivan offered a recipe in 1893 for "curry of kid or goat mutton" without making any connection to India, the British imperial route that curry followed must have been well known to her readers. Sullivan suggested using "the remains of a joint or the chops", cooking them in "a sauce of water, flour, butter, mustard, curry powder, a little lime juice, and a very little cocoanut milk". This was served with rice balls.[106]

In India, currying depended on freshly prepared spices and herbs, and down at least to the 1960s the "East Indians" of Jamaica mostly made their own curry for home consumption, "prepared basically with saffron or yellow ginger and a number of spices". But this seasoning had already been transformed into a portable dry powder by the English, many of whom wished to cook curry after they had returned from colonial India. The word itself came to be generalized broadly to seasoning rather than just traditional currying. In 1870 the *Gleaner* advertised tinned "Currine", a seasoning "composed of nothing but the purest vegetable spices of Mexico and the West Indies", for use with sauces, soups, gravies and meats. Only salt needed to be added.[107]

By the 1930s, curry goat was already a tradition. In 1933, when Mr J.B. Sutherland gave a lecture at Hope, he was able to advocate continuation of "the good old custom of planters making a 'curry goat feed' and inviting their friends". Sutherland told his audience that "a fat wether [a ram castrated when young] should always be buckled [caught] and curried at least once a year". The goat was to be killed early in the day, between seven and eight o'clock, and the "mutton" cut into small pieces, scalded and mixed with black pepper (100 grams per 15 kilograms of mutton), dannia (100 grams), beaten "challotte" (scallion, 500 grams), onion (500 grams), garlic (500 grams), larchi (100 grams), twelve peppers, "tamric" (turmeric, 250 grams) and coconut oil (4.5 litres). The pot with these ingredients was steamed down from 8 a.m. to 1 p.m., with salt added to taste. The dinner was to be "served after 4 drinks of rum and not before 1:30 when every man is right hungry". Each man got enough rice and bread, together with the curry goat, to make almost one kilogram of food, accompanied by half a pint (300 millilitres) of rum. As well as these plantation events, suppers of "curried goat and rice and peas" typically followed country cricket matches, horse races and fairs in the 1930s. Curried goat and rice was said to be "the most popular country dish", and "race meetings and curried goat" were "synonymous terms in St Mary".[108]

The centre of enthusiasm for curry goat began to shift in the 1930s from country to town. In Kingston, hotels offered curried goat as a "special feature" of vaudeville entertainments. By 1938, a little before the disturbances, the common Kingston rum shop was called "the poor people's club", where "you could get a clay pipe, a red-hot goat curry in the 'back room', or some of Jamaica's finest rum". A party held in Kingston in 1940 to raise funds for bombers served "curried goat and roast pork about which all are raving in these days", and the Queensbury Luncheonette on East Queen Street advertised "Mrs. Edith Guy's Curried-Goat Dish" as a "knockout". By the 1950s, curry goat could be called "one of the famous dishes of the country". Mary Manning Carley, shortly after Independence, confirmed curry goat as "the people's party food, always served at fairs and 'all-nite' dances".[109]

The other popular dish was "goat-belly soup" or "mannish water". Head, intestines and feet were the typical ingredients, with green banana, coco, yam, hot pepper, salt and dumplings added to the stock. White rum might also be added. One version of mannish water, published in 2002, was called "goat head soup" and used only the head. Increasing dependence on imported goat meat made the items needed to prepare mannish water scarce and more expensive, and by the 1990s curry goat too was becoming more of a luxury.[110]

Mannish water seems to be a relatively recent innovation. The earliest reference found in the *Gleaner* is from 1968, in a report of an event where "the usual curried goat was served and a truly Jamaican concoction 'mannish water'". The name retained its quotation marks for some years, down to about 1975, and appeared only in the supplement to the second edition of the *Dictionary of Jamaican English*, published in 1980, where the first citation for its use was from 1976. The recipe given there, supplied by a household helper, used head, feet and tripe, boiled with banana in its skin or with potatoes or breadfruit, and with scallion, pepper and butter, to make a soup. This was served at weddings "to fortify the male powers". Sullivan did not mention the soup, nor did Zora Hurston, who in 1938 attended a "curry goat feed" on a banana plantation in St Mary, an event that would have been favoured by Sutherland, with the food prepared by "Hindoos". But although there was no mannish water, Hurston described the event as "a masculine celebration", at which the men drank "cock soup", made from a rooster, rather than "chicken soup", followed by "ram (not nanny) goat and rice". After the cock soup and the curry goat, they ate "banana dumpling with dip-and-flash. That is, you dip your boiled banana in the suruwa sauce, flash off the surplus and take a bite."[111]

How was goat eaten before curry goat and mannish water? In the eighteenth century, Browne claimed that "a kid is generally thought as good, if not better than lamb, and frequently served up at the tables of every rank of people". Long noted the presence in Jamaica of the nanny goat, the rupi goat and the bastard ibex goat. The meat of the nanny goat, he said, when fat, was "not inferior to English mutton, and strongly resembles it in flavour", and "young kids, roasted whole, are justly esteemed a delicious regale [feast]". Sullivan, who saw "goat mutton" as characteristic of Jamaican meat cookery, gave only one recipe for curry. She began with "wet grill of kid or goat mutton", in which slices of cold, cooked meat were seasoned with pepper, butter, sauce, mustard, nutmeg and salt, then warmed in a frying pan in a sauce combining more of the same ingredients with water. She favoured Worcester sauce, and said some burnt sugar gave the sauce a nice colour. Sullivan's other goat recipes were for stews (including gungo peas), roasts, cutlets, grilled kidneys, a pie (including yam) and a timbale (using macaroni and cheese to make a boiled pudding in a mould). For roasts, Sullivan recommended that to tenderize a large, tough joint, the leg might first be wrapped in a towel and buried in a deep hole for two hours, by which process, she said, "the flavour will be immensely improved". On the other hand, Sullivan said she had "seen a small kid roasted and stuffed like a roasting pig". She commented that "if in good order, it is a dish by no means to be despised, but it is an ugly dish". Tastes had changed since Long's earlier appreciation. Whole roasted kid was an uncommon dish in the twentieth century, in contrast to the roast suckling pig with its head and tail intact. Claude McKay, writing of the early twentieth century, talked only of "stewed goat meat, the sauce highly-coloured with annatto". This was accompanied by "an assortment of native vegetables, the yellow and flowery [floury] afou yam, bourbon-pink cocoes and fine mashed cho-chos", served as the main dish in a meal that began with congo pea soup.[112]

Goat's milk has competed quite strongly with cow's milk. In the eighteenth century, the planters found it "pleasant", and Long claimed that it was "used here in common, and thought very nourishing and restorative". Stewart, in 1823, said that goats thrived in Jamaica, being hardier than sheep. Although few were kept by planters, because they damaged the young canes, he wrote, the free "small settlers" and "brown people" raised "great numbers, . . . for the purpose of supplying the inhabitants with milk". The milk of the goats was "sweet and much richer than cow's milk". Similarly, James Phillippo said in 1843 that goats were "kept chiefly for their milk".[113]

By the twentieth century, goat milk had fallen from favour and was replaced by imported condensed cow's milk. As a result, in 1917 it was argued that action was needed "to get a breed of milch goats established for the peasantry". Goats were "very scarce" and the "common goats" in the island were being slaughtered for their skins. After World War II, goat's milk was generally neglected, the peasantry choosing to market the animals as flesh and skin. Goat's milk was compared favourably with human milk, and nutritionists argued the advantage of easy digestion, the fat globules being smaller than those in cow's milk; it was also relatively rich in iron, and the animals rarely suffered from tuberculosis. And in the 1950s it was said that the "strong taste, which some people dislike in goat's milk", could be avoided by not running the ram with the herd and by keeping the animals clean.[114] Yet goat's milk – and even more so goat cheese – became an eccentric taste. Almost all alternative milks were driven from the field by the cow.

SHEEP

Early English assessments of the Jamaican flock suggested there was hope for both the meat and milk of the sheep, *Ovis aries*. By the late eighteenth century, however, milking a sheep was becoming increasingly improbable. As to the flesh of the Jamaican sheep, in the 1680s some said it was "very good", whereas others declared it "not generally so good as in England". In the eighteenth century, some thought that sheep bred well and grew large and tall, and the flock was numerous, but they were not competitive. Mutton and lamb meat was merely "tolerable". A few commentators were more positive. Long, for example, said the "grass mutton" raised in Jamaica was "at the proper seasons, . . . remarkably sweet, juicy, and well-tasted, but small; and would be much better meat if kept to a proper age, for it is generally slaughtered too young; nor is any care bestowed on the choice of pasturage". "Stall-fed" animals, on the other hand, were "as grossly fat as the Essex mutton, and the flesh whitish". Stewart was also enthusiastic, saying that "the sheep are very good, and the mutton excellent" though more expensive than beef, pork or goat. Phillippo, twenty years later, thought Jamaica's sheep had "a degenerated appearance compared with those of England, but their flesh is savoury".[115]

After the early Spanish introductions, most of the sheep of Jamaica were English breeds such as Southdown, Shropshire and Down, and their crosses. Little was done to improve the quality or to promote the meat, though, and the island's flock dwindled from about ten thousand at Independence to one thousand by the 1990s. Compared to the island's ever-present goats, sheep were near to invisible. Like the goat, they escaped the feedlot system. Unlike goats, the average weight of sheep increased, from twenty-one kilograms in 1961 to twenty-three kilograms in 2005, but by then the local animals killed for lamb and mutton each year numbered only a few hundred.

Sullivan distinguished sheep mutton from goat mutton but admitted that it was "undeniable that a good deal of the so-called 'mutton' offered for sale in Jamaica is nothing else than goat, either old or young". She defended the quality of Jamaica's sheep mutton, saying "nothing can be better than a saddle of mutton from Salt Ponds or the mutton on the grazing pens throughout the island". Apart from the confusion between sheep and goat (and indeed they are difficult to distinguish anatomically), there was the old deceit of mutton dressed up as lamb. A seventeenth-century law attempted to prevent such fraud by requiring that all meat brought to market "for lamb, weighing above eight pounds the quarter, shall be deemed mutton; and each sold by the quarter or joint". Further, "to prevent selling and putting off old and small mutton for lamb", it was enacted in 1693 that "all lamb shall be brought into the open market with the heads on, and shewn, before cut up, to the clerk thereof, with the usual signs and marks of distinction, that he, upon scruple, may determine the matter between buyer and seller".[116]

As to the fifth quarter of the sheep, nothing seems ever to have been said of it. Jamaica's numerous Scots were never tempted to try making haggis from the stomachs of the island's sheep (or any other animal), though the Burns Society might import it.

There was no specific interest in tail or head. Occasionally, around 1900, lamb tongues were imported in tins. In 1946, when the government set prices for "sheep mutton", it distinguished only between shoulders, chops and legs (1 shilling 4 pence per pound) and stew (1 shilling 1 pence). Suppliers were few and demand limited. By the 1970s the local product had trouble competing with frozen lamb from New Zealand. Jamaica's penkeepers, after complaining of imports of frozen beef in the early 1930s, accepted that there was no objection to New Zealand mutton, because Jamaica bred few sheep and was rather "a cattle-breeding country". Supply exceeded demand.[117] Even New Zealand legs of lamb, much in favour in the United Kingdom, languished in supermarket freezers for many months, while New Zealand goat was snapped up.

DEER

Jamaica briefly, in the early to mid-eighteenth century, imported "red deer" from "the Continent". Long noted, "They rarely grow fat here in their wild state, but their flesh has a good flavour." Philip Henry Gosse reported the continuing presence of "small herds of deer in feral state" near Caymanas. According to tradition, said Gosse, the deer had come originally from the Spanish Main. In 1841 a buck was caught and killed, and its meat sold in the Spanish Town market. In the 1870s deer came already processed: imported "hashed and roast venison" and "rein deer tongues" could be bought in Kingston. More strangely, in 1899 an advertiser offered "a male reindeer, a little over 6 months old, will make an excellent crossing in any gentleman's sheep fold, no better venison for table use".[118]

CAMEL

The camel, *Camelus dromedarius*, was known in West Africa by at least AD 500 but probably only as a pack animal and largely confined to the arid edge of the Sahara. The drinking of camel milk and the eating of camel meat seems to have been a rarity in West Africa. In modern Ethiopia, on the other hand, the camel is used for both milk and meat, and is indeed the preferred meat in the eastern region of the country. The characteristics of camel meat are there assessed "generally comparable to those of other red meats, including beef, lamb and goat and even of chicken". It is tougher than beef and has some undesirable flavours, especially in older animals, but is thought to have medicinal qualities and to offer good food value. Camel meat is low in fat and cholesterol. In Ethiopia, consumption is encouraged, particularly as a substitute for beef.[119]

Jamaica's experience with the camel was brief, and directed at transport rather than meat. Browne said in 1756 that "great numbers [of camels] have been lately imported into Jamaica" and reported that "the flesh of them is reckoned very tender and wholesome". Thistlewood had seen them in 1753, apparently soon after they had been landed at Savanna la Mar. By 1774, however, Long said the great expectations were not fulfilled, because the camels could not handle the steep rocky tracks of the island. The remaining animals roamed the roads, frightening horses. Long said, "The young ones are said to be good meat, and often used as such by the inhabitants of those countries where they are more common; but the epicures of Jamaica have not yet thought proper to introduce this Asiatic dainty into their bill of fare." He rated them "the most useless animals belonging to this island".[120]

HORSE, DONKEY

Although the eating of horse, *Equus caballus*, and donkey, *E. asinus*, occurred historically in some places, including West Africa, it was uncommon in Jamaica. Only the exigencies of wartime shortages brought the idea to the fore. In April 1918 a correspondent "seriously advocated the selling of horseflesh here for food", and the *Gleaner's* editor agreed. He believed that it might "take some moral courage for beef-eaters to demand a pound of horse-steak, so long as those beef-eaters were of the 'Better-class'", and that "humbler folk might also think that horse-flesh was too much like carrion for their taste". To overcome such prejudice, all that was needed, argued the editor, was for "a number of men" to "publicly determine to eat horse-steak and horse-stew", to set the example. He declared himself willing.[121]

Horses were plentiful enough and were being driven from the roads by motor vehicles, so the idea of a Jamaican industry breeding for meat appeared viable. During World War I observers noted that horse meat was already being sold and eaten in England, and that "the horse is quite as clean a feeder as the cow or sheep, and so long as he is in good condition, and certified free of disease", there was "no reason (except prejudice) why we should object to make use of him as food, especially as we eat with great relish a large quantity of imported sausages, which don't profess to be made of anything else". Penkeepers, however, expressed shock at the proposal, saying that they loved their horses too much to make food of them and that Jamaica had not reached the extremity faced by the English. Others predicted that "Jamaicans, after having beheld the slaughtering of horses, would never eat their flesh".[122]

The English themselves saw horse-eating as the outcome of calamity, having long found repugnant the enthusiasm of the French and Germans. In general, it can be argued that the meat and milk of horses has not been consumed consistently because the horse is an inefficient converter of feed compared to cattle and pigs, and that, particularly for the English, the problem of supply was solved by sourcing meat from the empire. Jamaica can also be considered part of the equation, with the goat easily coming ahead of the horse in the hierarchy of potential meat animals. The meat of imported, canned "Vienna" sausages was sometimes, particularly in wartime, suspected of coming from horses rather than cows or pigs. During World War II, donkey was sold for beef by a St James butcher, the meat "attractively fat". The butcher was arrested, but only after he had sold most of it, and, presumably, after the meat had been eaten. Stolen animals were sometimes slaughtered and the meat cooked in country restaurants. Although it was believed that Jamaicans would not knowingly have eaten donkey meat, they ate happily enough in ignorance.[123]

The milk of the donkey was thought good for pregnant women. Nugent drank it in 1802. Even in the 1980s it was said that "the milk of the donkey is highly nutritious and rich", though without examples of current consumption in Jamaica. In terms of its protein and lactose content, the milk of the horse (and presumably donkey) more closely approximates human milk than does that from any other mammal.[124]

RABBIT

Jamaica had rabbits in the seventeenth and eighteenth centuries, but the rabbits seem to have been used only for their skins, and the rabbit population suffered heavily from attacks by rats. References to enslaved people eating rabbits are few. Gosse noted that wild rabbits had long existed around Spanish Town and wondered "why so little progress has been made in stocking our fields with an animal supplying a delicate dish wherever it has been an object of home economy".[125]

Occasional farmers probably bred and ate rabbits, but the animals remained little heard of well into the twentieth century and rarely appeared in the markets. Only in the 1980s was breeding advanced with some trepidation and little success. A few small farmers raised rabbits but found only a limited market in spite of the economic pressures of the time, and it was by then almost impossible to compete with chicken. The earliest recipes traced also appeared in the 1980s, one cookbook proposing rabbit fricassee, roasted rabbit and "curried goat or rabbit". It was also suggested that a recipe for brawn, using a pig's head, might be "made also with rabbit using the whole animal".[126]

CAT

Leslie claimed in 1739 that the enslaved people of Jamaica ate cats, sometimes "fricasseed". Browne said much the same, and Long in 1774 held that the "Negroes" would eat "even cats, which, they alledge, are not at all inferior in taste and goodness to rabbits". Others said that for the deprived plantation slaves, a cat was "generally esteemed a peculiar dainty". As late as 1873 Rampini claimed, "Stewed cat is said to be considered a dainty dish", and in the 1930s, when feral cats were common in remote forests, the place name Corn-Puss Gap was attributed to the fact that "the Maroons once salted (corned) a wild cat in that pass".[127] Most of this evidence of the eating of cats by Jamaicans, down to the late nineteenth century, comes from prejudiced sources. At the same time, feral cats do grow large and troublesome, and are today valued as food in some parts of the world. Sometimes even people who keep cats as pets also eat them.

DOG

The Taino had domesticated dogs, and it is possible that dogs were eaten in Jamaica, as they were on the Caribbean mainland coasts. The practice was fairly widespread in West Africa until recent times, though long disapproved of by Muslims. The first English settlers in Jamaica, initially facing inadequate food supplies, ate stray dogs as well as iguanas and snakes. As to the enslaved, some of the commentators who claimed to know that cats were part of their occasional, opportunistic food said the same about dogs. But some did not, suggesting that the evidence for the eating of cats is stronger than that for dogs before the twentieth century.[128]

By the twentieth century, the eating of dogs was generally disapproved of in Jamaica, though Chinese people were, disparagingly, said to eat dogs, as in the "popular saying" reported in the 1980s, "Chiney people nyam dog".[129] In the 1970s it had been rumoured that some of the domestic dogs that went missing from upper St Andrew households ended up as patty meat, possibly at the hands of Chinese bakers. The contemporary eating of dogs in China was well known.

RAT

While the evidence for the eating of cats and dogs in Jamaica is not always convincing, there is no uncertainty about the rat. Sloane said rats were sold by the dozen in the 1680s, "and when they have been bred amongst the sugar-canes, are thought by some discerning people very delicious victuals". By the 1730s, rats were in plague proportions and planters gave a bottle of rum for every fifty trapped. Enslaved people, it was asserted, "broil them and eat them with a great deal of pleasure". Long said the largest was "commonly called the *Charles-price* rat, having been first observed here about the time when the late Sir Charles Price, Baronet, returned hither from Europe". It was presumed to have come from St Croix on a Danish ship, and had multiplied rapidly, preying on poultry and eggs. Later writers have guessed that it might have been a South American "ferret" or an opossum but it did not become established in the island.[130]

Jamaica also had the black house-rat, another import from Europe, and two species believed to be indigenous. One of these was probably the Jamaican rice rat, *Oryzomys antillarum*, an endemic rodent. It proved a pest in sugar fields and, along with other rats, was subjected to control by the mongoose, which was introduced from India in 1872. By 1900 the rice rat was effectively extinct. More important was the "cane rat" (or "cane-field rat"), which lived on sugar. This, said Long, gave its flesh a "luscious and very delicate flavour, . . . as I am informed by those who have eaten them, when roasted". The white inhabitants of Jamaica did not eat the cane rat, he observed, though it was "highly esteemed among the plantation Negroes, who spit half a dozen of them at a time, upon a long skewer, and broil them in this manner on their fires, leaving their heads on, but always cutting off the tail, close to the rump, which they think is not proper to be eaten". Stewart, in 1823, claimed similarly that "some of the Africans eat the cane-field rat, which they regard as a great luxury".[131]

During slavery, the white people of Jamaica often expressed disgust at the eating of rats but equally noticed that the cane-field rat had a clean diet, and occasionally claimed to know someone – a Frenchman perhaps – who had bravely tried rat and found it equal to a young chicken or rabbit. Another approach was to identify the cane-field rat as something other than a rat. Thus Gosse in 1846 found rats and mice "numerous" in all parts of Jamaica, but argued that "the Cane-piece Rat" was "manifestly a distinct species . . . distinguished by its size, by its rufous colour, and by the smallness of its ears". One Gosse inspected was forty-three centimetres long, from nose to tail, but he noted that Robinson had illustrated a specimen that reached fifty centimetres.[132]

Was the "cane-field rat" of Jamaica the same species as the "cane rat" or "cutting-grass", *Thryonomys swinderianus*, of West and Central Africa? According to D.R. Rosevear, writing in the 1960s, the more formal name "cane rat" was rarely used in West Africa; most people there referred simply to the "cutting-grass". The animal was also occasionally called a "ground-hog". The cane rat has a head-and-body length of forty-five centimetres or more, with a tail twenty centimetres long. Its head was small relative to the size of the body, with a squat shape and powerful incisors (Figure 10.8). Weights of four to six kilograms were typical, with some of the rodents weighing up to nine kilograms. One-year-olds reached weights of two to three kilograms. The cane rat was common throughout the region, from Senegal to southern Africa, wherever there was dense reedy grass in wet places. It was "chiefly notorious for cutting down tall graminaceous [grass-like] crops such as maize, guinea-corn and sugar-cane, neatly felling the stems by cutting through their bases". In West Africa the cane rat was often hunted, sometimes with dogs, partly because it was a pest, but equally "because of its tasty white flesh which, especially in view of its size, makes it one of the most commonly sought after sources of animal protein". In the seventeenth century, Dutch traders in West Africa called it a "delicacy". For Europeans who did not know what they were eating (with the head and tail removed), it was "a very grateful dish; for they are fat, tender and very agreeable". The cane rat was not the only rodent eaten in West Africa. Other large rodents "have long been recognised as providing a good meal of sweet-tasting flesh; and there are amongst the smaller species a number of clean, vegetable feeders that have been found acceptable". In West and Central Africa, the grass-cutter or cane rat is now eaten stewed, grilled or smoked, and is bred in captivity for human consumption.[133]

Figure 10.8 Cane-rat, grass-cutter

The eating of "cane rat" in Africa was known to some Jamaicans and was occasionally mentioned in newspapers, beginning in the 1960s. Soup "made from cane-piece rats" was said to be a cure for whooping cough. In 1987 C.J. Allen observed there were many Jamaicans "who once drank rat soup, for therapeutic reasons, not nutritional, but our systems didn't refuse the amino acids given". Allen, who had lived in West Africa, pointed out that there the cane rat was a "vegetarian", clean and healthy, weighing up to ten kilograms, and said that it "looked very delicious" roasted. He advocated its production and consumption in Jamaica. In West Africa, he said, "rat meat – the meat of their cane rat – is preferred to any other kind of domestic animal". Allen asked, "Would we be averse to eating rats? I doubt. Most of us are descendants of captured West Africans and . . . if our cousins over there relish them why shouldn't we?"[134]

CONEY

The coney, or Jamaican hutia (*Geocapromys browni*), grows to forty to sixty centimetres in length and weighs from one to nine kilograms (Figure 10.9). It was abundant before Columbus and was eaten by the Taino. It was probably the first Caribbean meat Columbus tasted.[135] In 1683 it was said that the "Indian coney, called raccoones", of Jamaica was "good meat, but of a distasteful shape, being something like an overgrown rat". It remained common into the nineteenth century, but by the 1890s the mongoose had much reduced "the toothsome conie". It was added to the list of protected animals in 1944 but down to the 1980s was "still hunted ardently in Portland and St. Thomas parishes", using dogs and nets, and considered by some "a rare and exotic delicacy". In 1992 it was described as simply "a kind of rodent", though it was claimed that "some people even today follow the Arawak example and eat coneys". The coney is both under pressure from hunters, though it is protected by law, and constrained by the reduction of its natural habitat. It is not often seen, partly because it rarely comes out in daylight. In 2003 a Maroon leader acknowledged that the coney was protected and said that "the animal is not hunted much but they make a nice stew".[136]

Figure 10.9 Coney

MANATEE

Like the turtle, the West Indian manatee, *Trichechus manatus*, is a large sea animal, but a mammal rather than a reptile. It grows to four metres long and five hundred kilograms in weight, with a thick, wrinkled, leathery skin, and lives for fifty years or more (Figure 10.10). It is rotund, with a small head and no neck. Apart from a thin layer of fat immediately under the skin, manatees have less blubber than most marine animals. They are now the only remaining plant-eating marine mammals, grazing on water plants such as seagrasses, water hyacinth and morass weeds, and generally spending more than eight hours a day feeding. The manatee bears only one calf every two or three years. Commonly called the sea cow, the manatee was formerly found most often along stretches of the southern coast of Jamaica, living in shallow saltwater bays, brackish estuaries and rivers. Species of sea cow also occurred along the coast of West Africa and may have been eaten there.[137]

The manatee represented a substantial resource of potential food for the Taino. It was harder to catch than the turtle, because its acute hearing alerted it to hunters, but it was lethargic and essentially defenceless against man. Its feeding habits identified habitual sites where it could be netted. Thomas Trapham said in 1679 that the manatee or sea cow was a feast, though already relatively rare. An anonymous writer of 1682 said that the flesh of the manatee was "by some esteemed the most delicate in the world,

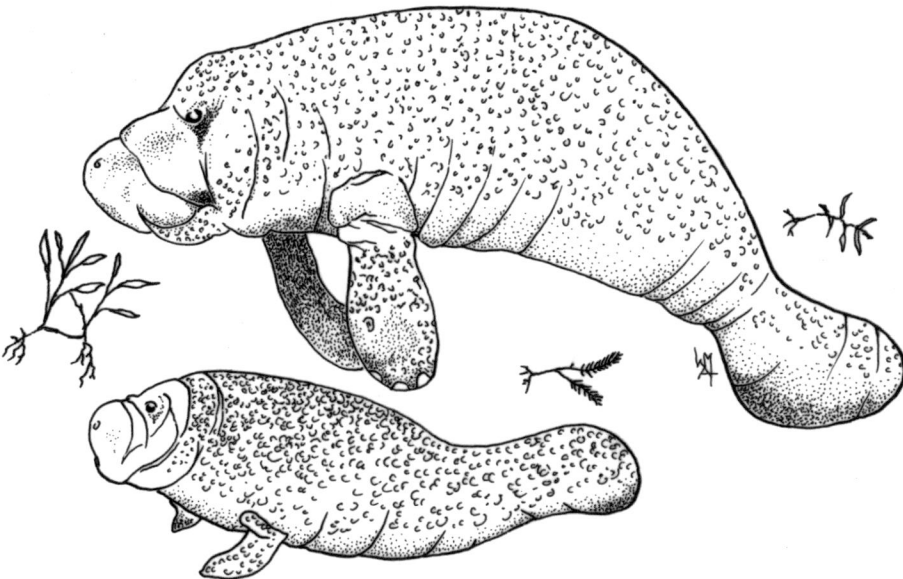

Figure 10.10 Manatee

sweeter than the tenderest veal, sold at Jamaica, where it's sometimes brought for 6d. the pound". Hans Sloane said, "They have formerly been frequent, but are, by the multitude of people and the hunters catching them, destroy'd." The manatee's meat was "reckon'd extraordinary food and are likewise salted as beef, and eaten as provision". Long said the "manatti or sea cow" was best salted, and tasted "like very white veal, but the skin has the rankness of pork".[138]

Manatee flesh was sold in Jamaica's markets into the 1840s, but was by then quite rare. In 1816 a "gentleman" told Lewis he had tasted the milk of the female manatee and "could not have distinguished it from the sweetest cow's milk". Lewis himself ate some of the flesh roasted and reported, "Except that its consistence was rather firmer, I should not have known it from veal." Gosse found a manatee butchered for sale in Savanna la Mar in 1844; the carcass was "eagerly bought up in joints, as a delicacy for the table". He himself "had the pleasure . . . of breakfasting on steaks of its flesh, which was of delicious flavour, without any oiliness: its taste was something between veal and pork, rather approaching the latter". Rampini claimed in 1873 that the manatee was "very common" around Bluefields Bay, but he could report only thirteen sightings in two years between Black River and Savanna la Mar. He found the flesh "delicious, in some parts resembling pork, in others beef", and said that "a splendid 'round of beef' can be cut from under the belly".[139]

In the first half of the twentieth century, manatees were sometimes taken up when fishing with a seine, along the south coast between Alligator Pond and Clarendon, and occasionally were still seen in dozens feeding in the shallow vegetated flats and fresh water outflows. The manatee was added to the list of protected animals in 1944. By 1980 the total stock was reduced to about one hundred, and by 2000 their numbers were perhaps fifty. Occasionally animals were killed by fishermen using explosives or caught in nets, inadvertently, but butchered and the meat sold as beef or veal.[140]

MONK SEAL

The Caribbean monk seal, *Monachus tropicalis*, was formally declared extinct in 1996, though it is possible that the species survives out of sight. Very few sightings were recorded in the twentieth century, the last being on the Seranilla Bank, south of Jamaica, in 1952. The first recorded sighting was that by Columbus in 1494 off Hispaniola. He had some killed for food. The monk seal was genetically tame, so that a human could easily club a resting animal to death. Continuing attack by mariners and fishermen, initially for meat and later oil, as well as reduction of habitat, led rapidly to the effective disappearance of the monk seal by about 1800, though there was a small colony at Pedro Cays until the 1840s.[141]

The monk seal reached 2.5 metres and weighed more than 200 kilograms. It ate fish and used its strong teeth to break mollusc shells. It had a thick layer of fat underneath the skin, and it was this fat that was exploited for oil. In the 1760s, Lindsay illustrated a group of monk seals, though without identifying either the animals or the location (Plate 40). Compared to other images of the monk seal, Lindsay's showed the head thrown back, and the body foreshortened and insufficiently rotund, but the teeth and nails are shown to be prominent. Lindsay made no mention of the monk seal as food. Little evidence exists for its consumption by Jamaican people, and it is uncertain how far it entered their diet rather than that of buccaneers and voyagers.

PART 3: INORGANIC MATTER

CHAPTER 11

SALT, EARTH, WATER

Although the life of human beings is sustained by the ingestion of living organisms, most of them plants and animals, inorganic materials are also important as supplements or cooking mediums. These inorganic materials are eaten sometimes self-consciously as food, while at other times they are inadvertently contained in the living organisms selected as food or consumed by accident. Several significant items enter the diet in these various ways, the most important by far for the history of the development of taste being salt, which is as much a centrepiece of Jamaican food history as is its apparent counterpoint, sugar.

SALT

Jamaicans have long been known for their love of salt and of the salty taste. Significantly, a rejection of salt was central to the development of ital Rastafarian foodways in the twentieth century, symbolizing a wider rejection of the dead and non-natural world. From the 1940s, Rasta criticized the use of salt as seasoning, along with shop-bought processed foods, and replaced it with an emphasis on ital, fresh, "raw" foods. However, whereas Rastafarian views on the importance of consuming "natural" or "living" things and the avoidance of meat from animals that feed on other animals have been influential, the avoidance of preserved and salted "dead" foods has not been able to overcome the long-standing craving for salt.[1]

The common Jamaican taste for salt is generally traced to the period of slavery and to the use of salted, cured fish and meat. It was fish that typically came heavily encrusted in salt. In 1707, the slaves of Longville Estate advanced as their primary complaint against a harsh overseer the fact that they "had not had a grain of salt" since the proprietor, Charles Long, had become an absentee. Another absentee planter, Matthew Gregory Lewis, visiting his Westmoreland plantation in 1816, observed the same desire. Although "vegetables form the basis of negro sustenance", he said, "the slaves . . . are so passionately fond of salted provisions, that, instead of giving them fresh beef (as at their festival of Saturday last), I have been advised to provide some hogsheads of salt fish, as likely to afford them more gratification, at such future additional holidays as I may find it possible to allow them in this busy crop season". By the 1830s, saltfish was often abbreviated to "salt", and obtaining "a supply of salt provisions" was commonly seen as the primary objective of trade at the markets during slavery. As argued in the discussion of fish and meat, this choice was both a matter of necessity and economics. Even in 1900 it was rational for the urban poor to add to their boiled yam and banana "a herring or two, or a bit of salted fish" rather than purchasing fresh meat. This was a choice driven by the development of a habitual, dominating taste for salt as much as it was a matter of simple cost and the practicality of preservation.[2]

When H.G. De Lisser investigated the grocery shops of Jones Pen, Kingston, in 1941, he observed that it was a custom for shopkeepers to give a handful of salt (or a little vinegar) to customers who made purchases like rice or codfish. This custom, he believed, had been established by the Chinese. But much of the people's salt still came from salted provisions. In 1955, Dr W.E. McCulloch identified "salted and pickled fish and meats" as "expensive luxuries". He complained that they had relatively little nutritional value and as a result, "we pay for a poor quality protein which is less than in fresh meats and buy salt at a high price which is wholly unjustifiable as salt may be as much as [one] quarter of the weight of the product". Further, in the pickled varieties, he mused, a high price was paid for the water. McCulloch discussed the body's need for minerals, arguing that the ordinary diet contained adequate amounts of phosphorous and potassium, and badly lacked calcium, but that there was "no shortage of salt". The great need in Jamaica, he believed, was to increase consumption of calcium. This would come best from milk, of which the island lacked a sufficient supply. The island's limestone and marl could help, "but we can't tell people to eat chalk". Calcium might be disguised, as in fortified bread, thought McCulloch, but instead he advocated the eating of more dark green leafy vegetables.[3]

By the late 1960s, the increasing shift to locally produced fresh chicken and pork and away from saltfish, pickled mackerel and pig's tail, salt beef and pickled pork was remarked as a fundamental change in food habits and taste. According to the satirical writer A.E.T. Henry, "The Jamaican, by virtue of inherited taste over several generations, is so convinced that the protein portion of his diet should be salted or pickled, he calls it 'salt'ing even when it is fresh." In this scheme, said Henry, writing prophetically in 1968, dumpling and breadfruit would "suffer a devastating loss of prestige", while rice would become the common companion of chicken. Ackee, callaloo and avocado all faced calamity if they lost their "boon companions, saltfish and mackerel".[4]

In the 1980s, when saltfish and salt meat were less regular items of diet, their capacity to supply the desired salt taste was replaced to some extent by packaged dried soup mixes and powdered stock. Thus cock soup and chicken and beef noodle soups could "make any meal a treat", serving to "flavour up, spruce up, spice up, or simply to add that dash of difference". Increasingly, the desire for salt taste was satisfied by snack foods. The traditional savoury items sold by vendors on the streets of Kingston were made with seasonings, and most with added salt. Most non-traditional savoury items also had doses of salt. The taste for sugar was strong as well. One fundamental kitchen tip offered to Jamaican cooks in 1993 was that "if you've added too much salt to a recipe", the first solution is to "add a little sugar". Conversely, if a dish was "too sweet", the best solution is to "add some salt".[5]

Of the five basic tastes, saltiness is the only one to derive its name directly from a particular substance or commodity. It is a "true" taste (detected in the mouth by salt-specific taste buds), created by the joint presence of monobasic anions and cations in solution. In food, saltiness normally comes from sodium chloride (NaCl) – commonly called "salt" – in the proportions 40 per cent sodium and 60 per cent chloride. Alternative chlorides exist, but they have unpleasant bitter tastes and are purgative or poisonous. Most of the salt ingested comes from this sodium chloride or common salt, but sodium *occurs in other compounds used in foods. Bicarbonate of soda (sodium hydrogen* carbonate), produced from salt or brine, is used along with sour milk (an acid) to raise soda bread, which became popular in the nineteenth century, and sodium nitrate is the saltpetre used to pickle meat. MSG (monosodium glutamate), commonly known in Jamaica as "seasoning salt", also has a high salt content. When large quantities of MSG were consumed in Jamaica in the late twentieth century, most of it in Chinese-style cooking, people with allergic reactions were encouraged to use "natural ingredient seasonings" or onions and sweet peppers.[6]

Salt is essential to life. Mammals naturally feel thirsty or desire salt when the balance between water and sodium in the body fluid is disrupted. What is not essential is "added" or "free" salt. Humans lived for hundreds of thousands of years without added salt in their diets, obtaining the salt they needed for survival from the small amounts absorbed with their food. In order to function efficiently, the body developed mechanisms to conserve these small doses. As long as hunting and fishing were dominant modes of economy, populations living on the flesh of freshly killed animals could obtain mineral salts in solution from the meat or blood. The shift to sedentary agriculture about five thousand years ago made people dependent on carbohydrates, which necessitate salt supplements. Equally important was the discovery that salt could be used to preserve meat and other foods, making food available out of season and enabling sedentary settlement. Salt preserves by killing or slowing down the growth of bacteria and by suppressing decay, drawing water from vegetables and meat by osmosis. Highly salted food, however, tends to suppress the salt taste receptors in the mouth, making natural foods seem insipid and unattractive. A craving developed, and added salt was used with unsalted food to achieve the concentration appreciated in preserved foods.

Most modern populations share this taste for salt, but many people crave salt far beyond what is necessary. Average daily salt consumption around the world is now about ten grams – ten times the amount humans are genetically programmed to consume. The current level is, however, not the historical peak of salt consumption. In the nineteenth century, salt consumption was twice as high in some countries, and in places such as sixteenth-century Sweden where there was a high consumption of salted fish, daily intake was as high as one hundred grams. The global decline in salt consumption over the last one hundred years can be traced largely to the use of refrigeration and to the concomitant decline in salt-preserved foods, which has been sufficient to counter the current trend to added salt in processed foods. Although a physiological need for salt exists, it is at a low level, and salt craving can be traced directly to cultural forces. It is an addiction, rooted in hedonism or the "pleasures of sensation".[7]

How do Jamaicans rate in terms of their supposed addiction to salt? Estimates of Jamaican salt consumption are difficult to obtain for the whole course of Jamaican history, and consumption was of course inflated by the vital role of salted and pickled fish, pork and beef in the diet from the seventeenth to the twentieth centuries. Per capita imports of salt provide a guide to the quantities of free salt added to food but must be added to the changing and largely unquantifiable amounts that come with preserved and processed goods. On the other side of the equation, an unknown but increasing proportion of the salt imported was used for purposes other than food, and local production must also be factored in. Yet even with these many caveats in mind, it is clear that imports per capita grew most rapidly between 1850 and 1865, increasing by four times over that short period. There was a slower growth (roughly a doubling) between the abolition of slavery and 1850, and another long period of slow and steady growth from 1865 to 1940 (another doubling), after which the data become too difficult of interpretation to be useful (Figure 11.1). It is striking that the period of greatest increase,

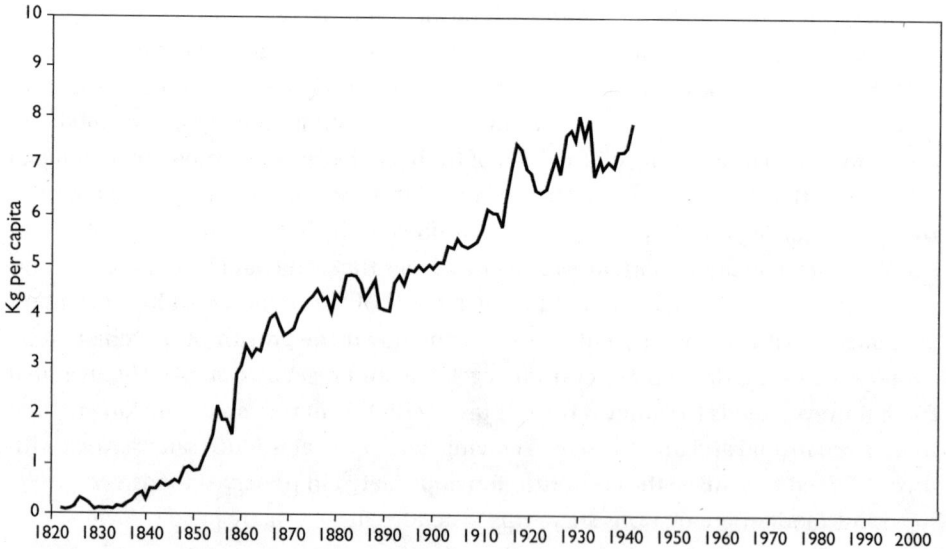

Figure 11.1 Salt imports per capita, 1820–1940. Source: Appendix 1.

1850–1865, matched closely the period in which saltfish imports declined most rapidly (to about one-third of the level in 1850), and that the long-term increase in salt imports broadly presents a counterpoint to the long-term decline in imports of salted and pickled fish and cured cow and pig meat (Figures 8.1, 10.5 and 10.6). Taking as a guide the peak salt import figures observed, in the interwar period, suggests a consumption of at least twenty grams per day per capita, double the ten grams in 1865. A rough estimate of total consumption, taking into account the salted fish and meat, suggest that twenty grams was typical of the longer-term trend.

Today, common salt is typically white, dry, pure and evenly grained. Rice is put into salt shakers to absorb any trace of moisture that might remain and make pouring difficult. In the past, everyday salt was often wet, coarse, lumpy, and dirty. Salt extracted from water (brine) is hard to dry completely, and hard to free of impurities. Seaside evaporation ponds, either natural or specially constructed, are dried by sun and wind. As the salt forms, it is raked up into piles, inevitably containing within it algae and seaweed that colour it grey. Salt obtained from underground, as rock or as brine, is difficult to grind and dry. The creation of free-pouring even-grained salt did not happen until the 1910s. This was achieved by adding first magnesium carbonate, then later calcium silicate. Technological change since the end of the eighteenth century vastly increased productivity and made salt inexpensive, thus enabling its use in a wide range of modern industries. Demand from chemical and other industries also increased dramatically during the twentieth century, so that culinary salt came to be a small proportion of the total salt output.[8]

In Jamaica, the Salt Ponds near Yallahs in St Thomas and the Great Salt Pond in St Catherine were formerly raked for salt. The Spanish made use of the salt deposits on the south coast, for the salt pork trade. According to Hughes, writing in 1672, good salt was produced easily by the evaporation of sea water in paved ponds, and was used to salt the island's beef and pork, "which will not keep sweet otherwise many hours after it is killed". John Collins said in 1682 that salt could be taken from Jamaica for little more than the cost of carriage but needed to be refined for the salting of North Atlantic fish. Edward Long believed "marine salt" was "easily manufactured, upon all the salina's in this island, by exsolation [evaporation]", and noted that a few coastal plantations still made their own salt by "coction" or boiling. Cauldrons could be filled using a wind-sail pump, and when the salt had been "boiled to a granulation, it is stowed in baskets, which are suspended in an airy, shaded place, to let the bittern drain off; after which, it is fit for consumption".[9] In spite of this enthusiasm, the salt resources of Jamaica came to be viewed sceptically. The sugar-plantation economy of the eighteenth century easily outproduced salt-making, which shifted its locus to the Bahamas and Anguilla. Imports then dominated until the early twentieth century.

The Jamaica Salt Company Limited was established in 1921 "to carry on the business of manufacturers of and dealers in salt and bye-products of salt manufacture", but not until the 1960s were factories set up in Kingston and Spanish Town to produce common and fine salt in quantity. In 1984 a Solar Salt Project, using the evaporation process, was begun in Clarendon and by 1991 produced 1,000 tonnes annually. But Jamaica consumed about 330,000 tonnes of salt, most of it imported from Bonaire and the Bahamas. The major users overall were ice factories and large farms.[10]

Why do Jamaicans crave salt? One argument is that perspiration is an important mechanism for excreting salt, and hard labour in the tropical sun meant great daily loss and hence a physiological need beyond the average to restore the balance. A further clue is that the great majority of Jamaica's people came from West Africa, one of the salt-deficient regions of the world. Small amounts of salt were produced there by evaporation from lagoon salines along the coast or by the boiling of seawater, and entered local trading systems, but it was not enough. An east–west trade in cloth and sea salt developed between cotton-growing, salt-starved Mali and downriver Senegambia.[11] A long-distance trade across the Sahara had also developed, beginning about AD 400, made possible by the introduction of camel transport: rock salt mined in what was then the western Sudan (the north of modern-day Mali) was exchanged for gold dust. In the period before Columbus, salt dominated trade across the Sahara, in combination with gold, slaves, kolanuts and expensive textiles. Salt sold for high prices, and for the Sudanese served as a currency alongside gold and silver, sometimes exchanging at parity by weight with gold. Rock salt was so expensive in West Africa, that people were said never to use it ground or sprinkled but rather to hold a lump in the hand and lick it while eating, to make it last. The trans-Saharan trade persisted to about 1800, when cheaply produced salt began to be imported from Europe and the price fell dramatically.[12]

Salt is now considered a simple and cheap commodity, but one unlikely to be assessed positively in the system of food, nutrition and health. Consumption is as much as twenty times greater than it was before the establishment of agricultural societies. The health hazard associated with this change is that because the body has difficulty unlearning the need to conserve salt, there is a consequent increase in blood pressure and heart disease. Comparison of modern populations suggests a correlation between salt intake and hypertension, and in this comparison Jamaica falls somewhere between West Africa and the United States. The controversial "slavery hypothesis" links modern hypertension in these populations with an original salt deficiency in West Africa, the trauma of the slave trade and the conditions of life of the enslaved.[13] Certainly, regardless of its origins, modern Jamaicans' hunger for salt is an unhealthy desire. By the 1990s, newspaper reports regularly warned of research findings that linked salt and high blood pressure and called on Jamaicans to reduce their consumption.[14]

In view of modern interpretations of the fundamental causes of salt-craving, Jamaican folk knowledge offers an interesting version. Zora Hurston, having attended a St Thomas nine-night (wake) in 1938, reported a variety of opinion on the question whether or not duppies (spirits) liked salt. Some people believed they did not like salt and were vexed by it, so that on seeing salt around a place they would go back to their graves. Others, according to Hurston, held an opposite opinion, saying that salt was not given to duppies because it made them too strong for mortals. It was argued that "salt gives 'temper' to mortal food and duppies are not mortal any longer so they do not need salt. When he leaves off being mortal, the duppy does not need anything to temper his vittles." Another voice said that salt was not given because "salt is heavy" and therefore would hold the duppy to the ground and prevent his flying away: "Once Africans could all fly because they never ate salt. Many of them were brought to Jamaica to be slaves, but they never were slaves. They flew back to Africa. Those who ate salt had to stay in Jamaica and be slaves, because they were too heavy to fly."[15]

EARTH

Earth and unwanted metals are regularly ingested along with food and drink. Washed or unwashed, vegetables retain persistent attachments that are not necessarily gritty in the mouth. Similarly, grain ground in a stone or clay vessel may include minerals. Most of this material is neither nutritious nor life-threatening. Liquids, on the other hand, can have long-term ill effects when polluted. In the Caribbean, the most dramatic example is lead poisoning caused by the drinking of rum that had been distilled in lead vessels and pipes, particularly "new rum", and particularly in the eighteenth century. Canned foods, soldered with lead, were a significant source for a long period but began to be eliminated in the 1970s. In recent times, lead has been more likely to come from contaminated land or from fish taken from polluted waters such as Kingston Harbour. In 2005, studies found worrying levels of lead in locally produced dutch pots, and users were encouraged not to scrub them but to rub them with vegetable oil.[16] Cadmium, a modern toxic metal, has also been shown recently to have high concentrations in some food crops, such as leafy vegetables and legumes, grown in uncontaminated Jamaican soils.[17]

On the positive side, minerals can be added to common foods with beneficial effects. Modern "iodized" table salt has added iodine to help prevent goitre, while fluoride is added to drinking water (as well as to toothpaste) to prevent dental decay. Modern milling practices in Jamaica and elsewhere produce "fortified" flour by adding minerals, notably iron, in minute proportions. Iron-fortified dried skimmed milk, by itself or mixed with cornmeal to make a porridge, has been found to offer health benefits to infants who are no longer breastfeeding. Long-grain white rice, an American product, was sold in Jamaica in 2005, "vitamin enriched (thiamine, niacin, folate) plus iron".[18] Similarly, chlorine has been added to the public supply of drinking water. All of these elements are ingested unwittingly.

But earth can also be deliberately eaten. The active, self-conscious eating of earth is an ancient and widespread practice, often called geophagy. The causes and effects of geophagy are debated. Some argue that the practice is an attempt to alleviate malnutrition or famine, or a response to specific mineral deficiencies, notably iron, and serving to detoxify plant food. Others claim it is the geophagy that causes malnutrition, including deficiencies of iron and zinc. Geophagy may also be understood as the cause of intestinal parasitism or alternatively as a response to the presence of worms in the belly. Further, geophagy may be seen as essentially an expression of cultural beliefs, separate from, or combined with, physiological responses.[19] In West Africa, clay has long been consumed as a regular food item, specially mined and prepared, sometimes mixed with salt, and sold in cakes in the market.[20]

The enslaved people of Jamaica carried with them from Africa an understanding of geophagy. They mined particular veins of "aboo earth", found in marl beds and, in the late eighteenth century, said Long, "*aboo*, or earth cakes are vended among the Negroes at Spanish Town", using a particular earth from the northeastern edge of the town, near the Rio Cobre. The earth was "apparently smooth, unctuous, and somewhat cohesive, of a sweetish taste, and dissolves readily in the mouth". Simon Taylor, writing in 1789, interpreted the eating of earth as a reaction to the treatment given by doctors of the European tradition. The enslaved people, he said, had "their blood broke down by the cursed quantity of mercury and antinomials the plantation doctors give them", creating "*a constant acid on their stomachs*". To remedy this, the people "if they can possibly get at it use a sort of whitish loam which allays the acid, but instantly bloats them, and when they cannot get at it they will eat cinders, ashes, or in short any sort of stuff". Taylor and Long thought the practice addictive and a cause of dropsy and other illnesses. Dovaston similarly said, "Some slaves are much addicted to eating of dirt and others will eat of chalk, and sooner chuse it than their food." John Stewart, writing in 1823, however, believed that "this diseased appetite proceeds from an insufficiency of wholesome and nourishing food" and needed to be solved by improved nutrition rather than by the harsh and barbarous treatment often meted out.[21]

In 1835 James Maxwell, surgeon to the Annotto Bay Marine Hospital, claimed that an absorbent clay eaten by enslaved people "occurs disseminated; colour chocolate brown; has an unctuous soapy feel; is soft; fractures roughly, and does not adhere to the tongue". Baked in cakes, said Maxwell, it was "used by many as a social habit, under the name of aboo", and "the moderate use of this earth is considered by the negroes neither dangerous nor disgraceful; and those who eat it, take it as much to gratify an acquired taste, similar to that of chewing tobacco or opium, as to satisfy any morbid desire". Favoured earths were excavated from the beds of rivers and from roadside banks. According to Maxwell, "many of the agricultural negroes, especially the women, who are well fed, habitually consume moderate quantities of steatite made up into balls like chocolate, which are baked and sold in the market amongst themselves at the rate of two for five pence". Some ate the clay "in its native state", he said, but "others mix it with a proportion of salt, and, after, baking, preserve it in the smoke for occasional use". In 1837 Joseph Sturge and Thomas Harvey similarly reported that "the alkaline earth which is so greedily sought for by dirt eaters, is sometimes made into cakes and sold in Kingston market".[22]

Modern accounts of geophagy in Jamaica are typically associated with the "strange appetites" and "outrageous cravings" of pregnant women for soap, ice, chalk and tooth-paste, as well as soil and wood-ash. Some also believed that drinking its own bathwater would make a baby strong. In 1983 a study found that when pregnant Jamaican women experienced a craving for earth, it was always for country dirt, rather than the "unclean" dirt of town, and generally identified as a specific type, such as the red dirt from a gully bank or the dirt attached to tubers. Occasionally the taste of the best earth was compared to that of chocolate.[23]

WATER

Jamaica's water resources were long regarded as bountiful, and indeed, the English called the island the "land of wood and water". Drinking and cooking only ever used small quantities compared to the demands of agriculture and industry, but the massive aqueducts, built during slavery, that carried large volumes of water long distances in order to power sugar and coffee mills, were tapped for domestic use one way or another. In the 1670s, before the earthquake, Port Royal was supplied with water from the Rio Cobre, carried in casks.[24] Only in the urban areas did government take an interest in providing piped water, and even there the first projects did not commence until the 1840s and drew on existing plantation aqueducts.

The Liguanea Plain, Kingston's site, was a dry place long dependent on wells. Rivers were tapped and dams and reservoirs built, but the supply was rarely adequate to demand, resulting in periodic lock-offs, particularly during droughts. Water quality was improved by filtration beginning in the 1870s, and later by sterilization (chlorammo-niation), to achieve a high level of purity. Outside Kingston, public supply and moni-toring developed more slowly. Down to the 1930s, few areas had piped supplies and the water was rarely purified. There were complaints that chlorination of the Kingston supply gave the water a bad taste. The most common source of water remained the open river or stream, and that too was often polluted by people and animals. Many people still had no latrines. Few of the sources were really safe for drinking, but still the impor-tance of "water as a food" was advocated.[25]

At the time of the 1943 census, piped water reached the dwellings of most people in Kingston and St Andrew. In the island overall, however, only 26 per cent had such access. Fully 40 per cent took their water direct from streams, while others depended on standpipes (9 per cent), public tanks (8 per cent), catchments (6 per cent), ponds (5 per cent) and wells (4 per cent). Only 41 per cent of dwellings had water to hand and the majority had to carry their water home, often more than a kilometre. The need for improved supplies of potable water was recognized as a major project at Independence. A National Water Commission, amalgamating earlier bodies, was established in 1980. By the 2001 census, the proportion of households with piped water had increased to 77 per cent, though one-third of those had to collect water from a standpipe or a pipe in a yard rather than having it come directly into their kitchens. Catchments supplied 12 per cent, and 5 per cent took their water from a river. Some rural water schemes did not meet the criteria for good quality, and a large proportion of country people stored water, thus creating another possibility of contamination. Street food cooks necessarily stored water and used it in preparing meals.[26]

At the turn of the century, water was generally not regarded as a "food", though it supplied the minerals sodium, calcium and magnesium and was therefore a vital nutrient. Bottled water, sometimes labelled "mineral water" or "spring water", became popular. By 2005, Jamaica was importing ten times as much water as it was exporting, with almost fifty brands on the market. More than 300,000 litres of "flavourless mineral water" was imported, some of it coming from as far away as Thailand. Although Jamaican producers concentrated on high-quality spring water, competition with cheaper imports proved difficult as price proved to be the major factor in water purchasing. Some producers attempted to identify themselves as local and superior through branding, like Jamaica Spring Water and Mek Yah Wata. In 2005 local producers of bottled water, most of it drawn from springs, bemoaned the fact that they were unable to compete success-fully in local and overseas markets. To succeed overseas, it was recognized, brand defi-nition was essential to convince consumers of "the uniqueness of our water".[27]

Water was also imported as ice. Attempts to bring ice to Jamaica from the frozen ponds of New England began in 1805, but the first two cargoes to actually reach the island were brought from Halifax, Nova Scotia, in 1813 or 1814. In this experiment, lobster, cod, salmon and all sorts of shellfish were imported, enveloped in ice. By the 1840s Kingston had a brick ice store and the trade was put on a permanent footing. In the 1870s, "ice-ships" brought fresh fruit from the United States. In 1880 ice-making machines were being advertised in Jamaica: the Atlas engine, made in Birmingham, England, produced "transparent ice as hard, clear and durable as natural ice, at less than half the price". It was not until 1884 that an ice factory was built in Kingston. A block of ice was considered an appropriate gift, to be hauled across the island by the affluent to present to a rural host. By 1900 there were ice factories in almost all the larger towns.[28]

One by-product of the new ready availability of ice was the making of shaved ice treats. By the 1930s, "snowballs" were being sold from little carts in Kingston, "small balls of shaved ice at a penny a ball, transformed into any brilliant color chosen from a score of bottles of synthetically colored syrup". Simple icicles on sticks, called "suck suck", were sold by vendors on bicycles. In the 1980s, "back and front" was remembered as a popular "olde time" drink, enjoyed perhaps with a fried dumpling and a saltfish fritter. The back and front was "a pint or half-pint tumbler of snow-ball topped with ice cream". The snowball and ice cream were mixed by stirring in alternating clockwise and anticlockwise sweeps, and might also contain evaporated milk and grated nutmeg. The snowball was gradually replaced by sno-cone (in which the syrup was poured over shaved ice in a paper cone), sky juice (the syrupy drink in a plastic container) and, later, box juice and box milk (the liquid in a sealed, coated card box).[29]

Another way of using water was to drink the liquid in which food had been cooked, the "pot water". Food cooked in water loses minerals by leaching. Thus it was recom-mended, in the 1990s, that the pot water be reused in order to benefit by the potassium and other minerals. "Banana water", meaning the water in which green bananas had been boiled, was already promoted in folklore as a means towards strength and health, perhaps because it contained traces of iron.[30] On the other hand, the pot water from boiling ackees was identified as a culprit in poisoning cases. The question of pot water was debated particularly during the world wars, when food resources were stretched. In some cases, the ackee pot water was used to make soup, with a beef bone, for example. In other cases the water was used to boil yam, and eating the yam was enough to cause "vomiting sickness". Children died rather than adults because they were given "the 'soup' or 'pot water'". The threat from pot water was argued at least as early as 1915. In 1940 Dr Eugene Gideon said that "the ackee was cooked in a common pot along with cocoa, yam, bread-fruit, and or other ground foods and often with a small piece of meat or relish in the form of salted pork. The pot water or soup was fed to the youngest members of the family whilst the solid portions of the pot were distributed to the older members." In 1961 it was noted that the additional iron obtained from the use of iron cooking pots was likely to diminish as aluminium became more fashionable, but later the locally made aluminium cooking pot was in turn to come under fire as a potential cause of illness.[31]

CHAPTER 12

CONCLUSION

It may appear ironic that of the many foods consumed by Jamaicans only a small proportion are indigenous. Most have their origins elsewhere: they have reached the island as imports or are the products of naturalized plants and animals introduced over the last several centuries. This pattern of introduction, adaptation and elaboration is not peculiar to the food system but typical of many elements of Jamaican culture. Indeed, modern conceptions of the character of "Jamaican food" centre not on unique, endemic species of plants and animals but rather on the creative, creole manipulation of resources and on the development of a central core of vital elements. Yet this is a relatively recent conception. In earlier times, the indigenous was far more important.

The food resources of the Taino came entirely from their own region; indeed, they had no other practical options. They did carry the bitter cassava to Jamaica, but the plant was already part of the culture of their people and travelled with its established technologies of processing and cooking. Europeans and Africans, on the other hand, confronting a whole new world of plants and animals, immediately added to them many of the plants and animals they had known and produced in often quite different environments. Down to the end of the seventeenth century, it was the indigenous that was most likely to be understood as "Jamaican" by Europeans and Africans, placed in contrast with the familiar of the Old World. In this pantheon, cocoa and avocado, pineapple and mammee apple held an important place as new-found fruits, but most esteemed as delicacies were the endemic wild animals, notably turtle, ringtail pigeon, black land crab and mountain mullet. These retained their status into the early twentieth century but are now almost completely forgotten, their populations dramatically depleted, often endangered.

Why were endemic and indigenous land animals so attractive as food sources and why were their numbers reduced so rapidly? Apart from the lure of the exotic, these indigenous animals offered a rich resource of protein that was not otherwise in large supply, and they did not need to be farmed. So long as their numbers remained abundant, substantial quantities of fresh flesh food could be obtained by hunting them. But the hunters generally had little regard for sustainability, and happily consumed eggs and young. Some of the animals, such as the manatee and the turtle, were poorly equipped to withstand the onslaught.

The endemic and indigenous plants of Jamaica, on the other hand, were much better placed to survive, so long as the human population remained relatively small. Few food plants disappeared. Even the cabbage tree palm fared better than the animals. The relative degree of survival of the plants was partly a result of their modes of reproduction and dispersal, but was also aided by their lower position in the scale of delicacies. Fruit emerged as a central marker of Jamaican food only in the nineteenth century, and by then the perception of what was indigenous was beginning to become fuzzy, as introduced fruits, such as the banana and the mango, took their place beside pine and mammee apple.

The twentieth century saw the definition of Jamaican food shift once again, this time to methods of processing, preparation and cooking. Before the late nineteenth century, the most distinctive methods of cooking associated with Jamaica were barbecue and jerk, which were founded on the abundant supply of feral animals, particularly cows and pigs, that were hunted in the seventeenth century in much the same way as were the endemic wild animals of Jamaica. Pepperpot soup also had some standing. These foods persisted but had only a tenuous hold as iconic dishes at the beginning of the twentieth century. More important was the emerging "national dish" ackee and saltfish and its close rival rice and peas, both of which used imported and introduced ingredients. These were joined by patty, bun and hard-dough bread, a completely new style of baked Jamaican foods, however firmly their origins were rooted in earlier traditions. Other products took on a more subtle Jamaican character, such as Jamaican cheese, Jamaican condensed milk and Jamaican margarine, all of which were made to particular specifications to suit Jamaican sweet and salty taste. As well as the beef in the patty, meat featured in the "Jamaican" dishes stew peas, curry goat and, most importantly, jerk pork and chicken. In every case, it was the method of preparation and cooking that distinguished these dishes. Not one of them used an indigenous plant or the meat of an indigenous animal.

The concept "Jamaican food" connects directly with the developing understanding of identity and what it means to be Jamaican. What people eat is not sufficient in itself to construct identity, of course, but for Jamaicans visiting or living overseas, or for Jamaicans seeking to distinguish themselves from other Caribbean peoples, food regularly proves a point of immediate connection and difference. Jamaicans are not unique in this. It is a characteristic of island peoples that parallels the often ethnic identifications associated with immigrant populations in continental societies. Jamaica's neighbour Cuba, for example, is equally focused on the idea of "Cuban food", which has travelled far and wide with the outpouring of people over the last fifty years. Yet although it has sometimes been argued that Jamaican food has much in common with that of the rest of the Caribbean, to the point that the national motto could be read as "Out of Many, One Cuisine", Jamaicans are more likely to agree with Bruce Geddes's contention that "of all the Caribbean countries it is in Jamaica that a truly national cuisine has developed".[1]

Independence encouraged reflection on the nature and distinctiveness of "Jamaican food", but the idea had its roots in a Creole enthusiasm that was firmly established by the eighteenth century. Creole taste, shared by black and white, enslaved and free, gave priority to pungent spice. Hot peppers were central.[2] The new peoples who came to Jamaica after 1838 accommodated to this preference and enhanced it. Indian cooking styles blended almost seamlessly, as is seen in the widespread adoption of curry goat. The Chinese tradition of cooking has remained more strictly separate and authentic, using many ingredients imported from Asia that have no equivalents in the Jamaican *food-supply system. At the same time, the essence of stir-fry cooking methods has been* accepted into the general system of food preparation in Jamaica. By 1940 hotels were offering their guests "Chinese chop suey". Yet many of the special ingredients of Chinese cooking are probably still eaten by Jamaicans, other than those of Chinese descent, only when they go to restaurants. On the other hand, beginning in the 1960s, Jamaican cookbooks sometimes included special sections on Chinese cooking and encouraged cooks to explore the "incomparable taste and flavour" found in authentic Chinese cuisine. A 1998 cookbook included in its section of "authentic Jamaican cuisine" a recipe for chow mein, explaining that the dish was "a favourite with Jamaicans although it is a Chinese authentic cuisine".[3]

While Jamaican food is not self-consciously labelled African, are its fundamentals in fact African taken as Jamaican? West Africans, it is said, prefer meals consisting of a bulky mash or paste of starchy food, eaten with a sauce to provide protein, vitamins and salt. The staple starch might be obtained from roots (yam, coco, cassava, potato), cereals (rice, Guinea corn, maize) or fruit (plantain, banana), with particular crops dominating locally to create strong regional contrasts. The protein might come from meat and fish but could also be found in oils from groundnuts, shea butter or palm oil. These patterns changed dynamically during the colonial period. Corn (maize) and cassava entered Africa from the Americas, changing the range of possible foods, so that it is easier to identify an "African" style of food preparation than to associate African food with specific ingredients. By the time of the abolition of the Atlantic slave trade, corn was already well established as a secondary crop in the forest regions of West Africa and in the intermediate zone between forest and savannah, serving as a supplement to the traditional yam staple. Cassava spread more slowly, probably because of the need to learn safe processing technologies. The significance of salt in the West African diet also had its counterpart in Jamaica. Spices seem to have been relatively rare in West Africa before Columbus, though they were quickly adopted and became a further element in the dynamic transfer of foods and cooking styles.[4]

Proponents of the Africanness of Jamaican food have been relatively few, though the origins of many of the ingredients and methods of preparation used in Jamaica obviously derive directly from West and Central Africa, the cultural homeland of most Jamaicans. In 1980 the African-Caribbean Institute of Jamaica published a cookbook titled *A Panorama of African Cuisine* which included a section on cooking rules for "African Jamaican Cuisine" but, apart from a reference to methods of pounding and grinding, the directions followed closely what was associated with "Jamaican" cooking generally (leaving out the curry and the stir-fry).[5] Generally speaking, cookbooks may have special sections for East Indian and Chinese dishes, but not for African dishes – or for English ones, for that matter. These dishes have been broadly assimilated and are now associated with the idea of a shared taste that makes everything Jamaican.

Why are salt, sugar and spice so important in the history of Jamaican taste? Salt and spice are often attributed their roles in the food system as a straightforward consequence of their long use as preservatives. Although they were important in this way, it is too simple an explanation. Salt was a scarce and valuable commodity in early colonial Jamaica, but much desired by the African people forced to labour on the island's plantations. It was even more scarce in most of West Africa. The great trans-Saharan trade that developed did not respond to a demand for preservatives but rather to an immediate dietary need or simple taste. Sugar too was a luxury initially but the development of the plantations shifted the balance to create abundance in all but the most refined versions of the commodity. It is equally incorrect to argue that spices ceased to be appealing once they stopped being "exotic" materials obtained from far away, the "paradise" of the spice islands and distant Asia.[6] Some of the spices remained luxuries for a very long period, and some indeed continue in that class, but Jamaica quickly became the home of many pungent foodstuffs, creating opportunities for the island's cooks that came to mark the cuisine more than salt and sugar could ever do.

Salt continued to be craved even when it had ceased to be vital as a preservative and when its deleterious effects on health had become well known. The love of salt can be traced to physiological demands, created by evolution in environments quite different from those now inhabited. The body cannot easily forget the hard-learned lesson that salt, originally obtained naturally in small quantities, needs to be conserved for long-term survival. Today the intake of salt is excessive but the body cannot easily expel it, with serious consequences for health. In this case, inherited taste can prove deleterious. A parallel might be drawn with sickle cell anaemia, in which the sickle cell trait had functionality as a protection against malaria but is simply debilitating in a modern society like Jamaica that has effectively defeated the disease.

The example of salt shows that it can be difficult for people to change their taste for particular foods or food types, and that the advice of nutritionists, dietitians and practitioners of medicine is routinely ignored. More broadly, it is sometimes also argued that Jamaicans are generally conservative in taste, unwilling to try new foods and dishes.[7] The truth of this might be found in the extent to which Jamaicans remain wedded to particular foods when they leave home and in their reluctance to eat the foods of the places to which they migrate. Are they unusually conservative in this way or is it just a characteristic of migrant peoples? Necessity is an important driver of changed food patterns among migrants generally, and the availability of exotic crops made possible by modern refrigerated and rapid air transport has reduced this necessity, facilitating the maintenance of established foods and food traditions. At the same time, it is the presence of "ethnic" and "national" foods within traditional national systems that has helped set off the former as special and unique. Thus the modern diaspora has both supported and amplified the concept of Jamaican food (by giving it a presence in overseas centres that it did not have before) and carried an awareness back to Jamaica, through return migration and tourism.

In the longer term, conservatism in taste and food systems was not viable. Certainly the Taino practised it effectively, but they lacked the impulse or opportunity for any true alternative. The history of modern Jamaican food, on the other hand, is founded on the introduction of a wide range of plants and animals from widely scattered parts of the world. These plants and animals had, in turn, a diverse series of centres of domestication, often distant from the places from which they were brought to Jamaica (Figures 12.1–12.4). Some of the plants and animals were known to the European colonizers but not to the Africans (cabbage and codfish, for example); others were known only to the Africans (ackee and Guinea corn); and some things were known by none of Jamaica's people (breadfruit and otaheite apple). These were added to equally unknown plants of the Americas introduced from the mainland, such as cocoa and the "Irish" potato. Other plants and animals known by both Europeans and Africans ultimately became dominant foods: rice, cow, goat, pig, chicken.

Many of the plants and land animals that entered the Jamaican food system depended for their introduction on active human intervention (Appendix 2). Only plants and animals with special characteristics easily found their own way to the island. Thus all of the important roots and tubers were brought to Jamaica by people who already knew the food value of these plants and already possessed appropriate technologies for cultivation and preparation. Further, although the roots and tubers were not able to survive long periods floating on the sea, they did possess storage qualities that made them an ideal choice for long-distance human voyaging. The consequence was that some roots (such as cassava) travelled with the migrant Taino, who self-consciously thought of the plants as their future food supply, while others (such as African and Asian varieties of yam) were the immediate food supply of voyagers, and their remnants entered the agricultural and food systems of Jamaica adventitiously and unremarked.

Some fruits arrived in much the same way, as unintended migrants or stowaways. The ackee is perhaps the best example, but several other of the plants introduced to Jamaica from Africa must have travelled similarly. Large live animals, on the other hand, required care while on a long voyage: forethought was essential. Like the roots, animals were carried alive as food for the voyage, and a few probably survived to live on the land

1400

Corn
Anatto
Yam (*D. trifida*)
Pineapple
Cassava
Arrowroot

Garlic

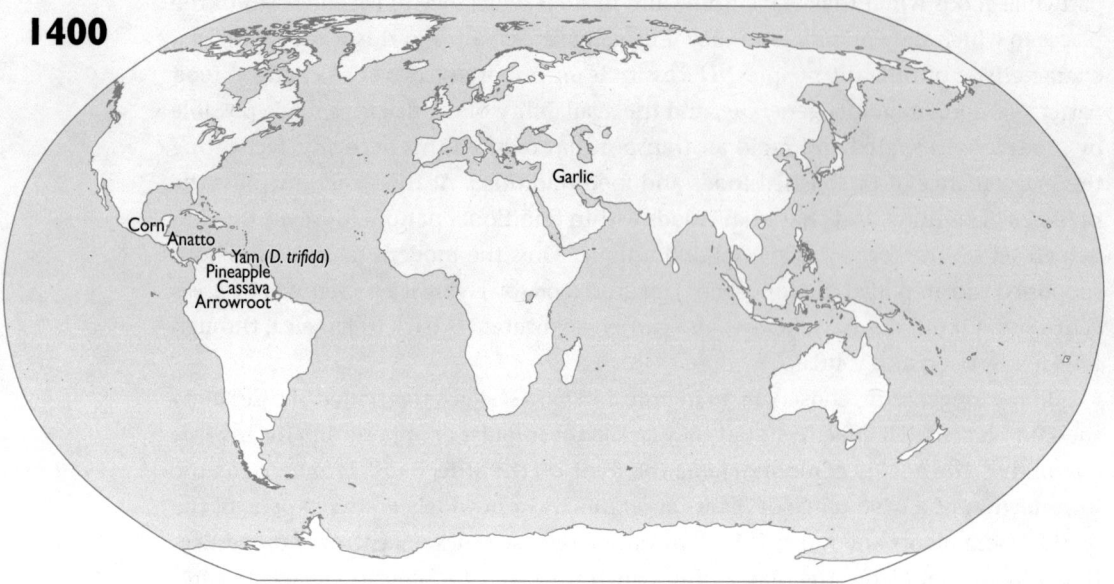

Figure 12.1 Origins of plants and animals introduced to Jamaica before 1400, indicating sites of domestication rather than the places from which the plants and animals were taken to Jamaica

1600

Cabbage
Lettuce Kale
Asparagus
Goose Pomegranate *Sheep*
Rabbit *Goat*
Cow, Pig *Duck*
(Bos taurus) Onion
Scallion

Red pea
Pawpaw
Avocado
Cocoa   Maiden plum
Broadbean
Vanilla

Cat
Donkey
Bonavist bean   *Guineafowl*
Gherkin *Cane rat*   Lemon   Citron
Rice (*Oryza glaberrima*)   Watermelon   Coco
Gungo pea Kolanut Pussley Guinea corn   Ginger
Tamarind Yam (*D. cayenensis*)
Yam (*D. rotundata*)
Peanut
Cowpea

Orange
Mandarin
Chicken Tangerine
Lime Yam (*D. esculenta*)
Yam (*D. alata*)
Plantain
Banana   Coconut

Sugar
cane

Irish
potato

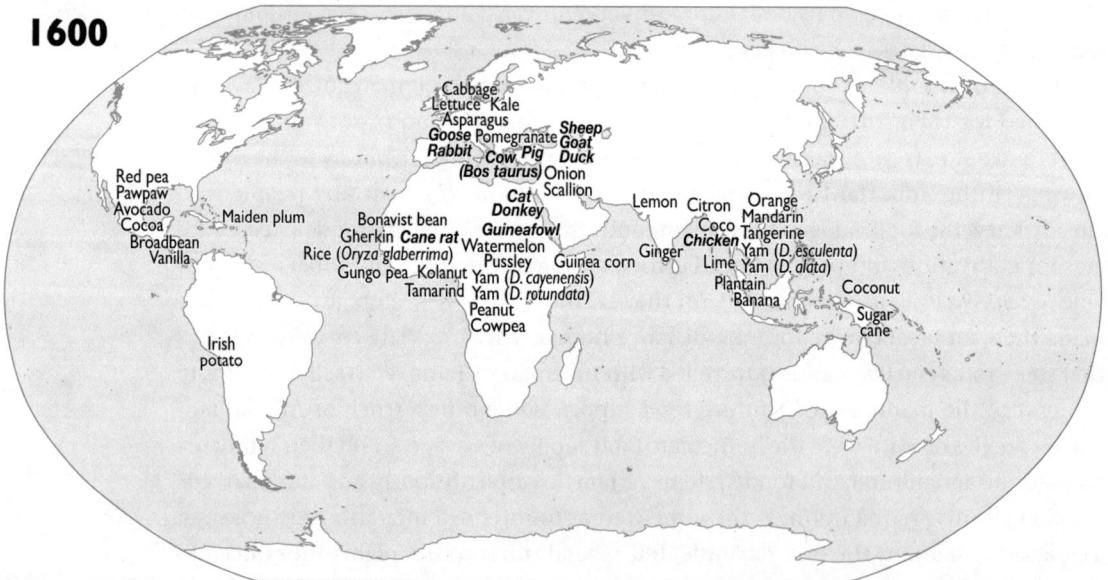

Figure 12.2 Origins of plants and animals introduced to Jamaica between 1400 and 1600, indicating sites of domestication rather than the places from which the plants and animals were taken to Jamaica

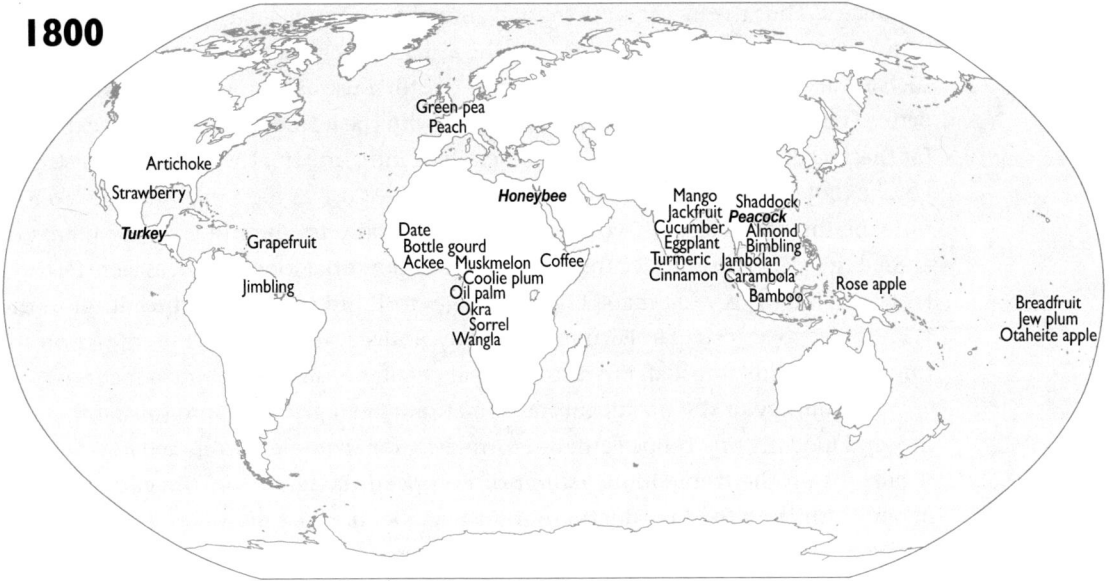

1800

Artichoke
Strawberry
Turkey
Grapefruit
Jimbling

Green pea
Peach

Honeybee

Date
Bottle gourd
Ackee Muskmelon Coffee
Coolie plum
Oil palm
Okra
Sorrel
Wangla

Mango Shaddock
Jackfruit *Peacock*
Cucumber Almond
Eggplant Bimbling
Turmeric Jambolan
Cinnamon Carambola
Bamboo

Rose apple

Breadfruit
Jew plum
Otaheite apple

Figure 12.3 Origins of plants and animals introduced to Jamaica between 1600 and 1800, indicating sites of domestication rather than the places from which the plants and animals were taken to Jamaica

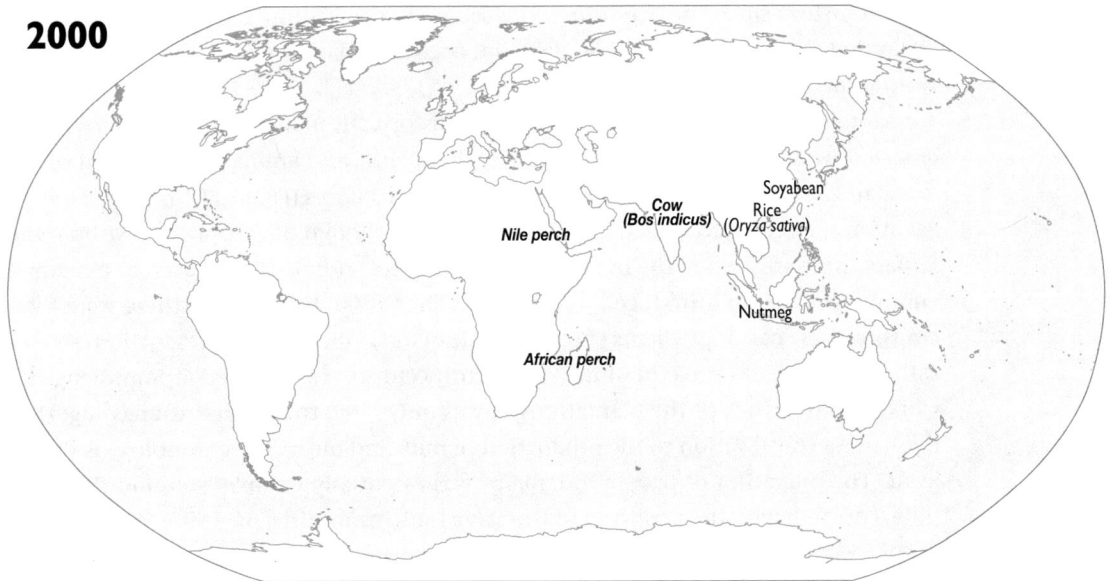

2000

Soyabean
Cow Rice
(Bos indicus) *(Oryza sativa)*
Nile perch

Nutmeg

African perch

Figure 12.4 Origins of plants and animals introduced to Jamaica between 1800 and 2000, indicating sites of domestication rather than the places from which the plants and animals were taken to Jamaica

of Jamaica. Thus the major modern food animals – cow, pig, goat, sheep and chicken – were all intentional introductions, arriving as part of regular voyages. Smaller animals such as cat and rat were regular stowaways, but their use as food was less common and petered out early. Something similar happened with the introduction of plants exploited for their seeds, the seeds themselves generally coming to Jamaica as stores for use on a voyage (notably African rice and Guinea corn) or for use as food in Jamaica, as well as for experimental planting. Voyages made specifically to obtain particular plants or animals in order to introduce them to Jamaica as potential food resources were few and far between. This is what made Bligh's voyages to Tahiti to bring the breadfruit to the West Indies so spectacular. Further, as already noticed, the introduction of the bread-fruit was not only unusual, but also the final chapter of significant introductions.

The journey of the breadfruit has sometimes been given a more substantial role in world food history. Felipe Fernández-Armesto, for example, has argued that "Bligh's saga sums up the tremendous labour of European navigators of the early modern period in shifting food products around the globe, not just by way of trade but also as samples for planting". The breadfruit symbolizes for Fernández-Armesto the ecolog-ical exchange that followed Columbus, making it an element in one of the most signif-icant revolutions in world history. Down to the sixteenth century, he contends, the drifting apart of the continents resulted in separate and divergent spheres of biolog-ical development, a process reversed by the European voyagers. To this extent, it is easy enough to agree with Fernández-Armesto that "the great ocean-borne exchange of biota of the last 500 years constituted the biggest human intervention in environ-mental history since the beginnings of species domestication". It is equally true that important food plants, including the yam, coco and plantain, were moved across the world long before Columbus.[8]

From the point of view of Jamaican food history, the period from 1500 to 1800 was crucial. It was during those three centuries that plants and animals were carried to the island most self-consciously and across the longest distances (Figures 12.1–12.4). Human agency was essential to all of these transplantations, though they happened without the fanfare that surrounded the breadfruit. Some new economic plants, such as cinchona and mulberry, were introduced to the island after 1800, but none of these were food crops, and few new ingredients entered Jamaican food culture. The introduction of Zebu cattle from India at the end of the nineteenth century was directed at improving the working-cattle stock of the plantations; it was only later, through cross-breeding, that there was a contribution to the production of milk and meat. The chronology is signif-icant. The migration of people to Jamaica was essentially complete around the same time, concluded by the abolition of the slave trade from Africa in 1807. Various other peoples arrived, and the Indians and the Chinese among them did have a significant impact on the food history of the island, but the basics were already firmly in place, both in demography and in food resources.

The first people forced from Africa to Jamaica found there few familiar plants and animals. But over the three hundred years of the Atlantic slave trade, the flora and to a lesser extent the fauna became more similar, as African plants were naturalized in Jamaica and plants from the Americas were introduced to West and Central Africa. On the other hand, many things were never successfully transferred and remained missing from the Jamaican environment. Jamaica never became a home for certain African food plants because it lacked the appropriate environment (millet and fonio, for example) and never introduced wild animals that might be hunted (such as antelope and gazelle) because the movement of undomesticated animals was always difficult.[9]

Alongside the introductions, items were regularly dropped from the list of foods eaten by Jamaicans. In part, this was a process of replacement. Things eaten only of "necessity" – arguably animals such as cat, dog and rat, for example – could be replaced by goat and cow, for reasons of economic or nutritional efficiency or to obey rules of healthy living or of religion. Similarly, leaves of trees and vines were dropped from the list once hardship did not drive people to eat them and as a wider variety of plant foods became available. In some cases, the dropping of items was the result of extinctions and problems of supply. As Frederick Simoons has shown, it is almost always easier to add an animal to the list of prohibited species than to remove one.[10]

In spite of the seeming increased availability of diverse foods, the range of foods eaten by Jamaicans has narrowed rather than widened. On the surface, modern commercial markets suggest a great proliferation of potential foods. However, the number of animals used for food has been dramatically reduced. Just three mammals – cow, pig and goat – matter in modern Jamaican meat and milk supply. Several mammals – cat, dog, rat, manatee – have ceased to seem appropriate as human food. Among the birds, the chicken now reigns supreme, produced and eaten in vast numbers, while other birds are forgotten or neglected. The narrowing is somewhat less for fish, but fish overall have become less important. Most dramatically, the reptiles have disappeared almost completely from Jamaican diet.

One striking difference between plant and animal resources is that very few of the plants exploited for food in Jamaica were heavily depleted or made extinct by overuse. Animals, on the other hand, regularly faced depletion and extinction. This was particularly true of indigenous reptiles (turtle), birds (flamingo, ringtail pigeon) and mammals (manatee, monk seal), but their extinction or depletion did not lead to reduced meat-eating. Rather, these animals were replaced by farmed, domesticated animals, the great weight of meat coming from a handful of mammals (cow, pig and goat) and a single bird (chicken). Three seeds (wheat, corn and rice) similarly came to dominate shelves and tables, processed into a myriad of forms but still limited in origin. Although many species of plants are edible and occasionally eaten, just twenty account for 90 per cent of the plant food consumed around the world, the three leading cereals alone – wheat, rice and corn – for more than 50 per cent.[11] This pattern of narrowing sources matched by elaborated processing ran parallel to the shift of the centre of Jamaican food from specific wild animals and luscious fruits to the modern emphasis on cooking styles that have helped make products derived from introduced, imported elements distinctively local.

Boiling and stewing in an iron pot over an open fire was typical for most Jamaicans for much of Jamaica's history, beginning in the late seventeenth century. The material of the pot might vary (ceramic or aluminium), as might its contents, and the construction of the fireplace (coal-pot or Caledonian stove), but the fundamentals remained quite stable. Boiling and stewing were not the practice of the Taino, nor were they usual under the Spanish, with different resources available and a differently structured society. It was the sugar plantation, based on slavery, that brought forth the bubbling, simmering iron pot. How far was this a result of choices made by the planters and imposed on the increasingly numerous community of enslaved people and how far was it a choice made by the people themselves?

Boiling was the primary cooking technique in most of the West African cultures from which the people of Jamaica came. Among the Yoruba, for example, "to cook" was the equivalent of "to boil", though frying, toasting, roasting and baking were all practised.[12] The planters of Jamaica made a different choice for themselves, feasting on meat as often as possible and roasting and frying whenever they could, though never totally neglecting the contents of the pot. Similarly, the Maroons were notorious for their jerked hog, but also ate from the pot a range of plant foods. Further, enslaved people were punished for consuming meat from plantation animals, and when the planters gave festival treats they killed and roasted oxen, sheep and hogs. After the abolition of slavery, the demand for meat increased rapidly when people could afford to purchase. It seems fair to conclude that enslaved people in Jamaica would have preferred tools and techniques that enabled different and varied styles of cooking. Their poor, though free, descendants no doubt felt the same. Only in the later twentieth century, when a counterculture emerged and nutritionists became advocates, did meat and salt, roasting and frying, begin to be viewed negatively.

Jamaicans have from time to time been encouraged to eat Jamaican, in order to demonstrate their nationalism and to support the local economy. Such campaigns have not always been realistic, in the midst of globalization and structural readjustment that have drawn the island into an era of intensified intercontinental food chains. In 1987, for example, when Jamaicans were urged to "put more local food on the table", the first recipes promoted used as their main ingredients coco, cassava, sweet potato, breadfruit, plantain and banana, all of them "food" crops.[13] This emphasis is appropriate. Globally it is these staples that have generally performed best as local resources. For example, about 85 per cent of total banana and plantain production is consumed domestically, with the banana dominant in Asia and the plantain in Africa. Like Jamaica, Africa has seen a recent decline in the starchy staples, which have been displaced by cereals and particularly by corn. Rice has also proved a strong rival to yams in West Africa, and it has even been asked "whether yams have any worthwhile future as food crops". In parts of Asia, the supposed process of "rizification" has been balanced by strong performance from roots and tubers, though the exotic sweet potato and cassava have generally displaced the indigenous taro and yam.[14]

Nationalism, nostalgia and the endemic or indigenous character of plants and animals might have helped construct the idea of "Jamaican food", but they have not driven decisions about what to eat each day. Economy of effort was vital in the long run, particularly in the context of slavery and the heavy demands on time from plantation labour that left little for the production and preparation of food among the working population. Although the rich planter class could, and did, devote considerable resources to their enjoyment of food and drink, and some of what they developed lasted in the longer term, for most people the costs and benefits of particular foods had to be carefully weighed. Price, availability, preparation time and energy use all help determine what people actually eat, but these everyday decisions are linked to the popularity of particular foods by the idea of taste.

Ideas about food are part of a larger understanding of the healthy human body, connecting nutrition with disease and taste. Decisions about what to eat and drink are made also, then, within the context of understandings of the potential short- and long-term effects of the substances ingested, some of them deleterious, others medicinal, curative or prophylactic. Rastafarians have expressed some of the strongest views on these matters. Some have even argued that death by disease is directly triggered by following a "European diet" that includes red meat, salt, white flour and rice.[15] This is a warning that has not been carefully regarded.

Marvin Harris has proposed a cost-benefit efficiency model to explain why particular animals are eaten and others not, and why the equation varies both from culture to culture and, historically, over time. Harris identifies a hierarchy of potential meat- and milk-producing animals, derived from an "optimal foraging theory" that looks to optimization rather than symbolism as a means of explaining what is eaten and what is not. The smallest animals are not worth the effort required to collect enough of them. Other animals drop off the list not because they are simply small (or large), but because they are relatively inefficient converters of feed, their ranking dependent on the available alternatives. Thus he concludes that cows, pigs and chickens come out on top of the hierarchy of potential meat-animals because of their efficiency as ruminants (and he might well have included goats in this list), whereas animals such as dogs, cats, horses, rats and goldfish are inefficient and therefore considered ideal as pets rather than food.[16]

A similar argument can be applied to the eating of insects. Although abundant in mass, they have to be collected in large numbers in order to deliver a substantial food benefit, and in addition they are often seasonal. Only where alternative, larger animals are not readily available do insects and other "small things" become attractive as food, and it is this that seems best to explain global differences in their consumption.[17] Unlike the Japanese, a food and nutrition conference was told in 1992, "Jamaicans would never eat grasshoppers for dinner", even though overcoming such taboos and eating "strange foods" could do much to solve global problems of malnutrition and starvation. Earlier, in 1938, when the question of nutrition and diet was much debated in the months leading up to the labour disturbances, there were questions raised about the association of nationality and food habits. The English national character could be traced to the eating of roast beef, but some also ate roast badger, and it was asked, "If an oyster, why not a snail; and if a rabbit, why not a badger? It is all a matter of our up-bringing." If some Jamaicans still regarded the macaca grub as a "delicacy", why not fricasseed mongoose?[18]

Why is it that animals rather than plants are the objects of disgust? It might seem that nutritional, health and moral considerations are at the root of this difference. The recognition of a shared animality between humans and other creatures leads to disgust at the killing of associated species and also to fear of the outcome of such "murder", a closeness not felt with other living organisms. Simoons also contends that "disgust derives from a primitive dread of being contaminated or debased", and that this fear is "generated principally by waste products of the human and animal body". Thus there is a fear of coming into contact with the excretions of the body, and an even greater fear of ingesting these unclean emissions, particularly dung. An extension of this argument is that herbivores are generally considered more acceptable than carnivores, while the most disgusting of the animals are generally omnivores (including humans) and eaters of filth and excrement, as can be seen in the widespread association of disgust with the pig and the dog. Beyond the general disgust associated with animals and the relatively open attitude to plant foods, certain types of animals (such as reptiles) are commonly thought repulsive, and many people find disgusting the thought of eating bodily excretions (such as saliva) and organs (such as eyes and intestines) even when these come from animals whose flesh is otherwise considered acceptable as food.[19] These attitudes are not always applied consistently, though, as seen in the easy consumption of honey and eggs.

Further, although animals or particular parts of animals may be regarded with disgust, meat plays a central role in modern diet. When Jamaicans ask "What's for dinner?" the reply expected will most likely be "mutton" or "chicken" or some other kind of meat. Ethical and economic difficulties, however, do often lead to a search for substitutes. Textured soybean products are served as meat-analogues, sometimes shaped to mimic particular animals and cuts of meat. In 2005 the medical technique of tissue engineering, in which individual cells are multiplied into whole tissues, was applied to food production, with the prospect that for some species a single cell could produce the world's annual meat supply. This "cultured meat" could be produced on an industrial scale, with muscle cells grown on large sheets and regularly stretched to ensure texture.[20] As well as having health and environmental advantages, such a development might seem to avoid ethical objections to the killing of farm animals.

The contemporary plethora of choice presented by the groaning shelves of the supermarket contains many hidden paradoxes and ambiguities. People are now confronted by a profusion of commercially prepared food products, processed materials not found in nature and whose natural origins are often obscure. Industrial-commercial processing has particular requirements that create foods that "commonly provide inapparent salt, refined flour, sugar or corn sweeteners, and trans fatty acids in extraordinary concentration".[21] Thus, although choice may appear almost unlimited and food energy can be obtained with relatively little effort, consumers are often unable or unwilling to make choices in assembling the elements of their diet but rather rely on combinations put together in factories. This has important implications for modern health patterns, of course, but here the significant conclusion is that modern Jamaicans find in prepared foods the loads of salt and sugar for which they long hankered, and this makes such prepared foods attractive choices even if they lack the "spice" fundamental to Jamaican taste.

ESTIMATES OF PRODUCTION, IMPORT AND CONSUMPTION OF SELECTED FOODS, 1822–2005

The charts of per capita production, import and consumption of particular food items in Jamaica (Figures 3.10, 4.6, 5.10, 6.2, 6.13, 8.1, 9.3, 10.2, 10.5, 10.6 and 11.1) are based on data from three major sources. For the period since 1960, the quantities used are those available at the Food and Agriculture Organization (FAO) statistical website, http://faostat.fao.org/. This database overlaps series in the *Yearbook of Food and Agricultural Statistics* published by FAO covering the period from 1940, though with gaps for some items in some periods. Supplementary statistics are found in another FAO publication, *World Crop Statistics: Area, Production and Yield, 1948–1964* (Rome: FAO, 1966). All of these FAO data derive from information supplied by the government of Jamaica, and generally match statistics found in official publications prepared by the Department of Statistics, including the *Statistical Abstract* (1960–1984), *Production Statistics* (1960–1984), the *Annual Abstract of Statistics* and the *Quarterly Digest of Statistics* (1938–1964). These sources depended in turn on data gathered by the Ministry of Agriculture and various commodity boards, data from the Kingston and St Andrew Corporation and parish councils supervising abattoirs, and data supplied by the larger manufacturers of food and beverages.

For the years before 1945, and commencing in 1822, the most complete data are found in the official *Blue Books* of Jamaica. Total imports in the period 1822–1856 represent goods on ships entering Jamaica's ports, without regard to re-export. Data were recorded port by port. Goods for home consumption were defined by the *Blue Books* as "goods (ex-ship and ex-warehouse) on which duty has been paid and which have passed into the hands of the consumer". Wherever possible, only goods consumed within Jamaica are included in the estimates.

Information recorded in the *Blue Books* used a variety of weights and measures. Some goods came in containers described only by their names, from bags and boxes, cans and casks, to hogsheads and puncheons, firkins and bundles. Others were recorded by uniform measure, as in bushels and quintals. All of these units have been standardized commodity by commodity, and converted to metric mass and volume, using indications found in the following: Accounts Current (Jamaica Archives, Spanish Town); advertisements in the *Gleaner*; R.D. Connor, *The Weights and Measures of England* (London: Her Majesty's Stationery Office, 1987); R.E. Zupko, *A Dictionary of Weights and Measures for the British Isles: The Middle Ages to the Twentieth Century* (Philadelphia: American Philosophical Society, 1985); William D. Johnstone, *For Good Measure: A Complete Compendium of International Weights and Measures* (New York: Holt, Rinehart, and Winston, 1975); Lester A. Ross, *Archaeological Metrology: English, French, American, and Canadian Systems of Weights and Measures for North American Historical Archaeology*, Historical Archaeology No. 68 (Ottawa: National Historic Parks and Sites Branch, Parks Canada, 1983); Lewes Roberts, *The Merchants Map of Commerce* (London, 1700); and *Sears, Roebuck, and Co., Catalog* (Chicago: Sears, Roebuck, and Co., 1900). Where necessary, as when hogsheads and puncheons came in different sizes, the standardized measures have been averaged to match the known distribution.

Annual population totals are taken from the censuses and estimated by interpolation for the intercensual years. The per capita rates shown in the charts are three-year moving averages.

ORIGINS AND DATES OF INTRODUCTION OF SELECTED JAMAICAN FOOD PLANTS AND ANIMALS

This table excludes foods that were imported and never produced in Jamaica, and migratory birds. The column "place of origin" identifies the original sites of growth and domestication, rather than the intermediate sites that sometimes supplied Jamaica. Dates of introduction are approximate in most cases. Plants and animals identified here as indigenous are sometimes referred to in the text as naturalized; "indigenous" here means that the plants and animals were found in Jamaica when Europeans arrived in 1494, whether or not they had been brought to the island by human agency. Generally, only one common Jamaican name is provided for each plant or animal, the one considered most popular.

PLANTS

Jamaican Name	Scientific Name	Place of Origin	Date of Introduction
Acerola cherry	*Malphigia punicifolia*	Caribbean	Indigenous
Ackee	*Blighia sapida*	West Africa	c. 1770
Almond	*Terminalia catappa*	Southeast Asia	c. 1700
Anatto	*Bixa orellana*	Tropical America	c. 700
Arrowroot	*Maranta arundinacea*	South America	c. 700
Artichoke	*Helianthus tuberosus*	North America	c. 1700
Asparagus	*Asparagus officinalis*	Europe	c. 1600
Avocado	*Persea americana*	Mexico	c. 1510
Badoo	*Colocasia esculenta*	India/Burma	c. 1520

Jamaican Name	Scientific Name	Place of Origin	Date of Introduction
Bamboo	*Bambusa vulgaris*	East Indies	c. 1650
Banana	*Musa acuminata*	Malaysia	1516
Bimbling	*Averrhoa bilimbi*	Southeast Asia	1793
Bonavist bean	*Lablab purpureus*	Africa	c. 1600
Bottle gourd	*Lagenaria vulgaris*	Africa	c. 1700
Breadfruit	*Artocarpus altilis*	Tahiti	1793
Breadnut	*Brosimum alicastrum*	Tropical America	Indigenous
Broad bean	*Phaseolus lunatus*	Tropical America	c. 1600
Cabbage	*Brassica oleracea*	Europe	c. 1600
Cabbage palm	*Roystonea* sp.	Jamaica	Endemic
Cacoon	*Entada gigas*	Tropical America	Indigenous
Calabash	*Crescentia cujete*	Tropical America	Indigenous
Callaloo	*Amaranthus viridis*	Tropics	Indigenous
Carambola	*Averrhoa carambola*	Malaysia	c. 1750
Cashew	*Anacardium occidentale*	Tropical America	Indigenous
Cassava	*Manihot esculenta*	Brazil	c. 700
Cerasee	*Momordica charantai*	Tropics	Indigenous
Chainy root	*Smilax balbisiana*	Cuba/Hispaniola	Indigenous
Cherimoya	*Annona cherimola*	Andes	Indigenous
Cherry	*Malphigia glabra*	Tropical America	Indigenous
Chewstick	*Gouania lupuloides*	Caribbean	Indigenous
Chocho	*Sechium edule*	Tropical America	Indigenous
Cinnamon	*Cinnamomum verum*	Sri Lanka	1780
Citron	*Citrus medica*	Himalayas	1494
Cobnut	*Omphalea triandra*	Jamaica	Endemic
Coco	*Colocasia esculenta*	India/Burma	c. 1520
	Xanthosoma sagittifolium	Caribbean	Indigenous
Cocoa	*Theobroma cacao*	Mesoamerica	c. 1520
Coconut	*Cocos nucifera*	Indo-Pacific Ocean	c. 1600
Cocoplum	*Chrysobalanus icaco*	Tropical America	Indigenous
Coffee	*Coffea arabica*	Ethiopia	1728
Coolie plum	*Ziziphus mauritiana*	Old World tropics	c. 1700
Corn	*Zea mays*	Mesoamerica	c. 1000
Country pepper	*Capsicum frutescens*	Tropical America	Indigenous
Cowpea	*Vigna sinensis*	Central Africa	c. 1600
Cucumber	*Cucumis sativus*	South Asia	c. 1700
Custard apple	*Annona reticulata*	Tropical America	Indigenous
Damson plum	*Chrysophyllum oliviforme*	Caribbean	Indigenous

Jamaican Name	Scientific Name	Place of Origin	Date of Introduction
Dasheen	*Colocasia esculenta*	India/Burma	c. 1520
Date	*Phoenix dactylifera*	West Africa	c. 1700
Dildo	*Cereus gracilis*	Caribbean	Indigenous
Eddoe	*Colocasia esculenta*	India/Burma	c. 1520
Eggplant	*Solanum melongena*	South Asia	c. 1700
Ganja	*Cannabis sativa*	India	c. 1850
Garlic	*Allium sativum*	Southwest Asia	c. 1400
Gherkin	*Cucumis anguria*	Africa	c. 1600
Ginger	*Zingiber officinale*	India	1525
Golden apple	*Passiflora laurifolia*	South America	Indigenous
Granadilla	*Passiflora ligularis*	South America	Indigenous
Grapefruit	*Citrus paradisi*	Barbados	c. 1700
Green pea	*Pisum sativum*	Europe	c. 1700
Guava	*Psidium guajava*	Tropical America	Indigenous
Guinea corn	*Sorghum bicolor*	East Africa	c. 1550
Guinep	*Melicoccus bijugatus*	Tropical America	Indigenous
Gungo pea	*Cajanus cajan*	South Asia/Africa	c. 1600
Hogplum	*Spondias mombin*	Tropical America	Indigenous
Horse bean	*Canavalia ensiformis*	Tropical America	Indigenous
Irish potato	*Solanum tuberosum*	Andes	c. 1600
Jackfruit	*Artocarpus heterophyllus*	India	1782
Jamaican plum	*Spondias purpurea*	Tropical America	Indigenous
Jambolan	*Syzygium cumini*	Indo-Malaysia	c. 1700
Jimbling	*Phyllanthus acidus*	Brazil	c. 1700
Jew plum	*Spondias dulcis*	Tahiti	1782
Kale	*Brassica oleracea*	Europe	c. 1600
Kolanut	Cola acuminata	West Africa	c. 1600
Lemon	*Citrus limon*	India/Pakistan	1494
Lettuce	*Lactuca* sp.	Europe	c. 1600
Lignum vitae	*Guaiacum officinale*	Tropical America	Indigenous
Lime	*Citrus aurantifolia*	Malaysia	1494
Maccafat	*Acrocomia spinosa*	Jamaica	Endemic
Maiden plum	*Comocladia pinnatifolia*	Hispaniola	c. 1510
Mammee apple	*Mammea americana*	Tropical America	Indigenous
Mammee sapota	*Pouteria sapota*	Central America	Indigenous
Mandarin	*Citrus reticulata*	Southeast Asia	c. 1600
Mango	*Mangifera indica*	India	c. 1770
Muskmelon	*Cucumis melo*	Africa	c. 1700

Jamaican Name	Scientific Name	Place of Origin	Date of Introduction
Naseberry	*Manilkara zapota*	Tropical America	Indigenous
Nutmeg	*Myristica fragrans*	Indonesia	c. 1840
Oil palm	*Elaeis guineensis*	West Africa	c. 1650
Okra	*Abelmoschus esculentus*	Tropical Africa	c. 1700
Onion	*Allium cepa*	Southwest Asia	c. 1510
Orange	*Citrus sinensis*	Southeast Asia	1494
Otaheite apple	*Syzygium malaccense*	Tahiti	1793
Passion fruit	*Passiflora edulis*	South America	Indigenous
Pawpaw	*Carica papaya*	Mesoamerica	c. 1520
Peach	*Prunus persica*	Europe	c. 1700
Peanut	*Arachis hypogaea*	Africa	c. 1600
Pimento	*Pimenta dioica*	Central America	Indigenous
Pineapple	*Ananas comosus*	South America	c. 700
Plantain	*Musa acuminata*	Malaysia	c. 1510
Pomegranate	*Punica granatum*	Mediterranean	c. 1550
Prickly pear	*Opuntia tuna*	Caribbean	Indigenous
Pumpkin	*Cucurbita* sp.	America	Indigenous
Pussley	*Portulaca oleracea*	Old World tropics	c. 1600
Red pea	*Phaseolus vulgaris*	Mesoamerica	c. 1600
Rice	*Oryza glaberrima*	West Africa	c. 1550
	O. sativa	Asia	c. 1850
Roseapple	*Syzygium jambos*	Indo-Pacific Ocean	c. 1750
Sarsaparilla	*Smilax regelii*	Brazil/Guyana	Indigenous
Scallion	*Allium fistulosum*	Southwest Asia	c. 1510
Scotch bonnet pepper	*Capsicum chinense*	Tropical America	Indigenous
Seaweed	*Chondrus* sp.	General	Indigenous
Seville orange	*Citrus aurantium*	Southeast Asia	1494
Shaddock	*Citrus grandis*	Southern China	c. 1650
Sorrel	*Hibiscus sabdariffa*	Old World tropics	c. 1650
Soursop	*Annona muricata*	Tropical America	Indigenous
Soybean	*Glycine max*	East Asia	c. 1940
Squash	*Cucurbita* sp.	America	Indigenous
Star apple	*Chrysophyllum cainito*	Greater Antilles	Indigenous
Strawberry	*Fragaria* sp.	America	c. 1800
Strawberry pear	*Cereus triangularis*	Caribbean	Indigenous
Sugar cane	*Saccharum officinarum*	New Guinea	c. 1510
Susumber	*Solanum torvum*	Tropics	Indigenous
Sweet cup	*Passiflora malformis*	South America	Indigenous

Jamaican Name	Scientific Name	Place of Origin	Date of Introduction
Sweet pepper	*Capsicum annum*	Tropical America	Indigenous
Sweet potato	*Ipomoea batatas*	Tropical America	Indigenous
Sweetsop	*Annona squamosa*	Tropical America	Indigenous
Tamarind	*Tamarindus indica*	Africa	c. 1600
Tangerine	*Citrus reticulata*	Southeast Asia	c. 1600
Tannia	*Xanthosoma sagittifolium*	Caribbean	Indigenous
Tomato	*Lycopersicon esculentum*	Tropical America	Indigenous
Trumpet tree	*Cecropia peltata*	Tropical America	Indigenous
Turmeric	*Curcuma domestica*	South Asia	1780
Vanilla	*Vanilla fragrans*	Central America	c. 1550
Wangla	Sesamum orientale	Old World tropics	c. 1700
Watermelon	*Citrullus vulagaris*	Tropical America	c. 1600
Wiss	*Vitis tiliifolia*	Tropical America	Indigenous
Yam	*Dioscorea alata*	Southeast Asia	c. 1550
	D. cayenensis	West Africa	c. 1510
	D. esculenta	Southeast Asia	c. 1550
	D. rotundata	West Africa	c. 1510
	D. trifida	Guyana/Brazil	c. 700
Zamia	*Cycas megacarpa*	America	Indigenous

ANIMALS

Jamaican Name	Scientific Name	Place of Origin	Date of Introduction
Alligator	*Crocodilus acutus*	Jamaica	Endemic
Anchovy	*Anchoa hepsetus*	Tropics	Indigenous
Baldpate	*Columba leucocephala*	Greater Antilles	Indigenous
Barracuda	*Sphyraena* sp.	Tropics	Indigenous
Black crab	*Gecarcinus ruricola*	Jamaica	Endemic
Brown noddy	*Anous stolidus*	Caribbean	Indigenous
Busu	*Neritina virginea*	Caribbean	Indigenous
Butterfish	*Peprilus triacanthus*	Atlantic	Indigenous
	Cephalopholis fulva	Caribbean	Indigenous
Calipever	*Mugil liza*	America	Indigenous
Cane rat	*Thryonomys swinderianus*	Africa	c. 1600
Cat	*Felis silvestris catus*	Europe	c. 1510
Chicken	*Gallus gallus*	Southeast Asia	c. 1550
Clucking hen	*Aramus guarauna*	Greater Antilles	Indigenous

Jamaican Name	Scientific Name	Place of Origin	Date of Introduction
Conch	*Strombus gigas*	Caribbean	Indigenous
Coney	*Geocapromys browni*	Jamaica	Endemic
Cow	*Bos indicus*	India	1850?
	B. taurus	Africa	1494?
Cutlassfish	*Trichiurus lepturus*	Atlantic	Indigenous
Deer	*Cervus elaphus*	North America	c. 1700
Doctorfish	*Acanthurus chirurgus*	Caribbean	Indigenous
Dog	*Canis familiaris*	Caribbean	Indigenous
Dolphin	*Tursiops truncatus*	Tropics	Indigenous
Donkey	*Equus asinus*	Middle East	c. 1550
Duck	*Anas platyrhynchos*	General	Indigenous
Goat	*Capra hircus*	Middle East	1494
Goatfish	*Upeneus maculatus*	Caribbean	Indigenous
Goose	*Anser anser*	Old World	c. 1550
Green turtle	*Chelonia mydas*	Caribbean	Indigenous
Ground dove	*Columbina passerina*	Caribbean	Indigenous
Grouper	*Epinephelus morio*	Caribbean	Indigenous
Grunt	*Haemulon* sp.	Caribbean	Indigenous
Guineafowl	*Numida meleagris*	Africa	c. 1600
Hawksbill turtle	*Thallasochelys imbricata*	Caribbean	Indigenous
Honeybee	*Apis mellifica*	Europe	c. 1660
Iguana	*Cyclura collei*	Jamaica	Endemic
Jabbering crow	*Corvus jamaicensis*	Jamaica	Endemic
Jackfish	*Seleve vomer*	Atlantic	Indigenous
Jewfish	*Epinephelus itajara*	Caribbean	Indigenous
Jonga	*Macrobrachium jamaicensis*	Caribbean	Indigenous
Kingfish	*Scomberomorus cavalla*	Atlantic	Indigenous
Land crab	*Gecarcinus* sp.	Caribbean	Indigenous
Loggerhead	*Tyrannus caudifasciatus*	Greater Antilles	Indigenous
Macaca	*Stenodontes damicornis*	Caribbean	Indigenous
Maccaback	*Gerres rhombeus*	Caribbean	Indigenous
Manatee	*Trichechus manatus*	Caribbean	Indigenous
Marlin	*Makaira nigricans*	Atlantic	Indigenous
Monk seal	*Monachus tropicalis*	Greater Antilles	Indigenous
Mountain mullet	*Agonostomus monticola*	Jamaica	Endemic
Mudfish	*Phylipnus dormitator*	Caribbean	Indigenous
Muscovy duck	*Cairina moschata*	Caribbean	Indigenous
Octopus	*Octopus vulgaris*	Caribbean	Indigenous

Jamaican Name	Scientific Name	Place of Origin	Date of Introduction
Oldwife	*Alosa pseudoharengus*	America	Indigenous
Oyster	*Crassostrea rizhoporae*	Caribbean	Indigenous
Parrot	*Amazona agilis*	Jamaica	Endemic
	A. collaria	Jamaica	Endemic
Parrotfish	*Scarus guacamaia*	America	Indigenous
Peacock	*Pavo* sp.	Asia	c. 1700
Pea dove	*Zenaida aurita*	Caribbean	Indigenous
Pelican	*Pelecanus occidentalis*	Greater Antilles	Indigenous
Petchary	*Tyrannus dominicensis*	Caribbean	Indigenous
Pig	*Sus scrofa*	North Africa	1494?
Plain pigeon	*Columba inornata*	Caribbean	Indigenous
Rabbit	*Oryctolagus cuniculus*	Europe	c. 1600
Ringtail pigeon	*Columba caribaea*	Jamaica	Endemic
Sea egg	*Diadema antillarum*	Caribbean	Indigenous
Sheep	*Ovis aries*	Middle East	c. 1510
Snapper	*Lutjanus* sp.	Tropics	Indigenous
Snook	*Centropomus undecimalis*	America	Indigenous
Sooty tern	*Sterna fuscata*	Caribbean	Indigenous
Spanish mackerel	*Scomberomorus maculatus*	Atlantic	Indigenous
Spiny lobster	*Panulirus argus*	Caribbean	Indigenous
Sprat	*Clupea sprattus*	Atlantic	Indigenous
Squid	*Sepioteuthis sepioidea*	Caribbean	Indigenous
Swordfish	*Xiphias gladius*	Caribbean	Indigenous
Tilapia	*Oreochromis mossambica*	Africa	1950
	O. nilotica	Africa	1978
Trunkfish	*Lactophrys quadricornis*	General	Indigenous
Turkey	*Meleagris gallopavo*	North America	c. 1700
Welchman	*Myripistris jacobus*	Caribbean	Indigenous
Whelk	*Cittarium pica*	Caribbean	Indigenous
Whistling duck	*Dendrocygna arborea*	Great Antilles	Indigenous
Whitebelly dove	*Leptotila jamaicensis*	Jamaica	Endemic
Whitewing dove	*Zenaida asiatica*	Caribbean	Indigenous
Yellow snake	*Epicrates subflavus*	Jamaica	Endemic
Yellowtail snapper	*Ocyurus chrysurus*	Caribbean	Indigenous

NOTES

Chapter 1

1. Warren Belasco and Philip Scranton, eds, *Food Nations: Selling Taste in Consumer Societies* (New York: Routledge, 2002); Alan Warde, *Consumption, Food and Taste: Culinary Antimonies and Commodity Culture* (London: Sage, 1997); Linda Keller Brown and Kay Mussell, eds, *Ethnic and Regional Foodways in the United States: The Performance of Group Identity* (Knoxville: University of Tennessee Press, 1984); Michael Ashkenazi and Jeanne Jacob, *The Essence of Japanese Cuisine: An Essay on Food and Culture* (Philadelphia: University of Pennsylvania Press, 2000); Alberto Capatti and Massimo Montanari, *Italian Cuisine: A Cultural History* (New York: Columbia University Press, 2003); Arjun Appadurai, "How to Make a National Cuisine: Cookbooks in Contemporary India", *Comparative Studies in Society and History* 30 (1988): 3–24; B.W. Higman, "Cookbooks and Caribbean Cultural Identity: An English-Language Hors d'Oeuvre", *New West Indian Guide* 72 (1998): 77–95.

2. Kenneth Gardnier, *Creole Caribbean Cookery* (London: Grafton, 1986); Sue Mullin, *Creole Cooking: The Taste of Tropical Islands* (London: Apple Press, 2000), 7; Stéphanie Ovide, *French Caribbean Cuisine* (New York: Hippocrene, 2002), 15; Richard R. Wilk, "Food and Nationalism: The Origins of 'Belizean Food' ", in *Food Nations: Selling Taste in Consumer Societies*, ed. Warren Belasco and Philip Scranton (New York: Routledge, 2002), 67–89; Richard Wilk, *Home Cooking in the Global Village: Caribbean Food from Buccaneers to Ecotourists* (Oxford: Berg, 2006), 19–21.

3. Kenneth F. Kiple and Kriemhild Coneè Ornelas, eds, *The Cambridge World History of Food* (Cambridge, UK: Cambridge University Press, 2000); *The Dictionary of Jamaican English*, 2nd ed., ed. F.G. Cassidy and R.B. Le Page (Cambridge, UK: Cambridge University Press, 1980) includes eighteen "Jamaica/n" food entries; *Gleaner*, 27 April 1877, 2, and 22 December 1886, 2.

4. *Gleaner*, 30 March 1962, 12; cf. ibid., 27 February 1959, 1.

5. *Gleaner*, 30 March 1962, 12; John Rashford, "Those That Do Not Smile Will Kill Me: The Ethnobotany of the Ackee in Jamaica", *Economic Botany* 55 (2001): 190–211.

6. Josephine Howard, "Jamaica and Jamaican Dishes", *American Cookery* 22, no. 6 (1918): 422; Mary Manning Carley, *Jamaica: The Old and the New* (London: George Allen and Unwin, 1963), 115; *Gleaner*, 8 February 1932, 16; 11 March 1935, 7; 5 January 1938, 5; *Jamaica Public Health* 11, no. 10 (1936): 82; 14, no. 2 (1939): 13.

7. *Gleaner*, 26 August 1939, 35.

8. Wilk, "Food and Nationalism", 80–81; *Gleaner*, 10 May 1930, 9; 27 August 1938, 12.

9. *Gleaner*, 13 July 1944, 7; 1 March 1956, 15; 28 January 1960, 7; 6 February 1960, 9; 8 February 1962, 22.

10. Norma Benghiat, *Traditional Jamaican Cookery* (Harmondsworth, UK: Penguin, 1985), 77; Heather Hope Royes and Gillian Royes Baccus, eds, *The Jamaica Farmer's Guide* (Kingston: Selectco Publications, 1988), 180; Valerie Facey, *Busha Browne's Indispensable Compendium of Traditional Jamaican Cookery* (Kingston: Mill Press, 1993), 102; Virginia Burke, *Walkerswood Caribbean Kitchen* (London: Simon and Schuster, 2000), 37; *Jamaica, Finest Taste for All Seasons: Sweet and Savoury Dishes, Cocktails and Desserts*, comp. Laurel Hepburn (Kingston: Laurel Hepburn and Associates, 2000), 2; Rashford, "Those That Do Not Smile", 210n2; *Gleaner*, 14 January 1968, 8; 6 June 1991, 3; 12 August 1995, 7B; *Gleaner, Food Supplement*, 15 May 1986, 26.

11. *Gleaner*, 31 August 1962, 15; 30 October 1963, 3; 4 April 1964, 12; 18 November 1964, 26; 25 November 1965, 28; 4 December 1965, 16; Carley, *Jamaica*, 114; Vivien Goldman, *Pearl's Delicious Jamaican Dishes: Recipes from Pearl Bell's Repertoire* (New York: Island Trading, 1992), 54.

12. John H. Parry, "Salt Fish and Ackee", *Caribbean Quarterly* 2 (1954): 29–35; *Gleaner*, 1 March 1956, 15.

13. Carley, *Jamaica*, 114; *Gleaner*, 4 August 1987, 8; 17 November 1987, 9; 17 December 1987, A6; 31 July 1988, 9A; 4 November 1990, 8A; 9 November 1990, 7; Barbara Gloudon, "In Celebration of the Patty", in *A Tapestry of Jamaica: The Best of Skywritings, Air Jamaica's Inflight Magazine*, ed. Linda Gambrill (Kingston: Creative Communications, 2003), 136.

14. Lady Maria Nugent, *Lady Nugent's Journal of Her Residence in Jamaica from 1801 to 1805*, ed. Philip Wright (Kingston: Institute of Jamaica, 1966), 88.

15. Philip Henry Gosse, *The Birds of Jamaica* (London: John Van Voorst, 1847), 293–94. See also Bernard Martin Senior, *Jamaica, as It Was, as It Is, and as It May Be* (London: T. Hurst, 1835), 68.

16. *Gleaner*, 22 December 1890, 4; 19 November 1895, 4; 3 May 1938, 8. See also Walter Jekyll, ed., *Jamaican Song and Story: Annancy Stories, Digging Sings, Ring Tunes, and Dancing Tunes* (London: David Nutt, 1907), 72.

17. *Gleaner*, 8 October 1878, 4; 1 March 1900, 9; *Gall's News Letter*, 2 February 1880; Jamaica Tourist Association, *Jamaica: "The Land of Streams and Woods"* (Kingston: Jamaica Tourist Association, 1911), 7.

18. Bessie Pullen-Bury, *Ethiopia in Exile: Jamaica Revisited* (1905; Freeport, New York: Books for Libraries Press, 1971), 98.

19. Jamaica Tourist Association, *Jamaica*, 52.

20. James Ramsey Ullman and Al Dinhofer, *Caribbean Here and Now: The Complete Vacation Guide to 52 Sunny Islands and Vacation Lands in the Caribbean Sea* (New York: Macmillan,

1968), 172; Richard Beamish, *Restaurants of Jamaica 1983–1984: Featuring Traditional Jamaican Recipes* (Montego Bay, Jamaica: privately printed, 1984), 1.

21. Clinton V. Black, *Jamaica Guide* ([London]: William Collins and Sangster (Jamaica), 1973), 29–32.

22. *Gleaner*, 31 May 1997, A12; 17 December 2000, 5; 14 November 2002, D3; 16 October 2003, C4; Jamaica Tourist Office website, 9 July 2004; *Jamaica Observer*, 21 May 2005, 11.

23. Novlet C. Jones, *Cook Up Jamaican Style* (Kingston: Information and Communications Unit, Ministry of Agriculture, 1977), 5.

24. *Jamaica, Finest Taste*, x; cf. Ian Cook and Michelle Harrison, "Cross Over Food: Re-materializing Postcolonial Geographies", *Transactions of the Institute of British Geographers* 28 (2003): 296–317.

25. Novlet C. Jones, *Cook Up Jamaican Style*, 3rd ed. (Kingston: Information and Communications Unit, Ministry of Agriculture, 2000), 5.

26. V.S. Campbell, D.P. Sinha and A.W. Patterson, "KAP Study on Project Lifestyle (Jamaica)", *Cajanus* 25 (1992): 40; Marcia Magnus, "Jamaican Fast Food Consumption Patterns", *Cajanus* 27 (1994): 91, 95; *Gleaner, Food Supplement*, 16 May 1985, 23; *Gleaner*, 23 September 1965, 19; *Gleaner, Pure Class*, 29 May 2005, 9.

27. *Gleaner, Food Supplement*, 24 September 1964, 18; Jane Dixon, *The Changing Chicken: Chooks, Cooks and Culinary Culture* (Sydney, Australia: University of New South Wales Press, 2002).

28. Pauline M. Samuda, Richard A. Cook, Cristanna M. Cook, and Fitzroy Henry, "Identifying Foods Commonly Consumed by the Jamaican Population: The Focus Group Approach", *International Journal of Food Sciences and Nutrition* 49 (1998): 81–82. See also J.A. Munroe, "Food Consumption Patterns in Jamaica", *Papers of the Workshop on Household Food Availability and Nutritional Status* (Kingston: Caribbean Food and Nutrition Institute, 1987), 51–64; Campbell, Sinha, and Patterson, "KAP Study", 39.

29. Dahlia Whitbourne, "The Ordinary Diet in Jamaica with Comments Thereon", *Jamaica Public Health* 11, no. 9 (1936): 68–71; British Medical Association, Jamaica Branch, Nutrition Committee, *Nutrition in Jamaica* (Kingston: Government Printer, 1945), 9.

30. Ann Ashworth and J.C. Waterlow, *Nutrition in Jamaica, 1969–70* (Mona, Jamaica: Extra-Mural Department, University of the West Indies, [1970]), 22; Department of Statistics, *Household Expenditure Survey 1958* ([Kingston]: Department of Statistics, 1960), 21–22, 49, 67; Donald J. Harris, "Econometric Analysis of Household Consumption in Jamaica", *Social and Economic Studies* 13 (1964): 471–87; Carley, *Jamaica*, 112; Jacques May and Donna L. McLellan, *The Ecology of Malnutrition in the Caribbean* (New York: Hafner, 1973), 118–20.

31. Brian L. Moore and Michele A. Johnson, eds, *"Squalid Kingston", 1890–1920: How the Poor Lived, Moved and Had Their Being* (Mona, Jamaica: Social History Project, Department of History, University of the West Indies, 2000), 85–86.

32. B.W. Higman, *Slave Populations of the British Caribbean, 1807–1834* (Baltimore, MD: Johns Hopkins University Press, 1984), 210–12, 251–55.

33. Virgil, *The Ploughman's Lunch: Moretum, a Poem Ascribed to Virgil*, trans. E.J. Kenney (Bristol: Bristol Classical Press, 1984), 10–11.

34. *Gleaner, Food Supplement*, 23 January 1964, 13; 24 September 1964, 11. Cf. James E. McWilliams, *A Revolution in Eating: How the Quest for Food Shaped America* (New York: Columbia University Press, 2005), 7–10.

35. Harold McGee, *On Food and Cooking: The Science and Lore of the Kitchen* (London: Unwin Hyman, 1984), 610–14; Cynthia Marchand, Inez Miles, Hyacinth Glen, Rubye Gayle, and Sadie Campbell, *Home Economics for Caribbean Schools: CXC Food and Nutrition, A Two Year Course*, 3rd ed. (Kingston: Jamaica Publishing House, 2002), 72–74.

36. Edmund Hickeringill, *Jamaica Viewed* (London: John Williams, 1661), 76; William F. Keegan, *The People Who Discovered Columbus: The Prehistory of the Bahamas* (Gainesville: University of Florida Press, 1992), 147; Irving Rouse, *The Tainos: Rise and Decline of the People Who Greeted Columbus* (New Haven, CT: Yale University Press, 1992), 171.

37. Cherry Brady, "'Drum Chicken'", in *A Tapestry of Jamaica: The Best of Skywritings, Air Jamaica's Inflight Magazine*, ed. Linda Gambrill (1983; Kingston: Creative Communications, 2003), 150; Helen Willinsky, *Jerk: Barbecue from Jamaica* (Freedom, CA: The Crossing Press, 1990), 4–11; Marchand et al., *Home Economics*, 82–83.

38. Jones, *Cook Up Jamaican Style* (1981), 45.

39. McGee, *On Food and Cooking*, 23, 268, 597–606.

40. *Gleaner*, 2 March 1962, 16; 11 March 1966, 11; McGee, *On Food and Cooking*, 619–24; Marchand et al., *Home Economics*, 124; E. Phyllis Clark, *West Indian Cookery* (London: Thomas Nelson, 1945), 59.

41. "Characteristic Traits of the Creolian and African Negroes in this Island, &c., &c.", *Columbian Magazine* 3 (September 1797): 252; C.L.G. Harris, "The True Traditions of My Ancestors", in *Maroon Heritage: Archaeological and Ethnographic Perspectives*, ed. E. Kofi Agorsah (Kingston: Canoe Press, 1994), 57; Claude McKay, *Banana Bottom* (New York: Harper and Row, 1933), 96.

42. *Gleaner, Food Supplement*, 21 May 1986, 25; McGee, *On Food and Cooking*, 615–16.

43. *Gleaner*, 18 October 1938, 12; James Walvin, *Fruits of Empire: Exotic Produce and British Taste, 1660–1800* (London: Macmillan, 1997), 194.

44. Enid Donaldson, *The Real Taste of Jamaica* (Kingston: Ian Randle, 1993), 118, 131; Enid Donaldson-Mignotte, "How Jamaicans Like Their Food", *Gleaner*, 3 October 1996, B8; 20 October 1996, 10C; Benghiat, *Traditional Jamaican Cookery*, 133; *Jamaica: Finest Taste*, 112; Campbell, Sinha, and Patterson, "KAP Study", 36.

45. Elsa Miller and Leonard "Sonny" Henry, *Creative Jamaican Cooking and Menus* (Kingston: Kingston Publishers, 1982), iv; Peggy Rankine, *Simply Delicious: A Collection of Original Recipes and Useful Kitchen Hints* (Mandeville, Jamaica: West Indies College Press, 1987), 2; Jill Hamilton, *A Little Jamaican Cookbook* (Kingston: Heinemann Caribbean, 1990), 3; Willinsky, *Jerk*, 19.

46. Carley, *Jamaica*, 113–14; Ullman and Dinhofer, *Caribbean Here and Now*, 172; *Gleaner*, 22 February 1998, 8C.

47. Esther Chapman, ed., *Pleasure Island: The Book of Jamaica* (Kingston: Arawak, 1952 [1951]), 97; *Gleaner*, 10 February 1988, 34.

48. B. Pullen-Burry, *Jamaica as It Is, 1903* (London: T. Fisher Unwin, 1903), 51. See also A. Hyatt Verrill, *Jamaica of Today* (New York: Dodd, Mead, 1931), 109.

49. Bryan Edwards, *The History, Civil and Commercial, of the British West Indies* (London: G. and W.B. Whittaker, 1819), 1: 255–56; Edward Brathwaite, *The Development of Creole Society in Jamaica 1770–1820* (Oxford: Clarendon, 1971), 302; McWilliams, *Revolution in Eating*, 38–40; Cynric R. Williams, *A Tour through the Island of Jamaica, from the Western to Eastern End, in the Year 1823* (London: Thomas Hurst, Edward Chance, 1827), 11.

50. Pullen-Burry, *Jamaica as It Is*, 198; H.G. De Lisser, "Behind the Scenes at the J.P.S.: Revelations, Personal, Social and Gastronomic", *Planters' Punch* 3, no. 2 (1933–34): 37.

51. Dolf Wyllarde, *Mafoota* (London: Hurst and Blackett, 1907), 175; Pullen-Burry, *Jamaica as It Is*, 55; Charles H. Eden, *The West Indies* (London: Sampson, Low, Marston, Searle and Rivington, 1880), 80; Mary Gaunt, *Reflection – In Jamaica* (London: Ernest Benn, 1932), 163–64; Edmund Wilson, *The Sixties: The Last Journal, 1960–1972*, ed. Lewis M. Dabney (New York: Farrar Straus Giroux, 1993), 766; John P. Homiak, "Dub History: Soundings on Rastafari Livity and Language", in *Rastafari and Other African-Caribbean Worldviews*, ed. Barry Chevannes (London: Macmillan, 1998), 149–50; Peter Farb and George Armelagos, *Consuming Passions: The Anthropology of Eating* (New York: Washington Square Press, 1983), 208; Joan P. Alcock, *Food in Roman Britain* (Stroud, UK: Tempus, 2001), 79–82.

52. John De Mers, *The Food of Jamaica: Authentic Recipes from the Jewel of the Caribbean* (Singapore: Periplus, 1999), 5; *A Panorama of African Recipes* (Kingston: African Caribbean Institute of Jamaica, 1980), ii; Benghiat, *Traditional Jamaican Cookery*, 27; Facey, *Busha Browne*, 5.

53. P.A.S. Breslin, "Human Gustation and Flavour", *Flavour and Fragrance Journal* 16 (2001): 439. See also Edmund T. Rolls, "Taste, Olfactory, and Food Texture Processing in the Brain, and the Control of Food Intake", *Physiology and Behavior*, 85 (2005): 47; David G. Laing and Anthony Jinks, "Flavour Perception Mechanisms", *Trends in Food Science and Technology* 7 (1996): 387–89; Elizabeth D. Capaldi, ed., *Why We Eat What We Eat: The Psychology of Eating* (Washington, DC: American Psychological Association, 1996); John L. Smith, *The Psychology of Food and Eating: A Fresh Approach to Theory and Method* (Basingstoke, UK: Palgrave, 2002), 54–59; Farb and Armelagos, *Consuming Passions*, 19–28; E.N. Anderson, *Everyone Eats: Understanding Food and Culture* (New York: New York University Press, 2005), 70–81; Carolyn Korsmeyer, "Introduction: Perspectives on Taste", in *The Taste Culture Reader: Experiencing Food and Drink*, ed. Carolyn Korsmeyer (Oxford: Berg, 2005), 6–8.

54. Frank N. Kotsonis, George A. Burdock, and W. Gary Flamm, "Food Toxicology", in *Casarett and Doull's Toxicology: The Basic Science of Poisons*, ed. Curtis D. Klaassen (New York: McGraw-Hill, 2001), 1050.

55. Ibid., 1051–52, 1068–71; Gary Paul Habhan, *Why Some Like It Hot: Food, Genes, and Cultural Diversity* (Washington, DC: Island Press, 2004), 10.

56. F.J. Francis, "Colour and Appearance as Dominating Sensory Properties of Foods", in *Sensory Properties of Foods*, ed. G.G. Birch, J.G. Brennan, and K.J. Parker (London: Applied Science Publishers, 1977), 27; R.D. Montgomery, "Observations on the Cyanide Content and Toxicity of Tropical Pulses", *West Indian Medical Journal* 13 (1964): 1; Douglas B. MacDougall,

"Colour in Meat", in *Sensory Properties of Foods*, 64–65; Peter G. Knight, Jose C. Jackson, Brendan Bain, and Denise Eldemire-Shearer, "Household Food Safety Awareness of Selected Urban Consumers in Jamaica", *International Journal of Food Sciences and Nutrition* 54 (2003): 312–13.

57. Breslin, "Human Gustation and Flavour", 439.

58. Constance Classen, David Howes and Anthony Synnott, *Aroma: The Cultural History of Smell* (London: Routledge, 1994), 104–7; Roberto A. Buffo and Claudio Cardelli-Freire, "Coffee Flavour: An Overview", *Flavour and Fragrance Journal* 19 (2004): 99.

59. A.C. Noble, "Taste-Aroma Interactions", *Trends in Food Science and Technology* 7 (1996): 439–44; Derek G. Land, "Perspectives on the Effects of Interactions of Flavor Perception: An Overview", in *Flavor-Food Interactions*, ed. Robert J. McGorrin and Jane V. Leland (Washington, DC: American Chemical Society, 1996), 3; M.W. Kearsley and P.J. Sicard, "The Chemistry of Starches and Sugars Present in Food", in *Dietary Starches and Sugars in Man: A Comparison*, ed. John Dobbing (London: Springer-Verlag, 1989), 21–23.

60. Jean Anthelme Brillat-Savarin, *The Physiology of Taste, or Meditations on Transcendental Gastronomy*, trans. M.F.K. Fisher (1949; New York: Knopf, 1972), 38; Kumiko Sugimoto and Yuzo Ninomiya, "Introductory Remarks on Umami Research: Candidate Receptors and Signal Transduction Mechanisms on Umami", *Chemical Senses* 30, suppl. 1 (2005): i21–22; Rolls, "Taste, Olfactory, and Food Texture", 46; J. Delwiche, "Are There 'Basic' Tastes?" *Trends in Food Science and Technology* 7 (1996): 411–15; Breslin, "Human Gustation and Flavour", 442–54; Jan H.A. Kroeze, "The Perception of Complex Taste Stimuli", in *Psychological Basis of Sensory Evaluation*, ed. R.L. McBride and H.J.H. MacFie (London: Elsevier Applied Science, 1990), 41–68; Anderson, *Everyone Eats*, 70.

61. Linda A. Mahabee and Milton L. Mahabee, *A Vegetarian Cookbook and Better Living Guide* (Mandeville, Jamaica: College Press, 1987), 25.

62. Breslin, "Human Gustation and Flavour", 440; Adam Drewnowski, "Fat and Sugar in the Global Diet: Dietary Diversity in the Nutrition Transition", in *Food in Global History*, ed. Raymond Grew (Boulder, CO: Westview, 1999), 197; Anderson, *Everyone Eats*, 34–38.

63. Marion E. Frank and Thomas P. Hettinger, "What the Tongue Tells the Brain about Taste", *Chemical Senses* 30, suppl. 1 (2005): i68; Makoto Sugita and Yoshiki Shiba, "Genetic Tracing Shows Segregation of Taste Neuronal Circuitries for Bitter and Sweet", *Science* 309 (July 29, 2005): 781–85; D. Eric Walters, "How Are Bitter and Sweet Tastes Related?" *Trends in Food Science and Technology* 7 (1996): 399–403; D. Eric Walters and Glenn Roy, "Taste Interactions of Sweet and Bitter Compounds", in *Flavor-Food Interactions*, ed. Robert J. McGorrin and Jane V. Leland (Washington, DC: American Chemical Society, 1996), 130–33; Paul A.S. Breslin, "Interactions among Salty, Sour and Bitter Compounds", *Trends in Food Science and Technology* 7 (1996): 390–99.

64. J. Landman and J. St E. Hall, "The Dietary Habits and Knowledge of Folklore of Pregnant Jamaican Women", *Ecology of Food and Nutrition* 12 (1983): 208–9.

65. John P. Bartley, "A New Method for the Determination of Pungent Compounds in Ginger (*Zingiber officinale*)", *Journal of the Science of Food and Agriculture* 68 (1995): 215.

66. B.G. Green, "Chemesthesis: Pungency as a Component of Flavor", *Trends in Food Science and Technology* 7 (1996): 415–16, 419; Henry B. Heath and Gary Reineccius, *Flavor Chemistry and Technology* (Basingstoke: Macmillan, 1986), 3; Wolfgang Schivelbusch, *Tastes of Paradise: A Social History of Spices, Stimulants, and Intoxicants* (New York: Pantheon, 1992), 7.

67. J.W. Purseglove, E.G. Brown, C.L. Green, and S.R.J. Robbins, *Spices* (London: Longman Scientific and Technical, 1981), 1: vii; Sara J. Risch, "Spices: Sources, Processing, and Chemistry" in *Spices: Flavor Chemistry and Antioxidant Properties*, ed. Sara J. Risch and Chi-Tang Ho (Washington, DC: American Chemical Society, 1996), 3.

68. Jan C.R. Demyttenaere, Ilse E.I. Koninckx, and Arvid Meersman, "Microbial Production of Bioflavours by Fungal Spores", in *Flavour Science: Recent Developments*, ed. A.J. Taylor and D.S. Mottram (Cambridge, UK: Royal Society of Chemistry, 1996), 105; H. Stam, A.L.G.M. Boog and M. Hoogland, "The Production of Natural Flavours by Fermentation", in Taylor and Mottram, *Flavour Science*, 122–25; Andreas Muheim, Alex Häusler, Boris Schilling, and Konrad Lerch, "The Impact of Recombinant DNA-Technology on the Flavour and Fragrance Industry", in *Flavours and Fragrances*, ed. Karl A.D. Swift (Cambridge, UK: Royal Society of Chemistry, 1997), 11–20.

69. Igor de Garine, Stephen Hugh-Jones and Armin Prinz, "Cultural Factors in Food Choices – Background", in *Tropical Forests, People and Food: Biocultural Interactions and Applications to Development*, ed. C.M. Hladik, A. Hladik, O.F. Linares, H. Pagezy, A. Semple, and M. Hadley (Paris: UNESCO, 1993), 525–32.

70. Sidney W. Mintz, *Tasting Food, Tasting Freedom* (Boston: Beacon, 1996), 13; Diva Sanjur, *Social and Cultural Perspectives on Nutrition* (Englewood Cliffs, NJ: Prentice-Hall, 1982), 27–34; Paul Fieldhouse, *Food and Nutrition: Customs and Culture* (London: Croom Helm, 1986), 23–25; Elaine N. McIntosh, *American Food Habits in Historical Perspective* (Westport, CT: Praeger, 1995), 141–49; Mark Conner and Christopher J. Armitage, *The Social Psychology of Food* (Buckingham, UK: Open University Press, 2002), 12–41; Edward C. Rosenthal, *The Era of Choice: The Ability to Choose and Its Transformation of Contemporary Life* (Cambridge, Massachusetts: MIT Press, 2005), 219–20.

71. Marjorie Grant Whiting, "Toxicity of Cycads", *Economic Botany* 17 (1963): 271; G.F. Asprey and Phyllis Thornton, "Medicinal Plants of Jamaica", *West Indian Medical Journal* 2 (1953): 233; Arvilla Payne-Jackson and Mervyn C. Alleyne, *Jamaican Folk Medicine: A Source of Healing* (Mona, Jamaica: University of the West Indies Press, 2004), 163–64; Timothy Johns, *With Bitter Herbs They Shall Eat It: Chemical Ecology and the Origins of Human Diet and Medicine* (Tucson: University of Arizona Press, 1990), 251; Nina L. Etkin, "The Cull of the Wild", in *Eating on the Wild Side: The Pharmacologic, Ecologic, and Social Implications of Using Nonculti-gens*, ed. Nina L. Etkin (Tucson: University of Arizona Press, 1994), 6–10; Andrew Dalby, *Dangerous Tastes: The Story of Spices* (Berkeley: University of California Press, 2000), 16.

72. Kotsonis, Burdock, and Flamm, "Food Toxicology", 1071–78.

73. Knight, Jackson, Bain, and Eldemire-Shearer, "Household Food Safety", 313.

74. Marvin Harris, *Good to Eat: Riddles of Food and Culture* (New York: Simon and Schuster, 1985), 13; Paul Colinvaux, *Ecology* (New York: Wiley, 1986), 18–19; Anderson, *Everyone Eats*, 11–39; National Research Council, Board on Science and Technology for International

Development, *Postharvest Food Losses in Developing Countries* (Washington, DC: National Academy of Sciences, 1978), 3.

75. Jack R. Harlan, *Crops and Man* (Madison, WI: American Society of Agronomy/Crop Science Society of America, 1975), 52–57; Dolores R. Piperno, "The Origins of Plant Cultivation and Domestication in the Neotropics", in *Behavioral Ecology and the Transition to Agriculture*, ed. Douglas J. Kennett and Bruce Winterhalder (Berkeley: University of California Press, 2006), 159; Sandrine Mignon-Grasteau, et al., "Genetics of Adaptation and Domestication in Livestock", *Livestock Production Science* 93 (2005): 4; Peter Bellwood, *First Farmers: The Origins of Agricultural Societies* (Oxford: Blackwell Publishing, 2005), 146–48; Jared Diamond, *Guns, Germs and Steel: A Short History of Everybody for the Last 13,000 Years* (London: Vintage, 1998), 158–75; Jack R. Harlan, *The Living Fields: Our Agricultural Heritage* (Cambridge, UK: Cambridge University Press, 1995), 54–57; L.T. Evans, *Crop Evolution, Adaptation and Yield* (Cambridge, UK: Cambridge University Press, 1993), 69–72; Juliet Clutton-Brock, ed., *The Walking Larder: Patterns of Domestication, Pastoralism, and Predation* (London: Unwin Hyman, 1989); Juliet Clutton-Brock, *Domesticated Animals from Earliest Times* (London: British Museum [Natural History] and Heinemann, 1981), 15–16.

76. Hans Sloane, *A Voyage to the Islands Madera, Barbados, Nieves, S. Christophers and Jamaica, with the Natural History of the last of those Islands* (London, 1707–25), 1: xxv.

77. Frederick J. Simoons, *Eat Not This Flesh: Food Avoidances from Prehistory to the Present* (Madison: University of Wisconsin Press, 1994), 297, 322; Farb and Armelagos, *Consuming Passions*, 197–210; Madeleine Ferrières, *Sacred Cow, Mad Cow: A History of Food Fears* (New York: Columbia University Press, 2006), 325–29.

78. Robb Walsh, *Are You Really Going to Eat That? Reflections of a Culinary Thrill Seeker* (New York: Counterpoint, 2003), 7–10; Jerry Hopkins, *Extreme Cuisine* (London: Bloomsbury, 2005), 90, 231–32.

79. Yvonne McCalla Sobers, *Delicious Jamaica! Vegetarian Cuisine* (Summertown, TN: Book Publishing Company, 1996), 113; Carol S. Holzberg, *Minorities and Power in a Black Society: The Jewish Community of Jamaica* (Lanham, MD: North-South Publishing, 1987), 49–55.

80. Margaret Ebanks, *The Rastafari Cookbook: Ital Recipes* (Kingston: Antilles Book Company, 1981), 11; Homiak, "Dub History", 144–48; Jacqueline Landman-Bogues, "Rastafarian Food Habits", *Cajanus* 9 (1976): 228–34; Joseph Owens, *Dread: The Rastafarians of Jamaica* (Kingston: Sangster, 1976), 166–69; Laura Osborne, *The Rasta Cookbook* (London: Macdonald, 1990), 8–9.

81. Nick Fiddes, *Meat: A Natural Symbol* (London: Routledge, 1991), 14; Roger Horowitz, *Putting Meat on the American Table: Taste, Technology, Transformation* (Baltimore, MD: Johns Hopkins University Press, 2006), 17; Marvin Harris, *Good to Eat*, 19–46; Simoons, *Eat Not This Flesh*, 5; Drewnowski, "Fat and Sugar in the Global Diet", 198.

Chapter 2

1. Robert J. Whittaker, *Island Biogeography: Ecology, Evolution, and Conservation* (Oxford: Oxford University Press, 1998), 20–21; Rudolf Diesel, Christoph D. Schubart, and Martina Schuh,

"A Reconstruction of the Invasion of Land by Jamaican Crabs (Grapsidae: Sesarminae)", *Journal of Zoology* 250 (2000): 141–43; Klaus Anger and Christoph D. Schubart, "Experimental Evidence of Food-Independent Larval Development in Endemic Jamaican Freshwater-Breeding Crabs", *Physiological and Biochemical Zoology* 78 (2005): 246–47.

2. Stewart B. Peck, "Historical Biogeography of Jamaica: Evidence from Cave Invertebrates", *Canadian Journal of Zoology* 77 (1999): 368–80; David Lack, *Island Biology Illustrated by the Land Birds of Jamaica* (Berkeley: University of California Press, 1976), 15–19, 81; Thomas A. Farr, "Land Animals of Jamaica: Origins and Endemism", *Jamaica Journal* 17, no. 1 (February 1984): 38.

3. Patrick L. Osborne, *Tropical Ecosystems and Ecological Concepts* (Cambridge, UK: Cambridge University Press, 2000), 358–62; Ivan Goodbody, "Avian Refuges", *Jamaica Journal* 25, no. 2 (1994), 59; Lack, *Island Biology*, 19, 81–83.

4. David Watts, *The West Indies: Patterns of Development, Culture and Environmental Change since 1492* (Cambridge, UK: Cambridge University Press, 1987), 38–40.

5. Thomas M. Whitmore and B.L. Turner II, *Cultivated Landscapes of Middle America on the Eve of Conquest* (Oxford: Oxford University Press, 2001), 102–4; Watts, *West Indies*, 41–65, 75–77; David Watts, "The Caribbean Environment and Early Settlement", in *General History of the Caribbean*, vol. 2, *New Societies: The Caribbean in the Long Sixteenth Century*, ed. P.C. Emmer (London: UNESCO Publishing/Macmillan, 1999), 29–36; Rouse, *Tainos*, 7, 17–19; John Rashford, "Arawak, Spanish and African Contributions to Jamaica's Settlement Vegetation", *Jamaica Journal* 24, no. 3 (1993): 18–19.

6. James W. Lee, "Arawak Burens", *Archaeology Jamaica* (second quarter 1980): 1–12.

7. Kathleen Deagan, "Reconsidering Taíno Social Dynamics after Spanish Conquest: Gender and Class in Culture Contact Studies", *American Antiquity* 69 (2004): 622; Watts, *West Indies*, 107; Troy S. Floyd, *The Columbus Dynasty in the Caribbean 1492–1526* (Albuquerque: University of New Mexico Press, 1973), 109–12.

8. Rashford, "Arawak, Spanish and African Contributions", 19–22; Watts, *West Indies*, 115; Kenneth R. Andrews, *The Spanish Caribbean: Trade and Plunder, 1530–1630* (New Haven, CT: Yale University Press, 1978), 222.

9. *A True Description of Jamaica, with the Fertility, Commodities, and Healthfulness of the Place* (London, 1657), 2; Hickeringill, *Jamaica Viewed*, 10, 14–15, 16, 18–25.

10. B.W. Higman, *Jamaica Surveyed: Plantation Maps and Plans of the Eighteenth and Nineteenth Centuries* (Kingston: Institute of Jamaica Publications, 1988), 8–9.

11. Watts, *West Indies*, 161–62.

12. John H. Parry, "Plantation and Provision Ground: An Historical Sketch of the Introduction of Food Crops into Jamaica", *Revista de Historia de America* 39 (1955): 1–20; *Jamaica Quarterly Journal*, no. 1 (July 1818): 6–8. Cf. George Dodd, *The Food of London* (London: Longman, Brown, Green, and Longmans, 1856), 276.

13. Sidney W. Mintz and Douglas Hall, *The Origins of the Jamaican Internal Marketing System* (New Haven, CT: Department of Anthropology, 1960, Yale University Publications in Anthropology, No. 57); "Characteristic Traits", 2 (April 1797): 702.

14. B.W. Higman, *Slave Population and Economy in Jamaica, 1807–1834* (Cambridge, UK: Cambridge University Press, 1976), 375–76; Higman, *Slave Populations of the British Caribbean*, 136–37; McWilliams, *Revolution in Eating*, 44–51.

15. Philip Henry Gosse, *A Naturalist's Sojourn in Jamaica* (London: Longman, Brown, Green, and Longmans, 1851), 132.

16. David Barker and Balfour Spence, "Afro-Caribbean Agriculture: A Jamaican Maroon Community in Transition", *Geographical Journal* 154 (1988): 204.

17. *Gleaner*, 2 January 1900, 1; 5 January 1900, 1, 7; Annie Manville Fenn, "Housekeeping in Jamaica", *The Youth's Companion*, 16 March 1893; Brian L. Moore and Michele A. Johnson, eds, *The Land We Live In: Jamaica in 1890* (Mona, Jamaica: Social History Project, Department of History, University of the West Indies, 2000), 105.

18. "Characteristic Traits" 3 (September 1797): 252.

19. Ibid., 252; John Taylor Papers, Powel Collection, Box 29F (Historical Society of Pennsylvania, Philadelphia); *Jamaica Quarterly Journal* (December 1818): 292; "Characteristic Traits" 3 (September 1797): 251–52; B.W. Higman, *Montpelier, Jamaica: A Plantation Community in Slavery and Freedom, 1739–1912* (Kingston: University of the West Indies Press, 1998), 216–19. Cf. Rachael Feild, *Irons in the Fire: A History of Cooking Equipment* (Marlborough, UK: Crowood, 1984), 8–12.

20. Henry Barham, *Hortus Americanus: Containing an Account of the Trees, Shrubs, and Other Vegetable Productions, of South-America and the West-India Islands, and Particularly of the Island of Jamaica* (Kingston: Alexander Aikman, 1794), 28; "Characteristic Traits" 3 (September 1797): 252; Edward Long, *The History of Jamaica* (London: T. Lowndes, 1774), 3: 752, 801–2; John Rashford, "Packy Tree, Spirits and Duppy Birds", *Jamaica Journal* 21, no. 3 (1988): 4; Rashford, "The Past and Present Uses of Bamboo in Jamaica", *Economic Botany* 49 (1995): 395–405.

21. "Characteristic Traits" 3 (September 1797): 252.

22. *Gleaner*, 10 November 1879, 3; 7 January 1884, 3; 2 January 1900, 3; 17 January 1900, 3; Feild, *Irons in the Fire*, 261; *Gall's News Letter*, 8 January 1880.

23. Douglas Hall, *Free Jamaica, 1838–1865: An Economic History* (New Haven, CT: Yale University Press, 1959), 124–37; Watts, *West Indies*, 504–5.

24. Anthony Trollope, *The West Indies and the Spanish Main* (1859; Gloucester, UK: Alan Sutton, 1985), 32; Alfred Leader, *Through Jamaica with a Kodak* (Bristol: John Wright, 1907), 142; M.A. Joslyn, "The Freezing Preservation of Vegetables", *Economic Botany* 15 (1961): 347; Jamaica: Agriculture – Economic Survey, 10 August 1933, C.O. 137/800/7 (National Archives, London); *Gleaner*, 30 December 1933, 12.

25. *Gleaner*, 2 June 1990, 13; 11 May 1991, 1; 26 July 1998, 1A; Belal Ahmed and Sultana Afroz, *The Political Economy of Food and Agriculture in the Caribbean* (Kingston: Ian Randle, 1996), 131–33.

26. Carley, *Jamaica*, 112; Colin Rickards, ed., *The West Indies and Caribbean Year Book 1975* (Toronto: Caribook, 1975), 249–51; Paulette Meikle, "Spatio-temporal Trends in Root Crop Production and Marketing in Jamaica", *Caribbean Geography* 3 (1992): 231; Jones, *Cook Up Jamaican Style* (2000), 4–5.

27. Cook and Harrison, "Cross Over Food", 296–317.

28. Clark, *West Indian Cookery*, 82–83; Marchand et al., *Home Economics*, 204.

29. Frederic G. Cassidy, *Jamaica Talk: Three Hundred Years of the English Language in Jamaica* (London: Macmillan, 1961), 85; Fenn, "Housekeeping in Jamaica"; Clark, *West Indian Cookery*, 63.

30. *Gleaner*, 21 December 1877, 2; 26 October 1894, 7; 22 February 1915, 10.

31. *Gleaner*, 11 October 1930, 26; 14 August 1934, 4; 6 February 1936, 18; Marchand et al., *Home Economics*, 106; Beryl Wood and Magda Pollard, *Caribbean Schools Home Economics: Book I* (Kingston: Longman Caribbean, 1983), 31–32; Henry Fraser, Sean Carrington, Addinton Forde and John Gilmore, *A–Z of Barbadian Heritage* (Kingston: Heinemann, 1990), 40, 61.

32. Zora Neale Hurston, *Voodoo Gods: An Inquiry into Native Myths and Magic in Jamaica and Haiti* (London: J.M. Dent, 1939), 25–26; Clark, *West Indian Cookery*, 63; *Gleaner*, 11 November 1992, 16.

33. *Charcoal for Fuel* (Kingston: Ministry of Mining, Energy and Tourism, 1988).

34. Jamaica Agricultural Society, *The Farmer's Food Manual: A Recipe Book for the West Indies* (Glasgow: University Press, 1957), 133–34; Marchand et al., *Home Economics*, 106; Clark, *West Indian Cookery*, 65–67.

35. *Gleaner*, 26 June 1940, 3; 5 July 1956, 2.

36. *Gleaner*, 11 June 1992, 2.

37. *Planters' Punch* 1, no. 1 (1920): 23; 3, no. 5 (1936–37): 78; 4, no. 1 (1938–39): 105; 4, no. 2 (1939–40): 106–7.

38. Sylvester Ayre, *Bush Doctor: Jamaica and the Caribbean's Almost Forgotten Folklore and Remedies* (Kingston: LHM Publishing, 2002), 63–64; *Gleaner, Supermarket Supplement*, 25 January 1990, xi; Jamaica Agricultural Society, *Farmer's Food Manual*, 293–306.

39. O.D. Scott, K. Moodie and R. Bissessar, "A Preliminary Quantitative Survey of the Bacterial Flora of Restaurants and Bakeries in the City of Kingston, Jamaica", *West Indian Medical Journal* 17 (1968): 158.

40. *Gleaner, Food Supplement*, 27 June 1968, 11; 24 April 1986, 28; *Gleaner*, 11 May 1986, 29; 28 October 1987, 23; *Gleaner, Pure Class*, 29 May 2005, 9.

41. *Pepperpot* 4 (1954): 63; *Gleaner, Food Supplement*, 23 January 1964, 9; Thomas L. Graham, *Kingston 100: 1872–1972* (Kingston: Tom Graham Publications, 1972), 117.

42. *Gleaner*, 9 April 2000, 2A.

43. Douglas Hall, *Grace, Kennedy and Company Limited: A Story of Jamaican Enterprise* (Kingston: Grace, Kennedy and Co., 1992), 8, 14, 75–76, 101–3, 155–57; Cook and Harrison, "Cross Over Food", 296–317; *Gleaner*, 27 July 1986; *Gleaner, Grace in Production*, 1 August 1990, 6.

44. Scott, Moodie, and Bissessar, "Preliminary Quantitative Survey", 158; *Gleaner*, 20 October 1993, 8; 11 November 1994, 12A; Dorian Powell, Eleanor Wint, Erna Brodber, and Versada Campbell, *Street Foods of Kingston* (Mona, Jamaica: Institute of Social and Economic Research, 1990), 21–23, 33–36.

45. *Gleaner*, 11 February 1985, 3; 17 July 1985, 21; 6 November 1994, 1–2; *Gleaner, Mother's Supplement*, 23 July 1991, 3; *Gleaner, Business and Industry Supplement*, 26 May 1992, 13; *Financial Gleaner*, 4 November 1994, 7; *Jamaica Observer, Food Digest*, 14 October 1994, 3B.

46. *Gleaner*, 6 December 1998, 6C, 11C, 15C; *Business Observer*, 11 May 2005, 1B; 22 February 2006, 7B.

47. *Financial Gleaner*, 20 May 2005, 24; Jack Ralph Kloppenburg, Jr, *First the Seed: The Political Economy of Plant Biotechnology, 1492–2000* (Cambridge, UK: Cambridge University Press, 1988).

48. See Eleanor Lowenstein, *Bibliography of American Cookery Books, 1742–1860*, 3rd ed. (Worcester, MA: American Antiquarian Society, 1972); Susannah Carter, *The Frugal Housewife, or Complete Woman Cook* (London: F. Newbery. Reprinted Boston: Edes and Gill, 1772); Richard Briggs, *The New Art of Cookery, According to the Present Practice* (Philadelphia: W. Spotswood, R. Campbell and B. Johnson, 1792); Isabella Beeton, *Mrs Beeton's Book of Household Management* (1859–61; facsimile ed., London: Chancellor Press, 1982); Kathryn Hughes, *The Short Life and Long Times of Mrs. Beeton* (New York: Knopf, 2006), 352–58; *Gleaner*, 18 October 1869, 4.

49. Caroline Sullivan, *The Jamaica Cookery Book* (Kingston: A.W. Gardner, 1893), iv; *Gleaner*, 18 December 1893, 2.

50. *Gleaner*, 27 November 1897, 2; 6 January 1892, 2; 15 August 1904, 6; 21 August 1905, 13; 5 September 1907, 5; 22 November 1990, 31.

51. *Gleaner*, 21 March 1906, 2; 11 January 1908, 11; 12 November 1908, 2; 13 November 1908, 3; 18 January 1909, 8; 3 December 1969, 3.

52. McKay, *Banana Bottom*, 53.

53. *The Best of Creative Cooking* (Kingston: Grace Kitchens and Consumer Services, 1993), ii.

54. *Gleaner*, 2 December 1938, 22; *Boonoonoonoos: A Collection of Recipes* (Kingston: American Women's Group, 1987); *Festival 70, National Culinary Arts Finals, July 22, 1970, Courtleigh Manor Hotel* (cyclostyled); *Festival 71, National Culinary Arts, Finals – July 21, 1971, Sheraton-Kingston Hotel* (cyclostyled).

55. Carl von Linné, *Flora Jamaicensis* (Uppsala, 1759), 7–10; Carl von Linné, *Plantarum Jamaicensium Pugillus* (Uppsala, 1759), 3; Barham, *Hortus Americanus*, 5–7.

56. Daniel L. Kelly and Timothy A. Dickinson, "Local Names for Vascular Plants in the John Crow Mountains, Jamaica", *Economic Botany* 39 (1985): 346–62.

57. Gosse, *Naturalist's Sojourn*, 421.

58. Parry, "Plantation and Provision Ground", 1; *Gleaner*, 1 March 1956, 15.

Chapter 3

1. *The West Indies and Caribbean Year Book 1967* (London: Thomas Skinner, 1966), 245; Byron Murray and Patrick Lewin, *The Jamaican Chef: Over a Century of Traditional Jamaican Dishes* (Montego Bay, Jamaica: Life Long Publishers, 1990); Medea Benjamin, Joseph Collins and Michael Scott, *No Free Lunch: Food and Revolution in Cuba Today* (San Francisco: Institute for Food and Development Policy, 1984), 3.

2. Lord [Sydney] Olivier, *Jamaica: The Blessed Island* (London: Faber and Faber, 1936), 312; Martha Warren Beckwith, *Black Roadways: A Study of Jamaican Folk Life* (1929; New York: Negro Universities Press, 1969), 15.

3. Peter Marsden, *An Account of the Island of Jamaica* (Newcastle, 1788), 19, 24; Sloane, *Voyage*, 1: xv; Charles Leslie, *A New and Exact Account of Jamaica* (Edinburgh: A. Kincaid, 1739), 33; *The Importance of Jamaica to Great-Britain, Consider'd: In a Letter to a Gentleman* (London: A. Dodd, c. 1740), 39; Patrick Browne, *The Civil and Natural History of Jamaica* (1756; New York: Arno, 1972), 24. Cf. Catherine Gallagher and Stephen Greenblatt, *Practicing New Historicism* (Chicago: University of Chicago Press, 2000), 114.

4. Versada Campbell and Dinesh P. Sinha, *Nutrition Made Simple* (Kingston: Caribbean Food and Nutrition Institute, 2002), 23; John Stewart, *An Account of Jamaica* (London: Longman, Hurst, Rees and Orme, 1808), 100; Trollope, *West Indies*, 25; Beckwith, *Black Roadways*, 17; *Statistical Yearbook of Jamaica* (1992), 272; Higman, *Montpelier*, 197.

5. Andrew Lack and David Evans, *Plant Biology*, 2nd ed. (New York: Taylor and Francis, 2005), 45–49; Peter R. Bell and Alan R. Hemsley, *Green Plants: Their Origins and Diversity* (1992; Cambridge, UK: Cambridge University Press, 2000), 270–73; J.C. Forbes and R.D. Watson, *Plants in Agriculture* (Cambridge, UK: Cambridge University Press, 1992), 241–44; John King, *Reaching for the Sun: How Plants Work* (Cambridge, UK: Cambridge University Press, 1997), 66, 116.

6. Errol Simms and Lloyd B. Rankine, "Factors Contributing to the Growth and Development of the Root Crop Industry in Jamaica", *Social and Economic Studies* 28 (1979): 61–65; Meikle, "Spatio-temporal Trends", 224.

7. *Gleaner, Food Supplement*, 5 July 1984, 21; *Statistical Yearbook of Jamaica* (1993), 443n; S. Chandra, "Tropical Root Crop Statistics: A World Perspective", *Proceedings of the Sixth Symposium of the International Society for Tropical Root Crops* (Lima: International Potato Center, 1984), 41–46.

8. Jamaica Agricultural Society, *Farmer's Food Manual*, 77; H.G. Muller, *An Introduction to Tropical Food Science* (Cambridge, UK: Cambridge University Press, 1988), 138.

9. Virginia Burke, *Eat Caribbean* (London: Simon and Schuster, 2005), 169-85; Jones, *Cook Up Jamaican Style* (2000), 3.

10. M.J.T. Norman, C.J. Pearson, and P.G.E. Searle, *The Ecology of Tropical Food Crops*, 2nd ed. (Cambridge, UK: Cambridge University Press, 1995), 90; Edward S. Ayensu and D.G. Coursey, "Guinea Yams: The Botany, Ethnobotany, Use and Possible Future of Yams in West Africa", *Economic Botany* 26 (1972): 314–16; David R. Harris, "Traditional Systems of Plant Food Production and the Origins of Agriculture in West Africa", in *Origins of African Plant Domestication*, ed. Jack R. Harlan, Jan M.J. De Wet, and Ann B. Stemler (The Hague: Mouton, 1976), 347.

11. Harris, "Traditional Systems", 335; D.G. Coursey, "The Origins and Domestication of Yams in Africa", in *Origins of African Plant Domestication*, ed. Harlan et al., 385.

12. Sloane, *Voyage*, 1: xxv; Johns, *With Bitter Herbs*, 52; Doyle McKey and Stephen Beckerman, "Chemical Ecology, Plant Evolution and Traditional Manioc Cultivation Systems", in

Tropical Forests, People and Food: Biocultural Interactions and Applications to Development, ed. C.M. Hladik, A. Hladik, O.F. Linares, H. Pagezy, A. Semple, and M. Hadley (Paris: UNESCO, 1993), 83–84.

13. Barbara S. Renvoize, "The Area of Origin of *Manihot esculenta* as a Crop Plant – A Review of the Evidence", *Economic Botany* 26 (1972): 352–60; Marianne Elias, Gilda Santos Mühlen, Doyle McKey, Ana Carolina Roa and Joe Tohme, "Genetic Diversity of Traditional South American Landraces of Cassava (*Manihot esculenta* Crantz): An Analysis Using Microsatellites", *Economic Botany* 58 (2004): 242–45.

14. David J. Rogers, "Some Botanical and Ethnological Considerations of *Manihot esculenta*", *Economic Botany* 19 (1965): 371; I.C. Onwueme, *The Tropical Tuber Crops: Yams, Cassava, Sweet Potato, and Cocoyams* (Chichester, UK: John Wiley, 1978), 145–47; Watts, *West Indies*, 57; Royes and Baccus, *Jamaica Farmer's Guide*, 208–9; McKey and Beckerman, "Chemical Ecology", 83–84.

15. Darna L. Dufour, "The Bitter Is Sweet: A Case Study of Bitter Cassava (*Manihot esculenta*) use in Amazonia", in *Tropical Forests, People and Food: Biocultural Interactions and Applications to Development*, ed. C.M. Hladik, A. Hladik, O.F. Linares, H. Pagezy, A. Semple, and M. Hadley (Paris: UNESCO, 1993), 575; McKey and Beckerman, "Chemical Ecology", 83; Gamini Seneviratne, "Processing Cassava to Improve Safety and Nutritional Value", *Cajanus* 19 (1986): 72–79; Curtis D. Klaassen, ed., *Casarett and Doull's Toxicology: The Basic Science of Poisons*, 6th ed. (New York: McGraw-Hill, 2001), 552, 971, 1072.

16. Neville L.R. King and J. Howard Bradbury, "Bitterness of Cassava: Identification of a New Apiosyl Glucoside and other Compounds That Affect Its Bitter Taste", *Journal of the Science of Food and Agriculture* 68 (1995): 223–30; O.L. Oke, "Processing and Detoxification of Cassava", *Proceedings of the Sixth Symposium of the International Society for Tropical Root Crops* (Lima: International Potato Center, 1984), 329–36; Dufour, "Bitter Is Sweet", 586.

17. William C. Sturtevant, "History and Ethnography of Some West Indian Starches", in *The Domestication and Exploitation of Plants and Animals*, ed. Peter J. Ucko and G.W. Dimbleby (Chicago: Aldine, 1969), 179; Anna Curtenius Roosevelt, *Parmana: Prehistoric Maize and Manioc Subsistence along the Amazon and Orinoco* (New York: Academic Press, 1980), 119–39; Jane Gregory Rubin and Ariana Donalds, eds, *Bread Made from Yuca: Selected Chronicles of Indo-Antillean Cultivation and Use of Cassava 1526–2002* (New York: InterAmericas, 2003); Onwueme, *Tropical Tuber Crops*, 109; William O. Jones, *Manioc in Africa* (Stanford, CA: Stanford University Press, 1959), 5; J. Howard Bradbury and Warren D. Holloway, *Chemistry of Tropical Root Crops: Significance for Nutrition and Agriculture in the Pacific* (Canberra: Australian Centre for International Agricultural Research, 1988), 27–29; Royes and Baccus, *Jamaica Farmer's Guide*, 208–11.

18. Sturtevant, "History and Ethnography", 179–81.

19. Sloane, *Voyage*, 1: xviii, 133; William Hughes, *The American Physitian; or, a Treatise of the Roots, Plants, Trees, Shrubs, Fruit, Herbs, &c. Growing in the English Plantations in America* (London: William Crook, 1672), 90–92; *The Present State of Jamaica* (London: Thomas Malthus, 1683), 21; Leslie, *New and Exact*, 33–34; P.A. Lancaster, J.S. Ingram, M.Y. Lim, and

D.G. Coursey, "Traditional Cassava-Based Foods: Survey of Processing Techniques", *Economic Botany* 36 (1982): 22–28.

20. Philip D. Curtin, *The Atlantic Slave Trade: A Census* (Madison: University of Wisconsin Press, 1969), 160; Jones, *Manioc in Africa*, 60–84; Long, *History*, 3: 778; Matthew Gregory Lewis, *Journal of a West India Proprietor, Kept during a Residence in the Island of Jamaica* (London: John Murray, 1834), 212.

21. Douglas Hall, *In Miserable Slavery: Thomas Thistlewood in Jamaica, 1750–86* (London: Macmillan, 1989), 161, 255; Cassidy, *Jamaica Talk*, 194, 392; *Gleaner*, 24 December 1866, 2; 17 November 1870, 4; Josias Cork, *Root Food Growth in Jamaica* (Kingston: George Henderson, 1881), 10–11; Jones, *Manioc in Africa*, 58, 173–75.

22. Sullivan, *Jamaica Cookery Book*, 38; Barham, *Hortus Americanus*, 34; *Gleaner*, 12 October 1914, 4; Hannah Glasse, *The Art of Cookery Made Plain and Easy* (1747; London: Prospect Books, 1983), 151; Clark, *West Indian Cookery*, 148.

23. Sullivan, *Jamaica Cookery Book*, 38–39, 89–90; *Gleaner*, 2 March 1899, 2.

24. Caroline Sullivan, *A Collection of 19th Century Jamaican Cookery and Herbal Recipes* (Kingston: The Mill Press, 1990), 42, 58.

25. *Gleaner*, 3 July 1918, 11; 14 January 1938, 4; Poppy Cannon, "The Cooking in Paradise", in *Ian Fleming Introduces Jamaica*, ed. Morris Cargill (London: Andre Deutsch, 1965), 190.

26. Beckwith, *Black Roadways*, 20–22.

27. Ibid., 20, 44–45; Clark, *West Indian Cookery*, 147; *Gleaner, Outlook Magazine*, 11 September 1994, 9.

28. Donaldson, *Real Taste*, 3–4, 49–50; *Jamaica, Finest Taste*, 128; *Gleaner, Supermarket Supplement*, 10 February 1994, 20; *Business Observer*, 18 May 2005, 3B.

29. Long, *History*, 3: 781; Jamaica Agricultural Society, *Farmer's Food Manual*, 180, 371; *Gleaner*, 25 March 1898, 3; 4 August 1908, 9.

30. Sullivan, *Jamaica Cookery Book*, 5–6; *Gleaner*, 7 June 1938, 16.

31. Donaldson, *Real Taste*, 4; *Importance of Jamaica*, 34–35; Long, *History*, 3: 781; Sullivan, *Jamaica Cookery Book*, 38–40, 49; *Gleaner*, 25 July 1989, 6; 5 August, 2001, 7B.

32. Sloane, *Voyage*, 1: xxix; Hughes, *American Physitian*, 90–92; *Present State of Jamaica*, 22.

33. Browne, *Civil and Natural*, 349–50.

34. P.A. Lancaster and J.E. Brooks, "Cassava Leaves as Human Food", *Economic Botany* 37 (1983): 331–48; David J. Rogers, "Cassava Leaf Protein", *Economic Botany* 13 (1959): 261–63; Long, *History*, 3: 778; *Importance of Jamaica*, 34–35.

35. Sturtevant, "History and Ethnography", 189–92; John W. Thieret, "Economic Botany of the Cycads", *Economic Botany* 12 (1957): 3; Whiting, "Toxicity of Cycads", 271–302; Klaassen, *Casarett and Doull's Toxicology*, 1072.

36. *Gleaner*, 11 September 1969, 3; 23 May 1971, 27.

37. Jerome S. Handler, "The History of Arrowroot and the Origin of Peasantries in the British West Indies", *Journal of Caribbean History* 2 (1971): 88–89; Sturtevant, "History and Ethnography", 184–89.

38. Ibid., 185; Handler, "History of Arrowroot", 49–51; Royes and Baccus, *Jamaica Farmer's Guide*, 207–8.

39. Barham, *Hortus Americanus*, 6–8; Long, *History*, 3: 759; John Lunan, *Hortus Jamaicensis, or a Botanical Description, (According to the Linnean System) and an Account of the Virtues, &c. of its Indigenous Plants Hitherto Unknown, as also of the most useful exotics* ([Spanish Town, Jamaica]: St Jago de la Vega Gazette, 1814), 1: 31–32. Cf. Thomas Roughley, *The Jamaica Planter's Guide* (London: Hurst, Longman, Rees, Orme and Brown, 1823), 417; Edward S. Ayensu, *Medicinal Plants of the West Indies* (Algonac, MI: Reference Publications, 1981), 122.

40. Sullivan, *Jamaica Cookery Book*, 33, 84–85; Clark, *West Indian Cookery*, 261; Jamaica Agricultural Society, *Farmer's Food Manual*, 179; Handler, "History of Arrowroot", 54–59.

41. M.D. Erdman and B.A. Erdman, "Arrowroot (*Maranta arundinacea*), Food, Feed, Fuel, and Fibre Resource", *Economic Botany* 38 (1984): 332–41; Handler, "History of Arrowroot", 75–87; *Gleaner*, 11 April 1870, 2; 6 February 1918, 10; *Gleaner, Food Supplement*, 13 December 1984, 41.

42. J. Alexander and D.G. Coursey, "The Origins of Yam Cultivation", in *The Domestication and Exploitation of Plants and Animals*, ed. Peter J. Ucko and G.W. Dimbleby (London: Duckworth, 1969), 422.

43. D.G. Coursey, *Yams: An Account of the Nature, Origins, Cultivation and Utilisation of the Useful Members of Dioscoreaceae* (London: Longmans, 1967), 5–19, 25–26; Coursey, "Origins and Domestication of Yams in Africa", 383–408; Bruce F. Johnston, *The Staple Food Economies of Western Tropical Africa* (Stanford, CA: Stanford University Press, 1958), 112; D.G. Coursey, "The Comparative Ethnobotany of African and Asian Yam Cultures", in *Proceedings of the Third Symposium of the International Society for Tropical Root Crops* (Ibadan, Nigeria: International Society for Tropical Root Crops, 1977), 164–68; Harris, "Traditional Systems", 340; Lucien Degras, *The Yam: A Tropical Root Crop* (Oxford: Macmillan Education, 1993).

44. I.H. Burkill, "The Rise and Decline of the Greater Yam in the Service of Man", *Advancement of Science* 7, no. 28 (1951): 447; John Alexander, "The Domestication of Yams: A Multidisciplinary Approach", in *Science in Archaeology: A Survey of Progress and Research*, ed. Don Brothwell and Eric Higgs (London: Thames and Hudson, 1969), 229–34.

45. Royes and Baccus, *Jamaica Farmer's Guide*, 216; Stephen D. Behrendt, "Markets, Transaction Cycles, and Profits: Merchant Decision Making in the British Slave Trade", *William and Mary Quarterly* 58 (2001): 182–85.

46. Royes and Baccus, *Jamaica Farmer's Guide*, 216–17; *Statistical Yearbook of Jamaica* (1982), 441.

47. Alexander and Coursey, "Origins of Yam Cultivation", 421–22; Onwueme, *Tropical Tuber Crops*, 4–6; Marie A. McAnuff, Felix O. Omoruyi, Angela Sotelo-López and Helen N. Asemota, "Proximate Analysis and Some Antinutritional Factor Constituents in Selected Varieties of Jamaican Yams (*Dioscorea* and *Rajana* spp.)", *Plant Foods for Human Nutrition* 60 (2005): 96.

48. Barham, *Hortus Americanus*, 211–12; Browne, *Civil and Natural*, 359; Long, *History*, 3: 781; Sullivan, *Jamaica Cookery Book*, 34; Beckwith, *Black Roadways*, 15.

49. Lunan, *Hortus Americanus*, 2: 308; Roughley, *Jamaica Planter's Guide*, 406–7.

50. Sullivan, *Jamaica Cookery Book*, 34; Lunan, *Hortus Americanus*, 2: 309–10; Beckwith, *Black Roadways*, 15; Cassidy, *Jamaica Talk*, 339–40; *Gleaner*, 2 July 1996, C1.

51. *Gleaner*, 5 September 1940, 9; Caribbean Research Council, Committee on Agriculture, Nutrition, Fisheries and Forestry, *Root Crops and Legumes in the Caribbean*, Crop Inquiry Series No. 4 (Washington, DC: Caribbean Research Council, 1947), 33; Black, *Jamaica Guide*, 29.

52. *Gleaner*, *Food Supplement*, 25 January 1990, 21; *Gleaner*, *Supermarket Supplement*, 25 January 1990, ix; *Gleaner*, *Home, Living and Food Guide*, 10 February 1994, 20; McAnuff et al., "Proximate Analysis", 96–97; Beckwith, *Black Roadways*, 16.

53. Onwueme, *Tropical Tuber Crops*, 12–13; Lunan, *Hortus Americanus*, 2: 308; *Gleaner*, 18 February 1941, 7; Coursey, *Yams*, 39–41, 74–77; Coursey, "Origins and Domestication", 385; Royes and Baccus, *Jamaica Farmer's Guide*, 219.

54. Browne, *Civil and Natural History*, 359–60; Long, *History*, 3: 781; Roughley, *Jamaica Planter's Guide*, 407–10; Coursey, "Origins and Domestication", 386.

55. Roughley, *Jamaica Planter's Guide*, 410–12; Long, *History*, 3: 781; Degras, *The Yam*, 222.

56. Browne, *Civil and Natural History*, 360; Long, *History*, 3: 781–82; Roughley, *Jamaica Planter's Guide*, 411; Ayre, *Bush Doctor*, 64; *Star*, 25 May 1989, 2; Coursey, *Yams*, 138–39.

57. Onwueme, *Tropical Tuber Crops*, 86; Sullivan, *Jamaica Cookery Book*, 34; McKay, *Banana Bottom*, 114; *Gleaner*, 18 February 1918, 8.

58. *Gleaner*, *Food Supplement*, 24 July 1986, 25; Donaldson, *Real Taste*, 9; Charles Hyatt, *When Me Was a Boy* (Kingston: Institute of Jamaica Publications, 1989), 153.

59. Sullivan, *Jamaica Cookery Book*, 34–36, 45.

60. *Recipes for Cooking West Indian Yams* (London: Imperial Department of Agriculture for the West Indies, 1902); *Gleaner*, *Farmer's Weekly*, 30 July 1955, 8; *Gleaner*, *Home, Food and Living Guide*, 2 May 1991, 22.

61. Clark, *West Indian Cookery*, 36–37, 128; Donaldson, *Real Taste*, 11, 29–30.

62. Patricia Cuff, *A Taste of the Old Home Place: Select Jamaican Recipes* (Mandeville: Pat Cuff Publications, 1989), 7–8; Mahabee and Mahabee, *Vegetarian Cookbook*, 30, 38, 90; Jones, *Cook Up Jamaican Style* (1981), 73, 87; Teresa E. Cleary, *Jamaica Run-dung: Over 100 Recipes* (Kingston: Brainbuster Publications, 1970), 14; Benghiat, *Traditional Jamaican Cookery*, 62.

63. *Gleaner*, 31 May 1997, A12.

64. Onwueme, *Tropical Tuber Crops*, 86; Coursey, *Yams*, 145–46. Cf. Sidney W. Mintz, *Sweetness and Power: The Place of Sugar in Modern History* (New York: Viking, 1985), 9–11; Cassidy, *Jamaica Talk*, 193; Ayre, *Bush Doctor*, 67–68.

65. "Characteristic Traits" 3 (July 1797): 107; Cassidy, *Jamaica Talk*, 193; *Gleaner*, *Food Supplement*, 1 August 1968, 17.

66. Sullivan, *Jamaica Cookery Book*, 3; Benghiat, *Traditional Jamaican Cookery*, 51.

67. Clark, *West Indian Cookery*, 293; Cassidy, *Jamaica Talk*, 192; *Panorama of African Recipes*, 14–15; Miller and Henry, *Creative Jamaican Cooking*, 35; Harris, "True Traditions of My Ancestors", 58.

68. Onwueme, *Tropical Tuber Crops*, 199; Jaw-Kai Wang, ed. *Taro: A Review of Colocasia esculenta and Its Potentials* (Honolulu: University of Hawaii Press, 1983).

69. Harlan, *Crops and Man*, 223–24; Jonathan D. Sauer, *Historical Geography of Crop Plants: A Select Roster* (Boca Raton, FL: CRC Press, 1993), 179–81. Cf. Peter Matthews and Ryohei

Terauchi, "The Genetics of Agriculture: DNA Variation in Taro and Yam", in *Tropical Archaeobotany: Applications and New Developments*, ed. Jon G. Hather (London: Routledge, 1994), 251–62; Janet H. Petterson, *Dissemination and Use of the Edible Aroids, with particular reference to Colocasia (Asian Taro) and Xanthosoma (American Taro)* (PhD. diss., University of Florida, 1977), xi.

70. Sauer, *Historical Geography*, 181; Onwueme, *Tropical Tuber Crops*, 199–201.

71. Onwueme, *Tropical Tuber Crops*, 201–6.

72. *Importance of Jamaica*, 39; Cassidy, *Jamaica Talk*, 338; Barham, *Hortus Americanus*, 56; Beckwith, *Black Roadways*, 17.

73. Royes and Baccus, *Jamaica Farmer's Guide*, 104, 211; *Statistical Yearbook of Jamaica* (1982), 441–43; (1993), 272; *Gleaner, Food Supplement*, 6 August 1987, 31; *Report of Committee on the Cost of Production of Certain Local Food Crops* (Kingston: Government Printer, 1946), 4.

74. Royes and Baccus, *Jamaica Farmer's Guide*, 211–12.

75. Simon Taylor, Kingston, to Chaloner Arcedeckne, London, 1 January 1786, 3A/1786/1 Vanneck/Arcedeckne Papers (Cambridge University Library); Lunan, *Hortus Americanus*, 1: 212.

76. Lunan, *Hortus Americanus*, 1: 212; Beckwith, *Black Roadways*, 17; Royes and Baccus, *Jamaica Farmer's Guide*, 212; Onwueme, *Tropical Tuber Crops*, 216–17.

77. Sullivan, *A Collection*, 4; Sullivan, *Jamaica Cookery Book*, 36; Donaldson, *Real Taste*, 15; Clark, *West Indian Cookery*, 99–101; Murray and Lewin, *Jamaican Chef*, 3–4; Cleary, *Jamaica Rundung*, 17, 23–24; Mahabee and Mahabee, *Vegetarian Cookbook*, 39, 90; Jones, *Cook Up Jamaican Style* (1981), 81. Cf. Benghiat, *Traditional Jamaican Cookery*, 60; *Jamaica, Finest Taste*, 5.

78. *Gleaner, Food Supplement*, 6 August 1987, 31; 25 January 1990, 21; *Gleaner*, 1 May 1997, B5; Harris, "Traditional Systems", 333; Roughley, *Jamaica Planter's Guide*, 404.

79. *Gleaner, Food Supplement*, 25 July 1985, 37; *Star*, 25 May 1989, 2; *Gleaner, Home, Food and Living Guide*, 28 February 1991, 24; *Gleaner*, 1 July 1995, 11A; 15 May 1997, B6.

80. Mahabee and Mahabee, *Vegetarian Cookbook*, 31; *Gleaner, Food Supplement*, 5 July 1984, 22; John Dovaston, "Agricultura Americana, or Improvements in West-India Husbandry Considered" (Codex Eng 60, John Carter Brown Library, Providence), 94; Long, *History*, 3: 769–70; Ayre, *Bush Doctor*, 88–89.

81. Long, *History*, 3: 769–70; Hall, *In Miserable Slavery*, 40, 283; Lunan, *Hortus Americanus*, 1: 213; H.A.P.C. Oomen and G.J.H. Grubben, *Tropical Leaf Vegetables in Human Nutrition* (Amsterdam: Koninklijk Instituut vor de Tropen, 1977), 79–81, 101; Sauer, *Historical Geography*, 179; Onwueme, *Tropical Tuber Crops*, 221.

82. Barham, *Hortus Americanus*, 56; Long, *History*, 3: 769–70.

83. *Gleaner*, 14 January 1905, 10; *Gleaner, Food Supplement*, 7 February 1985, 23; *Jamaica Observer*, 13 June 1993, 46; Benghiat, *Traditional Jamaican Cookery*, 61.

84. *Report of Committee on the Cost of Production of Certain Local Food Crops*, 9–10; Royes and Baccus, *Jamaica Farmer's Guide*, 214–16; Oomen and Grubben, *Tropical Leaf Vegetables*, 101; Onwueme, *Tropical Tuber Crops*, 181. Cf. Bradbury and Holloway, *Chemistry of Tropical Root Crops*, 18–20.

85. W.J. Fielding and K. Ryder, *The Biometry of Sweet Potato* (Ipomoea batatas): *Some Consider-ations for Field Experiments*, Special Publication No. 8 (Kingston: Ministry of Agriculture and Mining, 1995); Royes and Baccus, *Jamaica Farmer's Guide*, 216; *Gleaner, Food Supplement*, 7 February 1985, 23.

86. Chris Ballard, "Still Good to Think With: The Sweet Potato in Oceania", in *The Sweet Potato in Oceania: A Reappraisal*, Oceania Monograph 56, ed. Chris Ballard, Paula Brown, R. Michael Bourke and Tracy Harwood (Sydney: University of Sydney, 2005), 2–3; J.S. Cooley, "The Sweet Potato: Its Origin and Primitive Storage Practices", *Economic Botany* 5 (1951): 378–83; Redcliffe N. Salaman, *The History and Social Influence of the Potato* (Cambridge, UK: Cambridge University Press, 1949), 131; Watts, *West Indies*, 58; Onwueme, *Tropical Tuber Crops*, 167.

87. Leslie, *New and Exact*, 33; Cooley, "Sweet Potato", 383–86; Sauer, *Historical Geography*, 37–38.

88. Sloane, *Voyage*, 1: 150; Long, *History*, 3: 774; Beckwith, *Black Roadways*, 17–18; Cassidy, *Jamaica Talk*, 337; Royes and Baccus, *Jamaica Farmer's Guide*, 215.

89. Hughes, *American Physitian*, 12–15; *Certain Inducements to Well Minded People, who are here straitned in their estates or otherwise: or such as are willing out of noble and publike principles, to transport themselves, or some servants, or agents for them into the West-Indies, for the propa-gating of the Gospel, and increase of trade* (London, 1643), 4; Sloane, *Voyage*, 1: 151; *Present State of Jamaica*, 22; Dovaston, "Agricultura Americana", 94; Long, *History*, 3: 774.

90. Hughes, *American Physitian*, 12–15; Sloane, *Voyage*, 1: 150–51; Long, *History*, 3: 774–75; Lunan, *Hortus Americanus*, 2: 219; Sullivan, *A Collection*, 52.

91. *Jamaica Observer*, June 13, 1993, 46; Sullivan, *Jamaica Cookery Book*, 36, 45–46; "Myrtle and Money", *Planters' Punch* 4, no. 4 (1941–42): 16; Clark, *West Indian Cookery*, 188–89; Leila Brandon, *A Merry-Go-Round of Recipes from Jamaica* (Kingston: Novelty Trading, 1963), 64; Benghiat, *Traditional Jamaican Cookery*, 153; Donaldson, *Real Taste*, 107; Jamaica, *Finest Taste*, 133; Glasse, *Art of Cookery*, 59–105.

92. Sullivan, *Jamaica Cookery Book*, 36; Oomen and Grubben, *Tropical Leaf Vegetables*, 101.

93. Alfred W. Crosby, Jr, *The Columbian Exchange: Biological and Cultural Consequences of 1492* (Westport, CT: Greenwood, 1972); Henry Hobhouse, *Seeds of Change: Five Plants That Trans-formed Mankind* (New York: Harper and Row, 1985); Herman J. Viola and Carolyn Margolis, eds, *Seeds of Change: A Quincentennial Commemoration* (Washington, DC: Smithsonian Institu-tion Press, 1991); Walvin, *Fruits of Empire*; Burkill, "Rise and Decline of the Greater Yam", 448.

94. Long, *History*, 3: 774; Lunan, *Hortus Americanus*, 1: 92–93.

95. Sauer, *Historical Geography*, 145–50; Salaman, *History and Social Influence*, 99–100.

96. Cassidy, *Jamaica Talk*, 337; Royes and Baccus, *Jamaica Farmer's Guide*, 212–13.

97. Trollope, *West Indies*, 21, 39; Algernon E. Aspinall, *The British West Indies: Their History, Resources and Progress* (London: Pitman, 1912), 120; Cork, *Root Food Growth*.

98. *Gleaner*, 7 July 1938, 1; Clark, *West Indian Cookery*, 100, 117, 128, 131, 254, 278.

99. *Gleaner, Food Supplement*, 1 August 1968, 16; Benghiat, *Traditional Jamaican Cookery*, 61; Cork, *Root Food Growth*, 9; *Report of Committee on the Cost of Production of Certain Local Food Crops*, 11–12; Caribbean Research Council, Committee on Agriculture, Nutrition, Fisheries

and Forestry, *Root Crops and Legumes*, 33; J.G. Hawkes, *The Potato: Evolution, Biodiversity and Genetic Resources* (London: Belhaven, 1990); *Gleaner*, 4 December 1965, 16.

100. *Gleaner*, 2 January 1900, 2; 25 July 1900, 4.

101. *Gleaner*, 28 May 1988, 17–18; 19 April 1995, 3A; 1 July 1995, 12A; Hugo Weenen, J. Kerler, and J.G.M. van der Ven, "The Maillard Reaction in Flavour Formation", in *Flavours and Fragrances*, ed. Karl A.D. Swift (Cambridge, UK: Royal Society of Chemistry, 1997), 155–58.

102. Long, *History*, 3: 805–6; Lunan, *Hortus Jamaicensis*, 1: 34; Charles I.G. Rampini, *Letters from Jamaica: "The Land of Streams and Woods"* (Edinburgh: Edmonston and Douglas, 1873), 25.

103. J.W. Thieret, "Ginger in Jamaica", *Economic Botany* 15 (1959): 86; D.W. Rodriquez, *Ginger: A Short Economic History*, Commodity Bulletin No. 4 (Kingston: Ministry of Agriculture and Fisheries, 1971), 13; Purseglove et al., *Spices*, 2: 507; *Gleaner*, 27 April 1877, 2; 2 November, 1990, 31.

104. Purseglove et al., *Spices*, 2: 490–95; Bartley, "A New Method", 215–22; Yajing Shao, Philip Marriott, Robert Shellie and Helmut Hügel, "Solid-Phase Micro-extraction: Comprehensive Two-Dimensional Gas Chromatography of Ginger (*Zingiber officinale*) Volatiles", *Flavour and Fragrance Journal* 18 (2003): 12.

105. Richard Blome, *A Description of the Island of Jamaica* (London: J. Williams, Jr, 1672), 13; Long, *History*, 3: 700; Rodriquez, *Ginger*, 3–5.

106. Rodriquez, *Ginger*, 6; Purseglove et al., *Spices*, 2: 447–50, 460.

107. Sloane, *Voyage*, 1: lxviii–lxix; Long, *History*, 3: 701; Beckwith, *Black Roadways*, 25; Purseglove et al., *Spices*, 2: 465–66.

108. *Gleaner*, 4 May 1986; Purseglove et al., *Spices*, 2: 466–67, 477–79.

109. Rodriquez, *Ginger*, 10–11; Long, *History*, 3: 701; Sullivan, *Jamaica Cookery Book*, 69.

110. A. Cooper, *The Complete Distiller* (London: P. Vaillant and R. Griffiths, 1757), 162; Shao et al., "Solid-Phase Micro-extraction", 5.

111. Purseglove et al., *Spices*, 2: 532–37, 552, 569.

112. Hall, *In Miserable Slavery*, 86; "Characteristic Traits" 3 (July 1797): 108; *Gleaner*, 18 May 1892, 5; 6 April 1980, 14; 30 October 2002, B8; 12 March 2005, 24; *Gleaner, Flair Feature*, 13 September 1999, 6.

Chapter 4

1. Forbes and Watson, *Plants in Agriculture*, 8–11; King, *Reaching for the Sun*, 13–26; Bell and Hemsley, *Green Plants*, 272–81; Lack and Evans, *Plant Biology*, 41–58.

2. Cf. Erika E. Gaertner, "Breadstuff from Fir (*Abies balsamea*)", *Economic Botany* 24 (1970): 69–72.

3. *Gleaner, Food Supplement*, 24 October 1985, 22.

4. Oomen and Grubben, *Tropical Leaf Vegetables*, 13–15.

5. *Gleaner, Food Supplement*, 13 December 1984, 30.

6. Scientific Research Council, *Callalu: A Good Mixer* (Kingston: Scientific Research Council, 1971), 1; Whitbourne, "Ordinary Diet in Jamaica", 70; John Stewart, *A View of the Past and Present State of the Island of Jamaica* (Edinburgh: Oliver and Boyd, 1823), 66–67; *Gleaner*, 23 February 1940, 13; 28 March 1940, 16; Oomen and Grubben, *Tropical Leaf Vegetables*, 77.

7. G.J.A. Terra, *Tropical Vegetables: Vegetable Growing in the Tropics and Subtropics Especially of Indigenous Vegetables* (Amsterdam: Koninklijk Instituut voor de Tropen, 1973), 23; Royes and Baccus, *Jamaica Farmer's Guide*, 238–67.

8. Robert Becker and Robin M. Saunders, "New Uses for Amaranth", *Cajanus* 17 (1984): 213–14; Scientific Research Council, *Callalu*, 4; *Gleaner, Home, Living and Food Guide*, 11 May 1995, 8C.

9. *Gleaner, Home, Living and Food Guide*, 11 May 1995, 8C.

10. *Importance of Jamaica*, 34; Hall, *In Miserable Slavery*, 156; Browne, *Civil and Natural*, 232; Dovaston, "Agricultura Americana", 1: 94.

11. Long, *History*, 3: 771–72.

12. Lunan, *Hortus Jamaicensis*, 1: 35, 142; Sullivan, *Jamaica Cookery Book*, 2, 97–98.

13. Scientific Research Council, *Callalu*, 1; P.V. Devi Prasad, *Edible Fruits and Vegetables of the English-Speaking Caribbean* (Kingston: Caribbean Food and Nutrition Institute, 1986), 36; C.W. van Epenhuijsen, *Growing Native Vegetables in Nigeria* (Rome: Food and Agriculture Organization of the United Nations, 1974), 30–35.

14. Ayre, *Bush Doctor*, 88; *Gleaner*, 16 October 2003, C1; Carollin Carol, interview, 25 September 1989.

15. Sloane, *Voyage*, 1: 143–44; Barham, *Hortus Americanus*, 44.

16. Reverend John Lindsay, "Elegancies of Jamaica", 60 (Natural History Division, Bristol Museum and Art Gallery); *Importance of Jamaica*, 40.

17. *Columbian Magazine* (June 1797): 8. See also Lewis, *Journal*, 106.

18. Briggs, *New Art of Cookery*, 35–36.

19. Rampini, *Letters from Jamaica*, 64–65.

20. Beckwith, *Black Roadways*, 14; *Gleaner, Home, Living and Food Guide*, 21 January 1993, 25.

21. Chapman, *Pleasure Island*, 102; Jamaica Agricultural Society, *Farmer's Food Manual*, 142; Scientific Research Council, *Callalu*, 2.

22. *Gleaner, Food Supplement*, 23 January 1986, 25; *Gleaner, Home, Living and Food Guide*, 4 March 1993, 14; Donaldson, *Real Taste*, 15.

23. Sullivan, *Jamaica Cookery Book*, 98; Scientific Research Council, *Sample Menus of Meals Highlighting Jamaican Foods* (Kingston: Scientific Research Council, [1974], cyclostyled), 10; *Gleaner, Food Supplement*, 13 December 1984, 30; 23 January 1986, 25.

24. *Gleaner, Food Supplement*, 23 January 1986, 25; *Jamaica Observer*, 3 November 2002, 8.

25. Sullivan, *Jamaica Cookery Book*, 39; Barham, *Hortus Americanus*, 154–55; Tom Stobart, *Herbs, Spices and Flavorings* (New York: Overlook, 1982), 204.

26. *Gleaner, Food Supplement*, 1 August 1968, 17; *Gleaner*, 20 July 1963, 14; 18 September 1969, 16; *Gleaner, Tourism Supplement*, 5 July 1970, 103; Henry Lowe, Errol Morrison, Kenneth Magnus, and Ellen Campbell-Grizzle, *Poisonous Plants of Jamaica* (Kingston: Pelican, 2002), 81.

27. Accounts Current, Liber 1, ff. 24-36 (Jamaica Archives, Spanish Town); James M. Phillippo, *Jamaica: Its Past and Present State* (London: John Snow, 1843), 48.

28. Long, *History*, 3: 770–71; Barham, *Hortus Americanus*, 9; Lunan, *Hortus Jamaicensis*, 1: 35,

130; *Importance of Jamaica*, 34; Browne, *Civil and Natural History*, 273; Sullivan, *Jamaica Cookery Book*, 32.

29. Douglas Hall, "Botanical and Horticultural Enterprise in Eighteenth-Century Jamaica", in *West Indies Accounts: Essays on the History of the British Caribbean and the Atlantic Economy in Honour of Richard Sheridan*, ed. Roderick A. McDonald (Kingston: University of the West Indies Press, 1996), 111–13; Hall, *In Miserable Slavery*, 177; Trevor Burnard, *Mastery, Tyranny, and Desire: Thomas Thistlewood and His Slaves in the Anglo-Jamaican World* (Chapel Hill: University of North Carolina Press, 2004), 63.

30. *Gleaner*, 24 December 1931, 11; 11 March 1955, 6; *Gleaner, Food Supplement*, 4 April 1968, 11. See also *Gleaner*, 20 March 1900, 3; *Gleaner, Home, Food and Living Guide*, 31 January 1991, 21.

31. Stewart, *View*, 66.

32. W.J. Titford, *Sketches towards a Hortus Botanicus Americanus* (London: Sherwood, Neely and Jones, 1811), 55–56; Lunan, *Hortus Jamaicensis*, 1:316.

33. *Jamaica Observer*, 1–3 October 1993, 36.

34. Richard Blome, *The Present State of His Majesties Isles and Territories in America* (London: Dorman Newman, 1687), 23; *Importance of Jamaica*, 34; Browne, *Civil and Natural*, 260.

35. Browne, *Civil and Natural History*, 260; Barham, *Hortus Americanus*, 17; Titford, *Sketches*, 50.

36. Leader, *Through Jamaica with a Kodak*, 142; Sullivan, *Jamaica Cookery Book*, 102–14; *Financial Gleaner*, 20 November 1987, 3; Obiagele Lake, "Cultural Beliefs and Breastfeeding Practices among Jamaican Rastafarians", *Cajanus* 25, no. 4 (1992): 208.

37. Barham, *Hortus Americanus*, 186–91; Long, *History*, 3: 807–8.

38. *Gleaner*, 2 May 1896, 1; 2 March 1920, 2; 3 January 1948, 11; 7 March 1960, 19; *Gleaner, Food Supplement*, 13 June 1985, 23.

39. *Gleaner*, 6 April 1989, 1.

40. Lake, "Cultural Beliefs and Breastfeeding Practices", 208; Johannes Novak, Karin Zitterl-Eglseer, Stanley G. Deans, and Chlodwig M. Franz, "Essential Oils of Different Cultivars of *Cannabis sativa* L. and their Antimicrobial Activity", *Flavour and Fragrance Journal* 16 (2001): 259.

41. Henry Lowe and Errol Morrison, *Ganja: The Jamaican Connection* (Kingston: Pelican, 2001), 19–20; Eric, *Cooking with Ghanja* (Dorset, UK: Ghanja Press, 1995); Ebanks, *Rastafari Cookbook*, 21, 29, 45; *Gleaner*, 2 August 1972, 3; 20 August 1993, 1.

42. Lunan, *Hortus Jamaicensis*, 1: 43; Harris, *Good to Eat*, 13; Rampini, *Letters from Jamaica*, 65; Rashford, "Past and Present Uses of Bamboo", 401.

43. *Gleaner, PCJ 25th Anniversary Supplement*, 15 June 2004, 7.

44. Hughes, *American Physitian*, 79–80; Sloane, *Voyage*, vol. 1, Preface; Browne, *Civil and Natural History*, 343; Long, *History*, 3: 744; Hall, *In Miserable Slavery*, 104.

45. Long, *History*, 3: 744; Hall, *In Miserable Slavery*, 104; Gosse, *Naturalist's Sojourn*, 262.

46. *Gleaner*, 20 November 1926, 19; Sullivan, *Jamaica Cookery Book*, 32, 92–93; Herbert T. Thomas, *Untrodden Jamaica* (Kingston: A.W. Gardner, 1890), 17.

47. Nugent, *Lady Nugent's Journal*, 76; *Gleaner*, 17 June 1880.

48. *Gleaner*, 21 December 1985, 31; 25 March 1989, 15; *Gleaner*, *PCJ 25th Anniversary Supplement*, 15 June 2004, 7.

49. Mauro Galetti and José Carlos Fernandez, "Palm Heart Harvesting in the Brazilian Atlantic Forest: Changes in Industry Structure and the Illegal Trade", *Journal of Applied Ecology* 35 (1998): 294.

50. Barham, *Hortus Americanus*, 195; Long, *History*, 3: 757; "Trumpet Tree", *Jamaica Journal* 24, no. 3 (1993): 66; *Gleaner*, 29 July 1965, 42; 29 May 1969, 3.

51. Powers of Attorney, Liber 96, f. 175 (1B/11/24, Jamaica Archives, Spanish Town); Purseglove et al., *Spices*, 1: 100–103.

52. Long, *History*, 3: 705–6; Titford, *Sketches*, Plate VII; Lunan, *Hortus Jamaicensis*, 1: 195.

53. Long MSS, Add. 22678, ff. 3, 19, 24–27 (British Library, London); Lunan, *Hortus Jamaicensis*, 1: 191–92; Stewart, *View*, 62; *Falmouth Post*, 12 February 1850.

54. Leslie, *New and Exact*, 326; "Characteristic Traits" 3 (July 1797): 108; Hall, *In Miserable Slavery*, 86.

55. Long, *History*, 3: 847; Lunan, *Hortus Jamaicensis*, 1: 177; M. Adu-Tutu, Y. Afful, K. Asante-Appiah, Diana Lieberman, J.B. Hall, and Memory Elvin-Lewis, "Chewing Stick Usage in Southern Ghana", *Economic Botany* 33 (1979): 320.

56. Barham, *Hortus Americanus*, 207; Thomas Trapham, *A Discourse on the State of Health in the Island of Jamaica* (London: R. Boulter, 1679), 48; Lunan, *Hortus Jamaicensis*, 1: 137–38; Stewart, *View*, 314; Gosse, *Naturalist's Sojourn*, 125–26.

57. *Gleaner, Food Supplement*, 21 November 1985, iv; *Gleaner*, 5 July 1988, 19.

58. Beckwith, *Black Roadways*, 14; *Gleaner*, 24 March 1990, 13.

59. Powell et al., *Street Foods of Kingston*, 36.

60. *Coalpot Recipe Postcards* (Kingston: n.p., [c. 1980]); Benghiat, *Traditional Jamaican Cookery*, 144; Donaldson, *Real Taste*, 8; Miller and Henry, *Creative Jamaican Cooking*, 9.

61. Mintz, *Sweetness and Power*.

62. An Act to prevent hawking and peddling, and disposing of goods clandestinely, *Laws of Jamaica*, 1735, cap. VI; Marsden, *Account*, 19.

63. Betty Wood, ed., *The Letters of Simon Taylor of Jamaica to Chaloner Arcedekne, 1765–1775*, Camden Miscellany, Vol. 35 (London: Cambridge University Press for the Royal Historical Society, 2002), 38; Hall, *In Miserable Slavery*, 265.

64. Ibid., 47; Nugent, *Lady Nugent's Journal*, 50; Sullivan, *Jamaica Cookery Book*, 114.

65. Joseph Sturge and Thomas Harvey, *The West Indies in 1837* (London: Hamilton, Adams, 1838), 177; Beckwith, *Black Roadways*, 24; Moore and Johnson, *"Squalid Kingston"*, 59.

66. "Melinda", *Planters' Punch* 4, no. 2 (1939–40): 6; Whitbourne, "Ordinary Diet in Jamaica", 70; Hurston, *Voodoo Gods*, 272; Cannon, "Cooking in Paradise", 190; Donaldson, *Real Taste*, 11.

67. McKay, *Banana Bottom*, 189, 311; Sullivan, *Jamaica Cookery Book*, 106, 114; Dolf Wyllarde, *Tropical Tales and Others* (London: Stanley Paul, 1909), 314.

68. Sloane, *Voyage*, 1: lxix.

69. Williams, *Tour*, 6, 14; Hall, *In Miserable Slavery*, 86.

70. *Gleaner*, 8 May 1880, 3; 20 December 1893, 2; 20 March 1900, 3; 21 May 1985, 15; 1 February 2006, A8.

71. Donaldson, *Real Taste*, 135; *Planters' Punch* 4, no. 1 (1938–39): 28; Frederick H. Smith, *Caribbean Rum: A Social and Economic History* (Gainesville: University Press of Florida, 2005), 50–55.

72. Hughes, *American Physitian*, 34; George Smith, *The Nature of Fermentation Explain'd; with the Method of Opening the Body of any Grain or Vegetable Subject, so as to Obtain from It a Spiritous Liquor: Exemplified by the Process of Preparing Rum, as 'tis Manag'd in the West-Indies* (London: Bernard Lintot, 1729), 17.

73. Hall, *In Miserable Slavery*, 47; Frederick H. Smith, "Spirits and Spirituality: Enslaved Persons and Alcohol in West Africa and the British and French Caribbean", *Journal of Caribbean History* 38 (2004): 286–90.

74. *Gleaner*, 20 March 1880, 3; 1 January 1890, 2; 4 September 1918, 15; *Planters' Punch*, 4, no. 1 (1938–39), 57; *Jamaica Rum Book* (London: Macmillan Caribbean, 1986), 7–9.

75. *Planters' Punch* 4, no. 1 (1938–39): 118; *Gleaner*, 21 July 1915, 16; 11 March 1935, 3.

76. *Gleaner*, 12 February 1866, 5; 5 November 1866, 1; 18 June 1867, 3; 3 September 1995, 1A. On proof, see Noel Deerr, *Cane Sugar* (London: Norman Rodger, 1921), 582; Hugh Barty-King and Anton Massel, *Rum: Yesterday and Today* (London: Heinemann, 1983), 67.

77. *Gleaner*, 2 August 1985, 19; 23 July 1986, 3; 13 September 1991, 28.

78. Hughes, *American Physitian*, 34; Sloane, *Voyage*, 1: xxix; *Gleaner*, 10 May 1938, 3; Hamilton, *Little Jamaican Cookbook*, 57; Donaldson, *Real Taste*, 136, 141; *Jamaica Rum Book*, 31; Elaine R. McLean, *Jamaican Cooking* (Milwaukee, WI: privately printed, 1989), 8.

79. *Gleaner*, 24 January 1870, 2; 9 July 1938, 2; *Planters' Punch* 4, no. 2 (1939–40): 32.

80. *Gleaner*, 1 August 1986, 9.

81. *Gall's News Letter*, 7 January 1880; *Gleaner, Desnoes and Geddes 75th Anniversary Supplement*, 7 July 1993, 6–7.

82. *Gleaner, Desnoes and Geddes 75th Anniversary Supplement*, 7 July 1993, 6–7; *Planters' Punch* 4, no. 1 (1938–39): 52.

83. *Royal Gazette* (Spanish Town), 6 May 1820; *Gleaner*, 6 May 1870, 3; 20 June 1913, 15; 26 June 1914, 14.

84. *Gleaner*, 26 September 1985, 8; 23 September 1993, 1; *Gleaner, Desnoes and Geddes 75th Anniversary Supplement*, 7 July 1993, 7.

85. *Jamaica Rum Book*, 7–36; *Gleaner*, 31 July 1985.

86. *Gleaner, Home, Living and Food Guide*, 4 August 1994, 22; *Gleaner*, 12 May 2005, C1; Ebanks, *Rastafari Cookbook*, 87.

87. *Cooking with Red Stripe* (Kingston: Desnoes and Geddes, [1993]), 17, 56, 69; *Gleaner, Home, Living and Food Guide*, 6 January 1994, 18; *Jamaica Rum Book*, 44–48; Brandon, *Merry-Go-Round*, 55; Wenton O. Spence, *Jamaican Cookery: Recipes from Old Jamaican Grandmothers* (Kingston: Heritage Publishers, 1981), 11; Cuff, *Taste*, 13.

88. "The New Industry of Sweets", *Planters' Punch* 3, no. 2 (1933–34): 86; *Gleaner*, 16 July 1932, 21; 3 August 1940, 32; 24 December 1966, 7; 24 March 1992, 2; Olive Senior, *Arrival of the*

Snake-Woman and Other Stories (London: Longman, 1989), 51; Enid Donaldson, "Sweets for My Sweet", in *A Tapestry of Jamaica: The Best of Skywritings, Air Jamaica's Inflight Magazine*, ed. Linda Gambrill (1996; Kingston: Creative Communications, 2003), 151.

Chapter 5

1. Edgar Mayhew Bacon and Eugene Murray Aaron, *The New Jamaica* (New York: Walbridge, 1890), 117; Pullen-Burry, *Jamaica as It Is, 1903*, 51–54; Chapman, *Pleasure Island*, 103.

2. Lack and Evans, *Plant Biology*, 125–30; Bell and Hemsley, *Green Plants*, 295–300; Forbes and Watson, *Plants in Agriculture*, 179–85; King, *Reaching for the Sun*, 151–52.

3. Muller, *Introduction to Tropical Food Science*, 121.

4. Carley, *Jamaica*, 113; *Gleaner*, 27 May 1990, 14C.

5. N.W. Simmonds, *Bananas* (London: Longmans, 1959), 54; J.A. Samson, *Tropical Fruits* (London: Longman, 1980), 119; Sauer, *Historical Geography*, 198.

6. Edmond De Langhe and Pierre de Maret, "Tracking the Banana: Its Significance in Early Agriculture", in *The Prehistory of Food: Appetites for Change*, ed. Chris Gosden and Jon Hather (London: Routledge, 1999), 377–96; N.S. Price, "The Origin and Development of Banana and Plantain Cultivation", in *Bananas and Plantains*, ed. S. Gowen (London: Chapman and Hall, 1995), 3; Sauer, *Historical Geography*, 198–200; Watts, *West Indies*, 76.

7. Lunan, *Hortus Jamaicensis*, 2: 72; Simmonds, *Bananas*, 259; Samson, *Tropical Fruits*, 120–21.

8. *Gleaner*, 28 February 1933, 12; Sloane, *Voyage*, 1: xix.

9. Ibid., 1: xix; Long, *History*, 3: 782; Richard B. Sheridan, "The Maroons of Jamaica, 1730–1830: Livelihood, Demography and Health", *Slavery and Abolition* 6 (1985): 155; Roughley, *Jamaica Planter's Guide*, 412–15; *Importance of Jamaica*, 10.

10. Simmonds, *Bananas*, 9.

11. Marsden, *Account*, 64; *Importance of Jamaica*, 29; Sloane, *Voyage*, 1: xix; Sullivan, *Jamaica Cookery Book*, 108, italics in original.

12. Sloane, *Voyage*, 1: xix; Barham, *Hortus Americanus*, 44; Marsden, *Account*, 64; Browne, *Civil and Natural History*, 363; Lunan, *Hortus Jamaicensis*, 2: 72; Long, *History*, 3: 782; R.R. Madden, *A Twelvemonth's Residence in the West Indies* (London: James Cochrane, 1835), 1: 237.

13. Sullivan, *Jamaica Cookery Book*, 30; Beckwith, *Black Roadways*, 18.

14. Hall, *In Miserable Slavery*, 14; Clark, *West Indian Cookery*, 293; *Gleaner, Food Supplement*, 6 August 1987, 31; *Panorama of African Recipes*, 15–20.

15. *Gleaner*, 18 October 1938, 12; *Importance of Jamaica*, 29.

16. Simon Taylor, Kingston, to Chaloner Arcedeckne, London, 1 January and 19 March 1786, 3A/1786/1 and 6, Vanneck/Arcedeckne Papers. The original of the January 1 letter reads "coor cuntine"; the copy, in another hand, reads "concantine". Rampini, *Letters from Jamaica*, 73.

17. Browne, *Civil and Natural History*, 363; *Importance of Jamaica*, 29; Long, *History*, 3: 782; Lunan, *Hortus Jamaicensis*, 2: 72.

18. Brandon, *Merry-Go-Round*, 61; Cleary, *Jamaica Run-dung*, 49; Jones, *Cook Up Jamaican Style*

(1981), 76; Benghiat, *Traditional Jamaican Cookery*, 156; McLean, *Jamaican Cooking*, 74; Sullivan, *Jamaica Cookery Book*, 30.

19. *Importance of Jamaica*, 29; Harris, "True Traditions", 57; Sullivan, *Jamaica Cookery Book*, 87–88; *Gleaner, Home, Living and Food Guide*, 4 June 1992, 22; Jones, *Cook Up Jamaican Style* (2000), 52; Scientific Research Council, *Sample Menus*, 16.

20. Higman, *Jamaica Surveyed*, 274–75; Higman, *Montpelier*, 197; Sauer, *Historical Geography*, 199; Harris, "Traditional Systems", 332; Browne, *Civil and Natural History*, 364.

21. Long, *History*, 3: 783; Barham, *Hortus Americanus*, 15–16; Titford, *Sketches*, xv; Roughley, *Jamaica Planter's Guide*, 415; Douglas Hall, *Ideas and Illustrations in Economic History* (New York: Holt, Rinehart and Winston, 1964), 59.

22. Sauer, *Historical Geography*, 201; Olivier, *Jamaica*, 377–78; Hall, *Ideas and Illustrations*, 58.

23. Claude McKay, *The Dialect Poetry of Claude McKay* (Plainview, NY: Books for Libraries Press, 1972), 30.

24. Virginia Scott Jenkins, *Bananas: An American History* (Washington, DC: Smithsonian Institution Press, 2000).

25. Sir Sibbald David Scott, *To Jamaica and Back* (London: Chapman and Hall, 1876), 264; Hall, *Ideas and Illustrations*, 60–79; Olivier, *Jamaica*, 379; *Gleaner*, 22 December 1886, 2; 8 February 1897, 7.

26. Hall, *Ideas and Illustrations*, 65–66; Gisela Eisner, *Jamaica, 1830–1930: A Study in Economic Growth* (Manchester, UK: Manchester University Press, 1961), 304–5.

27. *Gleaner*, 2 May 1917, 8; 3 January 1941, 6; 5 February 1941, 10; 18 February 1941, 7; 21 February 1941, 9; 31 March 1941, 16; 21 May 1942, 1; 25 July 1942, 8; *Planters' Punch* 4, no. 4 (1941–42): 13–14.

28. Gabrielle J. Persley and Pamela George, eds, *Banana Improvement: Research Challenges and Opportunities* (Washington, DC: World Bank, 1996), 4; *Gleaner*, 31 January 2006, A4.

29. Sullivan, *Jamaica Cookery Book*, 47, 57–61, 73, 76; *Gleaner*, 3 January 1938, 17; 16 January 1941, 8; 28 January 1941, 6.

30. Clark, *West Indian Cookery*, 36, 46, 121, 197, 218; Brandon, *Merry-Go-Round*, 7; Cleary, *Jamaica Run-dung*, 12; Jamaica Information Service, *Banana Recipes* (1965; Kingston: Novelty Trading, 1975), 27; Jenkins, *Bananas*, 114–15.

31. Jones, *Cook Up Jamaican Style* (1981), 22; McLean, *Jamaican Cooking*, 5; Hughes, *American Physitian*, 76; Long, *History*, 3: 783.

32. Jones, *Cook Up Jamaican Style* (1981), 83–84; Mahabee and Mahabee, *Vegetarian Cookbook*, 72; *Gleaner, Chippies 25th Anniversary Supplement*, 25 November 1989, 5.

33. *Gleaner, Supermarket Shopping Guide*, 24 January 1991, 10D; *Gleaner, Home, Living and Food Guide*, 30 December 1993, 24.

34. *Gleaner, Farmer's Weekly*, 15 October 1955, 8; Murray and Lewin, *Jamaican Chef*, 27; McLean, *Jamaican Cooking*, 73; "Characteristic Traits" 3 (July 1797): 107.

35. Jenkins, *Bananas*, 118–20; *Gleaner*, 6 January 1912, 18; 21 August 1914, 10.

36. *Gleaner*, 23 June 1938, 4; 29 November 1940, 6; 3 December 1941, 6; 17 December 1941, 6; 30 November 1940, 12; 6 December 1940, 10; *Gleaner, Supermarket Supplement*, 10 February 1994, 20.

37. Edwards, *History*, 2: 512–15; Dulcie Powell, *The Voyage of the Plant Nursery, H.M.S.* Providence, *1791–1793* (Kingston: Institute of Jamaica, 1973), 8–9; Brathwaite, *Development of Creole Society*, 86; Richard B. Sheridan, "The Crisis of Slave Subsistence in the British West Indies during and after the American Revolution", *William and Mary Quarterly* 33 (1976): 625; Richard B. Sheridan, "Captain Bligh, the Breadfruit, and the Botanic Gardens of Jamaica", *Journal of Caribbean History* 23 (1989): 29–30.

38. Richard Drayton, *Nature's Government: Science, Imperial Britain, and the "Improvement" of the World* (New Haven, CT: Yale University Press, 2000); Sheridan, "Captain Bligh", 33–34.

39. Royes and Baccus, *Jamaica Farmer's Guide*, 186; Lunan, *Hortus Jamaicensis*, 1: 114; Nyree J.C. Zerega, "The Breadfruit Trail", *Natural History* 112, no. 10 (2003): 46–50; Nyree J.C. Zerega, Diane Ragone and Timothy J. Motley, "Complex Origins of Breadfruit (*Artocarpus altilis*, Moraceae): Implications for Human Migrations in Oceania", *American Journal of Botany* 91 (2004): 760–66.

40. J.C. Beaglehole, ed., *The* Endeavour *Journal of Joseph Banks 1768-1771* (Sydney, Australia: Angus and Robertson, 1962), 1: 341; J.C. Beaglehole, *The Life of Captain James Cook* (Stanford, CA: Stanford University Press, 1974), 179; David Mackay, "Banks, Bligh and Breadfruit", *New Zealand Journal of History* 8 (1974): 63; Edward Duyker, *Nature's Argonaut: David Solander, 1733–1782, Naturalist and Voyager with Cook and Banks* (Melbourne, Australia: Melbourne University Press, 1998), 153; Timothy Fulford, "The Taste of Paradise: The Fruits of Romanticism in the Empire", in *Cultures of Taste/Theories of Appetite: Eating Romanticism*, ed. Timothy Morton (New York: Palgrave Macmillan, 2004), 41–57; Tim Fulford, Debbie Lee, and Peter J. Kitson, *Literature, Science and Exploration in the Romantic Era: Bodies of Knowledge* (Cambridge, UK: Cambridge University Press, 2004), 108–26; Emma Spary and Paul White, "Food of Paradise: Tahitian Breadfruit and the Autocritique of European Consumption", *Endeavour* 28 (2004): 75–80.

41. Powell, *Voyage of the Plant Nursery*, 10; Mackay, "Banks, Bligh and Breadfruit", 71–72; Sheridan, "Captain Bligh", 39; Banks MSS, Add. 33, 978, ff. 217–21, Banks Correspondence, Vol. 2 (British Library, London).

42. William Bligh, *The Log of H.M.S.* Providence *1791–1793* (Guildford, UK: Genesis Publications, 1976), 18 July 1792, 3 March 1793; Powell, *Voyage of the Plant Nursery*, 15–31; Mackay, "Banks, Bligh and Breadfruit", 74–77; Madge Darby, "Bligh's Disciple: Matthew Flinders's Journals of HMS *Providence* (1791–3)", *Mariner's Mirror* 86 (2000): 401–11; Douglas Oliver, *Return to Tahiti: Bligh's Second Breadfruit Voyage* (Melbourne, Australia: Melbourne University Press, 1988); Drayton, *Nature's Government*, 79–81, 113–14; Alan Frost, *The Global Reach of Empire: Britain's Maritime Expansion in the Indian and Pacific Oceans 1764–1815* (Melbourne, Australia: Miegunyah Press, 2003), 203–4.

43. *Royal Gazette*, quoted in Powell, *Voyage of the Plant Nursery*, 26–27, 40–41.

44. Bligh, *Log*, 24.

45. Parry, "Plantation and Provision Ground", 19; Parry, "Salt Fish and Ackee", 34; J.H. Parry and P.M. Sherlock, *A Short History of the West Indies* (London: Macmillan, 1956), 149; Watts, *West Indies*, 505; Sheridan, "Captain Bligh", 45.

46. John Williamson, *Medical and Miscellaneous Observations, Relative to the West India Islands* (Edinburgh, 1817), 1: 173; Stewart, *Account of Jamaica*, 99–100; Robert Charles Dallas, *The History of the Maroons from Their Origin to the Establishment of Their Chief Tribe at Sierra Leone* (London: Longman, 1803), 2: 353–54; Sheridan, "Captain Bligh", 45–46.

47. Lunan, *Hortus Jamaicensis*, 1: 113; Nugent, *Lady Nugent's Journal*, 28, 67, 94–95; Titford, *Sketches*, xiii; Sheridan, "Captain Bligh", 99–100.

48. *Jamaica Magazine* (1812): 373–74.

49. Titford, *Sketches*, xiii; Lunan, *Hortus Jamaicensis*, 1: 113; Stewart, *View*, 62; Gosse, *Naturalist's Sojourn*, 258.

50. Beaglehole, *The* Endeavour *Journal of Joseph Banks*, 1: 344.

51. Powell, *Voyage of the Plant Nursery*, 36; Sturge and Harvey, *West Indies in 1837*, 179; Beaglehole, *The* Endeavour *Journal of Joseph Banks*, 1: 344; John H. Parry, "The Indies Richly Planted", *Terrae Incognitae* 1 (1969): 21; Paul Alan Cox, "Two Samoan Technologies for Breadfruit and Banana Preservation", *Economic Botany* 34 (1980): 181–85; Nancy J. Pollock, *These Roots Remain: Food Habits in Islands of the Central and Eastern Pacific since Western Contact* (Honolulu: Institute for Polynesian Studies, 1992), 93–98.

52. *Gleaner*, 2 May 1917, 8; 25 October 1945, 7; 8 June 1985, 1; Powell, *Voyage of the Plant Nursery*, 7; *Jamaican Herald*, 20 February 1994.

53. *Gleaner*, 24 December 1866, 2; 7 January 1918, 6; Sullivan, *Jamaica Cookery Book*, 75–76; Spence, *Jamaican Cookery*, 41.

54. Lunan, *Hortus Jamaicensis*, 1: 113; Clark, *West Indian Cookery*, 117, 139, 188; Sullivan, *Jamaica Cookery Book*, 57.

55. Brandon, *Merry-Go-round*, 47–49; Judy Cuninghame, *Some Fruits and Recipes of Jamaica* (Virgin Islands: Caribbean Natural Colour, 1971), 4; Benghiat, *Traditional Jamaican Cookery*, 37, 65–66, 205–6; *Gleaner, Food Supplement*, 6 August 1987, 31; Sandra Barnes, *The Breadfruit in the Caribbean, 1793–1993: Recipes from Caribbean Cookbooks* (St Augustine, Trinidad: Agriculture and Life Sciences Division, Main Library, University of the West Indies, 1993).

56. Jamaica Agricultural Society, *Farmer's Food Manual*, 251; Jamaica Information Service, *Jamaican Cuisine* (Kingston: Jamaica Information Service, 1964); *Gleaner, Home, Living and Food Guide*, 9 July 1992, 28.

57. Felipe Fernández-Armesto, *Food: A History* (London: Pan Books, 2002), 185–88; Jamaica Tourist Office website, 9 July 2004.

58. Edwards, *History* 3: 378–80, 401.

59. *Gleaner*, 4 August 1915, 10; 26 July 1915, 4; 27 August 1915, 11; Marjorie Davidson, "Ackees and Avocadoes", *Jamaica Journal* 5, no. 4 (1971): 28; *Gleaner, Sunday Magazine*, 29 July 1976, 8.

60. Powell, *Voyage of the Plant Nursery*, 31–35, 48, 67; C. Dennis Adams, *The Blue Mahoe and Other Bush* (Kingston: Sangster's Bookstores, 1971), 32.

61. C.D. Adams, *Flowering Plants of Jamaica* (Mona, Jamaica: University of the West Indies, 1972), 441; Rashford, "Those That Do Not Smile", 190–91; Royes and Baccus, *Jamaica Farmer's Guide*, 180–82.

62. Lady Brassey, *In the Trades, the Tropics, and the Roaring Forties* (London: Longmans, Green, 1885), 249; *Gleaner*, 26 December 1877, 2; 17 May 1917, 11; 19 February 1918, 13; 30 March

1940, 17; Kenneth R. Hill, "The Vomiting Sickness of Jamaica", *West Indian Medical Journal* 1 (1951–52): 243–44.

63. P.C. Feng, "Hypoglycin – from Ackee: A Review", *West Indian Medical Journal* 18 (1969): 238–43; J.I. Addae and G.N. Melville, "A Re-examination of the Mechanism of Ackee-Induced Vomiting Sickness", *West Indian Medical Journal* 37 (1988): 6–8; E.A. Kean, "Commentary on a Review on the Mechanism of Ackee-Induced Vomiting Sickness", *West Indian Medical Journal* 37 (1988): 139–42; Lowe et al., *Poisonous Plants*, 32–33; Orane A. Blake, José C. Jackson, Maria A. Jackson, and C.L. André Gordon, "Assessment of Dietary Exposure to the Natural Toxin Hypoglycin in Ackee (*Blighia sapida*) by Jamaican Consumers", *Food Research International* 37 (2004): 833–38.

64. Tadeusz Lewicki, *West African Food in the Middle Ages* (Cambridge, UK: Cambridge University Press, 1974), 67.

65. *Gleaner*, 16 September 1993, 24; 6 February 1960, 9; *Gleaner, Food Supplement*, 4 April 1968, 16.

66. Sullivan, *Jamaica Cookery Book*, 37 (italics in original); Adams, *Blue Mahoe*, 30–32; Rosemary Parkinson, *Culinaria, The Caribbean: A Culinary Discovery* (Cologne: Könemann, 1999), 78.

67. Ibid., 78; Hamilton, *Little Jamaican Cookbook*, 29; Lewicki, *West African Food*, 67; Titford, *Sketches*, xiv, 59; *Gleaner*, 6 June 1970, 9; Jill Roberts, *A Hamper of Recipes from Jamaica* (Kingston: Heinemann Educational (Caribbean), 1987), 95; *Jamaica, Finest Taste*, 2; Burke, *Eat Caribbean*, 88.

68. *Gleaner, Business and Industry Supplement*, 28 April 1992; Rashford, "Those That Do Not Smile", 193–97.

69. Lunan, *Hortus Jamaicensis*, 1: 9; Lewis, *Journal*, 152; Marianne North, *Recollections of a Happy Life: Being the Autobiography of Marianne North*, ed. Mrs John Addington Symonds (London: Macmillan, 1893), 99; Sullivan, *Jamaica Cookery Book*, 4–5, 37, 49, 96–97.

70. *Gleaner*, 5 April 1940, 10; Chapman, *Pleasure Island*, 275; *Gleaner, Food Supplement*, 1 October 1987, 24; *Gleaner, Home, Living and Food Guide*, 4 March 1993, 14; *Gleaner, Supermarket Supplement*, 24 June 1993, 11; *Gleaner*, 15 August 1999, 9C; [Ray Chen], *Cooking with Lasco: A Great Collection of Delicious, Nutritious and Affordable Recipes using Lasco Products* (Kingston: Periwinkle, 2003), 23.

71. *Gleaner*, 3 July 1893, 7; Sullivan, *Jamaica Cookery Book*, 17, 37.

72. Wyllarde, *Mafoota*, 175; *Gleaner*, 14 January 1905, 10.

73. *Gleaner*, 21 July 1915, 6; 27 August 1915, 11; 4 September 1918, 10, 14; 6 September 1918, 9.

74. H.G. De Lisser, "Christina's Dream", *Planters' Punch* 1, no. 1 (1920): 18; De Lisser, "Behind the Scenes at the J.P.S.", 37; Chapman, *Pleasure Island*, 279; Jamaica Agricultural Society, *Farmer's Food Manual*, 157.

75. *Gleaner*, 10 May 1930, 9; 5 January 1938, 5; Carley, *Jamaica*, 114; Jamaica Society for the Blind, *Recipe Round-up: A Book of Favourite Recipes* (1956; Mandeville, Jamaica: Jamaica Society for the Blind, 1968), 18; Cleary, *Jamaica Run-dung*, 27; Benghiat, *Traditional Jamaican Cookery*, 77; Donaldson, *Real Taste*, 66; *Jamaica, Finest Taste*, 82.

76. *Gleaner, Food Supplement*, 15 May 1986, 26; *Gleaner*, 31 July 1988, 9A; 6 June 1991, 3; Sobers, *Delicious Jamaica!*, 35.

77. Parry, "Salt Fish and Ackee", 33; Rashford, "Those That Do Not Smile", 194–96; McWilliams, *Revolution in Eating*, 48.

78. Nugent, *Lady Nugent's Journal*, 26; Rashford, "Those That Do Not Smile", 195.

79. Leslie, *New and Exact*, 54; Long, *History*, 3: 809; Sauer, *Historical Geography*, 94–95; Whitmore and Turner, *Cultivated Landscapes*, 102–4.

80. Louis O. Williams, "The Avocados, a Synopsis of the Genus *Persea*, subg. *Persea*", *Economic Botany* 31 (1977): 315–20; Robert W. Hodgson, "The Avocado: A Gift from the Middle Americas", *Economic Botany* 4 (1950): 253; Sauer, *Historical Geography*, 95–97.

81. Samson, *Tropical Fruits*, 201; Royes and Baccus, *Jamaica Farmer's Guide*, 184–86.

82. Hughes, *American Physitian*, 41–42; Barham, *Hortus Americanus*, 10; Long, *History*, 3: 808; Lunan, *Hortus Jamaicensis*, 1: 37; Nugent, *Lady Nugent's Journal*, 26; Stewart, *View*, 63. See also Titford, *Sketches*, xiv; Lewis, *Journal*, 241–42.

83. Long, *History*, 3: 809; Lunan, *Hortus Jamaicensis*, 1: 37; Dovaston, "Agricultura Americana", 2: 294.

84. Nugent, *Lady Nugent's Journal*, 26, 26n1; Cassidy, *Jamaica Talk*, 355; Sullivan, *Jamaica Cookery Book*, 75.

85. Royes and Baccus, *Jamaica Farmer's Guide*, 184; Clark, *West Indian Cookery*, 103, 139, 199; McLean, *Jamaican Cooking*, 18; Facey, *Busha Browne*, 12, 32; Donaldson, *Real Taste*, 38, 96.

86. Lal Behari Singh, *The Mango* (London: Leonard Hill, 1960), 79; S.K. Mukherjee, "Origin of Mango (*Mangifera indica*)", *Economic Botany* 26 (1972): 260–64; K.T. Achaya, *A Historical Dictionary of Indian Food* (New Delhi: Oxford University Press, 1998), 139; Samson, *Tropical Fruits*, 185–95; Sauer, *Historical Geography*, 17.

87. Singh, *Mango*, 1; Titford, *Sketches*, xiv; Whitbourne, "Ordinary Diet in Jamaica", 70; *Gleaner*, 6 June 1992, 3; Bacon and Aaron, *New Jamaica*, 116.

88. Hall, *In Miserable Slavery*, 232, 238, 245–46, 262. Cf. Burnard, *Mastery, Tyranny, and Desire*, 119; Bligh, *Log*, 18 February 1793; Singh, *Mango*, 8–9; Edwards, *History*, 3: 373; Drayton, *Nature's Government*, 80; Sauer, *Historical Geography*, 19.

89. Lunan, *Hortus Jamaicensis*, 1: 486; Stewart, *View*, 62; Sturge and Harvey, *West Indies in 1837*, 179; James Macfadyen, *The Flora of Jamaica: A Description of the Plants of that Island, Arranged According to the Natural Orders* (London: Longman, Orme, Brown, Green and Longmans, 1837), 222; Gosse, *Naturalist's Sojourn*, 258; Scott, *To Jamaica and Back*, 257; Singh, *Mango*, 9.

90. Macfadyen, *Flora*, 221; North, *Recollections of a Happy Life*, 81; *Gleaner*, 20 November 1926, 19; Brassey, *In the Trades*, 222.

91. Singh, *Mango*, 9; *Gleaner*, 9 August 1880, 2; *Colonial Standard and Jamaica Despatch*, 10 August 1880.

92. Sullivan, *Jamaica Cookery Book*, 80; *Gleaner*, 25 August 1938, 13; Cassidy, *Jamaica Talk*, 353; Royes and Baccus, *Jamaica Farmer's Guide*, 199; Verrill, *Jamaica of Today*, 111; *Gleaner*, 13 November 1985, 21; 6 June 1992, 3.

93. Long, *History*, 3: 810–11; Barham, *Hortus Americanus*, 3.

94. Sullivan, *Jamaica Cookery Book*, 62–64, 91–92, 102–3; Lunan, *Hortus Jamaicensis*, 1: 486; Macfadyen, *Flora*, 222; Achaya, *Historical Dictionary*, 141; *Gleaner*, 14 July 1938, 7.

95. Clark, *West Indian Cookery*, 184; Jones, *Cook Up Jamaican Style* (1981), 32, 40; Burke, *Walk-erswood*, 73.

96. Benghiat, *Traditional Jamaican Cookery*, 193, 203–4; Donaldson, *Real Taste*, 97; Achaya, *Historical Dictionary*, 141–42; Santha Rama Rau, *The Cooking of India* (Amsterdam: Time-Life International, 1972), 72, 94.

97. Edwards, *History*, 3: 401; Nugent, *Lady Nugent's Journal*, 28; Titford, *Sketches*, xiii; Lunan, *Hortus Jamaicensis*, 1: 388.

98. Homiak, "Dub History", 148; Jones, *Cook Up Jamaican Style* (1981), 40; *Jamaica Observer*, 10 September 1993, 36; Ayre, *Bush Doctor*, 82; C.A. Thomas, "Jackfruit, *Artocarpus heterophyllus* (Moraceae), as Source of Food and Income", *Economic Botany* 34 (1980): 155.

99. Sauer, *Historical Geography*, 188; Reginald Child, *Coconuts* (London: Longmans, 1964), 4–11; Harlan, *Crops and Man*, 241–43; Whitmore and Turner, *Cultivated Landscapes*, 82; Watts, *West Indies*, 76.

100. Hughes, *American Physitian*, 62; Browne, *Civil and Natural History*, 308; Long, *History*, 3: 738; Stewart, *View*, 60.

101. J.R.R. Suah, "The Elusive Lethal Yellowing Disease of Coconuts", *Jamaica Journal* 6, no. 4 (December 1972): 15–17; Rickards, *West Indies and Caribbean Year Book 1975*, 253; H.H. Harries, "The Natural History of the Coconut", *Jamaica Journal* 44 (1980): 61–65; *Jamaican Herald*, 12 February 2006, 9A.

102. Long, *History*, 3: 740. See also Hughes, *American Physitian*, 64; Barham, *Hortus Americanus*, 133; Child, *Coconuts*, 37–38.

103. Hickeringill, *Jamaica Viewed*, 18–19, 23; Hughes, *American Physitian*, 64; Long, *History*, 3: 739.

104. Sullivan, *Jamaica Cookery Book*, 73, 95; Child, *Coconuts*, 199.

105. Sullivan, *Jamaica Cookery Book*, 52; Brandon, *Merry-Go-Round*, 60; Donaldson, *Real Taste*, 124; *Gleaner*, 15 March 1932, 12; 26 August 1995, 10A.

106. Browne, *Civil and Natural History*, 308; Sullivan, *Jamaica Cookery Book*, 88–89; *Gleaner*, 15 March 1932, 12; *Gleaner, Food Supplement*, 28 March 1985, 27; Donaldson, *Real Taste*, 111.

107. Sullivan, *Jamaica Cookery Book*, 5, 65–67, 72.

108. *Gleaner*, 17 May 1963, 7; 27 October 1963, 27; 8 January 1964, 16; 4 February 1979, 30; *Gleaner, Food Supplement*, 14 April 1965, iv; Benghiat, *Traditional Jamaican Cookery*, 80; Brandon, *Merry-Go-Round*, 36; Cleary, *Jamaica Run-dung*, 29; *Peas Please!* (Kingston: Scientific Research Council, 1972), 15; Burke, *Walkerswood*, 31.

109. Ibid., 35; Jamaica Agricultural Society, *Farmer's Food Manual*, 145; recipe supplied by Carollin Carol, 25 September 1989.

110. *Gleaner*, 10 December 1880, 2; Child, *Coconuts*, 175.

111. Rickards, *West Indies and Caribbean Year Book 1975*, 253; *Gleaner*, 20 May 1985; 10 June 1992, 14; 19 December 1994, 2A; 26 August 1995, 10A.

112. C.W.S. Hartley, *The Oil Palm* (London: Longman, 1977), 1, 39–40; Long, *History*, 3: 740; Titford, *Sketches*, xvi.

113. Hartley, *Oil Palm*, 32.

114.   Browne, *Civil and Natural History*, 343; *Gleaner*, 15 March 1932, 12.

115.   Long, *History*, 3: 742; Lewicki, *West African Food*, 73–75.

116.   Long, *History*, 3: 800;. See also Daniel Zohary and Maria Hopf, *Domestication of Plants in the Old World: The Origin and Spread of Cultivated Plants in West Asia, Europe and the Nile Valley* (Oxford: Clarendon, 1988), 167–68; Thomas W. Whitaker and Glen N. Davis, *Cucurbits: Botany, Cultivation, and Utilization* (London: Leonard Hill, 1962), 2, 17; Long, *History*, 3: 801; Hughes, *American Physitian*, 22–23.

117.   Lewis, *Journal*, 50.

118.   Sullivan, *Jamaica Cookery Book*, 56–57.

119.   Whitaker and Davis, *Cucurbits*, 4; Long, *History*, 3: 800.

120.   Whitaker and Davis, *Cucurbits*, 2-3; Browne, *Civil and Natural History*, 353–55; Lunan, *Hortus Jamaicensis*, 1: 254.

121.   Titford, *Sketches*, xvi; Whitaker and Davis, *Cucurbits*, 3–4.

122.   Lunan, *Hortus Jamaicensis*, 1: 254; Long, *History*, 3: 801; *Gleaner*, 1 October 1880; Sullivan, *Jamaica Cookery Book*, 34, 96.

123.   Long, *History*, 3: 801.

124.   Ibid., 3: 772; Lindsay, "Elegancies of Jamaica", 136; Lewicki, *West African Food*, 61–62.

125.   Titford, *Sketches*, xiii, 53; Lunan, *Hortus Jamaicensis*, 1: 280; Sullivan, *Jamaica Cookery Book*, 37–38.

126.   Lindsay, "Elegancies of Jamaica", 60.

127.   *Importance of Jamaica*, 35; Barham, *Hortus Americanus*, 123; Long, *History*, 3: 775.

128.   Marsden, *Account*, 24–25; "Characteristic Traits" 3 (June 1797): 8; Lunan, *Hortus Jamaicensis*, 2: 12.

129.   *Marly, or the Life of a Planter in Jamaica* (Glasgow: R. Griffin, 1828), 211–12; Sullivan, *Jamaica Cookery Book*, 2, 38, 95; Franklin W. Martin, "Okra, Potential Multiple-Purpose Crop for the Temperate Zones and Tropics", *Economic Botany* 36 (1982): 341.

130.   James Saunt, *Citrus Varieties of the World* (Norwich, UK: Sinclair International, 2000), 109, 123–25, 131–32.

131.   J. Kumamoto, R.W. Scora, H.W. Lawton, and W.A. Clerx, "Mystery of the Forbidden Fruit: Historical Epilogue on the Origin of the Grapefruit, *Citrus paradisi* (Rutaceae)", *Economic Botany* 41 (1987): 98; T. Ralph Robinson, "Grapefruit and Pummelo", *Economic Botany* 6 (1952): 228; Lewis, *Journal*, 152.

132.   *Gleaner*, 11 March 1946, 8; Saunt, *Citrus Varieties*, 82–83; W.W. Guo, D. Prasad, P. Serrano, F.G. Gmitter, Jr, and J.W. Grosser, "Citrus Somatic Hybridization with Potential for Direct Tetraploid Scion Cultivar Development", *Journal of Horticultural Science and Biotechnology* 79 (2004): 401; Donaldson, *Real Taste*, 10. Sauer claims the ortanique is "evidently a hybrid . . . that originated in antiquity in Southeast Asia or southern China" (*Historical Geography*, 144).

133.   *Gleaner*, 22 March 1941, 21; 2 March 1943, 8; 4 September 1946, 17; Saunt, *Citrus Varieties*, 85.

134.   Ibid., 107; Sauer, *Historical Geography*, 138–44; Samson, *Tropical Fruits*, 64–66; *Gleaner*, 29 January 1938, 12; 4 May 1938, 11; 11 May 1938, 9; *West India Committee Circular* 53 (21 April 1938): 141.

135. Guo et al., "Citrus Somatic Hybridization", 400; Saunt, *Citrus Varieties*, 11–12.

136. Hickeringill, *Jamaica Viewed*, 10; Hughes, *American Physitian*, 48–49; *Present State of Jamaica*, 20; Leslie, *New and Exact*, 21, 32; An English Merchant, *Some Modern Observations upon Jamaica: As to Its Natural History, Improvement in Trade, Manner of Living, &c.* (London, 1727), 15; *Importance of Jamaica*, 33; Browne, *Civil and Natural History*, 308; Long, *History*, 3: 795; Macfadyen, *Flora of Jamaica*, 127.

137. Ibid., 129–30; *Importance of Jamaica*, 33; Long, *History*, 3: 797; James Anthony Froude, *The English in the West Indies or the Bow of Ulysses* (London: Longmans, Green, 1888), 211, 218; *Gleaner*, 26 March 1879, 2.

138. *Importance of Jamaica*, 33; Long, *History*, 3: 797; Titford, *Sketches*, xiii; Lunan, *Hortus Jamaicensis*, 2: 173; Saunt, *Citrus Varieties*, 99–100.

139. Hughes, *American Physitian*, 49–50; Long, *History*, 3: 795–99; *Jamaica Post*, 17 January 1890; Sullivan, *Jamaica Cookery Book*, 73.

140. Robert T. Hill, *Cuba and Porto Rico with the Other Islands of the West Indies* (London: T. Fisher Unwin, 1898), 210; *West Indies and Caribbean Year Book 1975*, 252.

141. *Gleaner, Home, Food and Living Guide*, 31 January 1991, 21; *Gleaner, Food Supplement*, 30 January 1986, 26; *Gleaner*, 1 July 1940, 15; Nugent, *Lady Nugent's Journal*, 63; Titford, *Sketches*, xv; Lewis, *Journal*, 79; John Hearne, *Stranger at the Gate* (London: Faber and Faber, 1956), 9

142. Sullivan, *Jamaica Cookery Book*, 44, 46–47, 74, 84–85, 90; Kim D. Bowman and Frederick G. Gmitter, Jr, "Forbidden Fruit (*Citrus* sp., Rutaceae) Rediscovered in St. Lucia", *Economic Botany* 44 (1990): 165–73; Titford, *Sketches*, xv; Kumamoto et al., "Mystery of the Forbidden Fruit", 97–107.

143. Donaldson, *Real Taste*, 131; *Gleaner, Food Supplement*, 20 February 1986, 22.

144. Long, *History*, 3: 729–30; Macfadyen, *Flora of Jamaica*, 335; Nugent, *Lady Nugent's Journal*, 27; Sullivan, *Jamaica Cookery Book*, 64–67.

145. Long, *History*, 3: 805. See also An English Merchant, *Some Modern Observations*, 19; *Importance of Jamaica*, 34; Browne, *Civil and Natural History*, 285.

146. Clark, *West Indian Cookery*, 211; *Gleaner, Food Supplement*, 8 January 1987, 24; Brandon, *Merry-Go-Round*, 42; Myrtle Marcelle, "Sorrel: A Truly Jamaican Tradition", *Jamaica Journal* 11, nos 3 and 4 (1978): 60–61; Benghiat, *Traditional Jamaican Cookery*, 180, 194, 196; Facey, *Busha Browne*, 100; *Gleaner*, 31 May 1998, 8E.

147. Gosse, *Naturalist's Sojourn*, 158; Sullivan, *Jamaica Cookery Book*, 70; Benghiat, *Traditional Jamaican Cookery*, 137, 142, 179.

148. Titford, *Sketches*, xiv; Sullivan, *Jamaica Cookery Book*, 68, 77; Samson, *Tropical Fruits*, 228; Benghiat, *Traditional Jamaican Cookery*, 38.

149. Sullivan, *Jamaica Cookery Book*, 81; Samson, *Tropical Fruits*, 228.

150. Sullivan, *Jamaica Cookery Book*, 82; Lunan, *Hortus Jamaicensis*, 1: 88.

151. Cleary, *Jamaica Run-dung*, 39; Benghiat, *Traditional Jamaican Cookery*, 138; Donaldson, *Real Taste*, 9; *Jamaica, Finest Taste*, 7.

152. Lewicki, *West African Food*, 69–70.

153. Hickeringill, *Jamaica Viewed*, 10; Lindsay, "Elegancies of Jamaica", 123; Titford, *Sketches*, xiv.

154. Long, *History*, 3: 852–56; Stewart, *View*, 65; Phillippo, *Jamaica*, 48.

155. Leslie, *New and Exact*, 32; Long, *History*, 3: 852; Stewart, *View*, 65.

156. Sullivan, *Jamaica Cookery Book*, 80; Leader, *Through Jamaica with a Kodak*, 150; Rampini, *Letters from Jamaica*, 25; *Gleaner*, 22 August 1991, 21.

157. *Gleaner*, 19 September 1873, 2; 3 January 1900, 1; 20 March 1900, 3; 17 August 1918, 7; Titford, *Sketches*, xv; Long, *History*, 3: 853; Stewart, *View*, 65.

158. Long, *History*, 3: 853–54; North, *Recollections of a Happy Life*, 89; Rampini, *Letters from Jamaica*, 25; *Gleaner*, 10 April 1890, 2; 10 and 17 May 1890, 2; Sullivan, *Jamaica Cookery Book*, 80.

159. Leader, *Through Jamaica with a Kodak*, 150; *Gleaner*, 22 June 1938, 16.

160. North, *Recollections of a Happy Life*, 89; Sullivan, *Jamaica Cookery Book*, 75; Lunan, *Hortus Jamaicensis*, 1: 98; Titford, *Sketches*, xv.

161. Powers of Attorney, Liber 96, f. 175; *Gleaner*, 2 February 1900, 2.

162. *Present State of Jamaica*, 20–21; Leader, *Through Jamaica with a Kodak*, 150; *Gleaner*, 17 August 1938, 5; Royes and Baccus, *Jamaica Farmer's Guide*, 189–97; Lewicki, *West African Food*, 75–76.

163. *Importance of Jamaica*, 32; Long, *History*, 3: 790–92; Lunan, *Hortus Jamaicensis*, 1: 335; *Gleaner*, 26 September 1985, 8.

164. Sloane, *Voyage*, 1: xxviii; *Royal Gazette* (Spanish Town), 29 January 1820, 6 May 1820, 20 May 1820, 14 October 1820; David Hancock, "Commerce and Conversation in the Eighteenth-Century Atlantic: The Invention of Madeira Wine", *Journal of Interdisciplinary History* 29 (1998): 197, 207.

165. J.L. Collins, *The Pineapple: Botany, Cultivation and Utilization* (London: Leonard Hill, 1960), 184; Sauer, *Historical Geography*, 196; Whitmore and Turner, *Cultivated Landscapes*, 87.

166. Collins, *The Pineapple*, 184.

167. Samson, *Tropical Fruits*, 163; Collins, *The Pineapple*, 71; Marsden, *Account*, 86; Higman, *Jamaica Surveyed*, 121–22.

168. *Importance of Jamaica*, 30; Long, *History*, 3: 792; Benghiat, *Traditional Jamaican Cookery*, 138; Scott, *To Jamaica and Back*, 264; Bacon and Aaron, *New Jamaica*, 116; Collins, *The Pineapple*, 73.

169. *A Book of the Continuation of Forreign Passages* (London: Thomas Jenner, 1657), 46; Sloane, *Voyage*, 1: 191; *Importance of Jamaica*, 30; *A Treatise on the Ananas or Pine-apple, Containing Plain and Easy Directions for Raising this Most Excellent Fruit Without Fire, and in Much Higher Perfection than from the Stove* (Devizes, UK, 1759), i.

170. Benghiat, *Traditional Jamaican Cookery*, 138.

171. Lieut.-Col. [Nathaniel] Newnham-Davis, *Dinners and Diners: Where and How to Dine in London*, rev. ed. (London: Grant Richards, 1901), 184; Sullivan, *Jamaica Cookery Book*, 47–48, 72; Beeton, *Mrs Beeton's*, 804.

172. Long, *History*, 3: 793; Scott, *To Jamaica and Back*, 77; Sullivan, *Jamaica Cookery Book*, 107.

173. Hall, *In Miserable Slavery*, 88; Lewis, *Journal*, 104–5; Sullivan, *Jamaica Cookery Book*, 42, 72; Clark, *West Indian Cookery*, 110, 197, 201, 208.

174. Browne, *Civil and Natural History*, 360; *Gleaner*, 15 February 1938, 15; Jorge A. Pino, Karina Almora and Rolando Marbot, "Volatile Components of Papaya (*Carica papaya* L., Maradol Variety) Fruit", *Flavour and Fragrance Journal* 18 (2003): 496.

175. Lindsay, "Elegancies of Jamaica", 48–49, 56–57.

176. *Importance of Jamaica*, 31; Hall, *In Miserable Slavery*, 170, 223; Browne, *Civil and Natural History*, 360; *Best of Creative Cooking*, 12.

177. Browne, *Civil and Natural History*, 360; Long, *History*, 3: 802–3; Dovaston, "Agricultura Americana", 2: 289.

178. Lunan, *Hortus Jamaicensis*, 2: 37; Sullivan, *Jamaica Cookery Book*, 78–79; Verrill, *Jamaica of Today*, 115.

179. *Gleaner*, 15 February 1938, 15; Gaunt, *Reflection*, 55; Jones, *Cook Up Jamaican Style* (1981), 23, 40; Donaldson, *Real Taste*, 130; *Jamaica, Finest Taste*, 135; Cleary, *Jamaica Run-dung*, 29–30; Facey, *Busha Browne*, 39; Burke, *Walkerswood*, 59.

180. Omer S. Lloyd Thomas, "The Current Status of Papaya Production in Jamaica", in *Proceedings of the Papaya and Mango Seminar* (Kingston: Inter-American Institute for Cooperation on Agriculture, 1993), 1–18; *Gleaner, Home, Living and Food Guide*, 10 February 1994, 20.

181. Lunan, *Hortus Jamaicensis*, 2: 245; *Jamaica Observer*, 5 November 1993, 36.

182. Sullivan, *Jamaica Cookery Book*, 20; Beckwith, *Black Roadways*, 14; Whitbourne, "Ordinary Diet in Jamaica", 70; *Gleaner, Food Supplement*, 12 June 1986, 18.

183. Benghiat, *Traditional Jamaican Cookery*, 62; Cleary, *Jamaica Run-dung*, 23, 43; *Gleaner, Food Supplement*, 12 June 1986, 18; *Gleaner*, 12 August 1995, 7B; 8 May 1997, A15.

184. Verrill, *Jamaica of Today*, 114; Samson, *Tropical Fruits*, 217; Prasad, *Edible Fruits*, 5; M.R.B. Franco and N.S. Janzantti, "Aroma of Minor Tropical Fruits", *Flavour and Fragrance Journal* 20 (2005): 362.

185. Dovaston, "Agricultura Americana", 2: 290; Titford, *Sketches*, xiii, xvi; Lunan, *Hortus Jamaicensis*, 1: 178, 256; Macfadyen, *Flora of Jamaica*, 10–11; Gosse, *Naturalist's Sojourn*, 62.

186. Sullivan, *Jamaica Cookery Book*, 72–73, 79, 107–108; Scott, *To Jamaica and Back*, 97; Gaunt, *Reflection*, 6.

187. Long, *History*, 3: 836; Dovaston, "Agricultura Americana", 2: 288; Titford, *Sketches*, xiv.

188. Titford, *Sketches*, xv, 57; Lunan, *Hortus Jamaicensis*, 1: 480; Sullivan, *Jamaica Cookery Book*, 70; Barham, *Hortus Americanus*, 98.

189. *Book of the Continuation of Forreign Passages*, 46; Samson, *Tropical Fruits*, 235.

190. Sullivan, *Jamaica Cookery Book*, 78, 80; Lunan, *Hortus Jamaicensis*, 2: 2; *Importance of Jamaica*, 31; Stewart, *View*, 61; Titford, *Sketches*, xiv; Gosse, *Naturalist's Sojourn*, 268; Verrill, *Jamaica of Today*, 112–13.

191. Hughes, *American Physitian*, 46; *Importance of Jamaica*, 32; Long, *History*, 3: 803; Titford, *Sketches*, xiv; Lunan, *Hortus Jamaicensis*, 1: 350; Sullivan, *Jamaica Cookery Book*, 44–45, 51.

192. Leslie, *New and Exact*, 21; Samson, *Tropical Fruits*, 215–16.

193. Lunan, *Hortus Jamaicensis*, 1: 319; Sullivan, *Jamaica Cookery Book*, 79.

194. Carlos G. Moscoso, "West Indian Cherry: Richest Known Source of Vitamin C", *Economic Botany* 10 (1956): 280–94; Franco and Janzantti, "Aroma of Minor Tropical Fruits", 358–59;

Long, *History*, 3: 790; Lunan, *Hortus Jamaicensis*, 1: 49; Royes and Baccus, *Jamaica Farmer's Guide*, 188; Benghiat, *Traditional Jamaican Cookery*, 176, 194; Samson, *Tropical Fruits*, 226.

195. Long, *History*, 3: 826–27; Lunan, *Hortus Jamaicensis*, 1: 259.

196. Chris S. Duvall, "On the Origin of the Tree *Spondias mombin* in Africa", *Journal of Historical Geography* 32 (2006): 249–66; Titford, *Sketches*, xiv; Benghiat, *Traditional Jamaican Cookery*, 195.

197. *Importance of Jamaica*, 53; Browne, *Civil and Natural History*, 372; Long, *History*, 3: 769; Lunan, *Hortus Jamaicensis*, 1: 115; Stewart, *View*, 56.

198. Sullivan, *Jamaica Cookery Book*, 80–81; *Gleaner*, 13 June 1907, 9; 27 April 1926, 15.

199. Lunan, *Hortus Jamaicensis*, 1: 203–4.

200. Macfadyen, *Flora of Jamaica*, 220; Franco and Janzantti, "Aroma of Minor Tropical Fruits", 367.

201. *Importance of Jamaica*, 32–33; Long, *History*, 3: 726; Macfadyen, *Flora of Jamaica*, 220; Sullivan, *Jamaica Cookery Book*, 62; Benghiat, *Traditional Jamaican Cookery*, 141, 172, 207; Royes and Baccus, *Jamaica Farmer's Guide*, 187–88; Gaunt, *Reflection*, 6.

202. Samson, *Tropical Fruits*, 218; Titford, *Sketches*, xiv; Lunan, *Hortus Jamaicensis*, 1: 159; Long, *History*, 3: 726; Macfadyen, *Flora of Jamaica*, 220.

203. Sullivan, *Jamaica Cookery Book*, 81; Clark, *West Indian Cookery*, 213; Facey, *Busha Browne*, 39; *Gleaner, Food Supplement*, 27 July 1989, 34.

204. Cassidy, *Jamaica Talk*, 198; John Rashford, "The Star Apple: A Symbol of Meanness in Jamaica", *Jamaica Journal* 24, no. 1 (1991): 49–53; Samson, *Tropical Fruits*, 233; Gosse, *Naturalist's Sojourn*, 91; Beckwith, *Black Roadways*, 44; Jorge Pino, Rolando Marbot and Aristides Rosado, "Volatile Constituents of Star Apple (*Chrysophyllum cainito* L.) from Cuba", *Flavour and Fragrance Journal* 17 (2002): 401.

205. Benghiat, *Traditional Jamaican Cookery*, 139–40. Cf. Cleary, *Jamaica Run-dung*, 36; *Jamaica Observer, Sparkle*, 12 March 1995, 12; Jamaica Agricultural Society, *Farmer's Food Manual*, 145; *Gleaner*, 11 July 1961, 16; 5 April 1962, 3; Roberts, *Hamper of Recipes*, 40; Miller and Henry, *Creative Jamaican Cooking*, 77; *Gifts from a Jamaican Kitchen* (Kingston: LHM Publishing, 2002), 58; Donaldson, *Real Taste*, 132.

206. Sullivan, *Jamaica Cookery Book*, 78; Titford, *Sketches*, xiii. Cf. Barham, *Hortus Americanus*, 183; Long, *History*, 3: 855–56.

207. *Gleaner*, 6 October 1922, 5; 9 March 1927, 5; North, *Recollections of a Happy Life*, 1: 94, 103; R.W. Thompson, *Black Caribbean* (London: Macdonald, 1946), 266; *Gleaner, Home, Living and Food Guide*, 1 April 1993, 33.

208. Sullivan, *Jamaica Cookery Book*, 76–77.

209. Lindsay, "Elegancies of Jamaica", 187–88; Titford, *Sketches*, xv; Lunan, *Hortus Jamaicensis*, 1: 343.

210. Lewis, *Journal*, 104; North, *Recollections of a Happy Life*, 85–86; Scott, *To Jamaica and Back*, 97; Sullivan, *Jamaica Cookery Book*, 43; *Gleaner*, 4 November 1893, 3.

211. Barham, *Hortus Americanus*, 92; Long, *History*, 3: 773; Andrew F. Smith, *The Tomato in America: Early History, Culture, and Cookery* (Urbana: University of Illinois Press, 2001), 20.

212. Long, *History*, 3: 773; J.A. Jenkins, "The Origin of the Cultivated Tomato", *Economic Botany* 2 (1948): 391–92; Smith, *Tomato in America*, 26.

213. *Gleaner*, 20 March 1900, 3; 24 December 1931, 11; 11 April 1938, 13; 21 April 1938, 8.

214. *Gleaner*, 26 July 1998, 2A; *Gleaner, Home, Living and Food Guide*, 10 February 1994, 20; 5 January 1995, 23.

215. Long, *History*, 3: 773; Titford, *Sketches*, xiv; Sullivan, *Jamaica Cookery Book*, 64, 67–68, 93.

216. Andrew F. Smith, *Pure Ketchup: A History of America's National Condiment* (Washington, DC: Smithsonian Institution Press, 2001), 42–45, 138–39; Sullivan, *Jamaica Cookery Book*, 100–101.

217. Whitaker and Davis, *Cucurbits*, 12; Browne, *Civil and Natural History*, 355; William Beckford, *A Descriptive Account of Jamaica* (London: T. and J. Egerton, 1790), 2: 190; *Gleaner*, 2 October 1880, 2.

218. Whitaker and Davis, *Cucurbits*, 1, 17; Thomas W. Whitaker and Hugh C. Cutler, "Cucurbits and Cultures in the Americas", *Economic Botany* 19 (1965): 344.

219. Browne, *Civil and Natural History*, 355; Long, *History*, 3: 802; Lunan, *Hortus Jamaicensis*, 1: 183; Titford, *Sketches*, xiv.

220. Long, *History*, 3: 802; Lunan, *Hortus Jamaicensis*, 1: 183; Sullivan, *Jamaica Cookery Book*, 95.

221. *Gleaner*, 2 October 1880, 2; Sullivan, *Jamaica Cookery Book*, 40–41, 53–56 (italics in original).

222. *Gleaner, Food Supplement*, 28 November 1985, xii; 8 January 1987, 19; 4 June 1987, 30; Chen, *Cooking with Lasco*, 22.

223. "Cerasee", *Jamaica Journal* 20, no. 4 (1987/88): 70; Lindsay, "Elegancies of Jamaica", 204; Sullivan, *Jamaica Cookery Book*, 114; Benghiat, *Traditional Jamaican Cookery*, 228; *Gleaner*, 8 May 1997, A15.

224. Whitaker and Davis, *Cucurbits*, 8–12.

225. Long, *History*, 3: 802; Titford, *Sketches*, xvi; *Gleaner, Food Supplement*, 9 July 1987, 36; Donaldson-Mignotte, "How Jamaicans Like Their Food", B8; Sullivan, *Jamaican Cookery Book*, 6; *Gleaner, Home, Living and Food Guide*, 7 October 1993, 21.

226. Sullivan, *Jamaica Cookery Book*, 31–32, 49; *Gleaner, Food Supplement*, 9 July 1987, 36.

227. Long, *History*, 3: 802.

228. Browne, *Civil and Natural History*, 266; Long, *History*, 3: 752; Rashford, "Packy Tree", 4; Sullivan, *Jamaica Cookery Book*, 93–94. Cf. Barham, *Hortus Americanus*, 67–68.

229. D.W. Rodriquez, *Pimento: A Short Economic History*, Commodity Bulletin No. 3 (Kingston: Ministry of Agriculture and Fisheries, 1969), 2–4; Purseglove et al., *Spices*, 1: 286; Dalby, *Dangerous Tastes*, 150.

230. Rodriquez, *Pimento*, 1.

231. *Book of the Continuation of Forreign Passages*, 46; Blome, *Description of the Island*, 13; Blome, *Present State*, 15; Long, *History*, 3: 705; Cooper, *Complete Distiller*, 139–40; Stewart, *View*, 268.

232. Ministry of Agriculture (Export Division), *Jamaica Pimento "Allspice": Uses and Recipes* (Kingston: Jamaica Information Service, 1987).

233. Barham, *Hortus Americanus*, 4–5; *Importance of Jamaica*, 35; Long, *History*, 3: 714–15; Lunan, *Hortus Jamaicensis*, 1: 29; *Gleaner, Food Supplement*, 24 October 1985, 19.

234. Barbara Pickersgill, "The Domestication of Chili Peppers", in *The Domestication and Exploitation of Plants and Animals*, ed. Peter J. Ucko and G.W. Dimbleby (London: Duckworth, 1969), 444–45.

235. Blome, *Present State*, 15; Hughes, *American Physitian*, 50–54; Barham, *Hortus Americanus*, 30; Lindsay, "Elegancies of Jamaica", 124–31; Long, *History*, 3: 722; Titford, *Sketches*, 46–47; Lunan, *Hortus Jamaicensis*, 1: 356–57.

236. Lindsay, Elegancies of Jamaica, 124; Long, *History*, 3: 722; *Importance of Jamaica*, 34; Purseglove et al., *Spices*, 1: 331–32, 341, 361, 423.

237. Lindsay, "Elegancies of Jamaica", 124.

238. Ibid., 124, 131; Browne, *Civil and Natural History*, 176; Long, *History*, 3: 722–23; Donaldson, *Real Taste*, 11; Purseglove et al., *Spices*, 1: 338.

239. Ibid., 1: 339–40; Don McGlashan, *Growing Scotch Bonnet Pepper* (Capsicum chinense Jacq.) *in Jamaica* (Kingston: Ministry of Agriculture, 2002).

240. Lindsay, "Elegancies of Jamaica", 124, 131; Lunan, *Hortus Jamaicensis*, 1: 356.

241. Long, *History*, 3: 723; Sullivan, *Jamaica Cookery Book*, 91, 103.

242. *Gleaner*, 11 March 1946, 2; 24 July 1994, 4E; 26 September 1996, A15.

243. M.A. Sumathykutty, J. Madhusudana Rao, K.P. Padmakumari, and C.S. Narayanan, "Essential Oil Constituents of Some Piper Species", *Flavour and Fragrance Journal* 14 (1999): 282.

244. Powers of Attorney, Liber 96, f. 175; J.F. Ward, *Black Pepper: A Review of Cultural Practices and Their Application to Jamaica* (Kingston: Government Printer, 1960); Purseglove et al., *Spices*, 1: 10, 66.

245. Lindsay, "Elegancies of Jamaica", 252, 256.

246. Gosse, *Naturalist's Sojourn*, 27.

247. Lindsay, "Elegancies of Jamaica", 236, 241, 248, 251.

248. Barham, *Hortus Americanus*, 68; Titford, *Sketches*, xvi.

249. Long, *History*, 3: 838–42; Barham, *Hortus Americanus*, 99–101; Nicola H. Strickland, "My Most Unfortunate Experience: Eating a Manchineel 'Beach Apple'", *British Medical Journal* 321 (12 August 2000): 428; J.F. Pitts, N.H. Barker, D.C. Gibbons, and J.L. Jay, "Manchineel Keratoconjunctivitis", *British Journal of Ophthalmology* 77 (1993): 284–88; W. Adolf and E. Hecker, "On the Active Principles of the Spurge Family, X: Skin Irritants, Cocarcinogens, and Cryptic Cocarcinogens from the Latex of the Manchineel Tree", *Journal of Natural Products* 47 (1984): 482–96; Lowe et al., *Poisonous Plants*, 65–66.

Chapter 6

1. Michael Fenner and Ken Thompson, *The Ecology of Seeds* (Cambridge, UK: Cambridge University Press, 2005), 97–99; Lack and Evans, *Plant Biology*, 125–28.

2. Fenner and Thompson, *Ecology of Seeds*, 23–31; Lack and Evans, *Plant Biology*, 135–36.

3. Norman, Pearson, and Searle, *Ecology of Tropical Food Crops*, 186–88.

4. Lack and Evans, *Plant Biology*, 249; Norman, Pearson, and Searle, *Ecology of Tropical Food Crops*, 89.

5. Evans, *Crop Evolution, Adaptation and Yield*, 141; Norman, Pearson, and Searle, *Ecology of Tropical Food Crops*, 89–91; K.K.P.N. Rao, "Nutritive Value of Cereals and Other Main Staple Foods", *Cajanus* 12 (December 1969): 486–89.

6. *Gleaner*, 3 April 1918, 4.

7. Blome, *Description of the Island*, 4; Hughes, *American Physitian*, 24–26; Sloane, *Voyage*, 1: xix; Browne, *Civil and Natural History*, 335; Long, *History*, 3: 762.

8. Long, *History*, 3: 762; Marvin P. Miracle, *Maize in Tropical Africa* (Madison: University of Wisconsin Press, 1966), 261; Lee A. Newsom and Kathleen A. Deagan, "*Zea mays* in the West Indies: The Archaeological and Early Historic Record", in *Corn and Culture in the Prehistoric New World*, ed. Sissel Johannessen and Christine A. Hastorf (Boulder, CO: Westview, 1994), 214–16; James C. McCann, *Maize and Grace: Africa's Encounter with a New World Crop, 1500–2000* (Cambridge, MA: Harvard University Press, 2005), 45–46.

9. Ibid., 3–6.

10. Whitmore and Turner, *Cultivated Landscapes*, 27.

11. Blome, *Description of the Island*, 4; Browne, *Civil and Natural History*, 335; Dovaston, "Agricultura Americana", 1: 37; Sloane, *Voyage*, 1: xix; Hughes, *American Physitian*, 26–27; Browne, *Civil and Natural History*, 25; Long, *History*, 3: 762–63; Lunan, *Hortus Jamaicensis*, 1: 336–37; Roughley, *Jamaica Planter's Guide*, 399.

12. *An Inquiry Concerning the Trade, Commerce, and Policy of Jamaica, Relative to the Scarcity of Money, and the Causes and Bad Effects of Such Scarcity, Peculiar to that Island* (London: T. Kinnersly and G. Woodfal, 1759), 16, 18; Long, *History*, 3: 764; Hall, *In Miserable Slavery*, 69.

13. *Gleaner*, 11 April 1870, 2; 18 August 1914; 3 January 1920, 15; 5 February 1941, 3; Beckwith, *Black Roadways*, 19, 44.

14. E.R.H. Martin, *Maize Investigation in Jamaica: A Review of Research 1940–1969* (Kingston: Agricultural Information Service, Ministry of Agriculture and Fisheries, 1971), 3–4, 69; C. Roy Reynolds, "Research in Corn Hybridization in Jamaica", *Jamaica Journal* 7, nos 1/2 (1973): 91–92; Walton C. Galinat, "The Domestication and Genetic Erosion of Maize", *Economic Botany* 28 (1974): 31.

15. Rickards, *West Indies and Caribbean Year Book 1975*, 253.

16. Sloane, *Voyage*, 1: xix; Dovaston, "Agricultura Americana", 1: 95; Marsden, *Account*, 13; Barbara Gloudon, "Gourmet Delights Jamaican-Style", *SkyWritings* 123 (July/August 1999): 39; Miracle, *Maize in Tropical Africa*, 5–6.

17. Long, *History*, 3: 764; Beckwith, *Black Roadways*, 19–20; Powell et al., *Street Foods of Kingston*, 33.

18. Leslie, *New and Exact*, 35; Hughes, *American Physitian*, 26–27; Browne, *Civil and Natural History*, 335; Long, *History*, 3: 762–64; Sullivan, *Jamaica Cookery Book*, 61–62.

19. Hughes, *American Physitian*, 26–27; Long, *History*, 3: 763–64; *Jamaica Times*, 19 January 1918, 6; 2 February 1918, 13; 23 February 1918, 4; *Gleaner*, 18 January 1918, 10; 31 January 1918, 13; 4 June 1941, 13; 17 June 1941, 14; 8 September 1941, 8; 26 March 1942, 1; 11 September 1942, 3.

20. *Coalpot Recipe Postcards*; *Best of Creative Cooking*, 29, 32; Sullivan, *Jamaica Cookery Book*, 85–86; Ebanks, *Rastafari Cookbook*, 45.

21. Sullivan, *Jamaica Cookery Book*, 86; *Gleaner*, 3 June 1941, 8; Beckwith, *Black Roadways*, 19; *Gleaner, Food Supplement*, 28 March 1985, 27.

22. *Gleaner*, 30 July 1991, 3; 15 August 1991, 20; 15 December 1991, 2.

23. Sullivan, *Jamaica Cookery Book*, 86; *Gleaner*, 3 June 1941, 8; 5 June 1941, 8; Brandon, *Merry-Go-Round*, 58; Sobers, *Delicious Jamaica*, 25.

24. *Gleaner, Food Supplement*, 20 June 1985, 26; 15 March 1990, 15; Roberts, *Hamper of Recipes*, 84; Cuff, *Taste*, 11; Hamilton, *Little Jamaican Cookbook*, 38; Clark, *West Indian Cookery*, 79; Beckwith, *Black Roadways*, 19–20; *Best of Creative Cooking*, 15.

25. Osborne, *Rasta Cookbook*, 121; Jamaica Agricultural Society, *Farmer's Food Manual*, 179; Spence, *Jamaican Cookery*, 41; Benghiat, *Traditional Jamaican Cookery*, 186; *Gleaner*, 20 October 1996, 10C; Sullivan, *Jamaica Cookery Book*, 87; Beckwith, *Black Roadways*, 19.

26. Ayre, *Bush Doctor*, 86; Jamaica Agricultural Society, *Farmer's Food Manual*, 179, 371.

27. Sullivan, *Jamaica Cookery Book*, 87–88; Jamaica Agricultural Society, *Farmer's Food Manual*, 180; *Gleaner*, 15 March 1911, 8.

28. Ayre, *Bush Doctor*, 89.

29. J.B. Wills, "Crops Other Than Cocoa and the Diseases and Pests Which Affect Them", in *Agriculture and Land Use in Ghana*, ed. J. Brian Wills (London: Oxford University Press, 1962), 370; W.B. Morgan and J.C. Pugh, *West Africa* (London: Methuen, 1969), 79.

30. Stewart, *View*, 65.

31. Browne, *Civil and Natural History*, 25; Simon Taylor, Kingston, to Chaloner Arcedeckne, London, 30 November 1799, 3A/1799/23 Vanneck/Arcedeckne Papers; Williams, *Tour*, 197.

32. Ibid., 66, 198; Long, *History*, 3: 761; Lunan, *Hortus Jamaicensis*, 1: 351–52; *Royal Gazette*, 26 February 1820.

33. Sloane, *Voyage*, 1: xix; Dovaston, "Agricultura Americana", 1: 96; Marsden, *Account*, 17, 37.

34. "Characteristic Traits" 2 (May 1797): 766.

35. *Gleaner*, 30 April 1870, 7; 29 June 1925, 3; Jamaica Agricultural Society, *Farmer's Food Manual*, 91.

36. *Gleaner*, 29 June 1925, 3.

37. *Gleaner*, 9 August 1979, 22.

38. Wood, *Letters of Simon Taylor*, 11; Hall, *In Miserable Slavery*, 33, 63, 68.

39. F.M. Dania Ogbe and J.T. Williams, "Evolution in Indigenous West African Rice", *Economic Botany* 32 (1978): 59–64; Morgan and Pugh, *West Africa*, 81–83; Judith Carney, "Landscapes and Technology Transfer: Rice Cultivation and African Continuities", *Technology and Culture* 37 (1996): 5–35; Carney, *Black Rice: The African Origins of Rice Cultivation in the Americas* (Cambridge, MA: Harvard University Press, 2001); Carney, "'With Grains in Her Hair': Rice in Colonial Brazil", *Slavery and Abolition* 25 (2004): 1–27; Behrendt, "Markets, Transaction Cycles, and Profits", 181.

40. Carney, "'With Grains in Her Hair'", 22; Carney, "African Rice in the Columbian Exchange", *Journal of African History* 42 (2001): 377–96; Carney, *Black Rice*, 158; Sloane, *Voyage*, 1: xix, 103.

41. Barham, *Hortus Americanus*, 159; Long, *History*, 3: 768; *Inquiry Concerning the Trade*, 16–17; *Royal Gazette* (Spanish Town), 20 May 1820.

42. Titford, *Sketches*, 58; Lunan, *Hortus Jamaicensis*, 1: 117; Stewart, *View*, 65; Williams, *Tour*, 66; *Gleaner*, 1 January 1890, 5; 6 January 1890, 1; 10 February 1890, 4; 1 March 1900, 8; 3 March 1900, 12; Moore and Johnson, *Land We Live In*, 71.

43. *Gleaner*, *Food Supplement*, 9 May 1985, 28; 19 October 1989, 20; *Gleaner*, 6 September 1989, 3; 1 May 1991, 29; Ahmed and Afroz, *Political Economy of Food*, 133–34; *Rice Cook Book* (Montego Bay: Grains Jamaica, [1991]), 2, 8, 17, 20.

44. Rao, "Nutritive Value of Cereals", 486–87; Merle Esmay, Soemangat, Eriyatno, and Allan Phillips, *Rice Postproduction Technology in the Tropics* (Honolulu: University Press of Hawaii, 1979), 105–6.

45. Muller, *Introduction to Tropical Food Science*, 109–12; Forbes and Watson, *Plants in Agriculture*, 179.

46. *Inquiry Concerning the Trade*, 16–17; Edward Long, *A Free and Candid Review of a Tract, Entitled, "Observations on the Commerce of the American States"* (London: T. and W. Lowndes, 1784), 45; West-India Planters and Merchants, *Considerations on the Present State of the Intercourse between his Majesty's Sugar Colonies and the Dominions of the United States of America* (London: 1784), 26, 34.

47. *Gleaner*, 28 March 1866, 4; 1 January 1890, 2, 5; 2 January 1890, 8; 6 January 1920, 7, 13; 2 March 1920, 7; 1 May 1920, 8.

48. *Gleaner*, 1 September 1942, 1; 22 June 1949, 8; Jamaica Agricultural Society, *Farmer's Food Manual*, 78.

49. Arnold Spicer, ed., *Bread: Social, Nutritional and Agricultural Aspects of Wheaten Bread* (London: Applied Science Publishers, 1975).

50. *Gleaner*, *Food Supplement*, 22 April 1965, 14–15; Kari Levitt and Alister McIntyre, *Canada–West Indies Economic Relations* (Montreal: Centre for Developing-Area Studies, McGill University, 1967), 65–69; *Gleaner*, *Bakers' Expo Supplement*, 22 January 1987, iii.

51. *Gleaner*, 2 April 1992, 27; *Gleaner*, *Jamaica Flour Mills 25th Anniversary Supplement*, 7 October 1993, 6–8.

52. *Gleaner*, 21 January 1995, 11; 17 February 1995, 4A; Aimee Webster, "Why the Shift to White Wheat Flour?", *Gleaner*, 30 October 1988; *Gleaner*, 31 January 1986, 8.

53. Leslie, *New and Exact Account*, 34; *Gleaner*, 28 January 1866, 3; Sullivan, *Jamaica Cookery Book*, 83.

54. *Jamaica Standard*, 27 July and 2 October 1839; Moore and Johnson, *"Squalid Kingston"*, 24, 87; *Gleaner*, 1 March 1947, 1.

55. McKay, *Banana Bottom*, 231; *Gleaner*, 8 February 1912, 4; 7 March 1912, 18; 17 October 1916, 12.

56. Elizabeth David, *English Bread and Yeast Cookery* (London: Penguin, 1979), 170; Rose Levy Beranbaum, *The Bread Bible* (New York: Norton, 2003), 85; *Gleaner*, 7 March 1912, 18; 21 July 1915, 5; 11 March 1946, 2; 16 May 1995, 8A.

57. John Burnett, "Trends in Bread Consumption", in *Our Changing Fare: Two Hundred Years of British Food Habits*, ed. T.C. Barker, J.C. McKenzie, and John Yudkin (London: MacGibbon and Kee, 1966), 62–64. Cf. Steven Laurence Kaplan, "Breadways", *Food and Foodways* 7 (1997): 9–12.

58. *Gleaner*, 4 January 1900, 1; 22 January 1900, 5; 24 October 1914; 27 February 1918, 4.

59. *Jamaica Public Health* 2, no. 8 (1927): 4; 2, no. 10 (1927): 2; 3, no. 11 (1928): 3–4; *Gleaner*, 4 September 1918, 12.

60. Michael Pawson and David Buisseret, *Port Royal, Jamaica* (Oxford: Clarendon, 1975), 103; *Gleaner*, 8 February 1912, 4; 19 November 1960, 17; 28 December 1986; 3 January 1987; *Gleaner, Bakers' Expo Supplement*, 22 January 1987, xiii; *Gleaner*, 16 May 1995, 8A.

61. Hughes, *American Physitian*, 132; *Gleaner*, 25 February 1929, 20.

62. Rampini, *Letters from Jamaica*, 18; *Gleaner*, 2 November 1918, 13; 2 January 1920, 12; "Biscuits – Once Upon a Time, and Now", *Planters' Punch* 1, no. 5 (1924–25): 37; *Gleaner*, 11 May 1969, 2; *Gleaner, Supplement*, 26 June 1986, 1.

63. H.G. De Lisser, "Haunted", *Planters' Punch* 4, no. 2 (1939–40): 24; *Planters' Punch*, 4, no. 1 (1938–39): 80; *Gleaner*, 25 February 1929, 20.

64. *Gleaner*, 17 August 1918, 10; 4 September 1918, 12; 4 March 1920, 12; 3 January 1920, 8; 22 December 1931, 5; 24 December 1931, 11; *Gleaner, Supplement*, 26 June 1986, 5–9; *Planters' Punch* 1, no. 1 (1920): 35; 4, no. 1 (1938–39): 80.

65. McKay, *Banana Bottom*, 77; *Gleaner*, 15 March 1932, 12; Hurston, *Voodoo Gods*, 12–13.

66. *Gleaner*, 6 March 1920, 13; 15 March 1932, 12; 23 March 1932, 12; Kenneth Pringle, *Waters of the West* (London: George Allen and Unwin, 1938), 40.

67. Brandon, *Merry-Go-Round*, 6; *Gleaner*, 7 April 1985, 12; Donaldson, *Real Taste*, 4; Benghiat, *Traditional Jamaican Cookery*, 125.

68. Brandon, *Merry-Go-Round*, 7; Roberts, *Hamper of Recipes*, 64, 68; Cuff, *Taste*, 13; *Gleaner, Supermarket Supplement*, 26 November 1992, 4; Donaldson, *Real Taste*, 111.

69. Cuff, *Taste*, 15; Lucinda Scala Quinn, *Jamaican Cooking: 140 Roadside and Homestyle Recipes* (New York: Macmillan, 1997), 141.

70. De Mers, *Food of Jamaica*, 50.

71. *Gleaner*, 12 April 1958, 12; 19 and 23 April 1987, 8; 14 May 1987, 32; Jamaica Agricultural Society, *Farmer's Food Manual*, 289–90.

72. Brandon, *Merry-Go-Round*, 6; Jones, *Cook Up Jamaican Style* (1981), 28; Benghiat, *Traditional Jamaican Cookery*, 124; *Gleaner*, 6 March 1920, 13; 25 February 1929, 20; *Gleaner, Food Supplement*, 14 March 1985, 21.

73. Donaldson, *Real Taste*, 114–16; *Gleaner, Food Supplement*, 20 March 1986, xi; *Jamaica Observer*, 11 April 1993, 29; *Gleaner, Flair Magazine*, 10 April 1995, 15; Chen, *Cooking with Lasco*, 31; Ebanks, *Rastafari Cookbook*, 60.

74. *Gleaner, Food Supplement*, 20 March 1986, xi; *Gleaner*, 19 and 23 April 1987, 8; 12 April 1993, 1.

75. *Gleaner*, 3 April 1928, 20; *Gleaner, Food Supplement*, 20 February 1986, 17; Miller and Henry, *Creative Jamaican Cooking*, 74; *Gleaner, Pre-Easter Feature*, 6 April 1990; *Gleaner, Supermarket Supplement*, 26 March 1992, 2; Murray and Lewin, *Jamaican Chef*, 24; McLean, *Jamaican Cooking*, 57; *Gleaner, Home, Food and Living Guide*, 7 March 1991, 26.

76. *Coalpot Recipe Postcards*; *Gleaner, Food Supplement*, 2 November 1989, 14; 9 November 1989, 19; 16 November 1989, 18; Donaldson, *Real Taste*, 108–9.

77. *Gleaner*, 3 May 1985, 1; Webster, "Why the Shift"; *Gleaner*, 12 May 2005, C1.

78. *Gleaner, Food Supplement*, 14 March 1985, 21; 15 January 1987, 19.

79. Glasse, *Art of Cookery*, 60; Briggs, *New Art of Cookery*, 35–36, 367–68.

80. Sullivan, *Jamaica Cookery Book*, 21.

81. *Gleaner*, 16 September 1926, 14; 19 February 1927, 2; 24 February 1928, 2 and 20; 15 March 1932, 12; 14 October 1939, 6; 23 December 1939, 2.

82. "Eating Goes Modern", *Planters' Punch* 4, no. 3 (1940–41): 12; "Myrtle and Money", 37; McKay, *Dialect Poetry*, 54, 81.

83. *Gleaner*, 2 July 1943, 1; 16 March 1946, 4; 21 August 1947, 2; Donaldson, *Real Taste*, 19.

84. *Gleaner*, 13 April 1945, 5; 8 April 1946, 2; 25 May 1947, 9; 16 November 1961, 13; 31 July 1962, 3; 20 July 1967, 11; 23 March 1968, 11; 8 April 1968, 14.

85. *Gleaner*, 20 December 1955, 20; *Gleaner, Tastee Supplement*, 25 June 1991, 2–4.

86. Donaldson, *Real Taste*, 19; *Gleaner, Bakers' Expo Supplement*, 22 January 1987, xvi; *Gleaner, Mother's Supplement*, 23 July 1991, 17; *Gleaner*, 24 October 1991; *Gleaner, Outlook*, 8 June 1997, 20.

87. *Gleaner*, 31 October 1944, 5; *Gleaner, Supermarket Supplement*, 27 February 1992, 14; Alex D. Hawkes, "In Search of the Perfect Patty", in *A Tapestry of Jamaica: The Best of Skywritings, Air Jamaica's Inflight Magazine*, ed. Linda Gambrill (1977; Kingston: Creative Communications, 2003), 137.

88. Hyatt, *When Me Was a Boy*, 18; Barbara Gloudon, "In Celebration of the Patty", 137.

89. McKay, *Banana Bottom*, 230.

90. *Gleaner*, 6 May 1969, 1; Scientific Research Council, *Sample Menus*, 15–16; *Gleaner, Food Supplement*, 5 February 1987, 18.

91. Sullivan, *Jamaica Cookery Book*, 90; H.G. De Lisser, "The Devil's Mountain", *Planters' Punch* 1, no. 2 (1921–23): 31; *Gleaner, Food Supplement*, 5 February 1987, 18; Scientific Research Council, *Sample Menus*, 11.

92. *Gleaner*, 15 July 1913, 5; 8 December 1927, 14; 22 November 1945, 13; 23 December 1957, 19; 10 December 1982, 37; *Jamaica Observer*, 24 May 2005, T2; Burke, *Eat Caribbean*, 169; Silvano Serventi and Françoise Sabban, *Pasta: The Story of a Universal Food* (New York: Columbia University Press, 2002).

93. *Gleaner*, 20 September 1876, 3; 21 April 1897, 5; 15 October 1903, 5; 25 February 1928, 16; Powell et al., *Street Foods of Kingston*, 36.

94. *Gleaner*, 18 October 1901, 3; 21 July 1915, 12; 2 July 1918, 3; 7 January 1920, 14.

95. *Gleaner, Food Supplement*, 11 January 1990, 17.

96. Sloane, *Voyage*, 1: 179; *Peas Please*, 1–2.

97. Sloane, *Voyage*, 1: 175.

98. Barham, *Hortus Americanus*, 19; Hughes, *American Physitian*, 20; Lunan, *Hortus Jamaicensis*, 1: 336–37; Long, *History*, 3: 787; Macfadyen, *Flora of Jamaica*, 297; *Jamaica Times*, 2 March 1918, 4; *Gleaner, Food Supplement*, 6 March 1986, 23.

99. Hughes, *American Physitian*, 20–21; Long, *History*, 3: 787; Macfadyen, *Flora of Jamaica*, 297; Beckwith, *Black Roadways*, 18–19.

100. Beckwith, *Black Roadways*, 19, 44; Lunan, *Hortus Jamaicensis*, 1: 433–34; Long, *History*, 3: 786; Donaldson, *Real Taste*, 91.

101. Hughes, *American Physitian*, 17–18; Barham, *Hortus Americanus*, 28; Browne, *Civil and Natural History*, 292; Long, *History*, 3: 786; Sloane, *Voyage*, 1: 184.

102. Sloane, *Voyage*, 1: 175–76; Macfadyen, *Flora of Jamaica*, 280; Caribbean Research Council, Committee on Agriculture, Nutrition, Fisheries and Forestry, *Root Crops and Legumes*, 33; Montgomery, "Observations on the Cyanide Content", 11.

103. Hughes, *American Physitian*, 19–20; Sloane, *Voyage*, 1: 177; Browne, *Civil and Natural History*, 291; McKay, *Dialect Poetry*, 17; Beckwith, *Black Roadways*, 19; Lewicki, *West African Food*, 164.

104. Lewicki, *West African Food*, 53–54.

105. Sloane, *Voyage*, 1: 178; Barham, *Hortus Americanus*, 19; Macfadyen, *Flora of Jamaica*, 292.

106. *Gleaner*, 8 October 1941, 8; Jamaica Agricultural Society, *Farmer's Food Manual*, 75; *Gleaner*, *Flair Magazine*, 3 March 1987, 4.

107. Chen, *Cooking with Lasco*, 4–16; *Healthy Eating for Better Living: A Caribbean Handbook* (Kingston: Caribbean Food and Nutrition Institute, 2002), 98; *Daily Observer, Thursday Life*, 12 May 2005, 3; Mahabee and Mahabee, *Vegetarian Cookbook*, 101–6; Helen Chin-See, *Tofu for Health and Pleasure as Cooked in Chinese Homes* (Kingston: Helen Chin-See, 2001), 7; Burke, *Walkerswood*, 33.

108. Sloane, *Voyage*, 1: lxxiii; Browne, *Civil and Natural History*, 295; Jamaica Agricultural Society, *Farmer's Food Manual*, 195.

109. *Gleaner*, 6 August 1940, 9; 5 September 1940, 9; 7 June 1985, 3; Simon Taylor, Kingston, to Chaloner Arcedeckne, London, 4 February 1794, 3A/1794/4 Vanneck/Arcedeckne Papers; Long, *History*, 3: 787.

110. *Gleaner*, 29 May 1879, 3; 25 May 1881, 3; 20 March 1900, 3; 15 July 1913, 5; 24 October 1940, 16; Jones, *Cook Up Jamaican Style* (1981), 28, 32.

111. Brandon, *Merry-Go-Round*, 54.

112. *Gleaner*, 7 May 1872, 4; 22 January 1892, 6; 5 January 1898, 7; 25 July 1904, 6.

113. Moore and Johnson, "*Squalid Kingston*", 78; *Gleaner*, 14 January 1905, 10; Beckwith, *Black Roadways*, 18–19; Whitbourne, "The Ordinary Diet in Jamaica", 69.

114. *Gleaner*, 28 January 1938, 10; 27 August 1938, 12; 1 May 1991. See also Chapman, *Pleasure Island*, 102; Carley, *Jamaica*, 114; Brandon, *Merry-Go-Round*, 54; Benghiat, *Traditional Jamaican Cookery*, 77; Cassidy, *Jamaica Talk*, 197; *Gleaner, Home, Living and Food Guide*, 3 September 1992, 17.

115. *Gleaner*, 27 August 1938, 12; 27 August 1938, 12; 24 September 1938, 3; Donaldson, *Real Taste*, 41.

116. *Gleaner*, 7 November 1938, 27; 8 March 1941, 26; 18 October 1946, 4; Cleary, *Jamaica Run-dung*, 46; *Gleaner*, 7 October 1946, 4.

117. Jonathan Norton Leonard, *Latin American Cooking* ([New York]: Time-Life International, 1970), 127; Margarette De Andrade, *Brazilian Cookery: Traditional and Modern* (Rio de Janeiro: A Casa do Livro Eldorado, 1978), 78–85; Alex D. Hawkes, *The Flavors of the Caribbean and Latin America: A Personal Collection of Recipes* (New York: Viking, 1978), 123–25; Manuelita Zepherin, Alison White, Wendy E. Clarke, and Rosie Jackman, *The Joys of Healthy Cooking*

in the Caribbean (Kingston: Ian Randle, 2005), 179; Jeffrey M. Pilcher, *Food in World History* (New York: Routledge, 2006), 67.

118. Cuff, *Taste*, 19; *Gleaner, Food Supplement*, 3 August 1989, 29; *Gleaner, Supermarket Supplement*, 25 November 1993, 7; Quinn, *Jamaican Cooking*, 50; Mahabee and Mahabee, *Vegetarian Cookbook*, 90; *Gleaner, Home, Living and Food Guide*, 3 September 1992, 17.

119. Sullivan, *Jamaica Cookery Book*, 2–3; *Peas Please*, 5; Donaldson, *Real Taste*, 33.

120. McKay, *Banana Bottom*, 53; *Gleaner*, 28 January 1938, 10; *Gleaner, Food Supplement*, 6 March 1986, 23; 8 January 1987, 23.

121. *Gleaner, Supermarket Shopping Guide*, 24 January 1991, 10D.

122. Long, *History*, 3: 789; Lunan, *Hortus Jamaicensis*, 1: 348–49; Sullivan, *Jamaica Cookery Book*, 81; Whitbourne, "Ordinary Diet in Jamaica", 69; *Gleaner*, 28 June 1940, 16; Jamaica Agricultural Society, *Farmer's Food Manual*, 75, 195–202; *Gleaner, Food Supplement*, 27 July 1989, 34.

123. Long, *History*, 3: 809–10; Browne, *Civil and Natural History*, 270.

124. *Gleaner*, 8 December 1870, 4; 11 September 1969, 11; 30 December 1962, 19; 7 January 1964, 14; 6 September 1966, 3; Sullivan, *Jamaica Cookery Book*, 81; Louise Bennett, *Jamaica Labrish* (Kingston: Sangster's Bookstores Jamaica, 1966), 28–29.

125. Lindsay, "Elegancies of Jamaica", 196; Barham, *Hortus Americanus*, 44; William Fawcett and Alfred Barton Rendle, *Flora of Jamaica* (London: British Museum, 1920), 4: 121–26; *Gleaner*, 16 October 2003, C1.

126. *Gleaner*, 6 August 1967, 11. Cf. *Gleaner*, 12 January 1994, 16; Harris, "True Traditions", 57.

127. Purseglove et al., *Spices*, 2: 644.

128. Ibid., 2: 645; Long, *History*, 3: 715–17; Sullivan, *Jamaica Cookery Book*, 54.

129. Andrew T. Weil, "Nutmeg as a Narcotic", *Economic Botany* 19 (1965): 194–215.

130. Long, *History*, 3: 735–36; Purseglove et al., *Spices*, 1: 174–77; Powers of Attorney, Liber 96, f. 175.

131. John Ellis, *An Historical Account of Coffee* (London: Edward and Charles Dilly, 1774), 13–14; Frederick L. Wellman, *Coffee: Botany, Cultivation and Utilization* (London: Leonard Hill, 1961), 16–26; D.W. Rodriquez, *Coffee: A Short Economic History with Special Reference to Jamaica* (Kingston: Ministry of Agriculture and Lands, 1961), 13; Sauer, *Historical Geography*, 131–33; S.D. Smith, "Accounting for Taste: British Coffee Consumption in Historical Perspective", *Journal of Interdisciplinary History* 27 (1996): 214.

132. Leslie, *New and Exact*, 313; Ellis, *Historical Account of Coffee*, 17; Long, *History*, 3: 681–83; Lunan, *Hortus Jamaicensis*, 1: 217; Rodriquez, *Coffee*, 13; Mario Samper and Radin Fernando, "Historical Statistics of Coffee Production and Trade from 1700 to 1960", in *The Global Coffee Economy in Africa, Asia, and Latin America, 1500–1989*, ed. William Gervase Clarence-Smith and Steven Topik (Cambridge, UK: Cambridge University Press, 2003), 412.

133. Rodriquez, *Coffee*, 1–4.

134. *Gleaner*, 26 July 1883, 2; 9 May 1887, 2; 20 February 1987, 1; Hill, *Cuba and Porto Rico*, 211; Jamaica Tourist Association, *Jamaica*, 7; Leader, *Through Jamaica with a Kodak*, 143; Scott, *To Jamaica and Back*, 101; Rodriquez, *Coffee*, 40, 57; Mary Banks, Christine McFadden, and Catherine Atkinson, *The World Encyclopedia of Coffee* (London: Lorenz, 1999), 85; Bennett

Alan Weinberg and Bonnie K. Bealer, *The World of Caffeine: The Science and Culture of the World's Most Popular Drug* (New York: Routledge, 2002), 206–7.

135. *Gleaner*, 4 November 2001, 8C; Hill, *Cuba and Porto Rico*, 211; Mario K. Samper, "The Historical Construction of Quality and Competitiveness: A Preliminary Discussion of Coffee Commodity Chains", in *The Global Coffee Economy in Africa, Asia, and Latin America, 1500–1989*, ed. William Gervase Clarence-Smith and Steven Topik (Cambridge, UK: Cambridge University Press, 2003), 85.

136. Buffo and Cardelli-Freire, "Coffee Flavour", 99–104; Werner Grosch, Michael Czerny, Robert Wagner, and Florian Mayer, "Studies on the Aroma of Roasted Coffee", in *Flavour Science: Recent Developments*, ed. A.J. Taylor and D.S. Mottram (Cambridge, UK: Royal Society of Chemistry, 1996), 200–205; Weenen, Kerler, and van der Ven, "Maillard Reaction in Flavour Formation", 155.

137. Rodriquez, *Coffee*, 13–16; Verene A. Shepherd and Kathleen E.A. Monteith, "Pen-Keepers and Coffee Farmers in a Sugar-Plantation Society", in *Slavery without Sugar: Diversity in Caribbean Economy and Society since the 17th Century* (Gainesville: University Press of Florida, 2002), 85–86; Higman, *Jamaica Surveyed*, 9; Higman, *Montpelier*, 197.

138. Sauer, *Historical Geography*, 134; Wellman, *Coffee*, 373–74.

139. Rodriquez, *Coffee*, 6; *Gleaner*, 9 September 1882, 2; 11 March 1955, 6; Mark Pendergrast, *Uncommon Grounds: The History of Coffee and How It Transformed Our World* (New York: Basic Books, 1999), 110, 147; *West Indies and Caribbean Year Book 1967*, 242.

140. Sullivan, *A Collection*, 56; Donaldson, *Real Taste*, 99.

141. Thompson, *Black Caribbean*, 233; *Gleaner*, 1 July 2002, A2. Cf. Claudia Roden, *Coffee* (Harmondsworth, UK: Penguin, 1981), 78–95.

142. *Gleaner, Food Supplement*, 28 March 1985, 21; Lunan, *Hortus Jamaicensis*, 1: 223, following Dr Fothergill's letter of 2 September 1773, quoted in Ellis, *Historical Account of Coffee*, 38; De Lisser, "Devil's Mountain", 31.

143. Clark, *West Indian Cookery*, 206–7. Cf. Wellman, *Coffee*, 396–98.

144. Facey, *Busha Browne*, 99; *Gleaner, Food Supplement*, 1 April 1965, 12.

145. Pendergrast, *Uncommon Grounds*, 108–9; Weinberg and Bealer, *World of Caffeine*, 186–90; *Gleaner*, 22 March 1941, 13; 9 January 1987, 8; *Gleaner, Desnoes and Geddes 75th Anniversary Supplement*, 7 July 1993, 6.

146. Philip D. Curtin, *Economic Change in Precolonial Africa: Senegambia in the Era of the Slave Trade* (Madison: University of Wisconsin Press, 1975), 228; *Importance of Jamaica*, 31; Long, *History*, 3: 855; Benghiat, *Traditional Jamaican Cookery*, 229.

147. *Gleaner*, 30 June 1898, 5; 2 January 1900, 3, 6; 9 March 1900, 2; Leader, *Through Jamaica with a Kodak*, 143; *Gleaner*, Brochure, 27 July 1991.

148. Allen M. Young, *The Chocolate Tree: A Natural History of Cacao* (Washington, DC: Smithsonian Institution Press, 1994).

149. Weenen, Kerler, and Van der Ven, "Maillard Reaction in Flavour Formation", 158.

150. Young, *Chocolate Tree*, 13.

151. Whitmore and Turner, *Cultivated Landscapes*, 87; Hickeringill, *Jamaica Viewed*, 18–20; Hughes, *American Physitian*, 112–13; Blome, *Description*, 16; Michael D. Coe and Sophie D. Coe, *The True History of Chocolate* (London: Thames and Hudson, 1996), 165–69; Henry Stubbe, *The Indian Nectar, or a Discourse Concerning Chocolata* (London: Andrew Crook, 1662), 125; Arthur MacGregor, "The Life, Character and Career of Sir Hans Sloane", in *Sir Hans Sloane: Collector, Scientist, Antiquary – Founding Father of the British Museum*, ed. Arthur MacGregor (London: British Museum, 1994), 15–16.

152. Dovaston, "Agricultura Americana", 2: 277–78; Long, *History*, 3: 695.

153. *Gleaner*, 2 January 1890, 8; Royes and Baccus, *Jamaica Farmer's Guide*, 145; G.A.R. Wood and R.A. Lass, *Cocoa* (London: Longman, 1985), 560.

154. D.H. Urquhart, *Cocoa*, 2nd ed. (London: Longmans, 1961), 3; Wood and Lass, *Cocoa*, 450–96, 523–26, 590–97.

155. Benoit Daviron, "Small Farm Production and the Standardization of Tropical Products", *Journal of Agrarian Change* 2 (2002): 177.

156. Hughes, *American Physitian*, 111, 119–20; Stubbe, *Indian Nectar*, preface; Marcy Norton, "Tasting Empire: Chocolate and the European Internalization of Mesoamerican Aesthetics", *American Historical Review* 111 (2006): 669; Coe and Coe, *True History of Chocolate*, 174.

157. Hughes, *American Physitian*, 127–33, 139.

158. Long, *History*, 3: 698–99; Sullivan, *Jamaica Cookery Book*, 112; *Gleaner*, 16 November 1898, 5; William Gervase Clarence-Smith, *Cocoa and Chocolate, 1765–1914* (London: Routledge, 2000), 29.

159. Beckwith, *Black Roadways*, 15; "Melinda", 6; Gaunt, *Reflection*, 134–35, 148; Clark, *West Indian Cookery*, 207.

160. Sauer, *Historical Geography*, 162–64; Wood and Lass, *Cocoa*, 1–8; Urquhart, *Cocoa*, 1–4; *Gleaner*, 31 August 1966, 1 and 8; 28 July 1969, 25; 2 December 1987, 33; *Gleaner, Highgate 15th Anniversary Supplement*, 27 October 1992, 2.

161. Clark, *West Indian Cookery*, 166, 180, 200, 203; Jones, *Cook Up Jamaican Style* (1981), 31.

Chapter 7

1. Phillippo, *Jamaica*, 231.

2. R. McNeill Alexander, *Animals* (Cambridge, UK: Cambridge University Press, 1990).

3. Douglas V. Armstrong, *The Old Village and the Great House: An Archaeological and Historical Examination of Drax Hall Plantation, St. Ann's Bay, Jamaica* (Urbana: University of Illinois Press, 1990), 227–33.

4. *Gleaner, Food Supplement*, 15 May 1986, 24; *Gleaner*, 15 January 1988, 11; Benghiat, *Traditional Jamaican Cookery*, 45; Donaldson, *Real Taste*, 55; De Mers, *Food of Jamaica*, 48.

5. Karl A. Aiken, G. Andre Kong, Stephen Smikle, Robin Mahon, and Richard Appeldoorn, "The Queen Conch Fishery on Pedro Bank, Jamaica: Discovery, Development, Management", *Ocean and Coastal Management* 42 (1999): 1069–81; *Gleaner*, 9 July 1995, 5C; 25 July 1999, 3C; 9 April 2000, 2A.

6. Burke, *Walkerswood*, 19; Hughes, *American Physitian*, 97–98; Long, *History*, 3: 868; Rampini, *Letters from Jamaica*, 18; Sullivan, *Jamaica Cookery Book*, 9.

7. *Gleaner*, 22 February 1871, 3; 2 January 1900, 2; 2 February 1900, 2; 3 March 1900, 5; 17 July 1993, 11.

8. Quinn, *Jamaican Cooking*, xix; *Gifts from a Jamaican Kitchen*, 38; Martin Moynihan and Arcadio F. Rodaniche, *The Behavior and Natural History of the Caribbean Reef Squid* Sepioteuthis sepioidea (Berlin: Verlag Paul Parey, 1982), 13.

9. L.B. Holthuis, *FAO Species Catalogue*, vol. 1, *Shrimps and Prawns of the World* (Rome: Food and Agriculture Organization of the United Nations, 1980), xvi; Frank Ross, "Aquaculture in Jamaica: A Growing Industry", *Jamaica Journal* 18, no. 4 (1985–86), 36; Long, *History*, 3: 869; Browne, *Civil and Natural History*, 424; Chapman, *Pleasure Island*, 100; Pringle, *Waters of the West*, 37, 47; Donaldson, *Real Taste*, 18.

10. Browne, *Civil and Natural History*, 421–22; Long, *History*, 3: 868.

11. Stewart, *View*, 82; Browne, *Civil and Natural History*, 423–24; Phillippo, *Jamaica*, 57–58; Sturge and Harvey, *West Indies in 1837*, 294; Wyllarde, *Tropical Tales*, 311; Carley, *Jamaica*, 115; *Gifts from a Jamaican Kitchen*, 23.

12. Browne, *Civil and Natural History*, 423–24; *Marly*, 211–12; Sullivan, *Jamaica Cookery Book*, 14–15; *Gleaner*, 29 March 1938, 2; Jekyll, *Jamaican Song and Story*, 72.

13. Phillippo, *Jamaica*, 58; *Jamaica Observer*, 13 May 1994, 42; Donaldson, *Real Taste*, 18.

14. Karl Aiken, "Lobsters: Their Biology and Conservation in Jamaica", *Jamaica Journal* 17, no. 4 (1984–85): 44–45; Browne, *Civil and Natural History*, 424; Sullivan, *Jamaica Cookery Book*, 3–4, 9–11.

15. Chapman, *Pleasure Island*, 100; Pringle, *Waters of the West*, 37, 47; Aiken, "Lobsters", 45–47; *Gleaner*, 9 July 1988, 22; 27 April 1990, 23; 20 March 1992, 23; Kingston *Star*, 25 May 1989, 1.

16. Sullivan, *Jamaica Cookery Book*, 4–5, 8; Browne, *Civil and Natural History*, 424; Elsa Miller, *Cook It My Way* (Discovery Bay, Jamaica: Northern Lithographers, [1970]), 2; *Gleaner*, 26 March 1975, 32; 15 October 1998, B13; Benghiat, *Traditional Jamaican Cookery*, 50.

17. David Nichols, *Echinoderms* (London: Hutchinson University Library, 1962), 65–75; J.D. Woodley, "Sea-Urchins Exert Top-Down Control of Macroalgae on Jamaican Coral Reefs", *Coral Reefs* 18 (1999): 192; Peter J. Edmunds and Robert C. Carpenter, "Recovery of *Diadema antillarum* Reduces Macroalgal Cover and Increases Abundance of Juvenile Corals on a Caribbean Reef", *Proceedings of the National Academy of Sciences* 98, no. 9 (2001): 5067-71; Anthony Clayton and Michael Haley, "The Management of Jamaica's Coral Reefs", *Jamaica Journal* 28, nos 2–3 (2004): 16.

18. J.B.C. Jackson, "Reefs since Columbus", *Coral Reefs* 16, suppl. (1997): S25; Gosse, *Naturalist's Sojourn*, 77; Klaassen, *Casarett and Doull's Toxicology*, 1079.

19. *Gleaner*, 10 October 1893, 3; 14 October 1893, 2.

20. *Gleaner*, 26 September 1941, 8; Miller and Henry, *Creative Jamaican Cooking*, 4; Elsa Miller and Leonard "Sonny" Henry, *Creative Bahamian Cooking and Menus* (Kingston: Kingston Publishers, 1982); Higman, "Cookbooks", 84–85.

21. F.S. Bodenheimer, *Insects as Human Food: A Chapter of the Ecology of Man* (The Hague: W. Junk, 1951), 5–8; Mark Q. Sutton, *Insects as Food: Aboriginal Entomophagy in the Great Basin*, Anthropological Papers No. 33 (Menlo Park, CA: Ballena Press, 1988), 83–86; Harris, *Good*

to Eat, 172; William C. McGrew, "The Other Faunivory: Primate Insectivory and Early Human Diet", in *Meat-Eating and Human Evolution*, ed. Craig B. Stanford and Henry T. Bunn (New York: Oxford University Press, 2001), 161–62.

22. Bodenheimer, *Insects as Human Food*, 22–25; McGrew, "Other Faunivory", 168–71.

23. Bodenheimer, *Insects as Human Food*, 301; Sloane, *Voyage*, 2: 193; Browne, *Civil and Natural History*, 429; Lindsay, "Elegancies of Jamaica"; Long, *History of Jamaica*, 3: 737.

24. Rampini, *Letters from Jamaica*, 42; *Gleaner, Special Magazine Section*, 22 May 1926, 3; *Gleaner*, 29 March 1938, 5.

25. McGrew, "Other Faunivory", 162–63; Sutton, *Insects as Food*, 1.

26. Mark L. Winston, *The Biology of the Honey Bee* (Cambridge, MA: Harvard University Press, 1987), 12; Tammy Horn, *Bees in America: How the Honey Bee Shaped a Nation* (Lexington: University Press of Kentucky, 2005), 6; Long, *History*, 3: 881–82; Hurston, *Voodoo Gods*, 35–36.

27. Sullivan, *Jamaica Cookery Book*, 118; Beckwith, *Black Roadways*, 25; Cannon, "Cooking in Paradise", 190; De Lisser, "Haunted", 24; *Gleaner*, 7 May 1941, 8.

28. Jamaica Agricultural Society, *Farmer's Food Manual*, 182–85.

29. *Gleaner, Outlook*, 28 May 2000, 11; *Business Observer*, 18 May 2005, 18B.

30. *Present State of Jamaica*, 19–20; Sloane, *Voyage*, 2: 333; Juliet Clutton-Brock, "Vertebrate Collections", in *Sir Hans Sloane: Collector, Scientist, Antiquary – Founding Father of the British Museum*, ed. Arthur MacGregor (London: British Museum Press, 1994), 226.

31. Nugent, *Lady Nugent's Journal*, 203–4n1; *Jamaica Observer*, 15 December 2005, 6; Bodenheimer, *Insects as Human Food*, 22; Lewicki, *West African Food*, 96–97.

32. Farr, "Land Animals of Jamaica", 43; Sloane, *Voyage*, 1: xx; *Present State of Jamaica*, 19; Lewicki, *West African Food*, 98–99; Watts, *West Indies*, 226.

33. Browne, *Civil and Natural History*, 461; *Importance of Jamaica*, 47; Long, *History*, 3: 880; "Characteristic Traits" 3 (July 1797): 108; Phillippo, *Jamaica*, 59; *Gleaner*, 19 November 1895, 4; J.D. Woodley, "A History of the Jamaican Fauna", *Jamaica Journal* 2, no. 3 (1968): 19.

34. *Present State of Jamaica*, 19; Long, *History*, 3: 869, 873; Lewicki, *West African Food*, 96.

35. Beckford, *Descriptive Account*, 1: 369–70; Lewis, *Journal*, 195–96; Long, *History*, 3: 871–73.

36. Peter L. Lutz and John A. Musick, eds, *The Biology of Sea Turtles*, vol. 1 (Boca Raton, FL: CRC Press, 1996); Peter L. Lutz, John A. Musick, and Jeanette Wyneken, eds, *The Biology of Sea Turtles*, vol. 2 (Boca Raton, FL: CRC Press, 2003); Robert M. Ingle and F.G. Walton Smith, *Sea Turtles and the Turtle Industry of the West Indies, Florida and the Gulf of Mexico, with Annotated Bibliography* (Miami, FL: University of Miami Press, 1949), 12–13; Beckford, *Descriptive Account*, 1: 376; Long, *History*, 3: 868; Stewart, *View*, 82.

37. Rampini, *Letters from Jamaica*, 167; Rhema Kerr, "Jamaica's Sea Turtles", *Jamaica Journal* 26, no. 1 (1996): 3; Jackson, "Reefs since Columbus", S26–28.

38. Watts, *West Indies*, 61; Ingle and Smith, *Sea Turtles*, 16, 21–30.

39. Cannon, "Cooking in Paradise", 189; Ingle and Smith, *Sea Turtles*, 37.

40. Watts, *West Indies*, 61–62; Karen A. Bjorndal, Alan B. Bolten, and Milani Y. Chaloupka, "Evaluating Trends in Abundance of Immature Green Turtles, *Chelonia mydas*, in the Greater Caribbean", *Ecological Applications* 15 (2005): 305; Lewicki, *West African Food*, 97–98.

41. *Present State of Jamaica*, 18; Sloane, *Voyage*, 1: xvii; An Act appointing the prices of meat, *Laws of Jamaica*, 1681, cap. IV.

42. Blome, *Description of the Island*, 24; Blome, *Present State*, 14, 21; Trapham, *Discourse on the State of Health*, 61; Sloane, *Voyage*, 1: lxxxviii; An Act appointing the price of meat, and regulating markets, *Laws of Jamaica*, 1693, cap. VI.

43. Edward Ward, *A Trip to Jamaica: With the True Character of the People and Island* (London: J. How, 1700), 13; Browne, *Civil and Natural History*, 465; *Importance of Jamaica*, 39; Leslie, *New and Exact*, 34; Long, *History*, 3: 868.

44. Carter, *Frugal Housewife*, 29–31.

45. Briggs, *New Art of Cookery*, 54–58.

46. Glasse, *Art of Cookery*, 167.

47. Rampini, *Letters from Jamaica*, 167; Sullivan, *Jamaica Cookery Book*, 1–2, 12–14; *Gleaner*, 14 January 1905, 10; Beckwith, *Black Roadways*, 33; Clark, *West Indian Cookery*, 106.

48. Caribbean Commission, Central Secretariat, *The Fish Trade of the Caribbean*, External Trade Bulletin No. 3 (Washington, DC: Caribbean Commission, 1948), 87; Ingle and Walton Smith, *Sea Turtles*, 51–52; Beckford, *Descriptive Account*, 1: 372–73; Rampini, *Letters from Jamaica*, 166–67; *Gleaner*, 27 April 1877, 2; 8 May 1880, 2.

49. Spence, *Jamaican Cookery*, 25; Miller and Henry, *Creative Jamaican Cooking*, 10; Benghiat, *Traditional Jamaican Cookery*, 48; *Gleaner*, 3 May 1985; *Boulevard News* (Kingston), 24 August 1989; Goldman, *Pearl's Delicious Jamaican Dishes*, 58; *Gleaner*, 15 November 1990; 5 July 1992; Kerr, "Jamaica's Sea Turtles", 3–6.

50. Sloane, *Voyage*, 1: xviii; Browne, *Civil and Natural History*, 465; Hall, *In Miserable Slavery*, 52, 57; Beckford, *Descriptive Account*, 1: 377; Lewis, *Journal*, 151; Gosse, *Naturalist's Sojourn*, 187–88.

51. Sullivan, *Jamaica Cookery Book*, 15–16; Wyllarde, *Tropical Tales*, 311.

Chapter 8

1. William H. Brown, *Marine Fisheries of the British West Indies*, ONR Report (Berkeley: Department of Geography, University of California, 1967), 1.

2. *Gleaner*, 24 May 1964, 8; Caribbean Commission, *Fish Trade*, 35–38; Levitt and McIntyre, *Canada-West Indies Economic Relations*, 70; Donaldson, *Real Taste*, 54.

3. Blome, *Present State*, 20; Blome, *Description of the Island*, 23; Sloane, *Voyage*, 2: 275; An English Merchant, *Some Modern Observations*, 9, 17; Marsden, *Account*, 12; Long, *History*, 3: 867.

4. An Act for regulating fowling and fishing, *Laws of Jamaica*, 1711, cap. XVI; *Gleaner*, 12 March 1885, 3; Jackson, "Reefs since Columbus", S28.

5. Burnard, *Mastery, Tyranny, and Desire*, 193–200; Nugent, *Lady Nugent's Journal*, 95; Williams, *Tour*, 79–80; Gosse, *Naturalist's Sojourn*, 205–11; Beckwith, *Black Roadways*, 33; J.L. Munro, "The Sea Fisheries of Jamaica: Past, Present and Future", *Jamaica Journal* 3, no. 3 (1969):

20–21; *Gleaner*, 14 March 1987; Clayton and Haley, "Management of Jamaica's Coral Reefs", 15–23.

6. Williams, *Tour through the Island*, 79–80; Lewicki, *West African Food*, 101–2; Curtin, *Economic Change in Precolonial Africa*, 213, 224–28; *Gleaner*, 14 March 1879, 2; 7 January 1896, 2–3.

7. *Gleaner*, 17 June 1880, 3; 28 March 1890, 2; 24 November 1890, 3; 28 December 1917, 9; 17 February 1933, 2; 14 August 1987.

8. Aspinall, *British West Indies*, 236–38; *Falmouth Post*, 3 June 1870; *Gleaner*, 17 January 1900, 3; 19 April 1918, 14; 11 October 1918, 4; Munro, "Sea Fisheries of Jamaica", 17.

9. *Gleaner*, 11 November 2001, 9B; Kent Gustavson, "Economic Production from the Artisanal Fisheries of Jamaica", *Fisheries Research* 57 (2002): 105–6.

10. *Gleaner*, 11 November 2001, 9B; Jones, *Cook Up Jamaican Style* (1981), 43; *West Indies and Caribbean Year Book 1967*, 246; Donaldson, *Real Taste*, 55.

11. Rampini, *Letters from Jamaica*, 66; Karl A. Aiken, "Reproduction, Diet and Population Structure of the Mountain Mullet, *Agonostomus monticola*, in Jamaica, West Indies", *Environmental Biology of Fishes* 53 (1998): 347–52.

12. Sloane, *Voyage*, 2: 288–89; Long, *History*, 3: 866; Nugent, *Lady Nugent's Journal*, 58; Lewis, *Journal*, 153; Stewart, *View*, 81; Gosse, *Birds of Jamaica*, 294; Gosse, *Naturalist's Sojourn*, 83–84.

13. Rampini, *Letters from Jamaica*, 65–66; Sullivan, *Jamaica Cookery Book*, 7-8; *Gleaner*, 20 November 1926, 19; Chapman, *Pleasure Island*, 100; Benghiat, *Traditional Jamaican Cookery*, 75; Pringle, *Waters of the West*, 37, 47.

14. *Gleaner*, 7 April 1919, 13; 26 October 1944, 4; 28 January 1949, 16; 8 November 1969, 3; 19 February 1995, 9A; *Gleaner, Special Magazine Section*, 21 January 1928, 1.

15. *Jamaica Post*, 17 January 1890; David K. Caldwell, *Marine and Freshwater Fishes of Jamaica*, Science Series Bulletin No. 17 (Kingston: Institute of Jamaica, 1966), 11–12; Ross, "Aquaculture in Jamaica", 29; Edward C. Migdalski and George S. Fichter, *The Fresh and Salt Water Fishes of the World* (New York: Knopf, 1976), 10.

16. *Festival 71, National Culinary Arts, Finals – July 21, 1971, Sheraton-Kingston Hotel* (cyclostyled), 18, 41; *Gleaner*, 15 March 1986; 30 March 1986; Ross, "Aquaculture in Jamaica", 34; *Gleaner, Feedtime Supplement*, 10 June 1989, 11; Wade O. Watanabe, Thomas M. Losordo, Kevin Fitzsimmons, and Fred Hanley, "Tilapia Production Systems in the Americas: Technological Advances, Trends, and Challenges", *Reviews in Fisheries Science* 10 (2002): 465–72.

17. *Gleaner*, 26 September 1987, 18; 10 December 1988, 12; 2 June 1990, 13; *Star*, 12 May 2005, 8; *Jamaica Observer*, 5 June 2005, 3.

18. Browne, *Civil and Natural History*, 450; Hall, *In Miserable Slavery*, 117, 170; Stewart, *View*, 81.

19. Caldwell, *Marine and Freshwater Fishes*, 78; Migdalski and Fichter, *Fresh and Salt Water Fishes*, 260–61.

20. Browne, *Civil and Natural History*, 451; Long, *History*, 3: 866; Reverend John Lindsay, Lindsay Drawings, Vol. VII, n.p. (Natural History Division, Bristol Museum and Art Gallery).

21. Stewart, *View*, 81; Sullivan, *Jamaica Cookery Book*, 8.

22. *Gleaner*, 25 July 1900, 1; 8 January 1906, 2; 11 May 1943, 8; 25 January 1908, 3; 14 March 1987.

23. Miller and Henry, *Creative Jamaican Cooking*, 11; Benghiat, *Traditional Jamaican Cookery*, 74; *Gleaner*, 3 March 1869, 4; 2 January 1900, 2; 2 February 1900, 2; 3 March 1900, 5; 20 March 1900, 3.

24. Browne, *Civil and Natural History*, 450; Stewart, *View*, 81; Hall, *In Miserable Slavery*, 127–28, 177; *Gleaner*, 14 March 1987, 9; Migdalski and Fichter, *Fresh and Salt Water Fishes*, 209.

25. Ibid., 108, 294–95; Mike Smylie, *Herring: A History of the Silver Darlings* (Stroud, UK: Tempus, 2004), 80; Lindsay Drawings, Vol. VII, n.p.

26. *Gleaner*, 6 January 1890, 3; Sullivan, *Jamaica Cookery Book*, 11.

27. Browne, *Civil and Natural History*, 441–42; Migdalski and Fichter, *Fresh and Salt Water Fishes*, 109.

28. Brandon, *Merry-Go-Round*, 34, 36; Munro, "Sea Fisheries of Jamaica", 19; Migdalski and Fichter, *Fresh and Salt Water Fishes*, 234–35.

29. Browne, *Civil and Natural History*, 449; Lindsay Drawings, Vol. VII, n.p.; Gosse, *Naturalist's Sojourn*, 209.

30. Lindsay Drawings, Vol. VII, n.p.; Migdalski and Fichter, *Fresh and Salt Water Fishes*, 237–38; Caldwell, *Marine and Freshwater Fishes*, 52–54.

31. Donaldson, *Real Taste*, 55.

32. Lindsay Drawings, Vol. VII, n.p.; Munro, "Sea Fisheries of Jamaica", 19; Migdalski and Fichter, *Fresh and Salt Water Fishes*, 210; Caldwell, *Marine and Freshwater Fishes*, 41.

33. Trapham, *Discourse on the State of Health*, 65; *Importance of Jamaica*, 39; Long, *History*, 3: 866; Migdalski and Fichter, *Fresh and Salt Water Fishes*, 211; Caldwell, *Marine and Freshwater Fishes*, 41.

34. Sullivan, *Jamaica Cookery Book*, 11; *Jamaica Post*, 17 January 1890; *Gleaner*, 24 November 1890; 27 October 1949, 10.

35. Jackson, "Reefs since Columbus", S27–28.

36. Browne, *Civil and Natural History*, 447; Lindsay Drawings, Vol. VII, n.p.; Migdalski and Fichter, *Fresh and Salt Water Fishes*, 28, 266–67.

37. Ibid., 246–47; Jones, *Cook Up Jamaican Style* (1981), 43.

38. Newnham-Davis, *Dinners and Diners*, 297; Sullivan, *Jamaica Cookery Book*, 7, 11–12; Jones, *Cook Up Jamaican Style* (1981), 45.

39. Cleary, *Jamaica Run-dung*, 29; Jones, *Cook Up Jamaican Style* (1981), 45; Benghiat, *Traditional Jamaican Cookery*, 82; *Gleaner*, *Food Supplement*, 24 October 1985, 19; *Gleaner*, *Home, Living and Food Guide*, 2 September 1993, 28; *Jamaica, Finest Taste*, 73; Donaldson, *Real Taste*, 58.

40. *Gleaner*, *Food Supplement*, 18 January 1990, 19; *Gleaner*, 15 May 1997, B6; Donaldson, *Real Taste*, 55; *Jamaica, Finest Taste*, 74.

41. Lindsay Drawings, Vol. VII, n.p.; Migdalski and Fichter, *Fresh and Salt Water Fishes*, 274–75.

42. *Gleaner*, 30 April 1967, vi.

43. Lindsay Drawings, Vol. VII, n.p.; Migdalski and Fichter, *Fresh and Salt Water Fishes*, 191.

44. Lindsay Drawings, Vol. VII, n.p.; *Gleaner*, 2 January 1930, 15; 3 January 1958, 9; 23 January 1959, 16; Scientific Research Council, *Sample Menus*, 2.

45. *Gleaner*, 5 June 1965, 6; Cleary, *Jamaica Run-dung*, 25; *Gleaner, Food Supplement*, 9 May 1985, 27; Cuff, *Taste*, 7; Donaldson, *Real Taste*, 8, 29, 54; *Jamaica Observer, Sparkle*, 12 March 1995, 12; Powell et al., *Street Foods of Kingston*, 33; *Gleaner, Home, Living and Food Guide*, 26 September 1991, 28.

46. Munro, "Sea Fisheries of Jamaica", 19; Migdalski and Fichter, *Fresh and Salt Water Fishes*, 285.

47. Sloane, *Voyage*, 2: 285; Browne, *Civil and Natural History*, 451; Clutton-Brock, "Vertebrate Collections", 77; Stewart, *View*, 81.

48. *Gleaner*, 5 February 1918, 14; Gaunt, *Reflection*, 14-16; A.L. Carnegie, "Poisoning by Barracuda Fish", *West Indian Medical Journal* 12 (1963): 217-18; Caldwell, *Marine and Freshwater Fishes*, 11.

49. Lindsay Drawings, Vol. VII, n.p.; Migdalski and Fichter, *Fresh and Salt Water Fishes*, 277, 282; Caldwell, *Marine and Freshwater Fishes*, 66-67.

50. Sullivan, *Jamaica Cookery Book*, 8.

51. Munro, "Sea Fisheries of Jamaica", 19; Migdalski and Fichter, *Fresh and Salt Water Fishes*, 227-29; *West Indies and Caribbean Year Book 1967*, 246; Jones, *Cook Up Jamaican Style* (1981), 43.

52. Williams, *Tour through the Island*, 79-80; *Gleaner*, 19 April 1918, 14; Chen, *Cooking with Lasco*, 8-9; *Jamaica Observer, Special Feature*, 12 May 2005, 7.

53. Benghiat, *Traditional Jamaican Cookery*, 75; Facey, *Busha Browne*, 14; De Mers, *Food of Jamaica*, 68; Donaldson, *Real Taste*, 55.

54. Browne, *Civil and Natural History*, 443-44; Gosse, *Naturalist's Sojourn*, 354, 357; Brassey, *In the Trades*, 209.

55. Lindsay Drawings, Vol. VI, n.p.; Migdalski and Fichter, *Fresh and Salt Water Fishes*, 22, 295-96.

56. Smylie, *Herring*, 10-11, 53.

57. Ibid., 24, 38-39; Migdalski and Fichter, *Fresh and Salt Water Fishes*, 104-5.

58. Smylie, *Herring*, 56-57, 180-82.

59. Wood, *Letters of Simon Taylor*, 11; Hall, *In Miserable Slavery*, 177; Stewart, *View*, 268; Philip Wright, *Knibb "the Notorious": Slaves' Missionary, 1803-1845* (London: Sidgwick and Jackson, 1973), 242.

60. *Gleaner*, 6 January 1890, 3; 10 February 1890, 4; 7 February 1900, 5; 20 March 1900, 3; Smylie, *Herring*, 81-83.

61. Sullivan, *Jamaica Cookery Book*, 18-19, 100; "From Herrings to Beef: Our Elevation to That Dietary Superiority, and How We Produce the Beef", *Planters' Punch* 4, no. 2 (1939-40): 13.

62. *Gleaner, Food Supplement*, 22 March 1990, 16; 12 July 1990, 31; *Gleaner, Home, Living and Food Guide*, 14 July 1994, 23; Smylie, *Herring*, 11.

63. Benghiat, *Traditional Jamaican Cookery*, 35; Donaldson, *Real Taste*, 21; Burke, *Walkerswood*, 19.

64. Sullivan, *Jamaica Cookery Book*, 97; Newnham-Davis, *Dinners and Diners*, 293-95; *Gleaner*, 17 August 1918, 11; Brandon, *Merry-Go-Round*, 30-31.

65. Smylie, *Herring*, 146-47; De Mers, *Food of Jamaica*, 123; www.Jamaican-recipes.com, 15 September 2005.

66. *The Times*, 23 July 1788; 1 January 1789, 2.

67. Glasse, *Art of Cookery*, 59–60, 84; Briggs, *New Art of Cookery*, 485–86.

68. Lindsay Drawings, Vol. VII, n.p.; Migdalski and Fichter, *Fresh and Salt Water Fishes*, 106.

69. Donaldson, *Real Taste*, 55; Sullivan, *Jamaica Cookery Book*, 99.

70. Migdalski and Fichter, *Fresh and Salt Water Fishes*, 278.

71. Sloane, *Voyage*, 1: xviii; Sullivan, *Jamaica Cookery Book*, 19; *Gleaner*, 19 January 1880.

72. *Gleaner, Food Supplement*, 27 June 1968, 11; 7 February 1985, 24; 14 November 1985, 19; *Gleaner*, 26 February 1987, 1; *Gleaner, Flair Magazine*, 24 March 1987, 6.

73. Lindsay Drawings, Vol. VII, n.p.; Browne, *Civil and Natural History*, 453; Sullivan, *Jamaica Cookery Book*, 7; *Gleaner*, 13 May 1946, 1; Chapman, *Pleasure Island*, 100; Donaldson, *Real Taste*, 55.

74. Browne, *Civil and Natural History*, 453; Jamaica Agricultural Society, *Farmer's Food Manual*, 158; Donaldson, *Real Taste*, 58.

75. *Gleaner*, 17 December 1867, 3; 17 January 1880; *Gleaner, Food Supplement*, 18 July 1985, 19; Migdalski and Fichter, *Fresh and Salt Water Fishes*, 106.

76. Harold A. Innis, *The Cod Fisheries: The History of an International Economy* (Toronto: University of Toronto Press, 1954), 3–6; Mark Kurlansky, *Cod: A Biography of the Fish That Changed the World* (London: Vintage, 1999), 32–33; Richard L. Haedrich and Lawrence C. Hamilton, "The Fall and Future of Newfoundland's Cod Fishery", *Society and Natural Resources* 13 (2000): 360.

77. Shannon Ryan, *Fish out of Water: The Newfoundland Saltfish Trade 1814-1914* (St John's, NL, Canada: Breakwater, 1986), 29; Innis, *Cod Fisheries*, 6.

78. Behrendt, "Markets, Transaction Cycles, and Profits", 179; Kurlansky, *Cod*, 80–81; Innis, *Cod Fisheries*, 118; Ryan, *Fish out of Water*, 30–33, 41–43.

79. *Gleaner*, 6 January 1890, 3; 2 March 1900, 2; 1 May 1900, 3; Ryan, *Fish out of Water*, 226–34; Innis, *Cod Fisheries*, 472.

80. Stewart, *View*, 268; Glasse, *Art of Cookery*, 114; Sullivan, *Jamaica Cookery Book*, 17–21, 99–100; Leader, *Through Jamaica with a Kodak*, 142.

81. De Lisser, "Christina's Dream", 18; Whitbourne, "Ordinary Diet in Jamaica", 69; *Gleaner*, 14 January 1905, 10; 23 November 1940, 16; 19 February 1942, 8; 26 September 1948, 6.

82. Kurlansky, *Cod*, 162–73; Haedrich and Hamilton, "Fall and Future", 359–66.

83. *Gleaner*, 5 March 1938, 24; 10 March 1986, 1; 31 July 1988, 9A; *Gleaner, Food Supplement*, 5 January 1989, 14; *Gleaner*, 6 June 1991, 3.

84. *Gleaner, Magazine*, 1 September 1991, x; *Gleaner*, 31 October 1991, 1 and 6.

85. *Gleaner*, 20 October 1993, 6; 18 January 1996, 11A; Donaldson, *Real Taste*, 55.

86. Sullivan, *Jamaica Cookery Book*, 17–18; De Lisser, "Haunted", 24; "Melinda", 6; *Gleaner*, 19 February 1942, 8; *Jamaica Observer*, 13 May 1994, 42; Kurlansky, *Cod*, 91.

87. *Gleaner*, 10 May 1930, 9; 15 March 1932, 12; Sullivan, *Jamaica Cookery Book*, 18–21, 87.

88. *Gleaner*, 4 September 1918, 5.

Chapter 9

1. Roger W. Smith, "Jamaica's Own Birds", *Jamaica Journal* 2, no. 4 (1968): 18; Goodbody, "Avian Refugees", 59; Gosse, *Birds of Jamaica*, 76.

2. Lady [R.G.] Taylor, *Introduction to the Birds of Jamaica* (London: Macmillan, 1955), v; Herbert Raffaele, James Wiley, Orlando Garrido, Allan Keith, and Janis Raffaele, *Birds of the West Indies* (London: Christopher Helm, 2003), 84–85.

3. Ajai Mansingh and Laurie Hammond, "The Invasion of the Cattle Egrets", *Jamaica Journal* 11, nos 3/4 (1978): 57–59; Audrey Downer and Robert Sutton, *Birds of Jamaica: A Photographic Field Guide* (Cambridge, UK: Cambridge University Press, 1990), 39.

4. Blome, *Present State*, 21; Sloane, *Voyage*, 1: xvii.

5. An Act for regulating fowling and fishing, *Laws of Jamaica*, 1711, cap. XVI; Stewart, *View*, 208; Gosse, *Birds of Jamaica*, 295.

6. Gosse, *Birds of Jamaica*, 390–94; W.E.D. Scott, "Observations on the Birds of Jamaica, West Indies", *Auk* 8 (1891): 256, 357, 365; 10 (1893): 342; *Gleaner*, 2 January 1914, 13; Beckwith, *Black Roadways*, 35.

7. *Gleaner, Home, Living and Food Guide*, 26 August 1993, 20; Facey, *Busha Browne*, 60.

8. Derek Goodwin, *Pigeons and Doves of the World*, 3rd ed. (Ithaca, NY: Cornell University Press, 1983), 9–11.

9. Gosse, *Birds of Jamaica*, 293–94; Long, *History*, 3: 864–65; Lewis, *Journal*, 103; Stewart, *View*, 78; Senior, *Jamaica, as It Was*, 68; Phillippo, *Jamaica*, 55.

10. Beckford, *Descriptive Account*, 1: 326; Gosse, *Birds of Jamaica*, 292–93; Thomas, *Untrodden Jamaica*, 17–18; Raffaele et al., *Birds of the West Indies*, 86; Allan M. Strong and Matthew D. Johnson, "Exploitation of a Seasonal Resource by Nonbreeding Plain and White-Crowned Pigeons: Implications for Conservation of Tropical Dry Forests", *Wilson Bulletin* 113 (2001): 73; *Gleaner, Home, Living and Food Guide*, 26 August 1993, 20.

11. Gosse, *Birds of Jamaica*, 298; Strong and Johnson, "Exploitation of a Seasonal Resource", 73–77; Raffaele et al., *Birds of the West Indies*, 86.

12. Gosse, *Birds of Jamaica*, 299–300, 319; Long, *History*, 3: 864–65; Strong and Johnson, "Exploitation of a Seasonal Resource", 73.

13. Miller and Henry, *Creative Jamaican Cooking*, 21; Benghiat, *Traditional Jamaican Cookery*, 112–13; Roberts, *Hamper of Recipes*, 19; Hall, *In Miserable Slavery*, 102; Sullivan, *Jamaica Cookery Book*, 23, 115–17.

14. Gosse, *Birds of Jamaica*, 312; Goodwin, *Pigeons and Doves*, 187–88.

15. Browne, *Civil and Natural History*, 469; Gosse, *Birds of Jamaica*, 308–9.

16. Ibid., 304–6; Goodwin, *Pigeons and Doves*, 183–84; Raffaele et al., *Birds of the West Indies*, 86; Miller and Henry, *Creative Jamaican Cooking*, 22.

17. Gosse, *Birds of Jamaica*, 315; Goodwin, *Pigeons and Doves*, 206–7.

18. Dovaston, "Agricultura Americana", 2: 240; Lewis, *Journal*, 394–95; Stewart, *View*, 100; Miller and Henry, *Creative Jamaican Cooking*, 20–21.

19. Nugent, *Lady Nugent's Journal*, 76; Rampini, *Letters from Jamaica*, 92; Gosse, *Birds of Jamaica*, 270.

20. Susan E. Konig, "The Breeding Biology of Black-Billed Parrot *Amazona agilis* and Yellow-Billed Parrot *Amazona collaria* in Cockpit Country, Jamaica", *Bird Conservation International* 11 (2001): 205; Stuart T. Danforth, "Birds Observed in Jamaica during the Summer of 1926", *Auk* 45 (1928): 485; Raffaele et al., *Birds of the West Indies*, 92.

21. *Importance of Jamaica*, 38; Gosse, *Birds of Jamaica*, 210, 217 (italics in original); Long, *History*, 3: 896; Downer and Sutton, *Birds of Jamaica*, 100.

22. Gosse, *Birds of Jamaica*, 170; Lack, *Island Biology*, 292; Downer and Sutton, *Birds of Jamaica*, 97.

23. Gosse, *Birds of Jamaica*, 178–80; *Gleaner*, 20 November 1926, 19; 13 September 1959, 18.

24. Long, *History*, 3: 864; Stewart, *View*, 80; Gosse, *Birds of Jamaica*, 229–30.

25. Long, *History*, 3: 864; Stewart, *View*, 79; Gosse, *Birds of Jamaica*, 353; Hall, *In Miserable Slavery*, 123, 127–28; Miller and Henry, *Creative Jamaican Cooking*, 23.

26. Downer and Sutton, *Birds of Jamaica*, 36, 56; Raffaele et al., *Birds of the West Indies*, 30.

27. Gosse, *Birds of Jamaica*, 434; *Gleaner*, 27 April 1883, 2; 24 April 1884, 2; 17 May 1884, 2; 23 April 1885, 2.

28. Scott, "Observations on the Birds of Jamaica", 360–61; Beckwith, *Black Roadways*, 52; Pringle, *Waters of the West*, 62; *Gleaner*, 24 January 1969, 2; 26 September 1984, 23.

29. Gosse, *Birds of Jamaica*, 414.

30. Nugent, *Lady Nugent's Journal*, 41.

31. Hall, *In Miserable Slavery*, 221, 223; Dovaston, "Agricultura Americana", 2: 240; Gosse, *Birds of Jamaica*, 396–99, 403.

32. *Present State of Jamaica*, 18; Stewart, *View*, 99–100; Benghiat, *Traditional Jamaican Cookery*, 114; Donaldson, *Real Taste*, 82; *Gleaner*, *Food Supplement*, 7 March 1985, 23; 25 July 1985, 31; *Gleaner*, 14 July 1989, 1.

33. Kevin C. MacDonald and Rachel Hutton MacDonald, "The Origins and Development of Domesticated Animals in Arid West Africa", in *The Origins and Development of African Livestock: Archaeology, Genetics, Linguistics and Ethnography*, ed. Roger M. Blench and Kevin C. MacDonald (London: UCL Press, 2000), 142–44; Mignon-Grasteau et al., "Genetics of Adaptation", 5.

34. Gosse, *Birds of Jamaica*, 325–27, 443; *Gleaner*, 2 January 1914, 13; Raffaele et al., *Birds of the West Indies*, 84.

35. Gosse, *Birds of Jamaica*, 327; Sullivan, *Jamaica Cookery Book*, 115–17; Miller and Henry, *Creative Jamaican Cooking*, 19–20; Benghiat, *Traditional Jamaican Cookery*, 115.

36. Stewart, *View*, 100; Long, *History*, 3: 864–65; Downer and Sutton, *Birds of Jamaica*, 48; Gosse, *Birds of Jamaica*, 361–63.

37. *Gleaner*, *Food Supplement*, 16 May 1985, 23; *Gleaner*, *Pure Class*, 29 May 2005, 9.

38. Akishinonomiya Fumihito et al., "One Subspecies of the Red Junglefowl (*Gallus gallus gallus*) Suffices as the Matriarchic Ancestor of all Domestic Breeds", *Proceedings of the National Academy of Sciences of the United States of America* 91 (1994): 12505–9; Kay Williamson, "Did Chickens Go West?", in *The Origins and Development of African Livestock: Archaeology, Genetics, Linguistics and Ethnography*, ed. Roger M. Blench and Kevin C. MacDonald (London: UCL

Press, 2000), 368–448; MacDonald and MacDonald, "Origins and Development of Domesticated Animals", 142; Mignon-Grasteau et al., "Genetics of Adaptation", 5.

39. Karin E. Schütz and Per Jensen, "Effects of Resource Allocation on Behavioural Strategies: A Comparison of Red Junglefowl (*Gallus gallus*) and Two Domesticated Breeds of Poultry", *Ethology*, 107 (2001): 754; International Chicken Genome Sequencing Consortium, "Sequence and Comparative Analysis of the Chicken Genome Provide Unique Perspectives on Vertebrate Evolution", *Nature* 432 (2004): 712.

40. *Present State of Jamaica*, 18; Browne, *Civil and Natural History*, 25, 470; Stewart, *View*, 268.

41. *Gleaner*, 11 January 1896, 8; 5 January 1938, 5; 13 May 1946, 1; Gaunt, *Reflection*, 215–16; Aspinall, *British West Indies*, 212.

42. Chapman, *Pleasure Island*, 98; *Gleaner*, 22 March 1941, 13; 2 January 1960, 9.

43. *Gleaner*, 16 January 1987, 15; 21 December 1994, 7D; *Gleaner, Food Supplement*, 12 July 1990, 33.

44. Dixon, *Changing Chicken*, 164; Horowitz, *Putting Meat on the American Table*, 103; *Gleaner, Home, Living and Food Guide*, 13 May 1993, 20.

45. *Gleaner, Food Supplement*, 22 April 1965, 10; *The Economics of Good Nutrition, No. 1: Budgeting*, Nutrition Education Series No. 1 (Kingston: Scientific Research Council, 1971), 12; Clark, *West Indian Cookery*, 133; Jamaica Agricultural Society, *Farmer's Food Manual*, 235; Holzberg, *Minorities and Power*, 51.

46. Cuff, *Taste*, 8; *Gleaner, Food Supplement*, 21 March 1985, 22; 24 September 1987, 32; 29 October 1987, 23.

47. *Gleaner*, 5 October 1988, 25; Clark, *West Indian Cookery*, 75–76, 132–33; Jamaica Agricultural Society, *Farmer's Food Manual*, 235.

48. *Peas Please*, 3, 33; *Best of Creative Cooking*, 2; Donaldson, *Real Taste*, 149.

49. Sullivan, *Jamaica Cookery Book*, 115–17; Lindsay, "Elegancies of Jamaica", 49; *Gleaner*, 9 September 1971, 19.

50. Chapman, *Pleasure Island*, 98; Donaldson, *Real Taste*, 70; *Gleaner, Home, Living and Food Guide*, 14 July 1994, 23; *Coalpot Recipe Postcards*.

51. *Gleaner, Home, Food and Living Guide*, 22 November 1990, 30; 19 December 1991, 8C; 21 April 1994, 30; *Gleaner*, 21 May 1995, 7C; *Jamaica Observer, Thursday Life*, 12 May 2005, 8.

52. *Gleaner, Food Supplement*, 23 January 1986, 20; 30 March 1989, 17; *Gleaner*, January–April 1938.

53. *Gleaner, Food Supplement*, 26 January 1989, 22; *Gleaner, Home, Food and Living Guide*, 17 January 1991, 20; 23 July 1991, 3; *Jamaican Herald*, 5 June 2005, 12B.

54. *Gleaner, Home, Food and Living Guide*, 17 January 1991, 20; *Gleaner*, 6 November 1994, 1; 28 May 2000, 1A.

55. *Gleaner, Food Supplement*, 1 February 1990, 20; *Gleaner, Supermarket Supplement*, 16 December 1993, 11; *Gleaner, Home, Living and Food Guide*, 16 March 1995, 8B; *Jamaica Observer, Thursday Life*, 12 May 2005, 8–9.

56. *Gleaner*, 25 January 1992, 6; 24 December 1993; 20 March 1996, 16A.

57. *Gleaner, Food Supplement*, 7 March 1985, 20; 21 March 1985, 26; *Gleaner*, 16 September 1991, 2; 18 January 1996, 11A.

58. Lewicki, *West African Food*, 112; Sullivan, *Jamaica Cookery Book*, 96–97, 115.

59. *Gleaner*, 2 January 1960, 9; 18 May 2005, D11; *Jamaica Observer*, 18 May 2005, 15B.

60. *Gleaner*, 21 December 1940, 3; Donaldson, *Real Taste*, 136; *Gleaner, Pure Class*, 29 May 2005, 9.

61. *Gleaner*, 12 May 2005, C3–4; 19 May 2005, A9; *Gleaner, Pure Class*, 29 May 2005, 9.

Chapter 10

1. Farr, "Land Animals of Jamaica", 41.

2. *Gleaner*, 18 October 1938, 12.

3. Moore and Johnson, *Land We Live In*, 37; *Gleaner*, 29 March 1938, 5.

4. An Act for preventing damages in plantations, preserving of cattle and regulating hunting, *Laws of Jamaica*, 1681, cap. X.

5. Diamond, *Guns, Germs and Steel*, 162–63; Mignon-Grasteau et al., "Genetics of Adaptation", 4–5.

6. Clutton-Brock, *Domesticated Animals*, 189–92; Diamond, *Guns, Germs and Steel*, 158–75; Mignon-Grasteau et al., "Genetics of Adaptation", 6; Stephen J.G. Hall, *Livestock Biodiversity: Genetic Resources for the Farming of the Future* (Oxford: Blackwell, 2004), 12–15.

7. J.C.T. van den Berg, *Strategy for Dairy Development in the Tropics and Subtropics* (Wageningen, Netherlands: PUDOC, 1990), 11–25; Long, *History*, 3: 865; Blome, *Present State*, 20.

8. Margaret C. Neville and Marianne R. Neifert, "An Introduction to Lactation and Breast-Feeding", in *Lactation: Physiology, Nutrition, and Breast-Feeding*, ed. Margaret C. Neville and Marianne R. Neifert (New York: Plenum, 1983), 3–5; G.J. Ebrahim, *Breast Feeding: The Biological Option* (London: Macmillan, 1978), 2, 39–41.

9. Stanley F. Gould, "Anatomy of the Breast", in *Lactation: Physiology, Nutrition, and Breast-Feeding*, ed. Margaret C. Neville and Marianne R. Neifert (New York: Plenum, 1983), 46–47; Derrick B. Jelliffe and E.F. Patrice Jelliffe, *Human Milk in the Modern World: Psychosocial, Nutritional, and Economic Significance* (Oxford: Oxford University Press, 1978), 9–25.

10. R. Perezescamilla, "Breast-Feeding in Africa and the Latin-American and Caribbean Region: The Potential Role of Urbanization", *Journal of Tropical Pediatrics* 40 (1994): 137–43; Herbert S. Klein and Stanley L. Engerman, "Fertility Differentials between Slaves in the United States and the British West Indies: A Note on Lactation Practices and Their Possible Implications", *William and Mary Quarterly* 35 (1978): 357–74; Jerome S. Handler and Robert S. Corruccini, "Weaning among West Indian Slaves: Historical and Bioanthropological Evidence from Barbados", *William and Mary Quarterly* 43 (1986): 111–17.

11. Simon Taylor, Kingston, to Chaloner Arcedeckne, London, 5 July 1789, 3A/1789/20 Vanneck/Arcedeckne Papers; Simon Taylor, Kingston, to Chaloner Arcedeckne, London, 5 August 1789, 3A/1789/24 Vanneck/Arcedeckne Papers; Helen K. Henderson and Richard N. Henderson, "Traditional Onitsha Ibo Maternity Beliefs and Practices", in *Anthropology of Human Birth*, ed. Margarita Artyschwager Kay (Philadelphia: F.A. Davis, 1982), 187–88;

Elisa Janine Sobo, *One Blood: The Jamaican Body* (Albany: State University of New York Press, 1993), 68–69.

12. Beckwith, *Black Roadways*, 58; *Jamaica Public Health* 3, no. 1 (1928): 3; Jamaica Agricultural Society, *Farmer's Food Manual*, 101.

13. Vernal S. Packard, *Human Milk and Infant Formula* (New York: Academic Press, 1982), 1–6; Jacqueline P. Landman and Violet Shaw-Lyon, "Breast-Feeding in Decline in Kingston, Jamaica, 1973", *West Indian Medical Journal* 25 (1976): 43–57; Jelliffe and Jelliffe, *Human Milk*, 213–19; Bernice L. Hausman, *Mother's Milk: Breastfeeding Controversies in American Culture* (New York: Routledge, 2003), 7–16.

14. Ebrahim, *Breast Feeding*; Caribbean Food and Nutrition Institute, *Breastfeeding – Before and After* (Kingston: Caribbean Food and Nutrition Institute and UNICEF, 1979); *Gleaner, Outlook*, 19 May 1996, 13.

15. Lake, "Cultural Beliefs and Breastfeeding Practices", 206, 209; Jamaica, Ministry of Health, "Jamaica Serious about Breastfeeding", *Cajanus* 27, no. 3 (1994): 119; *Gleaner*, 4 October 1996, D1; 24 May 1998, 11A; 9 April 2000, 8A; Diane Renaud, "Improving Childhood Nutrition: Breastfeeding and Beyond", *Cajanus*, 34, no. 4 (2001): 171–73; Leia M. Chatman, Hamisu M. Salihu, Michele E.A. Roofe, Patrick Wheatle, Donnadeen Henry, and Pauline E. Jolly, "Influence of Knowledge and Attitudes on Exclusive Breastfeeding Practice among Rural Jamaican Mothers", *Birth* 31, no. 4 (2004): 268; Lawrence M. Gartner, Jane Morton, Ruth A. Lawrence, Audrey J. Naylor, et al., "Breastfeeding and the Use of Human Milk", *Pediatrics* 115 (2005): 496–506.

16. Nugent, *Lady Nugent's Journal*, 169; Pringle, *Waters of the West*, 114.

17. Clark, *West Indian Cookery*, 241–45; *Planters' Punch* 4, no. 3 (1940–41): 25; Jamaica Agricultural Society, *Farmer's Food Manual*, 167–68.

18. Hickeringill, *Jamaica Viewed*, 59 (italics in original); Richard W. Bulliet, *Hunters, Herders, and Hamburgers: The Past and Future of Human-Animal Relationships* (New York: Columbia University Press, 2005), 106; Reay Tannahill, *Flesh and Blood: A History of the Cannibal Complex* (New York: Dorset, 1975), 154–58; W. Arens, *The Man-Eating Myth: Anthropology and Anthropophagy* (New York: Oxford University Press, 1979); Peggy Reeves Sanday, *Divine Hunger: Cannibalism as a Cultural System* (Cambridge, UK: Cambridge University Press, 1986); Fiddes, *Meat*, 123; Harris, *Good to Eat*, 220–21; Peter Hulme, *Colonial Encounters: Europe and the Native Caribbean, 1492–1797* (London: Methuen, 1986), 78–87.

19. MacDonald and MacDonald, "Origins and Development of Domesticated Animals", 129–35; Lewicki, *West African Food*, 81–86; Berg, *Strategy for Dairy Development*, 14–18.

20. G. Williamson and W.J.A. Payne, *An Introduction to Animal Husbandry in the Tropics* (London: Longmans, 1959), 146–47, 154; Aspinall, *British West Indies*, 210.

21. *Gleaner*, 5 December 1993, 9A; 14 November 1996, A4; Ministry of Agriculture, *The Development of the Jamaica Red Poll Breed of Cattle*, Animal Husbandry Bulletin No. 3 (Kingston: Ministry of Agriculture, Agricultural Information Service, 1979); Ministry of Agriculture, *The Development of the Jamaica Brahman Breed of Beef Cattle*, Animal Husbandry Bulletin No. 4 (Kingston: Ministry of Agriculture, Research and Development Division, 1983), 69.

22. Blome, *Description of the Island*, 4; Cattle and Dairy Industry, Report 20 December 1933, C.O. 137/803/12 (National Archives, London); *Gleaner*, 2 January 1960, 9.

23. Simon Taylor, Kingston, to Chaloner Arcedeckne, London, 1 May 1787, 3A/1787/6 Vanneck/Arcedeckne Papers; Nugent, *Lady Nugent's Journal*, 110; Ward, *Trip to Jamaica*, 13; Long, *History*, 3: 866; Aspinall, *British West Indies*, 211.

24. Jelliffe and Jelliffe, *Human Milk*, 172; Marie-Claude Mahias, "Milk and Its Transmutations in Indian Society", *Food and Foodways* 2 (1988): 266; Lewicki, *West African Food*, 124; Dovaston, "Agricultura Americana", 2: 230.

25. Jamaica Agricultural Society, *Farmer's Food Manual*, 75; E. Melanie Dupuis, *Nature's Perfect Food: How Milk Became America's Drink* (New York: New York University Press, 2002), 17–45; *Jamaica Public Health* 3, no. 7 (1928): 2; 5, no. 2 (1930): 19–20; 6, no. 10 (1931): 137; 8, no. 8 (1933): 106; *West India Committee Circular* 47 (29 September 1932): 391.

26. *Gleaner*, 27 June 1914, 1; 8 March 1933, 3; 7 February 1938, 13; 25 October 1938, 4; *Planters' Punch* 4, no. 1 (1938–39): 22; P.D.L. Guilbride, Viola Mae Young, and Jeanette Norsen, "A Bacteriological Survey of Milk and Milk Products in Jamaica", *West Indian Medical Journal* 4 (1955): 44; Hyatt, *When Me Was a Boy*, 95.

27. *Gleaner, Food Supplement*, 28 November 1968, vi; *Gleaner*, 3 May 1985, 1; 24 June 1989, 7; Henk Jan Bierling and Dick Vos, "Milk Distribution by Pushcart Vendors in Kingston, Jamaica", *Caribbean Geography* 2 (1988): 195–202.

28. Jamaica Agricultural Society, *Farmer's Food Manual*, 169; *Gleaner*, 14 September 1889, 1; 1 March 1900, 5.

29. *Gleaner, Business and Industry Supplement*, 25 August 1992, 6; Vin Lumsden, "Jamaica's Dairy Industry: A Perspective", *Cajanus* 26 (1993): 186–90; *Gleaner*, 13 May 1986, 15; 26 July 1998, 2A.

30. *Gleaner, Food Supplement*, 18 January 1990, 18; *Gleaner, Business and Industry Supplement*, 25 August 1992, 6; *Gleaner, Home, Living and Food Guide*, 1 October 1992, 30; *Gleaner*, 7 August 1994, 2A; Kevin Morgan, Terry Marsden, and Jonathan Murdoch, *Worlds of Food: Place, Power, and Provenance in the Food Chain* (Oxford: Oxford University Press, 2006), 30.

31. *Gleaner*, 3 March 2006, 3; Dupuis, *Nature's Perfect Food*, 215–19; Nicholas Scott Cardell and Mark Myron Hopkins, "The Effect of Milk Intolerance on the Consumption of Milk by Slaves in 1860", *Journal of Interdisciplinary History* 8 (1978): 507–13.

32. *Gleaner*, 10 November 1865, 2; 20 January 1866, 2; 18 March 1880, 4; 16 November 1880, 3.

33. *Gleaner*, 30 October 1890, 2; 2 January 1900, 5; 3 January 1900, 3.

34. *Gleaner*, 27 June 1914, 1; Moore and Johnson, *"Squalid Kingston"*, 110, 118; Cattle and Dairy Industry, Report; *Gleaner*, 26 August 1933, 1; 22 December 1933, 1, 6; 14 March 1938, 12.

35. *Gleaner*, 16 March 1938, 12; 18 March 1938, 12; *Jamaica Public Health*, 6, no. 10 (1931), 137; Jamaica Agricultural Society, *Farmer's Food Manual*, 168–69; *Gleaner*, 25 June 1994, 16.

36. *Gleaner*, 29 March 1940, 10; 24 August 1940, 6; 8 November 1940, 1; 6 September 1941, 1; *Planters' Punch* 4, no. 4 (1941–42): 19.

37. Jamaica Agricultural Society, *Farmer's Food Manual*, 168; Spence, *Jamaican Cookery*, 4; *Gleaner, Food Supplement*, 6 December 1984, 31; Cuff, *Taste*, 15; Murray and Lewin, *Jamaican Chef*, 36; Ebanks, *Rastafari Cookbook*, 58.

38. *Gleaner*, 15 June 1985, 1; *Gleaner, Business and Industry Supplement*, 25 August 1992, 7.

39. *Nestlé Quick 'n' Easy Desserts and Drinks* (Kingston: Food Specialities Jamaica, [c. 1988]), 3; Donaldson, *Real Taste*, 131; Pringle, *Waters of the West*, 42; *Planters' Punch* 4, no. 1 (1938–39): 27; *Gleaner*, 2 April 1943, 4.

40. Long, *History*, 3: 810; Long, *Free and Candid Review*, 71.

41. Sullivan, *Jamaica Cookery Book*, 118; *Gleaner*, 7 January 1918, 10; 11 April 1933, 6; Jamaica: Agriculture – Economic Survey: Cattle and Dairy Industry, 31 August 1934, C.O. 137/803/12 (National Archives, London).

42. *Planters' Punch* 4, no. 2 (1939–40): 41; 4, no. 3 (1940–41): 58, 83; *Gleaner*, 14 November 1993, 16A; 6 March 1920, 13.

43. Accounts Current, Liber 1, ff. 80–85; *Gleaner*, 3 January 1900, 1; Cattle and Dairy Industry, Report.

44. *Gleaner*, 9 July 1985, 2; *Gleaner, Food Supplement*, 20 March 1986, ii; *Jamaica Observer, Pure Class*, 23 January 1994, 6.

45. *A Jamaican Cheese Cookbook* (Kingston: Dairy Industries Jamaica, 1988); *Gleaner, Cheese Month Supplement*, 2 July 1988; *Gleaner*, 27 October 1988, 30–32.

46. *Gleaner*, 11 April 1866, 2; 5 March 1869, 4; Clarence Henry Eckles, Willes Barnes Combs, and Harold Macy, *Milk and Milk Products* (New York: McGraw-Hill, 1951), 290; Glasse, *Art of Cookery*, 168.

47. Rampini, *Letters from Jamaica*, 34–35; *Gleaner*, 8 February 1890, 2; 27 December 1890, 8; 3 April 1900, 5.

48. "Eating Goes Modern", 12; *Gleaner*, 24 January 1942, 9; 8 July 1945, 5; 20 April 1991, 3; 10 April 2005, J6; 7 October 2005, D2.

49. Aspinall, *British West Indies*, 210; Hall, *In Miserable Slavery*, 261; *Gleaner*, 30 January 1914.

50. *Gleaner*, 16 July 1914, 14; 26 January 1918, 3; N.T.M. Yeates, *Modern Aspects of Animal Production* (London: Butterworths, 1965), 171.

51. *Gleaner*, 15 January 1918, 3; 3 February 1933, 3; *Planters' Punch* 3, no. 3 (1934–35): 111; Restriction of Beef Importation, C.S.O. 1B/5/77/1933/251 (Jamaica Archives, Spanish Town).

52. Cattle and Dairy Industry, Report; *Gleaner*, 15 April 1933, 1; 30 December 1933, 12; 5 January 1943, 5; 8 May 1946, 8; Donaldson, *Real Taste*, 29.

53. *Gleaner, Feedtime Supplement*, 10 June 1989, 6; *Gleaner*, 7 October 1995, 12C; 14 February 2001, A2; 26 October 2002, A3. See also P.A. Barton-Gade, B.B. Chrystall, A.H. Kirton, G.R. Longdill, H.R. Cross and M. Jespersen, "Slaughter Procedures for Pigs, Sheep, Cattle and Poultry", in *Meat Science, Milk Science and Technology*, ed. H.R. Cross and A.J. Overby (Amsterdam: Elsevier Science, 1988), 33–82.

54. *Gleaner*, 23 April 1884, 1; 8 July 1889, 2; Holzberg, *Minorities and Power*, 51.

55. Sullivan, *Jamaica Cookery Book*, 15–22; An Act appointing the prices of meat, *Laws of Jamaica*, 1681, cap. IV; An Act appointing the price of meat, and regulating markets, *Laws of Jamaica*, 1693, cap. VI; *Gleaner*, 15 May 1946, 8.

56. Beeton, *Mrs Beeton's*, 276; Anissa Helou, *The Fifth Quarter* (Bath, UK: Absolute Press, 2004), 8–9; "From Herrings to Beef", 13; *Gleaner, Sunday Magazine*, 18 June 1989, ii.

57. *Gleaner, Food Supplement*, 24 September 1964, 12; 9 February 1984, 22; *Gleaner, Supermarket Shopping Guide*, 24 January 1991, 5D; *Gleaner*, 16 September 1991, 2.

58. Hall, *In Miserable Slavery*, 88, 261; *Festival 70*, 14.

59. *Gleaner*, 16 June 1871, 2; 9 August 1881, 3; 3 March 1900, 5; 20 March 1900, 3; Donaldson, *Real Taste*, 90; Benghiat, *Traditional Jamaican Cookery*, 95; Helou, *Fifth Quarter*, 56.

60. *Gleaner, Food Supplement*, 3 October 1985, 18; 25 June 1987, 16; *Gleaner, Home, Living and Food Guide*, 12 March 1992, 23; 1 July 1993, 29.

61. Moore and Johnon, *"Squalid Kingston"*, 68; *Gleaner*, 20 March 1900, 3; Beckwith, *Black Roadways*, 45; *Festival 70*, addendum 5; *Peas Please*, 26; Benghiat, *Traditional Jamaican Cookery*, 98; Murray and Lewin, *Jamaican Chef*, 14; *Gleaner, Home, Living and Food Guide*, 30 September 1993, 34; *Jamaica, Finest Taste*, 84; Donaldson, *Real Taste*, 91.

62. *Festival 70*, 6; Benghiat, *Traditional Jamaican Cookery*, 99, 144; *Gleaner, Food Supplement*, 20 August 1987, 19–20; 11 August 1988, 22; *Gleaner, Home, Living and Food Guide*, 1 October 1992, 30; Donaldson, *Real Taste*, 90; *Jamaica, Finest Taste*, 95.

63. Scientific Research Council, *Sample Menus*, 2; Quinn, *Jamaican Cooking*, xix; *Gleaner, Food Supplement*, 3 October 1985, 18; 6 March 1986, 22.

64. *Gleaner*, 30 September 1992, 1; *Gleaner, Outlook*, 21 May 1995, 4; Powell et al., *Street Foods of Kingston*, 33.

65. Williams, *Tour through the Island*, 14–15; Cleary, *Jamaica Run-dung*, 23; *Festival 70*, 6; *Festival 71*, 14, 24; Murray and Lewin, *Jamaican Chef*, 11.

66. Sloane, *Voyage*, 1: xvi; Marsden, *Account*, 12; *Gleaner*, 24 April 1942, 6; 13 May 1946, 1; Thompson, *Black Caribbean*, 227; Chapman, *Pleasure Island*, 98.

67. Sullivan, *Jamaica Cookery Book*, 15–22; Chapman, *Pleasure Island*, 98; Donaldson, *Real Taste*, 90; Donaldson-Mignotte, "How Jamaicans Like Their Food", B8; *Jamaica Observer*, 14 November 2002, 30.

68. Sloane, *Voyage*, 1: xv–xvii; An English Merchant, *Some Modern Observations*, 17; Leslie, *New and Exact*, 34; Stewart, *View*, 94; *Importance of Jamaica*, 40.

69. *Gleaner*, 10 May 1930, 9; *Gleaner, Food Supplement*, 21 May 1986, 25.

70. *Gleaner*, 24 September 1938, 3; 19 August 1945, 5; 28 February 1940, 14; 23 May 1940, 14; "Eating Goes Modern", 12; *Gleaner, Food Supplement*, 7 March 1985, 19; Horowitz, *Putting Meat on the American Table*, 80.

71. *Gleaner*, 11 February 1985, 3; 5 October 1997, 8B; 6 December 1998, 11C, 15C, 12F.

72. Browne, *Civil and Natural*, 25; Hall, *In Miserable Slavery*, 123; Leslie, *New and Exact*, 34; Sloane, *Voyage*, 1: xvi; *Importance of Jamaica*, 40.

73. *Gall's News Letter*, 7 February 1880; *Gleaner*, 17 June 1880, 3; 29 May 1940, 5; Cattle and Dairy Industry, Report; Brandon, *Merry-Go-Round*, 51.

74. *Gleaner*, 26 August 1896, 8; 20 March 1900, 3; 2 July 1943, 1; *Gleaner, Home, Food and Living Guide*, 31 January 1991, 21.

75. *Gleaner, Food Supplement*, 21 May 1986, 34; 18 May 1989, 28; *Gleaner, Home, Food and Living Guide*, 31 January 1991, 21; 20 June 1991, 25; Chen, *Cooking with Lasco*, 12–15.

76. *Gleaner*, 22 January 1938, 19; 2 January 1960, 2; *Planters' Punch* 4, no. 1 (1938–39): 36, 66; 4, no. 3 (1940–41): 58.

77. *Gleaner*, 28 February 1938, 5; 8 November 1938, 10; *Gleaner, Food Supplement*, 9 July 1987, 27.

78. *Gleaner, Home, Food and Living Guide*, 17 January 1991, 20; Donaldson, *Real Taste*, 90; *Gleaner*, 15 July 1938, 3; 7 February 1938, 18; 23 February 1938, 18; 9 March 1938, 10; 23 March 1938, 7; 2 April 1938, 23; 30 April 1938, 33.

79. *Gleaner*, 18 January 1945, 9; 24 January 1945, 9; 7 February 1945, 14; 13 February 1945, 9; 21 February 1945, 9; 8 March 1945, 5.

80. Roger M. Blench, "The History of Pigs in Africa", in *The Origins and Development of African Livestock: Archaeology, Genetics, Linguistics and Ethnography*, ed. Roger M. Blench and Kevin C. MacDonald (London: UCL Press, 2000), 355–67.

81. Hickeringill, *Jamaica Viewed*, 10, 13; Sloane, *Voyage*, 1: xvii; Blome, *Present State*, 20; Ward, *Trip to Jamaica*, 13.

82. Leslie, *New and Exact*, 34; Long, *History*, 3: 764, 866; Dovaston, "Agricultura Americana", 2: 240–41; Lunan, *Hortus Jamaicensis*, 1: 38; Williams, *Tour through the Island*, 198, 316; Stewart, *View*, 74–75, 98, 208; Pringle, *Waters of the West*, 36–37.

83. Aspinall, *British West Indies*, 212; *Gleaner*, 25 February 1918, 13; Chapman, *Pleasure Island*, 100; Cattle and Dairy Industry, Report.

84. *Gleaner, Feedtime Supplement*, 10 June 1989, 4, 12.

85. *Importance of Jamaica*, 40; Dovaston, "Agricultura Americana", 2: 243; Long, *History*, 3: 866.

86. Scott, *To Jamaica and Back*, 105; Stewart, *View*, 74–75, 208; Lewis, *Journal*, 151; Briggs, *New Art of Cookery*, 224; Senior, *Jamaica, as It Was*, 70.

87. Nugent, *Lady Nugent's Journal*, 156.

88. Sloane, *Voyage*, 1: xvi; Beckford, *Descriptive Account*, 1: 330; Scott, *To Jamaica and Back*, 177; *Gleaner*, 16 August 1892, 6; ibid., 8 May 1896, 4.

89. Thomas, *Untrodden Jamaica*, 87; *Gleaner*, 19 November 1895, 4.

90. C.J. Ward, *World's Fair, Jamaica at Chicago: An Account of the Colony of Jamaica, with Historical and Other Appendices* (New York: W.J. Pell, 1893), 71; *Gleaner*, 29 June 1895, 4; Jane Carson, *Colonial Virginia Cookery: Procedures, Equipment and Ingredients in Colonial Cooking* (Williamsburg, VA: Colonial Williamsburg Foundation, 1985), 115.

91. Hurston, *Voodoo Gods*, 33–40, 272; Norma Benghiat, "In Search of the Original 'Jerkers'", in *A Tapestry of Jamaica: The Best of Skywritings, Air Jamaica's Inflight Magazine*, ed. Linda Gambrill (1988; Kingston: Creative Communications, 2003), 146–47; *Gleaner*, 28 September 1940, 26; Willinsky, *Jerk*, 8–11.

92. *Gleaner*, 10 May 1930, 9; *Gleaner, Food Supplement*, 24 September 1964, 16; 9 February 1984, 22; *Jamaica Observer*, 27 May 1994, 42.

93. Brady, "Drum Chicken", 150; Willinsky, *Jerk*, 4–11; Marchand et al., *Home Economics*, 82–83; Burke, *Eat Caribbean*, 120–24; *Caribbean Week*, 2 October 1993, 51; *Jamaica Observer, Splash*, 3 June 2005, 30.

94. *Gleaner*, 1 October 1996, B5.

95. Hurston, *Voodoo Gods*, 33–40, 272; An Act appointing the prices of meat, *Laws of Jamaica*, 1681, cap. IV; An Act appointing the price of meat, and regulating markets, *Laws of Jamaica*, 1693, cap. VI; *Gleaner*, 15 May 1946, 8.

96. Hall, *In Miserable Slavery*, 170, 223; *Gleaner, Food Supplement*, 21 May 1986, 25; Miller and Henry, *Creative Jamaican Cooking*, 28.

97. *Gleaner, Farmer's Weekly*, 15 October 1955, 5; *Gleaner*, 22 October 1955, 8; *Gleaner, Home, Living and Food Guide*, 2 September 1993, 28; Miller and Henry, *Creative Jamaican Cooking*, 29.

98. Dovaston, "Agricultura Americana", 2: 243–44.

99. *Gleaner*, 20 March 1900, 3; 8 December 1933, 8.

100. Browne, *Civil and Natural History*, 25; Stewart, *View*, 98; *Gleaner*, 6 January 1890, 1, 3; *Gleaner, Food Supplement*, 25 January 1990, 21.

101. Hall, *In Miserable Slavery*, 133; *Gleaner*, 20 March 1900, 3; 25 February 1918, 13; 1 December 1931, 2.

102. Sullivan, *Jamaica Cookery Book*, 22–23.

103. Bendley Melville, "The Importance of Goats in Agricultural Development and Health and Nutrition", *Cajanus* 21 (1988): 203–4; Ministry of Agriculture, *Goat Production Handbook* (Kingston: Ministry of Agriculture and Goat Breeders Society of Jamaica, 2001), 2, 6–10; *Gleaner, Home, Food and Living Guide*, 17 January 1991, 21; *Gleaner*, 1 October 1992, 27.

104. Blome, *Present State*, 20; Sloane, *Voyage*, 1: xvi; Leslie, *New and Exact*, 178; Gosse, *Naturalist's Sojourn*, 440; *Gleaner*, 25 February 1918, 13.

105. *Gleaner*, 15 May 1946, 8.

106. Achaya, *Historical Dictionary*, 83; *Gleaner*, 31 August 1941, 20; 12 June 1945, 2; *Gleaner, Food Supplement*, 24 September 1964, 11; Sullivan, *Jamaica Cookery Book*, 27.

107. *Gleaner, Food Supplement*, 24 September 1964, 11; *Gleaner*, 18 March 1870, 2; Lizzie Collingham, *Curry: A Biography* (London: Chatto and Windus, 2005), 139–42.

108. *Gleaner*, 24 March 1932, 14; 20 June 1933, 14; 5 August 1933, 6; 4 October 1934, 23; 27 July 1948, 8; Pringle, *Waters of the West*, 49.

109. *Gleaner*, 22 August 1934, 2; 26 March 1938, 31; 26 January 1940, 8; 23 July 1940, 14; Chapman, *Pleasure Island*, 98; Carley, *Jamaica*, 115.

110. *Gleaner*, 15 January 1988; 3 June 1993, 36; Melville, "Importance of Goats", 206; Donaldson, *Real Taste*, 9, 34, 93; *Gifts from a Jamaican Kitchen*, 17.

111. *Gleaner*, 3 December 1968, 28; 29 August 1974, 28; 28 November 1974, 42; 4 July 1975, 13; Hurston, *Voodoo Gods*, 13–14, 272.

112. Browne, *Civil and Natural History*, 488; Long, *History*, 3: 866; Sullivan, *Jamaica Cookery Book*, 23–29; Donaldson, *Real Taste*, 93; *Gleaner, Home, Living and Food Guide*, 2 September 1993, 28; McKay, *Banana Bottom*, 53, 188.

113. Long, *History*, 3: 866; Dovaston, "Agricultura Americana", 2: 239; Browne, *Civil and Natural History*, 488; Stewart, *View*, 97; Phillippo, *Jamaica*, 87.

114. *Gleaner*, 2 April 1917, 7; *Jamaica Public Health* 9, no. 7 (1934): 100; 21, no. 1 (1946): 5; Carley, *Jamaica*, 112; Jamaica Agricultural Society, *Farmer's Food Manual*, 168; Melville, "Importance of Goats", 204; *Gleaner*, 4 April 1964, 12; 25 June 1994, 16.

115. Dovaston, "Agricultura Americana", 2: 239; Long, *History*, 3 :866; Blome, *Present State*, 20; *Present State of Jamaica*, 17; Leslie, *New and Exact*, 34; Dovaston, "Agricultura Americana", 2: 240; Long, *History*, 3: 865; Stewart, *View*, 97; Phillippo, *Jamaica*, 86.

116. Sullivan, *Jamaica Cookery Book*, 22–23; An Act appointing the price of meat, and regulating markets, *Laws of Jamaica*, 1693, cap. VI.

117. *Gleaner*, 20 March 1900, 3; 15 April 1933, 1; 15 May 1946, 8; Cattle and Dairy Industry, Report.

118. Blome, *Present State*, 20; *Present State of Jamaica*, 17; Long, *History*, 3: 866; Gosse, *Naturalist's Sojourn*, 433–34; *Gleaner*, 20 January 1873, 3; 12 April 1873, 3; 3 November 1888, 2; 1 March 1899, 6.

119. MacDonald and MacDonald, "Origins and Development of Domesticated Animals", 141–42; Lewicki, *West African Food*, 87–88; M.Y. Kurtu, "An Assessment of the Productivity for Meat and the Carcass Yield of Camels (*Camelus dromedarius*) and the Consumption of Camel Meat in the Eastern Region of Ethiopia", *Tropical Animal Health and Production* 36 (2004): 65–76.

120. Browne, *Civil and Natural History*, 488; Hall, *In Miserable Slavery*, 59; Long, *History*, 3: 898.

121. Robin Law, *The Horse in West African History: The Role of the Horse in the Societies of Pre-colonial West Africa* (Oxford: Oxford University Press, 1980), 170; Lewicki, *West African Food*, 88–89; MacDonald and MacDonald, "Origins and Development of Domesticated Animals", 140; *Gleaner*, 6 April 1918, 12.

122. *Gleaner*, 25 January 1918, 8; 5 April 1918, 10; 12 April 1918, 13; 22 April 1918, 4.

123. Dodd, *Food of London*, 291; Harris, *Good to Eat*, 92, 103; *Gleaner*, 25 January 1918, 8; 5 April 1918, 10; 5 August 1942, 3; 2 July 1943, 1; 25 September 1988.

124. Nugent, *Lady Nugent's Journal*, 115–16; Cross and Overby, *Meat Science*, 177.

125. Blome, *Present State*, 20; *Present State of Jamaica*, 17; Long, *History*, 3: 866; Nugent, *Lady Nugent's Journal*, 160; Stewart, *View*, 98–99; Long, *History*, 3: 901; Gosse, *Naturalist's Sojourn*, 442–43.

126. *Gleaner*, *Food Supplement*, 30 May 1985, 21–22; Miller and Henry, *Creative Jamaican Cooking*, 26, 28–29.

127. Leslie, *New and Exact*, 35; Browne, *Civil and Natural History*, 25, 485; Long, *History*, 3: 901; "Characteristic Traits" 3 (July 1797): 108; Phillippo, *Jamaica*, 218; Rampini, *Letters from Jamaica*, 92; Pringle, *Waters of the West*, 49.

128. Watts, *West Indies*, 61, 226; Lewicki, *West African Food*, 89–90; Browne, *Civil and Natural History*, 25; Stewart, *View*, 101; Phillippo, *Jamaica*, 87.

129. Mary F. Richardson, "*Out of Many, One People* – Aspiration or Reality? An Examination of the Attitudes to the Various Racial and Ethnic Groups within the Jamaican Society", *Social and Economic Studies* 32 (1983): 144.

130. Sloane, *Voyage*, 1: xx; Leslie, *New and Exact*, 35; Browne, *Civil and Natural History*, 25; Long, *History*, 3: 899; Woodley, "History of the Jamaican Fauna", 19.

131. Farr, "Land Animals of Jamaica", 41; Long, *History*, 3: 901–2; "Characteristic Traits" 3 (July 1797): 108; Stewart, *View*, 75, 268.

132. *Marly*, 52–53; Phillippo, *Jamaica*, 218; Gosse, *Naturalist's Sojourn*, 443–45; Rampini, *Letters from Jamaica*, 92.

133. D.R. Rosevear, *The Rodents of West Africa* (London: British Museum [Natural History], 1969), 33, 542–47; Jacques Hardouin, "Developing Minilivestock as Source of Human Food, Animal Feed or Revenue: A Brief Overview", *Ecology of Food and Nutrition* 36 (1997): 98; H. Ahissou, T. Lebreton de Vonne, F. Esnard, and H. Mouray, "Evolution of Grass-Cutter (*Thryonomys swinderianus*) Inflammation Markers: Comparison with Rabbit (*Oryctolagus cuniculus*) and Rat (*Rattus norvegicus*)", *Comparative Biochemistry and Physiology* 118A (1997): 1309.

134. *Gleaner*, 29 March 1938, 5; 23 July 1961, 7; C.J. Allen, "Producing Animal Protein in Your Backyard", *Gleaner*, 27 June 1987, 8; *Gleaner*, 21 May 1992.

135. Woodley, "History of the Jamaican Fauna", 17; Hardouin, "Developing Minilivestock", 98–100.

136. *Present State of Jamaica*, 19; Gosse, *Naturalist's Sojourn*, 468–81; *Gleaner*, 19 November 1895, 4; 6 December 1945, 16; 19 March 1979, 16; 26 July 1981, 7; 16 October 2003, C1 and C5.

137. Natural Resources Conservation Department, *Marine Mammal of Jamaica: The West Indian Manatee* (Kingston: Jamaica Information Service, 1991); Melissa Cole and Brandon Cole, *Manatees* (Woodbridge, CT: Blackbirch, 2001); Lewicki, *West African Food*, 96.

138. Watts, *West Indies*, 62–63; Trapham, *Discourse on the State of Health*, 64; Sloane, 2: 329; Long, *History*, 3: 868.

139. An English Merchant, *Some Modern Observations*, 17; Lewis, *Journal*, 198–99; Gosse, *Naturalist's Sojourn*, 345–46; Rampini, *Letters from Jamaica*, 170.

140. Beckwith, *Black Roadways*, 33; Wendy Shaul and Ann Haynes, "Manatees and Their Struggle for Survival", *Jamaica Journal* 19, no. 3 (1986): 29; *Gleaner*, 29 May 1928, 14; 6 December 1945, 16; 3 July 1989, 23; 4 September 1991, 13; 14 December 1997, D2.

141. Andrew R. Solow, "Inferring Extinction from a Sighting Record", *Mathematical Biosciences* 195 (2005): 47–48, 53; I.L. Boyd and M.P. Stanfield, "Circumstantial Evidence for the Presence of Monk Seals in the West Indies", *Oryx* 32 (1998): 310–16; J.A. Allen, "The West Indian Seal (*Monachus tropicalis* Gray)", *Bulletin of the American Museum of Natural History* 2 (1887): 1–34; Karl W. Kenyon, "Monk Seals", in *Handbook of Marine Mammals*, vol. 2, *Seals*, ed. Sam H. Ridgway and Richard J. Harrison (London: Academic Press, 1981), 201–3; Robert M. Timm, Rosa M. Salazar, and A. Townsend Peterson, "Historical Distribution of the Extinct Tropical Seal, *Monachus tropicalis* (Carnivora: Phocidae)", *Conservation Biology* 11 (1997): 549–51; Gosse, *A Naturalist's Sojourn*, 307–14.

Chapter 11

1. Ebanks, *Rastafari Cookbook*, 11; Homiak, "Dub History", 144–50; Versada Campbell, *Caribbean Foodways* (Kingston: Caribbean Food and Nutrition Institute, 1988), 22; Burke, *Eat Caribbean*, 155.

2. Robert Mowbray Howard, ed., *Records and Letters of the Family of the Longs of Longville, Jamaica, and Hampton Lodge, Surrey* (London: Simpkin, Marshall, Hamilton, Kent and Co., 1925), 1: 48; Lewis, *Journal*, 106; Phillippo, *Jamaica*, 275; Sturge and Harvey, *West Indies in 1837*, 256; Moore and Johnson, *"Squalid Kingston"*, 56; A.S. Forrest and John Henderson, *Jamaica* (London: Adam and Charles Black, 1906), 39–40; *Gleaner*, 30 December 1933, 12.

3. H.G. De Lisser, "H.G.D. Discovers Jones Penn", *Planters' Punch* 4, no. 4 (1941–42): 8; Jamaica Agricultural Society, *Farmer's Food Manual*, 74–76.

4. A.E.T. Henry, "Farewell Saltfish, Goodbye Mackerel and So-Long Salt Beef", *Gleaner*, 14 January 1968, 8.

5. *Gleaner, Food Supplement*, 20 August 1987, 26; Campbell, Sinha, and Patterson, "KAP Study", 36; Powell et al., *Street Foods of Kingston*, 33–36; *Best of Creative Cooking*, 54; Stobart, *Herbs*, 222; Mark Kurlansky, *Salt: A World History* (London: Vintage, 2003), 399–401.

6. *Jamaica Observer*, 9 April 1995, 3; S.A.M. Adshead, *Salt and Civilization* (London: Macmillan, 1992), 142–43; Graham A. MacGregor and Hugh E. de Wardener, *Salt, Diet and Health: Neptune's Poisoned Chalice – The Origins of High Blood Pressure* (Cambridge, UK: Cambridge University Press, 1998), 218–19; Stobart, *Herbs*, 221.

7. MacGregor and Wardener, *Salt, Diet and Health*, 1–5; Adshead, *Salt and Civilization*, 7; Jay Schulkin, *Sodium Hunger: The Search for a Salty Taste* (Cambridge, UK: Cambridge University Press, 1991), 3–4, 138–39; Derek Denton, *The Hunger for Salt: An Anthropological, Physiological and Medical Analysis* (Berlin: Springer-Verlag, 1982), 172–73; Richard H. Forsythe and Ralph A. Miller, "Salt in Processed Foods", in *Biological and Behavioral Aspects of Salt Intake*, ed. Morley R. Kare, Melvin J. Fregly, and Rudy A. Bernard (New York: Academic Press, 1980), 221–28; M.R. Bloch, "The Social Influence of Salt", *Scientific American*, July 1963, 89.

8. Kurlansky, *Salt*, 427; Adshead, *Salt and Civilization*, 142–45; Paul E. Lovejoy, *Salt of the Desert Sun: A History of Salt Production and Trade in the Central Sudan* (Cambridge, UK: Cambridge University Press, 1986), 3; Robert P. Multhauf, *Neptune's Gift: A History of Common Salt* (Baltimore, MD: Johns Hopkins University Press, 1978), 216.

9. Blome, *Description of the Island*, 12; Hughes, *American Physitian*, 35–36; John Collins, *Salt and Fishery* (London: A. Godbid and J. Playford, 1682), 67–72; Floyd, *Columbus Dynasty*, 110; Browne, *Civil and Natural History*, 55–56; Long, *History*, 3: 848.

10. Accounts Current, Liber 1, ff. 24-36; *West India Committee Circular* 36 (24 November 1921): 506; *Gleaner*, 9 June 1961, 1; 17 October 1969, 26; 6 June 1979, 17; 1 July 1991, 46.

11. Lovejoy, *Salt of the Desert Sun*, 1; Adshead, *Salt and Civilization*, 21–23; Bloch, "Social Influence of Salt", 94; Curtin, *Economic Change in Precolonial Africa*, 213, 224–28.

12. John Alexander, "The Salt Industries of West Africa: A Preliminary Study", in *The Archaeology of Africa: Food, Metals and Towns*, ed. Thurstan Shaw, Paul Sinclair, Bassey Andah, and Alex Okpoko (London: Routledge, 1993), 652–57; Lovejoy, *Salt of the Desert Sun*, 15–20; Lewicki, *West African Food*, 116–21; Toyin Falola, "'Salt Is Gold': The Management of Salt Scarcity in Nigeria during World War II", *Canadian Journal of African Studies* 26 (1992): 412–14.

13. Multhauf, *Neptune's Gift*; Schivelbusch, *Tastes of Paradise*, 4; MacGregor and Wardener, *Salt, Diet and Health*, 122–24; Thomas W. Wilson and Clarence E. Grim, "Biohistory of Slavery and Blood Pressure Differences in Blacks Today: A Hypothesis", *Hypertension* 17, suppl. 1 (1991): 122–29; Philip D. Curtin, "The Slavery Hypothesis for Hypertension among African Americans: The Historical Evidence", *American Journal of Public Health* 82 (1992): 1681–86; Jay S. Kaufman and Susan A. Hall, "The Slavery Hypertension Hypothesis: Dissemination and Appeal of a Modern Race Theory", *Epidemiology* 14 (2003): 111–18; Richard Cooper et

al., "The Prevalence of Hypertension in Seven Populations of West African Origin", *American Journal of Public Health* 87 (1997): 160–68; Edward D. Frohlich and Franz H. Messerli, "Sodium and Hypertension", in *Sodium: Its Biologic Significance*, ed. Solomon Papper (Boca Raton, FL: CRC Press, 1982), 143–74; R.A. Bernard, R.L. Doty, K. Engelman, and R.A. Weiss, "Taste and Salt Intake in Human Hypertension", in *Biological and Behavioral Aspects of Salt Intake*, ed. Morley R. Kare, Melvin J. Fregly, and Rudy A. Bernard (New York: Academic Press, 1980), 397–409.

14. *Gleaner*, 17 May 1996, B9.

15. Hurston, *Voodoo Gods*, 48.

16. *Jamaica Observer*, 18 May 2005, 34; Jerome S. Handler, Arthur C. Aufderheide, Robert S. Corruccini, Elizabeth M. Brandon, and Lorentz E. Wittmers, Jr, "Lead Contact and Poisoning in Barbados Slaves: Historical, Chemical, and Biological Evidence", *Social Science History* 10 (1986): 399–425; Smith, *Caribbean Rum*, 145–46; Klaassen, *Casarett and Doull's Toxicology*, 1073; S.C. Sheppard, "Geophagy: Who Eats Soil and Where do Possible Contaminants Go?" *Environmental Geology* 33 (1998): 109–14; Gerald Lalor, Robin Rattray, Mitko Vutchkov, Bertha Campbell, and Karen Lewis-Bell, "Blood Lead Levels in Jamaican School Children", *Science of the Total Environment* 269 (2001): 171–81; G.C.M. Harvey, Ivan Goodbody, and Karl A. Aiken, "The Artisanal Thread Herring Fishery of Kingston Harbour: A Review", *Bulletin of Marine Science* 73 (2003): 421–32.

17. Andrea Howe, Leslie Hoo Fung, Gerald Lalor, Robin Rattray, and Mitko Vutchkov, "Elemental Composition of Jamaican Foods 1: A Survey of Five Food Crop Categories", *Environmental Geochemistry and Health* 27 (2005): 28–29; Klaassen, *Casarett and Doull's Toxicology*, 1074.

18. Jamaica Agricultural Society, *Farmer's Food Manual*, 64–65; Ann Ashworth and Yvette March, "Iron Fortification of Dried Skim Milk and Maize-Soya-Bean-Milk Mixture (CSM): Availability of Iron in Jamaican Infants", *British Journal of Nutrition* 30 (1973): 577–84; *Gleaner*, 5 June 2005, F4.

19. B. Anell and S. Lagercrantz, *Geophagical Customs* (Uppsala, Sweden: Studia Ethnographica Upsaliensia, 1958); Kenneth F. Kiple and Virginia H. Kiple, "Deficiency Diseases in the Caribbean", *Journal of Interdisciplinary History* 11 (1980): 197–215; Carol J. Loveland, Thomas H. Furst, and Georgia C. Lauritzen, "Geophagia in Human Populations", *Food and Foodways* 3 (1989): 333; Peter W. Abrahams and Julia A. Parson, "Geophagy in the Tropics", *Geographical Journal* 162 (1996): 63–73; Gerald N. Callahan, "Eating Dirt", *Emerging Infectious Diseases* 9 (2003): 1016–21; Jacques Henry and Alicia Matthews Kwong, "Why Is Geophagy Treated Like Dirt?", *Deviant Behavior* 24 (2003): 353–71; S. Aufreiter, R.G.V. Hancock, W.C. Mahaney, A. Stambolic-Robb, and K. Sanmugadas, "Geochemistry and Mineralogy of Soils Eaten by Humans", *International Journal of Food Sciences and Nutrition* 48 (1997): 293–305; M.J. Wilson, "Clay Mineralogical and Related Characteristics of Geophagic Materials", *Journal of Chemical Ecology* 29 (2003): 1525–47.

20. Donald E. Vermeer, "Geophagy among the Tiv of Nigeria", *Annals of the Association of American Geographers* 56 (1966): 197–204; Vermeer, "Geophagy among the Ewe of Ghana", *Ethnology* 10 (1971): 56–72; John M. Hunter, "Geophagy in Africa and in the United States:

A Culture-Nutrition Hypothesis", *Geographical Review* 63 (1973): 170–95; P. Wenzel Geissler, "The Significance of Earth-eating: Social and Cultural Aspects of Geophagy among Luo Children", *Africa* 70 (2000): 653–82.

21. Edward Long, B.T. 6/10, 191-94 (Public Record Office, Kew); Long, *History*, 3: 851–52; Simon Taylor, Kingston, to Chaloner Arcedeckne, London, 5 July 1789, 3A/1789/20 Vanneck/Arcedeckne Papers; Dovaston, "Agricultura Americana", 2: 251; Stewart, *View*, 308. See also *Marly*, 97.

22. James Maxwell, "Pathological Enquiry into the Nature of Cachexia Africana, as it is Generally Connected with Dirt-Eating", *Jamaica Physical Journal* 2 (1835): 416–17; Sturge and Harvey, *West Indies in 1837*, 296.

23. Landman and Hall, "Dietary Habits and Knowledge", 206, 208; *Jamaica Record*, 4 June 1989; *Gleaner*, 15 May 1990, 1; 3 May 1992, 3A.

24. Trapham, *Discourse on the State of Health*, 44; Sloane, *Voyage*, 1: xxvii; Nugent, *Lady Nugent's Journal*, 66.

25. W. Kirkpatrick, *A Short History of the First One Hundred Years of the Public Water Supply in the Kingston and Liguanea Area, 1849–1949* (Kingston: Water Commission, 1949); *Gleaner*, 10 April 1933, 21; *Jamaica Public Health* 8, no. 5 (1933): 69–70; 8, no. 6 (1933): 86–87.

26. Helen McBain, "Towards a Viable Water Utility in Jamaica", *Social and Economic Studies* 34 (1985): 77–95; *Jamaica Record*, 2 September 1990, 3A.

27. *Gleaner*, 12 May 1996, 11A; 29 May 2005, C1, C3.

28. Gavin Weightman, *The Frozen Water Trade: How Ice from New England Lakes Kept the World Cool* (London: HarperCollins, 2001), 22, 130; *Gleaner*, 1 January 1890, 2; Rampini, *Letters from Jamaica*, 25; *Gall's News Letter*, 9 January 1880; Brassey, *In the Trades*, 259; Leader, *Through Jamaica with a Kodak*, 143.

29. Henry Albert Phillips, *White Elephants in the Caribbean: A Magic Journey through all the West Indies* (New York: Robert M. McBride, 1936), 126; *Gleaner*, 4 January 1933, 19; Hyatt, *When Me Was a Boy*, 155; *Gleaner*, *Food Supplement*, 25 June 1987, 31.

30. *Jamaica Observer*, 23 July 1993, 40; *Gleaner*, 12 May 1996, 11A.

31. *Gleaner*, 21 July 1915, 6; *Jamaica Times*, 2 March 1918, 1; *Gleaner*, 22 May 1918, 14; 30 March 1940, 7; 21 March 1944, 6; E.H. Back, "The Dietary of Small Farmers in Jamaica", *West Indian Medical Journal* 10 (1961): 34.

Chapter 12

1. Euridice Charon Cardona, "Yellow Cassavas, Purple Bananas", *Humanities Research* 10 (2003): 53–61; Bruce Geddes, *World Food Caribbean* (London: Lonely Planet Publications, 2001), 9, 131–36; Paris Permenter and John Bigley, *Jamaica: A Taste of the Island* (Edison, NJ: Hunter, 1999), 2.

2. Watts, *West Indies*, 165; Burnard, *Mastery, Tyranny, and Desire*, 22; Cannon, "Cooking in Paradise", 194; Titford, *Sketches*, 46; Burke, *Eat Caribbean*, 234.

3. *Gleaner*, 23 May 1940; Chin-See, *Tofu for Health*, 9; Brandon, *Merry-Go-Round*, 12; *Jamaica, Finest Taste*, 90.

4.   J.E. Flint, "Economic Change in West Africa in the Nineteenth Century", in *History of West Africa*, vol. 2, ed. J.F.A. Ajayi and Michael Crowder (Harlow, UK: Longman, 1974), 383; Lewicki, *West African Food*, 102-4, 121-22.

5.   *Panorama of African Recipes*, 1-2.

6.   Schivelbusch, *Tastes of Paradise*, 13-14.

7.   Owens, *Dread*, 166; Pilcher, *Food in World History*, 119.

8.   Fernández-Armesto, *Food*, 185-88; John L. Sorenson and Carl L. Johannessen, "Biological Evidence for Pre-Columbian Transoceanic Voyages", in *Contact and Exchange in the Ancient World*, ed. Victor H. Mair (Honolulu: University of Hawai'i Press, 2006), 242-74.

9.   Lewicki, *West African Food*, 24-32, 37-38, 93-96.

10. Simoons, *Eat Not This Flesh*, 297.

11. Lack and Evans, *Plant Biology*, 249; Hall, *Livestock Biodiversity*, 9-15.

12. William Bascom, "Yoruba Cooking", *Africa* 21 (1951): 125.

13. *Gleaner, Food Supplement*, 6 August 1987, 31; Tim Lang and Michael Heasman, *Food Wars: The Global Battle for Mouths, Minds and Markets* (London: Earthscan, 2004); Niels Fold and Bill Pritchard, eds, *Cross-continental Food Chains* (London: Routledge, 2005).

14. Price, "Origin and Development of Banana and Plantain Cultivation", 1; Miracle, *Maize in Tropical Africa*, 87-95; Richard Pearce, "Traditional Food Crops in Sub-Saharan Africa: Potential and Constraints", *Food Policy* 15, no. 5 (1990): 374; Ayensu and Coursey, "Guinea Yams", 313; Peter Boomgaard, "In the Shadow of Rice: Roots and Tubers in Indonesian History, 1500-1950", *Agricultural History* 77 (2003): 582-610.

15. Jean Besson, *Martha Brae's Two Histories: European Expansion and Caribbean Culture-Building in Jamaica* (Chapel Hill: University of North Carolina Press, 2002), 271.

16. Harris, *Good to Eat*, 198.

17. Ibid., 172; McGrew, "Other Faunivory", 161-62.

18. *Gleaner*, 20 November 1992, 8B; 29 March 1938, 5.

19. Simoons, *Eat Not This Flesh*, 309-10.

20. P.D. Edelman, D.C. McFarland, V.A. Mironov, and J.G.Matheny, "*In Vitro*-Cultured Meat Production", *Tissue Engineering* 11 (2005): 659-62; Fiddes, *Meat*, 15-17.

21. S. Boyd Eaton, Stanley B. Eaton III, and Loren Cordain, "Evolution, Diet, and Health", in *Human Diet: Its Origin and Evolution*, ed. Peter S. Ungar and Mark F. Telford (Westport, CT: Bergin and Garvey, 2002), 12.

BIBLIOGRAPHY

MANUSCRIPTS

Jamaica Archives (Spanish Town)
Accounts Current.
Colonial Secretary's Office.
Powers of Attorney.

John Carter Brown Library (Providence, Rhode Island)
Dovaston, John. "Agricultura Americana, or Improvements in West-India Husbandry Considered, wherein the Present System of Husbandry used in England is Applyed to the Cultivation or Growing of Sugar Canes to Advantage". 1774. (Codex Eng 60).

Historical Society of Pennsylvania (Philadelphia)
John Taylor papers, Powel Collection.

Bristol Museum and Art Gallery, Natural History Division
Lindsay, John. "Elegancies of Jamaica" and Drawings. c. 1762–75.

British Library (London)
Banks MSS, Add. 33978.
Long MSS, Add. 22678.
Sloane MSS, Sloane. 856.

National Archives (London)
B.T. 6/10.
C.O. 137.

Cambridge University Library
Vanneck/Arcedeckne papers.

NEWSPAPERS AND PERIODICALS

Boulevard News. Kingston.

Cajanus. Kingston.

Colonial Standard and Jamaica Despatch. Kingston.

Columbian Magazine. Kingston.

Falmouth Post. Falmouth, Jamaica.

Gleaner. Kingston.

Gall's News Letter. Kingston.

The Jamaica Magazine. Kingston.

Jamaican Herald. Kingston.

Jamaica Observer. Kingston.

Jamaica Post. Kingston.

Jamaica Public Health. Kingston.

The Jamaica Quarterly Journal, and Literary Magazine. Kingston.

Jamaica Record. Kingston.

Jamaica Standard. Kingston.

Jamaica Times. Kingston.

Nyam News. Kingston.

Pepperpot. Kingston.

Planters' Punch. Kingston.

Royal Gazette. Spanish Town.

Star. Kingston.

The Times. London.

West India Committee Circular. London.

BOOKS AND ARTICLES

Abrahams, Peter W., and Julia A. Parson. "Geophagia in the Tropics". *Geographical Journal* 162 (1996): 63–73.

Achaya, K.T. *A Historical Dictionary of Indian Food*. New Delhi: Oxford University Press, 1998.

Adams, C. Dennis. *The Blue Mahoe and Other Bush*. Kingston: Sangster's Bookstores, 1971.

———. *Flowering Plants of Jamaica*. Mona, Jamaica: University of the West Indies, 1972.

Addae, J.I., and G.N. Melville. "A Re-examination of the Mechanism of Ackee-Induced Vomiting Sickness". *West Indian Medical Journal* 37 (1988): 6–8.

Adolf, W., and E. Hecker. "On the Active Principles of the Spurge Family, X: Skin Irritants, Cocarcinogens, and Cryptic Cocarcinogens from the Latex of the Manchineel Tree". *Journal of Natural Products* 47 (1984): 482–96.

Adshead, S.A.M. *Salt and Civilization*. London: Macmillan, 1992.

Adu-Tutu, M., Y. Afful, K. Asante-Appiah, Diana Lieberman, J.B. Hall, and Memory Elvin-Lewis. "Chewing Stick Usage in Southern Ghana". *Economic Botany* 33 (1979): 320–28.

Ahissou, H., T. Lebreton de Vonne, F. Esnard, and H. Mouray. "Evolution of Grass-Cutter (*Thryonomys swinderianus*) Inflammation Markers: Comparison with Rabbit (*Oryctolagus cuniculus*) and Rat (*Rattus norvegicus*)". *Comparative Biochemistry and Physiology* 118A (1997): 1309–12.

Ahmed, Belal, and Sultanan Afroz. *The Political Economy of Food and Agriculture in the Caribbean.* Kingston: Ian Randle, 1996.

Aiken, Karl A. "Lobsters: Their Biology and Conservation in Jamaica". *Jamaica Journal* 17, no. 4 (1984–85): 44–47.

———. "Reproduction, Diet and Population Structure of the Mountain Mullet, *Agonostomus monticola*, in Jamaica, West Indies". *Environmental Biology of Fishes* 53 (1998): 347–52.

Aiken, Karl A., G. Andre Kong, Stephen Smikle, Robin Mahon, and Richard Appeldoorn. "The Queen Conch Fishery on Pedro Bank, Jamaica: Discovery, Development, Management". *Ocean and Coastal Management* 42 (1999): 1069–81.

Alcock, Joan P. *Food in Roman Britain.* Stroud, UK: Tempus, 2001.

Alexander, John. "The Domestication of Yams: A Multi-disciplinary Approach". In *Science in Archaeology: A Survey of Progress and Research*, edited by Don Brothwell and Eric Higgs, 229–34. London: Thames and Hudson, 1969.

———. "The Salt Industries of West Africa: A Preliminary Study". In *The Archaeology of Africa: Food, Metals and Towns*, edited by Thurstan Shaw, Paul Sinclair, Bassey Andah, and Alex Okpoko, 652–57. London: Routledge, 1993.

Alexander, J., and D.G. Coursey. "The Origins of Yam Cultivation". In *The Domestication and Exploitation of Plants and Animals*, edited by Peter J. Ucko and G.W. Dimbleby, 404–25. London: Duckworth, 1969.

Alexander, R. McNeill. *Animals.* Cambridge, UK: Cambridge University Press, 1990.

Allen, C.J. "Producing Animal Protein in Your Backyard". *Gleaner*, June 27, 1987, 8.

Allen, J.A. "The West Indian Seal (*Monachus tropicalis* Gray)". *Bulletin of the American Museum of Natural History* 2 (1887): 1–34.

Allsopp, Richard, ed. *Dictionary of Caribbean English Usage.* Oxford: Oxford University Press, 1996.

Anderson, E.N. *Everyone Eats: Understanding Food and Culture.* New York: New York University Press, 2005.

Andrews, Kenneth R. *The Spanish Caribbean: Trade and Plunder, 1530–1630.* New Haven, CT: Yale University Press, 1978.

Anell, B., and S. Lagercrantz. *Geophagical Customs.* Uppsala, Sweden: Studia Ethnographica Upsaliensia, 1958.

Anger, Klaus, and Christoph D. Schubart. "Experimental Evidence of Food-Independent Larval Development in Endemic Jamaican Freshwater-Breeding Crabs". *Physiological and Biochemical Zoology* 78 (2005): 246–58.

Appadurai, Arjun. "How to Make a National Cuisine: Cookbooks in Contemporary India". *Comparative Studies in Society and History* 30 (1988): 3–24.

Arens, W. *The Man-Eating Myth: Anthropology and Anthropophagy.* New York: Oxford University Press, 1979.

Armstrong, Douglas V. *The Old Village and the Great House: An Archaeological and Historical Examination of Drax Hall Plantation, St. Ann's Bay, Jamaica*. Urbana: University of Illinois Press, 1990.

Ashkenazi, Michael, and Jeanne Jacob. *The Essence of Japanese Cuisine: An Essay on Food and Culture*. Philadelphia: University of Pennsylvania Press, 2000.

Ashworth, Ann, and Yvette March. "Iron Fortification of Dried Skim Milk and Maize-Soya-Bean-Milk Mixture (CSM): Availability of Iron in Jamaican Infants". *British Journal of Nutrition* 30 (1973): 577–84.

Ashworth, Ann, and J.C. Waterlow. *Nutrition in Jamaica, 1969–70*. Mona, Jamaica: Extra-Mural Department, University of the West Indies, [1970].

Aspinall, Algernon E. *The British West Indies: Their History, Resources and Progress*. London: Pitman, 1912.

Asprey, G.F., and Phyllis Thornton. "Medicinal Plants of Jamaica". *West Indian Medical Journal* 2 (1953): 233–52; 3 (1954): 17–41; 4 (1955): 69–82; 4 (1955): 145–68.

Aufreiter, S., R.G.V. Hancock, W.C. Mahaney, A. Stambolic-Robb, and K. Sanmugadas. "Geochemistry and Mineralogy of Soils Eaten by Humans". *International Journal of Food Sciences and Nutrition* 48 (1997): 293–305.

Ayensu, Edward S. *Medicinal Plants of the West Indies*. Algonac, MI: Reference Publications, 1981.

Ayensu, Edward S., and D.G. Coursey. "Guinea Yams: The Botany, Ethnobotany, Use and Possible Future of Yams in West Africa". *Economic Botany* 26 (1972): 301–18.

Ayre, Sylvester. *Bush Doctor: Jamaica and the Caribbean's Almost Forgotten Folklore and Remedies*. Kingston: LHM Publishing, 2002.

Babb, Dalton. *Cooking the West Indian Way*. London: Macmillan Caribbean, 1986.

Back, E.H. "The Dietary of Small Farmers in Jamaica". *West Indian Medical Journal* 10 (1961): 28–43.

Bacon, Edgar Mayhew, and Eugene Murray Aaron. *The New Jamaica*. New York: Walbridge, 1890.

Baillie, Mrs. W. *The Peter Pan Book of Recipes*. Sold for the Benefit of the Jamaica Wesleyan Children's Home. Kingston: Daily Gleaner, 1928.

Ballard, Chris. "Still Good to Think With: The Sweet Potato in Oceania". In *The Sweet Potato in Oceania: A Reappraisal*, Oceania Monograph 56, edited by Chris Ballard, Paula Brown, R. Michael Bourke and Tracy Harwood, 1–13. Sydney: University of Sydney, 2005.

Banks, Mary, Christine McFadden, and Catherine Atkinson. *The World Encyclopedia of Coffee*. London: Lorenz, 1999.

Barham, Henry. *Hortus Americanus: Containing an Account of the Trees, Shrubs, and Other Vegetable Productions, of South-America and the West-India Islands, and Particularly of the Island of Jamaica*. Kingston: Alexander Aikman, 1794.

Barker, David, and Balfour Spence. "Afro-Caribbean Agriculture: A Jamaican Maroon Community in Transition". *Geographical Journal* 154 (1988): 198–208.

Barnes, Sandra. *The Breadfruit in the Caribbean, 1793–1993: Recipes from Caribbean Cookbooks*. St Augustine, Trinidad: University of the West Indies, Main Library, 1993.

Bartley, John P. "A New Method for the Determination of Pungent Compounds in Ginger (*Zingiber officinale*)". *Journal of the Science of Food and Agriculture* 68 (1995): 215–22.

Barton-Gade, P.A., B.B. Chrystall, A.H. Kirton, G.R. Longdill, H.R. Cross and M. Jespersen. "Slaughter Procedures for Pigs, Sheep, Cattle and Poultry". In *Meat Science, Milk Science and Technology*, edited by H.R. Cross and A.J. Overby, 33–82. Amsterdam: Elsevier Science, 1988.

Barty-King, Hugh, and Anton Massel. *Rum: Yesterday and Today*. London: Heinemann, 1983.

Bascom, William. "Yoruba Cooking". *Africa* 21 (1951): 125–37.

Bastyra, Judy. *Caribbean Cooking*. New York: Exeter, 1987.

Beaglehole, J.C., ed. *The Endeavour Journal of Joseph Banks 1768–1771*. 4 vols. Sydney, Australia: Angus and Robertson, 1962.

———. *The Life of Captain James Cook*. Stanford, CA: Stanford University Press, 1974.

Beamish, Richard. *Restaurants of Jamaica 1983–1984: Featuring Traditional Jamaican Recipes*. Montego Bay, Jamaica: privately printed, 1984.

Becker, Robert, and Robin M. Saunders. "New Uses for Amaranth". *Cajanus* 17 (1984): 213–14.

Beckford, William. *A Descriptive Account of the Island of Jamaica*. London: T. and J. Egerton, 1790.

Beckwith, Martha Warren. *Black Roadways: A Study of Jamaican Folk Life*. 1929. Reprint, New York: Negro Universities Press, 1969.

Beeton, Isabella. *Mrs Beeton's Book of Household Management*. 1859–61. Facsimile edition, London: Chancellor Press, 1982.

Behrendt, Stephen D. "Markets, Transaction Cycles, and Profits: Merchant Decision Making in the British Slave Trade". *William and Mary Quarterly* 58 (2001): 171–204.

Belasco, Warren, and Philip Scranton, eds. *Food Nations: Selling Taste in Consumer Societies*. New York: Routledge, 2002.

Bell, Peter R., and Alan R. Hemsley. *Green Plants: Their Origins and Diversity*. 1992. Cambridge, UK: Cambridge University Press, 2000.

Bellwood, Peter. *First Farmers: The Origins of Agricultural Societies*. Oxford: Blackwell, 2005.

Benghiat, Norma. "In Search of the Original 'Jerkers'". In *A Tapestry of Jamaica: The Best of Skywritings, Air Jamaica's Inflight Magazine*, edited by Linda Gambrill, 146–47. 1988. Kingston: Creative Communications, 2003.

———. *Traditional Jamaican Cookery*. Harmondsworth, UK: Penguin, 1985.

Benjamin, Medea, Joseph Collins, and Michael Scott. *No Free Lunch: Food and Revolution in Cuba Today*. San Francisco: Institute for Food and Development Policy, 1984.

Bennett, Louise. *Jamaica Labrish*. Kingston: Sangster's Bookstores Jamaica, 1966.

Beranbaum, Rose Levy. *The Bread Bible*. New York: Norton, 2003.

Berg, J.C.T. van den. *Strategy for Dairy Development in the Tropics and Subtropics*. Wageningen, Netherlands: PUDOC, 1990.

Bernard, R.A., R.L. Doty, K. Engelman, and R.A. Weiss. "Taste and Salt Intake in Human Hypertension". In *Biological and Behavioral Aspects of Salt Intake*, edited by Morley R. Kare, Melvin J. Fregly, and Rudy A. Bernard, 397–409. New York: Academic Press, 1980.

Besson, Jean. *Martha Brae's Two Histories: European Expansion and Caribbean Culture-Building in Jamaica*. Chapel Hill: University of North Carolina Press, 2002.

The Best of Creative Cooking. Kingston: Grace Kitchens and Consumer Services, 1993.

Bierling, Henk Jan, and Dick Vos. "Milk Distribution by Pushcart Vendors in Kingston, Jamaica". *Caribbean Geography* 2 (1988): 195–202.

"Biscuits – Once Upon a Time, and Now". *Planters' Punch* 1, no. 5 (1924–25): 37–39.

Bjorndal, Karen A., Alan B. Bolten, and Milani Y. Chaloupka. "Evaluating Trends in Abundance of Immature Green Turtles, *Chelonia mydas*, in the Greater Caribbean". *Ecological Applications* 15 (2005): 304–14.

Black, Clinton V. *Jamaica Guide*. [London]: William Collins and Sangster (Jamaica), 1973.

Blake, Orane A., José C. Jackson, Maria A. Jackson, and C.L. André Gordon. "Assessment of Dietary Exposure to the Natural Toxin Hypoglycin in Ackee (*Blighia sapida*) by Jamaican Consumers". *Food Research International* 37 (2004): 833–38.

Blench, Roger M. "The History of Pigs in Africa". In *The Origins and Development of African Livestock: Archaeology, Genetics, Linguistics and Ethnography*, edited by Roger M. Blench and Kevin C. MacDonald, 355–67. London: UCL Press, 2000.

Bligh, William. *The Log of H.M.S.* Providence *1791–1793*. Guildford, UK: Genesis Publications, 1976.

Bloch, M.R. "The Social Influence of Salt". *Scientific American*, July 1963, 89–98.

Blome, Richard. *A Description of the Island of Jamaica*. London: J. Williams, Jr, 1672.

———. *The Present State of His Majesties Isles and Territories in America*. London: Dorman Newman, 1687.

Blue Book for the Island of Jamaica. Kingston: Government Printing Office, 1822–1945. [Title varies].

Bodenheimer, F.S. *Insects as Human Food: A Chapter of the Ecology of Man*. The Hague: W. Junk, 1951.

A Book of the Continuation of Forreign Passages. London: Thomas Jenner, 1657.

Boomgaard, Peter. "In the Shadow of Rice: Roots and Tubers in Indonesian History, 1500–1950". *Agricultural History* 77 (2003): 582–610.

Boonoonoonoos: A Collection of Recipes. Kingston: American Women's Group, 1987.

Bowman, Kim D., and Frederick G. Gmitter, Jr. "Forbidden Fruit (*Citrus* sp., Rutaceae) Rediscovered in St. Lucia". *Economic Botany* 44 (1990): 165–73.

Boyd, I.L., and M.P. Stanfield. "Circumstantial Evidence for the Presence of Monk Seals in the West Indies". *Oryx* 32 (1998): 310–16.

Bradbury, J. Howard, and Warren D. Holloway. *Chemistry of Tropical Root Crops: Significance for Nutrition and Agriculture in the Pacific*. Canberra, Australia: Australian Centre for International Agricultural Research, 1988.

Brady, Cherry. "Drum Chicken". In *A Tapestry of Jamaica: The Best of Skywritings, Air Jamaica's Inflight Magazine*, edited by Linda Gambrill, 150. 1983. Kingston: Creative Communications, 2003.

Brandon, Leila. *A Merry-Go-Round of Recipes from Jamaica*. Kingston: Novelty Trading, 1963.

Brassey, Lady. *In the Trades, the Tropics, and the Roaring Forties*. London: Longmans, Green, 1885.

Brathwaite, Edward. *The Development of Creole Society in Jamaica 1770–1820*. Oxford: Clarendon, 1971.

Breslin, Paul A.S. "Interactions among Salty, Sour and Bitter Compounds". *Trends in Food Science and Technology* 7 (1996): 390–99.

———. "Human Gustation and Flavour". *Flavour and Fragrance Journal* 16 (2001): 439–56.

Briggs, Richard. *The New Art of Cookery, According to the Present Practice*. Philadelphia: Spotswood, 1792.

Brillat-Savarin, Jean Anthelme. *The Physiology of Taste, or Meditations on Transcendental Gastronomy*. Translated by M.F.K. Fisher. 1949. New York: Knopf, 1972.

British Medical Association, Jamaica Branch. Nutrition Committee. *Nutrition in Jamaica*. Kingston: Government Printer, 1945.

Brown, Linda Keller, and Kay Mussell, eds. *Ethnic and Regional Foodways in the United States: The Performance of Group Identity*. Knoxville: University of Tennessee Press, 1984.

Brown, William H. *Marine Fisheries of the British West Indies*. ONR Report. Berkeley: Department of Geography, University of California, 1967.

Browne, Patrick. *The Civil and Natural History of Jamaica*. London, 1756. Reprint, New York: Arno, 1972.

Buffo, Roberto A., and Claudio Cardelli-Freire. "Coffee Flavour: An Overview". *Flavour and Fragrance Journal* 19 (2004): 99–104.

Bulliet, Richard W. *Hunters, Herders, and Hamburgers: The Past and Future of Human-Animal Relationships*. New York: Columbia University Press, 2005.

Burke, Virginia. *Eat Caribbean*. London: Simon and Schuster, 2005.

———. *Walkerswood Caribbean Kitchen*. London: Simon and Schuster, 2000.

Burkill, I.H. "The Rise and Decline of the Greater Yam in the Service of Man". *The Advancement of Science* 7, no. 28 (1951): 443–48.

Burnard, Trevor. *Mastery, Tyranny, and Desire: Thomas Thistlewood and His Slaves in the Anglo-Jamaican World*. Chapel Hill: University of North Carolina Press, 2004.

Burnett, John. "Trends in Bread Consumption". In *Our Changing Fare: Two Hundred Years of British Food Habits*, edited by T.C. Barker, J.C. McKenzie, and John Yudkin, 61–75. London: MacGibbon and Kee, 1966.

Caldwell, David K. *Marine and Freshwater Fishes of Jamaica*. Science Series Bulletin No. 17. Kingston: Institute of Jamaica, 1966.

Callahan, Gerald N. "Eating Dirt". *Emerging Infectious Diseases* 9 (2003): 1016–21.

Campbell, Versada. *Caribbean Foodways*. Kingston: Caribbean Food and Nutrition Institute, 1988.

Campbell, Versada (Sadie), and Dinesh P. Sinha. *Nutrition Made Simple*. 1994. Kingston: Caribbean Food and Nutrition Institute, 2002.

Campbell, V.S., D.P. Sinha, and A.W. Patterson. "KAP Study on Project Lifestyle (Jamaica)". *Cajanus* 25 (1992): 25–48.

Cannon, Poppy. "The Cooking in Paradise". In *Ian Fleming Introduces Jamaica*, edited by Morris Cargill, 189–96. London: Andre Deutsch, 1965.

Capaldi, Elizabeth D., ed. *Why We Eat What We Eat: The Psychology of Eating*. Washington, DC: American Psychological Association, 1996.

Capatti, Alberto, and Massimo Montanari. *Italian Cuisine: A Cultural History*. New York: Columbia University Press, 2003.

Cardell, Nicholas Scott, and Mark Myron Hopkins. "The Effect of Milk Intolerance on the Consumption of Milk by Slaves in 1860". *Journal of Interdisciplinary History* 8 (1978): 507–13.

Cardona, Euridice Charon. "Yellow Cassavas, Purple Bananas". *Humanities Research* 10 (2003): 53–61.

Caribbean Commission. Central Secretariat. *The Fish Trade of the Caribbean*. External Trade Bulletin No. 3. Washington, DC: Caribbean Commission, Central Secretariat, 1948.

Caribbean Food and Nutrition Institute. *Breastfeeding – Before and After*. Kingston: Caribbean Food and Nutrition Institute and UNICEF, 1979.

Caribbean Research Council. Committee on Agriculture, Nutrition, Fisheries and Forestry. *Root Crops and Legumes in the Caribbean*. Crop Inquiry Series No. 4. Washington, DC: Caribbean Research Council, 1947.

Carley, Mary Manning. *Jamaica: The Old and the New*. London: George Allen and Unwin, 1963.

Carnegie, A.L. "Poisoning by Barracuda Fish". *West Indian Medical Journal* 12 (1963): 217-20.

Carney, Judith A. "African Rice in the Columbian Exchange". *Journal of African History* 42 (2001): 377–96.

———. *Black Rice: The African Origins of Rice Cultivation in the Americas*. Cambridge, MA: Harvard University Press, 2001.

———. "Landscapes and Technology Transfer: Rice Cultivation and African Continuities". *Technology and Culture* 37 (1996): 5–35.

———. "'With Grains in Her Hair': Rice in Colonial Brazil". *Slavery and Abolition* 25 (2004): 1–27.

Carson, Jane. *Colonial Virginia Cookery: Procedures, Equipment and Ingredients in Colonial Cooking*. Williamsburg, VA: Colonial Williamsburg Foundation, 1985.

Carter, Susannah. *The Frugal Housewife, or Complete Woman Cook*. London: F. Newbery. Reprinted Boston: Edes and Gill, 1772.

Cassidy, Frederic G. *Jamaica Talk: Three Hundred Years of the English Language in Jamaica*. London: Macmillan, 1961.

Cassidy, F.G., and R.B. Le Page, eds. *Dictionary of Jamaican English*. Cambridge, UK: Cambridge University Press, 1967.

———. *Dictionary of Jamaican English*. 2nd edition. Cambridge, UK: Cambridge University Press, 1980.

Census of Jamaica. 1943, 1960, 1970, 1982, 1991, 2001. [Title varies].

"Cerasee". *Jamaica Journal* 20, no. 4 (1987–88): 70.

Certain Inducements to Well Minded People, who are here straitned in their estates or otherwise: or such as are willing out of noble and publike principles, to transport themselves, or some servants, or agents for them into the West-Indies, for the propagating of the Gospel, and increase of trade. London: 1643.

Chandra, S. "Tropical Root Crop Statistics: A World Perspective". *Proceedings of the Sixth Symposium of the International Society for Tropical Root Crops*, 41–46. Lima, Peru: International Potato Center, 1984.

Chapman, Esther, ed. *Pleasure Island: The Book of Jamaica*. Kingston: Arawak, 1952 [1951].

"Characteristic Traits of the Creolian and African Negroes in this Island, &c., &c"., *Columbian Magazine* (Kingston), 2 (April 1797): 699–704; 2 (May 1797): 765–68; 3 (June 1797): 3–8; 3 (July 1797): 107–10; 3 (August 1797): 166–72; 3 (September 1797): 249–53; 3 (October 1797): 287–89.

Charcoal for Fuel. Kingston: Ministry of Mining, Energy and Tourism, 1988.

Chatman, Leia M., Hamisu M. Salihu, Michele E.A. Roofe, Patrick Wheatle, Donnadeen Henry, and Pauline E. Jolly. "Influence of Knowledge and Attitudes on Exclusive Breastfeeding Practice among Rural Jamaican Mothers". *Birth* 31, no. 4 (2004): 265–71.

[Chen, Ray]. *Cooking with Lasco: A Great Collection of Delicious, Nutritious and Affordable Recipes Using Lasco Products*. Kingston: Periwinkle, 2003.

Child, Reginald. *Coconuts*. London: Longmans, 1964.

Chin-See, Helen. *Tofu for Health and Pleasure as Cooked in Chinese Homes*. Kingston: privately printed, 2001.

Clarence-Smith, William Gervase. *Cocoa and Chocolate, 1765–1914*. London: Routledge, 2000.

Clarence-Smith, William Gervase, and Steven Topik, eds. *The Global Coffee Economy in Africa, Asia, and Latin America, 1500–1989*. Cambridge, UK: Cambridge University Press, 2003.

Clark, E. Phyllis. *West Indian Cookery*. London: Thomas Nelson, 1945.

Classen, Constance, David Howes, and Anthony Synnott. *Aroma: The Cultural History of Smell*. London: Routledge, 1994.

Clayton, Anthony, and Michael Haley. "The Management of Jamaica's Coral Reefs". *Jamaica Journal* 28, nos 2–3 (2004): 15–23.

Cleary, Teresa E. *Jamaica Run-dung: Over 100 Recipes*. Kingston: Brainbuster Publications, 1970.

Clutton-Brock, Juliet. *Domesticated Animals from Earliest Times*. London: British Museum (Natural History) and Heinemann, 1981.

———. "Vertebrate Collections". In *Sir Hans Sloane: Collector, Scientist, Antiquary —Founding Father of the British Museum*, edited by Arthur MacGregor, 77–92. London: British Museum Press, 1994.

Clutton-Brock, Juliet, ed. *The Walking Larder: Patterns of Domestication, Pastoralism, and Predation*. London: Unwin Hyman, 1989.

Coalpot Recipe Postcards. Kingston: n.p., [1980].

Coe, Michael D., and Sophie D. Coe. *The True History of Chocolate*. London: Thames and Hudson, 1996.

Cole, Melissa, and Brandon Cole. *Manatees*. Woodbridge, CT: Blackbirch, 2001.

Colinvaux, Paul. *Ecology*. New York: Wiley, 1986.

Collingham, Lizzie. *Curry: A Biography*. London: Chatto and Windus, 2005.

Collins, J.L. *The Pineapple: Botany, Cultivation and Utilization*. London: Leonard Hill, 1960.

Collins, John. *Salt and Fishery*. London: A. Godbid and J. Playford, 1682.

Conner, Mark, and Christopher J. Armitage. *The Social Psychology of Food*. Buckingham, UK: Open University Press, 2002.

Cook, Ian, and Michelle Harrison. "Cross Over Food: Re-materializing Postcolonial Geographies". *Transactions of the Institute of British Geographers* 28 (2003): 296–317.

Cooking with Red Stripe. Kingston: Desnoes and Geddes, [1993].

Cooley, J.S. "The Sweet Potato: Its Origin and Primitive Storage Practices". *Economic Botany* 5 (1951): 378–86.

Cooper, A. *The Complete Distiller*. London: P. Vaillant and R. Griffiths, 1757.

Cooper, Richard, C. Rotimi, S. Ataman, D. McGee, B. Osotimehin, S. Kadiri, et al. "The Prevalence of Hypertension in Seven Populations of West African Origin". *American Journal of Public Health* 87 (1997): 160–68.

Cork, Josias. *Root Food Growth in Jamaica*. Kingston: George Henderson, 1881.

Coursey, D.G. "The Comparative Ethnobotany of African and Asian Yam Cultures". In *Proceedings of the Third Symposium of the International Society for Tropical Root Crops*, 164–68. Ibadan, Nigeria: International Society for Tropical Root Crops, 1977.

———. "The Origins and Domestication of Yams in Africa". In *Origins of African Plant Domestication*, edited by Jack R. Harlan, Jan M.J. De Wet, and Ann B.L. Stemler, 383–408. The Hague: Mouton, 1976.

———. *Yams: An Account of the Nature, Origins, Cultivation and Utilisation of the Useful Members of Dioscoreaceae*. London: Longmans, 1967.

Cox, Paul Alan. "Two Samoan Technologies for Breadfruit and Banana Preservation". *Economic Botany* 34 (1980): 181–85.

Crosby, Alfred W., Jr. *The Columbian Exchange: Biological and Cultural Consequences of 1492*. Westport, CT: Greenwood, 1972.

Cross, H.R., and A.J. Overby, eds. *Meat Science, Milk Science and Technology*. Amsterdam: Elsevier Science, 1988.

Cuff, Patricia. *A Taste of the Old Home Place: Select Jamaican Recipes*. Mandeville, Jamaica: Pat Cuff Publications, 1989.

Cuninghame, Judy. *Some Fruits and Recipes of Jamaica*. Virgin Islands: Caribbean Natural Colour, 1971.

Curtin, Philip D. *The Atlantic Slave Trade: A Census*. Madison: University of Wisconsin Press, 1969.

———. *Economic Change in Precolonial Africa: Senegambia in the Era of the Slave Trade*. Madison: University of Wisconsin Press, 1975.

———. "The Slavery Hypothesis for Hypertension among African Americans: The Historical Evidence". *American Journal of Public Health* 82 (1992): 1681–86.

Dalby, Andrew. *Dangerous Tastes: The Story of Spices*. Berkeley: University of California Press, 2000.

Dallas, Robert Charles. *The History of the Maroons from Their Origin to the Establishment of Their Chief Tribe at Sierra Leone*. London: Longman, 1803.

Danforth, Stuart T. "Birds Observed in Jamaica during the Summer of 1926". *Auk* 45 (1928): 480–91.

Darby, Madge. "Bligh's Disciple: Matthew Flinders's Journals of HMS *Providence* (1791–3)". *Mariner's Mirror* 86 (2000): 401–11.

David, Elizabeth. *English Bread and Yeast Cookery*. London: Penguin, 1979.

Davidson, Alan. *The Penguin Companion to Food*. London: Penguin, 2002.

Davidson, Marjorie. "Ackees and Avocadoes". *Jamaica Journal* 5, no. 4 (1971): 28–31.

Daviron, Benoit. "Small Farm Production and the Standardization of Tropical Products". *Journal of Agrarian Change* 2 (2002): 162–84.

Deagan, Kathleen. "Reconsidering Taíno Social Dynamics after Spanish Conquest: Gender and Class in Culture Contact Studies". *American Antiquity* 69 (2004): 597–626.

De Andrade, Margarette. *Brazilian Cookery: Traditional and Modern*. Rio de Janeiro: A Casa do Livro Eldorado, 1978.

Deerr, Noel. *Cane Sugar*. London: Norman Rodger, 1921.

Degras, Lucien. *The Yam: A Tropical Root Crop*. Oxford: Macmillan Education, 1993.

De Langhe, Edmond, and Pierre de Maret. "Tracking the Banana: Its Significance in Early Agriculture". In *The Prehistory of Food: Appetites for Change*, edited by Chris Gosden and Jon Hather, 377–96. London: Routledge, 1999.

De Lisser, H.G. "Behind the Scenes at the J.P.S.: Revelations, Personal, Social and Gastronomic". *Planters' Punch* 3, no. 2 (1933–34): 35–38.

———. "Christina's Dream". *Planters' Punch* 1, no. 1 (1920): 16–18.

———. "The Devil's Mountain". *Planters' Punch* 1, no. 2 (1921–23): 1–31.

——— "Haunted". *Planters' Punch* 4, no. 2 (1939–40): 24.

———. "H.G.D. Discovers Jones Penn". *Planters' Punch* 4, no. 4 (1941–42): 8.

Delwiche, J. "Are There 'Basic' Tastes?" *Trends in Food Science and Technology* 7 (1996): 411–15.

De Mers, John. *The Food of Jamaica: Authentic Recipes from the Jewel of the Caribbean*. Singapore: Periplus, 1999.

Demyttenaere, Jan C.R., Ilse E.I. Koninckx, and Arvid Meersman. "Microbial Production of Bioflavours by Fungal Spores". In *Flavour Science: Recent Developments*, edited by A.J. Taylor and D.S. Mottram, 105–10. Cambridge, UK: Royal Society of Chemistry, 1996.

Denton, Derek. *The Hunger for Salt: An Anthropological, Physiological and Medical Analysis*. Berlin: Springer-Verlag, 1982.

Diamond, Jared. *Guns, Germs and Steel: A Short History of Everybody for the Last 13,000 Years*. London: Vintage, 1998.

Diesel, Rudolf, Christoph D. Schubart, and Martina Schuh. "A Reconstruction of the Invasion of Land by Jamaican Crabs (Grapsidae: Sesarminae)". *Journal of Zoology* 250 (2000): 141–60.

Dixon, Jane. *The Changing Chicken: Chooks, Cooks and Culinary Culture*. Sydney, Australia: University of New South Wales Press, 2002.

Dodd, George. *The Food of London*. London: Longman, Brown, Green, and Longmans, 1856.

Donaldson, Enid. *The Real Taste of Jamaica*. Kingston: Ian Randle, 1993.

———. "Sweets for My Sweet". In *A Tapestry of Jamaica: The Best of Skywritings, Air Jamaica's Inflight Magazine*, edited by Linda Gambrill, 151. 1996. Kingston: Creative Communications, 2003.

Donaldson-Mignotte, Enid. "How Jamaicans Like Their Food". *Gleaner*, October 3, 1996, B8.

Downer, Audrey, and Robert Sutton. *Birds of Jamaica: A Photographic Field Guide*. Cambridge, UK: Cambridge University Press, 1990.

Drayton, Richard. *Nature's Government: Science, Imperial Britain, and the "Improvement" of the World*. New Haven, CT: Yale University Press, 2000.

Drewnowski, Adam. "Fat and Sugar in the Global Diet: Dietary Diversity in the Nutrition Transition". In *Food in Global History*, edited by Raymond Grew, 194–206. Boulder, CO: Westview, 1999.

Dufour, Darna L. "The Bitter Is Sweet: A Case Study of Bitter Cassava (*Manihot esculenta*) Use in Amazonia". In *Tropical Forests, People and Food: Biocultural Interactions and Applications to Development*, edited by C.M. Hladik, A. Hladik, O.F. Linares, H. Pagezy, A. Semple, and M. Hadley, 575–88. Paris: UNESCO, 1993.

Duyker, Edward. *Nature's Argonaut: Daniel Solander, 1733–1782, Naturalist and Voyager with Cook and Banks*. Melbourne, Australia: Melbourne University Press, 1998.

Dupuis, E. Melanie. *Nature's Perfect Food: How Milk Became America's Drink*. New York: New York University Press, 2002.

Duvall, Chris S. "On the Origin of the Tree *Spondias mombin* in Africa". *Journal of Historical Geography* 32 (2006): 249–66.

"Eating Goes Modern". *Planters' Punch* 4, no. 3 (1940–41): 12.

Eaton, S. Boyd, Stanley B. Eaton III, and Loren Cordain. "Evolution, Diet, and Health". In *Human Diet: Its Origin and Evolution*, edited by Peter S. Ungar and Mark F. Telford, 7–17. Westport, CT: Bergin and Garvey, 2002.

Ebanks, Margaret. *The Rastafari Cookbook: Ital Recipes*. Kingston: Antilles Book Company, 1981.

Ebrahim, G.J. *Breast Feeding: The Biological Option*. London: Macmillan, 1978.

Eckles, Clarence Henry, Willes Barnes Combs, and Harold Macy. *Milk and Milk Products*. New York: McGraw-Hill, 1951.

The Economics of Good Nutrition, No. 1: Budgeting. Nutrition Education Series No. 1. Kingston: Scientific Research Council, 1971.

Edelman, P.D., D.C. McFarland, V.A. Mironov, and J.G. Matheny. "*In Vitro*–Cultured Meat Production". *Tissue Engineering* 11 (2005): 659–62.

Eden, Charles H. *The West Indies*. London: Sampson, Low, Marston, Searle and Rivington, 1880.

Edmunds, Peter J., and Robert C. Carpenter. "Recovery of *Diadema antillarum* Reduces Macroalgal Cover and Increases Abundance of Juvenile Corals on a Caribbean Reef". *Proceedings of the National Academy of Sciences* 98, no. 9 (2001): 5067–71.

Edwards, Bryan. *The History, Civil and Commercial, of the British West Indies*. 5 vols. London: G. and W.B. Whittaker, 1819.

Eisner, Gisela. *Jamaica, 1830–1930: A Study in Economic Growth*. Manchester, UK: Manchester University Press, 1961.

Elias, Marianne, Gilda Santos Mühlen, Doyle McKey, Ana Carolina Roa, and Joe Tohme. "Genetic Diversity of Traditional South American Landraces of Cassava (*Manihot esculenta* Crantz): An Analysis Using Microsatellites". *Economic Botany* 58 (2004): 242–56.

Ellis, John. *An Historical Account of Coffee*. London: Edward and Charles Dilly, 1774.

An English Merchant. *Some Modern Observations upon Jamaica: As to Its Natural History, Improvement in Trade, Manner of Living, &c*. London, 1727.

Epenhuijsen, C.W. van. *Growing Native Vegetables in Nigeria*. Rome: Food and Agriculture Organization of the United Nations, 1974.

Erdman, M.D., and B.A. Erdman. "Arrowroot (*Maranta arundinacea*), Food, Feed, Fuel, and Fibre Resource". *Economic Botany* 38 (1984): 332–41.

Eric. *Cooking with Ghanja*. Dorset, UK: Ghanja Press, 1995.

Esmay, Merle, Soemangat, Eriyatno, and Allan Phillips. *Rice Postproduction Technology in the Tropics*. East-West Center. Honolulu: University Press of Hawaii, 1979.

Etkin, Nina L. "The Cull of the Wild". In *Eating on the Wild Side: The Pharmacologic, Ecologic, and Social Implications of Using Noncultigens*, edited by Nina L. Etkin, 1–21. Tucson: University of Arizona Press, 1994.

Evans, L.T. *Crop Evolution, Adaptation and Yield*. Cambridge, UK: Cambridge University Press, 1993.

Facey, Valerie. *Busha Browne's Indispensable Compendium of Traditional Jamaican Cookery*. Kingston: Mill Press, 1993.

Falola, Toyin. "'Salt Is Gold': The Management of Salt Scarcity in Nigeria during World War II". *Canadian Journal of African Studies* 26 (1992): 412–36.

Farb, Peter, and George Armelagos. *Consuming Passions: The Anthropology of Eating*. New York: Washington Square Press, 1983.

Farr, Thomas A. "Land Animals of Jamaica: Origins and Endemism". *Jamaica Journal* 17, no. 1 (1984): 38–48.

Fawcett, William, and Alfred Barton Rendle. *Flora of Jamaica: Containing Descriptions of the Flowering Plants Known from the Island*. 7 vols. London: British Museum, 1920.

Feild, Rachael. *Irons in the Fire: A History of Cooking Equipment*. Marlborough, UK: Crowood, 1984.

Feng, P.C. "Hypoglycin – from Ackee: A Review". *West Indian Medical Journal* 18 (1969): 238–43.

Fenn, Annie Manville. "Housekeeping in Jamaica". *The Youth's Companion*, 16 March 1893.

Fenner, Michael, and Ken Thompson. *The Ecology of Seeds*. Cambridge, UK: Cambridge University Press, 2005.

Fernández-Armesto, Felipe. *Food: A History*. London: Pan Books, 2002.

Festival 70, National Culinary Arts Finals, July 22, 1970, Courtleigh Manor Hotel (cyclostyled).

Festival 71, National Culinary Arts, Finals – July 21, 1971, Sheraton-Kingston Hotel (cyclostyled).

A Festival of Jamaican Cuisine. Kingston: Jamaica Cultural Development Culinary Arts Department, 1983.

Fiddes, Nick. *Meat: A Natural Symbol*. London: Routledge, 1991.

Fielding, W.J., and K. Ryder. *The Biometry of Sweet Potato* (Ipomoea batatas): *Some Considerations for Field Experiments*. Special Publication No. 8. Kingston: Ministry of Agriculture and Mining, 1995.

Fieldhouse, Paul. *Food and Nutrition: Customs and Culture*. London: Croom Helm, 1986.

Ferrières, Madeleine. *Sacred Cow, Mad Cow: A History of Food Fears*. New York: Columbia University Press, 2006.

Flint, J.E. "Economic Change in West Africa in the Nineteenth Century". In *History of West*

Africa, vol. 2, edited by J.F.A. Ajayi and Michael Crowder, 380–401. Harlow, UK: Longman, 1974.

Floyd, Troy S. *The Columbus Dynasty in the Caribbean 1492–1526*. Albuquerque: University of New Mexico Press, 1973.

Fold, Niels, and Bill Pritchard, eds. *Cross-continental Food Chains*. London: Routledge, 2005.

Food and Agriculture Organization. *FAO Yearbook: Production*. Rome: FAO, 1948–2000.

——. *World Crop Statistics: Area, Production and Yield, 1948–64*. Rome: FAO, 1966.

Forbes, J.C., and R.D. Watson. *Plants in Agriculture*. Cambridge, UK: Cambridge University Press, 1992.

Forrest, A.S., and John Henderson. *Jamaica*. London: Adam and Charles Black, 1906.

Forsythe, Richard H., and Ralph A. Miller. "Salt in Processed Foods". In *Biological and Behavioral Aspects of Salt Intake*, edited by Morley R. Kare, Melvin J. Fregly, and Rudy A. Bernard, 221–28. New York: Academic Press, 1980.

Francis, F.J. "Colour and Appearance as Dominating Sensory Properties of Foods". In *Sensory Properties of Foods*, edited by G.G. Birch, J.G. Brennan, and K.J. Parker, 27–43. London: Applied Science Publishers, 1977.

Franco, M.R.B., and N.S. Janzantti. "Aroma of Minor Tropical Fruits". *Flavour and Fragrance Journal* 20 (2005): 358–71.

Frank, Marion E., and Thomas P. Hettinger. "What the Tongue Tells the Brain about Taste". *Chemical Senses* 30, suppl. 1 (2005): i68–69.

Fraser, Henry, Sean Carrington, Addinton Forde, and John Gilmore. *A–Z of Barbadian Heritage*. Kingston: Heinemann, 1990.

Frohlich, Edward D., and Franz H. Messerli. "Sodium and Hypertension". In *Sodium: Its Biologic Significance*, edited by Solomon Papper, 143–74. Boca Raton, FL: CRC Press, 1982.

"From Herrings to Beef: Our Elevation to That Dietary Superiority, and How We Produce the Beef". *Planters' Punch* 4, no. 2 (1939–40): 13–14.

Frost, Alan. *The Global Reach of Empire: Britain's Maritime Expansion in the Indian and Pacific Oceans 1764–1815*. Melbourne, Australia: Miegunyah Press, 2003.

Froude, James Anthony. *The English in the West Indies or the Bow of Ulysses*. London: Longmans, Green, 1888.

Fulford, Timothy. "The Taste of Paradise: The Fruits of Romanticism in the Empire". In *Cultures of Taste/Theories of Appetite: Eating Romanticism*, edited by Timothy Morton, 108–26. New York: Palgrave Macmillan, 2004.

Fulford, Tim, Debbie Lee, and Peter J. Kitson. *Literature, Science and Exploration in the Romantic Era: Bodies of Knowledge*. Cambridge, UK: Cambridge University Press, 2004.

Fumihito, Akishinonomiya, et al. "One Subspecies of the Red Junglefowl (*Gallus gallus gallus*) Suffices as the Matriarchic Ancestor of all Domestic Breeds". *Proceedings of the National Academy of Sciences of the United States of America* 91 (20 December 1994): 12505–9.

Gaertner, Erika E. "Breadstuff from Fir (*Abies balsamea*)". *Economic Botany* 24 (1970): 69–72.

Galetti, Mauro, and José Carlos Fernandez. "Palm Heart Harvesting in the Brazilian Atlantic Forest: Changes in Industry Structure and the Illegal Trade". *Journal of Applied Ecology* 35 (1998): 294–301.

Galinat, Walton C. "The Domestication and Genetic Erosion of Maize". *Economic Botany*, 28 (1974): 31–37.

Gallagher, Catherine, and Stephen Greenblatt. *Practicing New Historicism*. Chicago: University of Chicago Press, 2000.

Gardnier, Kenneth. *Creole Caribbean Cookery*. London: Grafton, 1986.

Garine, Igor de, Stephen Hugh-Jones, and Armin Prinz. "Cultural Factors in Food Choices – Background". In *Tropical Forests, People and Food: Biocultural Interactions and Applications to Development*, edited by C.M. Hladik, A. Hladik, O.F. Linares, H. Pagezy, A. Semple, and M. Hadley, 525–32. Paris: UNESCO, 1993.

Gartner, Lawrence M., Jane Morton, Ruth A. Lawrence, Audrey J. Naylor, et al. "Breastfeeding and the Use of Human Milk". *Pediatrics* 115 (2005): 496–506.

Gaunt, Mary. *Reflection – In Jamaica*. London: Ernest Benn, 1932.

Geddes, Bruce. *World Food Caribbean*. London: Lonely Planet Publications, 2001.

Geissler, P. Wenzel. "The Significance of Earth-Eating: Social and Cultural Aspects of Geophagy among Luo Children". *Africa* 70 (2000): 653–82.

Gifts from a Jamaican Kitchen. Kingston: LHM Publishing, 2002.

Glasse, Hannah. *The Art of Cookery Made Plain and Easy*. 1747. London: Prospect Books, 1983.

Gloudon, Barbara. "Gourmet Delights Jamaican-Style". *SkyWritings* 123 (July/August 1999): 38–39.

———. "In Celebration of the Patty". In *A Tapestry of Jamaica: The Best of Skywritings, Air Jamaica's Inflight Magazine*, edited by Linda Gambrill, 136–37. 2001. Kingston: Creative Communications, 2003.

Goldman, Vivien. *Pearl's Delicious Jamaican Dishes: Recipes from Pearl Bell's Repertoire*. New York: Island Trading, 1992.

Goodbody, Ivan. "Avian Refuges". *Jamaica Journal* 25, no. 2 (1994): 55–60.

Goodwin, Derek. *Pigeons and Doves of the World*. 3rd edition. Ithaca, NY: Cornell University Press, 1983.

Gosse, Philip Henry. *The Birds of Jamaica*. London: John van Voorst, 1847.

———. *A Naturalist's Sojourn in Jamaica*. London: Longman, Brown, Green, and Longmans, 1851.

Gould, Stanley F. "Anatomy of the Breast". In *Lactation: Physiology, Nutrition, and Breast-Feeding*, edited by Margaret C. Neville and Marianne R. Neifert, 23–47. New York: Plenum, 1983.

Graham, Thomas L. *Kingston 100: 1872–1972*. Kingston: Tom Graham Publications, 1972.

Green, B.G. "Chemesthesis: Pungency as a Component of Flavor". *Trends in Food Science and Technology* 7 (1996): 415–20.

Grosch, Werner, Michael Czerny, Robert Wagner, and Florian Mayer. "Studies on the Aroma of Roasted Coffee". In *Flavour Science: Recent Developments*, edited by A.J. Taylor and D.S. Mottram, 200–205. Cambridge, UK: Royal Society of Chemistry, 1996.

Guilbride, P.D.L., Viola Mae Young, and Jeanette Norsen. "A Bacteriological Survey of Milk and Milk Products in Jamaica". *West Indian Medical Journal* 4 (1955): 43–44.

Guo, W.W., D. Prasad, P. Serrano, F.G. Gmitter, Jr, and J.W. Grosser. "Citrus Somatic Hybridization with Potential for Direct Tetraploid Scion Cultivar Development". *Journal of Horticultural Science and Biotechnology* 79 (2004): 400–405.

Gustavson, Kent. "Economic Production from the Artisanal Fisheries of Jamaica". *Fisheries Research* 57 (2002): 103–15.

Habhan, Gary Paul. *Why Some Like It Hot: Food, Genes, and Cultural Diversity*. Washington, DC: Island Press, 2004.

Haedrich, Richard L., and Lawrence C. Hamilton. "The Fall and Future of Newfoundland's Cod Fishery". *Society and Natural Resources* 13 (2000): 359–72.

Hall, Douglas. "Botanical and Horticultural Enterprise in Eighteenth-Century Jamaica". In *West Indies Accounts: Essays on the History of the British Caribbean and the Atlantic Economy in Honour of Richard Sheridan*, edited by Roderick A. McDonald, 101–25. Kingston: University of the West Indies Press, 1996.

———. *Free Jamaica, 1838–1865: An Economic History*. New Haven, CT: Yale University Press, 1959.

———. *Grace, Kennedy and Company Limited: A Story of Jamaican Enterprise*. Kingston: Grace, Kennedy and Co., 1992.

———. *Ideas and Illustrations in Economic History*. New York: Holt, Rinehart and Winston, 1964.

———. *In Miserable Slavery: Thomas Thistlewood in Jamaica, 1750–86*. London: Macmillan, 1989.

Hall, Stephen J.G. *Livestock Biodiversity: Genetic Resources for the Farming of the Future*. Oxford: Blackwell, 2004.

Hamilton, Jill. *A Little Jamaican Cookbook*. Kingston: Heinemann Caribbean, 1990.

Hancock, David. "Commerce and Conversation in the Eighteenth-Century Atlantic: The Invention of Madeira Wine". *Journal of Interdisciplinary History* 29 (1998): 197–219.

Handler, Jerome S. "The History of Arrowroot and the Origin of Peasantries in the British West Indies". *Journal of Caribbean History* 2 (1971): 46–93.

Handler, Jerome S., Arthur C. Aufderheide, Robert S. Corruccini, Elizabeth M. Brandon, and Lorentz E. Wittmers, Jr. "Lead Contact and Poisoning in Barbados Slaves: Historical, Chemical, and Biological Evidence". *Social Science History* 10 (1986): 399–425.

Handler, Jerome S., and Robert S. Corruccini. "Weaning among West Indian Slaves: Historical and Bioanthropological Evidence from Barbados". *William and Mary Quarterly* 43 (1986): 111–17.

Hardouin, Jacques. "Developing Minilivestock as Source of Human Food, Animal Feed or Revenue: A Brief Overview". *Ecology of Food and Nutrition* 36 (1997): 95–107.

Harlan, Jack R. *Crops and Man*. Madison, WI: American Society of Agronomy/Crop Science Society of America, 1975.

———. *The Living Fields: Our Agricultural Heritage*. Cambridge, UK: Cambridge University Press, 1995.

Harries, H.H. "The Natural History of the Coconut". *Jamaica Journal* 44 (1980): 61–65.

Harris, C.L.G. "The True Traditions of My Ancestors". In *Maroon Heritage: Archaeological and Ethnographic Perspectives*, edited by E. Kofi Agorsah, 36–63. Kingston: Canoe Press, 1994.

Harris, David R. "Traditional Systems of Plant Food Production and the Origins of Agriculture in West Africa". In *Origins of African Plant Domestication*, edited by Jack R. Harlan, Jan M.J. De Wet, and Ann B.L. Stemler, 311–56. The Hague: Mouton, 1976.

Harris, Donald J. "Econometric Analysis of Household Consumption in Jamaica". *Social and Economic Studies* 13 (1964): 471–87.

Harris, Marvin. *Good to Eat: Riddles of Food and Culture.* New York: Simon and Schuster, 1985.

Hartley, C.W.S. *The Oil Palm.* London: Longman, 1977.

Harvey, G.C.M., Ivan Goodbody, and Karl A. Aiken. "The Artisanal Thread Herring Fishery of Kingston Harbour: A Review". *Bulletin of Marine Science* 73 (2003): 421–31.

Hausman, Bernice L. *Mother's Milk: Breastfeeding Controversies in American Culture.* New York: Routledge, 2003.

Hawkes, Alex D. *The Flavors of the Caribbean and Latin America: A Personal Collection of Recipes.* New York: Viking, 1978.

———. "In Search of the Perfect Patty". In *A Tapestry of Jamaica: The Best of Skywritings, Air Jamaica's Inflight Magazine,* edited by Linda Gambrill, 137. 1977. Kingston: Creative Communications, 2003.

Hawkes, J.G. *The Potato: Evolution, Biodiversity and Genetic Resources.* London: Belhaven, 1990.

Healthy Eating for Better Living: A Caribbean Handbook. Kingston: Caribbean Food and Nutrition Institute, 2002.

Hearne, John. *Stranger at the Gate.* London: Faber and Faber, 1956.

Heath, Henry B., and Gary Reineccius. *Flavor Chemistry and Technology.* Basingstoke, UK: Macmillan, 1986.

Helou, Anissa. *The Fifth Quarter.* Bath, UK: Absolute Press, 2004.

Henderson, Helen K., and Richard N. Henderson. "Traditional Onitsha Ibo Maternity Beliefs and Practices". In *Anthropology of Human Birth,* edited by Margarita Artyschwager Kay, 174–92. Philadelphia: F.A. Davis, 1982.

Henry, A.E.T. "Farewell Saltfish, Goodbye Mackerel and So-Long Salt Beef". *Gleaner,* 14 January 1968, 8.

Henry, Jacques, and Alicia Matthews Kwong. "Why Is Geophagy Treated Like Dirt?" *Deviant Behavior* 24 (2003): 353–71.

Hickeringill, Edmund. *Jamaica Viewed.* London: John Williams, 1661.

Higman, B.W. "Cookbooks and Caribbean Cultural Identity: An English-Language Hors d'Oeuvre". *New West Indian Guide* 72 (1998): 77–95.

———. *Jamaica Surveyed: Plantation Maps and Plans of the Eighteenth and Nineteenth Centuries.* Kingston: Institute of Jamaica Publications, 1988.

———. *Montpelier, Jamaica: A Plantation Community in Slavery and Freedom, 1739–1912.* Kingston: University of the West Indies Press, 1998.

———. *Slave Population and Economy in Jamaica, 1807–1834.* Cambridge, UK: Cambridge University Press, 1976.

———. *Slave Populations of the British Caribbean, 1807–1834.* Baltimore, MD: Johns Hopkins University Press, 1984.

Hill, Kenneth R. "The Vomiting Sickness of Jamaica". *West Indian Medical Journal* 1 (1951–52): 243–64.

Hill, Robert T. *Cuba and Porto Rico with the Other Islands of the West Indies.* London: T. Fisher Unwin, 1898.

Hobhouse, Henry. *Seeds of Change: Five Plants That Transformed Mankind*. New York: Harper and Row, 1985.

Hodgson, Robert W. "The Avocado: A Gift from the Middle Americas". *Economic Botany* 4 (1950): 253–93.

Holthuis, L.B. *FAO Species Catalogue*, vol. 1, *Shrimps and Prawns of the World*. Rome: Food and Agriculture Organization of the United Nations, 1980.

Holzberg, Carol S. *Minorities and Power in a Black Society: The Jewish Community of Jamaica*. Lanham, MD: North-South Publishing, 1987.

Homiak, John P. "Dub History: Soundings on Rastafari Livity and Language". In *Rastafari and Other African-Caribbean Worldviews*, edited by Barry Chevannes, 127–81. London: Macmillan, 1998.

Hopkins, Jerry. *Extreme Cuisine*. London: Bloomsbury, 2005.

Horn, Tammy. *Bees in America: How the Honey Bee Shaped a Nation*. Lexington: University Press of Kentucky, 2005.

Horowitz, Roger. *Putting Meat on the American Table: Taste, Technology, Transformation*. Baltimore, MD: Johns Hopkins University Press, 2006.

Howard, Josephine. "Jamaica and Jamaican Dishes". *American Cookery* 22, no. 6 (1918): 422–26.

Howard, Robert Mowbray, ed. *Records and Letters of the Family of the Longs of Longville, Jamaica, and Hampton Lodge, Surrey*. London: Simpkin, Marshall, Hamilton, Kent, 1925.

Howe, Andrea, Leslie Hoo Fung, Gerald Lalor, Robin Rattray, and Mitko Vutchkov. "Elemental Composition of Jamaican Foods 1: A Survey of Five Food Crop Categories". *Environmental Geochemistry and Health*, 27 (2005): 19–30.

Hughes, Kathryn. *The Short Life and Long Times of Mrs. Beeton*. New York: Knopf, 2006.

Hughes, William. *The American Physitian; or, a Treatise of the Roots, Plants, Trees, Shrubs, Fruit, Herbs, &c. Growing in the English Plantations in America*. London: William Crook, 1672.

Hulme, Peter. *Colonial Encounters: Europe and the Native Caribbean, 1492–1797*. London: Methuen, 1986.

Hunter, John M. "Geophagy in Africa and the United States: A Culture-Nutrition Hypothesis". *Geographical Review* 63 (1973): 170–95.

Hurston, Zora. *Voodoo Gods: An Inquiry into Native Myths and Magic in Jamaica and Haiti*. London: J.M. Dent, 1939.

Hyatt, Charles. *When Me Was a Boy*. Kingston: Institute of Jamaica Publications, 1989.

The Importance of Jamaica to Great-Britain, Consider'd: In a Letter to a Gentleman. London: A. Dodd, [c. 1740].

Ingle, Robert M., and F.G. Walton Smith. *Sea Turtles and the Turtle Industry of the West Indies, Florida and the Gulf of Mexico, with Annotated Bibliography*. Miami, FL: University of Miami Press, 1949.

Innis, Harold A. *The Cod Fisheries: The History of an International Economy*. Toronto: University of Toronto Press, 1954.

An Inquiry Concerning the Trade, Commerce, and Policy of Jamaica, Relative to the Scarcity of Money, and the Causes and Bad Effects of such Scarcity, Peculiar to that Island. London: T. Kinnersly and G. Woodfal, 1759.

International Chicken Genome Sequencing Consortium. "Sequence and Comparative Analysis of the Chicken Genome Provide Unique Perspectives on Vertebrate Evolution". *Nature* 432 (2004): 695–716.

Jackson, J.B.C. "Reefs since Columbus". *Coral Reefs* 16, suppl. (1997): S23–32.

Jamaica Agricultural Society. *The Farmer's Food Manual: A Recipe Book for the West Indies*. Glasgow: University Press, 1957.

Jamaica. Central Bureau of Statistics. *National Income of Jamaica for 1943*. Kingston: Bureau of Statistics, 1946.

Jamaica. Department of Statistics. *Annual Abstract of Statistics*. Kingston: Department of Statistics, 1938–64.

———. *Consumer Price Index*. Kingston: Department of Statistics, 1967–85.

———. *Household Expenditure Survey, 1958*. [Kingston]: Department of Statistics, 1960.

———. *Production Statistics*. Kingston: Department of Statistics, 1960–84.

———. *Rural Price Index*. Kingston: Department of Statistics, 1954–55.

Jamaica, Finest Taste for All Seasons: Sweet and Savoury Dishes, Cocktails and Desserts. Compiled by Laurel Hepburn. Kingston: Laurel Hepburn and Associates, 1998.

Jamaica Information Service. *Banana Recipes*. 1965. Reprint, Kingston: Novelty Trading, 1975.

———. *Jamaican Cuisine*. Kingston: Jamaica Information Service, 1964.

Jamaica. Ministry of Agriculture. *The Development of the Jamaica Brahman Breed of Beef Cattle*. Animal Husbandry Bulletin No. 4. Kingston: Ministry of Agriculture, Research and Development Division, 1983.

———. *The Development of the Jamaica Red Poll Breed of Cattle*. Animal Husbandry Bulletin No. 3. Kingston: Agricultural Information Service, 1979.

———. *Goat Production Handbook*. Kingston: Ministry of Agriculture and Goat Breeders Society of Jamaica, 2001.

Jamaica. Ministry of Agriculture (Export Division). *Jamaica Pimento "Allspice": Uses and Recipes*. Kingston: Jamaica Information Service, 1987.

Jamaica. Ministry of Health. "Jamaica Serious about Breastfeeding". *Cajanus* 27, no. 3 (1994): 119–22.

Jamaica Rum Book. London: Macmillan Caribbean, 1986.

Jamaica Society for the Blind. *Recipe Round-up: A Book of Favourite Recipes*. 1956. Mandeville, Jamaica: Jamaica Society for the Blind, 1968.

Jamaica Tourist Association. *Jamaica: "The Land of Streams and Woods"*. Kingston: Jamaica Tourist Association, 1911.

A Jamaican Cheese Cookbook. Kingston: Dairy Industries Jamaica, 1988.

Jekyll, Walter, ed. *Jamaican Song and Story: Annancy Stories, Digging Sings, Ring Tunes, and Dancing Tunes*. London: David Nutt, 1907.

Jelliffe, Derrick B., and E.F. Patrice Jelliffe. *Human Milk in the Modern World: Psychosocial, Nutritional, and Economic Significance*. Oxford: Oxford University Press, 1978.

Jenkins, J.A. "The Origin of the Cultivated Tomato". *Economic Botany* 2 (1948): 279–92.

Jenkins, Virginia Scott. *Bananas: An American History*. Washington, DC: Smithsonian Institution Press, 2000.

Johns, Timothy. *With Bitter Herbs Shall They Eat It: Chemical Ecology and the Origins of Human Diet and Medicine*. Tucson: University of Arizona Press, 1990.

Johnston, Bruce F. *The Staple Food Economies of Western Tropical Africa*. Stanford, CA: Stanford University Press, 1958.

Jones, Novlet C. *Cook Up Jamaican Style*. Kingston: Information and Communications Unit, Ministry of Agriculture, 1977. 2nd edition, 1981. 3rd edition, 2000.

Jones, William O. *Manioc in Africa*. Stanford, CA: Stanford University Press, 1959.

Joslyn, M.A. "The Freezing Preservation of Vegetables". *Economic Botany* 15 (1961): 347–75.

Kaplan, Steven Laurence. "Breadways". *Food and Foodways* 7 (1997): 1–44.

Kaufman, Jay S., and Susan A. Hall. "The Slavery Hypertension Hypothesis: Dissemination and Appeal of a Modern Race Theory". *Epidemiology* 14 (2003): 111–18.

Kean, E.A. "Commentary on a Review on the Mechanism of Ackee-Induced Vomiting Sickness". *West Indian Medical Journal* 37 (1988): 139–42.

Kearsley, M.W., and P.J. Sicard. "The Chemistry of Starches and Sugars Present in Food". In *Dietary Starches and Sugars in Man: A Comparison*, edited by John Dobbing, 1–33. London: Springer-Verlag, 1989.

Keegan, William F. *The People Who Discovered Columbus: The Prehistory of the Bahamas*. Gainesville: University of Florida Press, 1992.

Kelly, Daniel L., and Timothy A. Dickinson. "Local Names for Vascular Plants in the John Crow Mountains, Jamaica". *Economic Botany* 39 (1985): 346–62.

Kenyon, Karl W. "Monk Seals". In *Handbook of Marine Mammals*, vol. 2, *Seals*, edited by Sam H. Ridgway and Richard J. Harrison, 195–220. London: Academic Press, 1981.

Kerr, Rhema. "Jamaica's Sea Turtles". *Jamaica Journal* 26, no. 1 (1996): 2–6.

King, John. *Reaching for the Sun: How Plants Work*. Cambridge, UK: Cambridge University Press, 1997.

King, Neville L.R., and J. Howard Bradbury. "Bitterness of Cassava: Identification of a New Apiosyl Glucoside and Other Compounds That Affect Its Bitter Taste". *Journal of the Science of Food and Agriculture* 68 (1995): 223–30.

Kiple, Kenneth F., and Virginia H. Kiple. "Deficiency Diseases in the Caribbean". *Journal of Interdisciplinary History* 11 (1980): 197–215.

Kiple, Kenneth F., and Kriemhild Coneè Ornelas, eds. *The Cambridge World History of Food*. Cambridge, UK: Cambridge University Press, 2000.

Kirkpatrick, W. *A Short History of the First One Hundred Years of the Public Water Supply in the Kingston and Liguanea Area, 1849–1949*. Kingston: Water Commission, 1949.

Klaassen, Curtis D., ed. *Casarett and Doull's Toxicology: The Basic Science of Poisons*. 6th edition. New York: McGraw-Hill, 2001.

Klein, Herbert S., and Stanley L. Engerman. "Fertility Differentials between Slaves in the United States and the British West Indies: A Note on Lactation Practices and Their Possible Implications". *William and Mary Quarterly* 35 (1978): 357–74.

Kloppenburg, Jack Ralph, Jr. *First the Seed: The Political Economy of Plant Biotechnology, 1492–2000*. Cambridge, UK: Cambridge University Press, 1988.

Knight, Peter G., Jose C. Jackson, Brendan Bain, and Denise Eldemire-Shearer. "Household Food Safety Awareness of Selected Urban Consumers in Jamaica". *International Journal of Food Sciences and Nutrition* 54 (2003): 309–20.

Konig, Susan E. "The Breeding Biology of Black-Billed Parrot *Amazona agilis* and Yellow-Billed Parrot *Amazona collaria* in Cockpit Country, Jamaica". *Bird Conservation International* 11 (2001): 205–25.

Korsmeyer, Carolyn. "Introduction: Perspectives on Taste". In *The Taste Culture Reader: Experiencing Food and Drink*, edited by Carolyn Korsmeyer, 1–9. Oxford: Berg, 2005.

Kotsonis, Frank N., George A. Burdock, and W. Gary Flamm. "Food Toxicology". In *Casarett and Doull's Toxicology: The Basic Science of Poisons*, edited by Curtis D. Klaassen, 1049–88. New York: McGraw-Hill, 2001.

Kroeze, Jan H.A. "The Perception of Complex Taste Stimuli". In *Psychological Basis of Sensory Evaluation*, edited by R.L. McBride and H.J.H. MacFie, 41–68. London: Elsevier Applied Science, 1990.

Kumamoto, J., R.W. Scora, H.W. Lawton, and W.A. Clerx. "Mystery of the Forbidden Fruit: Historical Epilogue on the Origin of the Grapefruit, *Citrus paradisi* (Rutaceae)". *Economic Botany* 41 (1987): 97–107.

Kurlansky, Mark. *Cod: A Biography of the Fish That Changed the World*. London: Vintage, 1999.

———. *Salt: A World History*. London: Vintage, 2003.

Kurtu, M.Y. "An Assessment of the Productivity for Meat and the Carcass Yield of Camels (*Camelus dromedarius*) and the Consumption of Camel Meat in the Eastern Region of Ethiopia". *Tropical Animal Health and Production* 36 (2004): 65–76.

Lack, Andrew, and David Evans. *Plant Biology*. 2nd edition. New York: Taylor and Francis, 2005.

Lack, David. *Island Biology Illustrated by the Land Birds of Jamaica*. Berkeley: University of California Press, 1976.

Laing, David G., and Anthony Jinks. "Flavour Perception Mechanisms". *Trends in Food Science and Technology* 7 (1996): 387–89.

Lake, Obiagele. "Cultural Beliefs and Breastfeeding Practices among Jamaican Rastafarians". *Cajanus* 25 (4) (1992): 201–14.

Lalor, Gerald, Robin Rattray, Mitko Vutchkov, Bertha Campbell, and Karen Lewis-Bell. "Blood Lead Levels in Jamaican School Children". *The Science of the Total Environment* 269 (2001): 171–81.

Lancaster, P.A., and J.E. Brooks. "Cassava Leaves as Human Food". *Economic Botany* 37 (1983): 331–48.

Lancaster, P.A., J.S. Ingram, M.Y. Lim, and D.G. Coursey. "Traditional Cassava-Based Foods: Survey of Processing Techniques". *Economic Botany* 36 (1982): 12–45.

Land, Derek G. "Perspectives on the Effects of Interactions of Flavor Perception: An Overview". In *Flavor-Food Interactions*, edited by Robert J. McGorrin and Jane V. Leland, 2–11. Washington, DC: American Chemical Society, 1996.

Landman, Jacqueline P., and Violet Shaw-Lyon. "Breast-Feeding in Decline in Kingston, Jamaica, 1973". *West Indian Medical Journal* 25 (1976): 43–57.

Landman, J., and J. St E. Hall. "The Dietary Habits and Knowledge of Folklore of Pregnant Jamaican Women". *Ecology of Food and Nutrition* 12 (1983): 203–10.

Landman-Bogues, Jacqueline. "Rastafarian Food Habits". *Cajanus* 9 (1976): 228–34.

Lang, Tim, and Michael Heasman. *Food Wars: The Global Battle for Mouths, Minds and Markets.* London: Earthscan, 2004.

Law, Robin. *The Horse in West African History: The Role of the Horse in the Societies of Pre-colonial West Africa.* Oxford: Oxford University Press, 1980.

Laws of Jamaica. [Various editions].

Leader, Alfred. *Through Jamaica with a Kodak.* Bristol: John Wright, 1907.

Lee, James W. "Arawak Burens". *Archaeology Jamaica* (second quarter, 1980): 1–12.

Leonard, Jonathan Norton. *Latin American Cooking.* [New York]: Time-Life International, 1970.

Leslie, Charles. *A New and Exact Account of Jamaica.* Edinburgh: A. Kincaid, 1739.

Levitt, Kari, and Alister McIntyre. *Canada–West Indies Economic Relations.* Montreal: Centre for Developing-Area Studies, McGill University, 1967.

Lewicki, Tadeusz. *West African Food in the Middle Ages.* Cambridge, UK: Cambridge University Press, 1974.

Lewis, Matthew Gregory. *Journal of a West India Proprietor, Kept during a Residence in the Island of Jamaica.* London: John Murray, 1834.

Linné, Carl von. *Flora Jamaicensis.* Uppsala: 1759.

———. *Plantarum Jamaicensium Pugillus.* Uppsala: 1759.

Long, Edward. *A Free and Candid Review of a Tract, Entitled, "Observations on the Commerce of the American States".* London: T. and W. Lowndes, 1784.

———. *The History of Jamaica.* 3 vols. London: T. Lowndes, 1774.

Lovejoy, Paul E. *Salt of the Desert Sun: A History of Salt Production and Trade in the Central Sudan.* Cambridge, UK: Cambridge University Press, 1986.

Loveland, Carol J., Thomas H. Furst, and Georgia C. Lauritzen. "Geophagia in Human Populations". *Food and Foodways* 3 (1989): 333–56.

Lowe, Henry, and Errol Morrison. *Ganja: The Jamaican Connection.* Kingston: Pelican, 2001.

Lowe, Henry, Errol Morrison, Kenneth Magnus and Ellen Campbell-Grizzle. *Poisonous Plants of Jamaica.* Kingston: Pelican, 2002.

Lowenstein, Eleanor. *Bibliography of American Cookery Books, 1742–1860.* 3rd edition. Worcester, MA: American Antiquarian Society, 1972.

Lumsden, Vin. "Jamaica's Dairy Industry: A Perspective". *Cajanus* 26 (1993): 186–90.

Lunan, John. *Hortus Jamaicensis, or a Botanical Description, (According to the Linnean System) and an Account of the Virtues, &c. of its Indigenous Plants Hitherto Unknown, as also of the most useful exotics.* 2 vols. [Spanish Town, Jamaica]: St Jago de la Vega Gazette, 1814.

Lutz, Peter L., and John A. Musick, eds. *The Biology of Sea Turtles.* Vol. 1. Boca Raton, FL: CRC Press, 1996.

Lutz, Peter L., John A. Musick and Jeanette Wyneken, eds. *The Biology of Sea Turtles.* Vol. 2. Boca Raton, FL: CRC Press, 2003.

MacDonald, Kevin C., and Rachel Hutton MacDonald. "The Origins and Development of

Domesticated Animals in Arid West Africa". In *The Origins and Development of African Livestock: Archaeology, Genetics, Linguistics and Ethnography*, edited by Roger M. Blench and Kevin C. MacDonald, 127–62. London: UCL Press, 2000.

MacDougall, Douglas B. "Colour in Meat". In *Sensory Properties of Foods*, edited by G.G. Birch, J.G. Brennan, and K.J. Parker, 59–69. London: Applied Science Publishers, 1977.

Macfadyen, James. *The Flora of Jamaica: A Description of the Plants of That Island, Arranged According to the Natural Orders*. London: Longman, Orme, Brown, Green, and Longmans, 1837.

MacGregor, Arthur. "The Life, Character and Career of Sir Hans Sloane". In *Sir Hans Sloane: Collector, Scientist, Antiquary – Founding Father of the British Museum*, edited by Arthur MacGregor, 11–44. London: British Museum Press, 1994.

MacGregor, Graham A., and Hugh E. de Wardener. *Salt, Diet and Health: Neptune's Poisoned Chalice – The Origins of High Blood Pressure*. Cambridge, UK: Cambridge University Press, 1998.

Mackay, David. "Banks, Bligh and Breadfruit". *New Zealand Journal of History* 8 (1974): 61–77.

Madden, R.R. *A Twelvemonth's Residence in the West Indies*. London: James Cochrane, 1835.

Magnus, Marcia. "Jamaican Fast Food Consumption Patterns". *Cajanus* 27 (1994): 80–95.

Mahabee, Linda A., and Milton L. Mahabee. *A Vegetarian Cookbook and Better Living Guide*. Mandeville, Jamaica: College Press, 1987.

Mahias, Marie-Claude. "Milk and Its Transmutations in Indian Society". *Food and Foodways* 2 (1988): 265–88.

Mansingh, Ajai, and Laurie Hammond. "The Invasion of the Cattle Egrets". *Jamaica Journal* 11, nos 3–4 (1978): 57–59.

Marcelle, Myrtle. "Sorrel: A Truly Jamaican Tradition". *Jamaica Journal* 11, nos 3–4 (1978): 60–61.

Marchand, Cynthia, Inez Miles, Hyacinth Glen, Rubye Gayle, and Sadie Campbell. *Home Economics for Caribbean Schools: CXC Food and Nutrition, a Two Year Course*. 3rd edition. Kingston: Jamaica Publishing House, 2002.

Marly, or the Life of a Planter in Jamaica. Glasgow: R. Griffin, 1828.

Marsden, Peter. *An Account of the Island of Jamaica*. Newcastle, 1788.

Martin, E.R.H. *Maize Investigation in Jamaica: A Review of Research 1940–1969*. Kingston: Agricultural Information Service, Ministry of Agriculture and Fisheries, 1971.

Martin, Franklin W. "Okra, Potential Multiple-Purpose Crop for the Temperate Zones and Tropics". *Economic Botany* 36 (1982): 340–45.

Matthews, Peter, and Ryohei Terauchi. "The Genetics of Agriculture: DNA Variation in Taro and Yam". In *Tropical Archaeobotany: Applications and New Developments*, edited by Jon G. Hather, 251–62. London: Routledge, 1994.

Maxwell, James. "Pathological Enquiry into the Nature of Cachexia Africana, as It Is Generally Connected with Dirt-Eating". *Jamaica Physical Journal* 2 (1835): 409–35.

May, Jacques, and Donna L. McLellan. *The Ecology of Malnutrition in the Caribbean*. New York: Hafner, 1973.

McAnuff, Marie A., Felix O. Omoruyi, Angela Sotelo-López, and Helen N. Asemota. "Proximate

Analysis and Some Antinutritional Factor Constituents in Selected Varieties of Jamaican Yams (*Dioscorea* and *Rajana* spp.)". *Plant Foods for Human Nutrition* 60 (2005): 93–98.

McBain, Helen. "Towards a Viable Water Utility in Jamaica". *Social and Economic Studies* 34 (1985): 77–95.

McCann, James C. *Maize and Grace: Africa's Encounter with a New World Crop, 1500–2000*. Cambridge, MA: Harvard University Press, 2005.

McGee, Harold. *On Food and Cooking: The Science and Lore of the Kitchen*. London: Unwin Hyman, 1984.

McGlashan, Don. *Growing Scotch Bonnet Pepper* (Capsicum chinense Jacq.) *in Jamaica*. Kingston: Ministry of Agriculture, 2002.

McGrew, William C. "The Other Faunivory: Primate Insectivory and Early Human Diet". In *Meat-Eating and Human Evolution*, edited by Craig B. Stanford and Henry T. Bunn, 160–78. New York: Oxford University Press, 2001.

McIntosh, Elaine N. *American Food Habits in Historical Perspective*. Westport, CT: Praeger, 1995.

McKay, Claude. *Banana Bottom*. New York: Harper and Row, 1933.

———. *The Dialect Poetry of Claude McKay*. 1912. Plainview, NY: Books for Libraries Press, 1972.

McKey, Doyle, and Stephen Beckerman. "Chemical Ecology, Plant Evolution and Traditional Manioc Cultivation Systems". In *Tropical Forests, People and Food: Biocultural Interactions and Applications to Development*, edited by C.M. Hladik, A. Hladik, O.F. Linares, H. Pagezy, A. Semple, and M. Hadley, 83–112. Paris: UNESCO, 1993.

McLean, Elaine R. *Jamaican Cooking with Jamaican Talk*. Milwaukee: privately printed, 1989.

McWilliams, James E. *A Revolution in Eating: How the Quest for Food Shaped America*. New York: Columbia University Press, 2005.

Meikle, Paulette. "Spatio-temporal Trends in Root Crop Production and Marketing in Jamaica". *Caribbean Geography* 3 (1992): 223–35.

"Melinda". *Planters' Punch* 4, no. 2 (1939–40): 5–6.

Melville, Bendley. "The Importance of Goats in Agricultural Development and Health and Nutrition". *Cajanus* 21 (1988): 203–11.

Migdalski, Edward C., and George S. Fichter. *The Fresh and Salt Water Fishes of the World*. New York: Knopf, 1976.

Mignon-Grasteau, Sandrine, A. Boissy, J. Bouix, J.M. Faure, A.D. Fisher, G.N. Hinch, P. Jensen, et al. "Genetics of Adaptation and Domestication in Livestock". *Livestock Production Science* 93 (2005): 3–14.

Miller, Elsa. *Caribbean Cooking and Menus*. Kingston: Kingston Publishers, 1982.

———. *Cook It My Way*. Discovery Bay, Jamaica: Northern Lithographers, [1970].

Miller, Elsa, and Leonard "Sonny" Henry. *Creative Bahamian Cooking and Menus*. Kingston: Kingston Publishers, 1982.

———. *Creative Jamaican Cooking and Menus*. Kingston: Kingston Publishers, 1982.

Mintz, Sidney W. *Sweetness and Power: The Place of Sugar in Modern History*. New York: Viking, 1985.

———. *Tasting Food, Tasting Freedom: Excursions into Eating, Culture, and the Past*. Boston: Beacon, 1996.

Mintz, Sidney W., and Douglas G. Hall. *The Origins of the Jamaican Internal Marketing System*. Yale University Publications in Anthropology 57 (New Haven, CT: Yale University, Department of Anthropology, 1960): 3–26.

Miracle, Marvin P. *Maize in Tropical Africa*. Madison: University of Wisconsin Press, 1966.

Montgomery, R.D. "Observations on the Cyanide Content and Toxicity of Tropical Pulses". *West Indian Medical Journal* 13 (1964): 1–11.

Moore, Brian L., and Michele A. Johnson, eds. *The Land We Live In: Jamaica in 1890*. Mona, Jamaica: Social History Project, Department of History, University of the West Indies, 2000.

———. *"Squalid Kingston", 1890–1920: How the Poor Lived, Moved and Had Their Being*. Mona: Social History Project, Department of History, University of the West Indies, 2000.

Morgan, Kevin, Terry Marsden, and Jonathan Murdoch. *Worlds of Food: Place, Power, and Provenance in the Food Chain*. Oxford: Oxford University Press, 2006.

Morgan, W.B., and J.C. Pugh. *West Africa*. London: Methuen, 1969.

Morley, Laurel-Ann. *Cooking with Caribbean Rum*. London: Macmillan, 1991.

Moscoso, Carlos G. "West Indian Cherry: Richest Known Source of Natural Vitamin C". *Economic Botany* 10 (1956): 280–94.

Moynihan, Martin, and Arcadio F. Rodaniche. *The Behavior and Natural History of the Caribbean Reef Squid* Sepioteuthis sepioidea. Berlin: Verlag Paul Parey, 1982.

Muheim, Andreas, Alex Häusler, Boris Schilling, and Konrad Lerch. "The Impact of Recombinant DNA-Technology on the Flavour and Fragrance Industry". In *Flavours and Fragrances*, edited by Karl A.D. Swift, 11–20. Cambridge, UK: Royal Society of Chemistry, 1997.

Mukherjee, S.K. "Origin of Mango (*Mangifera indica*)". *Economic Botany* 26 (1972): 260–64.

Muller, H.G. *An Introduction to Tropical Food Science*. Cambridge, UK: Cambridge University Press, 1988.

Mullin, Sue. *Creole Cooking: The Taste of Tropical Islands*. London: Apple Press, 2000.

Multhauf, Robert P. *Neptune's Gift: A History of Common Salt*. Baltimore, MD: Johns Hopkins University Press, 1978.

Munro, J.L. "The Sea Fisheries of Jamaica: Past, Present and Future". *Jamaica Journal* 3, no. 3 (1969): 16–22.

Munroe, J.A. "Food Consumption Patterns in Jamaica". *Papers of the Workshop on Household Food Availability and Nutritional Status*, 51–64. Kingston: Caribbean Food and Nutrition Institute, 1987.

Murray, Byron, and Patrick Lewin. *The Jamaican Chef: Over a Century of Traditional Jamaican Dishes*. Montego Bay, Jamaica: Life Long Publishers, 1990.

"Myrtle and Money". *Planters' Punch* 4, no. 4 (1941–42): 37.

National Research Council. Board on Science and Technology for International Development. *Postharvest Food Losses in Developing Countries*. Washington, DC: National Academy of Sciences, 1978.

Natural Resources Conservation Department. *Marine Mammal of Jamaica: The West Indian Manatee*. Kingston: Jamaica Information Service, 1991.

Nenquin, Jacques. *Salt: A Study in Economic Prehistory*. Bruges, Belgium: De Tempel, 1961.

Nestlé Quick 'n' Easy Desserts and Drinks. Kingston: Food Specialities Jamaica Ltd, [c.1988].

Neville, Margaret C., and Marianne R. Neifert. "An Introduction to Lactation and Breast-Feeding". In *Lactation: Physiology, Nutrition, and Breast-Feeding*, edited by Margaret C. Neville and Marianne R. Neifert, 3–20. New York: Plenum, 1983.

"The New Industry of Sweets". *Planters' Punch* 3, no. 2 (1933–34): 86.

Newnham-Davis, Lieut.-Col. [Nathaniel]. *Dinners and Diners: Where and How to Dine in London*. Revised edition. London: Grant Richards, 1901.

Newsom, Lee A., and Kathleen A. Deagan. "*Zea mays* in the West Indies: The Archaeological and Early Historic Record". In *Corn and Culture in the Prehistoric New World*, edited by Sissel Johannessen and Christine A. Hastorf, 203–17. Boulder, CO: Westview, 1994.

Nichols, David. *Echinoderms*. London: Hutchinson University Library, 1962.

Noble, A.C. "Taste-Aroma Interactions". *Trends in Food Science and Technology* 7 (1996): 439–44.

Norman, M.J.T., C.J. Pearson, and P.G.E. Searle. *The Ecology of Tropical Food Crops*. 2nd edition. Cambridge, UK: Cambridge University Press, 1995.

North, Marianne. *Recollections of a Happy Life: Being the Autobiography of Marianne North*. Edited by Mrs John Addington Symonds. London: Macmillan, 1893.

Norton, Marcy. "Tasting Empire: Chocolate and the European Internalization of Mesoamerican Aesthetics". *American Historical Review* 111 (2006): 660–91.

Novak, Johannes, Karin Zitterl-Eglseer, Stanley G. Deans, and Chlodwig M. Franz. "Essential Oils of Different Cultivars of *Cannabis sativa* L. and Their Antimicrobial Activity". *Flavour and Fragrance Journal* 16 (2001): 259–62.

Nugent, Lady Maria. *Lady Nugent's Journal of Her Residence in Jamaica from 1801 to 1805*. Edited by Philip Wright. Kingston: Institute of Jamaica, 1966.

Ogbe, F.M. Dania, and J.T. Williams. "Evolution in Indigenous West African Rice". *Economic Botany* 32 (1978): 59–64.

Oke, O.L. "Processing and Detoxification of Cassava". *Proceedings of the Sixth Symposium of the International Society for Tropical Root Crops*, 329–36. Lima, Peru: International Potato Center, 1984.

Oliver, Douglas. *Return to Tahiti: Bligh's Second Breadfruit Voyage*. Melbourne, Australia: Melbourne University Press, 1988.

Olivier, Lord [Sydney]. *Jamaica: The Blessed Island*. London: Faber and Faber, 1936.

Onwueme, I.C. *The Tropical Tuber Crops: Yams, Cassava, Sweet Potato, and Cocoyams*. Chichester, UK: Wiley, 1978.

Oomen, H.A.P.C., and G.J.H. Grubben. *Tropical Leaf Vegetables in Human Nutrition*. Amsterdam: Koninklijk Instituut vor de Tropen, 1977.

Osborne, Laura. *The Rasta Cookbook*. London: Macdonald, 1990.

Osborne, Patrick L. *Tropical Ecosystems and Ecological Concepts*. Cambridge, UK: Cambridge University Press, 2000.

Ovide, Stéphanie. *French Caribbean Cuisine*. New York: Hippocrene, 2002.

Owens, Joseph. *Dread: The Rastafarians of Jamaica*. Kingston: Sangster, 1976.

Packard, Vernal S. *Human Milk and Infant Formula*. New York: Academic Press, 1982.

A Panorama of African Recipes. Kingston: African Caribbean Institute of Jamaica, 1980.

Parkinson, Rosemary. *Culinaria, The Caribbean: A Culinary Discovery.* Cologne: Könemann, 1999.

Parry, John H. "The Indies Richly Planted". *Terrae Incognitae* 1 (1969): 11–22.

———. "Plantation and Provision Ground: An Historical Sketch of the Introduction of Food Crops to Jamaica". *Revista de Historia de America* 39 (1955): 1–20.

———. "Salt Fish and Ackee". *Caribbean Quarterly* 2 (1954): 29–35.

Parry, J.H., and P.M. Sherlock. *A Short History of the West Indies.* London: Macmillan, 1956.

Pawson, Michael, and David Buisseret. *Port Royal, Jamaica.* Oxford: Clarendon, 1975.

Payne-Jackson, Arvilla, and Mervyn C. Alleyne. *Jamaican Folk Medicine: A Source of Healing.* Mona, Jamaica: University of the West Indies Press, 2004.

Pearce, Richard. "Traditional Food Crops in Sub-Saharan Africa: Potential and Constraints". *Food Policy* 15, no. 5 (1990): 374–82.

Peas Please! Kingston: Scientific Research Council, 1972.

Peck, Stewart B. "Historical Biogeography of Jamaica: Evidence from Cave Invertebrates". *Canadian Journal of Zoology* 77 (1999): 368–80.

Pendergrast, Mark. *Uncommon Grounds: The History of Coffee and How It Transformed Our World.* New York: Basic Books, 1999.

Perezescamilla, R. "Breast-Feeding in Africa and the Latin-American and Caribbean Region: The Potential Role of Urbanization". *Journal of Tropical Pediatrics* 40 (1994): 137–43.

Permenter, Paris, and John Bigley. *Jamaica: A Taste of the Island.* Edison, NJ: Hunter, 1999.

Persley, Gabrielle J., and Pamela George, eds. *Banana Improvement: Research Challenges and Opportunities.* Washington, DC: World Bank, 1996.

Petterson, Janet H. *Dissemination and Use of the Edible Aroids, with Particular Reference to Colocasia (Asian Taro) and Xanthosoma (American Taro).* Ph.D. diss., University of Florida, 1977.

Phillippo, James M. *Jamaica: Its Past and Present State.* London: John Snow, 1843.

Phillips, Henry Albert. *White Elephants in the Caribbean: A Magic Journey through all the West Indies.* New York: Robert M. McBride, 1936.

Pickersgill, Barbara. "The Domestication of Chili Peppers". In *The Domestication and Exploitation of Plants and Animals*, edited by Peter J. Ucko and G.W. Dimbleby, 443–50. London: Duckworth, 1969.

Pilcher, Jeffrey M. *Food in World History.* New York: Routledge, 2006.

Pino, Jorge, Rolando Marbot, and Aristides Rosado. "Volatile Constituents of Star Apple (*Chrysophyllum cainito* L.) from Cuba". *Flavour and Fragrance Journal* 17 (2002): 401–3.

Pino, Jorge A., Karina Almora, and Rolando Marbot. "Volatile Components of Papaya (*Carica papaya* L., Maradol Variety) Fruit". *Flavour and Fragrance Journal* 18 (2003): 492–96.

Piperno, Dolores R. "The Origins of Plant Cultivation and Domestication in the Neotropics". In *Behavioral Ecology and the Transition to Agriculture*, edited by Douglas J. Kennett and Bruce Winterhalder, 137–66. Berkeley: University of California Press, 2006.

Pitts, J.F., N.H. Barker, D.C. Gibbons, and J.L. Jay. "Manchineel Keratoconjunctivitis". *British Journal of Ophthalmology* 77 (1993): 284–88.

Pollock, Nancy J. *These Roots Remain: Food Habits in Islands of the Central and Eastern Pacific since Western Contact.* Honolulu: Institute for Polynesian Studies, 1992.

Powell, Dorian, Eleanor Wint, Erna Brodber, and Versada Campbell. *Street Foods of Kingston*. Mona: Institute of Social and Economic Research, 1990.

Powell, Dulcie. *The Voyage of the Plant Nursery, H.M.S.* Providence, *1791–1793*. Kingston: Institute of Jamaica, 1973.

Prasad, P.V. Devi. *Edible Fruits and Vegetables of the English-Speaking Caribbean*. Kingston: Caribbean Food and Nutrition Institute, 1986.

The Present State of Jamaica. London: Thomas Malthus, 1683.

Price, N.S. "The Origin and Development of Banana and Plantain Cultivation". In *Bananas and Plantains*, edited by S. Gowen, 1–12. London: Chapman and Hall, 1995.

Pringle, Kenneth. *Waters of the West*. London: George Allen and Unwin, 1938.

Pullen-Burry, Bessie. *Ethiopia in Exile: Jamaica Revisited*. 1905. Reprint, Freeport, NY: Books for Libraries Press, 1971.

———. *Jamaica as It Is, 1903*. London: T. Fisher Unwin, 1903.

Purseglove, J.W., E.G. Brown, C.L. Green, and S.R.J. Robbins. 2 vols. *Spices*. London: Longman Scientific and Technical, 1981.

Quinn, Lucinda Scala. *Jamaican Cooking: 140 Roadside and Homestyle Recipes*. New York: Macmillan, 1997.

Raffaele, Herbert, James Wiley, Orlando Garrido, Allan Keith, and Janis Raffaele. *Birds of the West Indies*. London: Christopher Helm, 2003.

Rampini, Charles I.G. *Letters from Jamaica: "The Land of Streams and Woods"*. Edinburgh: Edmonston and Douglas, 1873.

Rankine, Peggy. *Simply Delicious: A Collection of Original Recipes and Useful Kitchen Hints*. Mandeville, Jamaica: West Indies College Press, 1987.

Rao, K.K.P.N. "Nutritive Value of Cereals and Other Main Staple Foods". *Cajanus* 12 (December 1969): 486–91.

Rashford, John. "Ackee Poisoning and the Evolutionary Biology of Jamaica's Ackee Motif". *Proceedings of the Caribbean Food Crops Society* 32 (1996): 185–92.

———. "Arawak, Spanish and African Contributions to Jamaica's Settlement Vegetation". *Jamaica Journal* 24, no. 3 (1993): 17–23.

———. "Packy Tree, Spirits and Duppy Birds". *Jamaica Journal* 21, no. 3 (1988): 2–10.

———. "The Past and Present Uses of Bamboo in Jamaica". *Economic Botany* 49 (1995): 395–405.

———. "The Star Apple: A Symbol of Meanness in Jamaica". *Jamaica Journal* 24, no. 1 (June 1991): 49–53.

———. "Those That Do Not Smile Will Kill Me: The Ethnobotany of the Ackee in Jamaica". *Economic Botany* 55 (2001): 190–211.

Rau, Santha Rama. *The Cooking of India*. Amsterdam: Time-Life International, 1972.

Recipes for Cooking West Indian Yams. London: Imperial Department of Agriculture for the West Indies, 1902.

Renaud, Diane. "Improving Childhood Nutrition: Breastfeeding and Beyond". *Cajanus* 34, no. 4 (2001): 171–73.

Renvoize, Barbara S. "The Area of Origin of *Manihot esculenta* as a Crop Plant: A Review of the Evidence". *Economic Botany* 26 (1972): 352–60.

Report of Committee on the Cost of Production of Certain Local Food Crops. Kingston: Government Printer, 1946.

Reynolds, C. Roy. "Research in Corn Hybridization in Jamaica". *Jamaica Journal* 7, nos 1–2 (1973): 91–92.

Rice Cook Book. Montego Bay: Grains Jamaica Ltd, [1991].

Richardson, Mary F. "*Out of Many, One People*: Aspiration or Reality? An Examination of the Attitudes to the Various Racial and Ethnic Groups within the Jamaican Society". *Social and Economic Studies* 32 (1983): 143–67.

Rickards, Colin, ed. *The West Indies and Caribbean Year Book 1975*. Toronto: Caribook, 1975.

Risch, Sara J. "Spices: Sources, Processing, and Chemistry". In *Spices: Flavor Chemistry and Antioxidant Properties*, edited by Sara J. Risch and Chi-Tang Ho, 2–6. Washington, DC: American Chemical Society, 1996.

Risch, Sara J., and Chi-Tang Ho, eds. *Spices: Flavor Chemistry and Antioxidant Properties*. Washington, DC: American Chemical Society, 1996.

Roberts, Jill. *A Hamper of Recipes from Jamaica*. Kingston: Heinemann Educational (Caribbean), 1987.

Robinson, T. Ralph. "Grapefruit and Pummelo". *Economic Botany* 6 (1952): 228–45.

Roden, Claudia. *Coffee*. Harmondsworth, UK: Penguin, 1981.

Rodriquez, D.W. *Coffee: A Short Economic History with Special Reference to Jamaica*. Kingston: Ministry of Agriculture and Lands, 1961.

———. *Ginger: A Short Economic History*. Commodity Bulletin No. 4. Kingston: Ministry of Agriculture and Fisheries, 1971.

———. *Pimento: A Short Economic History*. Commodity Bulletin No. 3. Kingston: Ministry of Agriculture and Fisheries, 1969.

Rogers, David J. "Cassava Leaf Protein". *Economic Botany* 13 (1959): 261–63.

———. "Some Botanical and Ethnological Considerations of *Manihot esculenta*". *Economic Botany* 19 (1965): 369–77.

Rolls, Edmund T. "Taste, Olfactory, and Food Texture Processing in the Brain, and the Control of Food Intake". *Physiology and Behavior* 85 (2005): 45–56.

Roosevelt, Anna Curtenius. *Parmana: Prehistoric Maize and Manioc Subsistence along the Amazon and Orinoco*. New York: Academic Press, 1980.

Rosenthal, Edward C. *The Era of Choice: The Ability to Choose and Its Transformation of Contemporary Life*. Cambridge, MA: MIT Press, 2005.

Rosevear, D.R. *The Rodents of West Africa*. London: British Museum (Natural History), 1969.

Ross, Frank. "Aquaculture in Jamaica: A Growing Industry". *Jamaica Journal* 18, no. 4 (1985–86): 29–36.

Roughley, Thomas. *The Jamaica Planter's Guide*. London: Hurst, Longman, Rees, Orme and Brown, 1823.

Rouse, Irving. *The Tainos: Rise and Decline of the People Who Greeted Columbus*. New Haven, CT: Yale University Press, 1992.

Royes, Heather Hope, and Gillian Royes Baccus, eds. *The Jamaica Farmer's Guide*. Kingston: Selectco, 1988.

Rubin, Jane Gregory, and Ariana Donalds, eds. *Bread Made from Yuca: Selected Chronicles of Indo-Antillean Cultivation and Use of Cassava 1526–2002*. New York: InterAmericas, 2003.

Ryan, Shannon. *Fish out of Water: The Newfoundland Saltfish Trade 1814–1914*. St John's, NL, Canada: Breakwater, 1986.

Salaman, Redcliffe N. *The History and Social Influence of the Potato*. Cambridge, UK: Cambridge University Press, 1949.

Samper, Mario K. "The Historical Construction of Quality and Competitiveness: A Preliminary Discussion of Coffee Commodity Chains". In *The Global Coffee Economy in Africa, Asia, and Latin America, 1500–1989*, edited by William Gervase Clarence-Smith and Steven Topik, 120–53. Cambridge, UK: Cambridge University Press, 2003.

Samper, Mario, and Radin Fernando. "Historical Statistics of Coffee Production and Trade from 1700 to 1960". In *The Global Coffee Economy in Africa, Asia, and Latin America, 1500–1989*, edited by William Gervase Clarence-Smith and Steven Topik, 411–62. Cambridge, UK: Cambridge University Press, 2003.

Samson, J.A. *Tropical Fruits*. London: Longman, 1980.

Samuda, Pauline M., Richard A. Cook, Cristanna M. Cook, and Fitzroy Henry. "Identifying Foods Commonly Consumed by the Jamaican Population: The Focus Group Approach". *International Journal of Food Sciences and Nutrition* 49 (1998): 79–86.

Sanday, Peggy Reeves. *Divine Hunger: Cannibalism as a Cultural System*. Cambridge, UK: Cambridge University Press, 1986.

Sanjur, Diva. *Social and Cultural Perspectives on Nutrition*. Englewood Cliffs, NJ: Prentice-Hall, 1982.

Sauer, Jonathan D. *Historical Geography of Crop Plants: A Select Roster*. Boca Raton, FL: CRC Press, 1993.

Saunt, James. *Citrus Varieties of the World*. Norwich, UK: Sinclair International, 2000.

Schivelbusch, Wolfgang. *Tastes of Paradise: A Social History of Spices, Stimulants, and Intoxicants.* New York: Pantheon, 1992.

Schulkin, Jay. *Sodium Hunger: The Search for a Salty Taste*. Cambridge, UK: Cambridge University Press, 1991.

Schütz, Karin E., and Per Jensen. "Effects of Resource Allocation on Behavioural Strategies: A Comparison of Red Junglefowl (*Gallus gallus*) and Two Domesticated Breeds of Poultry". *Ethology* 107 (2001): 753–65.

Scientific Research Council. *Callalu: A Good Mixer*. Kingston: Scientific Research Council, 1971.

———. *Sample Menus of Meals Highlighting Jamaican Foods*. Kingston: Scientific Research Council, [1974].

Scott, O.D., K. Moodie, and R. Bissessar. "A Preliminary Quantitative Survey of the Bacterial Flora of Restaurants and Bakeries in the City of Kingston, Jamaica". *West Indian Medical Journal* 17 (1968): 158–62.

Scott, Sir Sibbald David. *To Jamaica and Back*. London: Chapman and Hall, 1876.

Scott, W.E.D. "Observations on the Birds of Jamaica, West Indies". *The Auk* 8 (1891): 249–56, 353–65; 9 (1892): 9–15, 369–75; 10 (1893): 177–81, 339–42.

Seneviratne, Gamini. "Processing Cassava to Improve Safety and Nutritional Value". *Cajanus* 19 (1986): 72–79.

Senior, Bernard Martin. *Jamaica, as It Was, as It Is, and as It May Be*. London: T. Hurst, 1835.

Senior, Olive. *Arrival of the Snake-Woman and Other Stories*. London: Longman, 1989.

———. *A–Z of Jamaican Heritage*. Kingston: Heinemann Educational/Gleaner, 1983.

———. *Encyclopedia of Jamaican Heritage*. Red Hills, St Andrew: Twin Guinep, 2003.

Serventi, Silvano, and Françoise Sabban. *Pasta: The Story of a Universal Food*. New York: Columbia University Press, 2002.

Shao, Yajing, Philip Marriott, Robert Shellie, and Hemut Hügel. "Solid-Phase Micro-extraction: Comprehensive Two-Dimensional Gas Chromatography of Ginger (*Zingiber officinale*) Volatiles". *Flavour and Fragrance Journal* 18 (2003): 5–12.

Shaul, Wendy, and Ann Haynes. "Manatees and Their Struggle for Survival". *Jamaica Journal* 19, no. 3 (1986): 29–36.

Shepherd, Verene A., and Kathleen E.A. Monteith. "Pen-Keepers and Coffee Farmers in a Sugar-Plantation Society". In *Slavery without Sugar: Diversity in Caribbean Economy and Society since the 17th Century*, edited by Verene A. Shepherd, 82–101. Gainesville: University Press of Florida, 2002.

Sheppard, S.C. "Geophagy: Who Eats Soil and Where Do Possible Contaminants Go?" *Environmental Geology* 33 (1998): 109–14.

Sheridan, Richard B. "Captain Bligh, the Breadfruit, and the Botanic Gardens of Jamaica". *Journal of Caribbean History* 23 (1989): 28–50.

———. "The Crisis of Slave Subsistence in the British West Indies during and after the American Revolution". *William and Mary Quarterly* 33 (1976): 615–41.

———. "The Maroons of Jamaica, 1730–1830: Livelihood, Demography and Health". *Slavery and Abolition* 6 (1985): 152–72.

Simmonds, N.W. *Bananas*. London: Longmans, 1959.

Simmons, Amelia. *American Cookery*. 1796. Reprint, Grand Rapids, MI: William B. Eerdmans, 1965.

Simms, Errol, and Lloyd B. Rankine. "Factors Contributing to the Growth and Development of the Root Crop Industry in Jamaica". *Social and Economic Studies* 28 (1979): 31–68.

Simoons, Frederick J. *Eat Not This Flesh: Food Avoidances from Prehistory to the Present*. Madison: University of Wisconsin Press, 1994.

Singh, Lal Behari. *The Mango*. London: Leonard Hill, 1960.

Slater, Mary. *Caribbean Cooking for Pleasure*. London: Hamlyn, 1970.

Sloane, Hans. *A Voyage to the Islands Madera, Barbados, Nieves, S. Christophers and Jamaica, with the Natural History of the Last of Those Islands*. London, 1707–25.

Smith, Andrew F. *Pure Ketchup: A History of America's National Condiment*. Washington, DC: Smithsonian Institution Press, 2001.

———. *The Tomato in America: Early History, Culture, and Cookery*. Urbana: University of Illinois Press, 2001.

Smith, Frederick H. *Caribbean Rum: A Social and Economic History*. Gainesville: University Press of Florida, 2005.

———. "Spirits and Spirituality: Enslaved Persons and Alcohol in West Africa and the British and French Caribbean". *Journal of Caribbean History* 38 (2004): 279–309.

Smith, George. *The Nature of Fermentation Explain'd; with the Method of Opening the Body of any Grain or Vegetable Subject, so as to Obtain from It a Spiritous Liquor: Exemplified by the Process of Preparing Rum, as 'tis Manag'd in the West-Indies.* London: Bernard Lintot, 1729.

Smith, John L. T*he Psychology of Food and Eating: A Fresh Approach to Theory and Method.* Basingstoke, UK: Palgrave, 2002.

Smith, Roger W. "Jamaica's Own Birds". *Jamaica Journal* 2, no. 4 (1968): 18–21.

Smith, S.D. "Accounting for Taste: British Coffee Consumption in Historical Perspective". *Journal of Interdisciplinary History* 27 (1996): 183–214.

Smylie, Mike. *Herring: A History of the Silver Darlings.* Stroud, UK: Tempus, 2004.

Sobers, Yvonne McCalla. *Delicious Jamaica! Vegetarian Cuisine.* Summertown, TN: Book Publishing Company, 1996.

Sobo, Elisa Janine. *One Blood: The Jamaican Body.* Albany: State University of New York Press, 1993.

Solow, Andrew R. "Inferring Extinction from a Sighting Record". *Mathematical Biosciences* 195 (2005): 47–55.

Sorenson, John L., and Carl L. Johannessen. "Biological Evidence for Pre-Columbian Transoceanic Voyages". In *Contact and Exchange in the Ancient World*, edited by Victor H. Mair, 238–97. Honolulu: University of Hawai'i Press, 2006.

Spary, Emma, and Paul White. "Food of Paradise: Tahitian Breadfruit and the Autocritique of European Consumption". *Endeavour* 28 (2004): 75–80.

Spence, Wenton O. *Jamaican Cookery: Recipes from Old Jamaican Grandmothers.* Kingston: Heritage Publishers, 1981.

Spicer, Arnold, ed. *Bread: Social, Nutritional and Agricultural Aspects of Wheaten Bread.* London: Applied Science Publishers, 1975.

Springer, Rita G. *Caribbean Cookbook.* 1968. London: Pan Books, 1979.

Stam, H., A.L.G.M. Boog, and M. Hoogland. "The Production of Natural Flavours by Fermentation". In *Flavour Science: Recent Developments*, edited by A.J. Taylor and D.S. Mottram, 122–25. Cambridge, UK: Royal Society of Chemistry, 1996.

Statistical Yearbook of Jamaica. 1982, 1992, 1993.

Stewart, John. *An Account of Jamaica.* London: Longman, Hurst, Rees and Orme, 1808.

———. *A View of the Past and Present State of the Island of Jamaica.* Edinburgh: Oliver and Boyd, 1823.

Stobart, Tom. *Herbs, Spices and Flavorings.* New York: Overlook, 1982.

Strickland, Nicola H. "My Most Unfortunate Experience: Eating a Manchineel 'Beach Apple'". *British Medical Journal* 321 (12 August 2000): 428.

Strong, Allan M., and Matthew D. Johnson. "Exploitation of a Seasonal Resource by Nonbreeding Plain and White-Crowned Pigeons: Implications for Conservation of Tropical Dry Forests". *Wilson Bulletin* 113 (2001): 73–77.

Stubbe, Henry. *The Indian Nectar, or a Discourse Concerning Chocolata.* London: Andrew Crook, 1662.

Sturge, Joseph, and Thomas Harvey. *The West Indies in 1837*. London: Hamilton, Adams, 1838.

Sturtevant, William C. "History and Ethnography of Some West Indian Starches". In *The Domestication and Exploitation of Plants and Animals*, edited by Peter J. Ucko and G.W. Dimbleby, 177–99. Chicago: Aldine, 1969.

Suah, J.R.R. "The Elusive Lethal Yellowing Disease of Coconuts". *Jamaica Journal* 6, no. 4 (1972): 15–17.

Sugimoto, Kumiko, and Yuzo Ninomiya. "Introductory Remarks on Umami Research: Candidate Receptors and Signal Transduction Mechanisms on Umami". *Chemical Senses* 30, suppl. 1 (2005): i21–22.

Sugita, Makoto, and Yoshiki Shiba. "Genetic Tracing Shows Segregation of Taste Neuronal Circuitries for Bitter and Sweet". *Science* 309 (July 29, 2005): 781–85.

Sullivan, Caroline. *The Jamaica Cookery Book: Three Hundred and Twelve Simple Receipts and Household Hints*. Kingston: Aston W. Gardner, 1893. Revised, expanded edition 1897. The 1897 edition is followed in *A Collection of 19th Century Jamaican Cookery and Herbal Recipes* (Kingston: The Mill Press, 1990). The 1893 edition is used in Caroline Sullivan, *Classic Jamaican Cooking: Traditional Recipes and Herbal Remedies* (London: Serif, 1996), and is freely adapted in Caroline Sullivan, *Jamaikanische Küche: Traditionelle Kochrezepte aus dem Jahre 1893* (Hamburg, Germany: Asfahani Verlag, 1997).

Sumathykutty, M.A., J. Madhusudana Rao, K.P. Padmakumari, and C.S. Narayanan. "Essential Oil Constituents of Some Piper Species". *Flavour and Fragrance Journal* 14 (1999): 279–82.

Sutton, Mark Q. *Insects as Food: Aboriginal Entomophagy in the Great Basin*. Anthropological Papers No. 33. Menlo Park, CA: Ballena Press, 1988.

Tannahill, Reay. *Flesh and Blood: A History of the Cannibal Complex*. New York: Dorset, 1975.

Taylor, Lady [R.G.]. *Introduction to the Birds of Jamaica*. London: Macmillan, 1955.

Terra, G.J.A. *Tropical Vegetables: Vegetable Growing in the Tropics and Subtropics Especially of Indigenous Vegetables*. Amsterdam: Koninklijk Instituut voor de Tropen, 1973.

Thieret, John W. "Economic Botany of the Cycads". *Economic Botany* 12 (1957): 3-41.

———. "Ginger in Jamaica". *Economic Botany* 15 (1959): 86.

Thomas, C.A. "Jackfruit, *Artocarpus heterophyllus* (Moraceae), as Source of Food and Income". *Economic Botany* 34 (1980): 154–59.

Thomas, Herbert T. *Untrodden Jamaica*. Kingston: A.W. Gardner, 1890.

Thomas, Omer S. Lloyd. "The Current Status of Papaya Production in Jamaica". In *Proceedings of the Papaya and Mango Seminar*. Kingston: Inter-American Institute for Cooperation on Agriculture, 1993, 1–18.

Thompson, Patricia Y. *Caribbean Style Eating for Disaster Conditions*. Kingston: Nutrition and Diet Services, 1990.

Thompson, R.W. *Black Caribbean*. London: Macdonald, 1946.

Timm, Robert M., Rosa M. Salazar, and A. Townsend Peterson. "Historical Distribution of the Extinct Tropical Seal, *Monachus tropicalis* (Carnivora: Phocidae)". *Conservation Biology* 11 (1997): 549–51.

Titford, W.J. *Sketches towards a Hortus Botanicus Americanus*. London: Sherwood, Neely and Jones, 1811.

Trapham, Thomas. *A Discourse on the State of Health in the Island of Jamaica*. London: R. Boulter, 1679.

A Treatise on the Ananas or Pine-apple, Containing Plain and Easy Directions for Raising This Most Excellent Fruit without Fire, and in Much Higher Perfection than from the Stove. Devizes, UK, 1759.

Trollope, Anthony. *The West Indies and the Spanish Main*. 1859. Gloucester, UK: Alan Sutton, 1985.

A True Description of Jamaica, with the Fertility, Commodities, and Healthfulness of the Place. London, 1657.

"Trumpet Tree". *Jamaica Journal* 24, no. 3 (1993): 66.

Ullman, James Ramsey, and Al Dinhofer. *Caribbean Here and Now: The Complete Vacation Guide to 52 Sunny Islands and Vacation Lands in the Caribbean Sea*. New York: Macmillan, 1968.

Urquhart, D.H. *Cocoa*. 2nd edition. London: Longmans, 1961.

Vaughan, J.G., and C.A. Geissler. *The New Oxford Book of Food Plants*. Oxford: Oxford University Press, 1997.

Vermeer, Donald E. "Geophagy among the Ewe of Ghana". *Ethnology*, 10 (1971): 56–72.

———. "Geophagy among the Tiv of Nigeria". *Annals of the Association of American Geographers* 56 (1966): 197–204.

Verrill, A. Hyatt. *Jamaica of Today*. New York: Dodd, Mead, 1931.

Viola, Herman J., and Carolyn Margolis, eds. *Seeds of Change: A Quincentennial Commemoration*. Washington, DC: Smithsonian Institution Press, 1991.

Virgil. *The Ploughman's Lunch: Moretum, a Poem Ascribed to Virgil*. Translated by E.J. Kenney. Bristol: Bristol Classical Press, 1984.

Walsh, Robb, *Are You Really Going to Eat That? Reflections of a Culinary Thrill Seeker*. New York: Counterpoint, 2003.

Walters, D. Eric. "How Are Bitter and Sweet Tastes Related?" *Trends in Food Science and Technology* 7 (1996): 399–403.

Walters, D. Eric, and Glenn Roy. "Taste Interactions of Sweet and Bitter Compounds". In *Flavor-Food Interactions*, edited by Robert J. McGorrin and Jane V. Leland, 130–42. Washington, DC: American Chemical Society, 1996.

Walvin, James. *Fruits of Empire: Exotic Produce and British Taste, 1660–1800*. London: Macmillan, 1997.

Wang, Jaw-Kai, ed. *Taro: A Review of Colocasia esculenta and Its Potentials*. Honolulu: University of Hawaii Press, 1983.

Ward, C.J. *World's Fair, Jamaica at Chicago: An Account of the Colony of Jamaica, with Historical and Other Appendices*. New York: W.J. Pell, 1893.

Ward, Edward. *A Trip to Jamaica: With the True Character of the People and Island*. London: J. How, 1700.

Ward, J.F. *Black Pepper: A Review of Cultural Practices and Their Application to Jamaica*. Kingston: Government Printer, 1960.

Warde, Alan. *Consumption, Food and Taste: Culinary Antimonies and Commodity Culture*. London: Sage, 1997.

Watanabe, Wade O., Thomas M. Losordo, Kevin Fitzsimmons, and Fred Hanley. "Tilapia Production Systems in the Americas: Technological Advances, Trends, and Challenges". *Reviews in Fisheries Science* 10 (2002): 465–98.

Watts, David. "The Caribbean Environment and Early Settlement". In *General History of the Caribbean, Vol. II, New Societies: The Caribbean in the Long Sixteenth Century*, edited by P. C. Emmer, 29–42. London: UNESCO Publishing/Macmillan, 1999.

———. *The West Indies: Patterns of Development, Culture and Environmental Change since 1492*. Cambridge, UK: Cambridge University Press, 1987.

Webster, Aimee. "Why the Shift to White Wheat Flour?" *Gleaner*, 30 October 1988.

Weenen, Hugo, J. Kerler, and J.G.M. van der Ven. "The Maillard Reaction in Flavour Formation". In *Flavours and Fragrances*, edited by Karl A.D. Swift, 153–70. Cambridge, UK: Royal Society of Chemistry, 1997.

Weightman, Gavin. *The Frozen Water Trade: How Ice from New England Lakes Kept the World Cool*. London: HarperCollins, 2001.

Weil, Andrew T. "Nutmeg as a Narcotic". *Economic Botany* 19 (1965): 194–217.

Weinberg, Bennett Alan, and Bonnie K. Bealer. *The World of Caffeine: The Science and Culture of the World's Most Popular Drug*. New York: Routledge, 2002.

Wellman, Frederick L. *Coffee: Botany, Cultivation and Utilization*. London: Leonard Hill, 1961.

West-India Planters and Merchants. *Considerations on the Present State of the Intercourse between his Majesty's Sugar Colonies and the Dominions of the United States of America*. London, 1784.

The West Indies and Caribbean Year Book 1967. London: Thomas Skinner, 1966.

Whitaker, Thomas W., and Hugh C. Cutler. "Cucurbits and Cultures in the Americas". *Economic Botany* 19 (1965): 344–49.

Whitaker, Thomas W., and Glen N. Davis. *Cucurbits: Botany, Cultivation, and Utilization*. London: Leonard Hill, 1962.

Whitbourne, Dahlia. "The Ordinary Diet in Jamaica with Comments Thereon". *Jamaica Public Health* 11, no. 9 (1936): 68–74.

White, Alison, and Patricia Y. Thompson. *The Caribbean Food and Nutrition Book*. London: Macmillan, 1989.

Whiting, Marjorie Grant. "Toxicity of Cycads". *Economic Botany* 17 (1963): 271–302

Whitmore, Thomas M., and B.L. Turner II. *Cultivated Landscapes of Middle America on the Eve of Conquest*. Oxford: Oxford University Press, 2001.

Whittaker, Robert J. *Island Biogeography: Ecology, Evolution, and Conservation*. Oxford: Oxford University Press, 1998.

Wilk, Richard R. "Food and Nationalism: The Origins of 'Belizean Food'". In *Food Nations: Selling Taste in Consumer Societies*, edited by Warren Belasco and Philip Scranton, 67–89. New York: Routledge, 2002.

———. *Home Cooking in the Global Village: Caribbean Food from Buccaneers to Ecotourists*. Oxford: Berg, 2006.

Williams, Cynric R. *A Tour through the Island of Jamaica, from the Western to Eastern End, in the Year 1823*. London: Thomas Hurst, Edward Chance, 1827.

Williams, Louis O. "The Avocados, a Synopsis of the Genus *Persea*, subg. *Persea*". *Economic Botany* 31 (1977): 315–20.

Williamson, G., and W.J.A. Payne. *An Introduction to Animal Husbandry in the Tropics*. London: Longmans, 1959.

Williamson, John. *Medical and Miscellaneous Observations, Relative to the West India Islands*. Edinburgh, 1817.

Williamson, Kay. "Did Chickens Go West?" In *The Origins and Development of African Livestock: Archaeology, Genetics, Linguistics and Ethnography*, edited by Roger M. Blench and Kevin C. MacDonald, 368–448. London: UCL Press, 2000.

Willinsky, Helen. *Jerk: Barbecue from Jamaica*. Freedom, CA: The Crossing Press, 1990.

Wills, J.B. "Crops Other Than Cocoa and the Diseases and Pests Which Affect Them". In *Agriculture and Land Use in Ghana*, edited by J. Brian Wills, 353–93. London: Oxford University Press, 1962.

Wilson, Edmund. *The Sixties: The Last Journal, 1960–1972*. Edited by Lewis M. Dabney. New York: Farrar Straus Giroux, 1993.

Wilson, M.J. "Clay Mineralogical and Related Characteristics of Geophagic Materials". *Journal of Chemical Ecology* 29 (2003): 1525–47.

Wilson, Thomas W., and Clarence E. Grim. "Biohistory of Slavery and Blood Pressure Differences in Blacks Today: A Hypothesis". *Hypertension* 17, suppl. 1 (1991): 122–29.

Winston, Mark L. *The Biology of the Honey Bee*. Cambridge, MA: Harvard University Press, 1987.

Wolfe, Linda, ed. *The Cooking of the Caribbean Islands*. 1970. London: Macmillan, 1985.

Wood, Beryl. *Caribbean Fruits and Vegetables: Selected Recipes*. Kingston: Longman Caribbean, 1973.

———. *Meal Planning and Preparation for Caribbean Students*. Kingston: Longman Caribbean, 1973.

Wood, Beryl, and Magda Pollard. *Caribbean Schools Home Economics: Book 1*. Kingston: Longman Caribbean, 1983.

Wood, Betty, ed. *The Letters of Simon Taylor of Jamaica to Chaloner Arcedekne, 1765–1775*. Camden Miscellany, Vol. 35. London: Cambridge University Press, for the Royal Historical Society, 2002.

Wood, G.A.R., and R.A. Lass. *Cocoa*. London: Longman, 1985.

Woodley, J.D. "A History of the Jamaican Fauna". *Jamaica Journal* 2, no. 3 (1968): 14–20.

———. "Sea-Urchins Exert Top-Down Control of Macroalgae on Jamaican Coral Reefs". *Coral Reefs* 18 (1999): 192.

Wright, Philip. *Knibb "the Notorious": Slaves' Missionary, 1803–1845*. London: Sidgwick and Jackson, 1973.

Wyllarde, Dolf. *Mafoota*. London: Hurst and Blackett, 1907.

———. *Tropical Tales and Others*. London: Stanley Paul, 1909.

Yeates, N.T.M. *Modern Aspects of Animal Production*. London: Butterworths, 1965.

Young, Allen M. *The Chocolate Tree: A Natural History of Cacao*. Washington, DC: Smithsonian Institution Press, 1994.

Zepherin, Manuelita, Alison White, Wendy E. Clarke, and Rosie Jackman. *The Joys of Healthy Cooking in the Caribbean*. Kingston: Ian Randle, 2005.

Zerega, Nyree J.C. "The Breadfruit Trail". *Natural History* 112, no. 10 (2003): 46–50.

Zerega, Nyree J.C., Diane Ragone, and Timothy J. Motley. "Complex Origins of Breadfruit (*Artocarpus altilis*, Moraceae): Implications for Human Migrations in Oceania". *American Journal of Botany* 91 (2004): 760–66.

Zohary, Daniel, and Maria Hopf. *Domestication of Plants in the Old World: The Origin and Spread of Cultivated Plants in West Asia, Europe, and the Nile Valley*. Oxford: Clarendon, 1988.

WEBSITES

http://faostat.fao.org/

http://www.gracefoods.com

http://www.jamaican-recipes.com

http://www.jamaicans.com/cooking

http://www.newspaperarchive.com

http://www.visitjamaica.com

INDEX